Yale Language Series, 6

BEGINNING

JAPANESE

PART II

by Eleanor Harz Jorden

with the assistance of Hamako Ito Chaplin

New Haven and London, Yale University Press

Set in IBM Documentary type and
printed in the United States of America by
The Murray Printing Company, Inc.
Westford, Mass.

Library of Congress catalog card number: 62–16235
ISBN: 0–300–00610–1 (cloth), 0–300–00136–3 (paper)

31 30 29 28 27

For

Temmy
Tabby
Telly

NOTE

This volume is a continuation of BEGINNING JAPANESE, Part I.
A description of romanization, special symbols, procedures, etc.
appears in the Introduction to that volume.

Contents

Contents   xiii

Lesson 21. Inns and Hotels

(a)

Clerk

1. Welcome.   I⌐rassyaima⌐se.

Smith

2. Do you have a room [for] tonight?   Ko⌐ṅbaṅ he⌐ya⌐ (ḡa) a⌐rima⌐su ka⌐

Clerk

promise <u>or</u> appointment   yakusoku <u>or</u> oyakusoku †
   <u>or</u> engagement
3. Are you expected?   O⌐yakusoku de gozaima⌐su ka⌐

Smith

4. No, I don't have a reservation   Iie, ya⌐kusoku wa arimase⌐ṅ ḡa⌐
(but)...

Clerk

Japanese-style room   nihoṅma
nothing but Japanese-style   nihoṅma sika /+ negative/
   rooms
5. We have nothing but Japanese-   Ni⌐hoṅma sika gozaimase⌐ṅ ḡa,
style rooms. How about [one of   i⌐ka⌐ḡa de gozaimasu ka⌐
them]?

being new   a⌐tara⌐sikute
is broad <u>or</u> wide <u>or</u> spacious   hi⌐ro⌐i /-ku/
   <u>or</u> big in area
is new and large   a⌐tara⌐sikute hi⌐ro⌐i
Japanese-style room <u>or</u>   za⌐siki⌐ <u>or</u> ozasiki †
   parlor
a Japanese-style room which   a⌐tara⌐sikute hi⌐ro⌐i zasiki
   is new and large
6. We have a new (and) large Japa-   A⌐tara⌐sikute hi⌐ro⌐i o⌐zasiki ḡa
nese-style room (but)...   gozaima⌐su ḡa⌐

Smith

being a Japanese-style room   nihoṅma de
7. A Japanese-style room will be   Ni⌐hoṅma de ke⌐kkoo desu.
fine.

(b)

Smith

with bath	huroba-tuki
room with bath	hu⌐roba-tuki no heya⌐

8. Do you have a room with bath?   Hu⌐roba-tuki no heya⌐ (ḡa) a⌐rima⌐su ka˩

Clerk

Western-style room	yooma
be free for use or unoccupied	aite (i)ru

9. We have Western-style rooms with bath, but tonight they're taken (lit. aren't free) (but) . . .   Huroba-tuki no yo⌐oma wa gozaima⌐su ḡa, ko⌐ṅbaṅ wa ⌐aite o⌐rimase⌐ṅ ḡa˩

quiet	si⌐zuka /na/
being quiet	si⌐zuka de
is quiet and large	si⌐zuka de hi⌐ro⌐i
a Japanese-style room that is quiet and large	si⌐zuka de hi⌐ro⌐i zasiki
one room	hi⌐to⌐-ma

10. There's one large, quiet Japanese-style room free (but) . . .   Si⌐zuka de hi⌐ro⌐i o⌐zasiki ḡa hito⌐-ma a⌐ite orima⌐su ḡa˩

Smith

being that	sore de

11. That will be fine.   So⌐re de ke⌐kkoo desu.

(c)

(Smith and Tanaka are stopping at a Japanese inn.)

Room-girl

bath	o⌐hu⌐ro +
go into the bath or take a bath	o⌐hu⌐ro ni ⌐ha⌐iru

12. Wouldn't you like to take a bath?   O⌐hu⌐ro ni o⌐hairi ni narimase⌐ṅ ka˩

Smith

be too hot	a⌐tusuḡi⌐ru /-ru/

13. I'd like to (go in) but it's too hot.   Ha⌐irita⌐i ṅ desu ḡa, a⌐tusuḡima⌐su yo.

Room-girl

usual or regular or ordinary	hutuu

14. It's [the] usual [temperature], isn't it?   Hutuu de gozaimasyoo?

Tanaka

is lukewarm	nu⌐ru⌐i /-ku/

15. Americans prefer a lukewarm bath (lit. alternative) (so . . .)   A⌐merika⌐ziṅ wa nu⌐ru⌐i hoo ḡa o⌐suki da⌐ kara˩

Room-girl

16. Well then, I'll make it lukewarm (so. . .)   Zya⌐a, nu⌐ruku i┗tasima┛su kara＿

. . .

Room-girl

17. Shall I serve dinner?[1] (Lit. Shall I make it dining?)   O⌐syokuzi ni itasimasyo⌐o ka.

Tanaka

Japanese eating tray   ozeñ +
18. Yes. Bring out the trays.   E⌐e. O⌐zeñ (o) da⌐site.

Room-girl

Japanese-style food   wasyoku
nothing but Japanese-style food   wasyoku sika /+ negative/
19. We have nothing but Japanese-style food (but) . . .   Wa⌐syoku sika gozaimase⌐ñ ḡa＿

Smith

being Japanese-style food   wasyoku de
20. Japanese-style food will be fine.   Wa⌐syoku de ke⌐kkoo desu.

drinking water   no⌐mi⌐mizu
21. Please bring some drinking water, too.   No⌐mi⌐mizu mo mo┗tte┛ kite kudasai.

. . .

Tanaka

is severe   hi⌐do⌐i /-ku/
wind   kaze
22. What an awful wind!   *Hi⌐do⌐i ka⌐ze de⌐su ⌐ne⌐e.

(to the room-girl)

brazier   hi⌐bati
23. Say, it's grown cold so bring a hibati, will you?   Tyo⌐tto; sa⌐muku ┗na┛tta kara, hi⌐bati (o) mo┗tte┛ kite ne?

(d)

Mr. Tanaka

is sleepy   nemui /-ku/
24. Oh, I'm sleepy!   A⌐a nemui.

Mr. Yamamoto

25. Me too.   Boku mo.

---

[1] Or breakfast or lunch, depending on the time of day.

(to room-girl)

go to bed <u>or</u> go to sleep	neru /-ru/
Japanese quilt	hutoñ
spread out (on the floor, ground, table, etc.)	siku /-u/

26. We're going to go to bed soon now (already) so spread out the quilts.

Mo⌐o ne⌐ru⌐ kara, hutoñ (o) siite.

bug <u>or</u> insect	musi
is frequent <u>or</u> is much <u>or</u> are many	o⌐o⌐i /-ku/
mosquito net	kaya

27. And we want a mosquito net too, because there are a lot of bugs.

Sore kara; mu⌐si (ḡa) oo⌐i kara, ka⌐ya mo tano⌐mu yo.

Room-girl

get up <u>or</u> wake up	o⌐ki⌐ru /-ru/

28. Certainly. What time will you get up?

Ha⌐i. Na⌐ñ-zi ni o⌐oki ni narima⌐su ka⌐

Mr. Yamamoto (to room-girl)

wake [someone] up	o⌐ko⌐su /-u/

29. Would you wake us at 7 o'clock? [That's] because we're taking an 8:30 train.

Si⌐ti⌐-zi ni o⌐ko⌐site ku⌐rena⌐i ka⌐ Ha⌐ti-zi-ha⌐ñ no ki⌐sya⌐ ni no⌐ru⌐ kara.

Mr. Tanaka (to room-girl)

shoes	ku⌐tu⌐
shine <u>or</u> polish	miḡaku /-u/
man's suit	sebiro
pressing iron <u>or</u> pressing	airoñ
apply <u>or</u> suspend <u>or</u> hang	ka⌐ke⌐ru /-ru/
press with an iron	a⌐iroñ o kake⌐ru
press a suit (lit. apply an iron to a suit)	sebiro ni a⌐iroñ o kake⌐ru

30. Say! I'd like to have these shoes shined and this suit pressed (but)...

Ano ne! Ko⌐no kutu⌐ (o) miḡaite, kono sebiro ni a⌐iroñ (o) ka⌐kete mo⌐raita⌐i ñ da kedo—

Room-girl

consent to <u>or</u> agree to	syooti-suru

31. Certainly.

Syo⌐oti-itasima⌐sita.

. . .

Mr. Tanaka

is noisy	ya⌐kamasi⌐i /-ku/

32. What a racket in the next room! (Lit. The next room is noisy, isn't it!)

To⌐nari no heya⌐ (wa) ya⌐kamasi⌐i ⌐ne⌐e.

Mr. Yamamoto

33. Yeah. They said this (place)   N̄. Koko (wa) ⌐si⌐zuka na he⌐ya⌐
     was a quiet room (but)...   da tte (i)┗tta⌐ kedo—

(e)

Smith

     rather good inn or inn on   i⌐i hoo no ryōkañ
        the good side
     one night   hi⌐to⌐-bañ
34. How much is the usual rather   Hutuu no ⌐i⌐i hoo no ryōkañ (wa)
     good inn, for one night?   hi⌐to⌐-bañ i⌐kura-ḡu⌐rai desyoo ka.

Tanaka

35. Hmm. I wonder if it wouldn't   Sa⌐a. Ni⌐señ-eñ-ḡu⌐rai kara zya
     be from about ¥2000 [up].   ┗na⌐i desyoo ka ┗ne⌐e.

Smith

     with meals   syokuzi-tuki
36. Is that with meals?   Sore (wa) syo⌐kuzi-tuki de⌐su ka⌐

Tanaka

     with two meals   nisyoku-tuki
37. It's with two meals.   Ni⌐syoku-tuki de⌐su yo⌐

Smith

     meaning   i⌐mi
     the expression (lit. one)   ni⌐syoku-tuki⌐ tte i┗u⌐ no
        said quote with two meals
     what meaning? (lit. mean-   do⌐o iu ┗i⌐mi
        ing said how?)
38. With two meals? What does   Nisyokutuki? Ni⌐syoku-tuki⌐ tte i┗u⌐
     'with two meals' mean?   no (wa) ⌐do⌐o iu ┗i⌐mi desu ka⌐

Tanaka

     be included   ha⌐itte (i)ru
     noon or daytime   hi⌐ru⌐
     separate   betu /na or no/
39. It means that (lit. it is the mean-   A⌐sa to ba⌐ñ no syokuzi (ḡa) ha⌐itte
     ing said quote) the morning and   (i)te, hiru no syokuzi wa be⌐tu da⌐
     evening meals are included and   tte iu ┗i⌐mi desu yo..
     the noon meal is separate.

NOTES ON THE BASIC DIALOGUES

1. Remember that -ma⌐se imperatives are used primarily by women and by
    service personnel.

3. Note also yakusoku-suru 'make a promise or appointment or engagement.'

4. 'but—is it possible to get a room anyway?'

6. 'but—would that be all right?'
The opposite of hi⌐ro¬i is se⌐ma¬i /-ku/ 'is narrow or cramped or small in area.'
Za⌐siki¬ refers to a Japanese-style room in an inn, and a Japanese-style parlor in a private home.

8. The -tuki of huroba-tuki is derived from tu⌐ku 'become attached.' Compare also syokuzi-tuki (Sentence 36) and nisyoku-tuki (Sentence 37).

9. 'but—would another kind of room be all right?'

10. 'but—would that be all right?'

12. The hot Japanese bath is an attraction of Japanese-style inns. A bath which the average American considers hot, a Japanese usually considers to be lukewarm (nu⌐ru¬i).
O⌐hu¬ro is used commonly by both men and women. The less polite equivalent is hu⌐ro¬.

15. 'so—the bath here seems too hot for him.'
With the polite osuki ⸸ alternant, this sentence would not be said by an American.

16. 'so—it will be all right then.'

18. The less polite zeñ is rarely used in conversation.

19. 'but—is that all right?'
With wasyoku compare yoosyoku 'Western-style food.'

21. When there is any doubt about sanitary conditions and the purity of the no⌐mi¬mizu, ask for yu⌐za¬masi 'water which has been boiled.'

26. Hutoñ refers to the large Japanese sleeping quilts which are spread out on the tatami each night and taken up each morning.

27. The opposite of o⌐o¬i is su⌐kuna¬i /-ku/ 'is rare or is scarce or are few.'
O⌐o¬i and su⌐kuna¬i do NOT precede the word they describe: thus, ya⌐ma¬ ḡa o⌐o¬i 'there are many mountains' (i.e. 'the mountains are many'), which is similar in meaning, though not in pattern, to ya⌐ma¬ ḡa ta⌐kusañ a¬ru. Note the following common patterns: X ḡa [or no] o⌐o¬i Y 'a Y with lots of X' (example: ya⌐ma¬ ḡa [or no] o⌐o¬i tokoro 'a place with lots of mountains' [lit. 'a mountains-are-many place']) and X ḡa [or no] su⌐kunai Y 'a Y with few or little X' (example: ya⌐ma¬ ḡa [or no] su⌐kuna¬i tokoro 'a place with few mountains' [lit. 'a mountains-are-few place']).

29. O⌐ko¬su is the transitive partner of intransitive o⌐ki¬ru (Sentence 28).

30. 'but—can it be done?'
Ka⌐kete mo⌐raita⌐i ñ da kedo is the informal equivalent of ka⌐kete mo⌐raita⌐i ñ desu keredo.

31. Syo⌐oti-(ita)sima¬sita is similar in meaning and usage to ka⌐sikomarima¬sita.

33. 'but—it isn't, is it!'

39. Hi⌐ru¬ has two meanings: it means 'daytime,' the opposite of yo⌐ru 'night-time'; it also means 'twelve o'clock noon.' With the latter meaning, it has a commonly occurring polite alternant o⌐hi¬ru+.

Betu is one of a limited group of nominals which may be followed by na or no when describing a following nominal.

GRAMMATICAL NOTES

1. Adjectivals: Gerund

The adverbial of adjectivals is made by dropping the -i of the citation form and adding -ku (cf. Lesson 2, Grammatical Note 1). If the citation form is unaccented, the adverbial is also unaccented. If the citation form is accented, the adverbial is accented. (With -nai negatives and -tai 'want to' words, the accent remains on the same syllable; with most other adjectivals, the accent usually moves one syllable closer to the beginning of the word—for example, wa⌐kara¬nai > wa⌐kara¬naku; no⌐mita¬i > no⌐mita¬ku; si⌐ro¬i > si⌐ro-ku. [1])

The gerund of adjectivals is made by adding -te to the adverbial. It is always accented: if the adverbial is accented, the derived gerund is accented on the same syllable; if the adverbial is unaccented, the derived gerund is regularly accented on the syllable immediately preceding the -kute ending.

Examples:

Citation Form (Informal Non-past)	Adverbial	Gerund
abunai 'is dangerous'	abunaku	a⌐buna¬kute
ti⌐isa¬i 'is small'	ti¬isaku	ti¬isakute
na⌐i 'isn't in a place,' 'haven't'	na¬ku	na¬kute
ta⌐be¬nai 'doesn't eat'	ta⌐be¬naku	ta⌐be¬nakute
ta⌐beta¬i 'want to eat'	ta⌐beta¬ku	ta⌐beta¬kute
oisii 'is delicious'	oisiku	o⌐isi¬kute
i¬i or yo⌐i 'is good'	yo¬ku	yo¬kute
nemui 'is sleepy'	nemuku	ne⌐mu¬kute
sa⌐mu¬i 'is cold'	sa¬muku	sa¬mukute
omoi 'is heavy'	omoku	o⌐mo¬kute
si⌐ro¬i 'is white'	si¬roku	si¬rokute

Like verbal and copula gerunds, an adjectival gerund occurs within a sentence, ending a sequence which is coordinate with what follows (cf. Lesson 7, Grammatical Note 5, and Lesson 10, Grammatical Note 3).

Examples:

Two sentences (informal style): Hi⌐ro¬i. 'It's large.'
                                                    Su⌐zusi¬i. 'It's cool.'
One sentence (informal style): Hi⌐rokute su⌐zusi¬i. 'It's large and it's cool.'

---

[1] Many adjectivals in this last group now occur with an alternate accent which follows the pattern of the first two groups. Thus: si¬roku ~ si⌐ro¬ku.

Two sentences (formal style): Hi⌐ro¬i desu. 'It's large.'
                               Su⌐zusi¬i desu. 'It's cool.'
One sentence (formal style): Hi⌐rokute su⌐zusi¬i desu. 'It's large and it's cool.'

Remember that words like si⌐zuka 'quiet,' ki¬ree 'pretty,' ge⌐nki 'healthy,' byooki 'sick,' etc., are nominals, and the -kute ending occurs only at the end of adjectivals. When the first of a pair of sentences ends in a nominal + √da, the first sequence of the corresponding compound sentence ends in nominal + de (the copula gerund) as described in Lesson 10, Grammatical Noté 3.

Compare: Two sentences: Si¬zuka desu. 'It's quiet.' (nominal + desu)
                          Su⌐zusi¬i desu. 'It's cool.'
          One sentence: Si¬zuka de su⌐zusi¬i desu. 'It's quiet and it's cool.'
and: Two sentences: Ya⌐kamasi¬i desu. 'It's noisy.' (adjectival + desu)
                          A⌐tu¬i desu. 'It's hot.'
          One sentence: Ya⌐kama¬sikute a⌐tu¬i desu. 'It's noisy and it's hot.'

A sentence modifier may include an adjectival gerund. In Basic Sentence 6 of this lesson, the nominal ozasiki 'room' is described by the single compound sentence a⌐tara¬sikute hi⌐ro¬i 'it is new and it is large,' i.e. 'a room that is new and large,' 'a new and large room.' With this, compare the sequence a⌐tarasi¬i hi⌐ro¬i ozasiki 'a new, large room,' in which ozasiki is described by two sentences—a⌐tarasi¬i 'it is new' and hi⌐ro¬i 'it is large.' Both kinds of sequence occur commonly.

Additional examples:

Ko⌐no koohi¬i wa o⌐isi¬kute ya⌐su¬i desu. 'This coffee is good and it's cheap.'

Otaku no oniwa wa ⌐hi¬rokute ⌐ki¬ree desu ⌐ne¬e. 'Your garden is large and beautiful, isn't it.'

Uti ḡa ⌐se¬makute, niwa ḡa hi⌐ro¬i. 'The house is small and the garden is big.'

I⌐ti-ḡatu¬ ḡa a⌐ttaka¬kute, ni-⌐ḡatu¬ ḡa ⌐sa¬mukatta. 'January was warm and February was cold.'

A¬tukute ⌐ko¬i otya ḡa su⌐ki⌐ desu. 'I like tea that's hot and strong.'

O¬okikute o⌐moi ni¬motu ḡa arimasu. 'I have some luggage that is big and heavy.'

2. Compound Verbals

A COMPOUND VERBAL consists of a verbal stem (the -ma¬su form minus -ma¬su) or adjectival stem (the citation form minus final -i) or a nominal, compounded with a following verbal. Compounds ending in su⌐ḡi¬ru 'exceed' (like a⌐tusuḡi¬ru 'be too hot') indicate excessive degree. For example:

ta¬be (stem of ta⌐be¬ru 'eat') + su⌐ḡi¬ru = ta⌐besuḡi¬ru 'overeat'
no¬mi (stem of no¬mu 'drink') + su⌐ḡi¬ru = no⌐misuḡi¬ru 'drink too much'
tukai (stem of tukau 'use') + su⌐ḡi¬ru = tu⌐kaisuḡi¬ru 'overuse'
ta¬ka (stem of ta⌐ka¬i 'is expensive') + su⌐ḡi¬ru = ta⌐kasuḡi¬ru 'be too expensive'

ooki (stem of ookii 'is big') + sugiru = ookisugiru 'be too big'
oo (stem of ooi 'is much' or 'are many') + sugiru = oosugiru 'be too much' or 'be too many'
geñki 'peppy' + sugiru = geñkisugiru 'be too peppy'

Note also:

nori (stem of noru 'ride') + kaeru[1] 'change [something]' = norikaeru 'change vehicles'
tori (stem of toru 'take') + kaeru[1] 'change [something]' = torikaeru 'exchange'

Included among compound verbals is the large group of words consisting of a nominal + suru 'make' or 'do': for example, kekkoñ 'marriage' + suru = kekkoñ-suru[2] 'marry'; beñkyoo 'study' [noun] + suru = beñkyoo-suru 'study' [verb].

Actually, formal verbals are compounds, consisting of a verbal stem + the verbal -masu (which differs from other verbals in that it never occurs independently, and has no meaning other than formality). Thus:

tabe (stem of taberu 'eat') + -masu (formality) = tabemasu 'eat (formal word)'

3. Particle sika 'only,' 'nothing but'

Particle sika following a nominal or a nominal + particle[3] occurs with negative (never affirmative) inflected expressions and is equivalent to English 'only + an affirmative,' 'nothing but + an affirmative,' or 'except + a negative.'

Examples:

a. (1) Sukosi arimasu. 'There's a little.'
(2) Sukosi sika arimaseñ. 'There's only a little.'

b. (1) Tanaka-sañ ḡa kimasita. 'Mr. Tanaka came.'
(2) Tanaka-sañ sika kimaseñ desita. 'No one came but Mr. Tanaka.'

c. (1) Teñpura o tabemasita. 'I ate tempura.'
(2) Teñpura sika tabemaseñ desita. 'I didn't eat anything but tempura.'

d. (1) Nihoñ ni arimasu. 'It's in Japan.'
(2) Nihoñ ni sika arimaseñ. 'It's only in Japan.'

---

1 Kaeru /-ru/ 'change [something],' not to be confused with kaeru /-u/ 'return.'

2 The hyphen in -suru compounds is an arbitrary convention which has no phonetic value.

3 The particle is not wa, ḡa, or o.

4. Ni⌐hoñma de ke⌐kkoo desu

A nominal (by itself or with following particles) + de (the gerund of da)+ √i⌐i or √yorosii or ke⌐kkoo or √ka⌐mawa⌐nai means 'being [the nominal], it's all right,' 'it will be fine if it's [the nominal],' '[the nominal] is agreeable (on this occasion) to me.' So⌐no mama⌐ de ⌐i⌐i (Lesson 16) is another example of this pattern.

Do not confuse X de ⌐i⌐i and X wa (or ḡa) ⌐i⌐i. Compare:

Te⌐ekoku-ho⌐teru wa ⌐i⌐i desu. 'The Imperial Hotel is good or nice or pleasant.'
Te⌐ekoku-ho⌐teru de ⌐i⌐i desu. 'The Imperial Hotel will be fine.' (used, for example, when deciding on a place to stay, or meet, or eat, etc.)

Ko⌐re wa i⌐i desu. 'This is good or nice or fine.'
Ko⌐re de i⌐i desu. 'If it's this, it will be agreeable.' or 'With this, I've had enough.' or 'This will be all right (on this occasion or in these circumstances).'

5. Informal Requests Ending in ku⌐rena⌐i ka

Requests ending in ku⌐dasaimase⌐ñ ka (Lesson 7, Grammatical Note 4) are polite and formal. An informal equivalent, ending in ku⌐dasara⌐nai?, occurs predominantly in women's speech. The plain equivalent of ku⌐dasaimase⌐ñ ka is ku⌐remase⌐ñ ka (Lesson 17, Grammatical Note 1), and two of its informal equivalents are ku⌐rena⌐i ka, which occurs in men's speech, and kurenai?, which occurs in both men's and women's speech. For example, all the following mean 'would you do it for me?' (lit. 'won't you give me doing?'):

	Formal	Informal
Polite	Si⌐te kudasaimase⌐ñ ka‿(MW)	Si⌐te kudasara⌐nai? (W)[1]
Plain	Si⌐te kuremase⌐ñ ka‿(MW)	Si⌐te kurena⌐i ka‿(M)
		Site kurenai? (MW)

Ku⌐rena⌐i ka is the first example of question particle ka ending an informal sentence. All informal questions introduced previously have ended in question intonation without ka: for example, Iku? 'Are you going?' I⌐i? 'Is it all right?' Kore? 'This?'

Informal questions ending with ka occur predominantly in men's speech, and except for a few combinations (ku⌐rena⌐i ka is one of them) are typical of abrupt speech.

Before ka, da is regularly lost. One informal equivalent of So⌐o desu ka is So⌐o ka.

---

[1] Predominantly.

6. Counters: -ma 'room,' -bañ 'night'

-Ma combines with numerals of Series II—but only rarely with numerals higher than seven—to count the number of room units. The numbers from one to seven are:

hi⌐to⌐-ma	'1 room'
hu⌐ta-ma⌐	'2 rooms'
mi⌐-ma	'3 rooms'
yo⌐-ma	'4 rooms'
i⌐tu⌐-ma	'5 rooms'
mu⌐-ma	'6 rooms'
na⌐na⌐-ma	'7 rooms'
i⌐ku-ma [1]	'how many rooms?'

The counter -bañ combines with numerals of Series II to count nights. Hi⌐to⌐-bañ '1 night' and huta-bañ '2 nights' occur commonly, and mi⌐-bañ '3 nights,' yo⌐-bañ '4 nights,' and i⌐tu⌐-bañ '5 nights' are heard occasionally, but the occurrence of this counter with higher numbers is rare. The corresponding question word is i⌐ku-bañ 'how many nights?'

DRILLS

A. Substitution Drill

1.	A Japanese-style room will be fine.	Ni⌐hoñma de ke⌐kkoo desu. [2]
2.	A Western-style room will be fine.	Yo⌐oma de ke⌐kkoo desu.
3.	Chopsticks will be fine.	Ha⌐si de ⌐ke⌐kkoo desu.
4.	The same will be fine.	O⌐nazi de ke⌐kkoo desu.
5.	One-way will be fine.	Ka⌐tamiti de ke⌐kkoo desu.
6.	An ordinary inn will be fine.	Hu⌐tuu no ryokañ de ke⌐kkoo desu.
7.	A small television will be fine.	Ti⌐isa⌐i ⌐te⌐rebi de ⌐ke⌐kkoo desu.
8.	Lukewarm, as it is, will be fine.	Nu⌐ru⌐i ma⌐ma⌐ de ⌐ke⌐kkoo desu.
9.	A Japanese one will be fine.	Ni⌐hoñ no⌐ de ⌐ke⌐kkoo desu.
10.	As far as the station will be fine.	E⌐ki made de ⌐ke⌐kkoo desu.

---

[1] Iku- regularly compounds with counters which combine with Series II numerals, to form the corresponding question word. (Compare i⌐ku-tu 'how many units?') Some Japanese also use iku- with other counters: for example, i⌐ku-niñ 'how many people?'

[2] Practice this drill with i⌐i desu and yo⌐rosi⌐i desu as well as ke⌐kkoo desu.

B. Substitution Drill

1. Are your children going to
    go to bed already?

    Okosañ (wa) ⌐mo⌐o ne⌐ma⌐su ka⌐

2. Are your children in bed
    (or asleep) already?

    Okosañ (wa) ⌐mo⌐o ne⌐te (i)ma⌐su
    ka⌐

3. Are your children up (or
    awake) already?

    Okosañ (wa) ⌐mo⌐o ⌐o⌐kite (i)masu
    ka⌐

4. Are your children going to
    get up already?

    Okosañ (wa) ⌐mo⌐o o⌐kima⌐su ka⌐

5. Are your children going to
    take a bath already?

    Okosañ (wa) ⌐mo⌐o o⌐hu⌐ro ni
    ha⌐irima⌐su ka⌐

6. Are your children taking a
    bath already?

    Okosañ (wa) ⌐mo⌐o o⌐hu⌐ro ni
    ⌐ha⌐itte (i)masu ka⌐

7. Are your children going to
    eat already?

    Okosañ (wa) ⌐mo⌐o ta⌐bema⌐su ka⌐

8. Are your children eating
    already?

    Okosañ (wa) ⌐mo⌐o ⌐ta⌐bete (i)masu
    ka⌐

C. Substitution Drill

1. It was a place with lots of
    bugs.

    Musi no [1] o⌐o⌐i to⌐koro⌐ desita
    yo⌐

2. It was a house with lots of
    windows.

    Ma⌐do no o⌐o⌐i u⌐ti de⌐sita yo⌐

3. It was a street with lots of
    shops.

    Mise no o⌐o⌐i mi⌐ti de⌐sita yo⌐

4. It was a school with lots of
    teachers.

    Se⌐ñse⌐e no o⌐o⌐i ga⌐kkoo de⌐sita
    yo⌐

5. It was an inn with lots of
    guests.

    Kyaku no o⌐o⌐i ryo⌐kañ de⌐sita
    yo⌐

6. It was an inn with few
    guests.

    Kyaku no su⌐kuna⌐i ryo⌐kañ de⌐-
    sita yo⌐

7. It was a station with few
    porters.

    Akaboo no su⌐kuna⌐i ⌐e⌐ki desita
    yo⌐

8. It was a room with few
    lights.

    De⌐ñki no su⌐kuna⌐i he⌐ya⌐ desita
    yo⌐

9. It was a spring with little
    rain.

    A⌐me no su⌐kuna⌐i ⌐ha⌐ru desita
    yo⌐

10. It was a hotel with few Jap-
    anese rooms.

    Zasiki no su⌐kuna⌐i ⌐ho⌐teru de-
    sita yo⌐

D. Substitution Drill

1. There's nothing but a West-
    ern-style room. Is that all
    right?

    Yo⌐oma sika arimase⌐ñ ḡa, ka⌐ma-
    imase⌐ñ ka⌐

---

[1] Particle no in all the sentences of this exercise may be replaced by ḡa.
Practice both alternants.

2. There's nothing but a Japanese-style room. Is that all right?

Ni⌐honˉma sika arimase⌐nˉ ḡa, ka-⌐maimase⌐nˉ ka↲

3. There's nothing but Western-style food. Is that all right?

Yo⌐osyoku sika arimase⌐nˉ ḡa, ka-⌐maimase⌐nˉ ka↲

4. There's nothing but cold water. Is that all right?

Mi⌐zu sika arimase⌐nˉ ḡa, ka⌐maimase⌐nˉ ka↲

5. There's nothing but a small room. Is that all right?

Se⌐ma⌐i he⌐ya⌐ sika a⌐rimase⌐nˉ ḡa, ka⌐maimase⌐nˉ ka↲

6. There's nothing but an old magazine. Is that all right?

Hu⌐ru⌐i za⌐ssi sika arimase⌐nˉ ḡa, ka⌐maimase⌐nˉ ka↲

7. There's nothing but a small hibachi. Is that all right?

Ti⌐isa⌐i ⌐hi⌐bati sika a⌐rimase⌐nˉ ḡa, ka⌐maimase⌐nˉ ka↲

8. There's nothing but a morning train. Is that all right?

A⌐sa no ki⌐sya⌐ sika a⌐rimase⌐nˉ ḡa, ka⌐maimase⌐nˉ ka↲

9. There's nothing but a ticket for next week. Is that all right?

Ra⌐isyuu no kippu sika arimase⌐nˉ ḡa, ka⌐maimase⌐nˉ ka↲

10. There's nothing but one from yesterday. Is that all right?

Ki⌐noo no⌐ sika a⌐rimase⌐nˉ ḡa, ka⌐maimase⌐nˉ ka↲

E. Substitution Drill

1. [He] said that this was a quiet room but . . . [1]

Koko (wa) ⌐si⌐zuka na he⌐ya⌐ da tte (i)⌐tta⌐ kedo‿

2. [He] said that the bath was lukewarm but . . .

O⌐hu⌐ro ḡa nu⌐ru⌐i tte (i)⌐tta⌐ kedo‿

3. [He] said that he would get up early this norning but . . .

Ke⌐sa ⌐ha⌐yaku o⌐ki⌐ru tte (i)⌐tta⌐ kedo‿

4. [He] said that there was plenty of gasoline left but . . .

Gasoriñ ḡa zyu⌐ubu⌐nˉ no⌐ko⌐tte (i)ru tte (i)⌐tta⌐ kedo‿

5. [He] said there were few bugs but . . .

Mu⌐si ḡa sukuna⌐i tte (i)⌐tta⌐ kedo‿

6. [He] said that he wouldn't go through Osaka but . . .

O⌐osaka (o) toora⌐nai tte (i)⌐tta⌐ kedo‿

7. [He] said that the winters here were severely cold but . . .

Ko⌐ko no huyu⌐ (wa) ⌐hi⌐doku sa-⌐mu⌐i tte (i)⌐tta⌐ kedo‿

8. [He] said that this was most important but . . .

Ko⌐re ḡa itibañ taisetu da⌐ tte (i)⌐tta⌐ kedo‿

9. [He] said that this room was large and cool but . . .

Ko⌐no heya⌐ (wa) ⌐hi⌐rokute su-⌐zusi⌐i tte (i)⌐tta⌐ kedo‿

10. [He] said that he would shine these shoes for me but . . .

Ko⌐no kutu⌐ (o) mi⌐ḡaite kureru⌐ tte (i)⌐tta⌐ kedo‿

---

[1] 'but—it isn't true, is it,' 'but—I'm not sure,' etc.

F. Substitution Drill

(Insert the substitution item in the model sentence as a modifier of
he⌐ya⌐, with or without no or na as required.)

1. It's a large room.   Hi⌐ro⌐i he⌐ya⌐ desu yo⌐
2. It's a quiet room.   Si⌐zuka na he⌐ya⌐ desu yo⌐
3. It's the next room.   To⌐nari no heya⌐ desu yo⌐
4. It's a ¥2000 room.   Ni⌐sen-en no heya⌐ desu yo⌐
5. It's a room with bath.   Hu⌐roba-tuki no heya⌐ desu yo⌐
6. It's a small room.   Se⌐ma⌐i he⌐ya⌐ desu yo⌐
7. It's a strange room.   He⌐n na he⌐ya⌐ desu yo⌐
8. It's a fine room.   Ri⌐ppa na heya⌐ desu yo⌐
9. It's a noisy room.   Ya⌐kamasi⌐i he⌐ya⌐ desu yo⌐
10. It's my room.   Wa⌐takusi no heya⌐ desu yo⌐

G. Substitution Drill

(Insert the substitution item in the model sentence in whatever form
or with whatever particle required.)

1. Shall I serve (lit. make [it])   Syo⌐kuzi ni simasyo⌐o ka.
    dinner?
2. Shall I make [it] lukewarm?   Nu⌐ruku si⌐masyo⌐o ka.
    /nu⌐ru⌐i/
3. Shall I make [it] the oppo-   Ha⌐ntai ni simasyo⌐o ka.
    site? /hantai/
4. Shall I separate [them]?   Be⌐tu ni simasyo⌐o ka.
    /betu/
5. Shall I put [them] together?   I⌐ssyo ni simasyo⌐o ka.
    /issyo/
6. Shall I make [it] hot?   A⌐tuku si⌐masyo⌐o ka.
    /a⌐tu⌐i/
7. Shall I fill [it]? /ippai/   I⌐ppai ni simasyo⌐o ka.
8. Shall I make [it] wide?   Hi⌐roku si⌐masyo⌐o ka.
    /hi⌐ro⌐i/
9. Shall I chill [it]? /tumetai/   Tu⌐metaku simasyo⌐o ka.
10. Shall I empty [it]? /ka⌐ra⌐/   Ka⌐ra⌐ ni si⌐masyo⌐o ka.

H. Substitution Drill (based on Grammatical Note 2)

1. I'd like to take a bath but   O⌐hu⌐ro ni ha⌐rita⌐i n desu ḡa,
    it's too hot.   a⌐tusuḡima⌐su yo.
2. I'd like to buy [it] but it's   Ka⌐ita⌐i n desu ḡa, ta⌐kasuḡima⌐su
    too expensive. /kau, ta-   yo.
    ⌐ka⌐i/
3. I'd like to go but it's too   I⌐kita⌐i n desu ḡa, to⌐osuḡima⌐su
    far. /iku, tooi/   yo.
4. I'd like to take [it] but it's   Mo⌐tte ikita⌐i n desu ḡa, o⌐mosu-
    too heavy. /motte iku,   ḡima⌐su yo.
    omoi/

5. I'd like to put [it] in but it's too big. /ireru, o˺oki˺i/

I˹reta˺i ñ desu ḡa, o˹okisuḡima˺su yo.

6. I'd like to read [it] but it's too difficult. /yo˺mu, mu-zukasii/

Yo˹mita˺i ñ desu ḡa, mu˹zukasisu-ḡima˺su yo.

7. I'd like to eat [it] but it's too spicy. /ta˹be˺ru, ka˹ra˺i/

Ta˹beta˺i ñ desu ḡa, ka˹rasuḡima˺su yo.

8. I'd like to drink [it] but it's too strong. /no˺mu, ko˺i/

No˹mita˺i ñ desu ḡa, ko˹suḡima˺su yo.

I. Grammar Drill (based on Grammatical Note 3)

Tutor: Ni˹hoñma ḡa arima˺su. 'There are Japanese-style rooms.'
Student: Ni˹hoñma sika arimase˺ñ. 'There are only Japanese-style rooms.'

1. A˹merika˺ziñ no to˞modati (ḡa) miema˞sita.

A˹merika˺ziñ no to˞modati sika miemase˞ñ desita.

2. A˹no hasi˺ (o) wa˞tarima˞-sita.

A˹no hasi˺ sika wa˞tarimase˞ñ de-sita.

3. Ho˺ñya e i˞kima˞sita.

Ho˺ñya e sika i˞kimase˞ñ desita.

4. Hi˹to˺-ma a˞ite (i)ma˞su yo⌐

Hi˹to˺-ma sika a˞ite (i)mase˞ñ yo⌐

5. Watakusi no ku˹ro˺i ku˞tu˞ (o) mi˞ḡakima˞sita.

Watakusi no ku˹ro˺i ku˞tu˞ sika mi˞ḡakimase˞ñ desita.

6. Ha˹ha ni i˞ima˞sita ḡa⌐

Ha˹ha ni sika i˞imase˞ñ desita ḡa⌐

7. A˹no siḡoto (o) nokosima˺-sita.

A˹no siḡoto sika nokosimase˺ñ de-sita.

8. Hi˹to˺-bañ to˞marima˞sita.

Hi˹to˺-bañ sika to˞marimase˞ñ de-sita.

J. Grammar Drill (based on Grammatical Note 1)

Tutor: A˹tarasi˺i desu. Hi˹ro˺i desu. 'It's new. It's large.'
         (two sentences)
Student: A˹tara˺sikute hi˹ro˺i desu. 'It's new and large.' (one sen-tence)

1. Se˹ma˺i desyoo? A˹tu˺i de-syoo?

Se˺makute a˹tu˺i desyoo?

2. Mi˹ti ḡa sema˺i. Zi˹doosya ḡa oo˺i.

Mi˹ti ḡa se˺makute, zidoosya ḡa o˹o˺i.

3. Hu˹yu˺ ḡa sa˞mu˞i desu. Na˹tu˺ ḡa a˞tu˞i desu.

Hu˹yu˺ ḡa ˞sa˞mukute, na˹tu˺ ḡa a˞tu˞i desu.

4. A˹no ryokañ no heya˺ wa ˹si˺zuka desu. Ge˺ñkañ wa ya˹kamasi˺i desu.

A˹no ryokañ no heya˺ wa ˹si˺zuka de, ge˺ñkañ wa ya˹kamasi˺i desu.

5. Kono mizu wa tu˹meta˺i. O˹isi˺i.

Kono mizu wa tu˹meta˺kute o˹isi˺i.

6. Ha⌐ya¬i a⌐tarasi¬i ⌐de⌐ꜙsya   Ha⌐yakute a⌐tarasi¬i ⌐de⌐ꜙsya ni
   ni no⌐rima⌐ꜙsita.   no⌐rima⌐ꜙsita.
7. Si⌐zuka na ⌐ki¬ree na ryo-   Si⌐zuka de ⌐ki¬ree na ryo⌐kañ ni
   ⌐kañ ni tomarima⌐ꜙsita.   tomarima⌐ꜙsita.
8. No⌐tta kisya¬ wa o⌐so⌐katta.   No⌐tta kisya¬ wa o⌐so⌐kute ki⌐tana¬-
   Ki⌐tana¬katta.   katta.

K. Level Drill[1] (based on Grammatical Note 5)

        Tutor: Ka¬ite ku⌐dasaimase⌐ꜙ ka⌐
                                  O⌐kaki ni na¬tte ku⌐dasaimase⌐ꜙ ka⌐
        Male student: Ka¬ite ku⌐rena⌐i ka⌐
        Male or female student: Ka¬ite kurenai?

1. Hu⌐toñ (o) siite kudasaima-   Hu⌐toñ (o) siite kurena¬i ka⌐
   se⌐ꜙ ka⌐
   Hu⌐toñ (o) osiki ni na¬tte   Hutoñ (o) siite kurenai?
   ku⌐dasaimase⌐ꜙ ka⌐
2. A⌐sita no a¬sa ⌐ha¬yaku   A⌐sita no a¬sa ⌐ha¬yaku o⌐ko¬site
   o⌐ko¬site ku⌐dasaimase⌐ꜙ   ku⌐rena⌐i ka⌐
   ka⌐
   A⌐sita no a¬sa ⌐ha¬yaku o⌐ó-   A⌐sita no a¬sa ⌐ha¬yaku o⌐ko¬site
   kosi ni na¬tte ku⌐dasaima-   kurenai?
   se⌐ꜙ ka⌐[2]
3. Mo⌐ó suko⌐si ⌐ma¬tte ku⌐da-   Mo⌐ó suko⌐si ⌐ma¬tte ku⌐rena⌐i ka⌐
   saimase⌐ꜙ ka⌐
   Mo⌐ó suko⌐si o⌐mati ni na¬-   Mo⌐ó suko⌐si ⌐ma¬tte kurenai?
   tte ku⌐dasaimase⌐ꜙ ka⌐
4. Gi⌐ñza ma¬de no⌐sete kuda-   Gi⌐ñza ma¬de no⌐sete kurena¬i ka⌐
   saimase⌐ꜙ ka⌐
   Gi⌐ñza ma¬de o⌐nose ni na¬-   Gi⌐ñza ma¬de no̅sete kurenai?
   tte ku⌐dasaimase⌐ꜙ ka⌐[2]
5. Ga⌐kkoo no ma¬e de o⌐ro¬-   Ga⌐kkoo no ma¬e de o⌐ro¬site ku-
   site ku⌐dasaimase⌐ꜙ ka⌐   ⌐rena⌐i ka⌐
   Ga⌐kkoo no ma¬e de o⌐oro-   Ga⌐kkoo no ma¬e de o⌐ro¬site ku-
   si ni na¬tte ku⌐dasaimase⌐ꜙ   renai?
   ka⌐[2]
6. O⌐tonari no Itoo-sañ (o)   O⌐tonari no Itoo-sañ (o) yoñde
   yoñde kudasaimase⌐ꜙ ka⌐   kurena¬i ka⌐
   O⌐tonari no Itoo-sañ (o)   Otonari no Itoo-sañ (o) yoñde
   oyobi ni na¬tte ku⌐dasaima-   kurenai?
   se⌐ꜙ ka⌐
7. Mo⌐ó suko⌐si ⌐o¬oki na ⌐ko⌐e   Mo⌐ó suko⌐si ⌐o¬oki na ⌐ko⌐e de
   de i⌐tte kudasaimase⌐ꜙ ka⌐   i⌐tte kurena⌐i ka⌐
   Mo⌐ó suko⌐si ⌐o¬oki na ⌐ko⌐e   Mo⌐ó suko⌐si ⌐o¬oki na ⌐ko⌐e de
   de o⌐ssya⌐tte ku⌐dasaima-   itte kurenai?
   se⌐ꜙ ka⌐

---

[1] In each case the sentences on the right are the plain informal equivalents
of the sentences on the left.

[2] In this alternate, the person addressed is being asked to have a third person
(exalted †) do something. For example: (2) 'Would you be kind enough to have
him (†) get up early?'

8. Si⌐o⌐ to ko⌐syo⌐o (o) ⌐to⌐-
   tte ku⌐dasaimase⌐ñ ka⌐
   Si⌐o⌐ to ko⌐syo⌐o (o) o⌐tori
   ni na⌐tte ku⌐dasaimase⌐ñ
   ka⌐

Si⌐o⌐ to ko⌐syo⌐o (o) ⌐to⌐tte ku⌐re-
na⌐i ka⌐
Si⌐o⌐ to ko⌐syo⌐o (o) ⌐to⌐tte kurenai?

L. Expansion Drill

1. I don't need [it].
   I don't need a mosquito net.
   There aren't many (lit.
   they are few) so I don't
   need a mosquito net.
   There aren't many bugs so
   I don't need a mosquito
   net.

I⌐rimase⌐ñ yo⌐
Ka⌐ya wa irimase⌐ñ yo⌐
Su⌐kuna⌐i kara, ka⌐ya wa irima-
se⌐ñ yo⌐

Mu⌐si ḡa sukuna⌐i kara, ka⌐ya wa
irimase⌐n yo⌐

2. I didn't go in.
   It was dirty so I didn't go
   in.
   It was lukewarm and dirty
   so I didn't go in.
   The bath was lukewarm
   and dirty so I didn't go in.
   The bath at that inn was
   lukewarm and dirty so I
   didn't go in.

Ha⌐irimase⌐ñ desita.
Ki⌐tana⌐katta kara, ha⌐irimase⌐ñ
desita.
Nu⌐rukute ki⌐tana⌐katta kara, ha⌐i-
rimase⌐ñ desita.
O⌐hu⌐ro wa ⌐nu⌐rukute ki⌐tana⌐katta
kara, ha⌐irimase⌐ñ desita.
A⌐no ryokañ no ohu⌐ro (wa) ⌐nu⌐ru-
kute ki⌐tana⌐katta kara, ha⌐irima-
se⌐ñ desita.

3. He says there isn't.
   He says there's only one
   room.
   I don't know but he says
   there's only one room.
   I don't know what kind of
   room it is but he says
   there's only one (room).
   I don't know what kind of
   room the room that's
   available is, but he says
   there's only one (room).
   I don't know what kind of
   room the room that's
   available tonight is, but
   he says there's only one
   (room).

A⌐rimase⌐ñ te.
Hi⌐to⌐-ma sika a⌐rimase⌐ñ te.

Si⌐rana⌐i kedo, hi⌐to⌐-ma sika a⌐ri-
mase⌐ñ te.
Do⌐ñna he⌐ya⌐ ka si⌐rana⌐i kedo,
hi⌐to⌐-ma sika a⌐rimase⌐ñ te.

A⌐ite (i)ru heya⌐ (wa) ⌐do⌐ñna he-
⌐ya⌐ ka si⌐rana⌐i kedo, hi⌐to⌐-ma
sika a⌐rimase⌐ñ te.

Ko⌐ñbañ a⌐ite (i)ru heya⌐ (wa) ⌐do⌐-
ñna he⌐ya⌐ ka si⌐rana⌐i kedo, hi-
⌐to⌐-ma sika a⌐rimase⌐ñ te.

4. It's bad.
   I don't feel well.
   I don't feel at all well.
   This morning I don't feel
   at all well.
   I drank too much so this
   morning I don't feel at
   all well.

Wa⌐ru⌐i desu yo⌐
Gu⌐ai ḡa waru⌐i desu yo⌐
To⌐ttemo guai ḡa waru⌐i desu yo⌐
Ke⌐sa wa to⌐ttemo guai ḡa waru⌐i
desu yo⌐
No⌐misuḡita⌐[1] kara, ke⌐sa wa to-
⌐ttemo guai ḡa waru⌐i desu yo⌐

---

[1] Alternate accent: no⌐misu⌐ḡita.

I drank too much sake so this morning I don't feel at all well.	Sa⌐ke (o) nomisu̅gita¬ kara, ke⌐sa wa to⌐ttemo guai g̅a waru⌐i desu yo⌐
I drank too much sake last night so this morning I don't feel at all well.	Yuube sa⌐ke (o) nomisu̅gita¬ kara, ke⌐sa wa to⌐ttemo guai g̅a waru⌐i desu yo⌐

5. It's all right.

I⌐i desu.

That one will be all right.

So⌐re de i⌐i desu.

There isn't [one] so that one will be all right.

Na⌐i kara, so⌐re de i⌐i desu.

There's nothing but that hibachi so that will be all right.

So⌐no hi⌐bati sika ⌐na⌐i kara, so⌐re de i⌐i desu.

Tonight there's nothing but that hibachi so that will be all right.

Ko⌐ñbañ wa so⌐no hi⌐bati sika ⌐na⌐i kara, so⌐re de i⌐i desu.

I'd like to buy [one] but tonight there's nothing but that hibachi so that will be all right.

Ka⌐ita⌐i ñ desu g̅a; ko⌐ñbañ wa so⌐no hi⌐bati sika ⌐na⌐i kara, so⌐re de i⌐i desu.

I'd like to buy a big heater but tonight there's nothing but that hibachi so that will be all right.

O⌐oki⌐i su⌐to⌐obu (g̅a) ka⌐ita⌐i ñ desu g̅a; ko⌐ñbañ wa so⌐no ⌐hi⌐bati sika ⌐na⌐i kara, so⌐re de i⌐i desu.

I'd like to buy a big heater tomorrow, but tonight there's nothing but that hibachi so that will be all right.

Asita o⌐oki⌐i su⌐to⌐obu (g̅a) ka⌐ita⌐i ñ desu g̅a; ko⌐ñbañ wa so⌐no ⌐hi⌐bati sika ⌐na⌐i kara, so⌐re de i⌐i desu.

It's grown cold so I'd like to buy a big heater tomorrow, but tonight there's nothing but that hibachi so that will be all right.

Sa⌐muku ⌐na⌐tta kara, asita o⌐oki⌐i su⌐to⌐obu (g̅a) ka⌐ita⌐i ñ desu g̅a; ko⌐ñbañ wa so⌐no ⌐hi⌐bati sika ⌐na⌐i kara, so⌐re de i⌐i desu.

It's grown awfully cold so I'd like to buy a big heater tomorrow, but tonight there's nothing but that hibachi so that will be all right.

Hi⌐doku ⌐sa⌐muku ⌐na⌐tta kara, asita o⌐oki⌐i su⌐to⌐obu (g̅a) ka⌐ita⌐i ñ desu g̅a; ko⌐ñbañ wa so⌐no ⌐hi⌐bati sika ⌐na⌐i kara, so⌐re de i⌐i desu.

SUPPLEMENTARY CONVERSATION

Smith: Go⌐meñ-kudasa⌐i. Ko⌐obe no ⌐Su⌐misu desu g̅a, ko⌐ñbañ o⌐negai-sima⌐su.

Clerk: I⌐rassyaima⌐se. Su⌐misu-sama de irassyaimasu ne? O⌐mati-site orima⌐sita. Do⌐ozo o⌐ag̅ari-kudasaima⌐se. Yooma wa ti⌐isa⌐i no sika go⌐zaimase⌐ñ g̅a, hurobatuki no ⌐i⌐i za⌐siki⌐ g̅a go⌐zaima⌐su g̅a—

Smith: Za⌐siki no ho⌐o g̅a ⌐i⌐i desu yo.

Room-girl: Do⌐ozo kotira e. O⌐ni⌐motu wa?

Smith: So⌐re dake⌐ desu.

Room-girl: Wa⌐takusi g̅a motte mairima⌐su. O⌐ni⌐kai de gozaimasu.

. . .

Room-girl: Ko⌐tira de gozaima¬su. Do¬ozo.
Smith: *Hi¬rokute ⌐ki¬ree na za⌐siki¬ desu ⌐ne¬e. A¬a, u¬mi ḡa mi⊦ema⌐su
    ⌐ne¬e.
Room-girl: O⌐ni¬motu wa ko⌐tira ni ooki-itasima¬su.
Smith: A¬a, do¬o mo.
Room-girl: Su¬ḡu ⌐hi¬bati o mo⊦tte mairima⌐su. Su⌐to⌐obu o o⊦tuke-itasi-
    masyo⁻o ka.
Smith: Hi¬bati de ⊦ke⁻kkoo desu.
Room-girl: O⌐so⌐reirimasu ḡa, kore ni o⌐namae o oneḡai-itasima¬su.
Smith: Nihoñḡo de?
Room-girl: Ha¬a, o⌐neḡai-itasima¬su.
Smith: *A⌐ñmari zyoozu¬ zya a⌐rimase¬ñ ḡa—

                          . . .

Room-girl: A⌐ri¬ḡatoo gozaimasita. *Zu¬ibuñ o⌐zyoozu de irassyaima¬su ⌐ne¬e.
    A⌐sita¬ wa na⌐ñ-zi-ḡo¬ro o⊦tati ni narima¬su ka⌐
Smith: Ha⌐to ni no⊦rima⁻su kara, ha⌐ti-zi-ha¬ñ ni ko⊦ko o tatita⁻i ñ desu.
Room-girl: Sa⌐yoo de gozaima¬su ka. Wa⌐karima¬sita. Su¬ḡu o⌐hu¬ro ni o⌐ha-
    iri ni narima¬su ka⌐
Smith: Iie, a¬to de hairimasu. Su¬ḡu o⌐zeñ o da¬site kudasai.
Room-girl: Osyokuzi wa yo⌐osyoku to wasyoku to ⌐do¬tira ḡa yo⊦rosi⁻i de-
    syoo ka.
Smith: Wa⌐syoku o oneḡai-sima¬su.
Room-girl: Ha¬a. Syo⌐oti-itasima¬sita. O⌐nomi¬mono wa?
Smith: Bi¬iru o. Sore kara, yu⌐za¬masi o mo⊦tte⁻ kite kudasai.
Room-girl: Syo⌐oti-itasima¬sita. Su¬ḡu o⊦zeñ o motte mairima⁻su. Go⌐meñ-
    kudasaima¬se.
Smith: O⌐neḡai-sima¬su.

                        English Equivalent

Smith: Excuse me. I'm [Mr.] Smith from Kobe. I'd like [a room for] to-
    night.
Clerk: (Welcome.) You're Mr. Smith, is that right? We were expecting you.
    Please come in. We have only a small Western-style room (lit. as for
    Western-style rooms, we have only a small one) but we have a nice Jap-
    anese-style room with bath . . .
Smith: I prefer the Japanese-style room.
Room-girl: This way please. Your luggage?
Smith: That is all I have.
Room-girl: I'll take it. [The room] is upstairs.

                          . . .

Room-girl: Here it is. Please [go in].
Smith: What a beautiful big (lit. large and beautiful) room. Oh, you can see
    the ocean, can't you.
Room-girl: I'll put your bag here.
Smith: Oh, thanks.
Room-girl: I'll bring a hibachi right away. Shall I turn on the heater?
Smith: A hibachi will be fine.

Room-girl: Excuse me but may I have your name on this [piece of paper]?
Smith: In Japanese?
Room-girl: Yes, please.
Smith: I'm not very good . . .

. . .

Room-girl: Thank you. [Looking at writing] You're very good [at writing]!
   About what time are you leaving tomorrow?
Smith: I'm taking the Hato so I'd like to leave here at 8:30.
Room-girl: Oh, I see. Are you going to take a bath right away?
Smith: No, I'll take it later. Please bring dinner right away.
Room-girl: For dinner which would you prefer—Western-style food or Jap-
   anese-style food?
Smith: I'd like Japanese food.
Room-girl: All right. What would you like to drink?
Smith: [I'd like] some beer. And would you bring some drinking water that
   has been boiled?
Room-girl: Certainly. I'll serve your dinner right away. Excuse me.
Smith: (Please do as I requested.)

EXERCISES

1. Practice asking and answering questions about meaning, using the patterns of Basic Sentences 38 and 39. (Warning: Don't attempt to say anything you aren't sure of!)

   Examples: Na⌐o⌐su to i⊦u⌐ no wa ⌐do⌐o iu ⊦i⌐mi desu ka⌟
                  Na⌐o⌐su to i⊦u⌐ no wa ⌐yo⌐ku suru to iu ⊦i⌐mi desu.
              Hu⌐robatuki to iu⌐ no wa ⌐do⌐o iu ⊦i⌐mi desu ka⌟
                  Hu⌐robatuki to iu⌐ no wa hu⌐roba⌐ ḡa ⌐tu⌐ite (i)ru to iu
                  ⊦i⌐mi desu.

2. At an inn

   a. Ask the clerk:

      (1) if he has a room with a bath.
      (2) if he has a quiet room.
      (3) if he has a large and cool room.
      (4) if he has a Western-style room.
      (5) how much it will be for one night.
      (6) if that includes meals.

   b. Tell the room-girl:

      (1) to shine your shoes.
      (2) to press this suit.
      (3) that you want to take a bath but you don't know where it is.
      (4) that the bath is too hot.
      (5) that you want some drinking water.
      (6) to bring dinner.

(7) that Japanese food will be fine.
(8) that you'd like sukiyaki.
(9) to spread the futon.
(10) that you'd like a mosquito net because there are a lot of bugs.
(11) that you don't need a mosquito net because there aren't many bugs.
(12) to wake you at 7:30 because you are going to take a 9 o'clock train.

Lesson 22. Services

BASIC DIALOGUES: FOR MEMORIZATION

(a)

Mr. Tanaka

hair (on the head)	ka⌐mi⌐
is long	na⌐ḡa⌐i /-ku/
barber or barbershop	tokoya
even going	i⌐tte⌐ mo
it's all right even if [some- one] goes or may go	i⌐tte⌐ mo ⌐i⌐i

1. My hair has grown long so I'd (just) like to go to the barber- shop. May I go now?

Ka⌐mi⌐ ḡa ⌐na⌐gaku ⌐na⌐tta kara, tyo⌐tto to⌐koya e ikita⌐i ñ desu ḡa; i⌐ma i⌐tte⌐ mo ⌐i⌐i desu ka⌐

Mr. Smith

2. Yes, that will be all right. E⌐e, i⌐i desu yo⌐

however or but	ke⌐redo
come back	ka⌐ette kuru

3. But I'd like you to come back by 3 o'clock.

Ke⌐redo, sa⌐ñ-zi made ni ⌐ka⌐ette kite mo⌐raita⌐i ñ desu yo.

business affairs or matter to attend to	yo⌐o or yoozi

4. [That's] because I have some- thing I must attend to, too, and I'm going out.

Bo⌐ku mo yoozi ḡa a⌐tte, de⌐ka- keru⌐ kara.

(at the barbershop)

Barber

what kind of style?	do⌐ñna huu /na/
into what kind of style?	do⌐ñna huu ni

5. How shall I cut (lit. do) it? Do⌐ñna huu ni i⌐tasimasyo⌐o ka.

Mr. Tanaka

is short	mi⌐zika⌐i /-ku/
clip or mow	karu /-u/

6. The front is fine as it is so clip [just] the sides and back short.

Ma⌐e wa ko⌐no mama⌐ de ⌐i⌐i kara, yoko to usiro (o) mi⌐zika⌐ku ka⌐tte kudasa⌐i.

Barber

7. Shall I wash your hair (lit. head) too?

A⌐tama⌐ mo a⌐raimasyo⌐o ka.

Mr. Tanaka

beard   hiḡe
shave   so⌉ru /-u/
8. Yes, wash my hair and give me   E⌉e, a⌐tama⌉ mo aratte, hi⌐ḡe mo
a good shave, too.   yo⌉ku ⌐so⌐tte.

(b)

Smith

bicycle   ziteñsya [1]
lend or rent (to someone)   kasu /-u/
look for   saḡasu /-u/
9. I'm looking for a place that   Zi⌐teñsya (o) kasu tokoro⌉ (o)
rents bicycles . . .   sa⌐ḡasite (i)ma⌐su ḡa—

Tanaka

bicycle shop or dealer   ziteñsyaya
it is the expectation that   kasu hazu da
    [someone] rents
10. They're supposed to rent [them]   A⌐no ziteñsyaya de kasu hazu
at that bicycle shop.   de⌉su yo—

(at the bicycle shop)

Smith

11. Is anyone here? (Lit. Excuse   Go⌐meñ-kudasa⌉i.
me.)

Shopkeeper (coming from back of shop)

12. (Welcome.)   Irassyai—

Smith

the report is that [someone]   ka⌐su so⌉o da
    rents
13. They say that you rent bicycles   Otaku de zi⌐teñsya (o) kasu so⌉o
at your place . . .   desu ḡa—

Shopkeeper

14. Yes, indeed. This way, please.   Ha⌉i ⌐ha⌐i. Do⌉ozo kotira e.

(c)

Customer (holding a ¥ 1000 bill)

15. Can you change this?   Ko⌐maka⌉ku de⌐kima⌐su ka—

Cab-driver (checking his money)

money   kane or okane +
it is the expectation that   a⌉tta hazu da
    there was
not at all   zeñzeñ / + negative/

---

[1] Has accented alternant: zi⌐te⌉ñsya.

16. I thought I had (lit. there ought to have been) some small change . . . I'm sorry but I don't have any at all.

Ko⌐maka⌐i okane (ḡa) ⌐a⌐tta ha⌐zu de⌐su ḡa— Su⌐mimase⌐ñ ḡa, zeñ-zeñ arimase⌐ñ.

(d)

Customer (Man)

use	tukau /-u/
deliver	to⌐doke⌐ru /-ru/

17. I want to use this on Tuesday morning so I'd like to have it delivered to my home by then . . .

Kore (wa) ka⌐yoo no a⌐sa tu⌐kaita⌐i kara, so⌐re ma⌐de ni ǔti e to⌐do-kete mo⌐raita⌐i ñ da ḡa ⌐ne⌐e.

Salesgirl

place where one lives	to⌐koro⌐ or otokoro †
onto this place	koko ni

18. Certainly. Would you please write your name and address here?

Syo⌐oti-itasima⌐sita. Onamae to oto-koro (o) kǒko ni o⌐kaki ni na⌐tte ku⌐dasaimase⌐ñ ka⌐

Customer

even borrowing	ka⌐rite⌐ mo
it's all right even if [some-one] borrows or may bor-row	ka⌐rite⌐ mo ⌐i⌐i

19. May I borrow this pencil?

Ko⌐no eñpitu (o) karite⌐ mo ⌐i⌐i?

Salesgirl

charge or cost	dai or odai +
even receiving	i⌐tadaite⌐ mo
whether receiving now or receiving at the time [someone] has delivered [it]	i⌐ma i⌐tadaite⌐ mo o⌐todoke-sita to⌐ki ni i⌐tadaite⌐ mo

20. Certainly. . . . You can pay now or when it's delivered (but) . . . (Lit. As for the charge, whether I receive it now or re-ceive it at the time I have de-livered, it's all right but . . .)

Do⌐ozo. . . . Odai wa ⌐i⌐ma i⌐ta-daite⌐ mo o⌐todoke-sita to⌐ki ni i⌐tadaite⌐ mo ⌐ke⌐kkoo de gozai-masu ḡa—

Customer

pay	ha⌐ra⌐u /-u/
receipt	uketori

21. I'll pay now so would you write a receipt?

I⌐ma ha⌐ra⌐u kara, uketori (o) ⌐ka⌐ite ku⌐rena⌐i ka⌐

(after receiving receipt)

don't forget	wa⌐surena⌐i de (kudasai)

22. Well then, by Tuesday morning
    —all right? Don't forget, will
    you?

    Zya⌐a, ka⌐yoo no a⌐sa made ni ne?
    Wa⌐surena⌐i de (kudasai) ne?

(e)
Mrs. Tanaka

    maid

    zyotyuu

    according to the talk of a
    maid

    zyo⌐tyuu no hanasi⌐ de wa

    the report is that it's de-
    licious

    o⌐isii so⌐o da

23. According to (the talk of) our
    maid, (the report is that) the
    meat at that store is cheap and
    good.

    U⌐ti no zyotyuu no hanasi⌐ de wa
    a⌐no mise no oni⌐ku (wa) ⌐ya⌐sukute
    o⌐isii so⌐o desu yo⌐

Mrs. Yamamoto

24. That's what they say!

    So⌐o desu tte ⌐ne⌐e.

    stop in

    yoru /-u/

25. I haven't gone [there] yet but
    shall we stop in and see?

    Ma⌐da i⌐kimase⌐n kedo, yo⌐tte mi-
    masyo⌐o ka.

    sell

    uru /-u/

    the report is that [some-
    one] is selling

    u⌐tte (i)ru so⌐o da

26. (Because) I hear they are al-
    ways selling good meat.

    I⌐tu mo ⌐i⌐i o⌐ni⌐ku (o) u⌐tte (i)ru
    so⌐o desu kara.

(at the butcher's)
Mrs. Tanaka (pointing)

    beef

    gyuuniku

    is soft <u>or</u> tender <u>or</u>
    pliable

    ya⌐waraka⌐i /-ku/

27. Is that beef tender?

    Sono gyuuniku (wa) ya⌐waraka⌐i
    desu ka⌐

Butcher

    is delicious <u>or</u> is skillful

    u⌐ma⌐i <u>or</u> n̄⌐ma⌐i /-ku/

28. Yes, indeed. It's very good.

    Ha⌐i ⌐ha⌐i. *N̄⌐ma⌐i desu yo⌐

Mrs. Tanaka

    one gram

    i⌐ti-gu⌐ramu

29. Well then, I'd like 500 grams.

    Zya⌐a, go⌐hyaku-gu⌐ramu onegai-
    simasu.

    use for sukiyaki

    sukiyaki ni tukau

    as much as possible

    narubeku

    is thin (of flat objects)

    usui /-ku/

    cut as thin as possible

    na⌐rubeku usuku ki⌐ru

30. I'm going to use [it] for sukiya-
    ki so please cut [it] as thin as
    possible.

    Su⌐kiyaki ni tukaima⌐su kara, na-
    ⌐rubeku usuku ki⌐tte kudasai.

NOTES ON THE BASIC DIALOGUES

3. Like particle keredo, this ke¬redo, which occurs at the beginning of sentences, also has alternants ke¬redomo and ke¬do.

6. Ka⌐mi¬ o kǎru is ordinarily used in reference to clipping hair, and ka⌐mi¬ o ⌐ki¬ru in reference to cutting hair. Karu is used more commonly by men, and ki¬ru by women.

9. 'but—do you know of one?'
   Compare: So⌐re o kasite ima¬su. 'I'm lending or renting that (to someone)'; So⌐re o karite ima¬su. 'I'm borrowing or renting that (from someone).'

11. See Lesson 12, Notes on the Basic Dialogues, 26.

13. 'but—is it true?'
    Note the use of otaku in reference to a shop.

15. Ko⌐maka¬ku de⌐ki¬ru means literally 'can make to occur in small units.'

16. 'but—I can't seem to find it.'
    The polite okane is the more common alternant in conversation.
    There are a few examples of zeñzeñ + an affirmative: for example, ze⌐ñzeñ tiḡa¬u 'be completely different'; ze⌐ñzeñ dame¬ da 'be no good at all,' 'be completely broken.'

17. 'but—you understand, don't you.'
    To⌐doke¬ru is the transitive partner of intransitive to⌐do¬ku /-u/ 'reach' or 'be delivered.'

20. 'but—which do you prefer?'
    Otodoke-sita is the humble equivalent of to⌐do¬keta (cf. Lesson 13, Grammatical Note 4).

27. Note also butaniku 'pork.'
    The opposite of ya⌐waraka¬i is katai /-ku/ 'is hard or tough or stiff or firm.'

28. U⌐ma¬i in some of its occurrences is equivalent to zyo⌐ozu¬ da and in others to oisii, but it is a less formal word.

30. The opposite of usui is atui 'is thick (of flat objects).' Note the difference in accent between this atui and a⌐tu¬i 'is hot'; but in some positions —for example, before √de¬su and kara, where non-past adjectivals are regularly accented on the next-to-last syllable—this distinction disappears: a⌐tu¬i desu 'it is thick' or 'it is hot,' a⌐tu¬i kara 'because it is thick' or 'because it is hot.'

GRAMMATICAL NOTES

1. hazu

Hazu 'expectation' is a nominal which is always preceded by a modifier

—usually a sentence modifier (cf. Lesson 19, Grammatical Note 1). It is regularly followed by √da (no before another nominal), or by particle wa or ḡa
+ √nai. Hazu implies expectation imposed by circumstances: the most common English equivalents in the affirmative are 'is expected to,' 'is supposed
to,' 'ought to,' 'should,' [1] etc.; for the negative hazu wa (or ḡa) nai, the
most common equivalents are 'there's no expectation,' 'there's no reason to
expect,' etc. The subject of a hazu modifier is rarely the speaker.

Examples:

Ko'ñbañ made ni ko're o yo'mu hazu desu. 'He's expected to read this
   by tonight.'
Wa'ka'tta ha'zu de'su ḡa_ 'He ought to have understood but . . .'
Ko're yo'ri so're no ho'o ḡa ta'ka'i hazu desu. 'That one should be
   more expensive than this one.'
Tanaka-sañ wa o'naka no guai ḡa he'ñ da kara, kyo'o wa na'ni mo ta-
   be'nai hazu desu. 'There's something wrong with Mr. Tanaka's
   stomach so he isn't expected to (lit. he is expected not to) eat any-
   thing today.'
A'ratta' kara, ki'ree na hazu desu. 'I washed [it] so it should be
   clean.'
Ku'ru hazu no hito ḡa 'ma'da ki'mase'ñ kara, tyo'tto 'ma'tte kudasai.
   'The man who is supposed to come hasn't come yet so just a minute.'
Byo'oki da' kara, ku'ru hazu wa 'na'i yo. 'He's sick so there's no reason to expect that he will come.' (Man talking)
Ya'kusoku da' kara, i'kanai hazu wa arimase'ñ. 'He has (lit. it is) an
   appointment, so there's no reason to expect he won't go.'
So'ñna hazu wa arimase'ñ yo_ 'There's no reason to expect anything
   like that.'

2. — so'o √da

So'o √da following a sentence ending in the informal style means that the
information contained in the sentence is being reported at second hand: 'it is
said that —,' 'I hear that —,' 'the report is that —,' etc. Following an
accented word or phrase, so'o regularly loses its accent.

Examples:

Tanaka-sañ wa a̅sita Yo'kohama e tu'ku soo desu. 'I hear that Mr.
   Tanaka is arriving in Yokohama tomorrow.'
A'tarasi'i zi'do'osya o ka'tta so'o desu. 'I hear you bought a new car.'
Ho'kka'idoo wa to'temo samu'i soo desu. 'They say that Hokkaido is
   very cold.'
Yo'katta soo da kara, mi'ta'i ñ desu yo_ 'I hear it was good so I want
   to see it.'
So'no kata' wa 'mo'o i'rassyara'nai soo desu. 'The report is that he
   isn't coming any more.'

---

[1] I. e. 'ought to,' or 'should' because it is natural and a matter of course,
not because it is a moral obligation.

So⌉o da soo desu ⌈ne⌉e. 'That's what they say!'
A⌈no zibiki⌉ wa ni⌈señ-eñ da⌉tta soo desu. 'They say that dictionary
    was ¥2000.'

When the information is attributed to a specific source, there is an introductory sequence like — no ha⌈nasi⌉ de wa 'according to the talk of —.'
The so⌉o √da following is further indication that information is being reported at second hand.

3. N e g a t i v e   R e q u e s t s

An informal non-past negative (i. e. a -nai adjectival) + copula gerund de
+ kudasai is a negative imperative meaning 'please don't —.'

Examples:

I⌈soḡa⌉nai de kudasai. 'Please don't hurry.'
Wa⌈surena⌉i de kudasai. 'Please don't forget.'
So⌈o ossyara⌉nai de kudasai. 'Please don't say that.'

Kudasai may be replaced by ku⌈rena⌉i ka, ku⌈dasaimase⌉ñ ka, etc., with
the same differences of politeness and formality that apply in affirmative requests.
A -nai adjectival + de (i. e. the pattern described above without kudasai)
in sentence-final position, or pre-final before a sentence particle, is an informal negative request.

Examples:

A⌈kena⌉i de. 'Don't open [it].'
Tu⌈kawana⌉i de yo. 'Don't use [it]!'
Mo⌉o si⌐na⌐i de ne? 'Don't do it any more — will you?'

4. G e r u n d + m o ;   P e r m i s s i o n

A gerund — verbal, adjectival, or copula — + mo means 'even being or doing so-and-so,' 'even if it is so-and-so,' 'even if [someone] does so-and-
so.' Before mo, a normally unaccented gerund acquires an accent on the
final syllable.

Examples:

Ki⌈ite⌉ mo wa⌈kara⌉nai. 'Even if I listen, I don't understand.'
A⌈na⌉ta ḡa i⌐tte⌐ mo wa⌈takusi wa ikimase⌉ñ. 'Even if you go, I'm not
    going.'
To⌈o⌉kute mo i⌈kita⌉i ñ desu. 'Even if it's far, I want to go.'
A⌈na⌉ta ḡa i⌐kana⌐kute mo wa⌈takusi wa ikima⌉su. 'Even if you don't
    go, I'm going.'
Yo⌈mita⌉kute mo mu⌈zukasisuḡima⌉su kara‿ 'Even if I want to read it,
    it's too difficult so . . .'

Ni-⌐too de⌐ mo ta⌐ka⌐i desu yo⌐ 'Even if it's second class it's expensive.'
O⌐mosi⌐roku ⌐na⌐kute mo ⌐yo⌐nde kudasai. 'Even if it's not interesting,
please read it.'
Su⌐ki⌐ zya ⌐na⌐kute mo ⌐ta⌐bete yo. 'Even if you don't like it, eat it!'

A pair of such gerund + <u>mo</u> phrases is equivalent to English 'whether it's
— or —,' 'whether [someone] does — or —.'

Examples:

Ki⌐ite⌐ mo ki⌐kana⌐kute mo wa⌐kara⌐nai. 'Whether I listen or don't listen, I don't understand.'
Ko⌐ohi⌐i wa ⌐a⌐tukute mo tu⌐meta⌐kute mo su⌐ki⌐ desu. 'Whether coffee is hot or cold, I like it.'
Go⌐zibun de site⌐ mo si⌐te moratte⌐ mo ka⌐maimase⌐n. 'It doesn't matter whether you do it yourself or have it done.'
Ka⌐ita⌐kute mo ka⌐itaku na⌐kute mo o⌐kane ḡa na⌐i kara⌐ 'Whether I
want to buy it or don't want to buy it, I have no money so . . . '
I⌐t-too de⌐ mo ni-⌐too de⌐ mo ta⌐ka⌐i desu yo⌐ 'Whether it's first class
or second class, it's expensive.'

Gerund + <u>mo</u> + $\begin{Bmatrix} \sqrt{i⌐i} \\ \sqrt{yorosii} \\ \sqrt{ka⌐mawa⌐nai} \end{Bmatrix}$ means 'even being <u>or</u> doing so-and-so,
it's all right <u>or</u> it doesn't matter.' This pattern is used in requesting and
granting permission: when the gerund is affirmative, permission to do or be
so-and-so is requested (in questions) or granted (in statements); when the
gerund is negative, permission not to do or be so-and-so is requested (in
questions) or granted (in statements).

Examples:

Tu⌐katte⌐ mo ⌐i⌐i desu ka⌐ 'May I use it?' (Lit. 'Even using, is it all
right?')
Ka⌐ette mo yo⌐rosi⌐i desu ka⌐ 'May I go home?'
So⌐re o ta⌐bete mo ⌐i⌐i desu. 'You may eat that.'
Sa⌐mukute mo ka⌐maimase⌐n. 'Even if it's cold, it doesn't matter.'
Ni-⌐too de⌐ mo ⌐i⌐i desu ka⌐ 'Will it be all right even if it's second
class?'
I⌐ma si⌐na⌐kute mo ⌐i⌐i desu ka⌐ 'Is it all right (even) if I don't do it
now?'
I⌐soḡa⌐nakute mo ⌐i⌐i desu. 'You don't have to hurry.' (Lit. 'Even if
you don't hurry it's all right.')
A⌐sita ko⌐nakute mo ka⌐maimase⌐n ka⌐ 'Do you mind (even) if I don't
come tomorrow?'

An affirmative answer to a request for permission may be <u>do⌐ozo</u> or <u>ha⌐i</u>
or √<u>i⌐i</u> or a repetition of all or part of the request without <u>ka,</u> etc.
The negative answer to a request for permission depends on whether the
request is affirmative or negative. In denying permission for someone to do
something, <u>tyo⌐tto⌐</u> or a negative imperative may be used:

Si⌐te⌐ mo ⌐i⌐i desu ka⌐ 'May I do [it]?'

Tyo⌐tto‿ 'I'm afraid not.' or Si⌐na⌐i de kudasai. 'Please don't do [it].'

In denying permission NOT to do something, tyo⌐tto‿ or an affirmative imperative or an appropriate affirmative gerund + moraitai may be used:

Si⌐na⌐kute mo ⌐i⌐i desu ka‿ 'Is it all right if I don't do [it]?'
Tyo⌐tto‿ 'I'm afraid not.' or Si⌐te kudasai. 'Please do [it].'
or Si⌐te moraita⌐i ñ desu ḡa‿ 'I'd like to have you do [it] . . .'

Other kinds of negative replies will be introduced later.

5. Counter -guramu

The counter -guramu combines with numerals of Series I to count grams.[1] The numbers from one to ten are:

i⌐ti-gu⌐ramu	'1 gram'	ro⌐ku-gu⌐ramu	'6 grams'
ni-⌐gu⌐ramu	'2 grams'	na⌐na-gu⌐ramu	'7 grams'
sa⌐ñ-gu⌐ramu	'3 grams'	ha⌐ti-gu⌐ramu	'8 grams'
yo⌐ñ-gu⌐ramu	'4 grams'	kyu⌐u-gu⌐ramu	'9 grams'
go-⌐gu⌐ramu	'5 grams'	zyu⌐u-gu⌐ramu	'10 grams'

na⌐ñ-gu⌐ramu   'how many grams?'

DRILLS

A. Substitution Drill

1. There isn't any of that at all.
   Sore wa ze⌐ñzeñ arimase⌐ñ.

2. I don't understand that at all.
   Sore wa ze⌐ñzeñ wakarimase⌐ñ.

3. There isn't enough of that at all.
   Sore wa ze⌐ñzeñ tarimase⌐ñ.

4. That doesn't matter at all.
   Sore wa ze⌐ñzeñ kamaimase⌐ñ.

5. That I don't use at all.
   Sore wa ze⌐ñzeñ tukaimase⌐ñ.

6. That doesn't hurt at all.
   Sore wa ze⌐ñzeñ ita⌐ku a⌐rimase⌐ñ.

7. That isn't heavy at all.
   Sore wa ze⌐ñzeñ omoku arimase⌐ñ.

8. That isn't tasty at all.
   Sore wa ze⌐ñzeñ u⌐maku a⌐rimase⌐ñ.

9. That isn't pretty at all.
   Sore wa ze⌐ñzeñ ki⌐ree zya a⌐rimase⌐ñ.

10. That isn't the same at all.
    Sore wa ze⌐ñzeñ onazi zya arimase⌐ñ.

---

[1] 500 grams = approximately 1.1 lbs.

B.   Substitution Drill

1. Can you change [it] (i. e. break it up into small pieces?	Ko⌐maka˥ku de⌐kima˥su ka↲
2. I changed [it].	Ko⌐maka˥ku <u>si⌐ma˥sita</u>.
3. I made [it] long.	<u>Na˥g̃aku</u> si⌐ma˥sita.
4. Can you make [it] long?	<u>Na˥g̃aku</u> de⌐kima˥su ka↲
5. Can you make [it] short?	<u>Mi⌐zika˥ku</u> de⌐kima˥su ka↲
6. I made [it] short.	<u>Mi⌐zika˥ku</u> si⌐ma˥sita.
7. I made [it] thin.	<u>U⌐suku</u> sima˥sita.
8. Can you make [it] thin?	<u>U⌐suku</u> dekima˥su ka↲
9. Can you make [it] thick?	<u>A⌐tuku</u> dekima˥su ka↲
10. I made [it] thick.	<u>A⌐tuku</u> sima˥sita.

C.   Substitution Drill

1. May I ask?	Ki⌐ite˥ mo ⌐i˥i desu ka↲
2. May I come?	Ki⌐te˥ mo ⌐i˥i desu ka↲
3. May I cut [it]?	Ki⌐tte mo ⌐i˥i desu ka↲
4. May I go up?	A⌐gatte˥ mo ⌐i˥i desu ka↲
5. May I give [it to him]?	A⌐g̃ete˥ mo ⌐i˥i desu ka↲
6. May I get up?	O˥kite mo ⌐i˥i desu ka↲
7. May I get off?	O˥rite mo ⌐i˥i desu ka↲
8. May I put [it down]?	O⌐ite˥ mo ⌐i˥i desu ka↲
9. May I go home?	Ka˥ette mo ⌐i˥i desu ka↲
10. May I apply [it]?[1]	Ka˥kete mo ⌐i˥i desu ka↲
11. May I write [it]?	Ka˥ite mo ⌐i˥i desu ka↲
12. May I do [it]?	Si⌐te˥ mo ⌐i˥i desu ka↲
13. May I spread [it] out?	Si⌐ite˥ mo ⌐i˥i desu ka↲
14. May I read [it]?	Yo˥ñde mo ⌐i˥i desu ka↲
15. May I call [him]?	Yo⌐ñde˥ mo ⌐i˥i desu ka↲

D.   Substitution Drill

(Insert the substitution item in its appropriate form.)

1. May I go now?	I˥ma i⌐tte˥ mo ⌐i˥i desu ka↲
2. May I use this telephone? /kono deñwa (o) tukau/	Ko⌐no deñwa (o) tukatte˥ mo ⌐i˥i desu ka↲
3. May I just stop in at that store? /tyo˥tto a⌐no mise˥ ni yŏru/	Tyo˥tto a⌐no mise˥ ni yo⌐tte˥ mo ⌐i˥i desu ka↲
4. May I spread the quilts now? /i˥ma hŭtoñ (o) siku/	I˥ma hu⌐toñ (o) siite˥ mo ⌐i˥i desu ka↲
5. May I get off at the next corner? /tu⌐g̃i˥ no ⌐ka˥do de o⌐ri˥ru/	Tu⌐g̃i˥ no ⌐ka˥do de ⌐o˥rite mo ⌐i˥i desu ka↲

---

[1] Or, depending on context, 'May I telephone?' 'May I press it?' etc.

6. May I smoke? /ta⌐bako (o) no⌐mu/

Ta⌐bako (o) no̅nde mo ⌐i⌐i desu ka⌟

7. May I throw away these little things? /kono ko⌐maka⌐i mo⌐no⌐ (o) su̅teru/

Kono ko⌐maka⌐i mo⌐no⌐ (o) su⌐tete⌐ mo ⌐i⌐i desu ka⌟

8. May I have a friend write it? /to⌐modati ni ka⌐ite morau/

To⌐modati ni ka⌐ite mo⌐ratte⌐ mo ⌐i⌐i desu ka⌟

9. May I go home early? /ha⌐yaku ⌐ka⌐eru/

Ha⌐yaku ⌐ka⌐ette mo ⌐i⌐i desu ka⌟

10. May I open the window? /ma⌐do (o) a̅keru/

Ma⌐do (o) a⌐kete⌐ mo ⌐i⌐i desu ka⌟

E. Substitution Drill

(Insert the substitution item in its appropriate form.)

1. It doesn't matter whether you go or not.

I⌐tte⌐ mo i⌐kana⌐kute mo ka⌐maimase⌐n̅ yo⌟

2. It doesn't matter whether you want to go or not. /ikitai/

I⌐kita⌐kute mo i⌐kitaku na⌐kute mo ka⌐maimase⌐n̅ yo⌟

3. It doesn't matter whether you use [it] or not. /tukau/

Tu⌐katte⌐ mo tu⌐kawana⌐kute mo ka⌐maimase⌐n̅ yo⌟

4. It doesn't matter whether you're good [at it] or not. /zyo⌐ozu⌐ da/

Zyo⌐ozu⌐ de mo zyo⌐ozu⌐ zya ⌐na⌐kute mo ka⌐maimase⌐n̅ yo⌟

5. It doesn't matter whether you write [it] or not. /ka⌐ku/

Ka⌐ite mo ka⌐ka⌐nakute mo ka⌐maimase⌐n̅ yo⌟

6. It doesn't matter whether you do [it] or not. /suru/

Si⌐te⌐ mo si⌐na⌐kute mo ka⌐maimase⌐n̅ yo⌟

7. It doesn't matter whether you want to do [it] or not. /sitai/

Si⌐ta⌐kute mo si⌐taku na⌐kute mo ka⌐maimase⌐n̅ yo⌟

8. It doesn't matter whether it's interesting or not. /o⌐mosiro⌐i/

O⌐mosi⌐rokute mo o⌐mosi⌐roku ⌐na⌐kute mo ka⌐maimase⌐n̅ yo⌟

9. It doesn't matter whether it's an express or not. /kyuukoo da/

Kyu⌐ukoo de⌐ mo kyu⌐ukoo zya na⌐kute mo ka⌐maimase⌐n̅ yo⌟

10. It doesn't matter whether it's heavy or not. /omoi/

O⌐mo⌐kute mo o⌐moku na⌐kute mo ka⌐maimase⌐n̅ yo⌟

F. Substitution Drill

1. I'm looking for a place where they rent bicycles.

Zi⌐te̅nsya (o) ka⌐su tokoro⌐ (o) sa⌐g̅asite (i)ma⌐su g̅a⌟

2. I'm looking for a place where they're selling braziers.

Hiˈbati (o) uˈtte (i)ru tokoroˈ (o) saˈg̅asite (i)maˈsu g̅a_

3. I'm looking for a place where they check baggage.

Niˈmotu (o) aˈzukaˈru toˈkoroˈ (o) saˈg̅asite (i)maˈsu g̅a_

4. I'm looking for a place where there aren't many bugs.

Muˈsi g̅a 1 sukunaˈi toˈkoroˈ (o) saˈg̅asite (i)maˈsu g̅a_

5. I'm looking for a place where the tempura is good.

Teˈñpura g̅a 1 umaˈi toˈkoroˈ (o) saˈg̅asite (i)maˈsu g̅a_

6. I'm looking for a place where the summers are cool.

Naˈtuˈ g̅a 1 suˈzusiˈi toˈkoroˈ (o) saˈg̅asite (i)maˈsu g̅a_

7. I'm looking for a place where the winters are warm.

Huˈyuˈ g̅a 1 aˈttakaˈi toˈkoroˈ (o) saˈg̅asite (i)maˈsu g̅a_

8. I'm looking for a place where it's all right to smoke.

Taˈbako (o) noˈñde mo ˈiˈi toˈkoroˈ (o) saˈg̅asite (i)maˈsu g̅a_

9. I'm looking for a place where it's all right to talk in a loud voice.

Oˈoki na ˈkoˈe de haˈnaˈsite mo ˈiˈi toˈkoroˈ (o) saˈg̅asite (i)maˈsu g̅a_

10. I'm looking for a place where I don't have to wait.

Maˈtaˈnakute mo ˈiˈi toˈkoroˈ (o) saˈg̅asite (i)maˈsu g̅a_

G. Substitution Drill

(Insert the substitution items in their appropriate forms.)

1. Please cut the meat as thin as possible.

Niˈkuˈ (o) naˈrubeku usuku kiˈtte kudasai.

2. Please clip the back as short as possible. /usiro, miˈzikaˈi, karu/

Usiro (o) naˈrubeku mizikaˈku kaˈtte kudasaˈi.

3. Please deliver the paper as early as possible. /siñbuñ, haˈyaˈi, toˈdokeˈru/

Siñbuñ (o) naˈrubeku haˈyaku toˈdoˈkete kudasai.

4. Please stop the car as near as possible. /kuruma, tiˈkaˈi, tomeru/

Kuruma (o) naˈrubeku tikaˈku toˈmete kudasaˈi.

5. Please draw the map as big as possible. /tiˈzu, oˈokiˈi, kaˈku/

Tiˈzu (o) naˈrubeku oˈokiku ˈkaˈite kudasai.

6. Please define this (lit. say the meaning of this) as simply as possible. /koˈno iˈmi, yasasii, iu/

Koˈno iˈmi (o) naˈrubeku yasasiku itte kudasaˈi.

---

1 Or no.

7. Please make the bath as hot as possible. /o⌐hu¬ro, a⌐tu¬i, suru/

O⌐hu¬ro (o) na⌐rubeku a¬tuku si˥te kudasa˥i.

8. Please make the coffee as strong as possible. /ko-⌐ohi¬i, ko¬i, suru/

Ko⌐ohi¬i (o) na⌐rubeku ko¬ku si˥te kudasa˥i.

9. Please cut the vegetables as fine as possible. /ya-sai, ko⌐maka¬i, ki¬ru/

Yasai (o) na⌐rubeku komaka¬ku ˥ki˥tte kudasai.

H. Grammar Drill (based on Grammatical Note 1)

Tutor: Kyo¬oto e ikimasu. 'He's going to go to Kyoto.'
Student: Kyo¬oto e i˥ku hazu de˥su. 'He's expected to go to Kyoto.'

1. Raineñ To⌐odai ni hairima¬-su.

Raineñ To⌐odai ni ha¬iru hazu desu.

2. Mo¬o Yo⌐kohama ni tukima¬-sita.

Mo¬o Yo⌐kohama ni tu¬ita hazu desu.

3. Ko⌐ko de¬ wa ni⌐hoñḡo (o) hanasima¬su.

Ko⌐ko de¬ wa ni⌐hoñḡo (o) hana¬-su hazu desu.

4. To⌐do¬keta toki ni ha⌐raima¬-sita.

To⌐do¬keta toki ni ha⌐ra¬tta hazu desu.

5. Osake to tabako (o) ya-⌐mema¬sita.

Osake to tabako (o) ya⌐meta hazu de¬su.

6. Mo⌐ratte¬ kara ⌐su¬ḡu wa-⌐tasima¬su.

Mo⌐ratte¬ kara ⌐su¬ḡu wa⌐tasu hazu de¬su.

7. Mo¬o ⌐ku¬-zi da kara, o¬kite (i)masu.

Mo¬o ⌐ku¬-zi da kara, ⌐o¬kite (i)ru hazu desu.

8. O⌐nazi gakkoo de¬su kara, mo¬o Ta⌐naka-sañ ni aima¬-sita.

O⌐nazi gakkoo de¬su kara, mo¬o Ta⌐naka-sañ ni a¬tta hazu desu.

I. Grammar Drill (based on Grammatical Note 2)

Tutor: Ni⌐hoñḡo ḡa yo¬ku dekimasu. 'He can speak Japanese well.'
Student: Ni⌐hoñḡo ḡa yo¬ku de˥ki˥ru soo desu. 'They say he can speak Japanese well.'

1. Su⌐ko¬si sika no˥ko˥tte (i)˥na˥i keredo, zyu⌐ubu¬ñ desu.

Su⌐ko¬si sika no˥ko˥tte (i)˥na˥i keredo, zyu⌐ubu¬ñ da soo desu.

2. Hu⌐yu¬ ḡa ˥na˥ḡakute, na⌐tu¬ ḡa mi⌐zika¬i desu.

Hu⌐yu¬ ḡa ˥na˥ḡakute, na⌐tu¬ ḡa mi⌐zika¬i soo desu.

3. Ro⌐ku-ḡatu¬ ni wa ⌐a¬me ḡa yo¬ku hurimasu.

Ro⌐ku-ḡatu¬ ni wa ⌐a¬me ḡa ⌐yo¬-ku ˥hu˥ru soo desu.

4. Yuube ga⌐iziñ sika miema-se¬ñ desita.

Yuube ga⌐iziñ sika mie¬nakatta soo desu.

5. Okane ḡa ta⌐rina¬katta kara, tomodati kara su⌐ko¬si ka⌐rima¬sita.

Okane ḡa ta⌐rina¬katta kara, to-modati kara su⌐ko¬si ka⌐rita so¬o desu.

6. Teⁿki no ⁺i⁺i hi ni wa ꜛu꜖mi ga̱ miemasu.

Teⁿki no ⁺i⁺i hi ni wa ꜛu꜖mi ga̱ mi⁺e⁺ru soo desu.

7. Koko no osasimi (wa) a꜖tara꜖sikute o꜖isi꜖i desu.

Koko no osasimi (wa) a꜖tara꜖si- kute o꜖isii so꜖o desu.

8. Ta꜖isi꜖kañ no sig̱oto (o) ya꜖meta꜖i desu.

Ta꜖isi꜖kañ no sig̱oto (o) ya꜖metai so꜖o desu.

9. Zya꜖ma ni na꜖ru kara, mo꜖tte ikimase꜖ñ.

Zya꜖ma ni na꜖ru kara, mo꜖tte ika- nai so꜖o desu.

10. Kyo꜖o wa ⁺ge⁺ñki da keredo, ki꜖no꜖o wa byo꜖oki de꜖sita.

Kyo꜖o wa ⁺ge⁺ñki da keredo, ki꜖no꜖o wa byo꜖oki da꜖tta soo desu.

11. Hutuu wa ꜖sa꜖ñ-zi made da keredo, kyo꜖o wa ꜖yo꜖-zi made desu.

Hutuu wa ꜖sa꜖ñ-zi made da keredo, kyo꜖o wa ꜖yo꜖-zi made da soo desu.

12. Okosañ (wa) mi꜖ñna ozyo꜖- osañ de, miñna ke꜖kkoñ- site (i)ma꜖su.

Okosañ (wa) mi꜖ñna ozyo꜖osañ de, miñna ke꜖kkoñ-site (i)ru so꜖o desu.

J. Grammar Drill (based on Grammatical Note 3)

Tutor: I꜖tte kudasa꜖i. 'Please go.'
Student: I꜖kana꜖i de kudasai. 'Please don't go.'

1. Mi꜖zika꜖ku ka⁺tte kudasa⁺i.

Mi꜖zika꜖ku ka꜖rana⁺i de kudasai.

2. So꜖o itte kudasa꜖i.

So꜖o iwana꜖i de kudasai.

3. A꜖merika no okane de ha- ra꜖tte kudasai.

A꜖merika no okane de harawa꜖nai de kudasai.

4. E꜖g̱o (o) hana꜖site kudasai.

E꜖g̱o (o) hanasa꜖nai de kudasai.

5. Ku꜖ruma no kag̱i꜖ (o) ꜖ka꜖- kete kudasai.

Ku꜖ruma no kag̱i꜖ (o) ka꜖ke꜖nai de kudasai.

6. Su꜖to꜖obu (o) ke꜖site kuda- sa꜖i.

Su꜖to꜖obu (o) ke꜖sana꜖i de kudasai.

7. Hu꜖ru꜖i sı̃ñbuñ ya zassi (o) su꜖tete kudasa꜖i.

Hu꜖ru꜖i sı̃ñbuñ ya zassi (o) su꜖te- na꜖i de kudasai.

8. Ko꜖maka꜖i mo⁺no⁺ (o) si- ꜖matte kudasa꜖i.

Ko꜖maka꜖i mo⁺no⁺ (o) si꜖mawana꜖i de kudasai.

K. Response Drill

Tutor: Kyo꜖oto e i꜖ku꜖ desyoo ka. 'Do you suppose he is going to go to Kyoto?'
Student: Ikanai hazu wa a꜖rimase꜖ñ yo⌐ 'There's no reason to ex- pect he won't go.'

1. Kyo꜖o ha꜖ra꜖u desyoo ka.

Ha꜖rawa꜖nai hazu wa a꜖rimase꜖ñ yo⌐

2. Okane (o) ka꜖site kureru꜖ desyoo ka.

Kasite kurenai hazu wa a꜖rima- se꜖ñ yo⌐

3. E꜖ki de ꜖ni꜖motu (o) a꜖zu- keta desyoo ka.

A꜖zuke꜖nakatta hazu wa a꜖rimase꜖ñ yo⌐

4. Kotosi dāig̱aku ni ꜖ha꜖iru desyoo ka.

Ha꜖ira꜖nai hazu wa a꜖rimase꜖ñ yo⌐

5. Koñna siḡoto (wa) de⌐ki⌐ru   De⌐ki⌐nai hazu wa a⌐rimase⌐ñ yo⌣
   desyoo ka.

6. Asuko kara ki⌐koeru⌐ de-   Kikoenai hazu wa a⌐rimase⌐ñ yo⌣
   syoo ka.

7. Uketori (o) ta⌐no⌐ñda de-   Ta⌐noma⌐nakatta hazu wa a⌐rima-
   syoo ka.   se⌐ñ yo⌣

8. Zyotyuu ni tu⌐taeta⌐ desyoo   Tu⌐taena⌐katta hazu wa a⌐rima-
   ka.   se⌐ñ yo⌣

L. Response Drill

Tutor: Si⌐te⌐ mo ⌐i⌐i desu ka⌣ 'May I do [it]?'
Student: E⌐e, si⌐te⌐ mo ⌐i⌐i desu yo⌣ 'Yes, you may do [it].' __or__
        Iie, si⌐na⌐i de kudasai. 'No, please don't do [it].'

1. Tomodati ni ⌐mi⌐sete mo   E⌐e, mi⌐sete mo ⌐i⌐i desu yo⌣
   ⌐i⌐i desu ka⌣ /e⌐e/

2. Ma⌐do (o) ⌐si⌐mete mo ⌐i⌐i   Iie, si⌐me⌐nai de kudasai.
   desu ka⌣ /iie/

3. Koko de ⌐ma⌐tte mo ⌐i⌐i   E⌐e, ma⌐tte mo ⌐i⌐i desu yo⌣
   desu ka⌣ /e⌐e/

4. Ha⌐itte mo ⌐i⌐i desu ka⌣   Iie, ha⌐ira⌐nai de kudasai.
   /iie/

5. Tukue no ue no zassi (o)   E⌐e, yo⌐nde mo ⌐i⌐i desu yo⌣
   ⌐yo⌐nde mo ⌐i⌐i desu ka⌣
   /e⌐e/

6. Ne⌐ko (o) ⌐da⌐site mo ⌐i⌐i   Iie, da⌐sa⌐nai de kudasai.
   desu ka⌣ /iie/

7. Kore (o) ko⌐no hako ni   E⌐e, i⌐rete⌐ mo ⌐i⌐i desu yo⌣
   irete⌐ mo ⌐i⌐i desu ka⌣
   /e⌐e/

8. Osara (o) ko⌐no todana ni   Iie, si⌐mawana⌐i de kudasai.
   simatte⌐ mo ⌐i⌐i desu ka⌣
   /iie/

9. Tyo⌐tto sa⌐ñpo-site⌐ mo   E⌐e, sa⌐ñpo-site⌐ mo ⌐i⌐i desu
   ⌐i⌐i desu ka⌣ /e⌐e/   yo⌣

10. A⌐ratte⌐ mo ⌐i⌐i desu ka⌣   Iie, a⌐rawana⌐i de kudasai.
    /iie/

M. Response Drill

Tutor: Si⌐na⌐kute mo ⌐i⌐i desu ka⌣ 'Is it all right if I don't do
       [it]?'
Student: E⌐e, si⌐na⌐kute mo ⌐i⌐i desu yo⌣ 'Yes, you don't have
        to do [it].' __or__ Iie, si⌐te kudasa⌐i. 'No, please do [it].'

1. Kyo⌐o gi⌐ñkoo e ikana⌐kute   E⌐e, i⌐kana⌐kute mo ⌐i⌐i desu
   mo ⌐i⌐i desu ka⌣ /e⌐e/   yo⌣

2. A⌐iroñ (o) kake⌐nakute mo   Iie, ka⌐kete kudasai.
   ⌐i⌐i desu ka⌣ /iie/

3. Tu⌐kue no ue⌐ (o) ka⌐tazuke-   E⌐e, ka⌐tazuke⌐nakute mo ⌐i⌐i
   ke⌐nakute mo ⌐i⌐i desu ka⌣   desu yo⌣
   /e⌐e/

4. Ni⌐hoñḡo (o) hanasa¬nakute
   mo ⌐i¬i desu ka↲ /iie/   Iie, ha⌐na¬site kudasai.

5. Asita i⌐na¬kute mo ⌐i¬i
   desu ka↲ /ee/   E¬e, i⌐na¬kute mo ⌐i¬i desu yo↲

6. Ko⌐ñbañ be⌐ñkyoo-sina¬kute
   mo ⌐i¬i desu ka↲ /iie/   Iie, be⌐ñkyoo-site kudasa¬i.

7. Si⌐buya de norikae¬nakute
   mo ⌐i¬i desu ka↲ /ee/   E¬e, no⌐rikae¬nakute mo ⌐i¬i desu
                                     yo↲

8. Si⌐ñbuñ (o) sikana¬kute mo
   ⌐i¬i desu ka↲ /iie/   Iie, si⌐ite kudasa¬i.

9. Asita ⌐ko¬nakute mo ⌐i¬i
   desu ka↲ /ee/   E¬e, ko⌐nakute mo ⌐i¬i desu yo↲

10. U⌐siro no ta¬iya o to⌐rikae-
    na¬kute mo ⌐i¬i desu ka↲   Iie, to⌐rikaete kudasa¬i.
    /iie/

N. Expansion Drill

1. Which shall we make it?   Do¬tira ni si⌐masyo¬o ka.
   It doesn't matter but which   Ka⌐maimase¬ñ ḡa, do¬tira ni si-
   shall we make it?   ⌐masyo¬o ka.
   Even if it's Thursday it   Mo⌐kuyo¬o de mo ka⌐maimase¬ñ
   doesn't matter but which   ḡa, do¬tira ni si⌐masyo¬o ka.
   shall we make it?
   Whether it's Wednesday or   Su⌐iyo¬o de mo mo⌐kuyo¬o de mo
   Thursday it doesn't mat-   ka⌐maimase¬ñ ḡa, do¬tira ni si-
   ter, but which shall we   ⌐masyo¬o ka.
   make it?

2. I hear it's a day off.   Ya⌐sumi¬ da soo desu.
   I hear that Friday is a day   Ki⌐ñyo¬o wa ya⌐sumi¬ da soo desu.
   off.
   I hear that next Friday is   Ra⌐isyuu no kiñyo¬o wa ya⌐sumi¬
   a day off.   da soo desu.
   According to what the   Se⌐ñse¬e no ha⌐nasi¬ de wa ra⌐i-
   teacher says, next Friday   syuu no kiñyo¬o wa ya⌐sumi¬ da
   is a day off.   soo desu.

3. He is expected to go . . .   I⌐ku hazu de¬su ḡa↲
   It's his job so he is ex-   Si⌐ḡoto da¬ kara, i⌐ku hazu de¬su
   pected to go . . .   ḡa↲
   Even if he doesn't want to   I⌐kitaku na¬kute mo; si⌐ḡoto da¬
   go, it's his job so he is   kara, i⌐ku hazu de¬su ḡa↲
   expected to go . . .
   Whether he wants to go or   I⌐kita¬kute mo i⌐kitaku na¬kute mo;
   not, it's his job so he is   si⌐ḡoto da¬ kara, i⌐ku hazu de¬su
   expected to go . . .   ḡa↲

4. There's no reason to ex-   Na¬i hazu wa a⌐rimase¬ñ yo↲
   pect that there isn't any.

There's no reason to ex- pect that there isn't any at all.	Ze⌐ñzeñ na⌐i hazu wa a⌐rimase⌐ñ yo⌐
I can't tell for sure but there's no reason to ex- pect that there isn't any at all.	Ha⌐kki⌐ri wa⌐karimase⌐ñ ḡa, ze⌐ñ- zeñ na⌐i hazu wa a⌐rimase⌐ñ yo⌐
I can't tell for sure how much is left but there's no reason to expect that there isn't any at all.	I⌐kura no⌐ko⌐tte (i)ru ka ha⌐kki⌐ri wa⌐karimase⌐ñ ḡa, ze⌐ñzeñ na⌐i hazu wa a⌐rimase⌐ñ yo⌐

5.

You'd better drink [it].	No⌐ñda hoo ḡa ⌐i⌐i desu yo⌐
You'd better drink [it] quickly.	Ha⌐yaku ⌐no⌐ñda hoo ḡa ⌐i⌐i desu yo⌐
It's medicine so you'd better take it quickly.	Ku⌐suri da⌐ kara, ha⌐yaku ⌐no⌐ñda hoo ḡa ⌐i⌐i desu yo⌐
Even if it's bitter, it's medicine, so you'd better take it quickly.	Ni⌐ḡakute mo; ku⌐suri da⌐ kara, ha⌐yaku ⌐no⌐ñda hoo ḡa ⌐i⌐i desu yo⌐
Whether it's sweet or bit- ter, it's medicine, so you'd better take it quickly.	A⌐ma⌐kute mo ⌐ni⌐ḡakute mo; ku- ⌐suri da⌐ kara, ha⌐yaku ⌐no⌐ñda hoo ḡa ⌐i⌐i desu yo⌐

6.

He is expected to come . . .	Ku⌐ru ha⌐zu de⌐su ḡa—
He is expected to come on ⌐time . . .	Zi⌐kañ-do⌐ori [ni] ⌐ku⌐ru ha⌐zu de⌐su ḡa—
Even if it doesn't rain (lit. fall) he is expected to come on time . . .	Hu⌐ra⌐nakute mo, zi⌐kañ-do⌐ori [ni] ⌐ku⌐ru ha⌐zu de⌐su ḡa—
Whether it rains (lit. falls) or not he is expected to come on time . . .	Hu⌐tte⌐ mo hu⌐ra⌐nakute mo, zi- ⌐kañ-do⌐ori [ni] ⌐ku⌐ru ha⌐zu de⌐su ḡa—
Whether it rains or not he is expected to come on time . . .	A⌐me ḡa hu⌐tte⌐ mo hu⌐ra⌐nakute mo, zi⌐kañ-do⌐ori [ni] ⌐ku⌐ru ha⌐zu de⌐su ḡa—
He has an appointment so whether it rains or not he is expected to come on time . . .	Ya⌐kusoku ḡa a⌐ru kara; a⌐me ḡa hu⌐tte⌐ mo hu⌐ra⌐nakute mo, zi- ⌐kañ-do⌐ori [ni] ⌐ku⌐ru ha⌐zu de⌐su ḡa—
He has a firm appointment so whether it rains or not he is expected to come on time . . .	Ka⌐tai yakusoku ḡa a⌐ru kara; a⌐me ḡa hu⌐tte⌐ mo hu⌐ra⌐nakute mo, zi⌐kañ-do⌐ori [ni] ⌐ku⌐ru ha⌐zu de⌐su ḡa—

QUESTION SUPPLEMENT

(based on the Basic Dialogues)

(a) 1. Tanaka-sañ wa ⌐do⌐ko e i⌐kima⌐sita ka⌐ Do⌐o site?
     2. Su⌐misu-sañ wa ⌐do⌐o site Tanaka-sañ ni ⌐sa⌐ñ-zi made ni ⌐ka⌐ette
         mo⌐raita⌐i ñ desu ka⌐
     3. Tanaka-sañ wa ⌐do⌐ñna huu ni to⌐koya ni site moraima⌐sita ka⌐

(b) 4. Su⌐misu-sañ wa ⌐na⌐ni o sa⌐ḡasite ima⌐sita ka⌐
     5. Ano ziteñsyaya de zi⌐teñsya o kasu so⌐o desu ḡa, ho⌐ñtoo de⌐su ka⌐

(d) 6. Okyakusañ wa ⌐do⌐o site ka⌐tta mono⌐ o ka⌐yo⌐o made ni to⌐do⌐kete
         mo⌐raita⌐i ñ desu ka⌐
     7. Okyakusañ wa ka̅rita eñpitu de ⌐na⌐ni o ka⌐kima⌐sita ka⌐
     8. Okyakusañ wa ⌐i⌐tu ha⌐raima⌐sita ka⌐
     9. Okyakusañ wa ⌐na⌐ni o ⌐ka⌐ite mo⌐raima⌐sita ka⌐

(e) 10. A⌐no mise⌐ wa ⌐do⌐ñna ni⌐ku⌐ o u⌐tte ima⌐su ka⌐
    11. Ta⌐naka-sañ no o⌐kusañ wa ⌐da⌐re kara so⌐o kikima⌐sita ka⌐
    12. Ta⌐naka-sañ no o⌐kusañ wa ⌐na⌐ni o ka⌐ima⌐sita ka⌐
    13. Ta⌐naka-sañ no o⌐kusan wa ⌐do⌐o site so⌐no niku⌐ o u⌐suku ki⌐tte
         mo⌐raima⌐sita ka⌐
    14. Da⌐re ḡa Ta⌐naka-sañ no o⌐kusañ to issyo ni ni⌐ku⌐ya ni yo⌐tte
         mima⌐sita ka⌐

SHORT SUPPLEMENTARY DIALOGUES

  1. Secretary: Ko⌐ñna hu⌐u ni si⌐ma⌐sita ḡa, i⌐ka⌐ḡa desyoo ka.
      Smith: A⌐a, to⌐temo ki⌐ree desu ⌐ne⌐e. Do⌐o mo go⌐ku⌐roosama⌐

  2. Smith: Ni⌐hoñzi⌐ñ wa ko⌐ñna hu⌐u na ⌐go⌐hañ ḡa o⌐suki da so⌐o desu
         ⌐ne⌐e.
      Tanaka: E⌐e. Da⌐isuki desu yo⌐

  3. A: Ka⌐sima⌐su ka⌐
      B: E⌐e. I⌐ti⌐-neñ dake ka⌐sita⌐i ñ desu ḡa⌐

  4. A: Ka⌐rima⌐su ka⌐
      B: E⌐e. I⌐ti⌐-neñ dake ka⌐rita⌐i ñ desu ḡa⌐

  5. A: Kinoo ⌐Sa⌐too-sañ kara de⌐ñwa ḡa arima⌐sita ḡa, o⌐ka⌐asañ ḡa byo-
         ⌐oiñ ni ha⌐itta soo desu.
      B: So⌐o desu ka. So⌐re wa ikemase⌐ñ ⌐ne⌐e.

  6. A: Yosida-sañ ⌐kyo⌐o ⌐ku⌐ru?
      Mr. B: Ko⌐nai soo da yo⌐
      A: So⌐o?
      Mr. B: Byo⌐oki da so⌐o da yo.

7. A: Kyo'o Ta'naka-sense'e ḡa mi'e'ru desyoo?
    B: Mo'o su'ḡu mi'e'ru ha'zu de'su ḡa ̄ Ni'-zi no ya'kusoku de'su ka-
       ra.
    A: Ta'naka-sense'e no hoka ni 'do'nata ḡa 'ku'ru ha'zu de'sita ka ̖
    B: Yo'sida-sañ mo ku'ru hazu desyoo?

8. A: O'tya a'ru?
    Mr. B: Na'i hazu wa 'na'i yo ̖ — i'tu mo 'a'ru kara.

9. Maid (coming from telephone): O'kusama ̖ Da'ñnasa'ma wa 'ma'da ka-
       'isya e otuki ni nara'nai soo desu.
    Mistress: Tu'ka'nai hazu wa a'rimase'ñ — ha'yaku u'ti o de'ta kara.
    He'ñ desu 'ne'e.

10. Teacher A: A'no ku'rasu[1] ko'marima'su 'ne'e. Ko'no ho'ñ o 'mo'o be'ñ-
       kyoo-sita hazu de'su ḡa, na'ni mo wakarimase'ñ 'ne'e.
    Teacher B: A'no ku'rasu no hi'to' wa u'ti de ze'ñzeñ beñkyoo-sina'i ka-
       ra, wa'ka'ru hazu wa a'rimase'ñ yo.

11. Student: O'zyama-site' mo yo'rosi'i desyoo ka.
    Teacher: Do'ozo 'do'ozo. Betu ni i'soḡa'siku 'na'i kara go'eñryo na'ku.

12. Smith: Ke'sa si'ḡoto ḡa ta'kusañ a'ru kara, o'kyakusa'ñ ḡa ki'te' mo
       a'imase'ñ yo ̖
    Secretary: U'eda-sañ no oyakusoku wa do'o nasaimasu ka ̖
    Smith: U'eda-sañ ni' wa a'ima'su ḡa, ho'ka no hito' wa da'me' desu.

13. Maid: I'ma 'pa'ñ o ka'tte mairima'su ḡa, mi'ruku wa ka'wana'kute mo
       yo'rosi'i desyoo ka.
    Mistress: A'a, mi'ruku mo ka'tte' kite kudasai.

14. A: Mo'o ta'no'ñda 'ho'ñ ḡa 'ki'ta ha'zu da' kara, ho'ñya e itte to'tte
       kima'su. I'ma ha'rawa'nakute mo 'i'i desyoo?
    Mr. B: E'e. A'to de 'bo'ku ḡa ha'ra'u kara, 'i'i desu yo ̖

15. A: A'tu'i desu 'ne'e. Ma'do o mi'ñna akete' mo su'zu'siku na'rimase'ñ
       'ne'e.
    B: Tu'metai mono' o 'no'ñde, su'ko'si ya'sumimasyo'o ka.
    A: So'o simasyo'o.

16. A: A'me ḡa hu'tte' iru kara, Tanaka-sañ 'ko'nai desyoo 'ne'e.
    B: Iie. Ku'ru hazu desu yo ̖ Hu'tte' mo hu'ra'nakute mo 'ku'ru tte
       i'tta' kara.

17. Employee: Asita yo'ozi ḡa gozaima'su kara, o'soku kite' mo yo'rosi'i
       desyoo ka.
    Employer: Tyo'tto ̖ A'sita' wa to'temo i'soḡasi'i kara. Hoka no hi wa?

───────────────

[1] 'Class.'

Employee: Zya⌐a, ki⌐ñyo⌐o de mo yo⌐rosi⌐i desu ḡa—
Employer: So⌐o site kudasa⌐i.

18. A: Mu⌐zukasi⌐i desyoo?
     B: Zeñzeñ. Kore wa ko⌐domo de⌐ mo de⌐ki⌐ru ñ desu yo⌐

English Equivalents

1. Secretary: I did it like this. How do you like it? (Lit. How is it?)
    Smith: Oh, that's very pretty! Thanks for your trouble.

2. Smith: They say that Japanese like this kind of (or style of) rice, don't
    they.
    Tanaka: Yes, we like it very much.

3. A: Are you going to rent it (i. e. to someone)?
    B: Yes, I'd like to rent it for just one year . . .

4. A: Are you going to rent it (i. e. from someone)?
    B: Yes, I'd like to rent it for just one year . . .

5. A: There was a telephone call from Mr. Sato yesterday. The report is
    that his mother has entered the hospital.
    B: Oh? That's too bad.

6. A: Is Mr. Yoshida coming today?
    Mr. B: They say he isn't coming.
    A: Oh?
    Mr. B: They say he's sick.

7. A: Dr. Tanaka is going to come today, isn't he?
    B: He should come any minute now . . . (Because) he has (lit. it is) a
    2 o'clock appointment.
    A: Who was supposed to come besides Dr. Tanaka?
    B: Mr. Yoshida is supposed to come too, isn't he?

8. A: Is there any tea?
    Mr. B: There should be (lit. there's no reason to expect that there isn't
    any)—since there always is some.

9. Maid: Madam. They say that Mr. —— (lit. the master) hasn't arrived
    at the office yet.
    Mistress: He should have arrived (lit. there's no reason to expect that
    he hasn't arrived)—since he left the house early. Isn't that strange!

10. Teacher A: That class is troublesome, isn't it. They're supposed to
    have studied this book already but they don't understand anything, do
    they.
    Teacher B: The people in that class don't study at home at all, so there's
    no reason to expect them to understand.

11. Student: May I interrupt you?
    Teacher: Certainly. I'm not especially busy so come right ahead.

12. Smith: I have a lot of work this morning so even if any visitors come, I
    won't see them.
    Secretary: What will you do about Mr. Ueda's appointment?
    Smith: Mr. Ueda I'll see, but not any other people.

13. Maid: I'm going to go and buy some bread now. I don't have to buy any
    milk, do I?
    Mistress: Oh, (go and) buy some milk too.

14. A: The books that were ordered should have come by now so I'll go to
    the bookstore and get them (lit. come having taken [them]). I don't
    have to pay now, do I?
    Mr. B: No (i.e. that's right). I'll pay later so don't bother.

15. A: Isn't it hot! Even if you open all the windows it doesn't get cool, does
    it.
    B: Shall we have something cold to drink and rest for a little while?
    A: Let's do that.

16. A: It's raining so Mr. Tanaka probably won't come, will he.
    B: Yes (i.e. that's not right), he should come. (Because) he said that
    he'd come whether it rained or not.

17. Employee: I have some business to attend to tomorrow so would it be all right if I came late?
    Employer: That's a bit inconvenient. (Because) tomorrow we're going
    to be very busy. How about another day?
    Employee: Well then, (even being) Friday will be all right . . .
    Employer: Please make it then (lit. that way).

18. A: It's difficult, isn't it?
    B: Not at all. This, even (being) a child can do.

EXERCISES

1. Tell the barber:

    a. to give you a shave.
    b. to cut your hair short.
    c. to wash your hair.

2. Tell the butcher:

    a. you want 500 grams of beef.
    b. to cut it as thin as possible.
    c. to deliver it as quickly as possible.

3. Ask the clerk in the store:

    a. if you may borrow his pencil.
    b. to write a receipt for you.
    c. to deliver these things to your home by 3 tomorrow.
    d. if he can change this (i. e. money).

4. Tell a friend that you have heard that:

    a. the barber next to the station is very good.
    b. the fish at that fish market is usually not fresh.
    c. they sell American newspapers and magazines at that bookstore.
    d. he is looking for a new house.

5. Ask permission to:

    a. come in.
    b. look at that.
    c. read that.
    d. smoke.
    e. use the telephone.
    f. come late tomorrow.
    g. go home early today.
    h. wait here.
    i. open the window.
    j. eat this.
    k. drink this.
    l. give this to the children.
    m. give this to the teacher.
    n. rest a little.
    o. pay now.

6. Practice the Basic Dialogues with appropriate variations, including variations in politeness and formality levels.

Lesson 23. Clothing

BASIC DIALOGUES: FOR MEMORIZATION

(a)

Maid

1. Are you going out tonight? Ko⌐ñbañ o⌐dekake de⌐su ka⌐

Mr. Tanaka

early evening	yuuḡata
it is a matter of going out	de⌐kakeru⌐ ñ da

2. Yes, I am going out toward evening (lit. from early evening on). A⌐a, yuᴸuḡata kara dekakeru⌐ ñ da yo⌐

change clothes	ki⌐ka⌐eru /-ru/ [1]
go having changed clothes	ki⌐ka⌐ete (i)ku
shirt	waisyatu
navy blue	ko⌐ñ

3. I'm going to change clothes before I go so get out a clean white shirt and my navy blue suit. Ki⌐ka⌐ete (i)⌐ku⌐ kara, si⌐ro⌐i ⌐ki⌐ree na waisyatu to ⌐ko⌐ñ no se⌐biro (o) da⌐site.

shoes on the new side <u>or</u> the newer shoes	a⌐tarasi⌐i hoo no kutu
put on <u>or</u> wear (on the feet or legs)	haku /-u/
go [somewhere] wearing (on the feet or legs)	haite (i)ku

4. And I'm going to wear my new(er) black shoes so shine them. Sore kara; a⌐tarasi⌐i hoo no ku⌐ro⌐i ku⌐tu⌐ (o) ha⌐ite (i)ku⌐ kara, miḡaite.

Maid

coat (full-length)	o⌐obaa
put on <u>or</u> wear (on the body)	kiru /-ru/
go [somewhere] wearing (on the body)	kite (i)ku

5. Are you going to wear an overcoat? O⌐obaa (o) ki⌐te (i)rassyaima⌐su ka⌐

---

[1] Alternate accent: ki⌐kae⌐ru.

45

Mr. Tanaka

snow	yu⌐ki⌐
6. Yes, of course I am (going to wear one). (Because) they say that tonight it's going to snow.	A⌐a, mo⌐ti⌐roñ kite (i)ku yo⌐ Koñ-bañ wa yu⌐ki⌐ ḡa ⌐hu⌐ru soo da kara.

Maid

hat	boosi or o⌐bo⌐osi +
put on <u>or</u> wear (on the head)	ka⌐bu⌐ru /-u/
go [somewhere] wearing (on the head)	ka⌐bu⌐tte (i)ku
7. Then you are going to wear a hat too, aren't you?	Zya⌐a, o⌐bo⌐osi mo ka⌐bu⌐tte (i)ra-ssyaimasu ka⌐

Mr. Tanaka

8. Yes, I am (going to wear one).	A⌐a, ka⌐bu⌐tte (i)ku yo⌐

. . .

umbrella	ka⌐sa
it is a matter of looking for	sa⌐ḡasite (i)ru⌐ ñ da
9. I'm looking for my umbrella. . . Oh! [This is where] it was.	Ka⌐sa (o) sa⌐ḡasite ru⌐ ñ da ḡa— A. A⌐tta.

(b)

Mrs. Tanaka

Western-style clothing	yoohuku or o⌐yo⌐ohuku +
dry [something] out <u>or</u> air [something]	ho⌐su /-u/
a matter of having [something] aired	ho⌐site mo⌐raita⌐i no
10. I want to have all the clothes that are over there aired to-day.	Kyo⌐o sŏko no yoohuku (o) mĩnna ⌐ho⌐site mo⌐raita⌐i no.

Maid

trousers	zu⌐boñ⌐
11. Do you mean these trousers too?	Ko⌐no zuboñ mo desu ka⌐

Mrs. Tanaka

dry cleaning	do⌐raikuri⌐iniñḡu
a matter of sending out for dry cleaning	do⌐raikuri⌐iniñḡu ni ⌐da⌐su no
12. No, the things that are on top of that chair are to be sent out for dry cleaning.	Iie, a⌐no isu no ue⌐ ni ⌐a⌐ru mo⌐no⌐ wa do⌐raikuri⌐iniñḡu ni ⌐da⌐su no yo⌐

Maid

sweater   se⌐etaa⌐
13. What are you going to do with   Ko⌐no se⌐etaa (wa) ⌐do⌐o nasaimasu
    this sweater?   ka⌐

Mrs. Tanaka

launder   señtaku-suru⌐
a matter of laundering   se⌐ñtaku-suru⌐ no
14. That's to be laundered at home.   So⌐re wa uti de señtaku-suru⌐ no.

Maid

socks or stockings   ku⌐tu⌐sita
gloves   te⌐bu⌐kuro
15. Shall I put away these socks   Kono ku⌐tu⌐sita ya te⌐bu⌐kuro (wa)
    and gloves and things?   si⌐maimasyo⌐o ka⌐

Mrs. Tanaka

16. Yes, in the top drawer.   E⌐e, ue no hikidasi ni.

. . .

a matter of not going in   ha⌐ira⌐nai no
17. Won't they go in?   Ha⌐ira⌐nai no?

    method or way of doing   sikata
    it can't be helped or   si⌐kata ḡa na⌐i or syo⌐o ḡa
        nothing can be done   na⌐i
    middle   mañnaka
18. If it's full it's full so put them   Si⌐kata ḡa na⌐i kara, ma⌐ñnaka
    in the middle drawer or the   no hikidasi de⌐ mo si⌐ta no⌐ de
    bottom one. (Lit. It can't be   mo ka⌐mawa⌐nai wa⌐
    helped so it will be all right
    whether it's the middle drawer
    or the bottom one.)

(c)

Tanaka

it is a matter of having   ka⌐tta⌐ ñ da
    bought
19. Excuse me but where did you   Si⌐tu⌐ree desu ḡa, sono sebiro
    buy that suit?   (wa) ⌐do⌐ko de ka⌐tta⌐ ñ desu ka⌐

Smith

send (of things)   okuru /-u/
it is a matter of having   o⌐kutte moratta⌐ ñ da
    had [something] sent
20. I had my mother in the States   A⌐merika no ha⌐ha ni o⌐kutte mo-
    send it [to me].   ratta⌐ ñ desu yo.

Tanaka

American-made	Amerika-see
it is a matter of being American-made	A⌐merika-see na⌐ ñ da
21. Oh, do you mean it's American-made?	A⌐a, A⌐merika-see na⌐ ñ desu ka.

material or cloth	ki⌐zi
22. What is this material?	Ko⌐no ki⌐zi (wa) ⌐na⌐ñ desyoo ka.

Smith

cotton	momeñ
dacron	da⌐kuroñ
23. It's cotton and dacron.	Momeñ to ⌐da⌐kuroñ desu yo.

Tanaka

synthetic fibers	kaseñ
strong or firm or durable or healthy	zyoobu /na/
it is strong and what is more—	zyo⌐obu da⌐ si
24. The synthetics nowadays are good because they are rugged and what is more they are cheap (isn't that true).	Kono-ḡoro no kaseñ wa zyo⌐obu da⌐ si, sono ue ya⌐su⌐i kara; i⌐i desu ⌐ne⌐e.

(d)

Smith

pattern	gara
gaudy or bright or loud[1]	ha⌐de⌐ /na/
plain or subdued or quiet[1]	zi⌐mi⌐ /na/
25. This pattern is a little loud (so) please show me one that's plainer.	Kono gara (wa) su⌐ko⌐si ha⌐de⌐ da kara, mo⌐tto zi⌐mi⌐ na no (o) ⌐mi⌐sete kudasai.

(looking at others brought by the clerk)

26. I wonder which one would be best.	Do⌐re ḡa i⌐tibañ i⌐i desyoo ka ⌐ne⌐e.

Clerk

solid color	mu⌐zi
suit or be becoming	ni⌐a⌐u /-u/
it is a matter of being becoming	ni⌐a⌐u ñ da
isn't it a matter of being becoming?	ni⌐a⌐u ñ zya nai? or o⌐niai ni na⌐ru ⌐ ñ zya nai?
27. Among these three, wouldn't the gray solid-color one be most becoming?	Ko⌐no mi-ttu⌐ no u⌐ti de⌐ wa, haii-ro no ⌐mu⌐zi no ḡa i⌐tibañ oniai ni na⌐ru ñ zya ⌐na⌐i desyoo ka.

---

[1] Of color, style, taste, etc.

Smith

decide <u>or</u> settle   kimeru /-ru/
decide on this one   kore ni kimeru
28. Well then, I'll take (lit. decide   Zya⌐a, ko⌐re ni kimemasyo⌐o.
     on) this one.

(e)

Smith

shape <u>or</u> style   katati <u>or</u> ka⌐ta⌐
make   tu⌐ku⌐ru /-u/
29. I'd like to have a suit of this   Koñna kata(ti) [1] no sebiro (o) tu-
     (kind of) style made.   Can you   ⌐ku⌐tte mo⌐raita⌐i ñ desu ḡa, su⌐ḡu
     do it right away?   de⌐kima⌐su ka⌐⌐

Tailor

30. Yes, I'll do it right away . . .   Ha⌐a, su⌐ḡu i⌐tasima⌐su ḡa⌐

Smith

[I] have decided and what   ki⌐meta⌐ si
  is more—
make the same as this   kore to onazi ni suru
it is a matter of making   su⌐ru⌐ ñ da
measurements   suñpoo
measure   ha⌐ka⌐ru /-u/
take measurements   su⌐ñpoo o haka⌐ru
31. The material I've decided on,   Ki⌐zi wa ki⌐meta⌐ si, kata(ti) [1]
     and the style is to be (made)   wa ko⌐re to onazi ni suru⌐ ñ da
     the same as this, so shall I   kara; i⌐ma su⌐ñpoo (o) haka⌐tte
     have the measurements taken   mo⌐raimasyo⌐o ka.
     now?

Tailor

32. Certainly.   Syo⌐oti-itasima⌐sita.

. . .

Smith (trying on the finished suit)

jacket   uwaḡi
length   na⌐ḡasa
is tight   kitui /-ku/
33. The length of the jacket is just   Uwaḡi no ⌐na⌐ḡasa wa tyo⌐odo i⌐i
     right but it's a little tight.   ñ desu ḡa, tyo⌐tto ki⌐tu⌐i ñ desu
                                            yo.

_____

[1] Accent of contracted alternant: <u>ka⌐ta⌐</u> wa.

Tailor

worry	siñpai or gosiñpai↑
34. I can make it bigger (lit. wide) so don't worry.	Hi⌉roku de⊦kima⊣su kara, go┌siñpai na⌉ku.

ADDITIONAL VOCABULARY

1. I'd like to buy a man's suit. What place would be good?		Se┌biro ḡa kaita⌉i ñ desu ḡa, do⌉ko ḡa ⊦i⊣i desyoo ka.
woman's suit		su⌉utu
skirt		su┌ka⌉ato
blouse		bu┌ra⌉usu
dress (one-piece)		wa┌ñpi⌉isu
handkerchief		hañkati
comb		ku┌si⌉
eyeglasses		me⌉ḡane
handbag		ha┌ñdoba⌉kku
necktie		ne⌉kutai
belt (man's)		bañdo
belt (woman's)		beruto
Japanese-style clothing		wahuku
underwear		sitaḡi
kimono		kimono
coat		haori
sash		o⌉bi
wooden clogs	Japanese-style clothing	geta
straw/rubber footgear		zoori
socks		ta⌉bi
summer kimono		yukata
quilted kimono		ta┌ñze⌉ñ
2. Is that suit [made of] synthetic fabric?		Ano sebiro wa ka┌señ de⌉su ka ◡
silk		ki⌉nu
wool		ke or u⌉uru
flax or linen		a┌sa⌉
3. Which necktie are you going to wear?		Do⌉no nekutai o si⊦te ikima⊣su ka ◡
wear a sash		o⌉bi o si⊦me⊣ru /-ru/
wear a belt		bañdo /or beruto/ o suru
wear eyeglasses		me⌉ḡane o ka⊦ke⊣ru /-ru/
wear gloves		te┌bu⌉kuro o hameru /-ru/

NOTES ON THE BASIC DIALOGUES

3. Ki⌐ka⌐eru: compare no⌐rika⌐eru 'change vehicles' and torikaeru 'exchange.' Ki⌐ka⌐eru is a compound of kiru 'wear' (sentence 5 below) and kaeru 'change.'
   Waisyatu usually refers to the kind of man's shirt worn with a necktie.

4. Compare a⌐tarasi⌐i kutu 'new shoes' and a⌐tarasi⌐i hoo no kutu 'shoes which are new compared with others.'
   In the combinations haite iku, kite iku (sentence 5), and ka⌐bu⌐tte iku (sentence 7), iku can of course be replaced by its polite equivalents ma⌐iru↓ and i⌐rassya⌐ru↑.

9. Note the use of the past tense a⌐tta 'it was [here].'

12. Do⌐raikuri⌐iningu is often shortened to dorai.

14. Sentaku is a nominal meaning 'laundering.' Note also sentakuya 'laundry (i.e. a store)' or 'laundryman' and sentakumono 'laundry (i.e. things to be washed).'

18. Syoo, a contraction of siyoo which is equivalent in meaning to sikata, is an informal word.

28. Kimeru is the transitive partner of intransitive kimaru /-u/ 'be decided.' Particle ni is the ni of goal. Compare: hi o kimeru 'decide the day' and sono hi ni kimeru 'decide on that day.'

31. Particle ni is the ni of goal: 'make into the same as this.'

34. Go⌐sinpai na⌐ku 'let there be no worry': compare go⌐enryo na⌐ku and o⌐kamai na⌐ku (Lesson 18, Grammatical Note 5). Sinpai also occurs in the compound verbal sinpai-suru 'worry.'

GRAMMATICAL NOTES

1. Extended Predicates

A major sentence (cf. Lesson 4, Grammatical Note 5) in Japanese is one which ends with, or consists of, an inflected word (non-past or past or tentative or imperative) with or without following sentence particles. The shortest possible major sentences belong to one of the following types:

(1) A verbal or adjectival alone.

   Examples: Wa⌐ka⌐ru. 'It's clear.' (Informal)
              Wa⌐karima⌐sita. 'It was clear.' (Formal)
              I⌐kimasyo⌐o. 'Let's go.' (Formal)
              I⌐rassyaima⌐se. 'Go!' or 'Come!' or 'Stay!' (Formal)
              Sa⌐mu⌐i. 'It's cold.' (Informal)
              A⌐tukatta. 'It was hot.' (Informal)

(2) The copula √da and what immediately precedes it, including one verbal, adjectival, or nominal (i.e. the sequence begins with a verbal, adjectival, or nominal, and ends with √da).

Examples: Wa⌐karimase⌐n desita. 'It wasn't clear.' (Formal)
Sa⌐mu⌐i desu. 'It's cold.' (Formal)
A⌐tukatta desyoo. 'It was probably hot.' (Formal)
So⌐o da. 'That's right.' (Informal)
Ho⌐n desu. 'It's a book.' (Formal)
Ko⌐re de⌐sita. 'It was this.' (Formal)
O⌐nazi desyo⌐o. 'It's probably the same.' (Formal)
Sa⌐n-zi made desu. 'It's until 3 o'clock.' (Formal)
So⌐re da⌐tta desyoo. 'It was probably that.' (Formal)

Such sequences will hereafter be referred to as PREDICATES. Longer major sentences end with—rather than consist of—a predicate, with or without following sentence particles.

For every non-past and past predicate, there is a corresponding form which will hereafter be called an EXTENDED PREDICATE. An extended predicate, meaning literally 'it is a matter of ——,' is a sequence consisting of two predicates: (1) a non-past or past predicate (usually informal) plus (2) an immediately following second predicate consisting of the nominal ñ (the contracted form of no[1]) 'matter,' 'case' + da (or a more formal/polite equivalent). Before this ñ/no, as before no meaning 'one(s),' the na alternant of da occurs. Accentuation before the two no's is also the same.

Thus, a formal predicate, non-past or past, has as its extended equivalent its informal equivalent (with da becoming na) + ñ desu.

Examples:

Formal Predicate	Formal Extended Predicate
wa⌐karima⌐su 'it's clear'	wa⌐ka⌐ru ñ desu 'it's a matter of being clear'[2]
wa⌐karima⌐sita 'it was clear'	wa⌐ka⌐tta ñ desu 'it's a matter of having been clear'
wa⌐karimase⌐n 'it isn't clear'	wa⌐kara⌐nai ñ desu 'it's a matter of not being clear'
wa⌐karimase⌐n desita 'it wasn't clear'	wa⌐kara⌐nakatta ñ desu 'it's a matter of not having been clear'
i⌐kita⌐i desu 'I want to go'	i⌐kita⌐i ñ desu 'it's a matter of wanting to go'
ta⌐ka⌐i desu 'it's expensive'	ta⌐ka⌐i ñ desu 'it's a matter of being expensive'
ta⌐kakatta desu } 'it was expensive' ta⌐ka⌐i desita	ta⌐kakatta ñ desu 'it's a matter of having been expensive'

---

[1] The uncontracted form often occurs in polite or precise speech, and also in some specific constructions—for example, in women's informal speech, as noted below.

[2] These are literal equivalents.

Formal Predicate	Formal Extended Predicate

to⌐modati de⌐su 'it's a friend'

to⌐modati de⌐sita 'it was a friend'

sa⌐ñ-zi made desu 'it's until 3 o'clock'

to⌐modati na⌐ ñ desu 'it's a matter of being a friend'

to⌐modati da⌐tta ñ desu 'it's a matter of having been a friend'

sa⌐ñ-zi made na ñ desu 'it's a matter of being until 3 o'clock'

The formal extended predicate can be made polite by replacing final desu with de gozaimasu.

The extended equivalent of an informal predicate, non-past or past, is formed by adding ñ da (but before ñ, da becomes na). Thus:

Informal Predicate [1]	Informal Extended Predicate [1]
wa⌐ka⌐ru	wa⌐ka⌐ru ñ da
wa⌐ka⌐tta	wa⌐ka⌐tta ñ da
wa⌐kara⌐nai	wa⌐kara⌐nai ñ da
wa⌐kara⌐nakatta	wa⌐kara⌐nakatta ñ da
ikitai	i⌐kita⌐i ñ da
ta⌐ka⌐i	ta⌐ka⌐i ñ da
ta⌐kakatta	ta⌐kakatta ñ da
tomodati da	to⌐modati na⌐ ñ da
to⌐modati da⌐tta	to⌐modati da⌐tta ñ da
sa⌐ñ-zi made da	sa⌐ñ-zi made na ñ da

Informal extended predicates ending in da are typical of men's speech. As equivalents in sentence-final position and before yo, ne⌐e, and ne, women [2] use extended predicates ending in uncontracted no without following da. Thus:

Informal Predicate [1]	Informal Extended Predicate [1] (alternate form)
wa⌐ka⌐ru	wa⌐ka⌐ru no
wa⌐ka⌐tta	wa⌐ka⌐tta no
wa⌐kara⌐nai	wa⌐kara⌐nai no
wa⌐kara⌐nakatta	wa⌐kara⌐nakatta no
ikitai	i⌐kita⌐i no
ta⌐ka⌐i	ta⌐ka⌐i no
ta⌐kakatta	ta⌐kakatta no

---

[1] The English equivalents are the same as for the formal predicates above.

[2] While the occurrence of any nominal + yo, ne⌐e, or ne is typical of women's speech, ordinarily nominals in sentence-final position occur in the speech of both men and women. However, the occurrence of this no in sentence-final position—particularly in statements—is more typical of women's speech.

Informal Predicate [1]	Informal Extended Predicate [1] (alternate form)
tomodati da	to⌐modati na¬ no
to⌐modati da¬tta	to⌐modati da¬tta no
sa¬ñ-zi made da	sa¬ñ-zi made na no

Women also use formal inflected forms in the first part of this kind of extended predicate. Wa⌐karima¬su no is more formal than wa⌐ka¬ru no, but less formal than wa⌐ka¬ru ñ desu.

Predicates ending with a tentative form of da (for example, de⌐syo¬o) also have extended equivalents. A formal predicate ending with de⌐syo¬o has as its extended equivalent the corresponding non-past or past informal predicate + ñ desyoo. Thus:

Formal Predicate	Formal Extended Predicate
wa⌐ka¬ru desyoo 'it's probably clear'	wa⌐ka¬ru ñ desyoo 'it's probably a matter of being clear' [2]
wa⌐ka¬tta desyoo 'it probably was clear'	wa⌐ka¬tta ñ desyoo 'it's probably a matter of having been clear'
wa⌐kara¬nai desyoo 'it probably isn't clear'	wa⌐kara¬nai ñ desyoo 'it's probably a matter of not being clear'
wa⌐kara¬nakatta desyoo 'it probably wasn't clear'	wa⌐kara¬nakatta ñ desyoo 'it's probably a matter of not having been clear'
i⌐kita¬i desyoo 'he probably wants to go'	i⌐kita¬i ñ desyoo 'it's probably a matter of wanting to go'
ta⌐ka¬i desyoo 'it's probably expensive'	ta⌐ka¬i ñ desyoo 'it's probably a matter of being expensive'
ta¬kakatta desyoo 'it probably was expensive'	ta¬kakatta ñ desyoo 'it's probably a matter of having been expensive'
to⌐modati desyo¬o 'it's probably a friend'	to⌐modati na¬ ñ desyoo 'it's probably a matter of being a friend'
to⌐modati da¬tta desyoo 'it probably was a friend'	to⌐modati da¬tta ñ desyoo 'it's probably a matter of having been a friend'
sa¬ñ-zi made desyoo 'it's probably until 3 o'clock'	sa¬ñ-zi made na ñ desyoo 'it's probably a matter of being until 3 o'clock'

---

[1] The English equivalents are the same as for the formal predicates above.

[2] These are literal equivalents.

An extended predicate ending in <u>desyoo</u> can be made polite by replacing <u>desyoo</u> with <u>de gozaimasyoo</u>.

Grammatically speaking, an extended predicate consists of a nominal n̄/<u>no</u> + √<u>da</u> predicate, with the nominal preceded by a sentence modifier.

Extended predicates occur both in sentence-final position and within a sentence. A predicate and its corresponding extended predicate are almost equivalent in meaning. However, the extended predicate is a more indirect form, and hence is often described as softer and less abrupt. Often, the extended predicate with n̄ is a pattern of familiarity (note that in the Basic Sentences of this lesson, the employer uses the extended-predicate pattern in addressing the maid, but not vice versa). Thus, the most significant difference between i⌐kima¬su and i⌐ku¬ n̄ desu, apart from a structural difference, is stylistic. It might be compared to the kind of difference that exists between English pairs like 'Why are you going?' and 'Why is it you're going?'; 'Who doesn't understand?' and 'Who is it that doesn't understand?'; etc.

Additional examples:

Do⌐ko e i⌐ku⌐ n̄ desu ka↲ 'Where are you going?'
Do⌐tira mo onazi na⌐ n̄ desu yo. 'They are both the same!'
Zu⌐ibuñ ta⌐ka¬i n̄ da yo. 'It is awfully expensive!' (man speaking)
So⌐o na no yo. 'That's the way it is!' (woman speaking)
O⌐mosiro¬i n̄ desyoo? 'It is interesting, isn't it?'
Kyo⌐oto e i⌐rassya⌐ru n̄ de gozaimasu ka↲ 'Do you mean you're going to Kyoto?'
I⌐ku¬ n̄ da ḡa, i⌐kitaku na¬i yo. 'I am going but I don't want to go!' (man speaking)
Te⌐ñpura wa tabe⌐ru n̄ desu ḡa, sa⌐simi¬ wa ta⌐be¬nai n̄ desu yo. 'I do eat tempura but I don't eat sashimi.'
U⌐ti da¬tta n̄ desu ḡa, i⌐ma wa ryo⌐ori¬ya ni ⌐na¬tte iru n̄ desu yo↲ 'It was a house but now it's become a restaurant.'

The negative of an extended predicate, with √<u>da</u> following n̄/<u>no</u> replaced by its negative equivalent, occurs in questions which expect agreement on the part of the person addressed. Thus: <u>ni⌐a¬u n̄ zya a⌐rimase¬n̄ ka</u> 'isn't it (a matter of being) becoming?' 'don't you agree that it's becoming?' and <u>ni⌐a¬u n̄ zya ⌐na¬i desyoo ka</u> 'wouldn't it be (a matter of being) becoming?' 'wouldn't you agree that it is becoming?'

2. Verbals: Honorific Equivalents Ending in √<u>da</u>

A nominal consisting of the polite prefix <u>o-</u> + a verbal stem (i.e. the -<u>ma¬su</u> form minus -<u>ma¬su</u>) [1] followed by √<u>da</u>, is an honorific replacement for the corresponding verbal. Like <u>o</u>-stem + <u>ni</u> √<u>na¬ru</u>, it is not used in reference to the speaker; however, the <u>o</u>-stem + <u>ni</u> √<u>na¬ru</u> construction is slightly more polite.

In its non-past form, the <u>o</u>-stem + √<u>da</u> pattern refers to present, future, or repeated action. Thus, <u>O⌐hanasi de¬su ka↲</u> means, depending on context, 'Are you talking?' or 'Are you going to talk?' or 'Do you talk?'; it is an honorific equivalent of both <u>Ha⌐na¬site imasu ka↲</u> and <u>Ha⌐nasima¬su ka↲</u> .

---

[1] The resulting nominal is unaccented.

Examples:

O⌐yobi de⌐su ka⌟ 'Are you calling me?'
O⌐wakari de⌐sita ka⌟ 'Did you understand?'
O⌐tanomi de gozaima⌐sita ka⌟ 'Did you order?'
O⌐tutome zya arimase⌐ñ ka⌟ 'Aren't you working?'
Oisoḡi desyoo? 'You're in a hurry, aren't you?'
O⌐dekake da⌐ kara_ 'Since you're going out . . .

WARNING: Not every verbal has this kind of polite equivalent. Use only those you have heard or checked with a native speaker.

3. Particle _si_ 'and'

The particle _si_ 'and,' 'and what is more' follows inflected words (verbals, adjectivals, and √da), non-past or past or tentative, informal or formal. It usually ends with comma intonation.

Compare the following three types of examples, all containing 'and' in their English equivalents:

(1) ho⌐ñ to za̅ssi 'books and magazines'
Tookyoo ya O̅osaka 'Tokyo and Osaka and such places'

(2) U⌐ti e ka⌐ette, ne⌐ma⌐sita. 'I returned home and went to bed.'
Se⌐makute a⌐tu⌐i. 'It is small and it is hot.'
Ko⌐re wa Ta⌐roo de, so⌐re wa Zi⌐roo desu. 'This is Taro and that is Jiro.'

(3) Ha⌐nasima⌐su si, ka⌐kima⌐su. 'He speaks and what is more, he writes.'
Se⌐ma⌐i si, a⌐tu⌐i. 'It's small and what is more, it's hot.'
Byo⌐oki da⌐ si, i⌐kitaku na⌐i. 'I'm sick and what is more, I don't want to go.'

In examples of the first kind, _to_ and _ya_ 'and' connect nominals.

In examples of the second kind, the gerund indicates an action or state co-ordinate with what follows: 'A is true AND B is true'; if, as in the first example under (2), the action of the gerund is not simultaneous with that of what follows, the order of inflected forms is chronological: 'A happens AND THEN B happens.' If a connective follows the gerund, it is often _sore kara_ 'and then,' 'after that.'

In examples of the third kind, an inflected word followed by particle _si_ furnishes one bit of evidence in a series, all of which are contributing to a single result: thus, in the examples above, 'he speaks and what is more, he writes—therefore he is proficient'; 'it's small and what is more, it's hot—therefore it's not a desirable room'; 'I'm sick and what is more, I don't want to go—therefore I'm not going.' There is not a chronological significance in the order of inflected words connected by _si_. If a connective occurs at the beginning of the second (or later) clause, it is often _sono ue_ 'on top of that,' 'what is more.'

Accentuation before _si_ is the same as accentuation before _kara_ 'so' and _desyoo_: in general, a normally unaccented verbal acquires an accent on its final syllable; a normally unaccented adjectival acquires an accent on its pre-final syllable; and √da following an unaccented word or phrase is accented.

Examples:

Yo˥ku ta˥bema˥su si, yo˥ku ne˥ma˥su kara; mo˥o su˥g̃u ˥ge˥ñki ni ˥na˥ru desyoo. 'He eats well and he sleeps well so he'll probably get strong very soon now.'

A˥no˥ hito wa ni˥hoñg̃o mo de˥kita si, e˥eg̃o mo dekima˥sita yo⌣ 'He could speak Japanese and could speak English too.'

Ko˥no apa˥ato wa sa˥mu˥i si, ti˥isa˥i desu. 'This apartment is cold, and what's more, it's small.'

Ni˥ku˥ mo ˥na˥i si, sa˥kana mo arimase˥ñ. 'There's no meat and there's no fish either.'

A˥no zi˥syo wa ˥o˥okikatta si, ta˥kakatta kara; ka˥imase˥ñ desita. 'That dictionary was big and it was expensive so I didn't buy it.'

Koko wa ˥ki˥ree da si, su˥zusi˥i si, si˥zuka da kara; su˥ki˥ desu. 'I like this place because it's pretty and it's cool and it's quiet.'

I˥i ˥ki˥zi datta si, ya˥sukatta kara; ta˥kusañ kaima˥sita. 'It was nice material and what's more it was cheap so I bought a lot.'

In all the above sentences, sono ue may be inserted following si.

4. Nominals Ending in -sa

An adjectival stem (i.e. the citation form minus its final -i) + -sa is a nominal indicating the extent of the adjectival quality. The accent of the -sa word is, with few exceptions, the same as the accent of the adverbial (-ku form) of the corresponding adjectival.

Examples:

na˥g̃a˥i 'is long'	na˥g̃asa 'length'
o˥oki˥i 'is big'	ookisa 'size'
a˥tu˥i 'is hot'	a˥tusa 'heat'
atui 'is thick'	atusa 'thickness'
hi˥ro˥i 'is big (in area)' or 'is wide'	hi˥rosa 'area' or 'width'
ko˥i 'is strong or thick (of liquids); is dark (of colors)'	ko˥sa 'strength or thickness (of liquids); darkness (of colors)'

5. Multiple Modifiers

A nominal may be described by more than one modifier, each of which retains its original form:

ta˥ka˥i bu˥ra˥usu 'an expensive blouse'; ko˥ñ no bu˥ra˥usu 'a navy blue blouse'; ta˥ka˥i ˥ko˥ñ no bu˥ra˥usu 'an expensive, navy blue blouse'

a˥tarasi˥i boosi 'a new hat'; ku˥ro˥i boosi 'a black hat'; a˥tarasi˥i ku˥ro˥i boosi 'a new, black hat'

wa˥takusi no se˥etaa 'my sweater'; mi˥dori no ˥se˥etaa 'a green sweater'; watakusi no ˥mi˥dori no ˥se˥etaa 'my green sweater' ki⌐ree na ⌐o⌐obaa 'a pretty coat'; ha⌐iiro no o⌐obaa 'a gray coat'; ki⌐ree na ha⌐iiro no o⌐obaa 'a pretty, gray coat'

In some cases, the modifier itself is modified. Thus:

u⌐sui haiiro no zido⌐osya 'a light gray car'
wa⌐takusi no tomodati no zido⌐osya 'my friend's car'

Compare the intonation patterns of the two preceding groups of examples. Given Modifier A + Modifier B + Nominal[1]: if Modifier A describes the nominal, then Modifier B is pronounced as if it were at the beginning of a new sentence; if Modifier A describes Modifier B, then both regularly belong to the same accent phrase. Thus:

usui hāiiro no waisyatu 'a thin, gray shirt' (i.e. a gray shirt that's thin; Modifier A [usui] modifies waisyatu and Modifier B [haiiro] is pronounced as if at the beginning of a new sentence)
usui haiiro no waisyatu 'a light gray shirt' (i.e. a shirt that's light gray; Modifier A [usui] modifies Modifier B [haiiro] and both belong to the same accent phrase)

o⌐oki⌐i tañsu no hikidasi 'a big, bureau drawer' (i.e. a bureau drawer that's big; Modifier A [o⌐oki⌐i] modifies hikidasi and Modifier B [tañsu] is pronounced as if at the beginning of a new sentence)
o⌐oki⌐i tañsu no hikidasi 'a drawer of the big bureau' (Modifier A [o⌐oki⌐i] modifies Modifier B [tañsu] and both belong to the same accent phrase)

The same distinction applies when Modifier A is a demonstrative (kono, sono, etc.) and Modifier B contains a nominal. Thus:

kono zi⌐do⌐osya no ⌐e⌐ñziñ 'this car-engine' (i.e. this engine that belongs to a car; Modifier A [kono] modifies e⌐ñziñ and Modifier B [zi⌐do⌐osya] is pronounced as if at the beginning of a new sentence)
ko⌐no zido⌐osya no ⌐e⌐ñziñ 'the engine of this car' (Modifier A [kono] modifies Modifier B [zi⌐do⌐osya] and both belong to the same accent phrase)

DRILLS

A. Substitution Drill

(Use whatever gerund is appropriate with the given substitution item.)

1. He's wearing a navy blue suit.	Ko⌐ñ no se⌐biro (o) kite (i)ma⌐su yo⌐
2. He's wearing black shoes.	Ku⌐ro⌐i ku⌐tu⌐ (o) ha⌐ite (i)ma⌐su yo⌐
3. He's wearing a funny hat.	O⌐kasi⌐i bo⌐osi (o) kabu⌐tte (i)masu yo⌐
4. He's wearing a loud necktie.	Ha⌐de⌐ na ⌐ne⌐kutai (o) si⌐te (i)ma⌐-su yo⌐

---

[1] With normal, non-contrastive intonation. Not included here are special cases comparable to English 'a BLUE car, not a GREEN car.'

5. He's wearing new gloves.   A⌐tarasi⌐i te⌐bu⌐kuro (o) ha⌐mete
                                      (i)ma⌐su yo⌐

6. She's wearing a pretty obi.   Ki⌐ree na ⌐o⌐bi (o) ⌐si⌐mete (i)ma-
                                      su yo⌐

7. He's wearing big glasses.   O⌐oki⌐i ⌐me⌐g̃ane (o) ⌐ka⌐kete
                                      (i)masu yo⌐

8. She's wearing a wide skirt.   Hi⌐ro⌐i su⌐ka⌐ato (o) ha⌐ite (i)ma⌐-
                                      su yo⌐

9. He's wearing a stunning   Ri⌐ppa na kimono (o) kite (i)ma⌐su
    kimono.   yo⌐

10. He's wearing woolen   U⌐uru no zu⌐bo⌐ñ (o) ha⌐ite (i)ma⌐-
    trousers.   su yo⌐

B. Substitution Drill

    (Use whatever gerund is appropriate with the given substitution item.)

1. Are you going to wear a   Gekizyoo e se⌐biro (o) kite iku⌐ ñ
    (man's) suit to the theater?   desu ka⌐

2. Are you going to wear a   Gekizyoo e ⌐su⌐utu (o) ki⌐te iku⌐ ñ
    (woman's) suit to the   desu ka⌐
    theater?

3. Are you going to wear   Gekizyoo e yo⌐ohuku (o) kite iku⌐ ñ
    Western-style clothing to   desu ka⌐
    the theater?

4. Are you going to wear Jap-   Gekizyoo e wa⌐huku (o) kite iku⌐ ñ
    anese-style clothing to the   desu ka⌐
    theater?

5. Are you going to wear a   Gekizyoo e ki⌐mono (o) kite iku⌐ ñ
    kimono to the theater?   desu ka⌐

6. Are you going to wear zori   Gekizyoo e zo⌐ori (o) haite iku⌐ ñ
    to the theater?   desu ka⌐

7. Are you going to wear a   Gekizyoo e bo⌐osi (o) kabu⌐tte i⌐ku⌐
    hat to the theater?   ñ desu ka⌐

8. Are you going to wear a   Gekizyoo e yu⌐kata (o) kite iku⌐ ñ
    yukata to the theater?   desu ka⌐

9. Are you going to wear a   Gekizyoo e ha⌐ori (o) kite iku⌐ ñ
    haori to the theater?   desu ka⌐

10. Are you going to wear a   Gekizyoo e wa⌐ñpi⌐isu (o) ki⌐te iku⌐
    dress to the theater?   ñ desu ka⌐

C. Substitution Drill

1. We decided on that teacher.   A⌐no señse⌐e ni ki⌐mema⌐sita.

2. We decided on the teacher   Se⌐ñse⌐e o ki⌐mema⌐sita.
    (i.e. who the teacher is to
    be).

3. The teacher decided [it].   Se⌐ñse⌐e g̃a ki⌐mema⌐sita.

4. The teacher has been de-   Se⌐ñse⌐e g̃a ki⌐marima⌐sita.
    cided on.

5. It was decided on Friday.[1]   Ki⌐ñyo⌐o ni ki⌐marima⌐sita.
6. We decided on Friday.[1]   Ki⌐ñyo⌐o ni ki⌐mema⌐sita.
7. We decided on the day   Hi ⌐o kimema⌐sita.
    (i.e. what day it is to be).

D. Substitution Drill

1. Is this to be put away?   Kore (wa) si⌐mau⌐ ñ desu ka⌐
    (Lit. As for this, is it a
    matter of putting it away?)
2. Is this to be put in?   Kore (wa) i⌐reru⌐ ñ desu ka⌐
3. Is this to be taken out?   Kore (wa) da⌐su ñ desu ka⌐
4. Is this to be aired?   Kore (wa) ⌐ho⌐su ñ desu ka⌐
5. Is this to be measured?   Kore (wa) ha⌐ka⌐ru ñ desu ka⌐
6. Is this to be sent?   Kore (wa) o⌐kuru⌐ ñ desu ka⌐
7. Is this to be laundered?   Kore (wa) se⌐ñtaku-suru⌐ ñ desu
                               ka⌐
8. Is this to be thrown away?   Kore (wa) su⌐teru⌐ ñ desu ka⌐
9. Is this to be wiped off?   Kore (wa) hu⌐ku⌐ ñ desu ka⌐
10. Is this to be fixed?   Kore (wa) na⌐o⌐su ñ desu ka⌐

E. Substitution Drill

(Insert the substitution item in its appropriate form.)

1. I want to have a (man's)   Sebiro (o) tu⌐ku⌐tte mo⌐raita⌐i
    suit made. Can you do it   ñ desu ḡa, su⌐ḡu de⌐kima⌐su ka⌐
    right away?
2. I want to have this watch   Kono tokee (o) na⌐o⌐site mo⌐rai-
    fixed. Can you do it right   ta⌐i ñ desu ḡa, su⌐ḡu de⌐kima⌐su
    away? /kono tokee (o)   ka⌐
    na⌐o⌐su/
3. I want to have this chair   Kono isu (o) to⌐do⌐kete mo⌐raita⌐i
    delivered. Can you do it   ñ desu ḡa, su⌐ḡu de⌐kima⌐su ka⌐
    right away? /kono isu (o)
    to⌐doke⌐ru/
4. I want to have this dress   Ko⌐no wañpi⌐isu (o) se⌐ñtaku-site
    laundered. Can you do it   moraita⌐i ñ desu ḡa, su⌐ḡu de-
    right away? /ko⌐no wañ-   ⌐kima⌐su ka⌐
    pi⌐isu (o) se⌐ñtaku-suru/
5. I want to have this car   Kono kuruma (o) mi⌐ḡaite morai-
    polished. Can you do it   ta⌐i ñ desu ḡa, su⌐ḡu de⌐kima⌐su
    right away? /kono kuruma   ka⌐
    (o) mi̅ḡaku/

---

[1] Two possible meanings, depending on context: (1) 'the day decided on was Friday' (ni = particle of goal); (2) 'the day the decision was made was Friday' (ni = particle of time).

6. I want to have my hair cut
    (i. e. clipped).   Can you do
    it right away? /ka⌐mi⌐ (o)
    ka̅ru/

Ka⌐mi⌐ (o) ka⌐tte moraita⌐i ñ desu
g̅a, su̅g̅u de⌐kima⌐su ka⌐⌐

7. I want to have my hair cut.
    Can you do it right away?
    /ka⌐mi⌐ (o) ⌐ki⌐ru/

Ka⌐mi⌐ (o) ⌐ki⌐tte mo⌐raita⌐i ñ
desu g̅a, su̅g̅u de⌐kima⌐su ka⌐⌐

8. I want to have these dishes
    washed.   Can you do it
    right away? /kono osara
    (o) a̅rau/

Kono osara (o) a⌐ratte moraita⌐i
ñ desu g̅a, su̅g̅u de⌐kima⌐su ka⌐⌐

9. I want to have this (man's)
    suit pressed.   Can you do
    it right away? /kono se-
    biro ni a⌐iroñ (o) kake⌐ru/

Kono sebiro ni a⌐iroñ (o) ka⌐kete
mo⌐raita⌐i ñ desu g̅a, su̅g̅u de-
⌐kima⌐su ka⌐⌐

10. I want to have a new cup-
    board made.   Can you do
    it right away? /a⌐tarasi⌐i
    todana (o) tu⌐ku⌐ru/

A⌐tarasi⌐i todana (o) tu⌐ku⌐tte mo-
⌐raita⌐i ñ desu g̅a, su̅g̅u de⌐ki-
ma⌐su ka⌐⌐

F.   Substitution Drill

1. The length is just right but
    it's a little tight.

Na⌐g̅asa wa tyo⌐odo i⌐i ñ desu g̅a,
tyo̅tto ki⌐tu⌐i ñ desu yo.

2. The size is just right but
    it's a little short.

O⌐okisa wa tyoodo i⌐i ñ desu g̅a,
tyo̅tto mi⌐zika⌐i ñ desu yo.

3. The thickness is just right
    but it's a little tough.

A⌐tusa wa tyoodo i⌐i ñ desu g̅a,
tyo̅tto ka⌐ta⌐i ñ desu yo.

4. It's just strong enough but
    it's a little cold.

Ko⌐sa wa tyo⌐odo i⌐i ñ desu g̅a,
tyo̅tto tu⌐meta⌐i ñ desu yo.

5. The speed is just right but
    it's a little expensive.

Ha⌐yasa wa tyo⌐odo i⌐i ñ desu g̅a,
tyo̅tto ta⌐ka⌐i ñ desu yo.

6. The color is just right but
    it's a little long.

I⌐ro⌐ wa tyo⌐odo i⌐i ñ desu g̅a,
tyo̅tto na⌐g̅a⌐i ñ desu yo.

7. The style is just right but
    it's a little big.

Ka⌐tati wa tyoodo i⌐i ñ desu g̅a,
tyo̅tto o⌐oki⌐i ñ desu yo.

8. The pattern is just right but
    it's a little small.

Ga⌐ra wa tyoodo i⌐i ñ desu g̅a,
tyo̅tto ti⌐isa⌐i ñ desu yo.

G.   Grammar Drill (based on Grammatical Note 1)

Tutor: I⌐kima⌐su. (regular predicate)   ⎫
Student: I⌐ku⌐ ñ desu. (extended predicate)   ⎬ 'I['ll] go.'
                                                  ⎭

1. A⌐merika e okurima⌐su ka⌐⌐   A⌐merika e okuru⌐ ñ desu ka⌐⌐
2. Ma⌐da to⌐dokimase⌐ñ ka⌐⌐   Ma⌐da to⌐doka⌐nai ñ desu ka⌐⌐
3. Mo̅o su⌐ñpoo (o) hakarima⌐-   Mo̅o su⌐ñpoo (o) haka⌐tta ñ desu
    sita yo⌐   yo⌐
4. A⌐tarasi⌐i sig̅oto (wa) a⌐si-   A⌐tarasi⌐i sig̅oto (wa) a⌐sita⌐ kara
    ta⌐ kara desu ka⌐⌐   na ñ desu ka⌐⌐

5. So⌐no niku⌐ (wa) ka⌐ta⌐i   So⌐no niku⌐ (wa) ka⌐ta⌐i ñ desu ka⌐
   desu ka⌐
6. So⌐no wañpi⌐isu (wa) Hu-   So⌐no wañpi⌐isu (wa) Hu⌐rañsu-see
   rañsu-see de⌐su ka⌐   na⌐ ñ desu ka⌐
7. O⌐ka⌐sikatta desu yo⌐   O⌐ka⌐sikatta ñ desu yo⌐   ·
8. Ka⌐maimase⌐ñ desita yo⌐   Ka⌐mawa⌐nakatta ñ desu yo⌐
9. Ki⌐no⌐o made byo⌐oki de⌐-   Ki⌐no⌐o made byo⌐oki da⌐tta ñ desu.
   sita.
10. Zyo⌐obu zya arimase⌐ñ ka⌐   Zyo⌐obu zya na⌐i ñ desu ka⌐

H. Grammar Drill[1] (based on Grammatical Note 1)

      Man: I⌐ku⌐ ñ da yo⌐ (extended predicate,
                informal men's speech)
                                                   'I['ll] go.'
      Woman: I⌐ku⌐ no yo⌐ (extended predicate,
                informal women's speech)

1. A⌐merika e okuru⌐ ñ da yo⌐   A⌐merika e okuru⌐ no yo⌐
2. Ma⌐da to⌐doka⌐nai ñ da yo⌐   Ma⌐da to⌐doka⌐nai no yo⌐
3. Mo⌐o su⌐ñpoo (o) haka⌐tta   Mo⌐o su⌐ñpoo (o) haka⌐tta no yo⌐
   ñ da yo⌐
4. A⌐tarasi⌐i si⌐goto (wa) a⌐si-   A⌐tarasi⌐i si⌐goto (wa) a⌐sita⌐ kara
   ta⌐ kara na ñ da yo⌐   na no yo⌐
5. So⌐no niku⌐ (wa) ka⌐ta⌐i ñ   So⌐no niku⌐ (wa) ka⌐ta⌐i no yo⌐
   da yo⌐
6. So⌐no wañpi⌐isu (wa) Hu-   So⌐no wañpi⌐isu (wa) Hu⌐rañsu-see
   ⌐rañsu-see na⌐ ñ da yo⌐   na⌐ no yo⌐
7. O⌐ka⌐sikatta ñ da yo⌐   O⌐ka⌐sikatta no yo⌐
8. Ka⌐mawa⌐nakatta ñ da yo⌐   Ka⌐mawa⌐nakatta no yo⌐
9. Ki⌐no⌐o made byo⌐oki da⌐-   Ki⌐no⌐o made byo⌐oki da⌐tta no yo⌐
   tta ñ da yo⌐
10. Zyo⌐obu zya na⌐i ñ da yo⌐   Zyo⌐obu zya na⌐i no yo⌐

I. Level Drill (based on Grammatical Note 2)

      Tutor: De⌐kakema⌐su ka⌐ (formal plain)
                                                'Are you going out?'
      Student: O⌐dekake de⌐su ka⌐ (formal honorific)

1. I⌐sogima⌐su ka⌐   O⌐isogi de⌐su ka⌐
2. Su⌐gu wa⌐karima⌐sita ka⌐   Su⌐gu o⌐wakari de⌐sita ka⌐
3. Ta⌐naka-señse⌐e (ga) yo⌐ñde   Ta⌐naka-señse⌐e (ga) o⌐yobi de⌐su
   (i)ma⌐su yo⌐   yo⌐
4. Do⌐nata (o) ⌐ma⌐tte (i)masu   Do⌐nata (o) o⌐mati de⌐su ka⌐
   ka⌐
5. Ra⌐zio (o) ki⌐ite (i)ma⌐su   Ra⌐zio (o) o⌐kiki de⌐su ka⌐
   ka⌐
6. Mo⌐o ka⌐erima⌐su ka⌐   Mo⌐o o⌐kaeri de⌐su ka⌐

---

[1] For a man student, the tutor gives the form on the right and the student gives
the form on the left. For a woman student, the opposite procedure is used.

J.   Expansion Drill

1. Do you have any material?
    Do you have any solid-color
      material?
    Do you have any white solid-
      color material?
    Do you have any white solid-
      color material that's
      linen?

    Ki¬zi ḡa a⌐rima¬su ka↲
    Mu¬zi no ⌐ki¬zi ḡa a⌐rima¬su ka↲
    Si⌐ro¬i ⌐mu¬zi no ⌐ki¬zi ḡa a⌐ri-
      ma¬su ka↲
    Asa no si⌐ro¬i ⌐mu¬zi no ⌐ki¬zi ḡa
      a⌐rima¬su ka↲

2. How much is one meter?
    How much is the material
      by the meter?
    How much is the woolen
      material by the meter?
    How much is the black
      woolen material by the
      meter?
    How much is that black
      woolen material by the
      meter?

    I⌐ti-me¬etoru ⌐i¬kura?
    Ki¬zi i⌐ti-me¬etoru ⌐i¬kura?
    U¬uru no ⌐ki¬zi i⌐ti-me¬etoru
      ⌐i¬kura?
    Ku⌐ro¬i ⌐u¬uru no ⌐ki¬zi i⌐ti-me¬-
      etoru ⌐i¬kura?
    Sono ku⌐ro¬i ⌐u¬uru no ⌐ki¬zi
      i⌐ti-me¬etoru ⌐i¬kura?

3. I'm looking for [it] (but). . .
    I'm looking for material
      (but). . .
    I'm looking for solid-color
      material (but). . .
    I'm looking for solid-color
      material of a conservative
      color (but). . .
    I'm looking for solid-color
      material of a more con-
      servative color (but). . .

    Sa⌐ḡasite (i)ru¬ ñ desu ḡa_
    Ki¬zi (o) sa⌐ḡasite (i)ru¬ ñ desu
      ḡa_
    Mu¬zi no ⌐ki¬zi (o) sa⌐ḡasite
      (i)ru¬ ñ desu ḡa_
    Zi⌐mi¬ na i⌐ro¬ no ⌐mu¬zi no ⌐ki¬zi
      (o) sa⌐ḡasite (i)ru¬ ñ desu ḡa_

    Mo¬tto zi⌐mi¬ na i⌐ro¬ no ⌐mu¬zi no
      ⌐ki¬zi (o) sa⌐ḡasite (i)ru¬ ñ desu
      ḡa_

4. Let's go to the sea[shore].
    It's hot so let's go to the
      sea[shore].
    It's a holiday and what's
      more it's hot so let's go
      to the sea[shore].
    Today it's a holiday and
      what's more it's hot so
      let's go to the sea[shore].

    ⌐U¬mi e i⌐kimasyo¬o.
    A⌐tu¬i kara, u¬mi e i⌐kimasyo¬o.
    O⌐yasumi da¬ si, a⌐tu¬i kara; u¬mi
      e i⌐kimasyo¬o.
    Kyo¬o wa o⌐yasumi da¬ si, a⌐tu¬i
      kara; u¬mi e i⌐kimasyo¬o.

5. It wore out. (Lit. It be-
      came no good.)
    It wore out right away.
    It's supposed to be durable
      but it wore out right away.

    Da⌐me¬ ni na⌐rima¬sita yo↲

    Su¬ḡu da⌐me¬ ni na⌐rima¬sita yo↲
    Zyo⌐obu na hazu de¬su ḡa, su¬ḡu
      da⌐me¬ ni na⌐rima¬sita yo↲

It's made of synthetic
fibers so it's supposed to
be durable but it wore
out right away.

Ka⌐señ de tukútte ˻a˧ru kara, zyo-
⌐obu na hazu de˥su ḡa; su̅ḡu da-
˻me˧ ni na˻rima˧sita yo⌐

This sweater is made of
synthetic fibers so it's
supposed to be durable
but it wore out right
away.

Ko⌐no se⌐etaa wa ka⌐señ de tukútte
˻a˧ru kara, zyo⌐obu na hazu de̅-
su ḡa; su̅ḡu da˻me˧ ni na˻rimạ˧-
sita yo⌐

6. I don't feel very well.

Tyo̅tto ki⌐moti ḡa warúi ñ desu
yo.

Today I don't feel very well.

Kyo̅o wa ⌐tyo̅tto ki⌐moti ḡa warúi ñ desu yo.

I ate a lot so today I don't
feel very well.

Ta⌐kusañ ta̅beta kara, kyo̅o wa
⌐tyo̅tto ki moti ḡa warúi ñ desu
yo.

On top of that I ate a lot so
today I don't feel very
well.

Sono ue ta⌐kusañ ta̅beta kara,
kyo̅o wa ⌐tyo̅tto ki⌐moti ḡa warúi ñ desu yo.

I drank a lot and on top of
that I ate a lot so today I
don't feel very well.

Ta⌐kusañ no̅ñda si, sono ue ta-
⌐kusañ ta̅beta kara; kyo̅o wa
⌐tyo̅tto ki⌐moti ḡa warúi ñ
desu yo.

I drank a lot and on top of
that I ate a lot, with a
friend, so today I don't
feel very well.

Tomodati to issyo ni ta⌐kusañ
no̅ñda si, sono ue ta⌐kusañ
ta̅beta kara; kyo̅o wa ⌐tyo̅tto
ki⌐moti ḡa warúi ñ desu yo.

Yesterday I drank a lot and
on top of that I ate a lot,
with a friend, so today I
don't feel very well.

Ki⌐no̅o wa to̅modati to issyo ni
ta⌐kusañ no̅ñda si, sono ue ta-
⌐kusañ ta̅beta kara; kyo̅o wa
⌐tyo̅tto ki⌐moti ḡa warúi ñ
desu yo.

SHORT SUPPLEMENTARY DIALOGUES

1. Guest: Sayoonara.
   Hostess: Mo̅o o˻kaeri de gozaima˧su ka⌐
   Guest: E˧e. Kyo̅o wa ⌐tyo̅tto i˻soḡima˧su kara⌐

2. Smith: Kinoo ha⌐zi̅mete Ta⌐naka-sañ no otaku e ikima˧sita ḡa, ano
   heñ wa *mi⌐ti ḡa yo̅ku a⌐rimase̅ñ he̅e.
   Yamamoto: Su̅ḡu o⌐wakari de˧sita ka⌐
   Smith: Iie. Zu̅ibuñ sa˻ḡasima˧sita yo.

3. Maid: Na̅ni o ki˻te irassyaima˧su ka⌐
   Mr. Tanaka: Ko̅ñ no sebiro kite, ku⌐ro̅i kutu haite iku yo.
   Maid: Waisyatu wa si⌐ro̅i no de gozaimasu ka⌐
   Mr. Tanaka: E˧e, so̅o.

4. Tanaka: Hiᶜdo˺i yuˣki˹ desu yo⌐
    Smith: Zya˺a, aᶜtui o˺obaa o kiˣte ikimasyo˹o.

5. Host: Yo˺ku iˣrassyaima˹sita. Do˺ozo oˣhairi-kudasa˹i.
    Smith (entering and removing overcoat): Siᶜtu˺ree-simasu.
    Host: A˺a, bo˺ku no uti wa saᶜmu˺i desu kara, do˺ozo ᶜo˺obaa o kiˣta
       mama˹ de⌐
    Smith: Sita ni taᶜkusañ kite orima˺su kara, do˺ozo goᶜsiñpai na˺ku.

6. Smith: Kyo˺o wa ūti kara ᶜta˺kusii de kiˣta˹ ñ desu yo⌐
    Tanaka: Kuruma wa?
    Smith: E˺ñziñ no guai ḡa ᶜhe˺ñ ni ˣna˹ttyatta kara, siᶜkata ḡa na˺katta
       ñ desu.

7. Smith: Sore Mᾱtumoto-sañ no otaku desyoo?
    Tanaka: Oᶜtaku da˺tta ñ desu ḡa, iˣma wa ryoᶜkañ ni na˺tta ñ desu yo⌐
       Matumoto-sañ wa kōko o kasite aᶜtarasi˺i uˣti ni ha˹itta soo desu.
    Smith: So˺o na ñ desu ka.

8. Mrs. Tanaka: Ano siᶜro˹i ᶜki˺ree na ˣse˹etaa taᶜka˺i no?
    Mrs. Yamamoto: Zu˺ibuñ taˣka˹i no yo⌐ Naᶜha-señ-eñ na˺ no yo⌐

9. Tanaka: Ano ᶜsi˺ro to ˣku˹ro no ˣse˹etaa taᶜka˺i?
    Mr. Yamamoto: Zu˺ibuñ taˣka˹i ñ da yo⌐ Naᶜhaseñ-eñ na˺ ñ da yo.

10. Tanaka: Waᶜka˺ru?
    Mr. Yamamoto: Bo˺ku wa waˣkara˹nai ñ da yo.
    Miss Itoo: Waᶜtakusi mo wakara˺nai no yo.

11. Customer: Aᶜo˹i ᶜki˺nu no ˣne˹kutai ˣmi˹sete⌐
    Salesgirl: Kore wa iᶜka˺ḡa de gozaimasu ka.
    Customer: Tyo˺tto haᶜde˺ zya ˣna˹i desyoo ka.
    Salesgirl: Zya˺a, mu˺zi no wa iᶜka˺ḡa de gozaimasu ka⌐
    Customer: A˺a, soᶜno ho˺o ḡa niˣaima˹su yo.

12. Tanaka: Kyo˺o ohima?
    Yamamoto: Kyo˺o wa ᶜgo˺ḡo deˣkakeru˹ si, yuuḡata toᶜmodati ḡa ku˺ru
       kara⌐
    Tanaka: Zya˺a mata.

13. Mr. Smith: Bo˺ku no ˣho˹ñ siᶜrimaseñ ka⌐
    Tanaka: Soᶜko ni arimaseñ ka⌐
    Mr. Smith: Koᶜre wa Tanaka-sañ no˹ da si, soᶜre wa Yosida-sañ no˺ da
       si⌐
    Tanaka: Zya˺a, toᶜnari no heya˺ zya ˣna˹i desyoo ka.

14. Mrs. Tanaka: Kinoo koᶜno ne˺kutai o kaˣima˹sita ḡa; syu˺ziñ ḡa haᶜde-
       suḡi˺ru tte iˣima˹sita kara, toᶜrikaete moraita˹i ñ desu ḡa⌐
    Salesgirl: Do˺ozo. Kotira ni ᶜmo˺tto ziᶜmi˺ na no ḡa taᶜkusañ gozai-
       ma˺su kara, oᶜsuki na˹ no o⌐

15. Smith: A⌐kai wañpi˩isu o kite ru a⌐no˥ hito ⌐To˥siko-sañ?
     Yamamoto: E˥e. Ha⌐de˥ na hito desyoo?
     Smith: Zu˥ibuñ.

16. Young Man A: Ku⌐ruma ḡa kaita˥i ñ da kedo; ti⌐ti˥ mo syo⌐oti-sina˩i si,
         o⌐kane mo na˥i si_ Syo⌐o ḡa na˥i ⌐ne˥e.
     Young Man B: Bo⌐ku mo so˥o datta kara, zi⌐teñsya o kattyatta˥ yo.

English Equivalents

1. Guest: Good-bye.
    Hostess: Are you going home already?
    Guest: Yes. (Because) today I'm in a bit of a hurry . . .

2. Smith: Yesterday I went to Mr. Tanaka's for the first time. The roads
        aren't good around there, are they.
    Yamamoto: Were you able to find it right away?
    Smith: No. I searched an awful lot.

3. Maid: What are you going to wear (lit. go wearing)?
    Mr. Tanaka: I'm going to wear my navy blue suit and (I'm going to wear)
        black shoes.
    Maid: And your shirt—will it be a white one?
    Mr. Tanaka: Yes, that's right.

4. Tanaka: It's snowing hard, you know. (Lit. It's severe snow, you know.)
    Smith: Then I guess I'll wear (lit. go wearing) a heavy (lit. thick) over-
        coat.

5. Host: I'm so glad you've come. Please come in.
    Smith: (Excuse me—i.e. for entering your home).
    Host: My house is cold so please leave your coat on (lit. please, being
        the condition of having put on a coat). [1]
    Smith: I'm wearing a lot underneath so please don't worry.

6. Smith: You know, I came from home by taxi today.
    Tanaka: What happened to your car?
    Smith: The engine went bad (lit. the condition of the engine became strange)
        so there was nothing I could do.

7. Smith: That's Mr. Matsumoto's house, isn't it?
    Tanaka: That was his house but now it's become an inn. They say that
        Mr. Matsumoto is renting this place (i.e. to someone) and he has gone
        into a new house.
    Smith: Is that the way it is.

---

[1] Japanese homes are usually much colder than American homes in winter.
When Americans visit Japanese homes, their hosts are often concerned about
the difference in temperature.

8. Mrs. Tanaka: Is that pretty, white sweater expensive?
    Mrs. Yamamoto: It's very expensive. Why, it's ¥ 7000.

9. Tanaka: Is that black and white sweater expensive?
    Mr. Yamamoto: It's very expensive. Why, it's ¥ 7000.

10. Tanaka: Do you understand?
     Mr. Yamamoto: I don't understand.
     Miss Ito: I don't understand either.

11. Customer: Let me see a blue silk necktie.
     Salesgirl: How about this one?
     Customer: Don't you think that's a little loud?
     Salesgirl: Then how about a solid-color one?
     Customer: Oh, that suits me better.

12. Tanaka: [Are you] free today?
     Yamamoto: Today I'm going out in the afternoon, and a friend is coming
         in the early evening, so . . .
     Tanaka: Then [I'll ask you] again [sometime].

13. Mr. Smith: Don't you know [where] my book [is]?
     Tanaka: Isn't it there?
     Mr. Smith: This is Mr. Tanaka's (one) and that is Mr. Yoshida's (one)
         and . . .
     Tanaka: Then wouldn't it be in the next room?

14. Mrs. Tanaka: I bought this necktie yesterday but my husband said that
         it's too loud so I'd like to have it exchanged . . .
     Salesgirl: Certainly. There are lots of more conservative ones [over]
         here so [please choose] one that you'd like.

15. Smith: [Is] that person wearing the red dress Toshiko?
     Yamamoto: Yes. She's quite a number, isn't she?
     Smith: Very much so!

16. Young Man A: I want to buy a car but my father won't say yes and I don't
         have the money and . . . There's nothing I can do!
     Young Man B: I was in the same boat so I ended up buying a bicycle.

EXERCISES

1. Ask the salesgirl to show you:

        a. that blue linen material.
        b. that black cotton skirt.
        c. that brown belt (man's).
        d. that red silk necktie.
        e. the gray umbrella in the middle.
        f. that obi on the bottom.

     g. that white wool sweater.
     h. some gray woolen trousers.
     i. that dark green furoshiki.
     j. some blue solid-color silk material.

2. Tell the tailor:

     a. that your jacket is too tight.
     b. that your trousers are too long.
     c. to make your coat smaller.
     d. to shorten your dress.
     e. that you want to have a suit made.
     f. that you want to have a black silk dress made.

3. Practice conversations between a customer and a clerk. Make your conversations as natural-sounding and as lively as possible. The customer is looking for the following:

     a. 3 1/2 meters of black woolen material, solid color, not more than ¥2500 a meter. [1]
     b. 5 meters of navy blue silk material, not more than ¥ 800 a meter. [1]
     c. a white cotton shirt for a six-year-old boy, for about ¥700.
     d. a silk necktie, conservative pattern, about ¥800.
     e. a large white sweater for a man, about ¥4000.

4. Ask someone (informally):

     a. to have your white suit dry-cleaned.
     b. to look for your old black umbrella.
     c. to air your brown overcoat.
     d. to iron your navy blue trousers as quickly as possible.
     e. to launder this sweater and these gloves.
     f. to shine all the shoes that are dirty.
     g. to get out your new gray sweater.
     h. to put your handkerchiefs in the top drawer.
     i. to put your socks in the middle drawer.
     j. to put your shirts in the bottom drawer.

5. Using colored pictures of people, practice describing in Japanese what they are wearing, within the limits of the vocabulary and constructions you have learned.

6. Practice the Basic Dialogues with appropriate variations, including variations in level.

---

[1] I⌐ti-me⌐etoru 'one meter.'

Lesson 24. Professions and Occupations

BASIC DIALOGUES: FOR MEMORIZATION

(a)

Smith

1. What kind of work are you doing?

Doⁿna si⌐ḡoto (o) site (i)ma⌐su
ka⌐

Tanaka

factory	ko⌐oba⌐ or ko⌐ozyo⌐o
work (verb)	hataraku /-u/

2. I'm working in a factory.

Ko⌐oba⌐ de ha⌐taraite (i)ma⌐su.

lens

re⌐ñzu

3. I'm employed (lit. it is a matter
   of) making lenses.

Re⌐ñzu (o) tu⌐ku⌐tte (i)ru ñ desu.

Smith

4. About how long have you been
   doing [this]?

Do⌐no-ḡurai site (i)ma⌐su ka⌐

Tanaka

since a long time ago or since way in the past	zu⌐tto ma⌐e kara
how many years it comes to	na⌐ñ-neñ ni ⌐na⌐ru ka
commit to memory	o⌐boe⌐ru /-ru/
remember clearly or remember exactly	ha⌐kki⌐ri o⌐bo⌐ete (i)ru

5. (It's) since a long time ago, but
   I don't remember exactly how
   many years it comes to.

Zu⌐tto ma⌐e kara desu ḡa,
na⌐ñ-neñ ni ⌐na⌐ru ka ha⌐kki⌐ri
o⌐bo⌐ete (i)⌐na⌐i ñ desu.

(b)

Smith

government employee	ko⌐omu⌐iñ
practice a profession	suru
work as a government employee	ko⌐omu⌐iñ o suru

6. You are working as a government employee, aren't you?

A⌐na⌐ta (wa) ko⌐omu⌐iñ (o) si⌐te
(i)ru⌐ ñ desyoo?

Tanaka

former time	mo⌐to
year before last	o⌐to⌐tosi
company employee	ka⌐isya⌐iñ

7. No. I used to (lit. as for for-   Iie. Mo⌐to wa ˻so⌐o desita ḡa;
   mer time it was that way), but   o˻to⌐tosi yamete, ka˻isya⌐iñ ni
   I quit the year before last and   na˻rima⌐sita.
   became a company employee.

Smith

   without interruption   zutto
8. Have you been in the same   Zu⌐tto onazi kaisya ni iru⌐ ñ
   company the whole time?   desu ka⌐

Tanaka

   beginning   hazime
   electric company   de˻ñkiḡa⌐isya
   employ   ya˻to⌐u /-u/
   receive employment or   ya˻to⌐tte morau
     be employed
   not even one year   i˻ti⌐-neñ mo / + negative/
   without doing or instead   si˻na⌐i de or se˻zu¹ ni
     of doing
   insurance company   ho˻keñḡa⌐isya
   undergo change   kawaru /-u/
   change to an insurance   ho˻keñḡa⌐isya ni kawaru
     company
9. No. At the beginning I was em-   Iie. Hazime wa de˻ñkiḡa⌐isya ni
   ployed by the electric company,   ya˻to⌐tte mo˻raima⌐sita ḡa; i˻ti⌐-
   but without working there (lit.   neñ mo so˻ko no siḡoto (o) si-
   without doing the work of that   na⌐i de, ho˻keñḡa⌐isya ni ka˻wa-
   place) even a year, I changed   tta⌐ ñ desu yo.
   to an insurance company.

Smith

   previous company   ma⌐e no kaisya
10. Excuse me [for asking] but why   Si˻tu⌐ree desu ḡa, do⌐o site ˻ma⌐e
   is it you quit the previous com-   no kaisya (o) ya˻meta⌐ ñ desu ka⌐
   pany?

Tanaka

   salary   kyu⌐uryoo
11. The salary was —you know!   Kyu⌐uryoo ḡa ˻ne⌐e.

(c)

Mr. Tanaka

12. Are you going to go to work at   Asoko ni ˻ha⌐iru ñ desu ka⌐
   (lit. enter) that place?

Yamamoto

   seem to be difficult or   mu˻zukasii yo⌐o da
     appear difficult

---

¹ Has unaccented alternant.

13. I want to (enter) but it seems
to be difficult.

Ha⌐irita⌐i ñ desu ḡa, mu⌐zukasii
yo⌐o desu.

    as many as ten days <u>or</u>
    all of ten days

    too-ka mo / + affirmative/

    a reply <u>or</u> answer

    he⌐ñzi⌐

14. I've been waiting for all of ten
days now but an answer hasn't
come yet.

Mo⌐o to⌐o-ka mo ma⌐tte (i)ru ñ
desu ḡa, ma⌐da he⌐ñzi⌐ ḡa ⌐ko⌐-
nai ñ desu yo⌐

    mail
    get in touch <u>or</u> contact
    story (<u>or</u> talk) that they'd
    get in touch with me

    yuubiñ
    reñraku-suru
    re⌐ñraku-site kureru tte iu
    hanasi⌐

15. The story was that they'd get
in touch with me by mail but . . .

Yu⌐ubiñ de reñraku-site kureru
tte iu hanasi⌐ datta ñ desu ḡa—

Mr. Tanaka

    can do [it] like you
    a person who can do work
    a person who is able to do
    the work like you
    surely <u>or</u> positively <u>or</u>
    certainly

    a⌐na⌐ta no yoo ni de⌐ki⌐ru
    si⌐ḡoto no deki⌐ru hito
    a⌐na⌐ta no yoo ni si⌐ḡoto
    no deki⌐ru hito
    kitto

16. People who are able to do the
work like you are few [and far
between] so certainly a favor-
able answer will come soon
now.

A⌐na⌐ta no yoo ni si⌐ḡoto no de-
ki⌐ru hito (wa) su⌐kuna⌐i kara,
kitto mo⌐o su⌐ḡu ⌐i⌐i he⌐ñzi⌐ ḡa
ki⌐ma⌐su yo.

    call to mind <u>or</u> recall

    o⌐moida⌐su /-u/

17. Oh, yes! Say! I just remembered—you know?

A⌐a, so⌐o da. Ano ⌐ne⌐e. I⌐ma
o⌐moida⌐sita ñ desu ḡa ne?

    secretary

    hi⌐syo⌐

18. A friend of mine is a secretary
at that place.

Boku no tomodati ḡa a⌐suko no
hisyo⌐ desu yo.

    in [such] a way that [some-
    one] tries asking
    tell [someone] to try asking

    ki⌐ite mi⌐ru yoo ni
    ki⌐ite mi⌐ru yoo ni ǐu

19. Shall I (just) tell her to try
asking?

Tyo⌐tto, a⌐no⌐ hito ni ki⌐ite mi⌐ru
yoo ni i⌐imasyo⌐o ka.

Yamamoto

    thing (intangible) <u>or</u> act
    <u>or</u> fact

    ko⌐to⌐

20. Would that (lit. that kind of
thing) be possible?

So⌐ñna koto⌐ (ḡa) de⌐ki⌐ru desyoo
ka.

Mr. Tanaka

21. Yes, of course.

E⌐e, mo⌐ti⌐roñ.

	without worrying <u>or</u> instead of worrying	si⌐ṅpai-sina⌐i de <u>or</u> si⌐ṅpai-se⌐zu [1] ni
22.	Wait (lit. be waiting) a minute and don't worry.	Si⌐ṅpai-sina⌐i de, tyo⌐tto ⌐ma⌐tte (i)te kudasai.
	ask [someone] to try asking	ki⌐ite mi⌐ru yoo ni ta⌐no⌐mu
23.	(Because) I'll telephone right now and ask her to try inquiring.	I⌐ma deṅwa-site, ki⌐ite mi⌐ru yoo ni ta⌐nomima⌐su kara.

Yamamoto

24.	Well, I'll leave it up to you (lit. I ask you [to treat me] favorably).	Zya⌐a, yo⌐rosiku oneḡai-sima⌐su.

(d)

(At a soba shop)

Mr. Yamamoto

	lunch not come any more (lit. become non-coming any more)	hirumesi [2] mo⌐o ⌐ko⌐naku ⌐na⌐ru
25.	Tanaka doesn't come for lunch any more, does he.	Tanaka-kuṅ ⌐mo⌐o hi⌐rumesi ni ko⌐naku ⌐na⌐tta ⌐ne⌐e.

Mr. Ito

	not a bit	ti⌐tto⌐ mo /+ negative/
26.	We don't see him a bit these days, do we.	Kono-ḡoro ti⌐tto⌐ mo a⌐wa⌐nai ⌐ne⌐e.
	finally <u>or</u> in the end seem to have ended up quit- ting	to⌐otoo ya⌐metyatta yo⌐o da
27.	He kept saying that he'd quit that place. It looks as if he finally did (quit)!	Asuko (o) yămeru yămeru tte i⌐tte (i)ta⌐ kedo, to⌐otoo ya⌐me- tyatta yo⌐o da ⌐ne⌐e.

Mr. Yamamoto

	is boring continue [something] without continuing <u>or</u> instead of continuing work that is more interest- ing and pays a good sal- ary almost (lit. as if) every day	tu⌐ma⌐ṅnai /-ku/ tuzukeru /-ru/ tu⌐zukena⌐i de <u>or</u> tuzu- kezu [3] ni mo⌐tto o⌐mosi⌐rokute ⌐kyu⌐- uryoo no ⌐i⌐i siḡoto ma⌐initi no yo⌐o ni [4]

---

[1] Has unaccented alternant.

[2] Man's word.

[3] Has accented alternant: tu⌐zuke⌐zu.

[4] Has alternate accent: ma⌐initi no ⌐yo⌐o ni.

28. You know, he used to say al-
    most every day that instead of
    continuing boring work like
    that, he wanted to do work that
    was more interesting and paid
    a good salary.

Añna tuˈmaˈñnai siḡoto (o) tuzu-
kezu ni, moˈtto oˈmosiˈrokute ˈkyu-
uryoo no ˈiˈi siˈḡoto ḡa sitaˈi tte;
maˈiniti no yoˈo ni iˈtte (i)taˈ ñ
da yo⏌

Mr. Ito

be(come) found
it is probably a case of
  having been found (in-
  formal)

mitukaru /-u/
miˈtukattaˈ ñ daroo

29. He must surely have found a
    good job. (Lit. It must surely
    be the case that good work has
    been found.)

Kitto ˈiˈi siḡoto ḡa miˈtukattaˈ ñ
daroo.

(e)

Tanaka

30. You are doing difficult work,
    aren't you! Isn't it a strain?

Muˈzukasii osiˈḡoto (o) siˈte
(i)rassyaˈru ñ desu ˈneˈe. Taiheñ desyoo?

Smith

finally or barely or
  with difficulty
make a mistake
without making a mistake
  or instead of making a
  mistake
in [such] a way that it is
  possible
reach the point where it
  is possible

yatto

maˈtiḡaeˈru /-ru/
maˈtiḡaeˈnai de or
  maˈtiḡaeˈzu ni

deˈkiˈru yoo ni

deˈkiˈru yoo ni ˈnaˈru

31. Yes. I have finally reached the
    point nowadays where I can do
    it without making mistakes
    but . . .

Eˈe. Kono-ḡoro yˈatto maˈtiḡaeˈzu ni deˈkiˈru yoo ni na-
ˈrimaˈsita keredo—

ADDITIONAL VOCABULARY

I don't remember for sure but isn't
he a bank employee?

Haˈkkiˈri oˈboˈete (i)ˈmaseˈñ
ḡa, giˈñkoˈoiñ zya aˈrimaseˈñ
ka⏌

carpenter
company president
dentist
diplomat

daˈiku
syatyoo
haˈisya
gaˈikoˈokañ

doctor (medical)	isya or oisyasañ †
driver or chauffeur	u⌐ñte¬ñsyu
eye doctor or oculist	me¬isya
factory worker	kooiñ
farmer	hya⌐kusyo¬o
fisherman	ryo¬osi
foreign trader	bo⌐oeki¬syoo
gardener	uekiya
laborer	ro⌐odo¬osya
lawyer	be⌐ñḡo¬si
manager	si⌐ha¬iniñ
missionary	se⌐ñkyo¬osi
newspaperman	ki⌐sya¬ or si⌐ñbuñki¬sya
nurse	ka⌐ñḡo¬hu
office worker	zi⌐mu¬iñ
professor	kyoozyu
pupil	se¬eto
salaried man or white-collar worker	sa⌐rari¬imañ
salesgirl	uriko
serviceman (i.e. member of the armed forces)	guñziñ
shop employee	mi⌐se no hito¬ or teñiñ
student	gakusee
waiter/waitress or steward/stewardess or barboy or office boy	kyu¬uzi [1] or booi [2]

NOTES ON THE BASIC DIALOGUES

2. <u>Koozyoo</u> usually refers to a large factory, whereas <u>ko⌐oba¬</u> often refers to a small factory or workshop.

Compare: <u>hataraku</u> 'work'
<u>siḡoto o suru</u> 'do work'
<u>tu⌐tome¬ru</u> 'become employed'

A place word + particle <u>de</u> occurs with the first two expressions, indicating the place where work is performed; an organizational word + particle <u>ni</u> with <u>tu⌐tome¬ru</u> indicates the organization for which one works:

<u>giñkoo de hataraite iru</u> 'be working at a bank'
<u>giñkoo de siḡoto o site iru</u> 'be doing work at a bank'
<u>gi⌐ñkoo ni tuto¬mete iru</u> 'be working for a bank'

4. Note the use of the non-past, indicating that an action or state is still continuing.

5. <u>Zu⌐tto ma¬e</u> means literally 'before by far,' i.e. 'way before.'

8. See 4 above.

---

[1] Male or female.

[2] Male.

Zutto 'by far' and zutto 'without interruption,' 'continuous' are distinguished only by context.

9. Particle wa following hazime is the wa of comparison.
Hazime also occurs followed by particle ni, indicating the time when something happens.
Kaisya ~ de⌐ṅkiḡa⌐isya, ho⌐keṅḡa⌐isya: There are many Japanese words beginning with k-, s-, t-, or h- whose initial sound changes when the word becomes the second part of a compound. The change, IF IT OCCURS (it is impossible to predict), is as follows:

   k > ḡ

       Example: Ku⌐tu⌐ 'shoes'
                 naḡaḠutu 'boots'

   s > z

       Example: Su⌐ki⌐ 'pleasing'
                 sakeZuki 'sake lover,' 'drinker'

   t before a, e, o > d; elsewhere, t > z

       Examples: Tana 'shelf'
                 ho⌐ṅDana 'bookshelf'

                 Tyawaṅ '(tea)cup'
                 ko⌐ohiiZya⌐waṅ 'coffee cup'

                 Ti 'blood'
                 hanaZi 'nosebleed'

   h > b (or, sometimes, p)

       Examples: Hako 'box'
                 ho⌐ṅBako 'bookcase'

                 Hya⌐ku⌐ '100'
                 sa⌐ṅByaku '300'
                 ro⌐pPyaku⌐ '600'

Kawaru is the intransitive partner of transitive kaeru 'change [something]' which has occurred in compounds no⌐rikae⌐ru 'change vehicles,' torikaeru 'exchange,' and ki⌐kae⌐ru 'change clothes.'

11. Ḡa here is the emphatic subject particle: 'It was the salary [that was the cause of my leaving].'

14. See 4 above.
He⌐ṅzi⌐: note also he⌐ṅzi⌐ (o) suru 'make an answer,' 'answer (verb).'

15. 'but—I haven't heard anything yet.'

17. O⌐bo⌐ete iru (sentence 5) means 'remember' in the sense of 'be in a state of having committed to memory,' whereas o⌐moida⌐su means 'remember' in the sense of 'call back to mind.'
Ḡa here indicates that the speaker is about to go on to explain what it is he just recalled.

25. Me⌐si⌐ is a less formal equivalent of go⌐hañ. Note also: asamesi 'break-fast' and bañmesi 'dinner' (i. e. 'evening meal').
    The use of na⌐ru indicates that a change has taken place: '[He used to come here for lunch but] he doesn't come any more.' See Lesson 10, Grammatical Note 4.

26. Titto is an alternant of tyo⌐tto which occurs before mo.

28. Tu⌐ma⌐ñnai is the contracted alternant of tu⌐mara⌐nai.
    Tuzukeru is the transitive partner of intransitive tuzuku /-u/ '[some-thing] continues.'

29. Mitukaru is the intransitive partner of transitive mitukeru /-ru/ 'find [something].'

31. 'but—it is still difficult.'
    Ma⌐tiḡae⌐ru is the transitive partner of intransitive ma⌐tiḡa⌐u /-u/ 'be wrong.'

GRAMMATICAL NOTES

1. yo⌐o

Yo⌐o is a nominal meaning 'manner' or 'likeness' or 'resemblance'; it is a na word, and it is always preceded by a modifier. It regularly loses its accent following an accented word or phrase.

Like other na words, yo⌐o occurs followed by √da or by the particle ni of manner (cf. Lesson 15, Grammatical Note 5).

A modifier preceding yo⌐o may be a sentence modifier, a nominal + par-ticle no, or a demonstrative (kono, sono, etc.).

Yo⌐o regularly indicates resemblance or approximation or what seems or appears to be; it has many different English equivalents depending upon the words that surround it. Study the following combinations carefully:

(1) —— yo⌐o √da 'it seems —— ,' 'it appears —— ,' 'it is like ——'

Examples:

Wa⌐ka⌐ru yoo da. 'He seems to understand.'
Ki⌐eta yo⌐o desu. 'It seems to have gone out.'
Ta⌐ka⌐i yoo desita. 'It seemed expensive.'
O⌐bo⌐ete i⌐nai yo⌐o desu. 'It appears that he doesn't remember.'
O⌐suki na yo⌐o de gozaimasu. 'It seems as if he likes it.'
Ki⌐nu no yoo desyoo? 'It's like silk, isn't it?'
So⌐no yo⌐o desita. 'It was like that.'

(2) —— yo⌐o na X[1] 'an X that seems —— ,' 'an X of the kind that —— ,' 'an X that is like ——'

---

[1] X, here, stands for any nominal.

Examples:

Ze⌐ñze̅ñ beñkyoo-sinai yo⌉o na gakusee desu. 'He's a student of the kind that never studies.'

Ta⌐naka-sañ no yo⌉o na tomodati wa su⌐kuna⌉i desu. 'Friends like Mr. Tanaka are rare.'

(3) —— yo⌉o ni 'in the manner of —— ,' 'like —— ,' 'as —— ,' 'in such a way that —— ,' 'so that —— '.

Examples:

Ma⌉e ni i⌐tta yo⌉o ni, sore wa da⌐me⌉ desu. 'As I said before, that's no good.'

Wa⌐surenai yo⌉o ni i⌐tte kudasa⌉i. 'Don't forget to go.' (Lit. 'Please go, in a manner of not forgetting.')

Ho⌐kka⌉idoo no yoo ni sa⌐mu⌉i desu. 'It's cold, like Hokkaido.'

A⌐na⌉ta no yoo ni wa de⌐kimase⌉ñ. 'I can't do it the way you can.'

Ko⌐ko kara mie⌉ru yoo ni ⌐o⌉okiku ⌐ka⌉ite kudasai. 'Please write large, in such a way that I can see it from here.'

Da⌐re mo oki⌉nai yoo ni ⌐ti⌉isa na ⌐ko⌉e de ha⌐na⌉site kudasai. 'Please talk in a low voice so that no one wakes up.'

Note the following special combinations containing —— yo⌉o ni:

(a) —— yo⌉o ni iu 'tell [someone] to —— '

Examples:

De⌐ñwa-suru yo⌉o ni i⌐tte kudasa⌉i. 'Please tell him to telephone.'

A⌐no⌉ hito ni ⌐ma⌉do o a⌐keru yo⌉o ni i⌐ima⌉sita. 'I told him to open the window.'

Na⌐ni mo iwanai yo⌉o ni i⌐tte kudasa⌉i. 'Tell him not to say anything.'

(b) —— yo⌉o ni ⌐na⌉ru 'reach the point where —— '

Examples:

Su⌐ko⌉si wa⌐ka⌉ru yoo ni na⌐rima⌉sita. 'I've reached the point where I understand a little.'

Mo⌐o⌉ hatarakanai yo⌉o ni na⌐rima⌉sita. 'He's reached the point where he doesn't work any more.'

(c) —— yo⌉o ni suru 'act in such a way that —— '

Example:

Ha⌉yaku zyo⌐ozu⌉ ni ⌐na⌉ru yoo ni si⌐te ima⌉su ḡa_ 'I'm trying to become proficient quickly but . . .' (Lit. 'I'm acting in such a way that I become proficient quickly but . . .')

When yo⌉o is preceded by a negative, and suru occurs in an imperative or request form, the combination is a polite negative request, less direct than the /a/nai de kudasai pattern.

Example: Tu⌐kawanai yo⌉o ni site kudasai. 'Please don't use it.'
(Lit. 'Please act in a not-using way.')

2. Alternate Negative Adverbial; -zu ni and -nai de

All adjectivals have an adverbial form ending in -ku, derived from the informal non-past (for example, o˦okiku from o˦oki˥i, ta˦beta˥ku from ta˦beta˥i, ta˦be˥naku from ta˦be˥nai, etc.). In addition, negative adjectivals (those ending in negative -nai) have a second adverbial form which will hereafter be referred to as the ALTERNATE NEGATIVE ADVERBIAL or, more simply, the -ZU FORM. It is made from a -nai form by replacing the final -nai with -zu (except for the irregular sezu from sinai).

Examples: [1]

VERBAL	NEGATIVE ADJECTIVAL		
Informal Non-past (= Citation form)	Informal Non-past	Adverbial	Alternate Adverbial[2]
ta˦be˥ru 'eat'	ta˦be˥nai	ta˦be˥naku	ta˦be˥zu
mi˥ru 'see'	mi˥nai	mi˥naku	mi˥zu
ma˥tu 'wait'	ma˦ta˥nai	ma˦ta˥naku	ma˥tazu
ka˥eru 'return'	ka˦era˥nai	ka˦era˥naku	ka˥erazu
kau 'buy'	kawanai	kawanaku	kawazu
ha˦na˥su 'talk'	ha˦nasa˥nai	ha˦nasa˥naku	ha˦na˥sazu
ka˥ku 'write'	ka˦ka˥nai	ka˦ka˥naku	ka˥kazu
i˦so˥gu 'be in a hurry'	i˦soga˥nai	i˦soga˥naku	i˦so˥gazu
yobu 'call'	yobanai	yobanaku	yobazu
yo˥mu 'read'	yo˦ma˥nai	yo˦ma˥naku	yo˥mazu
o˦ssya˥ru 'say'	o˦ssyara˥nai	o˦ssyara˥naku	o˦ssya˥razu
iku 'go'	ikanai	ikanaku	ikazu
ku˥ru 'come'	ko˥nai	ko˥naku	ko˥zu
suru 'do'	sinai	sinaku	sezu

The -zu form + particle ni of manner occurs within sentences meaning 'without doing so-and-so' or 'instead of doing so-and-so.'

Examples:

Beñkyoo-sezu ni Gi˦ñza e ikima˥sita. 'Instead of studying, he went to the Ginza.'
Nani mo iwazu ni de˦ma˥sita. 'He left, without saying anything.'
Su˦ñpoo o hakara˥zu ni tu˦ku˥tte simatta. 'He finished making it without taking the measurements.'

---

[1] There is no -zu form corresponding to the verbal a˥ru, in spoken Japanese.

[2] It is impossible to make any simple, meaningful statement about the accent of -zu forms. For some speakers, their accent coincides with that of the corresponding citation form, but many have alternate accents.

In the above examples, the -zu negative + ni may be replaced by the cor-responding -nai form + de (gerund of da), without any significant change in meaning. Thus:

> Be⌐nkyoo-sina⌐i de Gi⌐nza e ikima⌐sita.
> Na⌐ni mo iwana⌐i de de⌐ma⌐sita.
> Su⌐npoo o hakara⌐nai de tu⌐ku⌐tte simatta.

In this use, the two patterns are interchangeable except that -zu ni is less common in the spoken language, particularly in women's speech.

WARNING: -Nai de patterns—but NOT -zu ni patterns—also occur in nega-tive requests. (Example: Tu⌐kawana⌐i de (kudasai). 'Don't use it.' Cf. Les-son 22, Grammatical Note 3.)

3. da⌐ro⌐o

The informal equivalent of formal tentative de⌐syo⌐o is da⌐ro⌐o. Like de-⌐syo⌐o, da⌐ro⌐o loses its accent following an accented word or phrase, and the accent of words and phrases before da⌐ro⌐o is the same as before de⌐syo⌐o. Da⌐ro⌐o, like de⌐syo⌐o, may be preceded by informal verbals, non-past and past; adjectivals, non-past and past; informal da⌐tta; nominals; and particles.[1]

> Ku⌐ru daroo. 'He probably comes.' or 'He'll probably come.'
> Wa⌐ka⌐tta daroo. 'He probably understood.'
> Ta⌐ka⌐i daroo.[2] 'It's probably expensive.'
> Yo⌐katta daroo.[3] 'It probably was all right.'
> A⌐merika⌐ziñ datta daroo.[3] 'It probably was an American.'
> Ko⌐re daro⌐o. 'It's probably this one.'
> Kyo⌐oto kara daroo. 'It's probably from Kyoto.'

Da⌐ro⌐o occurs at the end of informal sentences, before sentence particles (including ka), and before ḡa 'but,' predominantly in men's speech. In formal and informal sentences, in the speech of men and women, it occurs in quotations and before certain particles, such as kara 'so.' Thus:

> De⌐ki⌐ru daroo? (M) 'You can do it, can't you?'
> Bo⌐ku daroo ka. (M) 'Do you think it's me?'
> Sa⌐mu⌐i daroo ḡa, o⌐obaa wa i⌐ranai. (M) 'It's probably cold, but I don't need a coat.'
> Mu⌐zukasi⌐i daroo to i⌐ima⌐sita. 'He said it would probably be diffi-cult.'
> Yo⌐ru daro⌐o tte. 'He says he'll probably stop in.'

---

[1] But unlike de⌐syo⌐o, da⌐ro⌐o does not also follow formal inflected forms.

[2] An alternate form of informal non-past adjectival tentative consists of an adjectival stem + -karo⌐o. Thus: ta⌐kakaro⌐o.

[3] The contracted equivalent of -katta daroo is -kattaroo and of da⌐tta daroo is da⌐ttaroo. Thus: yo⌐kattaroo, A⌐merika⌐ziñ dattaroo.

Sa⌈mu⌉i daroo kara, o⌉obaa o ki⊢masyo⊣o. 'It will probably be cold so I guess I'll wear a coat.'

Other uses of da⌈ro⌉o will be introduced later.

4. Particle mo Following a Number

An extent expression consisting of a number or quantity word + particle mo, followed by an affirmative, means 'as much as ——,' 'as many as ——,' 'all of ——,' indicating that in the given context, the amount is large.

Examples:

I⌈ti-zi⌉kañ mo ma⊢tima⊣sita. 'I waited all of an hour.'
Si⌈ti⌉-neñ mo i⊢ma⊣sita. 'I was there as long as seven years.'
Ni-⌈señ-eñ mo kakarima⌉su yo⌣ 'It will take as much as ¥2000.'
Sore o ha⌈ñbu⌉ñ mo tu⊢kaima⊣sita. 'I used as much as a half of that.'

An extent expression consisting of a number or quantity word + particle mo, followed by a negative, means 'not even ——,' indicating that in the given context, the amount is small.

Examples:

I⌉p-puñ mo ma⊢timase⊣ñ desita. 'I didn't wait even one minute.'
Su⌈kosi mo wakarimase⌉ñ. 'I don't understand at all (lit. even a little).'
Hi⌈to-ri mo kimase⌉ñ desita. 'Not a single person came.'
Isu wa hi⌈to-tu mo na⌉i. 'There isn't even one chair.'

5. ko⌈to⌉

Ko⌈to⌉, a nominal which is always preceded by a modifier, refers to 'things' in an intangible sense, whereas mo⌈no⌉ is a concrete 'thing.' Compare:

So⌈ñna koto⌉ wa o⌈mosiro⌉i. 'Things (i.e. facts or acts) like that are interesting.'

and:

So⌈ñna mono⌉ wa o⌈mosiro⌉i. 'Things (i.e. objects) like that are interesting.'

—— to (or [t] te) iu koto (lit. 'the thing said quote —— ') occurs as an equivalent of English 'the fact that ——.' Thus:

de⌈ki⌉ru to[1] iu koto 'the fact that it's possible'
a⌈tarasi⌉i to[1] iu koto 'the fact that it's new'
ko⌉nakatta to[1] iu koto 'the fact that [someone] didn't come'
to⌈modati da⌉ to[1] iu koto 'the fact that [someone] is a friend'

A nominal X + no + ko⌈to⌉ is an equivalent of English 'things pertaining to X,' '[things] about X.' Thus: u⌈ti no koto⌉ 'things pertaining to the house'; A⌈merika no koto⌉ '[things] about America.'

---

[1] Or tte.

Additional examples:

Ni⌐hoñ no koto⌐ wa ⌐yo⌐ku wa⌐karima⌐su ⌐ne⌐e. 'You understand a great
deal about Japan, don't you!'

Ni⌐hoñḡo o beñkyoo-site iru tte iu koto⌐ wa si⌐rimaseñ desita.'I didn't
know (the fact) that you were studying Japanese.'

Ko⌐syoo da to iu koto⌐ o wa⌐surema⌐sita. 'I forgot (the fact) that it was
(lit. is) broken.'

Ko⌐to⌐ directly preceded by an informal non-past verbal (meaning literally
'the act of —— ') occurs as an equivalent of English 'to do so-and-so' or
'doing so-and-so' in expressions like:

Sa⌐ñpo-suru koto⌐ ḡa su⌐ki⌐ desu. 'I like to take walks.'

Zi⌐te⌐ñsya ni no⌐ru koto⌐ ḡa ki⌐rai de⌐su. 'I hate to ride on bicycles.'

Ya⌐su⌐mu koto ḡa ta⌐isetu de⌐su. 'It is important to rest.'

DRILLS

A. Substitution Drill

1. He is (i.e. is working as) a government employee, isn't he?	A⌐no⌐ hito (wa) ko⌐omu⌐iñ (o) si⌐te (i)ru⌐ ñ desyoo?
2. He is (i.e. is working as) a teacher (or doctor), isn't he?	A⌐no⌐ hito (wa) <u>se⌐ñse⌐e</u> (o) si⌐te (i)ru⌐ ñ desyoo?
3. She is (i.e. is working as) a nurse, isn't she?	A⌐no⌐ hito (wa) <u>ka⌐ñḡo⌐hu</u> (o) si⌐te (i)ru⌐ ñ desyoo?
4. He is (i.e. is working as) a doctor, isn't he?	A⌐no⌐ hito (wa) i⌐sya (o) site (i)ru⌐ ñ desyoo?
5. He is (i.e. is working as) a dentist, isn't he?	A⌐no⌐ hito (wa) ⌐ha⌐isya (o) si⌐te (i)ru⌐ ñ desyoo?
6. He is (i.e. is working as) an oculist, isn't he?	A⌐no⌐ hito (wa) ⌐me⌐isya (o) si⌐te (i)ru⌐ ñ desyoo?
7. He is (i.e. is working as) a missionary, isn't he?	A⌐no⌐ hito (wa) <u>se⌐ñkyo⌐osi</u> (o) si⌐te (i)ru⌐ ñ desyoo?
8. He is (i.e. is working as) a carpenter, isn't he?	A⌐no⌐ hito (wa) <u>⌐da⌐iku</u> (o) si⌐te (i)ru⌐ ñ desyoo?
9. He is (i.e. is working as) a lawyer, isn't he?	A⌐no⌐ hito (wa) <u>be⌐ñḡo⌐si</u> (o) si⌐te (i)ru⌐ ñ desyoo?
10. He is (i.e. is working as) a newspaperman, isn't he?	A⌐no⌐ hito (wa) <u>ki⌐sya⌐</u> (o) si⌐te (i)ru⌐ ñ desyoo?

B. Substitution Drill

1. The work is fine but it's the salary [that's the problem].	Si⌐ḡoto wa i⌐i kedo, kyu⌐uryoo ḡa ⌐ne⌐e.
2. The teacher is fine but it's the pupils [that are the problem].	Se⌐ñse⌐e wa ⌐i⌐i kedo, <u>se⌐eto</u> ḡa ⌐ne⌐e.

3. The husband is fine but it's the wife [that's the problem].

Go⌐syu˧ziñ wa ⌐i˧i kedo, o˧kusañ ḡa ⌐he˧e.

4. The room is fine but it's the meals [that are the problem].

He⌐ya˥ wa ⌐i˧i kedo, syokuzi ḡa ⌐he˧e.

5. The style is fine but it's the pattern [that's the problem].

Ka⌐tati wa i˧i kedo, gara ḡa ⌐he˧e.

6. The material is fine but it's the color [that's the problem].

Ki˥zi wa ⌐i˧i kedo, i⌐ro˥ ḡa ⌐he˧e.

7. The inside is fine but it's the outside [that's the problem].

Na˥ka wa ⌐i˧i kedo, so˧to ḡa ⌐he˧e.

8. The house is fine but it's the furniture [that's the problem].

U⌐ti wa i˧i kedo, ka˥ḡu ḡa ⌐he˧e.

C. Substitution Drill

1. I worked for two years.

Ni˥-neñ ha⌐tarakima˧sita.

2. I worked for as long as two years.

Ni˥-neñ mo ha⌐tarakima˧sita.

3. I didn't work for even two years.

Ni˥-neñ mo ha⌐tarakimase˥ñ de-sita.

4. I worked for only two years.

Ni˥-neñ sika ha⌐tarakimase˥ñ de-sita.

5. I didn't work for two years (—but I did work).

Ni˥-neñ wa ha⌐tarakimase˥ñ de-sita.

6. I did work for two years.

Ni˥-neñ wa ha⌐tarakima˧sita.

7. I worked for just two years.

Ni˥-neñ dake ha⌐tarakima˧sita.

D. Substitution Drill

1. It appears that he's going to quit.

Ya⌐meru yo˥o desu.

2. They say that he's going to quit.

Ya⌐meru so˥o desu.

3. He's expected to quit.

Ya⌐meru hazu de˥su.

4. I plan to quit.

Ya⌐meru tumori de˥su.

5. He'll probably quit.

Ya⌐meru desyo˥o.

6. He said that he would quit.

Ya⌐meru to iima˥sita.

7. He said that he had quit.

Ya⌐meta to iima˥sita.

8. He probably quit.

Ya⌐meta desyo˥o.

9. He's supposed to have quit.

Ya⌐meta hazu de˥su.

10. They say he quit.

Ya⌐meta so˥o desu.

11. It appears that he quit.

Ya⌐meta yo˥o desu.

E.   Substitution Drill

1. He's like you.
2. It seems difficult.
3. It appears that he isn't coming any more.
4. It's like this.
5. He seems to have made a mistake.
6. It appears that he doesn't remember.
7. It seems to be strong.
8. He doesn't seem to be busy.
9. It doesn't seem to be full.
10. He seems to have changed to an American company.

A⌐na⌐ta no yoo desu.
Mu⌐zukasii yo⌐o desu.
Mo⌐o ⌐ko⌐nai yoo desu.
Ko⌐no yo⌐o desu.
Ma⌐tiḡa⌐eta yoo desu.

O⌐bo⌐ete (i)⌐nai yo⌐o desu.

Zyo⌐obu na yo⌐o desu.
I⌐soḡa⌐siku ⌐na⌐i yoo desu.

I⌐ppai zya na⌐i yoo desu.
A⌐merika no kaisya ni kawatta
   yo⌐o desu.

F.   Substitution Drill

1. Tell [him] to try asking.

2. Tell [him] to continue yesterday's work.
3. Tell [him] to send it as soon as possible.
4. Tell [him] to polish the car.
5. Tell [him] to check the luggage.
6. Tell [him] to (go) walk(ing).

7. Tell [him] to transfer to the bus.
8. Tell [him] not to overwork.

9. Tell [him] not to smoke here.
10. Tell [him] not to lock it.

Ki⌐ite mi⌐ru yoo ni i⌐tte kuda-
   sa⌐i.
Kinoo no siḡoto (o) tu⌐zukeru
   yo⌐o ni i⌐tte kudasa⌐i.
Na⌐rubeku ha⌐yaku o⌐kuru yo⌐o
   ni i⌐tte kudasa⌐i.
Zidoosya (o) mi⌐ḡaku yo⌐o ni
   i⌐tte kudasa⌐i.
Ni⌐motu (o) a⌐zuke⌐ru yoo ni
   i⌐tte kudasa⌐i.
A⌐ru⌐ite i⌐ku yo⌐o ni i⌐tte kuda-
   sa⌐i.
Ba⌐su ni no⌐rikae⌐ru yoo ni i⌐tte
   kudasa⌐i.
Ha⌐tarakisuḡi⌐nai yoo ni i⌐tte
   kudasa⌐i.
Koko de ta⌐bako (o) noma⌐nai
   yoo ni i⌐tte kudasa⌐i.
Ka⌐ḡi⌐ (o) ka⌐ke⌐nai yoo ni i⌐tte
   kudasa⌐i.

G.   Substitution Drill

1. Nowadays it's reached the point where he can do it.
2. Nowadays it's reached the point where he understands well.
3. Nowadays it's reached the point where it's upsetting.

Kono-ḡoro de⌐ki⌐ru yoo ni na-
   ⌐rima⌐sita.
Kono-ḡoro ⌐yo⌐ku wa⌐ka⌐ru yoo
   ni na⌐rima⌐sita.
Kono-ḡoro ko⌐ma⌐ru yoo ni na-
   ⌐rima⌐sita.

4. Nowadays it's reached the point where he studies hard.

Kono-ḡoro ⌐yo⌐ku be⌐ṅkyoo-suru yo⌐o ni na⌐rima⌐sita.

5. Nowadays it's reached the point where he drinks too much.

Kono-ḡoro no⌐misuḡi⌐ru yoo ni na⌐rima⌐sita.

6. Nowadays it's reached the point where he often makes mistakes.

Kono-ḡoro ⌐yo⌐ku ma⌐tiḡae⌐ru yoo ni na⌐rima⌐sita.

7. Nowadays it's reached the point where he uses Japanese a good deal.

Kono-ḡoro ni⌐hoṅḡo (o) yo⌐ku tu-⌐kau yo⌐o ni na⌐rima⌐sita.

8. Nowadays it's reached the point where it rains every day.

Kono-ḡoro ⌐a⌐me ḡa ⌐ma⌐initi ⌐hu⌐-ru yoo ni na⌐rima⌐sita.

H. Substitution Drill

1. Don't forget to write big.

Wa⌐surenai yo⌐o ni ⌐o⌐okiku ⌐ka⌐ite kudasai.

2. Write big, as I told you before.

Ma⌐e ni i⌐tta yo⌐o ni ⌐o⌐okiku ⌐ka⌐ite kudasai.

3. Write big, the same as this.

Ko⌐re to onazi yo⌐o ni ⌐o⌐okiku ⌐ka⌐ite kudasai.

4. Write big, the way Mr. Tanaka [does].

Ta⌐naka-saṅ no yo⌐o ni ⌐o⌐okiku ⌐ka⌐ite kudasai.

5. Write big, like this.

Ko⌐no yo⌐o ni ⌐o⌐okiku ⌐ka⌐ite ku-dasai.

6. Write big, so that I can see it from here.

Ko⌐ko kara mie⌐ru yoo ni ⌐o⌐okiku ⌐ka⌐ite kudasai.

I. Substitution Drill

1. I'd like to join [it] but it seems to be difficult.

Ha⌐irita⌐i ṅ desu ḡa, mu⌐zukasii yo⌐o desu.

2. I'd like to buy [it] but it seems to be expensive. /kau, ta⌐ka⌐i/

Ka⌐ita⌐i ṅ desu ḡa, ta⌐ka⌐i yoo desu.

3. I'd like to take [it] but it seems to be heavy. /mo-tte iku, omoi/

Mo⌐tte ikita⌐i ṅ desu ḡa, o⌐moi yo⌐o desu.

4. I'd like to wear [it] but it seems to be small. /kiru, ti⌐isa⌐i/

Ki⌐ta⌐i ṅ desu ḡa, ti⌐isa⌐i yoo desu.

5. I'd like to try riding [in it] but it seems to be dangerous. /no⌐tte mi⌐ru, abunai/

No⌐tte mita⌐i ṅ desu ḡa, a⌐bunai yo⌐o desu.

6. I'd like to use [it] but it seems to be dirty. /tukau, ki⌐tana⌐i/

Tu⌐kaita⌐i ṅ desu ḡa, ki⌐tana⌐i yoo desu.

J. Substitution Drill

1. I don't remember for sure how many years it comes to.	Na⌉ñ-neñ ni ⊢na⊣ru ka ha⌈kki⌉ri o⌈bo⌉ete (i)⌈na⌉i ñ desu.
2. I've already forgotten how many years it comes to.	Na⌉ñ-neñ ni ⊢na⊣ru ka ⌈mo⌉o wa⌈surete simaima⌉sita.
3. I don't know how many years it comes to.	Na⌉ñ-neñ ni ⊢na⊣ru ka si⌈rimase⌉ñ.
4. I can't tell how many years it comes to.	Na⌉ñ-neñ ni ⊢na⊣ru ka wa⌈karimase⌉ñ.
5. Shall I ask and see how many years it comes to?	Na⌉ñ-neñ ni ⊢na⊣ru ka ki⌈ite mimasyo⌉o ka.
6. Please say how many years it comes to.	Na⌉ñ-neñ ni ⊢na⊣ru ka i⌈tte kudasa⌉i.
7. Would you find out how many years it comes to?	Na⌉ñ-neñ ni ⊢na⊣ru ka si⌈ra⌉bete ku⊢remase⊣ñ ka_
8. He told me how many years it comes to.	Na⌉ñ-neñ ni ⊢na⊣ru ka o⌈siete kurema⌉sita.

K. Substitution Drill

1. He kept saying that he would quit. It looks as if he finally did (quit)!	Yameru yāmeru tte i⌈tte (i)ta⌉ kedo, to⌉otoo ya⊢metyatta yo⊣o desu ⌈ne⌉e.
2. He kept saying that he would go. It looks as if he finally did (go)! /iku/	Iku īku tte i⌈tte (i)ta⌉ kedo, to⌉otoo i⊢ttyatta yo⊣o desu ⌈ne⌉e.
3. He kept saying that he would sell [it]. It looks as if he finally did (sell)! /uru/	Uru ūru tte i⌈tte (i)ta⌉ kedo, to⌉otoo u⊢ttyatta yo⊣o desu ⌈ne⌉e.
4. He kept saying that he would do [it]. It looks as if he finally did (do)! /suru/	Suru sūru tte i⌈tte (i)ta⌉ kedo, to⌉otoo si⊢tyatta yo⊣o desu ⌈ne⌉e.
5. He kept saying that he would give [it to him]. It looks as if he finally did (give)! /aḡeru/	Aḡeru āḡeru tte i⌈tte (i)ta⌉ kedo, to⌉otoo a⊢ḡetyatta yo⊣o desu ⌈ne⌉e.
6. He kept saying that he would go home. It looks as if he finally did (go home)! /ka⌉eru/	Ka⌉eru ⌈ka⌉eru tte i⌈tte (i)ta⌉ kedo, to⌉otoo ⊢ka⊣ettyatta yoo desu ⌈ne⌉e.
7. He kept saying that he would decide. It looks as if he finally did (decide)! /kimeru/	Kimeru kīmeru tte i⌈tte (i)ta⌉ kedo, to⌉otoo ki⊢metyatta yo⊣o desu ⌈ne⌉e.
8. He kept saying that he would take [it]. It looks as if he finally did (take)! /to⌉ru/	To⌉ru ⌈to⌉ru tte i⌈tte (i)ta⌉ kedo, to⌉otoo ⊢to⊣ttyatta yoo desu ⌈ne⌉e.

L. Grammar Drill (based on Grammatical Note 1)

> Tutor: I⌐kana¬i de kudasai.   ⎫
> Student: I⌐kanai yo⌐o ni site kudasai. ⎬ 'Please don't go.'
>   ⎭

1. Ee͡go (o) tu⌐kawana¬i de kudasai.
    Ee͡go (o) tu⌐kawanai yo⌐o ni site kudasai.
2. Ma⌐tiḡae¬nai de kudasai.
    Ma⌐tiḡae¬nai yoo ni site kudasai.
3. Wa⌐surena¬i de kudasai.
    Wa⌐surenai yo⌐o ni site kudasai.
4. I⌐soḡa¬nai de kudasai.
    I⌐soḡa¬nai yoo ni site kudasai.
5. Ko⌐ko de¬ wa tǎbako (o) no⌐ma¬nai de kudasai.
    Ko⌐ko de¬ wa tǎbako (o) no⌐ma¬nai yoo ni site kudasai.
6. Okane (o) ka⌐rina¬i de kudasai.
    Okane (o) ka⌐rinai yo⌐o ni site kudasai.

M. Grammar Drill (based on Grammatical Note 2)

> Tutor: Ma⌐tiḡae¬nai de si˥ma˩sita. ⎫ 'He did it without making
> Student: Ma⌐tiḡae¬zu ni si˥ma˩sita.   ⎬   a mistake.'
>   ⎭

1. Ha⌐tarakana¬i de zu⌐tto nete (i)ma¬sita.
    Hatarakazu ni zu⌐tto nete (i)ma¬sita.
2. Ya⌐suma¬nai de zu⌐tto hataraite (i)ma¬sita.
    Ya⌐suma¬zu ni zu⌐tto hataraite (i)ma¬sita.
3. Ha⌐rawa¬nai de ⌐de¬te si˥maima˩sita.
    Ha⌐rawa¬zu ni ⌐de¬te si˥maima˩sita.
4. Wa⌐surena¬i de ǎsita ⌐ha¬yaku ki˥te˩ kudasai.
    Wasurezu ni ǎsita ⌐ha¬yaku ki˥te˩ kudasai.
5. Ho͡n (o) ˥mi˩nai de mo⌐o iti-do itte kudasa¬i.
    Ho͡n (o) ˥mi˩zu ni mo⌐o iti-do itte kudasa¬i.
6. O⌐yu (o) tukawana¬i´ de a⌐ratte kudasa¬i.
    Oyu (o) tukawazu ni a⌐ratte kudasa¬i.
7. Su⌐n̄poo (o) hakara¬nai de tu⌐ku¬tte si˥maima˩sita.
    Su⌐n̄poo (o) hakara¬zu ni tu⌐ku¬tte si˥maima˩sita.
8. Na⌐hi mo iwana¬i de de⌐ma¬sita.
    Nani mo iwazu ni de⌐ma¬sita.

N. Level Drill[1]

1. Zutto onazi kaisya ni iru?
    Zu⌐tto onazi kaisya ni ima¬su ka⤵
2. Ma⌐tiḡa¬eta daroo? (M)
    Ma⌐tiḡa¬eta desyoo?
3. Mo⌐o ⌐ko¬naku ˥na˩tta ⌐ne¬e. (M)
    Mo⌐o ⌐ko¬naku na⌐rima¬sita ⌐ne¬e.
4. Do⌐o site yameta no? (W)
    Do⌐o site ya˥meta˩ n̄ desu ka⤵
5. Ki⌐tto so⌐o daroo ˥ne˩e. (M)
    Ki⌐tto so⌐o desyoo ˥ne˩e.

----

[1] In each case the sentence on the right is the formal equivalent of the sentence on the left.

6. A⌐sita⌐ made ni re⌐ñraku-   A⌐sita⌐ made ni re⌐ñraku-site ku-
    site kurena⌐i ka↲ (M)   remase⌐ñ ka↲

7. Tu⌐ma⌐ñnakatta daroo?   Tu⌐mara⌐nakatta desyoo?
    (M)

8. O⌐kime ni na⌐tta? (W)   O⌐kime ni narima⌐sita ka↲

O. Expansion Drill

1. Please write.   Ka⌐ite kudasai.
    Please write your address.   O⌐tokoro (o) ka⌐ite kudasai.
    I'll get in touch with you   Re⌐ñraku-sima⌐su kara, o⌐tokoro
      so please write your   (o) ka⌐ite kudasai.
      address.
    I ll get in touch with you   Yu⌐ubiñ de reñraku-sima⌐su kara,
      by mail so please write   o⌐tokoro (o) ka⌐ite kudasai.
      your address.

2. [They]'re few [and far be-   Su⌐kuna⌐i daroo?
      tween], aren't they?
    Americans are few [and   A⌐merika⌐ziñ wa su⌐kuna⌐i daroo?
      far between], aren't
      they?
    Americans who can do [it]   De⌐ki⌐ru A⌐merika⌐ziñ wa su⌐ku-
      are few [and far between],   na⌐i daroo?
      aren't they?
    Americans who can [speak]   Ni⌐hoñḡo no deki⌐ru A⌐merika⌐-
      Japanese are few [and   ziñ wa su⌐kuna⌐i daroo?
      far between], aren't
      they?
    Americans who can [speak]   A⌐no oisyasañ no yo⌐o ni Ni⌐hoñ-
      Japanese like that doctor   ḡo no deki⌐ru A⌐merika⌐ziñ wa
      are few [and far between],   su⌐kuna⌐i daroo?
      aren't they?

3. It was the answer.   He⌐ñzi⌐ datta ñ desu yo.
    The answer was (lit. it   Ki⌐meta⌐ tte iu he⌐ñzi⌐ datta ñ
      was an answer which   desu yo.
      said) that they had de-
      cided.
    The answer was that they   Ho⌐ka no hito⌐ ni ki⌐meta⌐ tte iu
      had decided on another   he⌐ñzi⌐ datta ñ desu yo.
      person.
    I waited but the answer   Ma⌐tima⌐sita ḡa, ho⌐ka no hito⌐
      was that they had de-   ni ki⌐meta⌐ tte iu he⌐ñzi⌐ da-
      cided on another person.   tta ñ desu yo.
    I waited all of three weeks   Sa⌐ñ-syu⌐ukañ mo ma⌐tima⌐sita
      but the answer was that   ḡa, ho⌐ka no hito⌐ ni ki⌐meta⌐
      they had decided on   tte iu he⌐ñzi⌐ datta ñ desu yo.
      another person.

4. I've reached the point
   where I understand.

   I've reached the point
   where I understand a
   little.

   I've reached the point
   where I understand a
   little these days.

   It used to be difficult, but
   I've reached the point
   where I understand a
   little these days.

   At the beginning it was
   difficult, but I've
   reached the point where
   I understand a little
   these days.

Wa⌐ka⌐ru yoo ni na⌐rima⌐sita.

Su⌐ko⌐si wa⌐ka⌐ru yoo ni na⌐ri-
ma⌐sita.

Kono-ḡoro su⌐ko⌐si wa⌐ka⌐ru yoo
ni na⌐rima⌐sita.

Mu⌐zukasi⌐katta ñ desu ḡa, kono-
ḡoro su⌐ko⌐si wa⌐ka⌐ru yoo ni
na⌐rima⌐sita.

Ha⌐zime wa muzukasi⌐katta ñ
desu ḡa, kono-ḡoro su⌐ko⌐si wa-
⌐ka⌐ru yoo ni na⌐rima⌐sita.

5. I don't remember.
   I don't remember any more.
   I don't remember any
   more what year it was.
   I hired [her] but I don't
   remember any more
   what year it was.
   I hired [her] a long time
   ago but I don't remember
   any more what year it
   was.
   I hired that secretary a
   long time ago but I don't
   remember any more
   what year it was.

O⌐bo⌐ete (i)⌐na⌐i ñ desu.
Mo⌐o o⌐bo⌐ete (i)⌐na⌐i ñ desu.
Na⌐ñ-neñ datta ka ⌐mo⌐o o⌐bo⌐
(i)⌐na⌐i ñ desu.
Ya⌐toima⌐sita ḡa, na⌐ñ-neñ datta
ka ⌐mo⌐o o⌐bo⌐ete (i)⌐na⌐i ñ desu.

Zu⌐tto ma⌐e ni ya⌐toima⌐sita ḡa,
na⌐ñ-neñ datta ka ⌐mo⌐o o⌐bo⌐ete
(i)⌐na⌐i ñ desu.

So⌐no hisyo⌐ (o) zu⌐tto ma⌐e ni
ya⌐toima⌐sita ḡa, na⌐ñ-neñ datta ka ⌐mo⌐o o⌐bo⌐ete (i)⌐na⌐i ñ
desu.

6. I went to bed.
   I went to bed early.
   I went to bed early without
   studying.
   I had a headache so I went
   to bed early without
   studying.
   Last night I had a headache
   so I went to bed early
   without studying.

Ne⌐te simaima⌐sita.
Ha⌐yaku ne⌐te simaima⌐sita.
Beñkyoo-sezu ni ⌐ha⌐yaku ne⌐te
simaima⌐sita.
A⌐tama⌐ ḡa ⌐i⌐takatta kara, beñkyoo-sezu ni ⌐ha⌐yaku ne⌐te
simaima⌐sita.
Yuube a⌐tama⌐ ḡa ⌐i⌐takatta kara,
beñkyoo-sezu ni ⌐ha⌐yaku ne⌐te
simaima⌐sita.

SUPPLEMENTARY CONVERSATIONS

(with questions)

1. Smith: Hi⌐do⌉i ┖a┤me desu ⌐ne⌉e. Ki⌐no⌉o wa ┖do┤o desita ka⌐
    Tanaka: Ki⌐no⌉o mo ┖kyo┤o no yoo desita yo⌐ O⌐osaka wa do⌉o desita ka⌐
    Smith: Oosaka wa ki⌐no⌉o wa ⌐i⌉i ┖te┤ñki datta ñ desu ḡa ⌐ne⌉e.

    a. Kinoo ⌐Su⌉misu-sañ mo Tānaka-sañ mo ko⌐ko ni ima⌉sita
        ka⌐
    b. Kinoo kŏko wa ⌐do⌉ñna ┖te┤ñki desita ka⌐

2. Secretary: Otaku kara o⌐de⌉ñwa desu ḡa—
    Smith: I⌉ma i⌐soḡasi⌉i kara, sa┖ñ-zi suḡi⌉ ni ma⌐ta kake⌉ru yoo ni
                i┖tte kudasa┤i.

    a. Da⌉re ḡa sa┖ñ-zi suḡi┤ ni ma┖ta deñwa o kake┤ru desyoo
        ka.

3. Smith: A⌐tarasi⌉i hi┖syo┤ wa ⌐ma⌉da?
    Tanaka: E⌉e. Ke⌉sa hi⌐syo⌉ ni na┖rita┤i tte iu hito ḡa go-⌐ni⌉ñ mo ki┖ta┤
             ñ desu ḡa, i⌉i hito wa da⌐re mo ina⌉katta ñ desu.

    a. Tanaka-sañ wa ⌐mo⌉o a⌐tarasi⌉i hi┖syo┤ o ya⌐toima⌉sita ka⌐
    b. Ke⌉sa ┖ki┤ta hito wa ⌐do⌉ñna hi┖to de┤sita ka⌐

4. Tanaka: Hi⌐do⌉i yu┖ki┤ desita ⌐ne⌉e. Zi⌐mu⌉syo e i⌐kima⌉sita ka⌐
    Smith: Iie. Zi⌐mu⌉syo e ikazu ni u┖ti de siḡoto o sima⌉sita yo⌐

    a. Su⌉misu-sañ wa ⌐do⌉o site u┖ti de siḡoto o sita┤ ñ desyoo
        ka.

5. A: Na┖rubeku nihoñḡo o tukau yo⌉o ni si┖te iru┤ ñ desu ḡa, *mu⌐zukasi⌉i
        desu ⌐ne⌉e—nihoñḡo wa.
    B: Su⌉ḡu de┖ki┤ru yoo ni ┖na┤ru kara, da⌐izyo⌉obu desu yo.

    a. A⌉-sañ wa ni⌐hoñzi⌉ñ desyoo ka. Do⌉o site wa┖karima┤su ka⌐

6. Tanaka: Ko⌐no deñwa wa kosyoo da⌉ kara, tu┖kawanai yo⌉o ni site kuda-
             sai.
    Smith: Ko⌐ma⌉ru kara, ha⌉yaku na⌐o⌉site mo┖raimasyo┤o.
    Tanaka: Mo⌉o ta⌐no⌉ñda ñ desu ḡa; kyo⌉o wa i⌐soḡasi⌉i kara, a⌐sita ku⌉ru
             soo desu.

    a. Da⌉re ḡa a┖sita ku┤ru hazu desu ka⌐

7. Tanaka: Zyo⌉oñzu-sañ wa⌐ka⌉tta desyoo ka.
    Smith: Wa⌐kara⌉nakatta yoo desu ⌐ne⌉e.
    Tanaka: Zya⌉a, mo⌐o iti-do iimasyo⌉o ka.
    Smith: E⌉e, so⌐o site kudasa⌉i.

    a. Tanaka-sañ wa ⌐do⌉o site mo┖o iti-do iima┤su ka⌐

8. Smith: Zyo⌐oñzu-sañ wa nⁱhoñḡo ḡa ni⌐hoñziˀñ no yoo ni de⌐kimaˀsu
            ⌐neˀe. Do⌐ko de be⌐ñkyoo sitaˀ ñ desyoo ka⌐⌐

   Tanaka: Zyo⌐oñzu-sañ desu ka⌐⌐ O⌐kaˀasañ ḡa ni⌐hoñziˀñ de, zu⌐tto ko-
            domo no tokiˀ kara Ni⌐hoˀñ ni iˀmaˀsu kara; e⌐eḡo yoˀri ni-
            ⌐hoñḡo no hoˀo ḡa zyo⌐ozuˀ na ñ desu yo⌐⌐

   Smith: So⌐o desu ka. Zya⌐a, hoñtoo ni ni⌐hoñziˀñ to o⌐nazi yoˀo ni
            de⌐kiˀru ha⌐zu deˀsu ⌐neˀe.

            a. Zyo⌐oñzu-sañ no nihoñḡo wa ⌐doˀo desu ka⌐⌐
            b. Zyo⌐oñzu-sañ wa eˀeḡo to nihoñḡo to ⌐doˀtira ḡa zyo⌐ozuˀ
               desu ka⌐⌐
            c. Zyo⌐oñzu-sañ wa ⌐doˀko de ni⌐hoñḡo o naraˀtta ñ desu ka⌐⌐

9. Smith (conducting interview):   A⌐naˀta ⌐iˀma zyo⌐tyuu site ruˀ ñ desu ka⌐⌐
   Miss Yamamoto: Haˀa. O⌐toˀtosi made ko⌐oiñ o site ori-
                                   maˀsita ḡa; yamete, sore kara zyo⌐tyuu
                                   o site orimaˀsu.

   Smith: Iˀma ha⌐taraite imaˀsu ka⌐⌐
   Miss Yamamoto: Haˀa. Sibuya[1] no gi⌐ñko⌐oiñ no uti de ha-
                                   taraite orimasu.

   Smith: Do⌐o site ⌐iˀma no uti ya⌐metaˀi ñ desu
                                   ka⌐⌐

   Miss Yamamoto: Da⌐ñnasaˀma ḡa O⌐osaka no giñkoo ni oka-
                                   wari ni narimaˀsu kara.

   Smith: Aˀa, wa⌐karimaˀsita. Koko ni nⁱamae to
                                   de⌐ñwaba⌐ñḡoo ⌐kaˀite kudasai. Do⌐yoo
                                   maˀde ni de⌐ñwa de reñraku-simaˀsu
                                   kara.

   Miss Yamamoto: O⌐neḡai-itasimaˀsu.

            a. Yamamoto-sañ wa ⌐iˀtu kara zyo⌐tyuu
               o site imaˀsu ka⌐⌐
            b. Iˀma ⌐doˀko de ha⌐taraite imaˀsu ka⌐⌐
            c. Do⌐o site ya⌐metaˀi ñ desu ka⌐⌐
            d. Su⌐misu-sañ wa ⌐iˀtu made ni ⌐naˀñ de
               re⌐ñraku-simaˀsu ka⌐⌐

EXERCISES

1. Complete each of the following sentences with an appropriate ending:

            a. Mo⌐to wa A⌐merika de hataraite imaˀsita ḡa, iˀma wa ——— .
            b. Mo⌐to wa ni⌐hoñḡo o beñkyoo-site imaˀsita ḡa, iˀma wa ——— .
            c. Mo⌐to wa ke⌐kkoñ-site imaˀsita ḡa, iˀma wa ——— .
            d. Mo⌐to wa tu⌐toˀmete iˀmaˀsita ḡa, iˀma wa ——— .
            e. Mo⌐to wa ko⌐omuˀiñ o si⌐te imaˀsita ḡa, iˀma wa ——— .
            f. Mo⌐to wa gu⌐ñziñ deˀsita ḡa, iˀma wa ——— .
            g. Mo⌐to wa su⌐kiˀ desita ḡa, iˀma wa ——— .
            h. Mo⌐to wa o⌐mosiˀrokatta ñ desu ḡa, iˀma wa ——— .
            i. Mo⌐to wa ⌐yaˀsukatta ñ desu ḡa, iˀma wa ——— .

---

[1] Section of Tokyo.

　　　j. Mo⌐to wa a⌐buna⌐katta ñ desu ḡa, i⌐ma wa ───── .
　　　k. Mo⌐to wa o⌐so⌐katta ñ desu ḡa, i⌐ma wa ───── .
　　　l. Mo⌐to wa ya⌐sasi⌐katta ñ desu ḡa, i⌐ma wa ───── .

2.　Ask Mr. Tanaka what kind of work he does.
　　Mr. Tanaka answers that:

　　　a.　he is a bank employee.
　　　b.　he is a newspaperman.
　　　c.　he practices law in Yokohama.
　　　d.　he is a company employee but he wants to become a school
　　　　　teacher.
　　　e.　he used to work in a factory but now he is an embassy driver.
　　　f.　he works for the American Consulate in Kobe.
　　　g.　he isn't employed.
　　　h.　he is still a student, but in April, he will join the Bank of Japan.

3.　Interview a prospective employee. Find out his name, address, telephone
　　number, age, present place and kind of employment, reasons for wanting
　　to leave, salary, English ability. At the end of the interview, tell him you
　　will get in touch with him tomorrow morning.

4.　Give the substance of each of the Basic Dialogues in narrative, non-dia-
　　logue form, including as many details as possible. For example (Dia-
　　logue a):

　　　　　Tanaka-sañ wa ⌐re⌐ñzu o tu⌐ku⌐ru ko⌐oba⌐ de hataraite imasu.
　　　Zu⌐tto ma⌐e kara so⌐ñna siḡoto o site ima⌐su ḡa, nañ-neñ ni ⌐na⌐-
　　　ru ka Tānaka-sañ wa ha⌐kki⌐ri o⌐bo⌐ete i⌐mase⌐ñ.

Lesson 25. At the Office

BASIC DIALOGUES: FOR MEMORIZATION

(a)

Tanaka (to friend)

reception desk
1. I wonder where the reception desk is.

2. Oh, I see.

uketuke
Uketuke (wa) ⌈do⌉tira desyoo ⌐ne⌐e.

A, wa⌈karima⌉sita.

Receptionist

some business __or__ some matter to be attended to

3. Can I help you? (Lit. Is it some matter you wish to attend to?)

na⌉ni ka ⌈yo⌉o __or__ na⌉ni ka go⌈yo⌉o ↑
Na⌉ni ka go⌈yo⌉o desyoo ka.

Tanaka

4. We'd like to see Mr. Ueda . . .

U⌈eda-sañ ni ome ni kakarita⌉i ñ desu ḡa—

Ministry of Education
introduction

5. We've come through the introduction of Mr. Yamamoto at the Ministry of Education.

mo⌈ñbu⌉syoo
syookai __or__ gosyookai ↑
Mo⌈ñbu⌉syoo no Ya⌈mamoto-sañ no gosyookai de mairima⌉sita.

Receptionist

conference
in the middle of a conference
can receive __or__ can be received
can't I have you come?

ka⌉iḡi
kaiḡi-tyuu

moraeru /-ru/ __or__
itadakeru ↑ /-ru/
ki⌈te⌉ moraenai? __or__ i⌈ra⌉-
ssya⌉tte ↑ itadakenai ↓? __or__
i⌈ra⌉site ↑ itadakenai ↓?

6. He's in conference now so— I'm sorry but—would you come again [some other time]?

I⌉ma ka⌈iḡi⌉-tyuu de gozaima⌉su
kara; su⌈mimase⌉ñ ḡa, ma⌈ta ira⌉-
site i⌐tadakemase⌐ñ ka—

circumstances __or__
conditions

7. Is that convenient for you? (Lit. How are the conditions for you?)

tuḡoo __or__ gotuḡoo ↑

Gotuḡoo (wa) i⌈ka⌉ḡa de gozaiması
ka.

93

Tanaka

    can come   ko⌐rare⌐ru /-ru/

8. We can't come any more today   Kyo⌐o wa ⌐mo⌐o ko⌐raremase⌐ñ
    so I guess we'll come tomor-   kara, a⌐sita mairimasyo⌐o.
    row.

(b)

Tanaka

    come to see [someone]   a⌐i ni ⌐ku⌐ru or o⌐me ni
                                   kaka⌐ri ni ⌐ma⌐iru ‡

9. I've come to see Mr. Yama-   Ya⌐mamoto-sañ ni ome ni kaka⌐ri
    moto . . .   ni ma⌐irima⌐sita ḡa—

Secretary

    can't I have you wait?   ma⌐tte moraenai? or o⌐mati
                                 ni na⌐tte ‡ itadakenai ‡?

10. Mr. Yamamoto stepped out   Yamamoto-sañ (wa) ⌐tyo⌐tto o⌐de-
    for a moment but he'll be   kake ni narima⌐sita ḡa; su⌐ḡu o⌐ka-
    back soon so would you wait?   eri ni narima⌐su kara, o⌐mati ni
                                 na⌐tte i⌐tadakemase⌐ñ ka⌐

Tanaka

11. Yes, that will be all right.   E⌐e, ke⌐kkoo desu.

Secretary

    sit down (on a chair)   ka⌐ke⌐ru /-ru/
12. Please have a seat.   Do⌐ozo, o⌐kake-kudasa⌐i.

· · ·

Tanaka (to Yamamoto, after talking with him)

    various(ly)   iroiro
    helpful service   se⌐wa⌐ or o⌐sewa ‡
13. I'm much obliged to you.   Iroiro o⌐sewa ni na⌐rima⌐sita.

    a time when you are busy   o⌐isoḡasi⌐i ‡ tokoro
14. Thank you very much for your   O⌐isoḡasi⌐i to⌐koro⌐ (o) ⌐do⌐o mo
    time when you are [so] busy.   a⌐ri⌐ḡatoo gozaimasita.

(c)

Tanaka

    can read or can be   yo⌐me⌐ru /-ru/
        read
15. Can you read this?   Yo⌐mema⌐su ka⌐

Yamamoto

    letter   teḡami
16. It's a letter [written] in Eng-   Eeḡo no teḡami desyoo? Ze⌐ñ-
    lish, isn't it? I can't read   zeñ yome⌐nai ñ desu yo⌐
    it at all.

Tanaka

can read English
somebody who can read
   English

17. Well then, isn't there some-
    body here who can read
    English?

e⌐eḡo⌐ ḡa yome⌐ru
da⌐re ka e⌐eḡo ḡa yome⌐ru
hito <u>or</u> da⌐re ka e⌐eḡo
no yome⌐ru hito

Zya⌐a, koko ni ⌐da⌐re ka e⌐eḡo
(no) yome⌐ru hito (wa) i⌐mase⌐ñ
ka↲

Yamamoto

can speak <u>or</u> can be
   spoken

18. Hmmm. Mr. Matsuda can
    speak a little but I wonder
    who would be (the one) able
    to read that letter.

ha⌐nase⌐ru /-ru/

Sa⌐a. Ma⌐tuda-sañ wa suko⌐si
ha⌐nase⌐ru ñ desu ḡa, so⌐no te-
ḡami (ḡa) yome⌐ru no wa ⌐da⌐re
desyoo ⌐ne⌐e.

(d)

Tanaka

all day long
19. Are you going to work all
    day today too?

iti-niti-zyuu
Kyo⌐o mo i̅ti-niti-zyuu ha⌐taraki-
ma⌐su ka↲

Smith

half-day
20. No, today is just half-day . . .

ha⌐ññiti⌐
Iie, kyo⌐o wa ha⌐ññiti dake⌐ desu
ḡa—

Tanaka

movie
go to see
21. Then wouldn't you [like to] go
    to see a movie with me in the
    afternoon?

e⌐eḡa [1]
mi⌐ ni iku
Zya⌐a, go⌐ḡo i̅ssyo ni ⌐e⌐eḡa (o)
⌐mi⌐ ni i⌐kimase⌐ñ ka↲

Smith

somewhere <u>or</u> some
   place
go somewhere
go to eat
22. Yes, I'd like to. -After we see
    it, let's go somewhere to eat.

do⌐ko ka

do⌐ko ka e iku
ta⌐be ni iku
E⌐e, yo⌐roko⌐nde. Mi⌐te kara,
do⌐ko ka e ⌐ta⌐be ni i⌐kimasyo⌐o.

Tanaka

23. Yes, let's do that.

E⌐e, so⌐o simasyo⌐o.

(e)

Smith

overwork

ha⌐tarakisuḡi⌐ru /-ru/

---

[1] Has unaccented alternant.

must not overwork   ha⌈tarakisu⌉ḡite wa ĭkenai
                                       or ha⌈tarakisu⌉ḡitya ĭkenai
24. Mr. Yoshida. You know you   Yosida-sañ. Ha⌈tarakisu⌉ḡitya
     mustn't overwork, don't you?   i⌈kena⌉i ñ desyoo?

     can rest   ya⌈sume⌉ru /-ru/
25. Can't you rest for a little   Su⌈ko⌉si ya⌈sume⌉nai ñ desu ka⌄
     while?

                          Mr. Yoshida

     within today or before   kyoo-zyuu ni
          today is over
26. I want to finish doing all of   Kyoo-zyuu ni kŏno siḡoto (o)
     this work today so [I'll have   ⌈ze⌉ñbu si┗te simaita⌐i kara,
     to do] a little more.   mo⌈o suko⌉si⌐

     summer vacation   na⌈tuya⌉sumi
     take a summer vacation   na⌈tuya⌉sumi o ┗to⌐ru
27. I'm going to take my summer   A⌈sita⌉ kara ⌈bo⌉ku (wa) na⌈tuya⌉-
     vacation starting (lit. from)   sumi (o) ┗to⌐ru ñ desu yo.
     tomorrow, you know.

                          (f)

                          Mr. Tanaka

     must not drink or smoke   no⌉ñde wa ĭkenai or
                                          no⌉ñzya ĭkenai
28. You mustn't smoke here.   Koko de ta⌈bako (o) no⌉ñzya
                                       ĭkenai yo⌄

               Mr. Yamamoto

29. Why?   Na⌉ze?

               Mr. Tanaka

30. You say "Why?". . . It says   Na⌉ze tte⌐ Soo ⌈ka⌉ite ┗a⌐ru
     so—over there!   yo—asuko ni⌐

               Mr. Yamamoto

     notice   ki ⌈ḡa tu⌉ku
31. Oh! I didn't notice.   A, ki ⌈ḡa tuka⌉nakatta.

              NOTES ON THE BASIC DIALOGUES

   5. De here is the particle of means: 'we have come by means of the intro-
       duction——.'
       Note also the verbal syookai-suru 'introduce': A o B ni syookai-suru
       'introduce A to B.'

   6. With kaiḡi-tyuu compare hanasi-tyuu 'in the middle of talking' and si-
       ḡoto-tyuu 'in the middle of work.'

7. Note the common combinations tu⌐ɡoo ɡa i⌐i 'is convenient for someone' (lit. 'circumstances are good') and tu⌐ɡoo ga waru⌐i 'is inconvenient for someone' (lit. 'circumstances are bad').

8. Wa here is the particle of comparison: 'Today (in contrast with other
   days) we can't come any more so we'll come tomorrow.'

9. 'but—will it be possible for me to see him?'

12. Ka⌐ke⌐ru refers to sitting on a chair or other raised object, in contrast
    with the verbal suwaru /-u/, which refers to sitting Japanese-style on
    the floor or ground.

13. Iroiro, meaning 'in many ways,' 'variously,' can occur without a follow-
    ing particle as an expression of manner, modifying an inflected word or
    phrase. When it describes a following nominal, iroiro occurs with no
    or na and means 'various,' 'many kinds of.'

14. Note: X (o) a⌐ri⌐gatoo 'thank you for X.' The o is frequently omitted.
    To⌐koro⌐ is a nominal which sometimes refers to time and sometimes to
    place. Compare ma⌐e 'time before' or 'place in front.'

20. 'but—why do you ask?'

22. Particle e may be replaced by ni.

27. Na⌐tuya⌐sumi: note also a⌐kiya⌐sumi 'autumn vacation,' hu⌐yuya⌐sumi
    'winter vacation,' ha⌐ruya⌐sumi 'spring vacation.'

30. Tte is the quotative. See the latter part of Grammatical Note 1 in Les-
    son 18.

31. Note: X ni ki ⌐ga tu⌐ku 'notice X.'

GRAMMATICAL NOTES

1. The Potential

Yo⌐me⌐ru 'can read' or 'can be read'	is the POTENTIAL equivalent of	yo⌐mu 'read'
Ko⌐rare⌐ru 'can come'		ku⌐ru 'come'
Moraeru 'can receive' or 'can be received'		morau 'receive'
Itadakeru↓ 'can receive' or 'can be received'		itadaku↓ 'receive'

Most verbals have corresponding potential verbals meaning 'can do so-and-
so' or 'so-and-so can be done.' To make the citation form of the potential
of:

      -ru verbals: Substitute -rare-ru for final -ru
        Example: akeru 'open' ~ akerareru 'can open' or 'can be
           opened'
      -u verbals: Substitute -e-ru for final -u[1]
        Example: ka⌐ku 'write' ~ ka⌐ke⌐ru 'can write' or 'can be written'

---

[1] But for iku 'go' there are alternate potential forms: ikareru and ikeru.

-aru verbals: [1] Substitute -ar-e-ru for final -aru
     Example: oˢsyaˈru 'say' ~ oˢsyareˈru 'can say' or 'can be said'
Irregular verbals: kuˈru 'come' ~ koˈrareˈru or koˈreˈru 'can come'
     suru 'do' ~ deˈkiˈru 'is possible' or 'can do'
     (Deˈkiˈru is regularly used as the potential equivalent
     not only of independent suru but also of suru at the
     end of compounds.)

A potential is accented if the verbal from which it is derived is accented. The accent of the citation form is on the next-to-last syllable.

All potentials are themselves verbals of the -ru group. Thus, the potential of akeru has such forms as:

Informal non-past (= citation form): akerareru
Stem: akerare
Informal past: akerareta
Gerund: akerarete
Formal non-past: akeraremasu

Although there is some variation, in the speech of most Japanese, potentials are intransitive — that is, their usage parallels that of waˈkaˈru 'be clear,' iru 'be necessary,' zyoˈozu da 'be proficient,' suˈkiˈ da 'be pleasing,' etc., in occurring with particles wa and ḡa but not o (direct object particle). Study the following pairs of examples:

Taˈnaka-sañ ḡa yomimaˈsita. 'Mr. Tanaka read [it].'
Taˈnaka-sañ ḡa yomemaˈsita. 'Mr. Tanaka was able to read [it].'

Siˈñbuñ o yomimaˈsita. 'I read the newspaper.'
Siˈñbuñ ḡa yomemaˈsita. 'I was able to read the newspaper.' (Lit.'The newspaper could be read.'

Tanaka-sañ wa siˈñbuñ o yomimaˈsita. 'Mr. Tanaka read the newspaper.'
Tanaka-sañ wa siˈñbuñ ḡa yomemaˈsita. 'Mr. Tanaka was able to read the newspaper.' (Lit. 'As for Mr. Tanaka, the newspaper was able to be read.')

Siñbuñ wa Taˈnaka-sañ ḡa yomimaˈsita. 'Mr. Tanaka read the newspaper (in contrast with other things).'
Siñbuñ wa Taˈnaka-sañ ḡa yomemaˈsita. 'Mr. Tanaka was able to read the newspaper (in contrast with other things)'

Additional examples:

Kyoˈo wa iˈkaremaˈsu ḡa, aˈsitaˈ wa iˈkaremaseˈñ. 'Today I can go but tomorrow I can't (go).'
Niˈhoñḡo ḡa kakemaˈsu ka⌉ 'Can you write Japanese?'
Iˈsoḡasiˈi soo desu kara, aˈeˈnai desyoo. 'They say he's busy so you probably won't be able to see him.'
Aˈsita korareˈnai hito ˈdaˈre? 'Who [is] the person who can't come tomorrow?'
Kiˈppu ḡa kaenaˈkatta kara, koˈñbañ uˈti ni iru tumori deˈsu. 'I couldn't buy a ticket so I plan to stay at home tonight.'

---

[1] Potentials of -aru verbals are comparatively rare.

A verbal gerund + √moraenai or √itadakenai [1] 'cannot receive' occurs in questions as a request, meaning literally 'can't I receive the doing of something (by someone)?' In many—but not all—contexts, the 'someone' is 'you,' i.e. the person addressed.

Thus:

	Informal	Formal
Plain	Katte moraenai?	Ka⌐tte moraemase⌐ñ ka⌐
Polite	Katte itadakenai?	Ka⌐tte itadakemase⌐ñ ka⌐
	(Women's speech)	
or (more polite)	O⌐kai ni na⌐tte itadakenai? (Women's speech)	O⌐kai ni na⌐tte iᴴtadakemaseᴴñ ka⌐

All the above examples mean 'Could I have [you] [1] buy it for me?' 'Would [you] [1] buy it for me?' (Lit. 'Can't I receive buying?').

Compare:

Plain	Katte kurenai?	Ka⌐tte kuremase⌐ñ ka⌐
Polite	Ka⌐tte kudasara⌐nai?	Ka⌐tte kudasaimase⌐ñ ka⌐
	(Women's speech)	
or (more polite)	O⌐kai ni na⌐tte kuᴴdasa-ra⌐nai? (Women's speech)	O⌐kai ni na⌐tte kuᴴdasaima-se⌐ñ ka⌐

All of these examples mean 'Would you buy it for me?' (Lit. 'Won't you give me buying?')

These patterns closely resemble each other and are often interchangeable, but those using √moraenai and √itadakenai are less direct and more impersonal. Compare tu⌐ku⌐tte moraitai 'I want to have it made (i.e. by someone)' (lit. 'I want to receive making') and tu⌐ku⌐tte kudasai 'please make it (i.e. YOU make it)' (lit. 'give me making').

NOTE: There is an alternant for the potential, consisting of a non-past informal verbal[2] (citation form) + ko⌐to⌐ ḡa/wa √de⌐ki⌐ru (lit. 'the act of doing so-and-so is possible'). Compare:

Su⌐misu-sañ wa ni⌐hoñḡo ḡa yomema⌐su ka⌐ 'Can Mr. Smith read Japanese?' (Lit. 'As for Mr. Smith, can Japanese be read?')

Su⌐misu-sañ wa ni⌐hoñḡo o yo⌐mu koto ḡa de⌐kima⌐su ka⌐ 'Can Mr. Smith read Japanese?' (Lit. 'As for Mr. Smith, is the act of reading Japanese possible?')

Ha⌐nasema⌐su ḡa, ze⌐ñzeñ kakemase⌐ñ ᴴneᴴe. 'He can talk but he can't write at all, can he.'

Ha⌐na⌐su koto wa deᴴkima⌐su ḡa, ze⌐ñzeñ ka⌐ku koto wa de⌐kimase⌐ñ ᴴneᴴe. 'He can talk but he can't write at all, can he.'

In conversation, the potential forms discussed at the beginning of this note are more common than the corresponding expressions ending in —— ko⌐to⌐ ḡa/wa √de⌐ki⌐ru.

---

[1] Or someone else, depending on context.

[2] I.e. a verbal which is not a potential.

2. Prohibition: Gerund + <u>wa</u> + √<u>ikenai</u>

A gerund (verbal, adjectival or copula) + particle <u>wa</u> + √<u>ikenai</u> 'it won't do' is an expression of prohibition: '[you] must not do so-and-so' or 'it must not be so-and-so' (lit. 'as for doing or being so-and-so, it won't do'). In normal rapid speech, a -<u>te</u> + <u>wa</u> sequence is usually contracted to -<u>tya</u> or -<u>tyaa</u>, and a -<u>de</u> + <u>wa</u> sequence to -<u>zya</u> or -<u>zyaa</u>.

Examples:

Si⌐te⌐¹ wa ikenai. <u>or</u> (more commonly) Si⌐tya⌐a ikenai. 'You must not do it.'
So⌐re o ta⌐betya ikenai. 'You must not eat that.'
Ko⌐tira ni ha⌐ittya i⌐kemase⌐n. 'You must not come in here.'
Si⌐rokutya i⌐kemase⌐n. 'It must not be white.'
Sa⌐n-too zya⌐a² i⌐kemase⌐n. 'It must not be third class.'

This pattern occurs in strong negative replies to affirmative requests for permission. Thus:

Tu⌐katte⌐ mo ⌐i⌐i desu ka⌐ 'May I use it?'
Tu⌐kattya⌐a i⌐kemase⌐n. 'You must not (use).'

The pattern also occurs in questions. The most common English conversational equivalent is 'can't I do so-and-so?' <u>or</u> 'can't it be so-and-so?' (lit. as for doing or being so-and-so, won't it do?'). Note the affirmative and negative replies:

Tu⌐kattya⌐a i⌐kemase⌐n ka⌐ 'Can't I use it?'
(a) E⌐e. Tu⌐kattya⌐a i⌐kemase⌐n. 'No (i.e. that's right). You can't (<u>or</u> must not) use it.'
(b) Iie. Tu⌐katte⌐ mo ⌐i⌐i desu. 'Yes (i.e. that's wrong). You may (<u>or</u> can) use it.'

3. Indefinites: Interrogatives + <u>ka</u>

The indefinite particle <u>ka</u> following an interrogative makes the interrogative into its corresponding indefinite. Thus:

<u>na⌐ni</u> 'what?' and <u>na⌐ni ka</u> 'something,' 'anything'
<u>da⌐re</u> 'who?' and <u>da⌐re ka</u> 'someone,' 'somebody,' 'anyone,' 'anybody'
<u>do⌐ko</u> 'where?' and <u>do⌐ko ka</u> 'somewhere,' 'anywhere,' 'some place'
<u>i⌐tu</u> 'when?' and <u>i⌐tu ka</u> 'some time'
<u>do⌐tira</u> 'which (of two)?' and <u>do⌐tira ka</u> 'either one'
<u>do⌐re</u> 'which (of three or more things)?' and <u>do⌐re ka</u> 'some one <u>or</u> any one (of three or more things)'

---

¹ Before <u>wa</u>, a normally unaccented gerund acquires a final-syllable accent. The contraction of -te⌐ <u>wa</u> is usually tya⌐a.

² Here <u>zya⌐a</u> is a contraction of gerund de⌐ (from <u>da</u>) + <u>wa</u>. Elsewhere in this pattern, it is a contraction of the -de⌐ ending of a verbal gerund + <u>wa</u>.

These indefinites usually occur without a following particle as subjects and objects, but they are regularly followed by particles other than wa, g̃a, and o. Thus:

Da⌐re ka ki⌐ma⌐sita. 'Someone has come.'
Na⌐ni ka ta⌐bemasyo⌐o. 'Let's eat something.'
Do⌐tira ka ku⌐dasa⌐i. 'Please give me either one.'

but:

Da⌐re ka kara ki⌐kima⌐sita. 'I heard it from someone.'
Do⌐ko ka e i⌐kima⌐sita. 'He went somewhere.'
Da⌐re ka ni tu⌐ku⌐tte mo⌐raima⌐sita. 'He had it made by someone.'

When an appropriate indefinite describes a nominal—or, more commonly, a phrase ending with a nominal—it makes the nominal indefinite. Thus:

na⌐ni ka o⌐mosiro⌐i ⌐ho⌐n̄ 'some interesting book'
da⌐re ka ⌐yo⌐ku hataraku hito 'some person who works hard'
do⌐ko ka ⌐si⌐zuka na ryokañ 'some quiet inn'
i⌐tu ka i⌐sog̃a⌐siku ⌐na⌐i toki 'some time when you're not busy'

4. Questions without ka

It was mentioned in Lesson 1, Grammatical Note 2, that while all sentences ending with question particle ka are questions, not all questions end with ka.

Questions without ka are of two basic kinds. In the first type—which has occurred frequently in previous lessons—the sign of the question is final question-mark intonation.

Compare: Wa⌐ka⌐ru. 'It's clear.'
          Wa⌐ka⌐ru? 'Is it clear?'

Examples of this kind also occur in formal style, particularly in the speech of women:

Wa⌐karima⌐su. 'It's clear.'
Wa⌐karima⌐su?[1] 'Is it clear?'

In the second kind of question without ka—occurring in this lesson for the first time—the sign of the question is an interrogative word (for example, na⌐n̄, do⌐ko, do⌐tira, do⌐re, etc.). Such questions usually end with a tentative form and period intonation.

Examples:

Da⌐re desyoo. 'Who would that be?' 'Who is it?'
Sore ⌐na⌐n̄ daroo. 'What would that be?' 'What is that?'
Do⌐o simasyoo. 'What'll we do?'

5. Verbal Stems in Purpose Expressions

A verbal stem (the -ma⌐su form minus -ma⌐su) occurs as an independent

---

[1] In such cases, final syllable -su regularly has its voiced alternant instead of -sᵤ.

word preceding the particle <u>ni</u> of purpose. A word of motion —√iku, √ku⁷ru, etc.—always follows. The combination is a purpose expression: 'go, come, etc. in order to do so-and-so.' Thus:

> mi⁷ ni iku 'go to see'
> ka⌐i ni ku⁷ru 'come to buy'
> ku⌐ruma o nao⁷si ni iku 'go to fix the car'
> be⌐ñkyoo-si ni ku⁷ru 'come to study'
> to⁷ri ni i⌐rassya⁷ru 'go <u>or</u> come to pick up'
> i⌐tadaki ni ma⁷iru 'go <u>or</u> come to get'
> ta⁷be ni ⌐ka⁷eru 'return home to eat'

6. -<u>zyuu</u> 'throughout'

A time or place nominal X compounded with -<u>zyuu</u> (or -<u>tyuu</u>) means 'throughout X' or 'all through X.' A -<u>zyuu</u> compound is unaccented. Thus:

> kotosi-zyuu 'throughout this year'
> iti-g̃atu-zyuu 'all through January'
> ik-kag̃etu-zyuu 'all month long' (lit. 'throughout one month')
> hito-bañ-zyuu 'all night long' (lit. 'throughout one night')
> Nihoñ-zyuu 'throughout Japan'

When the particle <u>ni</u> of time follows a -<u>zyuu</u> compound of time, [1] the combination means 'within such-and-such a period of time,' i.e. before the stated time is over. Thus:

> kotosi-zyuu ni 'within this year'
> koñsyuu-zyuu ni 'within this week'

Additional examples:

> Gu⌐ai g̃a wa⌐rukatta kara, iti-niti-zyuu ya⌐suñde imasita.
>   'I didn't feel well so I took it easy all day long.'
> Kyoneñ-zyuu O⌐osaka de hataraite ima⁷sita.
>   'I was working in Osaka all last year.'
> Koñna ⌐ti⁷isa na mi⌐se⁷ wa Ni⌐hoñ-zyuu ni arima⁷su.
>   'Small shops like these are all over Japan.'
> Kotosi-zyuu ni a⌐tarasi⁷i uti o tu⌐ku⁷tte mo⌐raita⁷i ñ desu g̃a_
>   'I want to have a new house built within this year . . . '
> Ko⌐no hoñ wa kyo⌐o-zyuu ni yomita⁷i ñ desu g̃a_
>   'I'd like to read this book before the day is over . . . '

DRILLS

A. Substitution Drill

1. Thank you very much for your time when you are [so] busy.

   O⌐isog̃asi⁷i tokoro ⌐do⁷o mo a⌐ri⁷g̃atoo gozaimasita.

---

[1] Usually NOT a number compound.

2. Thank you very much for the letter.

Teḡami ⌐doꞌo mo a⌐ri⌐ḡatoo gozaimasita.

3. Thank you very much for the interesting book.

O⌐mosiroꞌi ˥ho˥ñ ⌐doꞌo mo a⌐ri⌐ḡatoo gozaimasita.

4. Thank you very much for the new magazine.

A⌐tarasiꞌi zassi ⌐doꞌo mo a⌐ri⌐ḡatoo gozaimasita.

5. Thank you very much for the pretty furoshiki.

Ki˥ree na hurosiki ⌐doꞌo mo a⌐ri˥ḡatoo gozaimasita.

6. Thank you very much for the telephone call.

O⌐deñwa ⌐doꞌo mo a⌐ri⌐ḡatoo gozaimasita.

7. Thank you very much for the English newspaper.

Eeḡo no siñbuñ ⌐doꞌo mo a⌐ri⌐ḡatoo gozaimasita.

8. Thank you very much for the delicious candy.

O⌐isii okaꞌsi ⌐doꞌo mo a⌐ri⌐ḡatoo gozaimasita.

B. Substitution Drill

1. I'd like to do this work (within) today . . .

Kyo⌐ꞌo-zyuu ni kono siḡoto (o) sitaꞌi ñ desu ḡa—

2. I'd like to do this work (within) this week . . .

Ko⌐ñsyuu-zyuu ni kono siḡoto (o) sitaꞌi ñ desu ḡa—

3. I'd like to do this work (within) this month . . .

Ko⌐ñḡetu-zyuu ni kono siḡoto (o) sitaꞌi ñ desu ḡa—

4. I'd like to do this work (within) this year . . .

Ko⌐tosi-zyuu ni kono siḡoto (o) sitaꞌi ñ desu ḡa—

5. I'd like to do this work all day long . . .

I⌐ti-niti-zyuu kono siḡoto (o) sitaꞌi ñ desu ḡa—

6. I'd like to do this work all week long . . .

I⌐s-syuukañ-zyuu kono siḡoto (o) sitaꞌi ñ desu ḡa—

7. I'd like to do this work all month long . . .

I⌐k-kaḡetu-zyuu kono siḡoto (o) sitaꞌi ñ desu ḡa—

8. I'd like to do this work all year long . . .

I⌐ti-neñ-zyuu kono siḡoto (o) sitaꞌi ñ desu ḡa—

C. Substitution Drill

1. Could(n't) I have you read the letter from Mr. Tanaka?

Tanaka-sañ kara no teḡami (o) ⌐yoꞌñde i˥tadakemase˥ñ ka⌣ [1]

2. Could(n't) I have you read the letter from Mr. Tanaka?

Tanaka-sañ kara no teḡami (o) ⌐yoꞌñde mo˥raemase˥ñ ka⌣ [2]

3. I had [him] read the letter from Mr. Tanaka.

Tanaka-sañ kara no teḡami (o) ⌐yoꞌñde mo˥raimaꞌsita. [2]

4. [He] read the letter from Mr. Tanaka for me.

Tanaka-sañ kara no teḡami (o) ⌐yoꞌñde ku˥remaꞌsita. [2]

5. Would(n't) you read the letter from Mr. Tanaka for me?

Tanaka-sañ kara no teḡami (o) ⌐yoꞌñde ku˥remase˥ñ ka⌣ [2]

---

[1] Polite.

[2] Plain.

6. Would(n't) you read the
    letter from Mr. Tanaka
    for me?

Tanaka-sañ kara no teḡami (o)
⌐yo⌐nde ku⌐dasaimase⌐ñ ka⌐ [1]

7. Please read the letter
    from Mr. Tanaka.

Tanaka-sañ kara no teḡami (o)
⌐yo⌐nde kudasai.

8. I had [him] read the
    letter from Mr. Tanaka.

Tanaka-sañ kara no teḡami (o)
⌐yo⌐nde i⌐tadakima⌐sita. [1]

D. Substitution Drill

1. Would you come again
    tomorrow?

Ma⌐ta asita irassya⌐tte i⌐tadake-
mase⌐ñ ka⌐

2. Would you wait a moment?

Syo⌐osyoo o⌐mati ni na⌐tte i⌐tada-
kemase⌐ñ ka⌐

3. Would you sit here?

Ko⌐tira ni ka⌐kete i⌐tadakemase⌐ñ
ka⌐

4. Would you get in touch
    [with me] today?

Kyo⌐o-zyuu ni reñraku-site itada-
kemaseñ ka⌐

5. Would you lend me a little
    money?

Okane (o) su⌐ko⌐si ka⌐site itada-
kemase⌐ñ ka⌐

6. Would you wake me early
    tomorrow morning?

A⌐sita no a⌐sa ⌐ha⌐yaku o⌐ko⌐site
i⌐tadakemase⌐ñ ka⌐

7. Would you show me the
    letter from the teacher?

Se⌐ñse⌐e kara no teḡami (o) ⌐mi⌐-
sete i⌐tadakemase⌐ñ ka⌐

8. Would you say it once
    more?

Mo⌐o iti-do itte itadakemase⌐ñ
ka⌐

9. Would you speak in Jap-
    anese?

Ni⌐hoñḡo de hana⌐site i⌐tadake-
mase⌐ñ ka⌐

10. Would you call Mr. Ueda
    who is next door?

O⌐tonari no Ueda-sañ (o) yoñde
itadakemase⌐ñ ka⌐

a. Repeat the above drill, substituting mo⌐raemase⌐ñ for i⌐tadakemase⌐ñ.

b. Repeat the above drill, substituting an honorific gerund for each of the
    plain gerunds. For example, in the third sentence ka⌐kete will be re-
    placed by o⌐kake ni na⌐tte.

E. Substitution Drill (based on Grammatical Note 2)

1. You mustn't overwork.

Ha⌐tarakisu⌐ḡityaa i⌐kemase⌐ñ yo⌐

2. You mustn't use [it].
    /tukau/

Tu⌐kattya⌐a i⌐kemase⌐ñ yo⌐

3. You mustn't open [it].
    /akeru/

A⌐ketya⌐a i⌐kemase⌐ñ yo⌐

4. You mustn't close [it].
    /simeru/

Si⌐metyaa i⌐kemase⌐ñ yo⌐

5. You mustn't go in.
    /ha⌐iru/

Ha⌐ittyaa i⌐kemase⌐ñ yo⌐

---

[1] Polite.

6. You mustn't wash [it].   A⌐rattya⌐a i⌐kemase⌐n̄ yo⌐
    /arau/

7. You mustn't drink [it].   No⌐n̄zyaa i⌐kemase⌐n̄ yo⌐
    /no⌐mu/

8. You mustn't quit.   Ya⌐metya⌐a i⌐kemase⌐n̄ yo⌐
    /yameru/

a. Repeat the above drill using the uncontracted gerund + <u>wa</u> sequences
    (for example, ha⌐tarakisu⌐ḡite wa).

F. Response Drill (based on Grammatical Note 2)

    Tutor: Si⌐te⌐ mo ⌐i⌐i desu ka⌐ 'May I do it?'
    Student: Iie. Si⌐tya⌐a i⌐kemase⌐n̄ yo⌐ 'No. You must not do it.'

1. Kodomo (o) o⌐ko⌐site mo   Iie. O⌐ko⌐sityaa i⌐kemase⌐n̄ yo⌐
    ⌐i⌐i desu ka⌐
2. Asita ⌐o⌐kite mo ⌐i⌐i desu   Iie. O⌐kityaa i⌐kemase⌐n̄ yo⌐
    ka⌐
3. A⌐merika no okane de   Iie. Ha⌐ra⌐ttyaa i⌐kemase⌐n̄
    hara⌐tte mo ⌐i⌐i desu ka⌐   yo⌐
4. I⌐ma no siḡoto (o) tu-   Iie. Tu⌐zuketya⌐a i⌐kemase⌐n̄
    ⌐zukete⌐ mo ⌐i⌐i desu ka⌐   yo⌐
5. Kyo⌐o ⌐ha⌐yaku ⌐ka⌐ette   Iie. Ka⌐ettyaa i⌐kemase⌐n̄ yo⌐
    mo ⌐i⌐i desu ka⌐
6. A⌐no⌐ hito ni ki⌐ite⌐ mo   Iie. Ki⌐itya⌐a i⌐kemase⌐n̄ yo⌐
    ⌐i⌐i desu ka⌐
7. Pe⌐n̄ de ⌐ka⌐ite mo ⌐i⌐i   Iie. Ka⌐ityaa i⌐kemase⌐n̄ yo⌐
    desu ka⌐
8. Ki⌐mono (o) kite⌐ mo ⌐i⌐i   Iie. Ki⌐tya⌐a i⌐kemase⌐n̄ yo⌐
    desu ka⌐
9. Ta⌐kusan̄ katte⌐ mo ⌐i⌐i   Iie. Ka⌐ttya⌐a i⌐kemase⌐n̄ yo⌐
    desu ka⌐
10. Ka⌐ḡi⌐ (o) ⌐ka⌐kete mo   Iie. Ka⌐ketyaa i⌐kemase⌐n̄ yo⌐
    ⌐i⌐i desu ka⌐

G. Response Drill (based on Grammatical Note 2)

    What does the <u>Ha⌐i</u>. or <u>Iie</u>. answer (as indicated by the tutor) mean,
    in response to the following questions? Use the <u>-te mo ⌐i⌐i desu</u>
    or <u>-tyaa i⌐kemase⌐n̄</u> pattern.

1. Ko⌐no sakana (o) ta⌐betyaa   Ta⌐bete mo ⌐i⌐i desu.
    i⌐kemase⌐n̄ ka⌐ . . . Iie.
2. O⌐hu⌐ro ni ⌐ha⌐itte mo ⌐i⌐i   Ha⌐ittyaa i⌐kemase⌐n̄.
    desu ka⌐ . . . Iie.
3. U⌐e no hikidasi ni iretya⌐a   I⌐retya⌐a i⌐kemase⌐n̄.
    i⌐kemase⌐n̄ ka⌐ . . . Ha⌐i.
4. Ta⌐bako (o) non̄de mo ⌐i⌐i   No⌐n̄de mo ⌐i⌐i desu.
    desu ka⌐ . . . Ha⌐i.

5. Asita ya⌐suꝫzyaa i⌐kema-   Ya⌐suꝫde mo ⌐i⌐i desu.
    seꝫ ka⌐ . . . Iie.

6. Tu⌐ḡi⌐ no ⌐ka⌐do (o) ma-   Ma⌐ḡattya⌐a i⌐kemaseꝫ.
    ⌐ḡatte⌐ mo ⌐i⌐i desu
    ka⌐ . . . Iie.

7. Ko⌐ko no mizu (o) noꝫ-   Noꝫzyaa i⌐kemase⌐ꝫ.
    zyaa i⌐kemase⌐ꝫ ka⌐ . . .
    Ha⌐i.

8. Ko⌐no teḡami (o) sutete⌐   Su⌐tete⌐ mo ⌐i⌐i desu.
    mo ⌐i⌐i desu ka⌐ . . . Ha⌐i.

H. Grammar Drill (based on Grammatical Note 3)

        Tutor: Da⌐re ḡa si⌐ma⌐sita ka⌐ 'Who did it?'
        Student: Da⌐re ka si⌐ma⌐sita ka⌐ 'Did somebody do it?'

1. Do⌐ko de ha⌐taraite (i)ru⌐   Do⌐ko ka de ha⌐taraite (i)ru⌐ ꝫ
    ꝫ desu ka⌐   desu ka⌐
2. Do⌐nata ḡa so⌐o ossyaima⌐-   Do⌐nata ka so⌐o ossyaima⌐sita
    sita ka⌐   ka⌐
3. Do⌐re (o) tu⌐kaimasyo⌐o   Do⌐re ka tu⌐kaimasyo⌐o ka.
    ka.
4. I⌐tu o⌐me ni kakarimasyo⌐o   I⌐tu ka o⌐me ni kakarimasyo⌐o
    ka.   ka.
5. Na⌐ni (o) sa⌐ḡasite (i)ru⌐   Na⌐ni ka sa⌐ḡasite (i)ru⌐ ꝫ desu
    ꝫ desu ka⌐   ka⌐
6. Do⌐ko e i⌐kimasyo⌐o ka.   · Do⌐ko ka e i⌐kimasyo⌐o ka.

I. Grammar Drill (based on Grammatical Note 5)

        Tutor: A⌐soko de sima⌐sita. 'He did it'
        Student: Asoko e si ⌐ni ikima⌐sita. 'He went there to do it.'

1. A⌐tarasi⌐i ⌐re⌐sutoraꝫ de   A⌐tarasi⌐i ⌐re⌐sutoraꝫ e ⌐go⌐haꝫ
    ⌐go⌐haꝫ (o) ta⌐bema⌐sita.   (o) ⌐ta⌐be ni i⌐kima⌐sita.
2. Se⌐ꝫse⌐e no otaku de o⌐tya   Se⌐ꝫse⌐e no otaku e o⌐tya (o)
    (o) nomima⌐sita.   no⌐mi ni i⌐kima⌐sita.
3. Kyo⌐oto de ha⌐tarakima⌐-   Kyo⌐oto e ha⌐taraki ni ikima⌐-
    sita.   sita.
4. A⌐no eeḡa⌐kaꝫ de Hu⌐raꝫsu   A⌐no eeḡa⌐kaꝫ e Hu⌐raꝫsu no eeḡa
    no eeḡa (o) mima⌐sita.   (o) mi⌐ ni i⌐kima⌐sita.
5. Ho⌐keꝫḡa⌐isya de to⌐modati   Ho⌐keꝫḡa⌐isya e to⌐modati ni a⌐i
    ni aima⌐sita.   ni i⌐kima⌐sita.
6. De⌐pa⌐ato de a⌐tarasi⌐i bo-   De⌐pa⌐ato e a⌐tarasi⌐i bo⌐osi (o)
    ⌐osi (o) kaima⌐sita.   kai ni ikima⌐sita.
7. Giꝫkoo de o⌐kane (o) ka-   Giꝫkoo e o⌐kane (o) kari ni iki-
    rima⌐sita.   ma⌐sita.
8. Yu⌐ubi⌐ꝫkyoku de te⌐ḡami   Yu⌐ubi⌐ꝫkyoku e te⌐ḡami (o) da⌐si
    (o) dasima⌐sita. [1]   ni i⌐kima⌐sita.

---

[1] Te⌐ḡami o da⌐su 'mail a letter.'

J. Grammar Drill (based on Grammatical Note 1)

    Tutor: To (o) si˹mema˺sita ka⤵ 'Did you shut the door?'
    Student: To (ḡa) si˹merarema˺sita ka⤵ 'Were you able to shut the door?'

1. Asita mata ki˹ma˺su ka⤵   Asita mata ko˹rarema˺su ka⤵
2. Nihoñḡo (o) yo˹mima˺su ka⤵   Nihoñḡo (ḡa) yo˹mema˺su ka⤵
3. So˹ñna mono˺ (wa) ˹do˺ko de ka⊦ima⁴su ka⤵   So˹ñna mono˺ (wa) ˹do˺ko de ka⊦ema⁴su ka⤵
4. Syo˹kudoo no ma˺do (o) a˹kema˺sita ka⤵   Syo˹kudoo no ma˺do (ḡa) a˹kerarema˺sita ka⤵
5. A˹sita˺ made ni re˹ñraku-sima˺su ka⤵   A˹sita˺ made ni re˹ñraku-dekima˺su ka⤵
6. A˹na˺ta (wa) byo˹oki de˺ mo ko˹no sigoto (o) tu-zukema˺su ka⤵   A˹na˺ta (wa) byo˹oki de˺ mo ko˹no sigoto (ḡa) tuzukerarema˺su ka⤵
7. Ni˹hoñ no okane de ha-raima˺sita ka⤵   Ni˹hoñ no okane de haraema˺sita ka⤵
8. Sono sigoto (wa) o˹taku de sima˺sita ka⤵   Sono sigoto (wa) o˹taku de deki-ma˺sita ka⤵
9. Ko˹ñsyuu mo raisyuu mo ikima˺su ka⤵   Ko˹ñsyuu mo raisyuu mo ikare-ma˺su ka⤵
10. Ka˹ḡi˺ (ḡa) ka˹ka˺tte (i)ta kara, ha˹ira˺nakatta.   Ka˹ḡi˺ (ḡa) ka˹ka˺tte (i)ta kara, ha˹ire˺nakatta.

K. Substitution Drill

1. Isn't there someone here who can read English?   Koko ni ˹da˺re ka e˹eḡo ḡa˺ [1] yo-me˹ru hito (wa) i˹mase˺ñ ka⤵
2. Isn't there someone here who knows (lit. can do) French?   Koko ni ˹da˺re ka hu˹rañsuḡo ḡa deki˺ru hito (wa) i˹mase˺ñ ka⤵
3. Isn't there someone here who can write Chinese?   Koko ni ˹da˺re ka tyu˹uḡokuḡo ḡa˺ [1] kake˹ru hito (wa) i˹mase˺ñ ka⤵
4. Isn't there someone here who understands German?   Koko ni ˹da˺re ka do˹ituḡo ḡa˺ [1] waka˹ru hito (wa) i˹mase˺ñ ka⤵
5. Isn't there someone here who is studying Spanish?   Koko ni ˹da˺re ka su˹peiñḡo (o) beñkyoo-site (i)ru hito˺ (wa) i˹mase˺ñ ka⤵
6. Isn't there someone here who wants to study English?   Koko ni ˹da˺re ka e˹eḡo ḡa˺ [1] beñ-kyoo-sitai hito˺ (wa) i˹mase˺ñ ka⤵
7. Isn't there someone here who can teach Japanese?   Koko ni ˹da˺re ka ni˹hoñḡo ḡa osierareru hito˺ (wa) i˹mase˺ñ ka⤵
8. Isn't there someone here who can speak Russian?   Koko ni ˹da˺re ka ro˹siaḡo ḡa ha-naseru hito (wa) i˹mase˺ñ ka⤵

---

[1] Or no.

L. Expansion Drill

1. [He] can't speak, can he.   Haˈnasemaseˈn ˈneˈe.
    [He] can't speak very   Aˈnmari hanasemaseˈn ˈneˈe.
    well, can he.

    [He] can read but he   Yoˈmemaˈsu ḡa, aˈnmari hanase-
    can't speak very well,   maseˈn ˈneˈe.
    can he.

    [He] can read English   Eˈeḡo wa yomemaˈsu ḡa, aˈnmari
    but he can't speak very   hanasemaseˈn ˈneˈe.
    well, can he.

    That student can read   Ano gakusee (wa) eˈeḡo wa yome-
    English but he can't   maˈsu ḡa, aˈnmari hanasemaseˈn
    speak very well, can   ˈneˈe.
    he.

2. I probably can't do it.   Deˈkiˈnai desyoo.
    I probably can't do it all.   Zeˈnbu wa deˈkiˈnai desyoo.
    I probably can't do it all   Koˈnsyuu-zyuu niˈ wa ˈzeˈnbu wa
    within this week.   deˈkiˈnai desyoo.
    I am doing [it] but I prob- Siˈte (i)ruˈ n desu ḡa, koˈnsyuu-
    ably can't do it all   zyuu niˈ wa ˈzeˈnbu wa deˈkiˈ-
    within this week.   nai desyoo.
    I am doing [it] all day long, Iˈti-niti-zyuu site (i)ruˈ n desu
    but I probably can't do   ḡa, koˈnsyuu-zyuu niˈ wa ˈzeˈn-
    it all within this week.   bu wa deˈkiˈnai desyoo.
    I am doing [it] every day Maˈiniti iˈti-niti-zyuu site (i)ruˈ
    all day long, but I   n desu ḡa, koˈnsyuu-zyuu niˈ
    probably can't do it all   wa ˈzeˈnbu wa deˈkiˈnai desyoo.
    within this week.

    That work I am doing   Sono siḡoto (wa) ˈmaˈiniti iˈti-
    every day all day long,   niti-zyuu site (i)ruˈ n desu ḡa,
    but I probably can't do   koˈnsyuu-zyuu niˈ wa ˈzeˈnbu
    it all within this week.   wa deˈkiˈnai desyoo.

3. I wasn't able to borrow   Kaˈriraremaseˈn desita.
    [it].

    He was out so I wasn't   Ruˈsu datta kara, kaˈriraremaseˈn
    able to borrow [it].   desita.
    I went but he was out so Iˈkimaˈsita ḡa; ruˈsu datta kara,
    I wasn't able to borrow   kaˈriraremaseˈn desita.
    [it].

    I went to borrow [it] but Kaˈri ni ikimaˈsita ḡa; ruˈsu datta
    he was out so I couldn't kara, kaˈriraremaseˈn desita.
    (borrow).

    I went to borrow a book Hoˈn (o) kaˈri ni ikimaˈsita ḡa;
    but he was out so I   ruˈsu datta kara, kaˈriraremaseˈn
    couldn't (borrow).   desita.

    I went to a friend's house Tomodati no uti e ˈhoˈn (o) kaˈri
    to borrow a book but he ni ikimaˈsita ḡa; ruˈsu datta kara,
    was out so I couldn't   kaˈriraremaseˈn desita.
    (borrow).

4. It would be good,
    wouldn't it.

    It would be best,
    wouldn't it.

    I wonder who would be
    best.

    I'd like to be taught (but)
    I wonder who would be
    best.

    I'd like to be taught
    French (but) I wonder
    who would be best.

    I'd like to be taught
    French by a person
    who's good at it (but)
    I wonder who would
    be best.

    I'd like to be taught
    French by some person
    who's good at it (but) I
    wonder who would be
    best.

I⌐i desyoo ⌐ne⌐e.

I⌐tibañ i⌐i desyoo ⌐ne⌐e.

Da⌐re ḡa i⌐tibañ i⌐i desyoo ⌐ne⌐e.

O⌐siete moraita⌐i ñ desu ḡa,
    da⌐re ḡa i⌐tibañ i⌐i desyoo
    ⌐ne⌐e.

Hu⌐rañsuḡo (o) osiete moraita⌐i
    ñ desu ḡa, da⌐re ḡa i⌐tibañ
    i⌐i desyoo ⌐ne⌐e.

Zyo⌐ozu⌐ na hito ni hu⌐rañsuḡo
    (o) osiete moraita⌐i ñ desu ḡa,
    da⌐re ḡa i⌐tibañ i⌐i desyoo
    ⌐ne⌐e.

Da⌐re ka zyo⌐ozu⌐ na hito ni
    hu⌐rañsuḡo (o) osiete moraita⌐i
    ñ desu ḡa, da⌐re ḡa i⌐tibañ
    i⌐i desyoo ⌐ne⌐e.

5. I've become upset.

    I've become upset be-
    cause [he] doesn't
    listen.

    I've become upset be-
    cause [he] doesn't
    listen at all.

    I've become upset be-
    cause that child doesn't
    listen at all.

    [I] said it but I've become
    upset because that child
    doesn't listen at all.

    [I] said that he mustn't,
    but I've become upset
    because that child
    doesn't listen at all.

    [I] told him that he
    mustn't forget, but I've
    become upset because
    that child doesn't lis-
    ten at all.

    [I] told him that he
    mustn't forget because
    it is important, but
    I've become upset be-
    cause that child doesn't
    listen at all.

Ko⌐ma⌐ttyatta.
Ki⌐kana⌐i kara, ko⌐ma⌐ttyatta.

Ze⌐ñzeñ kikana⌐i kara, ko⌐ma⌐-
    ttyatta.

A⌐no⌐ ko (wa) ze⌐ñzeñ kikana⌐i
    kara, ko⌐ma⌐ttyatta.

I⌐tta⌐ kedo; a⌐no⌐ ko (wa) ze⌐ñzeñ
    kikana⌐i kara, ko⌐ma⌐ttyatta.

I⌐kena⌐i tte i⌐tta⌐ kedo; a⌐no⌐ ko
    (wa) ze⌐ñzeñ kikana⌐i kara,
    ko⌐ma⌐ttyatta.

Wa⌐suretya⌐a i⌐kena⌐i tte i⌐tta⌐
    kedo; a⌐no⌐ ko (wa) ze⌐ñzeñ
    kikana⌐i kara, ko⌐ma⌐ttyatta.

Ta⌐isetu da⌐ kara, wa⌐suretya⌐a
    i⌐kena⌐i tte i⌐tta⌐ kedo; a⌐no⌐
    ko (wa) ze⌐ñzeñ kikana⌐i kara,
    ko⌐ma⌐ttyatta.

I told him that he
  mustn't forget because
  it is important, but
  I've become upset be-
  cause that child doesn't
  listen at all.

Bo⌐ku (wa); ta⌐isetu da⌐ kara, wa-
⌐suretya⌐a i⌐kena⌐i tte i⌐tta⌐ kedo;
a⌐no⌐ ko (wa) ze⌐ñzeñ kikana⌐i
kara, ko⌐ma⌐ttyatta.

6. Would you come?

Ki⌐te⌐ i⌐tadakemase⌐ñ ka⌐

    Would you come again?

Ma⌐ta kite⌐ i⌐tadakemase⌐ñ ka⌐

    Would you come again
      after three?

Sa⌐ñ-zi sugi⌐ ni ma⌐ta kite⌐
i⌐tadakemase⌐ñ ka⌐

    He's supposed to come
      back about three so
      would you come again
      after three?

Sa⌐ñ-zi-go⌐ro ⌐ka⌐eru ha⌐zu de⌐su
kara, sa⌐ñ-zi sugi⌐ ni ma⌐ta
kite⌐ i⌐tadakemase⌐ñ ka⌐

    He isn't in but he's sup-
      posed to come back
      about three so would
      you come again after
      three?

I⌐mase⌐ñ ga; sa⌐ñ-zi-go⌐ro ⌐ka⌐eru
ha⌐zu de⌐su kara, sa⌐ñ-zi sugi⌐
ni ma⌐ta kite⌐ i⌐tadakemase⌐ñ
ka⌐

    He isn't at his desk (lit.
      seat) but he's supposed
      to come back about
      three so would you
      come again after three?

O⌐se⌐ki ni i⌐mase⌐ñ ga, sa⌐ñ-zi-
go⌐ro ⌐ka⌐eru ha⌐zu de⌐su kara,
sa⌐ñ-zi sugi⌐ ni ma⌐ta kite⌐ i⌐ta-
dakemase⌐ñ ka⌐

    He isn't at his desk [just]
      now but he's supposed
      to come back about
      three so would you
      come again after three?

I⌐ma o⌐se⌐ki ni i⌐mase⌐ñ ga; sa⌐ñ-
zi-go⌐ro ⌐ka⌐eru ha⌐zu de⌐su
kara, sa⌐ñ-zi sugi⌐ ni ma⌐ta
kite⌐ i⌐tadakemase⌐ñ ka⌐

QUESTION SUPPLEMENT

(based on the Basic Dialogues)

(a) 1. Tanaka-sañ wa ⌐da⌐re ni a⌐ita⌐i ñ desu ka⌐
      2. Da⌐re no syookai de ki⌐ma⌐sita ka⌐
      3. Yamamoto-sañ wa ⌐do⌐ko ni tu⌐to⌐mete imasu ka⌐
      4. Ueda-sañ wa ⌐i⌐ma hi⌐ma de⌐su ka⌐
      5. Tanaka-sañ wa ⌐kyo⌐o ma⌐ta korarema⌐su ka⌐ I⌐tu ma⌐ta ku⌐ru
          desyoo ka.

(b) 6. Yamamoto-sañ wa zi⌐mu⌐syo ni i⌐ma⌐sita ka⌐
      7. Yamamoto-sañ wa ⌐kyo⌐o zi⌐mu⌐syo e ⌐ka⌐eru ha⌐zu de⌐sita ka⌐
      8. Tanaka-sañ wa Ya⌐mamoto-sañ ni awa⌐nai de so⌐no⌐ hito no zi-
          ⌐mu⌐syo o de⌐ma⌐sita ka⌐
      9. Tanaka-sañ wa Ya⌐mamoto-sañ to hana⌐site kara ⌐na⌐ñ te i⌐ima⌐-
          sita ka⌐

(c) 10. Yamamoto-sañ wa eego ga yo⌐mema⌐su ka⌐
      11. Ma⌐tuda-sañ wa do⌐o desu ka⌐
      12. Tanaka-sañ wa ⌐na⌐ni o ⌐yo⌐ñde mo⌐raita⌐i ñ desu ka⌐

(d) 13. Su┐misu-sañ wa ┌kyo┐o na┌ñ-zi-ḡo┐ro made ha⊢taraku⊣ desyoo ka.
14. Tanaka-sañ wa ┌go┐ḡo ┌do┐ko e i⊢ku tumori de⊣su ka⌣
15. Su┐misu-sañ mo i┌kima┐su ka⌣
16. E┌eḡa o mi┐te kara ┌na┐ni o su⊢ru tumori de⊣su ka⌣

(e) 17. Yosida-sañ wa ┌do┐o site ya⊢sumemase⊣ñ ka⌣
18. Yosida-sañ wa a┌sita┐ mo ha⊢taraku⊣ desyoo ka.
19. I┐ma hu┌yu┐ desyoo ka. Do┐o site wa⊢karima⊣su ka⌣

(f) 20. Koko de ┌na┐ni o si⊢te⊣ wa i⊢kemase⊣ñ ka⌣
21. Tanaka-sañ wa ┌do┐o site wa⊢karima⊣sita ka⌣
22. Ya┌mamoto-sañ mo sono koto┐ o si⊢tte ima⊣sita ka⌣
23. Tanaka-sañ to Yamamoto-sañ wa o┌toko┐ desyoo ka, o┌ñna┐ desyoo ka. Do┐o site wa⊢karima⊣su ka⌣

SHORT SUPPLEMENTARY DIALOGUES

1. Hotel guest: Ma┐da o⊢hu⊣ro ni ⊢ha⊣ittya īkenai?
Room-girl: A┐tuku ⊢na⊣tta yoo de go⊢zaima⊣su kara, mo┐o o┌hairi ni na┐tte mo yo┌rosi┐i desyoo.

2. Mr. Tanaka: Tadaima.
Maid: O┌kaeri-nasaima┐se. Ni-┌zi-ḡo┐ro ┌do┐nata ka i┌rassyaima┐sita yo⌣
Mr. Tanaka: Da┐re daroo.
Maid: O┌namae wa ukaḡaimase┐ñ desita ḡa, ha┌tati-ḡu┐rai no o┌ñna no kata┐ desita.
Mr. Tanaka: A┐a ┌so┐o. Zya┐a, Yo┌sida-sañ daro┐o.

3. Smith: Ti┌isa┐i ha⊢iza⊣ra mo┌o hito┐-tu ┌do┐ko ka ni ┌a┐ru ha⊢zu de⊣su ḡa_ Aa_ A┌rima┐sita.
Tanaka: A┐a, so┌re o saḡasite┐ ta ñ desu ka.

4. Smith: Asita ┌bo┐ku no zi⊢mu⊣syo e ki┌mase┐ñ ka⌣
Tanaka: A┌sita┐ desu ka⌣ A┌sita┐ yori ki┌ñyo┐o no hoo ḡa tu┌ḡoo ḡa i┐i ñ desu ḡa_
Smith: Zya┐a ki┌ñyo┐o ni ⊢do⊣ozo.

5. Smith: Do┐ko ka ┌si┐zuka na ki⊢ssa⊣teñ de o┌tya o nomimase┐n ka⌣
Tanaka: E┐e, so┌o simasyo┐o. A┌no yotukado ni a┐ru no ḡa ⊢i⊣i desyoo?

6. Smith: Kono mizu no┌mema┐su ka⌣
Tanaka: Iie, da┌me┐ desu yo. Zyotyuusañ o yoñde, no┌mi┐mizu o mo⊢raimasyo⊣o.

7. Smith: So┌no hako no na┐ka ni ┌mo┐tto i⊢rerareru⊣ desyoo?
Tanaka: Iie. Mo┐o i┌ppai de┐su kara.

8. Customer: Uketori ┌ka┐ite mo⊢raemase⊣ñ ka⌣
Salesgirl: Su┐ḡu o⊢kaki-sima⊣su kara, syo┐osyoo o⊢mati-kudasa⊣i.

9. Smith: Ki⌐koemase⌐n desita kara; su⌐mimase⌐n ḡa, mo⌐o iti-do ossya⌐tte
    i⌐tadakemase⌐n ka⌐
    Tanaka: To⌐nari no heya⌐ ḡa ya⌐kamasi⌐i desu ⌐ne⌐e. Si⌐zuka ni su⌐ru
    yo⌐o ni i⌐imasyo⌐o.

10. Smith: Sa⌐too-san wa?
    Tanaka: Tyo⌐tto ta⌐bako o kai ni ikima⌐sita. Su⌐ḡu ka⌐erima⌐su yo⌐

English Equivalents

1. Hotel guest: Can't I take a bath yet?
    Room-girl: It seems to be (lit. have become) hot so you may go in now.

2. Mr. Tanaka: I'm back.
    Maid: (Welcome back.) Someone came here at about two o'clock.
    Mr. Tanaka: Who would that be?
    Maid: I didn't ask her name . . . It was a woman about twenty years old.
    Mr. Tanaka: Oh. In that case, it must be Miss Yoshida.

3. Smith: There should be one more small ashtray somewhere . . . Uh . . .
        Here it is.
    Tanaka: Oh, is that what you were looking for?

4. Smith: Will (lit. won't) you come to my office tomorrow?
    Tanaka: Tomorrow? Friday is more convenient than tomorrow but . . .
    Smith: Then [come] on Friday, by all means.

5. Smith: Wouldn't you [like to] have tea at some quiet tearoom?
    Tanaka: Yes, let's do that. The one at that intersection would be nice,
        wouldn't it?

6. Smith: Can you drink this water?
    Tanaka: No, that's no good. Let's call the maid and get some drinking
        water.

7. Smith: You can put more into that box, can't you?
    Tanaka: No. (Because) it's full already.

8. Customer: Would you write a receipt for me?
    Salesgirl: I'll write it right away (so) just a moment please.

9. Smith: I couldn't hear so—I'm sorry but—could I have you say it once
        more?
    Tanaka: Isn't the next room noisy! Let's tell them to be quiet.

10. Smith: [Where is] Mr. Sato?
    Tanaka: He just went to buy some cigarettes. He'll be back in a minute.

EXERCISES

1. Make up conversations appropriate to the following situations. Keep your conversations lively — within the limits of the Japanese you have drilled on. Be careful to use appropriate politeness and formality levels.

   a. Mr. Smith from the American Embassy arrives at Mr. Tanaka's office to find that Mr. Tanaka has gone to the Embassy to see him.
   b. A lone American who speaks Japanese, but obviously cannot read it, is smoking in an area where several signs are posted which read "Danger! No Smoking!"
   c. A Russian who speaks only Russian arrives in Mr. Tanaka's office and is greeted by a Japanese-speaking receptionist and other office workers who discuss what is best to do.

2. (a) Ask if it is forbidden to:

   a. come in.
   b. smoke.
   c. look at that.
   d. eat this.
   e. drink this.
   f. go home early.
   g. come again tomorrow.
   h. open the window.
   i. turn on the radio.
   j. throw away these letters.
   k. use the telephone.
   l. show this to a friend.
   m. borrow this pencil.
   n. stay here.
   o. listen.
   p. wait here.
   q. rest for a while.
   r. put these things away.
   s. write on this paper.
   t. have (lit. receive) this.
   u. exchange this.
   v. deliver the desk tonight.
   w. park (lit. stop) the car here.
   x. remove the ashtrays.
   y. board the train now.

   (b) Give the iie answer for each of the questions in the preceding exercise.

Lesson 26. Weather

(a)

Tanaka

climate	kikoo
think	o⌐mo⌐u /-u/
what do you think?	do⌐o o⌐mo⌐u

1. What do you think of the climate here?　Koko no kikoo (wa) ⌐do⌐o omoimasu ka⌐

Smith

think that it's good	i⌐i to o⌐mo⌐u

2. I don't think it's very pleasant (but)...　A⌐ñmari i⌐i to wa o⌐moimase⌐ñ ḡa—

Tanaka

is muggy or sultry	mu⌐siatu⌐i /-ku/

3. The summers are awfully muggy, aren't they?　Na⌐tu⌐ (wa) ⌐zu⌐ibuñ mu⌐siatu⌐i ñ desyoo?

Smith

mildew	kabi
come out or spring up or grow	ha⌐e⌐ru /-ru/

4. Yes. [Things] get moldy (and)...　E⌐e. Ka⌐bi ḡa hae⌐ru si—

(b)

Smith

rainy season	tuyu

5. It will be the rainy season soon now, won't it?　Mo⌐o su⌐ḡu tu⌐yu ni narima⌐su ne?

Tanaka

middle	na⌐kaba⌐
begin [something]	hazimeru /-ru/
begin falling	hu⌐rihazime⌐ru /-ru/
think that it probably begins (or will begin) falling	hu⌐rihazime⌐ru daroo to o⌐mo⌐u

6. Yes. I think that it will probably begin raining (lit. falling) (from) about the middle of this month.　E⌐e. Koñḡetu no na⌐kaba-ḡo⌐ro kara hu⌐rihazime⌐ru daroo to omoimasu.

Smith

[something] continues   tuzuku /-u/
7. About how long does it last?   Do⌐no-g̃urai tuzukima⌐su ka⌐

Tanaka

year   to⌐si⌐
depend <u>or</u> rely   yoru /-u/
depending on the year   to⌐si⌐ ni yotte
   <u>or</u> according to the
   year
think that it was about   ha⌐tu-ka-g̃u⌐rai datta to
   20 days   o⌐mo⌐u
8. It's different depending on   To⌐si⌐ ni yotte ti⌐gaima⌐su g̃a,
   the year, but I think that it   kyo⌐nen wa ha⌐tu-ka-g̃u⌐rai datta
   was about 20 days last year.   to omoimasu.

Smith

unpleasant   i⌐ya⌐ /na/
9. Isn't it awful—the rainy   I⌐ya⌐ desu ⌐ne⌐e—tuyu wa.
   season.

(c)

Tanaka

begin to fall   hu⌐tte⌐ kuru
10. It's begun to rain.   A⌐me g̃a hu⌐tte⌐ kimasita yo⌐

. . .

cease   yamu /-u/
11. It has stopped already.   Mo⌐o ya⌐mima⌐sita.

   clear up   ha⌐re⌐ru /-ru/
   looking as if it is   ha⌐reso⌐o /na/
     about to clear up
   appear <u>or</u> seem   mi⌐e⌐ru /-ru/
     <u>or</u> look
   sun   hi
   emerge   de⌐te kuru
12. It looks as if it's going to   Ha⌐reso⌐o ni mi⌐ema⌐su yo⌐—hi
   clear—since the sun has   ⌐g̃a de⌐te ki⌐ma⌐sita kara.
   come out.

Smith

   think that it doesn't   hu⌐ra⌐nai to o⌐mo⌐u
     (<u>or</u> will not) fall
13. I don't think that it's going   Mo⌐o hu⌐ra⌐nai to o⌐moima⌐su
   to rain any more so let's   kara, de⌐kakemasyo⌐o.
   go out.

14. Won't you stop in at my   Tyo⌐tto u⌐ti ni yorimase⌐n ka⌐
   house for a minute?

Tanaka

let's go or I guess I'll go (informal)	ikoo
think I'll go	i⌈koo to omo⌉u
with much trouble or on purpose or with special kindness	se⌈kkaku⌉
it's kind of you to ask me but	se⌈kkaku⌉ desu ḡa

15. I'm thinking of going to the bank now (lit. from this point) so—it's kind of you to ask me but—I'm afraid not, today.

Kore kara gi⌈ñkoo e ikoo to omo⌉tte (i)masu kara; se⌈kkaku⌉ desu ḡa, kyo⌉o wa ⌐tyo⌉tto—

last week	señsyuu
be about to go or try to go	ikoo to suru
when I was about to go or when I tried to go	i⌈koo to sita to⌉ki [ni]
whatever happens or by all means	do⌈o site⌉ mo

16. Last week when I was about to go to the bank a friend came and I couldn't go, so today no matter what happens [I must go].

Señsyuu gi⌈ñkoo e ikoo to sita to⌉ki [ni] to̅modati ḡa kite, i⌈ka- rena⌉katta kara; kyo⌉o wa do⌈o site⌉ mo—

(d)

Mrs. Tanaka

blow	⌈hu⌉ku /-u/
cold-looking	sa⌈muso⌉o /na/

17. An awful wind is blowing and it looks cold, doesn't it.

Hi⌈do⌉i ka⌐ze ḡa hu⌐ite (i)te, sa- ⌈muso⌉o ⌈ne⌉e.

Mr. Tanaka

cloud up	ku⌈mo⌉ru /-u/
begin to cloud up	ku⌈mo⌉tte kuru

18. It's begun to cloud up, hasn't it.

Ku⌈mo⌉tte kita ⌐ne⌐e.

looking as if it is about to fall	hu⌈riso⌉o /na/

19. It looks as if it's going to snow.

Yu⌈ki⌉ ḡa hu⌐riso⌉o da yo⌐

Mrs. Tanaka

freeze	kooru /-u/
be frozen	kootte (i)ru
think that it probably is (or will be) dangerous	a⌈buna⌉i to o⌐mo⌐u

20. The roads are frozen so I   Mi⌈ti ḡa kootte (i)ru⌉ kara, a⌈bu-
    think it will probably be   na⌉i to o⌐mo⌐u ñ da kedo⌣
    dangerous . . .

Mr. Tanaka

21. Don't worry. I'll be careful   Da⌈izyo⌉obu da⌈izyo⌉obu. Ki⌈otu-
    (lit. because I'll go care-   ke⌉te (i)⌐ku⌉ kara.
    fully).

22. Well, goodbye.   Zya⌉a, i⌈tte kima⌉su.

Mrs. Tanaka

23. Goodbye.   I⌈tte (i)rassya⌉i.

(e)

Mrs. Tanaka

24. Good morning.   O⌈hayoo gozaima⌉su.

Mrs. Yamamoto

25. Good morning.   O⌈hayoo gozaima⌉su.

    is cold   o⌈samuu gozaima⌉su +
26. It's awfully cold. Is every-   Zu⌉ibuñ o⌐samuu gozaima⌉su ḡa,
    one [in your family] well?   mi⌈na⌉sama o⌈ge⌉ñki de (i)rassyai-
                                   masu ka⌣

Mrs. Tanaka

27. Yes, thank you.   A⌈ri⌉ḡatoo gozaimasu. Okaḡesa-
                                   ma de.

    a cold   kaze
    become fashionable or   ha⌊ya⌉ru /-u/
      popular or prevalent
    be fashionable or   ha⌊ya⌉tte (i)ru
      popular or prevalent
    baby   a⌉katyañ
28. There are a lot of colds going Kotosi wa ka⌈ze ḡa haya⌉tte ori-
    around this year. [Is] your   masu ḡa, o⌈taku no a⌉katyañ wa?
    baby [all right]?

Mrs. Yamamoto

    is big   o⌉okyuu gozaimasu +
    is weak or frail or   yo⌈wa⌉i /-ku/
      delicate or poor in
      health
    worry   siñpai-suru
29. He (lit. our child) is big,   Uti no ko wa ⌈o⌉okyuu gozaimasu
    but he's delicate so I am   ḡa; yo⌈wa⌉i kara, i⌉tu mo siñpai-
    always worrying . . .   site⌣

Mrs. Tanaka

    sturdy-looking or   zyoobusoo /na/ or
    healthy-looking   ozyoobusoo + /na/

30. He looks sturdy but . . .   O˹zyoobusoo de (i)rassyaima˺su
                                              keredo—

                    Mrs. Yamamoto

     shopping   kaimono or okaimono +
31. Are you going shopping now?   Kore kara o˹kaimono ni irassyai-
                                              ma˺su ka⌟

                    Mrs. Tanaka

     take the trouble to come   se˹kkaku ku˺ru
     finish [something]   su˻mase˺ru /-ru/
     want to finish   su˻maseto˺o gozaimasu +
32. Yes. Since I took the trouble   Ha˺a. Sekkaku Gi˹nza ma˺de ma-
     to come all the way to the   ˥irima˺sita kara, ka˹imono (o)
     Ginza, I'd like to finish my   sumaseto˺o gozaimasu.
     shopping.

                    ADDITIONAL VOCABULARY

1. Wasn't the <u>heavy rain</u> yes-   Ki˹noo no <u>ooa˺me</u> (wa) ta˹iheñ
    terday terrible!   de˺sita ˻ne˺e.

        sudden shower   ni˹wakaa˺me
        sudden (evening) shower   yuudati
        strong wind   o˹oka˺ze [1]
        storm   a˺rasi
        gale   bo˹ohu˺u
        typhoon   ta˹ihu˺u
        heavy snow   ooyuki
        snow storm   hu˺buki
        hail   arare or hyo˺o
        thunder   ka˹minari˺
        lightning   i˹nabi˺kari

2. Look at the <u>sky</u>.   So˺ra o ˥mi˥te kudasai.

        cloud   ku˺mo
        moon (<u>or</u> month)   tu˹ki˺
        star   hosi
        rainbow   ni˹zi˺

3. It's thundering, isn't it.   Ka˹minari˺ ḡa na˥tte [2] (i)ma˺su
                                              ˻ne˺e.

4. There's lightning, isn't there.   I˹nabi˺kari ḡa si˥te (i)ma˺su
                                              ˻ne˺e.

---

[1] Alternate accents: o˹okaze˺, ookaze.

[2] <u>Naru</u> /-u/ 'sound,' 'ring,' 'roar,' 'rumble.'

NOTES ON THE BASIC DIALOGUES

2. 'but—that is just my opinion.'

4. 'and—various other things happen that prove it's muggy.'
   Note also: ha⌐ ḡa ha⌐e⌐ru 'cut a tooth.'

5. The rainy season in Japan begins about the middle of June and usually lasts for three or four weeks.

6. Na⌐kaba⌐ is regularly used in reference to the middle of a period of time. The intransitive partner of transitive hazimeru is hazimaru /-u/ '[something] begins.' Both these verbals may be preceded by a time expression + kara ('begin at [lit. from] a given time') or, less commonly, a time expression + ni ('begin at a given time').

7. The transitive partner of intransitive tuzuku is tuzukeru /-ru/ 'continue [something]' (Lesson 24).

11. Yamu '[it] ceases' is the intransitive partner of transitive yameru /-ru/ 'stop doing [something]' (Lesson 14).

15. With kore kara 'from this point,' 'after this,' compare sore kara 'from that point,' 'after that.'
    Se⌐kkaku⌐ desu ḡa_ occurs as an apologetic refusal of an invitation or offer: 'you took the trouble to ask me but . . .' or 'you showed special kindness in asking me but . . .'
    Se⌐kkaku⌐ also occurs (cf. Sentence 32, following) as an expression of manner, without following particle: se⌐kkaku ku⌐ru 'come on purpose,' 'take the trouble to come,' 'come specially.' In such occurrences, it regularly loses its accent.

28. The more formal alternant of a⌐katyañ is akañboo.
    Note also kaze o hiku /-u/ 'catch a cold.'

31. Ni here is the ni of purpose: 'go for shopping.'

32. Su⌐mase⌐ru is a transitive verbal derived from the intransitive verbal su⌐mu /-u/ 'come to an end.'

GRAMMATICAL NOTES

1. Verbals: Informal Tentative

The formal tentative of verbals ends in -masyo⌐o and means 'let's do so-and-so' or 'I guess I'll do so-and-so.' To make the informal equivalent:

> -ru Verbals: Drop final -ru of the citation form and add -yoo.
> -u Verbals: Drop final -u of the citation form and add -oo.
> Irregular Verbals: ku⌐ru — ko⌐yo⌐o
>   suru — siyoo

If the citation form of a verbal is accented, the informal tentative is accented, on the next-to-last syllable. The informal tentative of an unaccented verbal occurs with unaccented and accented alternants.

Examples:

INFORMAL NON-PAST	TENTATIVE	
(= Citation form)	Informal	Formal
akeru 'open'	akeyoo [1]	a⌐kemasyo¬o
ta⌐be¬ru 'eat'	ta⌐beyo¬o	ta⌐bemasyo¬o
iru 'be in a place'	iyoo [1]	i⌐masyo¬o
mi¬ru 'see'	mi⌐yo¬o	mi⌐masyo¬o
ma¬tu 'wait'	ma⌐to¬o	ma⌐timasyo¬o
ka⌐e¬ru 'return'	ka⌐ero¬o	ka⌐erimasyo¬o
kau 'buy'	kaoo [1]	ka⌐imasyo¬o
ha¬na¬su 'talk'	ha¬naso¬o	ha¬nasimasyo¬o
kiku 'ask,' 'listen'	kikoo [1]	ki⌐kimasyo¬o
i⌐so¬g̱u 'be in a hurry'	i⌐sog̱o¬o	i⌐sog̱imasyo¬o
yobu 'call'	yoboo [1]	yo⌐bimasyo¬o
yo¬mu 'read'	yo⌐mo¬o	yo⌐mimasyo¬o

In informal sentences, the informal tentative occurs in sentence-final position and pre-final before particles. In these positions, it occurs more
commonly in the speech of men than of women. In formal and informal sentences, in the speech of men and women, it occurs in quotations. Thus:

Ikoo. 'Let's go.' or 'I guess I'll go.'
Do¬o siyoo. 'What'll we do?' or 'What'll I do?'
Mo⌐o suko¬si no⌐mo¬o yo. 'Let's drink a little more!'
Ta⌐beyo¬o ne? 'Let's eat, shall we?'
I¬ma dekakeyoo to i⊦ima⁴sita. 'He suggested we leave now.' (Lit.'He
    said quote let's leave now.')
I⌐sog̱o¬o tte. 'He suggested we hurry.' (Lit. 'Quote let's hurry.')

For additional uses, see Notes 2 and 3 following.

2. ——— to √o⌐mo¬u

A sentence ending with an informal non-past or past or tentative followed
by the quotative to[2] + √o⌐mo¬u means 'think [that] ——— .'

Examples:

I⌐ku to omoima¬su. 'I think I (or someone) will go.'
Wa⌐ka¬tta to omoimasu. 'I think I (or someone) understood.'
To⌐ttemo i¬i to o⊦moima⁴sita. 'I thought it was very good.'
Mu⌐zukasi¬katta to omoimasu. 'I think it was difficult.'
Ta¬naka-sañ wa byooki da to omoima¬su. 'I think Mr. Tanaka is sick.'

---

[1] Has accented alternant, with accent on the next-to-last syllable.

[2] Before √o⌐mo¬u, the quotative to is not interchangeable with [t] te.
For some speakers, accentuation before to˘ is the same as before kara, no,
etc., with all verbal tentative forms accented on the next-to-last syllable.

Bo⌐ku no datta to omoimasu. 'I think it was mine.'
Ko⌐nai daroo to o⌐moima⌐sita. 'I thought he probably wouldn't come.'
Ni⌐hoñzi⌐ñ daroo to omoimasu. 'I think he's probably a Japanese.'

In examples like the first two above, context usually determines whether
the subject of the quotation and the subject of √o⌐mo⌐u are the same or different; but there is often a contrast in meaning between (a) verbal non-past or
past + <u>daroo to √o⌐mo⌐u</u> 'think that someone (else) probably does <u>or</u> will do
<u>or</u> did so-and-so' (subject of the first inflected expression different from the
subject of √o⌐mo⌐u), and (b) verbal tentative + <u>to √o⌐mo⌐u</u> 'think of doing so-
and-so,' 'plan to do so-and-so' (subject of tentative and <u>o⌐mo⌐u</u> the same):

(a) Ka⌐u daro⌐o to omoimasu. 'I think he'll probably buy [it].'
(b) Ka⌐oo to omoima⌐su. 'I think I'll probably buy [it].' or 'I plan to
    buy [it].'
    Ka⌐oo to omo⌐tte imasu. 'I'm thinking of buying [it].'

The examples under (b) are similar to, but less definite than, <u>Ka⌐u tumori</u>
<u>de⌐su</u>. 'I intend to buy [it].'

When a tentative question precedes <u>to √o⌐mo⌐u</u>, the most common English
equivalent is 'I wonder if —— .' Thus:

Ta⌐bako o yameyo⌐o [1] ka to o⌐mo⌐tte imasu. 'I'm wondering if I should
    give up smoking.' (Lit. 'I'm thinking, "Shall I give up tobacco?"')
Mo⌐o ka⌐ero⌐o ka to o⌐mo⌐tte imasu. 'I'm wondering if I should go
    home (already) now.'

Note the following two types of negatives:

Byo⌐oki ni nara⌐nai to omoimasu. 'I don't think he'll get sick'—i.e.
    my thought is that he will not get sick.
Byo⌐oki ni na⌐ru to wa o⌐moimase⌐ñ. 'I don't think he'll get sick'—
    i.e. that he will get sick is not what I think.

3. Verbal Tentative + <u>to</u> + √suru

An informal tentative verbal + <u>to</u> + √suru means 'be about to —— ,' 'make
as if to —— ,' 'try (unsuccessfully) to —— .' It often occurs in the middle
of a sentence, followed by a statement of what prevented the completion of the
action.

Examples:

De⌐yo⌐o to si⌐ta to⌐ki [ni], a⌐me ḡa hu⌐rihazimema⌐sita.
    'Just as I was about to go out, it began to rain.'
Si⌐ñbuñ o kaoo to sita to⌐ki [ni], to⌐modati ni a⌐tte ka⌐imase⌐ñ desita.
    'Just as I was about to buy a paper, I met a friend and I didn't buy
    it.'

─────────────

[1] Before some particles—for example, <u>ka</u>—a normally unaccented informal
tentative regularly acquires an accent on its pre-final syllable.

A⌐ma˥do o a⌐keyoo to sima˥sita ḡa, ze⌐ñzeñ akeraremase˥ñ desita.
'I tried to open the shutters but I couldn't open them at all.'
Ha⌐iro˥o to si⌐ma˥sita ḡa, ka⌐ḡi˥ ḡa ka⌐ka˥tte ita kara—
'I tried to go in but it was locked so . . .'
Wa⌐takusi ḡa kaoo to sita zido˥osya wa, go⌐zyuu hati˥-neñ no ⌐Si⌐bo-
ree desu.
'The car I tried to buy is a '58 Chevrolet.'

With this pattern, compare gerund + √mi˥ru (Lesson 19, Grammatical Note 3):

Ha˥itte mi⌐ma˥sita.
'I tried going in'—i.e. I did actually go in.
Ha⌐iro˥o to si⌐ma˥sita ḡa—
'I tried to go in but [I couldn't].'

4. Polite Adjectivals

To make a formal polite adjectival:

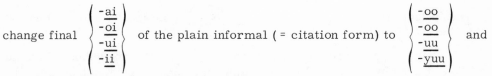

change final $\left\{\begin{matrix}-\underline{ai}\\ -\underline{oi}\\ -\underline{ui}\\ -\underline{ii}\end{matrix}\right\}$ of the plain informal (= citation form) to $\left\{\begin{matrix}-\underline{oo}\\ -\underline{oo}\\ -\underline{uu}\\ -\underline{yuu}\end{matrix}\right\}$ and

add <u>gozaimasu</u> (or <u>gozaimasita</u> or <u>gozaimasyoo</u>). Some adjectivals also add
the polite prefix <u>o-</u> in the polite form. In most cases, an adjectival which
has an accent in the plain informal is also accented in the polite, one syllable
nearer the beginning of the word.

Examples:

Informal Plain	Formal Plain	Formal Polite
itadakitai	i⌐tadakita˥i desu	i⌐tadakitoo gozaima˥su 'I'd like to receive'
hi⌐ro˥i	hi⌐ro˥i desu	hi˥roo gozaimasu 'it's wide'
ya⌐su˥i	ya⌐su˥i desu	ya˥suu gozaimasu 'it's cheap'
yorosii	yo⌐rosi˥i desu	yo⌐rosyuu gozaima˥su 'it's all right'

Some polite adjectivals occur very commonly: <u>o⌐hayoo gozaima˥su</u> (from
<u>ha⌐ya˥i</u> 'is early'), <u>o⌐medetoo gozaima˥su</u> (from <u>me⌐deta˥i</u> 'is auspicious'),
<u>a⌐ri˥ḡatoo gozaimasu</u> (from <u>a⌐riḡata˥i</u> 'is grateful'), <u>o⌐atuu gozaima˥su</u> (from
<u>a⌐tu˥i</u> 'is hot'), <u>o⌐samuu gozaima˥su</u> (from <u>sa⌐mu˥i</u> 'is cold'). Many adjec-
tivals have a polite equivalent which occurs only rarely in actual conversation.

The formal polite negative of adjectivals is the formal plain negative,
with <u>a⌐rimase˥ñ</u> replaced by <u>go⌐zaimase˥ñ</u>. Thus:

Informal Plain	Formal Plain	Formal Polite
a˥tuku ˥na˩i	⌐a˥tuku a⌐rimase˥ñ	a˥tuku go⌐zaimase˥ñ 'it isn't hot'

Except for those which are used as special greetings, polite adjectivals are used much more commonly by women than by men.

5. Nominals Ending in -soo

A nominal consisting of a verbal stem (the -ma⌝su form minus -ma⌝su) or an adjectival stem (the non-past minus -i) or a nominal (usually a na word) + -soo means '—— looking,' 'looking as if [it] would or will be ——.' The compound is accented on its pre-final syllable.[1] Thus:

> de⌜kiso⌝o 'looking [as if it would be] possible'
>   (from de⌜ki⌝ru 'be possible')
> a⌜tuso⌝o 'hot-looking,' 'looking as if it would be hot'
>   (from a⌜tu⌝i 'is hot')
> i⌜kitaso⌝o 'looking as if he would want to go'
>   (from ikitai 'want to go')
> zyoobusoo 'strong-looking,' 'looking as if it would be strong'
>   (from zyoobu 'strong')

Two irregular formations must be noted: (1) the -soo word derived from i⌝i/yo⌝i 'is good' is yo⌜saso⌝o 'looking [as if it would be] good'; (2) -soo words derived from informal negatives ending in -nai end in -nasasoo (and the -soo word derived from na⌝i 'there isn't any' is na⌜saso⌝o 'looking as if there wouldn't be any').

-Soo words are na words: they occur followed by √da (including na before a following nominal) or the particle ni of manner. Thus:

> O⌜isiso⌝o desu. 'It's delicious-looking.' 'It looks [as if it would be] delicious.'
> O⌜isiso⌝o na o⌐ka⌐si desu. 'It's delicious-looking cake.'
> O⌜isiso⌝o ni miemasu. 'It looks as if it would be delicious.' (Lit. 'It appears in a delicious-looking manner.')

Note the following negative constructions, which differ grammatically but can be used almost interchangeably:

> De⌜kinasaso⌝o desu. 'It looks [as if it will be] impossible.'
> De⌜kiso⌝o zya a⌐rimase⌐ñ. 'It doesn't look [as if it will be] possible.'
> De⌜kiso⌝o ni wa mi⌐emase⌐ñ. 'It doesn't look as if it will be possible.'
>   (Lit. 'It doesn't appear in a possible-looking manner.')

-Soo words imply evidence based on the senses — particularly sight — and usually indicate an action or state that has not yet occurred or been realized, in reference to the given context. Patterns with yo⌝o 'manner,' on the other hand, include various kinds of evidence (including sight) and usually refer to an already occurring action or already existing state. Compare:

> De⌜kiso⌝o desu ⌜ne⌝e. 'He looks as if he will be able to do it, doesn't he!' (said, perhaps, because he looks bright, capable, strong, etc.)

---

[1] However, the -soo derivative of an unaccented verbal or adjectival or nominal sometimes occurs without an accent.

De⌐ki⌐ru yoo desu ⌐ne⌐e. 'He seems to be able to do it, doesn't he!' (based on some kind of evidence I have—perhaps the results of his first attempt)

A⌐tuso⌐o desu ⌐ne⌐e. It looks /as if it would be/ hot!' (for example, said of a winter coat on a hot summer's day)

A⌐tu⌐i yoo desu ⌐ne⌐e. 'It seems to be hot, doesn't it.' (for example, said of something that is steaming)

Ya⌐metaso⌐o desu ⌐ne⌐e. 'He looks as if he is going to want to quit, doesn't he!' (said, perhaps, on the basis of the expression of his face)

Ya⌐metai yo⌐o desu ⌐ne⌐e. 'He seems to want to quit, doesn't he!' (said, perhaps, because of rumors I have heard)

WARNING: Do not confuse compounds in -soo with informal sentences followed by so⌐o da (Lesson 22, Grammatical Note 2). Thus:

Sa⌐muso⌐o desu. 'It looks /as if it would be/ cold.'
but:
Sa⌐mu⌐i soo desu. 'They say it's cold.'

Ge⌐ñkiso⌐o desu. 'He's healthy-looking.'
but:
Ge⌐ñki da soo desu. 'They say he's well.'

6. Intransitive Verbals + √ku⌐ru

The gerund of an intransitive verbal (i.e. one that never takes a direct object) + √ku⌐ru 'come' indicates the gradual coming into being of an action or state. (Compare English 'I've come to like it here'; 'You'll come to regret it'; etc.)

Examples:

tu⌐ka⌐rete kuru 'grow tired,' 'begin to tire'
wa⌐ka⌐tte kuru 'come to understand,' 'reach understanding'
ko⌐otte ku⌐ru 'begin to freeze'

In this pattern, √ku⌐ru must follow the gerund immediately. Compare:

Koko e i⌐so⌐ide ki⌐ma⌐sita. 'I came here in a hurry,' which has an alternant (differing only in emphasis):
I⌐so⌐ide ko⌐ko e kima⌐sita. Here the gerund is the gerund of manner (Lesson 20, Grammatical Note 1).

7. Compound Verbals Ending in √-hazimeru

A compound verbal consisting of a transitive or intransitive verbal stem (the -ma⌐su form minus -ma⌐su) + √-hazimeru 'begin' means 'begin doing so-and-so.' The compound is accented on the next-to-last syllable. Examples: ternate accent/ is unaccented). Examples:

ta⌐be⌐ru 'eat'	ta⌐behazime⌐ru 'begin eating'
a⌐ru⌐ku 'walk'	a⌐rukihazime⌐ru 'begin walking'
yo⌐mu 'read'	yo⌐mihazime⌐ru 'begin reading'
suru 'do'	si⌐hazime⌐ru 'begin doing'

The combination of a verbal gerund + √ku⌐ru, described in the previous note, indicates a more gradual beginning than a √-hazimeru compound.

DRILLS

A. Substitution Drill

1. It's different depending on the year.   To⌐si⌐ ni yotte tiḡaimasu.

2. It's different depending on the month.   Tu⌐ki⌐ ni yotte tiḡaimasu.

3. It's different depending on the day.   Hi ⌐ni yotte tiḡaima⌐su.

4. It's different depending on the time.   Zi⌐kañ ni yotte tiḡaima⌐su.

5. It's different depending on the place.   To⌐koro ni yotte tiḡaima⌐su.

6. It's different depending on the person.   Hi⌐to ni yotte tiḡaima⌐su.

7. It's different depending on the thing.   Mo⌐no⌐ ni yotte tiḡaimasu.

8. It's different depending on the store.   Mi⌐se⌐ ni yotte tiḡaimasu.

9. It's different depending on the weather.   Te⌐ñki ni yotte tiḡaimasu.

B. Grammar Drill (based on Grammatical Note 7)

Tutor: Mo⌐o si⌐ḡoto o sima⌐sita. 'I've done the work already.'
Student: Mo⌐o si⌐ḡoto o sihazimema⌐sita. 'I've begun to do the work already.'

1. A⌐me ḡa hu⌐rima⌐sita.   A⌐me ḡa hu⌐rihazimema⌐sita.

2. A⌐katyañ (wa) ⌐mo⌐o ⌐go⌐hañ o ta⌐bema⌐sita.   A⌐katyañ (wa) ⌐mo⌐o ⌐go⌐hañ o ta-⌐behazimema⌐sita.

3. Ho⌐ñ (o) ⌐ka⌐ita desyoo ka.   Ho⌐ñ (o) ka⌐kihazimeta⌐ desyoo ka.

4. A⌐tarasi⌐i ka⌐mi⌐ (o) tu⌐kaimasyo⌐o ka.   A⌐tarasi⌐i ka⌐mi⌐ o tu⌐kaihazi-memasyo⌐o ka.

5. Mo⌐o Ta⌐naka-sañ ḡa ka⌐-ita ⌐ho⌐ñ (o) yo⌐mima⌐-sita.   Mo⌐o Ta⌐naka-sañ ḡa ka⌐ita ⌐ho⌐ñ (o) yo⌐mihazimema⌐sita.

6. Mo⌐o si⌐taku (o) sima⌐-sita.   Mo⌐o si⌐taku (o) sihazimema⌐sita.

C. Grammar Drill (based on Grammatical Note 5)

Tutor: Sa⌐mu⌐i desu ⌐ne⌐e. 'Isn't it cold!'
Student: Sa⌐muso⌐o desu ⌐ne⌐e. 'Doesn't it look cold!'

1. Wa⌐karima⌐su ⌐ne⌐e—ano   Wa⌐kariso⌐o desu ⌐ne⌐e—ano kodo-
   kodomo wa.   mo wa.
2. So⌐re wa dekima⌐su ḡa—   So⌐re wa dekiso⌐o desu ḡa—
3. So⌐re wa dekimase⌐n ḡa—   So⌐re wa dekinasaso⌐o desu ḡa—
4. A⌐no mise no oka⌐si (wa)   A⌐no mise no oka⌐si (wa) o⌐isiso⌐o
   o⌐isi⌐i desu ⌐ne⌐e.   desu ⌐ne⌐e.
5. O⌐taku no bo⌐ttyan (wa)   O⌐taku no bo⌐ttyan (wa) ge⌐nkiso⌐o
   ⌐ge⌐nki desu ⌐ne⌐e.   desu ⌐ne⌐e.
6. Ke⌐sa ka⌐tta ho⌐n (wa)   Ke⌐sa ka⌐tta ho⌐n (wa) o⌐mosiro-
   o⌐mosiro⌐i desu ⌐ne⌐e.   so⌐o desu ⌐ne⌐e.
7. Te⌐gami (wa) arimase⌐n   Te⌐gami (wa) nasaso⌐o desu ḡa—
   ḡa—
8. Ko⌐nna ki⌐zi (wa) zyo-   Ko⌐nna ki⌐zi wa zyo⌐obusoo de⌐su
   ⌐obu de⌐su ⌐ne⌐e.   ⌐ne⌐e.

D. Level Drill [1] (based on Grammatical Note 4)

1. Uti no ko (wa) o⌐oki⌐i   Uti no ko (wa) ⌐o⌐okyuu gozai-
   desu ḡa—   masu ḡa—
2. Kyo⌐o wa ⌐a⌐tuku a⌐rima-   Kyo⌐o wa ⌐a⌐tuku go⌐zaimase⌐n
   se⌐n ⌐ne⌐e.   ⌐ne⌐e.
3. Kono sakana (wa) o⌐isi⌐i   Kono osakana (wa) o⌐isyuu gozai-
   desyoo?   masyoo?
4. Otaku no niwa (wa) hi⌐ro⌐i   Otaku no oniwa (wa) ⌐hi⌐roo go-
   desu ⌐ne⌐e.   zaimasu ⌐ne⌐e.
5. A⌐nna mono⌐ (wa) ta⌐ka⌐i   A⌐nna mono⌐ (wa) ⌐ta⌐koo gozai-
   desu ⌐ne⌐e.   masu ⌐ne⌐e.
6. Yo⌐rosi⌐i desyoo?   Yorosyuu gozaimasyoo?
7. Tu⌐ka⌐rete (i)masu kara,   Tu⌐ka⌐rete orimasu kara, su⌐ko⌐si
   su⌐ko⌐si ya⌐sumita⌐i desu.   ya⌐sumito⌐o gozaimasu.
8. So⌐no ho⌐n (wa) a⌐nmari   So⌐no ho⌐n (wa) a⌐nmari omosi⌐-
   omosi⌐roku a⌐rimase⌐n.   roku go⌐zaimase⌐n.

E. Substitution Drill

1. Since I took the trouble   Se⌐kkaku kita⌐ kara, su⌐maseta⌐i
   to come, I'd like to   n desu ḡa—
   finish [it].
2. Since I took the trouble   Se⌐kkaku tuku⌐tta kara, tu⌐kaita⌐i
   to make [it], I'd like to   n desu ḡa—
   use [it]. /tu⌐ku⌐ru,
   tukau/
3. Since I took the trouble   Se⌐kkaku katta⌐ kara, yo⌐mita⌐i
   to buy [it], I'd like to   n desu ḡa—
   read [it]. /kau, yo⌐mu/

---

[1] Each sentence on the right is the polite equivalent of the corresponding
sentence on the left.

4. Since I took the trouble
   to write [it], I'd like to
   show [it to him]. /ka⌐ku,
   mi⌐se⌐ru/

   Se⌐kkaku ka⌐ita kara, mi⌐seta⌐i ñ
   desu ḡa—

5. Since I took the trouble
   to fix [it], I'd like to sell
   [it]. /na⌐o⌐su, uru/

   Se⌐kkaku nao⌐sita kara, u⌐rita⌐i ñ
   desu ḡa—

6. Since I took the trouble
   to get [it] out, I'd like
   to take [it]. /da⌐su,
   motte iku/

   Se⌐kkaku da⌐sita kara, mo⌐tte iki-
   ta⌐i ñ desu ḡa—

7. Since I took the trouble
   to come, I'd like to see
   [it]. /ku⌐ru, mi⌐ru/

   Se⌐kkaku kita⌐ kara, mi⌐ta⌐i ñ
   desu ḡa—

F. Level Drill [1] (based on Grammatical Note 1)

1. Zya⌐a, i⌐kimasyo⌐o.
2. To⌐nari no heya⌐ de sa-
   ⌐ḡasite mimasyo⌐o.
3. Asita ⌐ha⌐yaku o⌐kima-
   syo⌐o.
4. Mu⌐koo no seki⌐ ni ka-
   ⌐kemasyo⌐o.
5. O⌐soku na⌐tta kara, ka-
   ⌐erimasyo⌐o.
6. Se⌐ñse⌐e kara mo⌐ratta
   zibiki⌐ (o) tu⌐kaimasyo⌐o.
7. Bi⌐iru (o) ⌐i⌐p-pai no-
   ⌐mimasyo⌐o.
8. Iya⌐ da kara, ya⌐mema-
   syo⌐o.
9. Ko⌐ñbañ yo⌐ohuku (o)
   kimasyo⌐o.
10. A⌐sita no a⌐sa ⌐ta⌐kusii
    de ki⌐masyo⌐o.

Zya⌐a, i⌐ko⌐o.
To⌐nari no heya⌐ de sa⌐ḡasite
   miyo⌐o.
Asita ⌐ha⌐yaku o⌐kiyo⌐o.

Mu⌐koo no seki⌐ ni ka⌐keyo⌐o.

O⌐soku na⌐tta kara, ka⌐ero⌐o.

Se⌐ñse⌐e kara mo⌐ratta zibiki⌐
   (o) tu⌐kao⌐o.
Bi⌐iru (o) ⌐i⌐p-pai no⌐mo⌐o.

Iya⌐ da kara, ya⌐meyo⌐o.

Ko⌐ñbañ yo⌐ohuku (o) kiyo⌐o.

A⌐sita no a⌐sa ⌐ta⌐kusii de ko-
   ⌐yo⌐o.

G. Substitution Drill (based on Grammatical Note 3)

1. I tried to go but I
   couldn't (go).

   I⌐koo to sima⌐sita ḡà, i⌐karema-
   se⌐ñ desita.

2. I tried to open [it] but I
   couldn't (open). /akeru/

   A⌐keyoo to sima⌐sita ḡa, a⌐kera-
   remase⌐ñ desita.

3. I tried to close [it] but I
   couldn't (close).
   /si⌐me⌐ru/

   Si⌐meyo⌐o to si⌐ma⌐sita ḡa, si⌐me-
   raremase⌐ñ desita.

4. I tried to continue [it]
   but I couldn't (continue).
   /tuzukeru/

   Tu⌐zukeyoo to sima⌐sita ḡa, tu⌐zu-
   keraremase⌐ñ desita.

---

[1] Each sentence on the right is the informal equivalent of the corresponding
sentence on the left.

5. I tried to get up but I
   couldn't (get up).
   /oˈkiˈru/

   Oˈkiyoˈo to siˈmaˈsita ḡa, oˈkira-
   remaseˈñ desita.

6. I tried to read [it] but
   I couldn't (read).
   /yoˈmu/

   Yoˈmoˈo to siˈmaˈsita ḡa, yoˈme-
   maseˈñ desita.

7. I tried to cut [it] but I
   couldn't (cut). /kiˈru/

   Kiˈroˈo to siˈmaˈsita ḡa, kiˈrema-
   seˈñ desita.

8. I tried to put [it] on but
   I couldn't (put on).
   /kiru/

   Kiˈyoo to simaˈsita ḡa, kiˈrarema-
   seˈñ desita.

9. I tried to come but I
   couldn't (come). /kuˈru/

   Koˈyoˈo to siˈmaˈsita ḡa, koˈrare-
   maseˈñ desita.

10. I tried to fix [it] but
    I couldn't (fix).
    /naˈoˈsu/

    Naˈosoˈo to siˈmaˈsita ḡa, naˈose-
    maseˈñ desita.

H. Substitution Drill (based on Grammatical Note 3)

1. Just as I was about to
   go, a friend came and
   I couldn't (go).

   Iˈkoo to sita toˈki /ni/ tŏmodati
   ḡa kite, iˈkarenaˈkatta ñ desu
   yo.

2. Just as I was about to
   go out, a friend came
   and I couldn't (go out).
   /deˈru/

   Deˈyoˈo to siˈta toˈki /ni/ tŏmodati ḡa kite, deˈrareˈnakatta ñ
   desu yo.

3. Just as I was about to
   go in, a friend came and
   I couldn't (go in).
   /haˈiru/

   Haˈiroˈo to siˈta toˈki /ni/ tŏ--
   modati ḡa kite, haˈireˈnakatta
   ñ desu yo.

4. Just as I was about to
   begin [it], a friend came
   and I couldn't (begin).
   /hazimeru/

   Haˈzimeyoo to sita toˈki /ni/ tŏmodati ḡa kite, haˈzimerarenaˈ-
   katta ñ desu yo.

5. Just as I was about to
   telephone, a friend
   came and I couldn't
   (telephone). /deˈñwa
   (o) kakeˈru/

   Deˈñwa (o) kakeyoˈo to siˈta toˈ-
   ki /ni/ tŏmodati ḡa kite, kaˈke-
   rareˈnakatta ñ desu yo.

6. Just as I was about to
   write [it], a friend came
   and I couldn't (write).
   /kaˈku/

   Kaˈkoˈo to siˈta toˈki /ni/ tŏmodati ḡa kite, kaˈkeˈnakatta ñ
   desu yo.

7. Just as I was about to
   look at [it], a friend
   came and I couldn't
   (look). /miˈru/

   Miˈyoˈo to siˈta toˈki /ni/ tŏmodati ḡa kite, miˈrareˈnakatta ñ
   desu yo.

8. Just as I was about to
   eat [it], a friend came
   and I couldn't (eat).
   /taˈbeˈru/

   Taˈbeyoˈo to siˈta toˈki /ni/ tŏmodati ḡa kite, taˈberareˈnaka-
   tta ñ desu yo.

9. Just as I was about to   Ya⌐sumo⌉o to si⊦ta to⊣ki /ni/ tō-
    rest, a friend came and   modati ḡa kite, ya⌐sume⌉nakatta
    I couldn't (rest).   ñ desu yo.
    /ya⌐su⌉mu/

10. Just as I was about to   Tu⌐kuro⌉o to si⊦ta to⊣ki /ni/ tō-
    make [it], a friend   modati ḡa kite, tu⌐kure⌉nakatta
    came and I couldn't   ñ desu yo.
    (make). /tu⌐ku⌉ru/

I. Substitution Drill (based on Grammatical Note 2)

1. I'm thinking of going to-   Ko⌉ñbañ i⌐koo to omo⌉tte (i)masu
    night . . .   ḡa—

2. I'm thinking of going out   Ko⌉ñbañ de⌐kakeyoo to omo⌉tte
    tonight . . . /dekakeru/   (i)masu ḡa—

3. I'm thinking of studying   Ko⌉ñbañ be⌐ñkyoo-siyoo to omo⌉tte
    tonight . . .   (i)masu ḡa—
    /beñkyoo-suru/

4. I'm thinking of stopping   Ko⌉ñbañ yo⌐roo to omo⌉tte (i)masu
    in tonight . . . /yoru/   ḡa—

5. I'm thinking of wearing   Ko⌉ñbañ yo⌐ohuku (o) kiyoo to
    Western-style clothing   omo⌉tte (i)masu ḡa—
    tonight . . . /yoohuku
    (o) kiru/

6. I'm thinking of going to   Ko⌉ñbañ ⌐ha⌉yaku ne⊦yoo to omo⊣tte
    bed early tonight . . .   (i)masu ḡa—
    /ha⌉yaku neru/

7. I'm thinking of listening   Ko⌉ñbañ ⌐ra⌉zio (o) ki⊦koo to omo⊣-
    to the radio tonight . . .   tte (i)masu ḡa—
    /ra⌉zio (o) kiku/

8. I'm thinking of watching   Ko⌉ñbañ ⌐te⌉rebi (o) mi⊦yo⊣o to
    television tonight . . .   o⊦mo⊣tte (i)masu ḡa—
    /te⌉rebi (o) ⊦mi⊣ru/

9. I'm thinking of writing   Ko⌉ñbañ te⌐ḡami (o) kako⌉o to o⊦mo⊣-
    letters tonight . . .   tte (i)masu ḡa—
    /te⌐ḡami (o) ka⌉ku/

10. I'm thinking of going   Ko⌉ñbañ ⌐ha⌉yaku ka⊦ero⌉o to o⊦mo⊣-
    home early tonight . . .   tte (i)masu ḡa—
    /ha⌉yaku ⊦ka⊣eru/

J. Grammar Drill (based on Grammatical Note 2)

    Tutor: I⌐koo to omoima⌉su. 'I think I'll probably go.'
    Student: I⌐ku daro⌉o to omoimasu. 'I think he'll probably go.'

1. I⌉ma no siḡoto (o) ya-   I⌉ma no siḡoto (o) ya⌐meru daro⌉o
    ⌐meyoo to omoima⌉su.   to omoimasu.

2. Zi⌐mu⌉syo (o) ka⌐tazu-   Zi⌐mu⌉syo (o) ka⌐tazuke⌉ru daroo
    keyo⌉o to omoimasu.   to omoimasu.

3. Ko⌐domo ni yaroo to   Ko⌐domo ni yaru daro⌉o to omoi-
    omoima⌉su.   masu.

4. Se⌐ñse¬e ni a⌐geyoo to   Se⌐ñse¬e ni a⌐geru daro⌐o to
   omoima¬su.   omoimasu.

5. O⌐hu¬ro ni ha⌐iro⌐o to   O⌐hu¬ro ni ⌐ha⌐iru daroo to omo-
   omoimasu.   imasu.

6. Ge⌐ta (o) hakoo to omo-   Ge⌐ta (o) haku daro⌐o to omoi-
   ima¬su.   masu.

7. Bo⌐osi (o) kaburo⌐o to   Bo⌐osi (o) kabu⌐ru daroo to omo-
   omoimasu.   imasu.

8. Kodomo (o) o⌐ite ikoo [1]   Kodomo (o) o⌐ite iku daro⌐o to
   to omoima¬su.   omoimasu.

K. Grammar Drill (based on Grammatical Note 2)

          Tutor: Wa⌐karima¬sita. 'I've understood.'
          Student: Wa⌐ka¬tta to omoimasu. 'I think I've understood.'

1. A⌐me ga ya⌐mima¬sita.   A⌐me ga ya⌐ñda to omoima¬su.

2. Kotosi ka⌐ze ga haya⌐tte   Kotosi ka⌐ze ga haya⌐tte (i)ru to
   (i)masu.   omoimasu.

3. Ko⌐ñna ho⌐ñ (wa) tu⌐ma-   Ko⌐ñna ho⌐ñ (wa) tu⌐mara⌐nai
   ra⌐nai desu.   to omoimasu.

4. Koñgetu no na⌐kaba⌐   Koñgetu no na⌐kaba⌐ kara da
   kara desu.   to omoimasu.

5. Mo⌐o rok-ka⌐getu tuzu-   Mo⌐o rok-ka⌐getu tuzuku to omo-
   kimasu.   imasu.

6. So⌐no ka⌐igi (wa) o⌐to⌐-   So⌐no ka⌐igi (wa) o⌐to⌐tosi datta
   tosi desita.   to omoimasu.

7. Ta⌐naka-sañ no yo⌐o na   Ta⌐naka-sañ no yo⌐o na se⌐ñse⌐e
   se⌐ñse⌐e wa su⌐kuna⌐i   wa su⌐kuna⌐i to omoimasu.
   desu.

8. Kinoo no sigoto (wa)   Kinoo no sigoto (wa) mu⌐zukasi⌐-
   mu⌐zukasi⌐katta desu.   katta to omoimasu.

L. Response Drill (based on Grammatical Note 2)

          Tutor: A⌐tu⌐i desu ka⌐ 'Is it hot?'
          Student: (a) A⌐tu⌐i to wa o⌐moimase⌐ñ ga⌐ ⎱
                   (b) A⌐tuku ⌐na⌐i to omoimasu.   ⎰ 'I don't think it's hot.'

1. Asuko no kikoo (wa)   I⌐i to wa o⌐moimase⌐ñ ga⌐
   ⌐i⌐i desu ka⌐   Yo⌐ku ⌐na⌐i to omoimasu.

2. Tanaka-sañ no eego   U⌐ma⌐i to wa o⌐moimase⌐ñ ga⌐
   (wa) u⌐ma⌐i desu ka⌐   U⌐maku ⌐na⌐i to omoimasu.

3. Are wa ko⌐oba⌐ desu   Ko⌐oba⌐ da to wa o⌐moimase⌐ñ ga⌐
   ka⌐   Ko⌐oba⌐ zya ⌐na⌐i to omoimasu.

4. Ko⌐ñna ki⌐zi (wa) yo-   Yo⌐wa⌐i to wa o⌐moimase⌐ñ ga⌐
   ⌐wa⌐i desu ka⌐   Yo⌐waku ⌐na⌐i to omoimasu.

---

[1] Oite iku 'leave behind (i. e. go having left [something]).'

5. Ki⌈marima⌉sita ka⌟   Ki⌈matta⌉ to wa o⌈moimase⌉ñ ḡa_
                               Ki⌈marana⌉katta to omoimasu.

6. A⌈ñna mono⌉ (wa) zyo-   Zyo⌈obu da⌉ to wa o⌈moimase⌉ñ ḡa_
   ⌈obu de⌉su ka⌟   Zyo⌈obu zya na⌉i to omoimasu.

7. A⌈suko no natu⌉ (wa) mu-   Mu⌈siatu⌉i to wa o⌈moimase⌉ñ ḡa_
   ⌈siatu⌉i desu ka⌟   Mu⌈sia⌉tuku ⌐na⌐i to omoimasu.

8. Ko⌈no wañpi⌉isu (wa) ha-   Ha⌈desuḡi⌉ru to wa o⌈moimase⌉ñ
   ⌈desuḡima⌉su ka⌟   ḡa_
                               Ha⌈desuḡi⌉nai to omoimasu.

M. Expansion Drill

1. [It] continues.   Tu⌈zukima⌉su.
   [It] lasts about 20 days.   Ha⌈tu-ka-ḡu⌉rai tuzukimasu.
   [It] begins about the   Na⌈kaba-ḡo⌉ro kara hazimatte,
      middle and lasts about   ha⌈tu-ka-ḡu⌉rai tuzukimasu.
      20 days.
   [It] begins about the   Roku-ḡatu no na⌈kaba-ḡo⌉ro kara
      middle of June and   hazimatte, ha⌈tu-ka-ḡu⌉rai tuzu-
      lasts about 20 days.   kimasu.
   The rainy season be-   Tuyu wa rōku-ḡatu no na⌈kaba-
      gins about the middle   ḡo⌉ro kara hazimatte, ha⌈tu-ka-
      of June and lasts   ḡu⌉rai tuzukimasu.
      about 20 days.

2. I go shopping.   Ka⌈imono ni ikima⌉su.
   I go shopping about 9   Ku-⌈zi-ḡo⌉ro kaimono ni ikimasu.
      o'clock.
   I usually go shopping   Taitee ku-⌈zi-ḡo⌉ro kaimono ni
      about 9 o'clock.   ikimasu.
   It's different depending   Hi ⌐ni yotte tiḡaima⌉su ḡa, taitee
      on the day but I usually   ku-⌈zi-ḡo⌉ro kaimono ni ikimasu.
      go shopping about 9
      o'clock.

3. It looks as if there   Na⌈saso⌉o desu ⌐ne⌐e.
      weren't any.
   There's no reason to   Na⌐i hazu wa ⌐na⌐i kedo, na⌈sa-
      expect that there   so⌐o desu ⌐ne⌐e.
      isn't any, but it looks
      as if there weren't
      any.
   Since he said that a lot   Ta⌈kusañ noko⌉tte (i)ru tte i⌐tta⌐
      was left there should   kara, na⌐i hazu wa ⌐na⌐i kedo;
      be some, but it looks   na⌈saso⌉o desu ⌈ne⌐e.
      as if there weren't
      any.

4. I think it's good.   I⌐i to omoimasu.
   I think it would be   Si⌈ta ho⌐o ḡa ⌈i⌐i to omoimasu.
      better to do it.

I think it would be better
  to make it tomorrow.

Instead of going today,
  I think it would be
  better to make it to-
  morrow.

Since it's begun to cloud
  up, instead of going
  today I think it would
  be better to make it
  tomorrow.

A⌐sita¬ ni si⌐ta ho⌐o ḡa ⌐i¬i to
  omoimasu.

Kyo⌐o wa i⌐kana⌐i de, a⌐sita¬ ni
  si⌐ta ho⌐o ḡa ⌐i¬i to omoimasu.
  masu.

Ku⌐mo¬tte ⌐ki⌐ta kara; kyo⌐o wa
  i⌐kana⌐i de, a⌐sita¬ ni si⌐ta
  ho⌐o ḡa ⌐i¬i to omoimasu.

5. Is that all right?

  I'd like to talk. Is that
    all right?

  I'd like to talk Japanese.
    Is that all right?

  I'd like to talk Japanese
    as much as possible.
    Is that all right?

  Since I've studied, I'd
    like to talk Japanese
    as much as possible.
    Is that all right?

  Since I've studied Jap-
    anese, I'd like to talk
    Japanese as much as
    possible. Is that all
    right?

  Since I took the trouble
    to study Japanese,
    I'd like to talk Japanese
    as much as possible.
    Is that all right?

Ka⌐maimase⌐ñ ka⌐⌐

Ha⌐nasita⌐i ñ desu ḡa, ka⌐mai-
  mase⌐ñ ka⌐⌐

Ni⌐hoñḡo de hanasita⌐i ñ desu
  ḡa, ka⌐maimase⌐ñ ka⌐⌐

Narubeku ni⌐hoñḡo de hanasita⌐i
  ñ desu ḡa, ka⌐maimase⌐ñ ka⌐⌐

Be⌐ñkyoo-sita⌐ kara, narubeku
  ni⌐hoñḡo de hanasita⌐i ñ desu
  ḡa; ka⌐maimase⌐ñ ka⌐⌐

Ni⌐hoñḡo (o) beñkyoo-sita⌐ kara,
  na⌐rubeku nihoñḡo de hanasita⌐i
  ñ desu ḡa; ka⌐maimase⌐ñ ka⌐⌐

Se⌐kkaku nihoñḡo (o) beñkyoo-
  sita⌐ kara, na⌐rubeku nihoñḡo
  de hanasita⌐i ñ desu ḡa; ka⌐mai-
  mase⌐ñ ka⌐⌐

6. It's unpleasant, isn't it.

  It's unpleasant because
    it rains (lit. falls) a
    lot.

  It's unpleasant because
    it rains a lot.

  [Things] get moldy and
    it rains a lot so it's un-
    pleasant, isn't it.

  It's muggy and [things]
    get moldy and it rains
    a lot so it's unpleasant,
    isn't it.

  The summer is unpleasant
    because it's muggy and
    [things] get moldy and
    it rains a lot.

I⌐ya¬ desu ⌐ne¬e.

Yo⌐ku ⌐hu⌐ru kara, i⌐ya¬ desu
  ⌐ne¬e.

A⌐me ḡa ⌐yo⌐ku ⌐hu⌐ru kara,
  i⌐ya¬ desu ⌐ne¬e.

Ka⌐bi ḡa hae⌐ru si, a⌐me ḡa
  ⌐yo⌐ku ⌐hu⌐ru kara; i⌐ya¬ desu
  ⌐ne¬e.

Mu⌐siatu⌐i si, ka⌐bi ḡa hae⌐ru
  si, a⌐me ḡa ⌐yo⌐ku ⌐hu⌐ru
  kara; i⌐ya¬ desu ⌐ne¬e.

Na⌐tu¬ wa, mu⌐siatu⌐i si, ka⌐bi ḡa
  hae⌐ru si, a⌐me ḡa ⌐yo⌐ku ⌐hu⌐ru
  kara; i⌐ya¬ desu ⌐ne¬e.

The summer here is un-
pleasant because it's
muggy and [things] get
moldy and it rains a lot.

Ko˹ko no natu˺ wa, mu˹siatu˺i si,
ka˹bi ga hae˹ru si, a˺me ga
˹yo˺ku ˻hu˻ru kara; i˹ya˺ desu
˹ne˺e.

SHORT SUPPLEMENTARY DIALOGUES

1. Smith: Ma˹da yu˻ki˼ ga hu˻tte˼ imasu ka⏌
   Tanaka: Yu˹ki˺ wa ya˻mima˼sita ga, ˹a˺me ni na˻rima˼sita.
   Smith: I˹ya˺ desu ˹ne˺e.

2. Mr. Yamamoto: Tanaka-sañ o˹soi ˹ne˺e.
   Mr. Okada: Si˹tu˺ree-site no˹mihazimeyo˺o ka.
   Mr. Yamamoto: So˹o siyo˺o.

3. Mrs. Tanaka: So˹no oka˹si o˹isisoo ˹ne˺e.
   Mr. Tanaka: Yo˹saso˺o da ˻ne˼e. Ta˹beyo˺o ka.
   Mrs. Tanaka: E˺e, ta˹bemasyo˺o.

4. Mr. Tanaka: So˺to a˹tuso˺o da kara, u˹ti ni iyo˺o yo.
   Mrs. Tanaka: So˺o ˹ne˺e.

5. Mr. Tanaka: Sa˺mukatta daroo?
   Mr. Yamamoto: Asi ko˹orisoo da˺tta yo.

6. Ueda: Da˺re ka ˹ma˺tte ru ñ desu ka⏌
   Yamamoto: E˺e. Ta˹naka-señse˺e o.
   Ueda: A˺a, mo˹o su˺gu ˻de˼te kuru to o˻moima˼su yo⏌

7. Smith: Mi˹na˺sañ o˹hirugo˺hañ ˹do˺o suru ñ desu ka⏌
   Tanaka: Hi˹to ni yotte tiḡaima˼su ga, taitee ka˹isya no so˺ba ni ˻a˼ru
            su˹si˼ya ya so˹ba˺ya de ta˻be˼ru ñ desu yo.

8. Tanaka: Asita se˹ñse˺e no otaku e i˻rassya˼ru soo desu ga; a˹ru˺ite
            i˻rassyaima˼su ka, ku˹ruma de irassyaima˼su ka.
   Smith: Sore wa ˹te˺ñki ni yotte ki˻mema˼su kara⏌

9. Smith: Sekkaku Ni˹ho˺ñ made ki˻ta˼ ñ da kara, Kyo˹oto ya ˹Na˺ra e
            i˻kita˼i ñ desu yo.
   Tanaka: Do˺ozo ˻do˼ozo. O˹mosiro˺i daroo to omoimasu.

10. Tanaka: Asita Ka˹makura e iko˺o to o˻mo˼tte ru ñ desu ga, a˹na˺ta mo
             i˹kimase˺ñ ka⏌
    Smith: Se˹kkaku˺ desu ga, a˹sita˺ wa ˹yo˺o ga a˻rima˼su kara⏌

11. Tanaka: Hu˹ru˼i kuruma ka˻o˼o ka to o˻mo˼tte ru ñ desu ga⏌
    Yamamoto: Ya˹sukute ˹i˼i no ga ˻a˼ru daroo to o˻moima˼su yo⏌

12. Tanaka: O˹matase-itasima˼sita. De˹kakeyo˺o to sita toki ˹a˺me ga hu-
             ˻rihazimema˼sita kara; ka˹sa o saḡasite⏌
    Smith: Do˺o itasimasite. *I˹ya˺ na ˹te˺ñki desu ˹ne˺e.

13. Smith: Ni˹motu ku˹ruma no na˺ka ni i˻reta˼ ñ desu ka⏌
    Tanaka: I˹reyoo to sita ñ desu ga, ka˹ḡi˺ ka˻ka˼tte ru yoo da kara⏌
    Smith: So˺o ˻so˼o. Ma˺e ni ka˹ḡi ˹ka˺keta ñ desu ˹ne˺e.

14. Tanaka: Koñgetu kara e⌐ego o beñkyoo-sihazimeyo⌐o to o⌐mo⌐tte ru ñ
desu ḡa, da⌐re ka zyo⌐ozu⌐ na se⌐ñse⌐e go⌐zo⌐ñzi desyoo ka.
　　 Smith: Sa⌐a. Betu ni zyo⌐ozu⌐ da to wa o⌐moimase⌐ñ ḡa, ka⌐nai wa—
　 Tanaka: O⌐kusama desu ka. O⌐siete kudasaima⌐su ka⌡
　　 Smith: E⌐e, yo⌐roko⌐ñde. So⌐ñna siḡoto ḡa suki⌐ desu kara—
　 Tanaka: Zya⌐a, koñsyuu o̅taku e de⌐ñwa o ka⌐kete, ki⌐mete itadakima-
syo⌐o.

English Equivalents

1. Smith: Is it still snowing?
　 Tanaka: The snow has stopped but it has turned to rain.
　 Smith: How awful!

2. Mr. Yamamoto: Isn't Tanaka late!
　 Mr. Okada: Shall we go ahead and have a drink? (Lit. Shall we be
                   rude and start drinking?)
　 Mr. Yamamoto: Let's do that.

3. Mrs. Tanaka: Doesn't that cake look delicious!
　 Mr. Tanaka: It looks good, doesn't it. Shall we have some?
　 Mrs. Tanaka: Yes, let's.

4. Mr. Tanaka: It looks hot outside so let's stay home.
　 Mrs. Tanaka: That's right.

5. Mr. Tanaka: It was cold, wasn't it?
　 Mr. Yamamoto: My feet felt as if they'd freeze!

6. Ueda: Are you waiting for someone?
　 Yamamoto: Yes. For Dr. Tanaka.
　 Ueda: Oh, I think he'll come out any minute now.

7. Smith: What do all of you do for lunch?
　 Tanaka: It depends on the person but we usually eat at places like sushi
           shops and soba shops that are near the office.

8. Tanaka: I hear that you are going to go to the teacher's house tomorrow.
           Are you going to walk there or go by car?
　 Smith: That I'll decide depending on the weather so [I don't know yet].

9. Smith: Since I've come all the way to Japan, I'd like to go to places
           like Kyoto and Nara.
　 Tanaka: Please do. I think that you'd probably enjoy it.

10. Tanaka: I'm thinking of going to Kamakura tomorrow. Wouldn't you like
            to go too?
　　 Smith: It's kind of you to ask me but tomorrow I have some business I
            must attend to so . . .

11. Tanaka: I'm wondering if I should buy a used (lit. old) car . . .
　 Yamamoto: I think there are probably some good cheap ones.

12. Tanaka: I'm sorry to have kept you waiting. Just as I was about to start
            out, it began to rain, so I looked for an umbrella and . . .
　　 Smith: Don't mention it. Isn't it awful weather!

13. Smith: Did you put the luggage in the car?
     Tanaka: I tried to put it in, but it seems to be locked so [I couldn't].
     Smith: That's right. I locked it a while ago, didn't I.

14. Tanaka: I've been thinking that I'd start studying English this month.
              Do you know some good teacher?
     Smith: I don't think she's especially good, but my wife . . .
     Tanaka: Your wife? Will she teach me?
     Smith: Yes, she'd be glad to. (Because) she likes that kind of work.
     Tanaka: Well then, I'll telephone your home this week and have it set-
              tled.

EXERCISES

1. Take turns asking and answering questions based on the Basic Dialogues.
    The student who is answering questions should do so without referring to
    the text.

2. Take turns asking and answering questions about the climate of places
    you know. Practice using words from the Additional Vocabulary as well
    as those which occur in the Basic Dialogues.

3. You have just returned from a trip. Give the following replies to Mr. Ta-
    naka's question, 'How was the weather?':

        a. It was very pleasant.
        b. It rained every day.
        c. It was awfully muggy.
        d. It was snowy and cold.
        e. It was hot.

4. Tell Mr. Tanaka that:

        a. it's raining.
        b. it's snowing.
        c. it has started to rain.
        d. it has stopped snowing.
        e. it has begun to cloud up.
        f. it has begun to clear up.
        g. it is very windy.

Lesson 27. Outings

BASIC DIALOGUES: FOR MEMORIZATION

(a)

Tanaka

1. Doesn't it rain (lit. fall) a lot!

*Yo⌐ku hu⌐rima⌐su ⌐ne⌐e.

Smith

2. There really is a great deal of rain this year, isn't there!

*Hoñtoo ni ko̅tosi wa ⌐a⌐me ḡa o⌐o⌐i desu ⌐ne⌐e.

   is amazing <u>or</u> unusual <u>or</u> unexpected

   me⌐zurasi⌐i /-ku/

   is unusually good

   me⌐zura⌐siku ⌐i⌐i

3. Yesterday was unusually nice (weather) but [we haven't had much weather like that].

Ki⌐no⌐o wa me⌐zura⌐siku ⌐i⌐i ⌐te⌐ñki desita ḡa—

Tanaka

   the country

   inaka

   cherry tree <u>or</u> cherry blossom

   sakura

4. Yesterday I went to the country to see the cherry blossoms . . .

Kinoo inaka e sa⌐kura (o) mi⌐ ni itte ⌐ne⌐e.

Smith

5. Oh.

A⌐a, so⌐o.

Tanaka

   completely

   su⌐kka⌐ri

   bloom

   saku /-u/

   be in bloom

   saite (i)ru

6. They were in full bloom already so they were beautiful.

Mo⌐o su⌐kka⌐ri sa⌐ite (i)ta⌐ kara, ki⌐ree desita yo⌐

Smith

   go out (for a special occasion)

   de⌐ru /-ru/

   be out

   de⌐te (i)ru

7. A lot of people were out (to see them), weren't they?

Hito (ḡa) ta⌐kusañ de⌐te (i)ta desyoo?

Tanaka

cherry-blossom viewing	ha⌐nami¬ or ohanami+
people looking at the cherry blossoms	ha⌐nami no hito¬
filled with people	hi⌐to¬ de ippai

8. Yes. The park was filled with people looking at the cherry blossoms.

E¬e. Kooeñ (wa) ha⌐nami no hito¬ de i⌐ppai de¬sita yo.

song	u⌐ta¬
sing	utau /-u/
make noise or be boisterous	sa⌐wa¬gu /-u/
do such things as drinking, singing, and making a racket	no¬ñdari u⌐tatta¬ri sa⌐wa¬i-dari suru

9. They were all drinking sake and singing songs and making a racket . . .

Miñna o⌐sake (o) no¬ñdari, u⌐ta¬ (o) u⌐tatta⌐ri, sa⌐wa¬idari site_

Smith

10. Oh, my goodness! or You don't say! or Really!

Sore wa sore wa.

Tanaka

box lunch	be⌐ñto¬o
tree	ki¬

11. We took our lunch and ate under the trees . . .

Be⌐ñto¬o (o) motte (i)tte, ki¬ no sita de ⌐ta⌐bete_

and or then or and then	sosite
play or amuse oneself	asobu /-u/
come after playing or go and play	a⌐soñde ku¬ru
return (noun)	ka⌐eri¬
the return train	ka⌐eri no de¬ñsya

12. And we amused ourselves (lit. came after amusing ourselves) until evening. The return train was crowded . . .

Sosite yu⌐u̅ata ma¬de a⌐soñde kima⌐sita ḡa, *ka⌐eri no de¬ñsya (ḡa) ⌐koñde ⌐ne¬e.

until arriving	tu¬ku made
stand up	ta¬tu /-u/
be standing	ta¬tte (i)ru

13. We were standing all the way until we arrived in Tokyo.

To⌐okyoo e tu¬ku made, zu⌐tto ta¬tte (i)masita.

Smith

14. How awful!

So⌐re wa taiheñ de¬sita ⌐ne⌐e.

Tanaka

therefore or and so   da⌐ kara or de⌐su kara
  or for that reason
  or that is why
15. That is why I got completely   Da⌐ kara su⌐kka⌐ri tu⌐ka⌐rete si-
    tired out, and today I don't   matte, kyo⌐o wa zēnzeñ ⌐geñki
    have any pep at all.   (ḡa) ⌐na⌐i ñ desu.

(b)

(Mr. Tanaka is talking to his good friend, Mr. Yamamoto.)

Mr. Tanaka

wherever [someone]   do⌐ko e i⌐tte⌐ mo
  goes
16. Nowadays wherever you go   Kono-ḡoro wa ⌐do⌐ko e i⌐tte⌐ mo
    it's crowded; (so) isn't it   ⌐ko⌐mu kara ko⌐ma⌐ru ⌐he⌐e.
    awful!

Mr. Yamamoto

on days off   ya⌐sumi no hi⌐ ni wa or
                                           ya⌐sumi no hi⌐ nyaa

not go anywhere   do⌐ko e mo ikanai
do such things as read   yo⌐ñdari ⌐mi⌐tari suru
  and see
17. Uh huh. On days off, instead   N̄. Ya⌐sumi no hi⌐ nyaa; doko e
    of going anywhere, it's better   mo ikazu ni; uti de ⌐hoñ ya za-
    to loaf around at home, read-   ⌐ssi yo⌐ñdari, te⌐rebi ⌐mi⌐tari
    ing books and magazines and   site; a⌐sobu ho⌐o ḡa ⌐i⌐i yo.
    watching television.

Mr. Tanaka

not do anything or   nani mo sinai
  do nothing
nap   hirune
take a nap   hirune (o) suru
do something like   hi⌐rune (o) sita⌐ri suru
  take a nap
18. Me—I take a nap or some-   Boku wa na⌐ni mo sina⌐i de, uti
    thing at home instead of do-   de hi⌐rune sita⌐ri site_
    ing anything.

Mr. Yamamoto

whatever [someone] says   na⌐ñ te i⌐tte⌐ mo
the act of resting   ya⌐su⌐mu koto
resting is best   ya⌐su⌐mu koto ḡa i⌐ti⌐bañ
                                           da
19. Whatever you say, on days   Na⌐ñ te i⌐tte⌐ mo; ya⌐sumi no
    of rest, rest is best.   hi⌐ nyaa, ya⌐su⌐mu koto ḡa i⌐ti-
                                         bañ da yo.

Mr. Tanaka

is young	wa⌐ka⌉i /-ku/
the interval during which [someone] is young	wa⌐ka⌉i uti
unconcerned <u>or</u> indifferent <u>or</u> unmoved	heeki /na/

20. Uh huh. While we were young we were a match for everything (but), weren't we.
N̄, wa⌐ka⌉i uti wa, na⌐n̄ de⌉ mo he⌐eki da⌐tta ḡa n̄e⌉e.

old person	to⌐siyori⌉ [1]
for an old person	to⌐siyori⌉ ni wa <u>or</u> to⌐siyori⌉ nyaa
care-taking	rusuban̄
take care of the house during the absence of others	rusuban̄ (o) suru

21. For old people, it's better to take care of the house while the others are away, than to go out to look at the cherry blossoms.
To⌐siyori⌉ nyaa, ha⌐nami⌉ ni de-⌐kakeru yo⌉ri ru⌐suban̄ suru ho⌉o ḡa ⌐i⌉i yo.

we <u>or</u> us	bo⌉kutati
gradually	dan̄dan̄
is troublesome <u>or</u> tiresome	me⌐n̄dookusa⌉i /-ku/

22. I suppose we aren't old yet but gradually cherry-blossom viewing has grown to be tiresome, hasn't it.
Bo⌉kutati wa ⌐ma⌉da to⌐siyori⌉ zya ⌐na⌉i daroo kedo, dan̄dan̄ ha⌐nami⌉ ḡa me⌐n̄dookusa⌉ku ⌐na⌉tta n̄e⌉e.

(c)

(A young man is talking to his girl friend.)

Taro

you	kimi
any number of times	na⌉n̄-do mo

23. I telephoned your place any number of times yesterday but no one answered.
Kinoo ki̇⌉mi no toko e ⌐na⌉n̄-do mo de⌐n̄wa-sita⌉ kedo, da⌐re mo de⌉nakatta yo⌄

24. What happened?
Do⌉o sita no? [2]

Haruko

25. Oh, we were (gone) on an excursion to Kamakura.
A⌉a, Ka⌐makura e asobi ni itte⌉ ta no yo⌄

---

[1] Alternate accent: to⌐siyo⌉ri.

[2] Note the use of the ―― no? pattern by a man in talking to his girl friend.

	is hard of hearing	mi⌐mi⌐ g̃a tōoi
26.	My grandfather was watch-ing the house but he's hard of hearing so he probably couldn't hear the phone.	O⌐zi⌐isañ g̃a ru⌐subañ site⌐ ta kedo; a⌐no⌐ hito mi⌐mi⌐ g̃a to⌐oi⌐ kara, deñwa ki⌐koena⌐katta ñ desyoo.

Taro

27.	Oh.	So⌐o ka.
28.	How was Kamakura?	Kamakura ⌐do⌐o datta?

Haruko

29.	It was lots of fun.	To⌐ttemo omosi⌐rokatta wa⌐
	swim	o⌐yo⌐g̃u /-u/
	go sight-seeing	keñbutu-suru
	do such things as swim and go sight-seeing	o⌐yo⌐idari ke⌐ñbutu-sita⌐ri suru
30.	We swam and went sight-seeing . . .	O⌐yo⌐idari ke⌐ñbutu-sita⌐ri site⌐

Taro

	whenever [someone] goes	i⌐tu i⌐tte⌐ mo
31.	Whenever you go there, that place is always fun, isn't it.	Asuko wa ⌐i⌐tu i⌐tte⌐ mo o⌐mo-siro⌐i ⌐ne⌐e.

NOTES ON THE BASIC DIALOGUES

12. Asobu is the opposite of hataraku. Depending on context, it can mean 'play,' 'be at leisure,' 'have a good time,' 'visit (for pleasure),' 'loaf,' 'be unemployed,' etc.

17. Nya or nyaa is the contracted equivalent of ni wa, used more commonly by men.

20. Uti 'interval' also follows nominals of time + no meaning 'the interval of ——,' 'within ——,' 'during ——.' Examples: i⌐k-kag̃etu no uti 'within a month'; sono hi no uti 'during that day.' Compare also A to B to C no uti 'among A and B and C' (Lesson 15, Grammatical Note 3).
   Note: heeki de suru 'do [it] with unconcern,' 'make nothing of it'; heeki na kao o suru 'look unconcerned' (lit. 'make an unconcerned face [i.e. expression]').

23. Kimi is the informal equivalent of a⌐na⌐ta, more typical of men's speech. A person addressed as kimi is always a close friend or an inferior of the speaker.

25. Asobi ni iku 'go for fun.' See the note on sentence 12 above.

26. Note the use of the honorific (⌐) o⌐zi⌐isañ in reference to one's own grandfather. This is normal usage among young people, as a sign of re-spect for age.

GRAMMATICAL NOTES

1. The Representative

Mi⌐tari		mi⌐ru 'see.'
Yo⌐ndari		yo⌐mu 'read.'
No⌐ndari	is the REPRESENTATIVE of	no⌐mu 'drink.'
Sa⌐wa⌐idari		sa⌐wa⌐gu 'make noise.'
O⌐yo⌐idari		o⌐yo⌐gu 'swim.'
Si⌐ta⌐ri		suru 'do.'

Inflected words (verbals, adjectivals, and copula) have REPRESENTATIVE forms which are made by adding -ri to the corresponding past. If the past is accented, the representative is accented on the same syllable; if the past is unaccented, the representative is accented on the next-to-last syllable (ta). Thus:

	Non-past	Past	Representative
Verbals	ta⌐be⌐ru 'eat'	ta⌐beta	ta⌐betari
	kau 'buy'	katta	ka⌐tta⌐ri
	o⌐ssya⌐ru 'say'	o⌐ssya⌐tta	o⌐ssya⌐ttari
	ku⌐ru 'come'	ki⌐ta⌐ [1]	ki⌐ta⌐ri
Adjectivals	a⌐tu⌐i 'is hot'	a⌐tukatta	a⌐tukattari
	akai 'is red'	a⌐ka⌐katta	a⌐ka⌐kattari
	i⌐i/yo⌐i 'is good'	yo⌐katta	yo⌐kattari
	ta⌐be⌐nai 'doesn't eat'	ta⌐be⌐nakatta	ta⌐be⌐nakattari
	ta⌐beta⌐i 'want to eat'	ta⌐beta⌐katta	ta⌐beta⌐kattari
Copula	da	da⌐tta	da⌐ttari

A formal verbal ending in -ma⌐su has a corresponding representative ending in -ma⌐sitari.

The representative is a tenseless form. It is used to indicate one action or state among several;[2] these may or may not be specifically mentioned. Most commonly, representatives occur in pairs, A and B, followed by √suru 'do.' A and B may follow each other directly (in which case they are never the same word) or they may be preceded by modifiers (in which case they may be the same or different words).

Such a combination of representatives plus √suru may refer (1) to typical actions or states (that is, those mentioned represent a longer list of similar actions or states): 'do (or be) such things as A and B,' 'do (or be) A and B and so on.'

Examples:

Sa⌐ra o aratta⌐ri, he⌐ya⌐ o ka⌐tazu⌐ketari site imasu.
'She's washing the dishes, straightening up the rooms, and so on.'

---

[1] Alternate accent: ki⌐ta.

[2] The several actions or states may be different or the same one repeated.

Be⌐ñkyoo-sita⌐ri, te⌐gami o ka⌐itari si┕ma┛sita.
'I did things like studying and writing letters.'
Ho⌐ñ o ┕yo┛ñdari, za⌐ssi o yo⌐ñdari simasu.
'I read books and (I read) magazines and so on.'

And/or the combination may refer (2) to repeated or alternating actions or
states: 'keep doing A and B' or 'do A and B, A and B.'

Examples:

De⌐tari ⌐ha⌐ittari si┕ma┛sita.
'He kept going out and coming in.'
A⌐tukattari ⌐sa⌐mukattari simasu.
'It's hot and cold, hot and cold.'
A⌐tuku ┕na┛ttari, sa⌐muku ┕na┛ttari simasu.
'It gets hot and (gets) cold, hot and cold.'

And/or the combination may refer (3) to differing actions or states of members of a group, occurring at the same time: 'some do A while others do
B.'

Example:

Tomodati wa; de⌐ñsya ni no┕tta┛ri, zi⌐buñ no kuruma ni notta⌐ri site
i┕kima┛sita.
My friends went, some in the (electric) train and some in their own
cars.'

Representative forms may also occur singly or in groups of three or more,
with the same kinds of meanings.[1] Thus:

U⌐ti -o soozi-sita⌐ri si┕ma┛sita.
'She cleaned the house and so on.'
Ko⌐nakattari si┕ma┛su kara, ko⌐ma⌐tte imasu.
'It's annoying because time and again he doesn't come.'
Be⌐ñkyoo-sita⌐ri, ho⌐ñ o ┕yo┛ñdari, te⌐gami o ka⌐itari si┕ma┛sita.
'I did things like studying and reading books and writing letters.'
Sara wa, ka⌐tta⌐ri tu⌐katta⌐ri ko⌐wa⌐sitari site imasu.
'I keep buying, using, and breaking plates.'
Tomodati wa; de⌐ñsya ni no┕tta┛ri, ba⌐su ni no┕tta┛ri, zi⌐buñ no ku-
ruma ni notta⌐ri site i┕kima┛sita.
'My friends went, some in (electric) trains, some in busses, and
some in their own cars.'

A representative form—or a sequence of such forms—is not always immediately followed by √suru. It sometimes occurs at the end of an accent
phrase without following particle, as a modifier of an inflected word or phrase,
and sometimes it immediately precedes √da. The uses of the representa-
tive(s) in such cases are the same—to indicate typical, repeated, alternating,
and/or distributive actions or states. Thus:

Be⌐ñkyoo-sita⌐ri, te⌐gami o ka⌐itari, to⌐temo isoga⌐sikatta.
'What with studying and writing letters (and so on), I was very busy.'

---

[1] Obviously there are no examples of a single representative form having
the last-mentioned kind of meaning.

Aˈme dattari, yuˈkiˈ dattari desu.
    'It's (being) rain and snow, rain and snow.'

Additional examples:

Niˈhoñ e kiˈteˈ kara, maˈiniti niˈhoñgo o hanaˈsitari ˈyoñdari siˈte
    imaˈsu kara; zuˈibuñ zyoˈozuˈ ni naˈrimaˈsita.
    'Ever since coming to Japan, he's been speaking and reading Jap-
    anese every day, so he's grown to be awfully good at it.'
Okaḡesama de ˈzuˈibuñ ˈgeˈñki ni ˈnaˈtte; neˈtaˈri ˈoˈkitari deˈkiˈru
    yoo ni naˈrimaˈsita.
    'I'm much better, thank you, and I've reached the point where I can
    alternate between being in bed and getting up.'
Aˈno mise no monoˈ wa; toˈkiˈ ni yotte, yaˈsukattari ˈtaˈkakattari su-
    ˈru yoˈo desu.
    'The things in that store seem to be sometimes cheap and some-
    times high, depending on the time.'
Aˈnoˈ hito wa; hi ni yotte, yoˈku beˈñkyoo-sitaˈri zeˈñzeñ sinaˈkattari
    suˈruˈ ñ desu.
    'He goes back and forth between studying hard and not studying at
    all, depending on the day.'
Kono-ḡoro wa; aˈme dattari yuˈkiˈ dattari site, iˈi ˈteˈñki no hi wa
    zeˈñzeñ naˈi ñ desu.
    'It keeps raining and snowing these days, and there are no pleasant
    days at all.'
Hoˈka no hito no heyaˈ o, kikazu ni aˈketaˈri siˈteˈ wa iˈkemaseˈñ.
    'You mustn't open [the door of] other people's rooms (or do other
    such things) without asking.'

2. Interrogative + mo

In previous lessons, there have been a few occurrences of interrogatives
(question words like daˈre 'who?' doˈko 'where?' etc.) followed by particle
mo:

    Daˈre mo demaseˈñ. 'Nobody answers.'
    Iˈtu mo go-ˈzi-hañ-ḡoˈro kaerimasu. 'I always go home at about 5:30.'

In general, it can be said that an interrogative + mo before a negative has
an all-exclusive meaning, and before an affirmative an all-inclusive meaning; but occurrences before negatives are more numerous.

The following chart includes the more frequent kinds of occurrence:

Interrogative	+ mo	+ Negative	+ Affirmative
daˈre 'who?'	daˈre mo	'nobody,' 'not anybody'	
naˈni 'what?'	naˈni mo	'nothing,' 'not anything'	
doˈko 'what place?'	doˈko mo	'no place,' 'not any place'	
iˈtu 'when?'	iˈtu mo		'always'
doˈtira 'which (of 2)?'	doˈtira mo	'neither one,' 'not either one'	'both'

1
Interrogative + mo often occurs with an unaccented alternant.

Interrogative	+ _mo_	+ Negative	+ Affirmative
do⌐re 'which (of 3 or more)?'	do⌐re mo	'not one (of 3 or more)'	'every one (of 3 or more)'
i⌐kura 'how much?'	i⌐kura mo	'no large amount'	'ever so much'
i⌐ku-tu 'how many?'	i⌐ku-tu mo	'no large number'	'a large number, ever so many'
do⌐no eñpitu [1] 'which pencil?'	do⌐no eñpi-tu [1] mo	'no pencil'	'every pencil'
do⌐ñna eñpitu [1] 'what kind of pencil?'	do⌐ñna eñ-pitu [1] mo	'no kind of pencil'	'every kind of pencil'
na⌐ñ-boñ [2] 'how many long cylin-drical units?'	na⌐ñ-boñ mo	'no large num-ber of long cy-lindrical units'	'a large number of long cylin-drical units'

Remember that _mo_ replaces particles _ḡa_, _wa_, and _o_ but follows other particles. Compare:

Da⌐re ḡa ki⌐ma⌐sita ka⌐
  'Who came?'
Na⌐ni o ta⌐bema⌐sita ka⌐
  'What did you eat?'
Da⌐re ni ki⌐kima⌐sita ka⌐
  'Whom did you ask?'
Do⌐ko e i⌐kima⌐sita ka⌐
  'Where did you go?'

Da⌐re mo kimase⌐ñ desita.
  'Nobody came.'
Na⌐ni mo tabemase⌐ñ desita.
  'I didn't eat anything.'
Da⌐re ni mo kikimase⌐ñ desita.
  'I didn't ask anybody.'
Do⌐ko e mo ikimase⌐ñ desita.
  'I didn't go anywhere.'

Additional Examples:

Da⌐re mo wakarimase⌐ñ. 'Nobody understands.'
Na⌐ni mo wakarimase⌐ñ. 'I don't understand anything.'
Do⌐ko de mo hataraite imase⌐ñ. 'I'm not working anywhere.'
I⌐tu mo de⌐ki⌐ru tte i⌐ima⌐su ḡa, de⌐kimase⌐ñ ⌐ne⌐e. 'He always says that he can do it, but he can't, can he!'
Hu⌐ta-tu kaima⌐sita ḡa, do⌐tira mo yo⌐ku a⌐rimase⌐ñ. 'I bought two but neither one is [any] good.'
Uti no ko wa do⌐tira mo oñna⌐ desu. 'Our children are both girls.'
Kinoo a⌐tarasi⌐i zassi o ta⌐kusañ kaima⌐sita ḡa, ma⌐da do⌐re mo yomi-mase⌐ñ. 'Yesterday I bought lots of new magazines but I haven't read any of them yet.'
Koko ni ni⌐hoñḡo no ho⌐ñ ḡa ta⌐kusañ arima⌐su ḡa, dore mo mu⌐zuka-si⌐i desu. 'There are lots of Japanese books here but every one of them is difficult.'
Su⌐ko⌐si wa a⌐rima⌐su ḡa, i⌐kura mo arimase⌐ñ. 'There is a little but there isn't any large amount.'
Mi-⌐ttu-ḡu⌐rai i⌐rima⌐su ḡa, i⌐ku-tu mo i⌐rimase⌐ñ. 'I need about three but I don't need a large number.'

---

[1] _Eñpitu_ represents any nominal.

[2] _Hoñ_ /-_boñ_/ represents any counter.

Hoꞟ wa i⌐ku-tu mo arima⌐su ḡa, yo⌐mu zikañ ḡa a⌐rimaseꞟ kara_ 'I have any number of books but I have no time to read so. . . .'

Koko no ⌐do⌐no kimono mo ⌐ki⌐ree zya a⌐rimaseꞟ ⌐ne⌐e. 'Not one of the kimonos here is pretty, is it!'

Ko⌐re mo simaita⌐i ñ desu ḡa, do⌐no hako mo i⌐ppai de⌐su kara_ 'I'd like to put these away too, but every box is full so. . . .'

Kono-ḡoro ⌐do⌐nna zi⌐do⌐osya mo ⌐ya⌐suku a⌐rimaseꞟ. 'Nowadays no kind of car is cheap.'

Si⌐ro⌐i ka⌐mi⌐ wa ⌐ma⌐da a⌐rima⌐su ḡa, a⌐o⌐i ka⌐mi⌐ wa ⌐mo⌐o na⌐ñ-mai mo arimase⌐ñ. 'There is still some white paper but there aren't many more sheets of blue paper.'

E⌐ꞟpitu wa na⌐ñ-boñ mo a⌐rima⌐su ḡa, pe⌐ñ wa ⌐i⌐p-poñ sika a⌐rima-se⌐ñ. 'I have any number of pencils but I have only one pen.'

3. do⌐ko e i⌐tte⌐ mo

Reread Lesson 15, Grammatical Note 4.

A verbal or adjectival gerund plus particle <u>mo</u> — as well as the copula gerund <u>de</u> plus <u>mo</u> — may follow an interrogative; the sequence has a generalized rather than an interrogative meaning, and is tenseless.

Compare the following pairs:

Na⌐ñ desu ka_ 'What is it?'	na⌐ñ de mo 'whatever it is,' 'no matter what it is'
Na⌐ni ḡa a⌐rima⌐su ka_ 'What is there?'	na⌐ni ḡa ⌐a⌐tte mo 'whatever there is,' 'no matter what there is'
Na⌐ni o ta⌐bema⌐su ka_ 'What are you going to eat?'	na⌐ni o ⌐ta⌐bete mo 'whatever [someone] eats,' 'no matter what [someone] eats'
Do⌐ko e i⌐kima⌐su ka_ 'Where are you going?'	do⌐ko e i⌐tte⌐ mo 'wherever [some-one] goes,' 'no matter where [someone] goes'
Do⌐ko kara ki⌐ma⌐su ka_ 'Where do you come from?' [1]	do⌐ko kara ki⌐te⌐ mo 'wherever [someone] comes from,' 'no matter where [someone] comes from'
Da⌐re ḡa ki⌐ma⌐su ka_ 'Who is coming?'	da⌐re ḡa ki⌐te⌐ mo 'whoever comes,' 'no matter who comes'
Da⌐re ni a⌐ita⌐i ñ desu ka_ 'Who is it you want to see?'	da⌐re ni a⌐ita⌐kute mo 'whomever [someone] wants to see,' 'no matter whom [someone] wants to see'
Na⌐ñ-zi ni i⌐kita⌐i ñ desu ka_ 'At what time do you want to go?'	na⌐ñ-zi ni i⌐kita⌐kute mo 'at what-ever time [someone] wants to go,' 'no matter what time [some-one] wants to go'

---

[1] I. e. in general, whenever you come here.

Examples:

Do⌐ko e i⌐tte⌐ mo To⌐okyoo wa yakamasi⌐i kara, su⌐ki⌐ zya ⌐na⌐i ñ desu.
'No matter where I go Tokyo is noisy so I don't like it.'
Mo⌐o yo⌐ku na⌐rima⌐sita kara, na⌐ni o si⌐te⌐ mo ka⌐maimase⌐ñ.
'I've recovered now so whatever I do it's all right.'
Do⌐no zi⌐biki⌐ o ⌐mi⌐te mo, ko⌐no i⌐mi wa wa⌐karimase⌐ñ desita.
'No matter what dictionary I looked at, I couldn't tell the meaning of this.'
I⌐tu ko⌐no depa⌐ato ni ki⌐te⌐ mo, hi⌐to⌐ de i⌐ppai de⌐su ⌐ne⌐e.
'No matter when you come to this department store it's filled with people, isn't it!'
I⌐kura ⌐ma⌐tte mo, a⌐no⌐ hito wa ki⌐mase⌐ñ desita.
'No matter how long I waited, he didn't come.'
I⌐kura ⌐ta⌐kakute mo, a⌐re ḡa kaita⌐i ñ desu.
'No matter how (much) expensive it is, that's the one I want to buy.'

4. Sentence-final Gerund [+ ne⌐e] in Non-request Sentences

Reread the note on fragments (Lesson 4, Grammatical Note 5).

In conversation, a gerund (verbal, adjectival, or copula) ending in suspensive intonation (‿) or a gerund + ne⌐e often occurs in sentence-final position, when the speaker is about to say more that is coordinate with what has just been said ('X is true and—Y is true'), or when the speaker assumes that the listener understands something coordinate without his continuing ('X is true and—you know the rest').

Usually each such occurrence of ne⌐e following a gerund is acknowledged by the listener either by word or gesture.

For examples, see Basic Sentences 4, 9, 11, 12, 18, and 30 in this lesson.

5. Verbal + made

Made was introduced previously, following a nominal of place meaning 'as far as,' and following a nominal of time meaning 'until,' 'up to and including.'

In this lesson, it follows a verbal in its informal non-past (NEVER past) form, meaning 'until.' The subject of the verbal, if expressed, is usually followed by particle ḡa. Thus:

ku⌐ru made 'until [someone] comes or came'
se⌐ñse⌐e ḡa ⌐ku⌐ru made 'until the teacher comes or came'

A sequence consisting of a verbal + made is accented on the verbal; the verbal acquires an accent on its final syllable if it is normally unaccented.

Examples:

Ta⌐naka-sañ ḡa ku⌐ru made ⌐ma⌐tte kudasai.
'Please wait until Mr. Tanaka comes.'
Hu⌐ne ḡa ⌐de⌐ru made Yo⌐kohama ni ima⌐sita.
'I stayed in Yokohama until the ship left.'

A⌐tarasi⌐i no o mo⌐rau⌐ made hu⌐ru⌐i no o tukaimasu.
'Until I get a new one I'll use the old one.'

6. Particle <u>ni</u> of Reference

The particle <u>ni</u> follows a nominal indicating the person in reference to
whom something is true.

Examples:

A⌐na⌐ta ni ti⌐isasuḡi⌐ru kara_
   'Since it's too small for you . . .'
To⌐siyori⌐ ni wa mu⌐zukasi⌐i desyoo ḡa, wa⌐ka⌐i hito ni wa he⌐eki de⌐su.
   'For old people it's probably difficult but for young people it's noth-
      ing at all.'

7. Pluralizing Suffixes

Most Japanese nominals do not distinguish between singular and plural;
but <u>bo⌐ku</u> 'I,' <u>watukusi</u> 'I,' <u>kimi</u> 'you,' and <u>a⌐na⌐ta</u> 'you,' which are always singular, are exceptions. The plural of these words is made by adding one of a
number of pluralizing suffixes, for example <u>-tati</u> or the honorific <u>-ḡata</u> ↑. [1]
Other nominals denoting persons, which in their basic form refer to one or
more than one without distinction, may also occur with these suffixes to de-
note specific plurals. Thus:

hi⌐to⌐ 'person' or 'persons' or 'people'—but hi⌐to⌐tati 'persons' or
   'people'
<u>kodomo</u> 'child' or 'children'—but <u>ko⌐domo⌐tati</u> 'children'
<u>hya⌐kusyo⌐o</u> 'farmer' or 'farmers'—but <u>hya⌐kusyo⌐otati</u> 'farmers'
<u>ka⌐ta⌐</u>↑ 'person' or 'persons' or 'people'—but <u>ka⌐ta⌐ḡata</u> ↑ 'persons'
   or 'people'

Note also: <u>Tanaka-sañ-tati</u> 'Mr. Tanaka and the others (of a particular
group).'

DRILLS

A. Substitution Drill

1. For old people it's in-   To⌐siyori⌐ ni wa o⌐mosiro⌐i de-
   teresting (but) . . . [2]   su ḡa_
2. For old people it's dif-   To⌐siyori⌐ ni wa <u>mu⌐zukasi⌐i</u>
   ficult (but) . . .   <u>desu</u> ḡa_
3. For old people it's bor-   To⌐siyori⌐ ni wa <u>tu⌐marana⌐i</u>
   · ing (but) . . .   <u>desu</u> ḡa_

---

[1] -<u>Ḡata</u> is never added to <u>bo⌐ku,</u> <u>watakusi,</u> or <u>kimi</u> since it is an honorific (↑)
suffix. Note that bo⌐kutati 'we' can include females (i.e. 'I [male] and others').

[2] 'but—not for everyone.'

4. For old people it's easy (but) . . .

To⌐siyori⌐ ni wa ya⌐sasi⌐i desu ḡa—

5. For old people it doesn't matter (but) . . .

To⌐siyori⌐ ni wa ka⌐maimase⌐n̄ ḡa—

6. For old people it's important (but) . . .

To⌐siyori⌐ ni wa ta⌐isetu de⌐su ḡa—

7. For old people it's possible (but) . . .

To⌐siyori⌐ ni wa de⌐kima⌐su ḡa—

8. For old people it's clear (but) . . .

To⌐siyori⌐ ni wa wa⌐karima⌐su ḡa—

B. Substitution Drill

1. There's really a lot of rain, isn't there.

A⌐me ḡa ho⌐n̄too ni oo⌐i desu ⌐ne⌐e.

2. There's really a lot of snow, isn't there.

Yu⌐ki⌐ ḡa ho⌐n̄too ni oo⌐i desu ⌐ne⌐e.

3. There's an amazing amount of snow, isn't there.

Yu⌐ki⌐ ḡa me⌐zura⌐siku o⌐o⌐i desu ⌐ne⌐e.

4. There's unusually little snow, isn't there.

Yu⌐ki⌐ ḡa me⌐zura⌐siku su⌐kuna⌐i desu ⌐ne⌐e.

5. There are unusually few cherry trees, aren't there.

Sakura ḡa me⌐zura⌐siku su⌐kuna⌐i desu ⌐ne⌐e.

6. There are very few cherry trees, aren't there.

Sakura ḡa to⌐ttemo sukuna⌐i desu ⌐ne⌐e.

7. The cherry trees are very pretty, aren't they.

Sakura ḡa to⌐ttemo ki⌐ree desu ⌐ne⌐e.

8. The trees are very pretty, aren't they.

Ki⌐ ḡa to⌐ttemo ki⌐ree desu ⌐ne⌐e.

9. The trees are awfully pretty, aren't they.

Ki⌐ ḡa ⌐zu⌐ibun̄ ⌐ki⌐ree desu ⌐ne⌐e.

10. There are an awful lot of trees, aren't there.

Ki⌐ ḡa ⌐zu⌐ibun̄ o⌐o⌐i desu ⌐ne⌐e.

C. Substitution Drill (based on Grammatical Note 5)

1. I waited until I arrived in Tokyo.

To⌐okyoo e tu⌐ku made ma⌐tima⌐-sita.

2. I waited until a friend came.

To⌐modati ḡa ku⌐ru made ma⌐ti-ma⌐sita.

3. I waited until the ship went out.

Hu⌐ne ḡa ⌐de⌐ru made ma⌐tima⌐-sita.

4. I waited until the movie began.

E⌐eḡa ḡa hazimaru⌐ made ma⌐ti-ma⌐sita.

5. I waited until everyone stood up.

Mi⌐n̄na⌐ ḡa ⌐ta⌐tu made ma⌐tima⌐-sita.

6. I waited until the candy got hard.

O⌐ka⌐si ḡa ka⌐taku na⌐ru made ma⌐tima⌐sita.

   7. I waited until my car   Ku⌐ruma ḡa hu⌐ruku ⌐na⌐ru made
       got old.   ma⌐tima⌐sita.

   8. I waited until I recovered.   Ge⌐ñki ni ⌐na⌐ru made ma⌐tima⌐-
                                  sita.

D. Substitution Drill

   1. It's best to rest.   Ya⌐su⌐mu koto ḡa i⌐ti⌐bañ desu.

   2. It's important to rest.   Ya⌐su⌐mu koto ḡa ta⌐isetu de⌐su.

   3. It's important to go to   Ha⌐yaku ne⌐ru koto⌐ ḡa ta⌐isetu
       bed early.   de⌐su.

   4. It's important to study   U⌐ti de beñkyoo-suru koto⌐ ḡa ta-
       at home.   ⌐isetu de⌐su.

   5. I like to study at home.   U⌐ti de beñkyoo-suru koto⌐ ḡa su-
                               ⌐ki⌐ desu.

   6. I like to swim.   O⌐yo⌐ḡu koto ḡa su⌐ki⌐ desu.

   7. I like to sing (songs).   U⌐ta⌐ (o) u⌐tau koto⌐ ḡa su⌐ki⌐ de-
                               su.

   8. I like to take baths.   O⌐hu⌐ro ni ⌐ha⌐iru koto ḡa su⌐ki⌐
                               desu.

   9. I like to eat with chop-   O⌐ha⌐si de ta⌐be⌐ru koto ḡa su⌐ki⌐
       sticks.   desu.

  10. Can you eat with chop-   O⌐ha⌐si de ta⌐be⌐ru koto ḡa de⌐ki-
       sticks?   ma⌐su ka⌐

  11. Can you read Japanese?   Ni⌐hoñḡo (o) yo⌐mu koto ḡa d ⌐ki-
                               ma⌐su ka⌐

  12. Can you fix this watch?   Ko⌐no tokee (o) nao⌐su koto ḡa de-
                               ⌐kima⌐su ka⌐

  13. Can you walk?   A⌐ru⌐ku koto ḡa de⌐kima⌐su ka⌐

E. Substitution Drill (based on Grammatical Note 1)

   1. Singing songs and making U⌐ta⌐ (o) u⌐tatta⌐ri sa⌐wa⌐idari
       a racket—you know!   site ⌐ne⌐e.

   2. Eating and drinking—you Ta⌐betari ⌐no⌐ñdari site ⌐ne⌐e.
       know! /ta⌐be⌐ru, no⌐mu/

   3. Swimming and taking   O⌐yo⌐idari sa⌐ñpo-sita⌐ri site
       walks —you know!   ⌐ne⌐e.
       /o⌐yo⌐ḡu, sañpo-suru/

   4. Going on and off—you   Ki⌐eta⌐ri ⌐tu⌐itari site ⌐ne⌐e.
       know! /kieru, tu⌐ku/

   5. Coming and going—you   I⌐tta⌐ri ⌐ki⌐tari site ⌐ne⌐e.
       know! /iku, ku⌐ru/

   6. Going out and coming in De⌐tari ⌐ha⌐ittari site ⌐ne⌐e.
       —you know! /de⌐ru,
       ha⌐iru/

   7. Sometimes understand-   Wa⌐ka⌐ttari wa⌐kara⌐nakattari
       ing and sometimes not   site ⌐ne⌐e.
       understanding—you
       know! /wa⌐ka⌐ru, wa⌐ka-
       ra⌐nai/

8. Being hot and cold, hot
   and cold—you know!
   /a⌐tu˥i, sa⌐mu˥i/

   A˥tukattari ⌐sa˥mukattari site ⌐ne˥e.

9. Sometimes tasting good
   and sometimes tasting
   awful—you know!
   /oisii, ma⌐zu˥i/

   O⌐isi˥kattari ⌐ma˥zukattari site ⌐ne˥e.

10. Raining and snowing,
    raining and snowing—
    you know! /a˥me da,
    yu⌐ki˥ da/

    A˥me dattari yu⌐ki˥ dattari site ⌐ne˥e.

F. Grammar Drill (based on Grammatical Note 3)

Tutor: To⌐okyoo e itte˥ mo ka⌐maimase˥ñ. 'Even if you go to To-
          kyo, it doesn't matter.'
Student: Do˥ko e i⌐tte˥ mo ka⌐maimase˥ñ. 'Wherever you go it
          doesn't matter.'

1. So⌐ko ni oite˥ mo ka⌐mai-
   mase˥ñ.

   Do˥ko ni o⌐ite˥ mo ka⌐maimase˥ñ.

2. To⌐modati ḡa itte˥ mo
   ka⌐maimase˥ñ.

   Da˥re ḡa i⌐tte˥ mo ka⌐maimase˥ñ.

3. Si⌐ḡoto (o) site˥ mo ka-
   ⌐maimase˥ñ.

   Na˥ni (o) si⌐tte˥ mo ka⌐maimase˥ñ.

4. Ti⌐isa˥i hoo ni si⌐te˥ mo
   ka⌐maimase˥ñ.

   Do˥tira ni si⌐te˥ mo ka⌐maima-
   se˥ñ.

5. I⌐tibañ tiisa˥i no ni si⌐te˥
   mo ka⌐maimase˥ñ.

   Do˥re ni si⌐te˥ mo ka⌐maimase˥ñ.

6. Ni-⌐do mi˥te mo ka⌐mai-
   mase˥ñ.

   Na˥ñ-do ⌐mi˥te mo ka⌐maimase˥ñ.

7. A˥sita mi˥te mo ka⌐mai-
   mase˥ñ.

   I˥tu ⌐mi˥te mo ka⌐maimase˥ñ.

G. Substitution Drill (based on Grammatical Note 3)

1. Wherever I go it's crowded
   (so) it's annoying.

   Do˥ko e i⌐tte˥ mo ⌐ko˥mu kara,
   ko⌐marima˥su.

2. No matter what kind of
   Western-style clothes I
   wear they aren't becoming (so) it's annoying.
   /do⌐ñna yoohuku (o) kiru,
   ni⌐awa˥nai/

   Do˥ñna yo⌐ohuku (o) kite˥ mo
   ni⌐awa˥nai kara, ko⌐marima˥su.

3. Whatever I learn I forget (so) it's annoying.
   /na˥ni (o) o⌐boe˥ru, wa-
   sureru/

   Na˥ni (o) o⌐bo˥ete mo wa⌐sure-
   ru˥ kara, ko⌐marima˥su.

4. Whenever I telephone
   he's out (so) it's annoying. /i˥tu deñwa-suru,
   ⌐ru˥su da/

   I˥tu de⌐ñwa-site˥ mo ⌐ru˥su da
   kara, ko⌐marima˥su.

5. However he says it I
   don't understand (so)
   it's annoying. /do⌐o
   iu, wa⌐kara⌐nai/

   Do⌐o i⌐tte⌐ mo wa⌐kara⌐nai kara,
   ko⌐marima⌐su.

6. Whatever I ask he
   doesn't know (so) it's
   annoying. /na⌐ni (o)
   kiku, siranai/

   Na⌐ni (o) ki⌐ite⌐ mo si⌐rana⌐i kara,
   ko⌐marima⌐su.

7. No matter what kind of
   work I do I get tired
   (so) it's annoying.
   /do⌐ñna siḡoto (o) suru,
   tu⌐kare⌐ru/

   Do⌐ñna si⌐ḡoto (o) site⌐ mo tu⌐ka-
   re⌐ru kara, ko⌐marima⌐su.

8. No matter how many
   hours I study I can't
   remember (so) it's
   annoying. /na⌐ñ-zi⌐-
   kañ beñkyoo-suru, o⌐bo-
   erare⌐nai/

   Na⌐ñ-zi⌐kañ be⌐ñkyoo-site⌐ mo
   o⌐boerare⌐nai kara, ko⌐marima⌐su.

H. Response Drill (based on Grammatical Note 2)

   Tutor: Do⌐ko e i⌐kima⌐sita ka⌐ 'Where did you go?'
   Student: Do⌐ko e mo ikimase⌐ñ desita. 'I didn't go anywhere.'

1. Da⌐re o ya⌐toima⌐sita ka⌐   Da⌐re mo yatoimase⌐ñ desita.
2. Da⌐re ḡa ru⌐subañ (o)   Da⌐re mo rusubañ (o) simase⌐ñ.
   sima⌐su ka⌐
3. Do⌐re o tu⌐kaima⌐sita   Do⌐re mo tukaimase⌐ñ desita.
   ka⌐
4. Do⌐tira ḡa su⌐ki⌐ desu   Do⌐tira mo suki⌐ zya a⌐rima-
   ka⌐   se⌐ñ.
5. Do⌐ko de ha⌐taraite   Do⌐ko de mo hataraite (i)mase⌐ñ.
   (i)ma⌐su ka⌐
6. Do⌐re ni i⌐rema⌐sita ka⌐   Do⌐re ni mo iremase⌐ñ desita.
7. Na⌐ni ḡa i⌐rima⌐su ka⌐   Na⌐ni mo irimase⌐ñ.
8. Do⌐ñna ha⌐na⌐ ḡa sa⌐ite   Do⌐ñna ha⌐na⌐ mo sa⌐ite (i)ma-
   (i)ma⌐su ka⌐   se⌐ñ.

I. Response Drill (based on Grammatical Note 2)

   Tutor: Na⌐ñ-do de⌐ñwa-sita⌐ desyoo ka⌐ 'How many times do
            you suppose he called?'
   Student: Na⌐ñ-do mo de⌐ñwa-sita⌐ to omoimasu. 'I think he called
            any number of times.'

1. Do⌐tira ḡa o⌐isi⌐i desyoo   Do⌐tira mo oisi⌐i to omoimasu.
   ka.
2. I⌐ku-tu mo⌐ratta⌐ desyoo   I⌐kutu mo mo⌐ratta⌐ to omoi-
   ka.   masu.

3. I⌐tu a⌐ite (i)ru⌐ desyoo ka.

   I⌐tu mo a⌐ite (i)ru⌐ to omoimasu.

4. Na⌐ñ-mai tu⌐kau⌐ de-syoo ka.

   Na⌐ñ-mai mo tu⌐kau⌐ to omoima-su.

5. Mo⌐o na⌐ñ-neñ i⌐ru⌐ de-syoo ka.

   Mo⌐o na⌐ñ-neñ mo i⌐ru⌐ to omoi-masu.

6. Mo⌐o nañ-ka⌐ḡetu tu⌐zu-ku⌐ desyoo ka.

   Mo⌐o nañ-ka⌐ḡetu mo tu⌐zuku⌐ to omoimasu.

7. Na⌐ñ-niñ ⌐de⌐ru desyoo ka.

   Na⌐ñ-niñ mo ⌐de⌐ru to omoimasu.

J. Level Drill [1]

1. To⌐siyori⌐ nyaa o⌐mosi-ro⌐i daroo kedo—

   To⌐siyori⌐ ni wa o⌐mosiro⌐i da-roo keredo.

2. Zya⌐a, tu⌐zukemasyo⌐o.

   De⌐ wa, tu⌐zukemasyo⌐o.

3. Tu⌐ma⌐ñnai desyoo—ko-⌐ñna e⌐eḡa ḡa.

   Tu⌐mara⌐nai desyoo—ko⌐ñna e⌐eḡa ḡa.

4. A⌐tta⌐kaku na⌐rima⌐sita ⌐ne⌐e.

   A⌐tata⌐kaku na⌐rima⌐sita ⌐ne⌐e.

5. I⌐tte rassya⌐i.

   I⌐tte irassya⌐i.

6. Sa⌐wa⌐izyaa i⌐kemase⌐ñ yo—

   Sa⌐wa⌐ide wa i⌐kemase⌐ñ yo—

7. Sakura wa ⌐mo⌐o sa⌐ite ma⌐su ka—

   Sakura wa ⌐mo⌐o sa⌐ite ima⌐su ka—

8. Ki⌐noo tukattyatta⌐ kara, mo⌐o a⌐rimase⌐ñ.

   Ki⌐noo tukatte simatta⌐ kara, mo⌐o a⌐rimase⌐ñ.

K. Expansion Drill

1. I don't go out.
   I don't go out very much.
   I don't go out very much these days.
   I worry so I don't go out very much these days.
   Even if I have someone stay at the house for me I worry, so I don't go out very much these days.
   No matter who stays at the house for me I worry, so I don't go out very much these days.

   De⌐kakemase⌐ñ.
   A⌐ñmari dekakemase⌐ñ.
   Kono-ḡoro wa a⌐ñmari dekake-mase⌐ñ.
   Si⌐ñpai-suru⌐ kara, kono-ḡoro wa a⌐ñmari dekakemase⌐ñ.
   Ru⌐subañ (o) site moratte⌐ mo, si⌐ñpai-suru⌐ kara; kono-ḡoro wa a⌐ñmari dekake-mase⌐ñ.

   Da⌐re ni ru⌐subañ (o) site moratte⌐ mo, si⌐ñpai-suru⌐ kara; kono-ḡoro wa a⌐ñ-mari dekakemase⌐ñ.

2. I plan to do it.
   I plan to do things like going sight-seeing.

   Su⌐ru tumori de⌐su.
   Ke⌐ñbutu-sita⌐ri suru tumori desu.

---

[1] In each case the sentence on the right contains the uncontracted equivalent of contractions in the sentence on the left.

I plan to do things like going to the country and go-
sight-seeing.

Iⁿaka e itta⌐ri keⁿbutu-sita⌐ri
suru tumori desu.

When I am free I plan to do
things like going to the
country and going sight-
seeing.

Hi⌐ma na toki⌐ [ni], iⁿaka e itta⌐-
ri keⁿbutu-sita⌐ri suru tumori
desu.

Since I took the trouble to
come here, when I am free
I plan to do things like going to the country and going sight-seeing.

Se⌐kkaku kima⌐sita kara; hi⌐ma na
toki⌐ [ni], iⁿaka e itta⌐ri keⁿ-
butu-sita⌐ri suru tumori desu.

Since I came all the way to
Japan, when I am free I
plan to do things like going
to the country and going
sight-seeing.

Sekkaku Niⁿhoⁿ e ki⌐ma⌐sita kara;
hi⌐ma na toki⌐ [ni], iⁿaka e itta⌐ri
keⁿbutu-sita⌐ri suru tumori desu.

3. I stay home.

U⌐ti ni ima⌐su.

I stay home, looking
after the children
and so on.

Ko⌐domo (o) mi⌐tari site, u⌐ti ni
ima⌐su.

I stay home, watching
the house, looking
after the children,
and so on.

Ru⌐subañ (o) sita⌐ri ko⌐domo (o)
mi⌐tari site, u⌐ti ni ima⌐su.

I stay home, always
watching the house,
looking after the
children, and so on.

I⌐tu mo ru⌐subañ (o) sita⌐ri ko-
⌐domo (o) mi⌐tari site, u⌐ti ni
ima⌐su.

Instead of going any-
where, I stay home,
always watching the
house, looking after
the children, and so
on.

Do⌐ko e mo ikana⌐i de; i⌐tu mo
ru⌐subañ (o) sita⌐ri ko⌐domo (o)
mi⌐tari site, u⌐ti ni ima⌐su.

I'm an old man [1] so in-
stead of going any-
where, I stay home,
always watching the
house, looking after
the children, and so
on.

To⌐siyori⌐ da kara, do⌐ko e mo
ikana⌐i de; i⌐tu mo ru⌐subañ (o)
sita⌐ri ko⌐domo (o) mi⌐tari site,
u⌐ti ni ima⌐su.

4. I think it's impossible.

De⌐ki⌐nai to omoimasu.

For old people I think
it's impossible.

To⌐siyori⌐ ni wa de⌐ki⌐nai to
omoimasu.

For young people it's
nothing at all, but for
old people I think it's
impossible.

Wa⌐ka⌐i hito ni wa he⌐eki de⌐su
ḡa, to⌐siyori⌐ ni wa de⌐ki⌐nai
to omoimasu.

---

[1] Or, of course, 'old woman.

This kind of work is nothing at all for young people, but for old people I think it's impossible.	Koñna siḡoto wa wa⌐ka¬i hito ni wa he⌐eki de⌐su ḡa, to⌐siyori¬ ni wa de⌐ki¬nai to omoimasu.

5.
I've reached the point where I understand.	Wa⌐ka¬ru yoo ni na⌐rima⌐sita.
I've gradually reached the point where I understand.	Dañdañ wa⌐ka¬ru yoo ni na⌐ri-ma⌐sita.
I'm doing things like listening to the Japanese radio so I've gradually reached the point where I understand.	Ni⌐hoñ no ra¬zio (o) ki⌐ita¬ri si⌐te (i)ru¬ kara, dañdañ wa-⌐ka¬ru yoo ni na⌐rima⌐sita.
I'm doing things like talking with Japanese and listening to the Japanese radio so I've gradually reached the point where I understand.	Ni⌐hoñzi¬ñ to ha⌐na¬sitari, Ni⌐hoñ no ra¬zio (o) ki⌐ita¬ri si⌐te (i)ru¬ kara; dañdañ wa⌐ka¬ru yoo ni na⌐rima⌐sita.
I'm doing things like studying and talking with Japanese and listening to the Japanese radio so I've gradually reached the point where I understand.	Be⌐ñkyoo-sita¬ri, ni⌐hoñzi¬ñ to ha⌐na¬sitari, Ni⌐hoñ no ra¬zio (o) ki⌐ita¬ri si⌐te (i)ru¬ kara; dañdañ wa⌐ka¬ru yoo ni na⌐ri-ma⌐sita.
I didn't understand but I'm doing things like studying and talking with Japanese and listening to the Japanese radio so I've gradually reached the point where I understand.	Wa⌐kara¬nakatta keredo; be⌐ñkyoo-sita¬ri, ni⌐hoñzi¬ñ to ha⌐na¬sitari, Ni⌐hoñ no ra¬zio (o) ki⌐ita¬ri si⌐te (i)ru¬ kara; dañdañ wa⌐ka¬-ru yoo ni na⌐rima⌐sita.
I didn't understand at all but I'm doing things like studying and talking with Japanese and listening to the Japanese radio so I've gradually reached the point where I understand.	Ze⌐ñzeñ wakara¬nakatta keredo; be⌐ñkyoo-sita¬ri, ni⌐hoñzi¬ñ to ha⌐na¬sitari, Ni⌐hoñ no ra¬zio (o) ki⌐ita¬ri si⌐te (i)ru¬ kara; dañdañ wa⌐ka¬ru yoo ni ⌐a⌐ri-ma⌐sita.
At the beginning I didn't understand at all but	Hazime wa ze⌐ñzeñ wakara¬na-katta keredo; be⌐ñkyoo-sita¬ri,

I'm doing things like studying and talking with Japanese and listening to the Japanese radio so I've gradually reached the point where I understand.

niˈhoñziˈñ to haˈnaˈsitari, Niˈhoñ no raˈzio (o) kiˈitaˈri siˈte (i)ruˈ kara, dañdañ waˈkaˈru yoo ni naˈrimaˈsita.

BASIC DIALOGUES: RESTATEMENT

(with questions)

Dialogue (a)

Kotosi wa ˈaˈme ḡa oˈoˈi desu ḡa, kiˈnoˈo wa meˈzuraˈsiku ˈiˈi ˈteˈñki desita. Tanaka-sañ wa kĭnoo ĭnaka e saˈkura o miˈ ni iˈkimaˈsita. Sakura wa ˈmoˈo saˈite itaˈ kara, kiˈree desita. Kooeñ wa haˈnami no hitoˈ de ĭppai de; miñna oˈsake o noˈñdari, uˈtaˈ o uˈtattaˈri siˈte imaˈsita. Tanaka-sañ wa ŏbeñtoo o motte itte, kiˈ no sita de taˈbemaˈsita. Yuˈuḡata maˈde asoñde, sore kara kaˈerimaˈsita. Kaˈeri no deñsya ḡa koˈñde, Toˈokyoo e tuˈku made zuˈtto taˈtte imasita. Daˈ kara; Tanaka-sañ wa suˈkkaˈri tuˈkaˈrete simatte, kyoˈo wa zeˈñzeñ geˈñki ḡa ˈnaˈi soo desu.

Questions:

1. Koˈtosi no teˈñki wa ˈdoˈo desu ka⌐
2. Kĭnoo no teˈñki wa ˈdoˈo desita ka⌐
3. Tanaka-sañ wa kĭnoo ˈnaˈni o siˈmaˈsita ka⌐
4. Haˈnami no hitoˈ wa ˈnaˈni o siˈte imaˈsita ka⌐
5. Tanaka-sañ wa ˈdoˈko de ˈnaˈni o taˈbemaˈsita ka⌐
6. Tanaka-sañ wa ˈkyoˈo wa ˈgeˈñki ḡa ˈnaˈi soo desu ḡa, doˈo site desu ka⌐

Dialogue (c)

Taˈroo-sañ wa kĭnoo ˈHaˈruko-sañ no uti e ˈnaˈñ-do mo deˈñwa-simaˈsita ḡa, daˈre mo demaseˈñ desita. Haˈruko-sañ wa Kǎmakura e ǎsobi ni itte ite, ruˈsu desita. Haˈruko-sañ no oˈziˈisañ ḡa ruˈsubañ o site imaˈsita keredo; miˈmiˈ ḡa toˈoiˈ kara, deñwa ḡa kiˈkoenaˈkatta ñ desyoo. Haˈruko-sañ wa Kǎmakura de oˈyoˈidari keˈñbutu-sitaˈri site aˈsobimaˈsita ḡa, toˈtemo omosiˈrokatta soo desu.

Questions:

1. Taˈroo-sañ wa kĭnoo ˈHaˈruko-sañ to haˈnasimaˈsita ka⌐ Doˈo site desu ka⌐
2. Daˈre ḡa ruˈsubañ o site imaˈsita ka⌐
3. Doˈo site soˈnoˈ hito wa deˈñwa ni deˈnakatta desyoo ka.
4. Haˈruko-sañ wa Kǎmakura de ˈnaˈni o siˈmaˈsita ka⌐

SHORT SUPPLEMENTARY DIALOGUES

1. Teacher A: He⌐ñ⌐ desu ⌐ne⌐e. Su⌐misu-sañ wa, hi ni yotte, yo⌐ku waʰkaˑ-
   ttari ze⌐ñzeñ wakaraˑnakattari suʰruˑ ñ desu yo⌐ Do⌐o site
   desyoo.
   Teacher B: Hi ni yotte ⌐yo⌐ku beʰñkyoo-sitaˑri ze⌐ñzeñ sinaˑkattari suʰruˑ kara desyoo?
   Teacher A: So⌐o desyoo ⌐ne⌐e.

2. Taro: Nitiyoo ni U⌐eno-ko⌐oeñ e itte ʰneˑe.
   Yukio: A⌐a ⌐so⌐o.
   Taro: *Zu⌐ibuñ hiʰto ḡa de⌐te ta yo⌐
   Yukio: So⌐o daroo. Haʰnami no hito⌐ daroo? Sakura ⌐do⌐o datta?
   Taro: Ma⌐da su⌐ko⌐si sika saʰite inaˑkatta ḡa ⌐ne⌐e. Ki⌐ no sita de hĭto
   ḡa taʰkusañ no⌐ñdari sa⌐wa⌐idari site ʰneˑe.
   Yukio: Kimi mo?
   Taro: Bo⌐ku wa sake wa dame⌐ da kara ʰneˑe. Beʰñto⌐o ʰtaˑbete kita
   yo.

3. Smith: A⌐nataḡata ni⌐ wa koʰñna zassi ḡa omosiro⌐i desyoo ḡa, waʰta-
   kusi⌐tati ni wa mu⌐zukasisuḡi⌐ru kara, ze⌐ñzeñ omosi⌐roku ⌐ha⌐i
   ñ desu yo.
   Tanaka: Mo⌐tto ya⌐sasii zassi mo a⌐ru kara, so⌐ñna⌐ no o ʰyo⌐ñda hoo ḡa
   ʰiˑi desyoo ⌐ne⌐e.

4. Mr. Tanaka: Koñna siḡoto wa na⌐ñ-zi⌐kañ mo kaʰkaˑru kara, ko⌐ñbañ ⌐ka⌐-
   eru made hŏka no siḡoto wa deʰki⌐nai to oʰmoˑu yo⌐
   Secretary: A⌐a, so⌐o desu ka.
   Mr. Tanaka: Da⌐ kara, da⌐re ḡa kiʰteˑ mo a⌐e⌐nai ñ da yo.
   Secretary: Wa⌐karima⌐sita.

5. Tanaka: Kono tuḡi na⌐ñyo⌐obi ni kiʰmasyoˑo ka.
   Smith: Na⌐ñyo⌐obi ni kiʰteˑ mo kaʰmaimaseˑñ ḡa, a⌐sa no uti ni kite⌐
   kudasai. Go⌐ḡo wa da⌐re mo ina⌐i kara.
   Tanaka: Wa⌐karima⌐sita. Zya⌐a, a⌐sa ʰha⌐yaku kimasu.

English Equivalents

1. Teacher A: Isn't it strange! Depending on the day, Mr. Smith either
   understands very well or doesn't understand at all.   Why
   would that be?
   Teacher B: Wouldn't it be because, depending on the day, he either studies hard or doesn't study at all?
   Teacher A: I guess that's it.

2. Taro: I went to Ueno Park on Sunday . . .
   Yukio: Oh.
   Taro: There were an awful lot of people out.
   Yukio: I guess so. You mean people looking at the cherry blossoms, don't
   you? How were the cherry blossoms?
   Taro: There were still only a few in bloom but lots of people were drink-
   ing and making a racket under the trees and . . .

Yukio: You too?
Taro: I can't drink sake so . . . I went and ate my lunch.

3. Smith: For you this kind of magazine is probably interesting, but for us
              it isn't at all interesting because it's too difficult.
    Tanaka: There are some easier magazines too so it would probably be
              better to read one like that, wouldn't it.

4. Tanaka: Work like this takes any number of hours so I don't think I can
              do any other work [right up] until I go home tonight.
    Secretary: Oh.
    Tanaka: That's why — no matter who comes — I won't be able to see him.
    Secretary: I see.

5. Tanaka: What day shall I come the next time?
    Smith: It doesn't matter what day you come but please come during the
              morning — since no one is here in the afternoon.
    Tanaka: I see.   Then I'll come early in the morning.

EXERCISES

1. Describe a weekend trip — where, how, and with whom you went, what you
    did, what you saw, the weather, etc. Include as many details as possible,
    but restrict yourself to those you are sure you can express in natural Jap-
    anese.

2. Suggest to a Japanese friend that you:

    (a) go to see the cherry blossoms on Sunday.
    (b) go swimming on Saturday.
    (c) go sight-seeing tomorrow afternoon.
    (d) take a box lunch.
    (e) sing some Japanese songs.
    (f) wait here until Taro comes.
    (g) stop in at a tearoom on the way home and have something cold
         to drink.
    (h) telepnone Mr. Ueda instead of writing a letter, because letters
         are a chore.

3. Make up ten short dialogues, each one of which contains one of the follow-
    ing:

    a. sosite
    b. da⌐kara
    c. ta⌐betari
    d. su⌐kka⌐ri
    e. me⌐zura⌐siku
    f. wa⌐takusi⌐tati
    g. na⌐ni mo
    h. na⌐ñ-zi⌐kañ mo
    i. na⌐ñ te i⌐tte⌐ mo
    j. ku⌐ru made

Lesson 28. Theater

BASIC DIALOGUES: FOR MEMORIZATION

(a)

Smith

a play or a show	sibai
see (a thing) or look at	haikeñ-suru ⁺ or
	go⌐rañ ni na⌐ru ⁺

1. Is that a theatrical magazine? Si⌐bai no zassi de⌐su ka⌐ Tyo⌐-
   I'll have a look at it. tto haikeñ-simasu.

Tanaka

(form of traditional	kabuki
Japanese theater)	

2. Have you seen kabuki? Ka⌐buki (o) gorañ ni narima⌐-
   sita ka⌐

Smith

by all means	ze⌐hi
lead	tureru /-ru/
take (people and animals)	turete (i)ku

3. Not yet; (so) do take me some Ma⌐da desu kara, ze⌐hi i⌐ti-do
   (lit. one) time. turete (i)⁴tte kudasai.

Tanaka

4. Yes, any time at all, when E⌐e, i⌐tu de⌐ mo, go⌐tuḡoo no i⌐i
   it's convenient for you. toki ni.

Smith

readily or easily	su⌐ḡu

5. Can tickets be bought easily? Kippu (wa) ⌐su⌐ḡu ka⌐eru⌐ ñ desu
   ka⌐

Tanaka

problem	moñdai

6. The tickets are the problem Ki⌐ppu ḡa mondai de⌐su ḡa ⌐ne⁴e.
   but—you know how it is.

advance sale	maeuri
not easily or not readily	nakanaka /+ negative/

7. It's better to buy [tickets] in ad- Ma⌐euri (o) katt(e) o⌐ita hoo ḡa
   vance but you can't buy them ⌐i⁴i ñ desu ḡa, na⌐kanaka kaena⌐i
   easily. ñ desu yo.

Smith

is difficult to buy	ka⌐iniku⌐i /-ku/

159

8. In America too, tickets for good shows are hard to buy. — A⌐merika de⌐ mo, i⌐i sibai no kippu (wa) ka⌐iniku⌐i n̄ desu yo.

    the act of buying — ka⌐u⌐ no
    in the process of buying or for buying — ka⌐u⌐ no ni
    if or when [someone] does — si⌐ta⌐ra
    how or what should [someone] do — do⌐o sitara ⌐i⌐i

9. What should you do to buy tickets? — Ki⌐ppu (o) kau⌐ no ni (wa), do⌐o sitara ⌐i⌐i n̄ desyoo ka.

                Tanaka

    if or when [someone] sees — mi⌐tara
    if or when [someone] tries telephoning — de⌐n̄wa-site mi⌐tara

10. You inquire by telephone. How would it be if I tried telephoning now? or Why don't I try telephoning now? — De⌐n̄wa de kiku⌐ n̄ desu ḡa, i⌐ma de⌐n̄wa-site mi⌐tara ⌐do⌐o desyoo.

                Smith

11. Would you? — O⌐neḡai-sima⌐su.

                (b)

        Ticket-seller (on the telephone)

    (kabuki theater in Tokyo) — Kabukiza
12. Hello. (This is the) Kabukiza. — Mo⌐simosi. Ka⌐bukiza de gozaima⌐su.

                Tanaka

    evening — yo⌐ru
    evening performance — yo⌐ru no bu
13. Do you still have two first-class [tickets] for the evening performance on the tenth? — Too-ka no ⌐yo⌐ru no bu, it-too ⌐ni⌐-mai, ma⌐da ⌐a⌐ru desyoo ka.

                Ticket-seller

    sellout — urikire
14. We're entirely sold out through the twentieth. — Ha⌐tu-ka ma⌐de ⌐ze⌐n̄bu u⌐rikire de gozaima⌐su.

    after that or later than that — so⌐re-i⌐ḡo
    being after that is all right — so⌐re-i⌐ḡo de yorosii
    if it's all right — yo⌐rosi⌐kattara
15. If after that is all right, there are still a few left (but) . . . — So⌐re-i⌐ḡo de yo⌐rosi⌐kattara, ma⌐da su⌐ko⌐si no⌐ko⌐tte orimasu ḡa_

Tanaka

	discuss <u>or</u> talk over	soodañ-suru
16.	Well, I'll talk it over; (so) just a moment please.	Zya⌐a, so⌐odañ-suru⌐ kara, tyo⌐-tto ⌐ma⌐tte kudasai.

. . .

| 17. | Hello. I'm sorry to have kept you waiting. It will be all right even if it's after the 'twentieth (but). . . | Mo⌐simosi. O⌐matase-sima⌐sita. Ha⌐tu-ka-i⌐ḡo de mo ⌐i⌐i ñ desu ḡa— |

Ticket-seller

	adjoin	tuzuku /-u/
18.	We have two first-class [seats] for the twenty-fourth but the seats aren't adjoining. Would they be all right?	Ni⌐zyuu yo-kka no it-too ⌐ni⌐-mai go⌐zaima⌐su ḡa, o⌐se⌐ki (ḡa) tu⌐zu-ite orimaseñ ḡa; yo⌐rosi⌐i desyoo ka.

Tanaka

	supposing adjoining seats if <u>or</u> when there are	mo⌐si tu⌐zuita se⌐ki a⌐ttara
19.	If there are adjoining seats, even second class will be all right (but). . .	Mo⌐si tu⌐zuita se⌐ki ḡa ⌐a⌐ttara, ni-⌐too de⌐ mo ⌐i⌐i desu ḡa—
20.	I'd like seats as near the center as possible.	Narubeku ma⌐ññaka no ho⌐o no ⌐se⌐ki (o) oneḡai-simasu.

Ticket-seller

| 21. | We have adjoining second-class seats for the twenty-sixth (but). . . | Ni⌐zyuu ro⌐ku-niti⌐ no ni⌐-too no tu⌐zuita ose⌐ki (ḡa) go⌐zaima⌐su ḡa— |

Tanaka

	put aside for future use	to⌐tte oku
22.	Then would you put them aside for me? (Because) I'll come (lit. go) to pick them up right away.	Zya⌐a, so⌐re (o) to⌐tt(e) oite ku-⌐remase⌐ñ ka⌐ Su⌐ḡu ⌐to⌐ri ni i⌐ku⌐ kara.
23.	I'm Yukio Tanaka.	Ta⌐naka Yukio de⌐su.

Ticket-seller

| 24. | Certainly. I'll be waiting (so). . . | Ka⌐sikomarima⌐sita. Zya⌐a, o⌐mati-site orima⌐su kara. |

(c)

Smith

	come to an end	owaru /-u/

the time (lit. one) when
   it ends

25. About what time does it end?

owaru⌐ no

O⌐waru⌐ no (wa) na⌐n̄-zi-ḡo⌐ro desyoo ka.

Tanaka

the end

26. If you see it from beginning
   to end it takes all of five
   hours.

27. Therefore it must end about
   eleven o'clock. (Lit. As for
   the time when it ends, it
   must get to be about
   11 o'clock.)

owari

Ha⌐zime kara owari ma⌐de ⌐mi⌐-
tara, go-⌐zi⌐kan̄ mo ka⌐ka⌐ru n̄
desu yo⌐

Da⌐ kara, o⌐waru⌐ no (wa) zyu-
⌐uiti-zi-ḡo⌐ro ni ⌐na⌐ru desyoo
⌐ne⌐e.

Smith

to that extent

28. Do you mean it takes that long?

son̄na ni

So⌐n̄na ni kaka⌐ru n̄ desu ka.

Tanaka

if it isn't interesting

29. If it isn't interesting you
   don't have to see it through
   to the end.

various dining rooms

curtain or act
between acts

30. There are all kinds of dining
   rooms inside the Kabukiza
   and you can eat between the
   acts (but). . .

o⌐mosi⌐roku ⌐na⌐kattara

O⌐mosi⌐roku ⌐na⌐kattara, o⌐wari
ma⌐de ⌐mi⌐nakute mo ⌐i⌐i n̄ desu yo⌐

iroiro na syokudoo or
  iron̄ na syokudoo

ma⌐ku⌐
maku no aida or makuai
Ka⌐bukiza no na⌐ka ni i⌐ron̄ na
syokudoo ḡa a⌐tte, makuai ni
ta⌐berare⌐ru n̄ desu ḡa—

Smith

if or when [someone]
  goes
as soon as [someone]
  goes
reserve
reserve in advance
if or when [someone]
  reserves in advance

31. How would it be if we reserved
   a table as soon as we got
   there (lit. went)?

i⌐tta⌐ra

i⌐tta⌐ra ⌐su⌐ḡu

yoyaku-suru
yoyaku-site oku
yo⌐yaku-sit(e) o⌐itara

I⌐tta⌐ra ⌐su⌐ḡu te⌐eburu (o) yo-
yaku-sit(e) o⌐itara ⌐do⌐o desyoo.

Tanaka

32. Let's do that.

So⌐o simasyo⌐o.

Smith

this time (i.e. this next	ko⌐ndo
time or this last time)	
plot	su⌐zi
simple or brief	kañtañ /na/
explain	setumee-suru

33. Some time when you're free,   I⌐tu ka o⌐hima na to⌐ki /ni/,
     would you explain briefly the   ko⌐ndo ⌐mi⌐ru si⌐bai no su⌐zi
     plot of the play we're going   (o) ka⌐ñtañ ni setumee-site ita-
     to see this time?   dakemase⌐ñ ka.

Tanaka

| complicated | hukuzatu /na/ |
| anyway or at any rate | to⌐nikaku |

34. It's rather complicated so I   Na⌐kanaka hukuzatu de⌐su kara,
     can't explain it very briefly   a⌐ñmari kañtañ ni⌐ wa se⌐tumee-
     but. . . Anyway I'll try (do-   dekimase⌐ñ ga ⌐ne⌐e. To⌐nikaku
     ing).   si⌐te mimasyo⌐o.

ADDITIONAL VOCABULARY

1. Have you seen <u>ballet</u> yet?   Mo⌐o ⌐ba⌐ree (o) go⌐rañ ni nari-
                                        ma⌐sita ka⌐

(a form of classical	no⌐o [1]
Japanese drama)	
(traditional Japanese	bu⌐ñraku
puppet theater)	
modern drama	siñḡeki
dance or dancing	odori
(Japanese style)	
dance or dancing	da⌐ñsu
(Western style)	

2. Do you like this kind of <u>music</u>?   Ko⌐ñna o⌐ñḡaku (wa) o⌐suki de⌐su
                                            ka⌐

concert	o⌐ñḡaku⌐kai [2]
orchestra	o⌐oke⌐sutora
opera	ka⌐ḡeki or o⌐pera

3. Isn't he good—that <u>musician</u>!   U⌐ma⌐i desu ⌐ne⌐e — ano <u>oñḡakuka</u> [3]
                                         wa.

actor or actress	yakusya or haiyuu
actress	zyoyuu
star (i.e. leading player)	su⌐ta⌐a

---

[1] Women usually use polite <u>onoo</u>+.

[2] Has contracted alternant: o⌐ñḡa⌐kkai.

[3] Has contracted alternant: oñḡakka.

NOTES ON THE BASIC DIALOGUES

1. Haikeñ-suru ꜛ and goꜛrañ ni naꜛru ꜛ are the polite equivalents of miꜛru. Haikeñ-suru is polite in a humbling sense, and is used most commonly when the thing looked at belongs to the person addressed (i.e. 'I look at something of yours'). Goꜛrañ ni naꜛru is polite in an honorific sense. Haikeñ and gorañ occur alone and at the end of longer sentences as informal polite requests: Haikeñ. 'Let me see!'; Gorañ. 'Look!'

3. Zeꜛhi occurs most frequently in request sentences and with -tai 'want to —— ' words.
Note also: tuꜛrete kuꜛru 'bring (people and animals).'

10. Note the use of ḡa connecting a statement and a closely related question.

13. Yoꜛru occurs both as a slightly more formal equivalent of bañ meaning 'evening' or 'night,' and as the opposite of hiꜛruꜛ 'daytime' meaning 'night-time.'
Hiru no bu and maꜛtinee both occur as equivalents of 'daytime performance.'

15. 'but—would that be all right?'
The opposite of -iꜛḡo is -iꜛzeñ 'before.' Both words occur directly following time expressions (which lose their accents). Thus: saꜛñ-zi-iꜛḡo 'after 3 o'clock'; geꜛtuyoobi-iꜛḡo 'after Monday'; goꜛzyuu roku-neñ-iꜛzeñ 'before '56.'

16. Note also the nominal soodañ 'discussion.'

17. 'but—what seats do you have?'

18. See the note on Sentence 10 above.

19. 'but—do you have any of those?'

21. 'but—would they be all right?'

24. 'so—be sure to come.'

26. The nominal owari is derived from the verbal owaru. A nominal derived from a verbal is regularly the verbal stem (the -maꜛsu form minus -maꜛsu), with one accent difference: normally a nominal derived from an accented verbal is also accented, but on its final syllable. Thus: haꜛnasiꜛ 'talk (noun)' or 'speech' from haꜛnaꜛsu 'talk (verb),' yaꜛsumiꜛ 'rest (noun),' or 'vacation' from yaꜛsuꜛmu 'rest (verb),' kaꜛeriꜛ 'return (noun)' from kaꜛeru 'return (verb),' and koori 'ice (noun)' from kooru 'freeze (verb).'

28. Note also koñna ni 'to this extent,' añna ni 'to that extent,' and doꜛñna ni 'to what extent?'

30. 'but—would you like to do that?'
Iroñ na (+ nominal) is the less formal, more conversational equivalent of iroiro na (+ nominal). Remember that when iroiro modifies an inflected expression, it occurs without a following particle. Thus: Iꜛroiro na kotoꜛ o iꜛimaꜛsita. 'I said various things.' But: Iꜛroiro hanasimaꜛsita. 'I talked about all sorts of things (lit. variously).' The iroñ alternant occurs only before na.

33. Note also the nominal setumee 'explanation.'

GRAMMATICAL NOTES

1. The Conditional

Mi˥tara		mi˥ru 'see.'
O˹ita˺ra		oku 'place.'
A˥ttara		a˥ru 'be (in a place)'
	is the CONDITIONAL of	or 'have.'
I˹tta˺ra		iku 'go.'
Si˹ta˺ra		suru 'do.'
Yo˹rosi˺kattara		yorosii 'is all right.'
Na˹kattara		na˥i 'there isn't.'

Inflected words (verbals, adjectivals, and copula) have CONDITIONAL forms, meaning 'if or when so-and-so happens or happened or had happened' or 'if it is or was or had been so-and-so.' A conditional form regularly refers to a single instance; it is never equivalent to 'whenever ——.'

To form the conditional of any inflected word, add -ra to its past. The accent of a past and its corresponding conditional are the same, except that a verbal conditional derived from an unaccented past is accented on its next-to-last syllable (-ta). Thus:

Verbal: tu˥ku 'arrive'; past, tu˥ita; conditional, tu˥itara [1] 'if or when [someone] arrives or arrived or had arrived'

Adjectival: sa˹mu˺i 'is cold'; past, sa˥mukatta; conditional, sa˥mukattara 'if it is or was or had been cold'

Copula: da; past, da˥tta; conditional, da˥ttara [1]

as in: so˹re da˺ttara 'if it is or was or had been that'

To˹okyoo kara da˺ttara 'if it is or was or had been from Tokyo'

i˹ku˺ ñ dattara 'if it is or was or had been a matter of going'

Like the gerund, the conditional is tenseless. Study the following examples, noting particularly how the final inflected forms determine the time:

(a) Kyo˥oto e i˪tta˥ra, Ta˹naka-sañ ni aima˥su.
    'If (or when) I go to Kyoto, I'll see Mr. Tanaka.'

(b) Kyo˥oto e i˪tta˥ra, Ta˹naka-sañ ni aima˥sita.
    'When I went to Kyoto, I saw Mr. Tanaka.'

(c) Kyo˥oto e i˪tta˥ra, Ta˹naka-sañ ni a˥tta ñ desu ḡa_
    'If I had gone to Kyoto, I would have seen Mr. Tanaka (but)...'

Compare example (b) with:

(d) Kyo˥oto e i˪tta toki˥ ni, Ta˹naka-sañ ni aima˥sita.
    'When I went to Kyoto, I saw Mr. Tanaka.'

Sentence (b) states a condition or set of circumstances and the result, whereas sentence (d) tells at what time an action took place. Sentence (b) answers the question 'under what circumstances?' and (d) answers the question 'when?'

Mo˥si 'supposing' may occur at the beginning of a condition. It is an advance signal of the condition, and emphasizes its suppositional character.

---

[1] A more formal conditional is made by adding -ra to the formal past of of verbals and the copula: thus, tu˹kima˥sitara, de˥sitara.

A condition, consisting of or ending with a conditional, plus do⌐o desu ka, do⌐o desyoo ka, etc. is a suggestion: 'how will or would it be if someone does or did so-and-so?' It is the Japanese equivalent of English 'why don't [you] do so-and-so?' used as a suggestion.

Examples:

Te⌐ḡami o ka⌐itara ⌐do⌐o desu ka.
'Why don't [you] write a letter?' or
'How will it be if [you] write a letter?'
Se⌐ñse⌐e ni ki⌐ita⌐ra ⌐do⌐o desyoo ka.
'Why don't [you] ask the teacher?' or
'How would it be if [you] asked the teacher?'

A condition, consisting of or ending with a conditional, plus √i⌐i 'it's good' is equivalent to English '[someone] should do so-and-so,' i.e. 'if [someone] does so-and-so, it will be good.' This construction frequently occurs with a question word in the condition.

Examples:

Kono miti o ma⌐ssu⌐ḡu i⌐tta⌐ra ⌐i⌐i desyoo.
'[You] should probably go straight along this street.' (Lit. 'It will probably be good if [you] go straight along this street.')
Do⌐o sitara ⌐i⌐i.
'What should [I] do?' (Lit. If [I] do what, will it be good?)
Do⌐ko de ki⌐ita⌐ra ⌐i⌐i desyoo ka.
'Where should [I] ask?' (Lit. 'If [I] asked where, would it be good?')

Do not confuse the following three kinds of patterns, all of which may contain 'should' in their English equivalents:

Do⌐o i⌐tta⌐ra ⌐i⌐i desyoo ka.
'How should I go?' (Lit. 'If I go how would it be good?')
Ha⌐yaku i⌐tta ho⌐o ḡa ⌐i⌐i desu yo⌐
'You should go early.' (I.e. 'It would be better to go early.')
Mo⌐o i⌐ru hazu de⌐su ḡa⌐
'He should be there already but [I don't know whether he is or not].'
(I.e. 'It is expected that he is there already.')

When a conditional is followed by a past form of i⌐i plus ḡa [⌐ne⌐e] or ke(re)do [⌐ne⌐e], the combination is equivalent to an English past wish: 'I wish so-and-so had happened.' Thus:

Tanaka-sañ ḡa ⌐ha⌐yaku ⌐ki⌐tara ⌐yo⌐katta ñ desu ḡa ⌐ne⌐e.
'I wish Mr. Tanaka had come early.' (Lit. 'If Mr. Tanaka had come early it would have been good but [he didn't], isn't that right.')
Mo⌐tto ⌐hu⌐ttara ⌐yo⌐katta keredo⌐
'I wish it had rained more.' (Lit. 'Although it would have been good if it had rained more [it didn't].')

Additional examples:

Ta⌐naka-sañ ḡa irassya⌐ttara, de⌐ñwa o ka⌐kete kudasai.
'If (or when) Mr. Tanaka comes, please telephone me.'

A⌐merika┐ e itta⌐ra┐ ⌐su┐gu e⌐e┐go ḡa zyoozu┐ ni ⌐na┐ru desyoo.

'As soon as you go to America, you will probably become proficient in English.' (Lit. 'When you go to America, immediately your English will probably become skillful.')

A⌐ñmari ta┐kakattara, ka⌐wana┐i de ne?

'If it's too expensive, don't buy it, will you?'

Ta⌐beta┐ku ⌐na┐kattara, ta⌐be┐nakute mo ka⌐maimase┐ñ.

'If you don't want to eat, you don't have to.'

O⌐dekake ni narita┐kattara, do⌐ozo go⌐eñryo na┐ku.

'If you want to go out, please don't hesitate.'

I┐i ⌐te┐ñki dattara i⌐kima┐su ḡa, a┐me ḡa ⌐hu┐ttara ya⌐mema┐su.

'If it's nice weather I'll go, but if it rains, I'll give up [the idea].'

Si⌐tte ita┐ra si⌐na┐katta to omoimasu.

'I think that if he had known, he wouldn't have done it.'

A⌐no sakana o tabe⌐nakattara, byo⌐oki ni nara┐nakatta desyoo.

'If I hadn't eaten that fish, I probably wouldn't have gotten sick.'

Ko⌐ra┐retara, ze┐hi ki⌐te┐ kudasai.

'If you can come, by all means do (come).'

Zi⌐do┐osya de i⌐ku┐ ñ dattara, bo┐ku mo i⌐kita┐katta ñ desu yo⌐

'If it had been a case of going by car, I'd have wanted to go too.'

2. More About Nominal no 'one[s]'

The nominal no 'one' or 'ones' may refer to a person, thing, place, time, or act, depending on context.

Compare the following examples:

(no referring to person)   O⌐sieru┐ no wa ⌐da┐re desu ka⌐
   'Who is it who teaches?'

(no referring to thing)   O⌐sieru┐ no wa ⌐na┐ñ desu ka⌐
   'What is it you teach?'

(no referring to place)   O⌐sieru┐ no wa ⌐do┐ko desu ka⌐
   'Where is it you teach?'

(no referring to time)   O⌐sieru┐ no wa na⌐ñyo┐o desu ka⌐
   'What day is it you teach?'

(no referring to act)   O⌐sieru┐ no wa o⌐mosiro┐i desyoo?
   'Teaching (i. e. the act of teaching) is interesting, isn't it?'

The nominal no referring to 'act,' with an appropriate preceding sentence modifier, may occur as a grammatical subject, object, topic, goal, etc. Note the last example above and study the following pairs:

Ko⌐ñna sibai ḡa omosiro┐i desu. 'This kind of play is interesting.'

Ko⌐ñna sibai o mi┐ru no ḡa o⌐mosiro┐i desu. '(The act of) seeing this kind of play is interesting.'

Ni⌐hoñgo no beñkyoo o yamema┐sita. 'I've given up the study of Japanese.'

Ni⌐hoñgo o beñkyoo-suru┐ no o ya⌐mema┐sita. 'I've given up (the act of) studying Japanese.'

Su⌐zi wa hu⌐kuzatu de⌐su. 'The plot is complicated.'
Su⌐zi o se⌐tumee-suru⌐ no wa hu⌐kuzatu de⌐su. '(The act of) explain-
   ing the plot is complicated.'

   The nominal no referring to an act closely resembles ko⌐to⌐ in meaning
and general usage, but depending upon the particular pattern, no may be preferred, or ko⌐to⌐ may be preferred, or either one may be used (with the ko-
⌐to⌐ alternative slightly more formal). In general, no is more common in
conversation except in a few fixed expressions: for example, —— ko⌐to⌐ ḡa
de⌐ki⌐ru (Lesson 25, Grammatical Note 1, end).

   Examples:

      A⌐ru⌐ku no wa i⌐ya⌐ desu.
         'I dislike walking.' (Lit. 'The act of walking is displeasing.')
      Ni⌐hoñḡo o beñkyoo-suru⌐ no wa mu⌐zukasi⌐i desu ⌐ne⌐e.
         '(The act of) studying Japanese is difficult, isn't it.'
      Ha⌐yaku ne⌐ru⌐ no ḡa su⌐ki⌐ desu.
         'I like going to bed early.' (Lit. 'The act of going to bed early is
         pleasing.')
      Ha⌐ya⌐i no wa ⌐ke⌐kkoo desu ḡa, o⌐so⌐i no wa ko⌐marima⌐su.
         '(The act of) being early is fine but (the act of) being late causes
         problems.'

3. —— no ni (wa)

   The nominal no occurs preceded by an informal non-past verbal and followed by particles ni (wa), meaning 'in the process of doing so-and-so.' This
pattern is especially common in general statements.

   Examples:

      O⌐taku e iku⌐ no ni (wa) Si⌐ñbasi⌐-eki no ⌐so⌐ba o to⌐orima⌐su ka↲
         'In going to your house, do you pass near Shimbashi Station?'
      Kore wa ⌐zu⌐ibuñ a⌐tu⌐i kara, tu⌐metaku suru⌐ no ni (wa) ko̅ori ḡa ta-
      ⌐kusañ irima⌐su.
         'This is very hot so in making it cold you need lots of ice.'
      Ni⌐hoñḡo o oboe⌐ru no ni (wa) zi⌐kañ ḡa kaka⌐ru desyoo?
         'It takes time—doesn't it—to learn Japanese?'

4. tu⌐zuita se⌐ki

   Intransitive verbals, particularly those meaning 'become so-and-so,' often
occur in the informal past as sentence modifiers of nominals. Thus:

      tuzuku 'adjoin'; tu⌐zuita se⌐ki 'adjoining seats' (lit. 'seats that have ad-
         joined')
      tu⌐kare⌐ru 'become tired'; tu⌐ka⌐reta hito 'tired person' (lit. 'person
         who has become tired')
      aku '[something] opens'; a⌐ita ma⌐do 'open window'
      no⌐ko⌐ru 'become left behind'; no⌐ko⌐tta mono 'left-over things'
      ti⌐ḡa⌐u 'be different' or 'be wrong'; ti⌐ḡa⌐tta hito 'different person' or
         'wrong person'

Less frequently, the corresponding gerund + (i)ru occurs, with about the same meaning (for example, tu⌐ka⌐rete (i)ru hito 'tired person'—lit. 'person who is tired').

5. Compound Adjectivals Ending in √-niku⌐i and √-yasu⌐i/ -i⌐i

The stem of a verbal (the -ma⌐su form minus -ma⌐su) compounded with -niku⌐i is an adjectival meaning 'cause difficulty in doing so-and-so.' The stem of a verbal + -yasu⌐i or -i⌐i [1] has the exact opposite meaning. Thus:

ka⌐kiniku⌐i 'cause difficulty   ka⌐kiyasu⌐i or ka⌐kii⌐i 'make
    in writing'   writing easy'
yo⌐miniku⌐i 'cause difficulty   yo⌐miyasu⌐i or yo⌐mii⌐i 'make
    in reading'   reading easy'
wa⌐kariniku⌐i 'cause difficulty   wa⌐kariyasu⌐i or wa⌐karii⌐i
    in understanding'   'make understanding easy'
o⌐boeniku⌐i 'cause difficulty   o⌐boeyasu⌐i or o⌐boei⌐i 'make
    in remembering'   remembering easy'

Examples:

Ko⌐no kami⌐ wa ka⌐kiyasu⌐i desu. 'This paper is easy to write on.'
Ko⌐no peñ wa ka⌐kiyasu⌐i desu. 'This pen is easy to write with.'
Koñna tori wa ta⌐beniku⌐i desu ⌐ne⌐e. 'This kind of chicken is hard to
    eat, isn't it!'
Ko⌐ñna ha⌐si wa ta⌐beniku⌐i desu ⌐ne⌐e. 'Chopsticks like these are hard
    to eat with, aren't they!'
Ne⌐niku⌐i ⌐be⌐tto desu ⌐ne⌐e. 'It's a bed that's hard to sleep in, isn't it!'
Tu⌐kaii⌐i zi⌐biki⌐ o ka⌐ima⌐sita yo⌐ 'Say, I bought a dictionary that's
    easy to use.'

With some verbal stems, the -yasu⌐i compound indicates ease in the sense of likelihood of occurrence. Thus:

ko⌐boreyasu⌐i 'is likely to   ka⌐wariyasu⌐i 'is likely to
    spill,' 'spill easily'   change,' 'change readily'

Such compounds do not have an alternant with -i⌐i.

DRILLS

A. Substitution Drill

1. I want to go and see, by all   Ze⌐hi i⌐tte mita⌐i ñ desu.
   means.
2. At any rate, I want to go   To⌐nikaku i⌐tte mita⌐i ñ desu.
   and see.
3. That is why I want to go   Da⌐ kara i⌐tte mita⌐i ñ desu.
   and see.
4. After this, I want to go   Kore kara i⌐tte mita⌐i ñ desu.
   and see.
5. However, I want to go   Ke⌐redo i⌐tte mita⌐i ñ desu.
   and see.
6. I want to go and see (al-   Mo⌐o i⌐tte mita⌐i ñ desu.
   ready) now.

------

[1]
The inflection of -i⌐i is the same as that of i⌐i 'is good': -yo⌐ku, -yo⌐kute, etc.

B. Substitution Drill

1. He doesn't readily under-   Na⌐kanaka wakarimase⌐ñ ⌐ne⌐e.
    stand, does he.

2. He doesn't understand at   Ze⌐ñzeñ wakarimase⌐ñ ⌐ne⌐e.
    all, does he.

3. He doesn't understand   A⌐ñmari wakarimase⌐ñ ⌐ne⌐e.
    very well, does he.

4. He doesn't understand   Ma⌐da wa⌐karimase⌐ñ ⌐ne⌐e.
    yet, does he.

5. He doesn't understand   Mo⌐o wa⌐karimase⌐ñ ⌐ne⌐e.
    any more, does he.

6. He doesn't understand   Ti⌐tto⌐ mo wa⌐karimase⌐ñ ⌐ne⌐e.
    a bit, does he.

C. Substitution Drill

1. It would be better to buy   Ma⌐euri (o) katt(e) o⌐ita hoo ḡa
    tickets in advance but I   ⌐i⌐i ñ desu ḡa, na⌐kanaka kae-
    can't buy them easily.   na⌐i ñ desu yo.

2. It would be better to for-   Wa⌐sureta ho⌐o ḡa ⌐i⌐i ñ desu
    get but I can't forget   ḡa, na⌐kanaka wasurerarena⌐i
    easily. /wasureru/   ñ desu yo.

3. It would be better to   O⌐bo⌐eta hoo ḡa ⌐i⌐i ñ desu ḡa,
    learn it but I can't learn   na⌐kanaka oboerare⌐nai ñ desu
    it easily. /o⌐boe⌐ru/   yo.

4. It would be better to fix   Ha⌐yaku na⌐o⌐sita hoo ḡa ⌐i⌐i ñ
    it quickly but I can't fix   desu ḡa, na⌐kanaka naose⌐nai
    it easily. /ha⌐yaku   ñ desu yo.
    na⌐o⌐su/

5. It would be better to quit   Tabako (o) ya⌐meta ho⌐o ḡa ⌐i⌐i
    smoking but I can't quit   ñ desu ḡa, na⌐kanaka yamera-
    easily. /tabako (o)   rena⌐i ñ desu yo.
    yāmeru/

6. It would be better to turn   A⌐no suto⌐obu (o) ke⌐sita ho⌐o ḡa
    off that heater but I can't   ⌐i⌐i ñ desu ḡa, na⌐kanaka ke-
    turn it off easily. /a⌐no   sena⌐i ñ desu yo.
    suto⌐obu (o) kēsu/

D. Substitution Drill (based on Grammatical Note 1)

1. If (or when) my friend   To⌐modati ḡa ki⌐tara, so⌐odañ-
    comes, we'll talk it over.   sima⌐su.

2. If my friend had come,   To⌐modati ḡa ki⌐tara, so⌐odañ-
    we would have talked it   sita⌐ ñ desu ḡa—
    over . . .

3. If (or when) my friend   To⌐modati ḡa ki⌐tara, so⌐odañ-
    comes, let's talk it   simasyo⌐o.
    over.

4. If (or when) my friend   To⌐modati ḡa ki⌐tara, so⌐odañ-
    comes, I'd like to talk   sita⌐i ñ desu ḡa—
    it over . . .

5. If (or when) my friend   To⌐modati ḡa ki⌐tara, so⌐odañ-
   comes, I think I'll talk   siyoo to omoima⌐su.
   it over.

E. Substitution Drill (based on Grammatical Note 1)

1. If you study, you'll   Be⌐ñkyoo-sita⌐ra, yo⌐ku wa⌐ka⌐ru
   probably understand   desyoo.
   very well.

2. If you ask the teacher,   Se⌐ñse⌐e ni ki⌐ita⌐ra, yo⌐ku wa-
   you'll probably under-   ⌐ka⌐ru desyoo.
   stand very well.
   /se⌐ñse⌐e ni kiku/

3. If you have the plot ex-   Su⌐zi (o) se⌐tumee-site moratta⌐ra,
   plained, you'll probably   yo⌐ku wa⌐ka⌐ru desyoo.
   understand very well.
   /su⌐zi (o) setumee-site
   morau/

4. If you read this, you'll   Ko⌐re (o) yo⌐ndara, yo⌐ku wa⌐ka⌐-
   probably understand   ru desyoo.
   very well. /ko⌐re (o)
   yo⌐mu/

5. If you continue until the   O⌐wari ma⌐de tu⌐zuketa⌐ra, yo⌐ku
   end, you'll probably   wa⌐ka⌐ru desyoo.
   understand very well.
   /o⌐wari ma⌐de tuzukeru/

6. If you see it again, you'll   Ma⌐ta mi⌐tara, yo⌐ku wa⌐ka⌐ru
   probably understand very   desyoo.
   well. /ma⌐ta mi⌐ru/

F. Substitution Drill (based on Grammatical Note 1)

1. How would it be if [you]   I⌐ma de⌐ñwa-site mi⌐tara ⌐do⌐o
   tried telephoning now?   desyoo.

2. How would it be if YOU   A⌐na⌐ta ḡa go⌐rañ ni na⌐ttara
   looked at it? /a⌐na⌐ta   ⌐do⌐o desyoo.
   ḡa go⌐rañ ni na⌐ru/

3. How would it be if I   Wa⌐takusi ḡa haikeñ-sita⌐ra ⌐do⌐o
   looked at it? /watakusi   desyoo.
   ḡa haikeñ-suru/

4. How would it be if [you]   To⌐modati (o) turete (i)⌐ttara
   took a friend? /tomodati   ⌐do⌐o desyoo.
   (o) turete (i)ku/

5. How would it be if [you]   O⌐yo⌐ḡi ni i⌐tta⌐ra ⌐do⌐o desyoo.
   went swimming? /o⌐yo⌐ḡi
   ni iku/

6. How would it be if [you]   U⌐ti ni yotta⌐ra ⌐do⌐o desyoo.
   stopped in at my house?
   /uti ni yoru/

7. How would it be if [you]   Da⌐re ka ni ki⌐ita⌐ra ⌐do⌐o desyoo.
   asked someone? /da⌐re
   ka ni kī̄ku/

8. How would it be if [you]   A｢kaboo (o) tanoꜜndara ꜛdoꜜo de-
    hired a porter? /a｢kaboo   syoo.
    (o) tanoꜜmu/

G. Substitution Drill (based on Grammatical Note 1)

    1. What should I do?   Doꜜo sitara ꜛiꜜi ñ desyoo ka.
    2. When should I take him?   Iꜜtu tu｢rete (i)ꜛttara ꜛiꜜi ñ de-
        /iꜜtu turete (i)ku/   syoo ka.
    3. Where should we discuss   Doꜜko de so｢odañ-sitaꜜra ꜛiꜜi ñ
        it? /doꜜko de soodañ-   desyoo ka.
        suru/
    4. Which song should I sing?   Doꜜno u｢taꜛ (o) u｢tattaꜛra ꜛiꜜi ñ
        /doꜜno u｢taꜛ (o) utau/   desyoo ka.
    5. What should I make?   Naꜜni (o) tu｢kuꜛttara ꜛiꜜi ñ de-
        /naꜜni (o) tu｢kuꜛru/   syoo ka.
    6. Whom should I ask?   Daꜜre ni ki｢itaꜛra ꜛiꜜi ñ desyoo
        /daꜜre ni kiku/   ka.
    7. What kind of things   Doꜜnna mo｢noꜛ (o) ta｢beꜛtara ꜛiꜜi
        should I eat? /doꜜnna   ñ desyoo ka.
        mo｢noꜛ (o) ta｢beꜛru/
    8. How many should I buy?   Iꜜku-tu ka｢ttaꜛra ꜛiꜜi ñ desyoo
        /iꜜku-tu kau/   ka.

H. Substitution Drill (based on Grammatical Note 3)

    1. What should I do to buy   Ki｢ppu (o) kauꜜ no ni (wa), doꜜo
        tickets?   sitara ꜛiꜜi ñ desyoo ka.
    2. What should I do to re-   Te｢eburu (o) yoyaku-suruꜜ no ni
        serve a table?   (wa), doꜜo sitara ꜛiꜜi ñ desyoo
                                     ka.
    3. What should I do to put   Ko｢nna obiꜜ (o) si｢meꜛru no ni
        on this kind of obi?   (wa), doꜜo sitara ꜛiꜜi ñ desyoo
                                     ka.
    4. What should I do to re-   Ni｢hoñḡo (o) oboeꜛru no ni (wa),
        member Japanese?   doꜜo sitara ꜛiꜜi ñ desyoo ka.
    5. What should I do to join   So｢ñna kaisya ni haꜛiru no ni (wa),
        that kind of company?   doꜜo sitara ꜛiꜜi ñ desyoo ka.
    6. What should I do to   Taꜜiya (o) to｢rikaeruꜛ no ni (wa),
        change a tire?   doꜜo sitara ꜛiꜜi ñ desyoo ka.
    7. What should I do to open   Ko｢no hikidasi (o) akeruꜜ no ni
        this drawer?   (wa), doꜜo sitara ꜛiꜜi ñ desyoo
                                     ka.
    8. What should I do to check   Niꜜmotu (o) a｢zukeꜛru no ni (wa),
        baggage?   doꜜo sitara ꜛiꜜi ñ desyoo ka.

I. Substitution Drill (based on Grammatical Note 1)

    1. I wish it had rained.   Aꜜme ḡa ꜛhuꜜttara ꜛyoꜛkatta ke-
                                     redo_
    2. I wish it hadn't rained.   Aꜜme ḡa hu｢raꜛnakattara ꜛyoꜛkatta
        /aꜜme ḡa hu｢raꜛnai/   keredo_

3. I wish he had come early. /haˈyaku ˈkuˈru/

Haˈyaku ˈkiˈtara ˈyoˈkatta keredo—

4. I wish he hadn't come late. /oˈsoku koˈnai/

Oˈsoku koˈnakattara ˈyoˈkatta keredo—

5. I wish it had been interesting. /oˈmosiroˈi/

Oˈmosiˈrokattara ˈyoˈkatta keredo—

6. I wish it hadn't been dull. /tuˈmaraˈnaku ˈnaˈi/

Tuˈmaraˈnaku ˈnaˈkattara ˈyoˈkatta keredo—

7. I wish it had been near. /tiˈkaˈi/

Tiˈkaˈkattara ˈyoˈkatta keredo—

8. I wish it hadn't been far. /toˈoku naˈi/

Toˈoku naˈkattara ˈyoˈkatta keredo—

9. I wish it had been simple. /kañtañ da/

Kaˈñtañ daˈttara ˈyoˈkatta keredo—

10. I wish it hadn't been complicated. /huˈku-zatu zya naˈi/

Huˈkuzatu zya naˈkattara ˈyoˈkatta keredo—

J. Substitution Drill (based on Grammatical Note 2)

1. About when is it you're going to buy it?

Kaˈuˈ no wa iˈtu-g̃oro deˈsu ka⌐

2. Who is it who's going to buy it?

Kaˈuˈ no wa ˈdaˈre desu ka⌐

3. What is it you're going to buy?

Kaˈuˈ no wa ˈnañ desu ka⌐

4. Which (of three or more) is it you're going to buy?

Kaˈuˈ no wa ˈdoˈre desu ka⌐

5. Which (of two) is it you're going to buy?

Kaˈuˈ no wa ˈdoˈtira desu ka⌐

6. How much is the one you're going to buy?

Kaˈuˈ no wa ˈiˈkura desu ka⌐

7. Where is the one you're going to buy? or Where is the one who's going to buy it? or Where is it you're going to buy it?

Kaˈuˈ no wa ˈdoˈko desu ka⌐

K. Substitution Drill (based on Grammatical Note 2)

1. I like to see plays.

Siˈbai (o) miˈru no wa suˈkiˈ desu.

2. I like to go sight-seeing.

Keˈñbutu-suruˈ no wa suˈkiˈ desu.

3. I dislike going sight-seeing.

Keˈñbutu-suruˈ no wa iˈyaˈ desu.

4. I dislike cleaning.

Soˈozi-suruˈ no wa iˈyaˈ desu.

5. Cleaning is a chore.

Soˈozi-suruˈ no wa meˈñdookusaˈi desu.

6. Doing that kind of work is
   a chore.

   So˹ńna siḡoto (o) suru˺ no wa
   me˹ńdookusa˺i desu.

7. Doing that kind of work is
   difficult

   So˹ńna siḡoto (o) suru˺ no wa
   mu˺zukasi˺i desu.

8. Studying Japanese is difficult.

   Ni˹hoñḡo (o) beñkyoo-suru˺ no wa
   mu˺zukasi˺i desu.

L. Response Drill (based on Grammatical Note 5)

Tutor: Ta˹beniku˺i ñ desu ka↲ 'Is it hard to eat?'

Student: Iie, { ta˹beyasu˺i
                ta˹bei˺i } ñ desu. 'No, it's easy to eat.'

1. Sibai no kippu (wa) ka-
   ˹iniku˺i ñ desu ka↲

   Iie, { ka˹iyasu˺i
          ka˹ii˺i } ñ desu.

2. Are (wa) si˹yasu˺i ñ desu
   ka↲

   Iie, si˹niku˺i ñ desu.

3. So˹ńna kutu˺ (wa) ha˹ki-
   niku˺i ñ desu ka↲

   Iie, { ha˹kiyasu˺i
          ha˹kii˺i } ñ desu.

4. Ano kusuri (wa) no˹mi-
   i˺i ñ desu ka↲

   Iie, no˹miniku˺i ñ desu.

5. A˹ńna ha˺si (wa) tu˹kai-
   niku˺i ñ desu ka↲

   Iie, { tu˹kaiyasu˺i
          tu˹kaii˺i } ñ desu.

6. Ano zassi (wa) yo˹miya-
   su˺i ñ desu ka↲

   Iie, yo˹miniku˺i ñ desu.

M. Expansion Drill

1. Would it be good?
   What should I do?
   What should I do with the
   meat?
   What should I do with the
   left-over meat?

   I˺i desyoo ka.
   Do˺o sitara ⌐i⌐i desyoo ka.
   Ni˹ku˺ wa ⌐do˺o sitara ⌐i⌐i de-
   syoo ka.
   No˹ko˺tta ni⌐ku˺ wa ⌐do˺o sitara
   ⌐i⌐i desyoo ka.

2. It's all right.
   You don't have to read it.
   You don't have to read it
   to the end.
   If it's difficult you don't
   have to read it to the
   end.
   (Supposing) if it's difficult you don't have to
   read it to the end.

   I˺i ñ desu yo.
   Yo˹ma˺nakute mo ˹i˺i ñ desu yo.
   O˹wari ma˺de yo⌐ma⌐nakute mo
   ˹i˺i ñ desu yo.
   Mu˹zukasi˺kattara, o˹wari ma˺de
   yo⌐ma⌐nakute mo ˹i˺i ñ desu
   yo.
   Mo˺si mu˹zukasi˺kattara, o˹wari
   ma˺de yo⌐ma⌐nakute mo ˹i˺i ñ
   desu yo.

3. How would it be?
   Why don't you buy [them]
   in advance?

   Do˺o desyoo.
   Ka˹tt(e) o˺itara ⌐do⌐o desyoo.

Why don't you buy the tickets in advance?

Kippu (o) ka⌐tt¬(e) o⌐itara ⌐do⌐o de-syoo.

Why don't you buy the return tickets in advance?

Kaeri no kippu (o) ka⌐tt¬(e) o⌐itara ⌐do⌐o desyoo.

Why don't you buy the return tickets (in advance) right away?

Su͟gu kăeri no kippu (o) ka⌐tt¬(e) o⌐itara ⌐do⌐o desyoo.

Why don't you buy the return tickets in advance as soon as you arrive?

Tu⌐itara ⌐su͟gu⌐ kăeri no kippu (o) ka⌐tt¬(e) o⌐itara ⌐do⌐o desyoo.

4. It will probably be(come) late, won't it.

O⌐soku na⌐ru desyoo ⌐ne⌐e.

It will probably end late too, won't it.

O⌐waru⌐ no mo o⌐soku na⌐ru desyoo ⌐ne⌐e.

If it's late, it will probably end late too, won't it.

O⌐so⌐kattara, o⌐waru⌐ no mo o⌐soku na⌐ru desyoo ⌐ne⌐e.

If it's that late, it will probably end late too, won't it.

So⌐ñna ni oso⌐kattara, o⌐waru⌐ no mo o⌐soku na⌐ru desyoo ⌐ne⌐e.

If it starts that late, it will probably end late too, won't it.

Ha⌐zimaru⌐ no ͟ga so⌐ñna ni oso⌐-kattara, o⌐waru⌐ no mo o⌐soku na⌐ru desyoo ⌐ne⌐e.

5. I can't go.

I⌐karemase⌐ñ.

I can't go very easily.

Na⌐kanaka ikaremase⌐ñ.

Before that I can't go very easily.

So⌐no ma⌐e wa na⌐kanaka ikare-mase⌐ñ.

It's all right but before that I can't go very easily.

I⌐i ñ desu ͟ga, so⌐no ma⌐e wa na⌐kanaka ikaremase⌐ñ.

If it's after the tenth it's all right but before that I can't go very easily.

To⌐o-ka-i⌐͟go dattara ⌐i⌐i ñ desu ͟ga, so⌐no ma⌐e wa na⌐kanaka ikaremase⌐ñ.

6. How would it be?

Do⌐o desyoo.

Why don't you buy [it]?

Ka⌐tta⌐ra ⌐do⌐o desyoo.

Why don't you buy a new one?

A⌐tarasi⌐i no (o) ka⌐tta⌐ra ⌐do⌐o desyoo.

It takes money so why don't you buy a new one?

O⌐kane ͟ga kaka⌐ru kara, a⌐tara-si⌐i no (o) ka⌐tta⌐ra ⌐do⌐o de-syoo.

It takes an awful lot of money so why don't you buy a new one?

Zu⌐ibuñ o⌐kane ͟ga kaka⌐ru kara, a⌐tarasi⌐i no (o) ka⌐tta⌐ra ⌐do⌐o desyoo.

It takes an awful lot of money to fix [it] so why don't you buy a new one?

Na⌐o⌐su no ni (wa) ⌐zu⌐ibuñ o⌐kane ͟ga kaka⌐ru kara, a⌐tarasi⌐i no (o) ka⌐tta⌐ra ⌐do⌐o desyoo.

It takes an awful lot of
money to fix this so
why don't you buy a
new one?

Ko⌐re (o) nao⌐su no ni (wa) ⌐zu⌐i-
buñ o⌐kane ḡa kaka⌐ru kara,
a⌐tarasi⌐i no (o) ka⌐tta⌐ra ⌐do⌐o
desyoo.

QUESTION SUPPLEMENT

(based on the Basic Dialogues)

(a) 1. Su⌐misu-sañ wa ⌐mo⌐o kābuki o mi⌐ma⌐sita ka⌐
     2. Su⌐misu-sañ wa ka⌐buki ḡa mita⌐i ñ desu ka⌐ Do⌐o site wa⌐kari-
         ma⌐su ka⌐
     3. Kabuki no kippu wa ⌐su⌐ḡu ka⌐eru⌐ ñ desu ka⌐ Amerika no ⌐i⌐i si-
         bai no kippu wa ⌐do⌐o desu ka⌐

(b) 4. Na⌐ñ-niti made u⌐rikire de⌐su ka⌐
     5. Ni⌐zyuu yo-kka no ī⌐t-too no kippu wa, do⌐o site i⌐rimase⌐ñ ka⌐
     6. Na⌐ñ-niti no kippu ni ki⌐mema⌐sita ka⌐ I⌐t-too no kippu de⌐su ka,
         ni-⌐too no kippu de⌐su ka⌐
     7. Tanaka-sañ wa kore kara ⌐na⌐ni o si⌐ma⌐su ka⌐

(c) 8. Ka⌐buki no owaru⌐ no wa na⌐ñ-zi-ḡo⌐ro desu ka⌐
     9. Ha⌐zime kara owari ma⌐de ⌐mi⌐tara, na⌐ñ-zi⌐kañ ka⌐karima⌐su ka⌐
    10. Ha⌐zimaru⌐ no wa ⌐na⌐ñ-zi desu ka⌐
    11. Tanaka-sañ to ⌐Su⌐misu-sañ wa ⌐do⌐ko de ta⌐be⌐ru tumori desu ka⌐
    12. Ge⌐kizyoo e itta⌐ra ⌐su⌐ḡu, na⌐ni o su⌐ru⌐ desyoo ka.
    13. Su⌐misu-sañ wa Ta̅naka-sañ ni ⌐do⌐ñna koto o ta⌐nomima⌐sita ka⌐
    14. Do⌐o site Tanaka-sañ wa a⌐ñmari kañtañ ni⌐ wa se⌐tumee-deki⌐-
         nai to i⌐ima⌐sita ka⌐

SUPPLEMENTARY CONVERSATION

Tanaka: Su⌐misu-sañ. A⌐zuma-o⌐dori[1] o go⌐rañ ni narima⌐sita ka⌐
Mr. Smith: Iie. Na⌐ñ desu ka⌐ —A⌐zuma-o⌐dori tte i⌐u⌐ no wa. Ni⌐hoñ no
            odori de⌐su ka⌐
Tanaka: O⌐dori dake⌐ zya ⌐ha⌐i ñ desu yo⌐ Ge⌐esya[2] ḡa suru kabuki
            de⌐su yo.
Mr. Smith: So⌐o desu ka. Zya⌐a, o⌐ñna⌐ ḡa su⌐ru kabuki de⌐su ka⌐
Tanaka: E⌐e. Hutuu no kabuki wa o⌐toko⌐ sika si⌐na⌐i ñ desu ḡa, A⌐zu-
            ma-o⌐dori wa ⌐Si⌐ñbasi no ge⌐esya ḡa suru⌐ ñ desu. Ki⌐ree de-
            su yo⌐
Mr. Smith: So⌐o desyoo ⌐ne⌐e. Ze⌐hi tu⌐rete i⌐tte kudasai. Ka⌐bukiza de
            site iru⌐ ñ desu ka⌐
Tanaka: Iie. Ka⌐bukiza no so⌐ba desu ḡa, Si⌐ñbasi-eñbuzyoo[3] tte iu
            gekizyoo de ⌐i⌐ma si⌐te iru⌐ ñ desu yo⌐

---

[1] A special spring entertainment performed in Tokyo.

[2] 'Geisha.'

[3] Name of a Tokyo theater.

Mr. Smith: Kippu wa suḡu kaeru ñ desu ka

Tanaka: Iie. Hutuu wa nakanaka kaenai ñ desu yo.

Mr. Smith: Sore wa komarimasu nee. Doo simasyoo ka.

Tanaka: Tuḡi no doyoobi, gotuḡoo ḡa yokattara; kippu ḡa ni-mai aru ñ desu yo Tomodati kara moratta ñ desu ḡa

Mr. Smith: Tuḡi no doyoobi desu ne? Nañ-zi kara desyoo ka.

Tanaka: Zyuuiti-zi kara desu ḡa

Mr. Smith: Yoru zya nai ñ desu ne? Zyaa, tyoodo ii desu. Doyoobi wa siti-zi kara yakusoku ḡa aru ñ desu ḡa

Tanaka: Yo-zi-hañ-ḡoro owaru to omoimasu ḡa, mosi omosiroku nakattara owari made minakute mo ii desyoo.

Mr. Smith: Omosiroi to omoimasu yo Boku wa kabuki ḡa suki de, yoku mi ni iku ñ desu yo

Tanaka: Zyaa Doyoobi ni doko de aimasyoo ka. Ima soodañ-site okimasyoo. Gozoñzi desu ka —Siñbasi-eñbuzyoo o.

Mr. Smith: Iie, sirimaseñ ḡa

Tanaka: Zyaa, zyuuiti-zi zyuugo-huñ mae ni Siñbasi-eki no mae de omati-simasyoo.

Mr. Smith: Zyaa, zyuugo-huñ mae made ni Siñbasi-eki no mae ni aru takusii no noriba no soba ni ikimasu kara, oneḡai-simasu.   . . .
             A, soo soo. Ohiru wa gekizyoo de tabemasu ka

Tanaka: Soo desu nee. Sañdoitti[1] to koohii o motte itte, makuai ni tabemasyoo ka.

Mr. Smith: Zyaa, boku ḡa motte ikimasu kara

Tanaka: Sore wa doo mo.

             (Gekizyoo de)

Mr. Smith: Hoñtoo ni kiree na odori desita nee.

Tanaka: Kimono mo kiree desita nee. Suzi owakari desita ka

Mr. Smith: Ee. Mae ni mimasita kara. Tuḡi wa sibai desu ne?

Tanaka: Ee, soo desu. Naḡai sibai no owari no hoo no hañbuñ o suru ñ desu yo

Mr. Smith: Aa, soo desu ka. Zyaa, sumimaseñ ḡa, suzi o kañtañ ni setumee-site kuremaseñ ka.

Tanaka: Yoku oboete imaseñ kara, tyotto matte kudasai Puroguramu[2] o yoñde mimasu kara

English Equivalent

Tanaka: Mr. Smith. Have you seen the Azuma-odori?

Mr. Smith: No. What is it —(the thing called) the Azuma-odori? Is it Japanese dancing?

Tanaka: It isn't just dancing. It's kabuki that geisha perform.

Mr. Smith: Really? Then do you mean that it's kabuki that women perform?

Tanaka: Yes. Only men do ordinary kabuki but the Shimbashi geisha do the Azuma-odori. It's beautiful, you know.

---

[1] 'Sandwich.'

[2] 'Program.'

Mr. Smith: It must be. Do take me. Are they performing it at the Kabukiza?
Tanaka: No. It's near the Kabukiza but they're performing it now at a theater called the Shimbashi-Embujo.
Mr. Smith: Can you buy tickets easily?
Tanaka: No. Usually you can't buy them easily [at all].
Mr. Smith: That's annoying. What shall we do?
Tanaka: If next Saturday is convenient, I have two tickets. I got them from a friend . . .
Mr. Smith: That's next Saturday you say? What time would it start?
Tanaka: It starts at 11:00 . . .
Mr. Smith: That's not the evening, is it? Then it's just fine. On Saturday, I have an appointment from 7 o'clock [on] but . . .
Tanaka: I think it will be over at about 4:30, but if it's not interesting we won't have to watch it until the end.
Mr. Smith: I think it will be interesting. I like kabuki and I often go to see it.
Tanaka: Then [you'll probably like this]. Where shall we meet on Saturday? Let's talk it over now (in advance). Do you know it—the Shimbashi-Embujo?
Mr. Smith: No, I don't (know it) . . .
Tanaka: Well then, I'll wait [for you] in front of Shimbashi Station at a quarter to eleven.
Mr. Smith: Well then, I'll be (lit. go) near the taxi stand that's in front of Shimbashi Station by a quarter of, so please [look for me].
              . . . Oh, yes.—At noontime will we eat in the theater?
Tanaka: Let me see . . . Shall we take sandwiches and coffee and eat between the acts?
Mr. Smith: In that case, I'll bring [the food] so [don't you bother].
Tanaka: That's very [kind of you].

(At the theater)

Mr. Smith: It was really beautiful dancing, wasn't it.
Tanaka: The kimono were beautiful too, weren't they. Did you understand the plot?
Mr. Smith: Yes, because I've seen it before. [1] The next is a play, isn't it?
Tanaka: Yes, that's right. They're going to do the second (lit. end) half of a long play.
Mr. Smith: Oh really? In that case, I'm sorry [to bother you] but would you explain the plot to me briefly?
Tanaka: I don't remember it very well so just a moment. (Because) I'll read the program and see.

EXERCISES

1. Plan a trip to see kabuki with a friend: decide when you will go, who will buy the tickets, what kind of seats you wish, where you will eat, etc.

2. Using the pattern of Basic Sentence 25 of this lesson, ask Mr. Tanaka:

---

[1] I. e. a performance using the same plot, probably in regular kabuki.

    a.   what time he begins work.
    b.   what time the show starts.
    c.   when it gets to be the rainy season.
    d.   when this work will end.
    e.   when he will return to Japan.

3.   Tell Mr. Tanaka that:

    a.   you dislike walking.
    b.   you think riding in Tokyo taxis is dangerous.
    c.   you think reading Japanese newspapers is difficult.
    d.   you like to eat at Japanese restaurants.
    e.   you think seeing kabuki is interesting.
    f.   going from here to your house is simple.

4.   You ask the theater employee: She replies:

a. if there are still three first-class [tickets] for the afternoon performance on the 14th.	There are but the seats are not together.
b. if the evening performance on the 20th is sold out already.	No, there are still a few second-class seats left.
c. if these seats [i.e. those for which you have tickets] are together.	Yes, they are.
d. if these seats are in the middle section.	No, they're on the side.
e. what time the show begins.	At 5 o'clock.
f. if there is an English program (puroguramu).	They should be selling them over there.
g. how long the intermission is.	Twenty minutes.
h. if it's all right even if you don't reserve a table in the dining room.	If you want to eat during the intermission, it's better to reserve a table now.

Lesson 29. Renting a House

BASIC DIALOGUES: FOR MEMORIZATION

(a)

Smith

being cool or because
  it's cool
is nice and cool

1. It's nice and cool here, isn't it!

su⌐zu⌐sikute

su⌐zu⌐sikute ⌐i⌐i

*Koko (wa) su⌐zu⌐sikute ⌐i⌐i desu ⌐ne⌐e.

house for rent

2. Aren't there houses for rent around here?

kasiya

Kono heñ ni ka⌐siya (ḡa) na⌐i de-syoo ka.

thus or this way
a place like this
being a case of wanting
  to rent or because
  [someone] wants to rent

3. (Because) I'd like to rent a summer home in a place like this.

ko⌐o

ko⌐o iu tokoro⌐

ka⌐rita⌐i no de

Ko⌐o iu tokoro⌐ ni na⌐tu no uti⌐ (o) ka⌐rita⌐i no de—

Tanaka

be pleasing or appeal
isn't clear whether there
  are or not
become vacant

4. Let me see. I can't tell whether or not there's a house of the kind that will appeal to you, but there certainly are vacant houses.

ki ni iru /-u/

a⌐ru ka ⌐do⌐o ka wa⌐kara⌐-nai

aku /-u/

So⌐o desu ⌐ne⌐e. Ki ⌐ni iru yo⌐o na uti (ḡa) ⌐a⌐ru ka ⌐do⌐o ka wa⌐karimase⌐ñ ḡa, aite (i)ru uti wa ki⌐tto arima⌐su yo—

Smith

being a case of being
  far or because it
  is far
town
a town like this

5. I wanted to go to Karuizawa but it's too far so I've been looking for a closer place. I think that a town like this is just right.

to⌐oi⌐ no de

ma⌐ti⌐

ko⌐o iu mati⌐

Ka⌐ruizawa e ikita⌐katta keredo; a⌐ñmari tooi⌐ no de, mo⌐tto ti-⌐ka⌐i to⌐koro⌐ (o) sa⌐ḡasite (i)ma⌐-su ḡa; ko⌐o iu mati⌐ ḡa tyo⌐odo i⌐i to omoimasu.

180

Tanaka (pointing to a house)

6. How would that house be?
   Would that be a little [too]
   small?

   Ano uti (wa)|do⌐o desyoo.[1] Tyo⌐-
   tto ti⌐isa⌐i desyoo ka.

Smith

even as a house

u⌐ti⌐ to si⌐te⌐ mo

7. Yes. Even as just a summer
   home that's too small so I'm
   afraid that wouldn't do.

   E⌐e. Na⌐tu dake⌐ no u⌐ti⌐ to si⌐te⌐
   mo, ti⌐isasuḡima⌐su kara ⌐tyo⌐tto—

Tanaka (pointing to another house)

inconvenient

hu⌐beñ /na/

8. It's a slightly inconvenient
   location but how would that
   house be?

   Tyo⌐tto ⌐hu⌐beñ na to⌐koro⌐ desu
   ḡa, a⌐no uti wa do⌐o desyoo.

isn't clear whether it's
   a house for rent or not

ka⌐siya ka do⌐o ka wa⌐ka-
   ra⌐nai

9. I can't tell whether it's (a
   house) for rent or not but I
   think it's vacant.

   Ka⌐siya ka do⌐o ka wa⌐karimase⌐ñ
   ḡa, a⌐ite (i)ru to omoima⌐su.

Smith

scenery

ke⌐siki

10. [In] back are the mountains
    and [in] front is the ocean
    so the scenery is lovely,
    isn't it.

   U⌐siro ḡa yama⌐ de, ma⌐e ḡa
   ⌐u⌐mi da kara; *ke⌐siki wa ⌐i⌐i
   desu ⌐ne⌐e.

as a house

u⌐ti⌐ to site

11. As a summer house it would
    probably be quite nice!

   Na⌐tu no uti⌐ to si⌐te⌐ wa, na-
   ⌐kanaka i⌐i desyoo ⌐ne⌐e.

Tanaka

home-owner or landlord
acquaintance
introduce

ya⌐nusi [2]
siriai
syookai-suru or gosyookai-
   suru[+]

12. The owner is an acquaintance
    of mine. Shall I introduce
    you?

   Ya⌐nusi (wa) si⌐riai de⌐su ḡa, go-
   ⌐syookai-simasyo⌐o ka.

Smith

13. Yes, please. (Because) I do
    want to see that house (lit.
    have that house shown to
    me).

   E⌐e oneḡai-simasu. Ze⌐hi a⌐no
   uti⌐ (o) ⌐mi⌐sete mo⌐raita⌐i kara.

---

[1] For explanation of special symbol |, see Part I, page xxxvii.

[2] Has unaccented alternant.

(b)

Smith

after it gets to be
    summer vacation
even if it's just two
    months

14. I'd like to come here after
     my summer vacation starts.
     Would you rent [the house]
     (even) for just two months?

na⌐tuya⌐sumi ni ⌐na⌐tte kara

ni-⌐ka⌐ḡetu da⌐ke⌐ de mo

Na⌐tuya⌐sumi ni ⌐na⌐tte kara ki⌐ta⌐i
ñ desu ḡa, ni-⌐ka⌐ḡetu da⌐ke⌐ de
mo ka⌐site itadakeru⌐ desyoo ka.

Landlord

the rent
being July, August,
    September
it has become or been
    decided or been set
    at or been made into

15. The rent has been set at
     ¥ 70,000 for July, August,
     and September (but) . . .

ya⌐tiñ

siti-ḡatu hăti-ḡatu ⌐ku⌐-ḡatu
de
na⌐tte (i)ru

Ya⌐tiñ (wa); siti-ḡatu hăti-ḡatu
⌐ku⌐-ḡatu de, na⌐namañ-eñ ni na⌐tte
orimasu ḡa—

Smith

commute

16. Would it be possible to com-
     mute as far as Tokyo?

kayou /-u/
To⌐okyoo ma⌐de ka⌐yoeru⌐ desyoo
ka.

Landlord

17. Yes. It's a little far but
     there are people who com-
     mute.

E⌐e. Tyo⌐tto to⌐oi⌐ keredo, ka-
⌐you hito⌐ mo i⌐ma⌐su yo⌐

Smith

the remaining one month

18. Well then, I guess it would
     be all right if I rented it for
     three months, took my vaca-
     tion for two months, and
     commuted during the re-
     maining month.

a⌐to no i⌐k-ka⌐ḡetu
Zya⌐a, sa⌐ñ-ka⌐ḡetu karite; ni-
⌐ka⌐ḡetu wa ya⌐su⌐ñde, a⌐to no
i⌐k-ka⌐ḡetu wa ka⌐yotta⌐ra ⌐i⌐i
desyoo ⌐ne⌐e.

(c)

Smith

being hot or because
    it's hot
be annoying because it's
    hot

19. Tokyo summers are bad be-
     cause of the heat. How is it
     here?

a⌐tukute

a⌐tukute ko⌐ma⌐ru

To⌐okyoo no natu⌐ wa ⌐a⌐tukute
ko⌐marima⌐su ḡa, ko⌐ko wa do⌐o
desyoo ka.

Landlord

being a case of having
   been special <u>or</u> because it was special

to⌐kubetu da⌐tta no de

20. Last year was special so it
     was hot here too, but usually
     it's very cool.

Kyo⌐neñ wa to⌐kubetu da⌐tta no
de, ko⌐ko mo a⌐tukatta ñ desu ḡa;
hutuu wa to⌐temo suzusi⌐i ñ desu
yo⌐

Smith

vehicle

norimono

21. What about transportation?

Norimono wa?

Landlord

it's nothing

na⌐ñ de mo na⌐i

22. [To go] to the station it
     takes about thirty minutes
     if you walk, but in the sum-
     mer there's a bus so it's
     nothing at all.

E⌐ki made (wa) a⌐ru⌐ite sa⌐ñzyup-
puñ-ḡu⌐rai ka⌐karima⌐su ḡa; na-
⌐tu⌐ wa ⌐ba⌐su ḡa ⌐a⌐ru kara, na⌐ñ
de mo arimase⌐ñ yo.

Smith

23. How far do you go for shop-
     ping?

Kaimono (wa) ⌐do⌐ko made i⌐ki-
ma⌐su ka⌐

Landlord

there's everything
sake shop
fish market, vegetable
   store, sake shop

na⌐ñ de mo a⌐ru
sakaya
sakanaya yāoya sākaya

24. Near the station there's
     everything, but we have a
     fish market, vegetable
     store, and sake shop right
     there.

E⌐ki no ⌐so⌐ba ni wa na⌐ñ de mo
arima⌐su ḡa, sakanaya yāoya sākaya wa ⌐su⌐ḡu so⌐ko ni arima⌐su
yo⌐

(d)

Smith

commodity prices

bukka

25. What about prices?

Bukka wa|do⌐o desu ka⌐

Landlord

never

kessite / + negative/

26. They're never high.

Ke⌐ssite ta⌐kaku wa a⌐rimase⌐ñ.

in particular
be surprised <u>or</u> amazed
   <u>or</u> startled
being cheap <u>or</u> because
   it's cheap
be amazed because it's
   so cheap

to⌐ku ni
bi⌐kku⌐ri-suru

ya⌐sukute

a⌐ñmari ya⌐sukute bi⌐kku⌐-
   ri-suru

27. In particular, the fish is so   To⌐ku ni sa⌐kana ⌐ga añmari ya⌐-
     cheap that you'll probably   sukute ḅi⌐kku⌐ri-nasaru desyoo.
     be amazed.

                              Smith

     however or but or   de⌐ mo
          even so
28. But isn't it the case that   De⌐ mo, na⌐tu⌐ wa ḅŭkka (⌐ga)
     prices go up in summer?   a⌐garu⌐ ñ zya ⌐na⌐i desyoo ka.

                          Landlord

     merchant or shopkeeper   syo⌐oniñ
     honest   syo⌐oziki⌐ /na/
     being a case of being   syo⌐oziki⌐ na no de
          honest or because
          [someone] is honest
29. The shopkeepers around   Ko⌐no heñ no syo⌐oniñ wa syo-
     here are honest so there's   ⌐oziki⌐ na no de, si⌐ñpai arima-
     nothing to worry about.   se⌐ñ.

     non-rice field or dry   hatake
          field
     in spite of the fact   su⌐kuna⌐i no ni
          that it is scarce
30. And in spite of the fact that   Sosite; ha⌐take ⌐ga sukuna⌐i no
     there aren't many farms   ni, ya⌐sai mo yasu⌐i ñ desu.
     (lit. fields) the vegetables
     are cheap too.

                              Smith

     consider or think over   ka⌐ñḡae⌐ru /-ru/
     whether I rent it or not   o⌐kari-site⌐ mo si⌐na⌐kute
                                            mo
31. In any case, I'll think it   To⌐nikaku ⌐tyo⌐tto ka⌐ñḡa⌐ete,
     over for a while, and whether   o⌐kari-site⌐ mo si⌐na⌐kute mo
     I rent [the house] or not, I'll   go⌐reñraku-sima⌐su.
     get in touch [with you].

     week end   syuumatu
32. This week end I plan to come   Ko⌐no syuumatu ni⌐ (wa) ma⌐ta
     here again so [I'll see you]   kotira e ku⌐ru tu⌐mori da⌐ kara,
     again then . . .   so⌐no to⌐ki /ni/ mata—

                              (e)
                          Tanaka

     in spite of the fact that   ki⌐ta⌐ no ni
          [someone] came
33. We went to the trouble of   Se⌐kkaku kita⌐ no ni, i⌐i kasiya
     coming here but there   (wa) a⌐rimase⌐ñ desita ⌐ne⌐e.
     wasn't a good house for
     rent, was there.

Smith

34. It can't be helped so let's
    look for one again, next
    week.

Si⌐kata ḡa na¹i kara, mata ra-
⌐isyuu saḡasimasyo¹o.

NOTES ON THE BASIC DIALOGUES

3. Note: ko¹o 'this way,' so¹o and a¹a 'that way,' do¹o 'what way?' or
    'how?'

8. The opposite of hu¹beñ is be¹ñri /na/
    Do not confuse be¹ñri 'convenient' in the sense of 'handy, accessible,
    convenient to use' with tu⌐ḡoo ḡa i¹i 'is convenient' indicating that
    stated conditions are convenient for someone on a particular occasion.
    A refrigerator is be¹ñri; having the picnic next Saturday, tu⌐ḡoo ḡa i¹i.

15. 'but—would this be agreeable to you?'
    Note the polite use of o⌐rima¹su following a gerund, with an inanimate
    subject.

17. Note particle mo: '[Most people don't commute but] there are also
    people who do commute.'

22. Do not confuse na⌐ñ de mo na¹i 'it is nothing' with na⌐ñi mo na¹i 'there
    is nothing' and na⌐ñ de mo a¹ru 'there is everything'

24. Sakaya refers to a shop where sake is sold in bottles to be taken out.
    Sakaba is a place where sake is drunk. The change of final -e to -a,
    when a word occurs as the first part of a compound, is common. Com-
    pare a¹me with a⌐maḡa¹sa 'rain umbrella' and a⌐ma¹do 'storm shutters.'

26. The wa of comparison may occur within a negative adjectival expres-
    sion: ta¹kaku wa ⌐na¹i '[whatever else they may be] expensive they're
    not.'

28. Ke¹redo (or more formal ke¹redomo or more informal ke¹do) 'however'
    is more often used when one speaker adds to what he has previously
    said, whereas de¹ mo (lit. 'even being [so]') often accompanies a shift
    of speaker.
    The opposite of aḡaru is sa⌐ḡa¹ru 'go down.' Both are intransitive
    verbals. Their transitive equivalents are aḡeru 'raise [something]' and
    sa⌐ḡe¹ru 'lower [something].'

30. Hatake contrasts with ta¹ 'rice field.' Ta¹ is a paddy field, while ha-
    take is a dry field where things other than rice are grown.

31. O⌐kari-site¹ mo si⌐na¹kute mo is the humble equivalent of ka⌐rite¹ mo
    ka⌐rina¹kute mo.

GRAMMATICAL NOTES

1. Gerund Meaning 'because'

    A gerund (or a phrase ending with a gerund) that is coordinate with what follows may explain the reason for what follows. Thus:

> O⌐hu⌐ro ḡa a⌐tusu⌐ḡite ha⌐irimase⌐n̄ desita. 'The bath was too hot and
> [so] I didn't go in.' (Lit. 'The bath being too hot, I didn't go in.'
> Sa⌐mukute i⌐ya⌐ desu. 'It's cold and [so] I don't like it.' (Lit. 'Being
> cold, I don't like it.')
> Byooki de ki⌐mase⌐n̄ desita. 'He was sick and [so] he didn't come.'
> (Lit. 'Being sick, he didn't come.')

An extended predicate (cf. Lesson 23, Grammatical Note 1) may also occur
in its gerund form as a causal expression: a non-past or past verbal, adjectival, or copula [1] is followed by no [2] + gerund de 'being the case that ——— ,'
'inasmuch as ——— ,' 'because ——— .' Thus:

> Ki⌐noo itta⌐ no de, kyo⌐o wa i⌐kimase⌐n̄. 'Inasmuch as I went yesterday,
> I'm not going today.' (Lit. 'Being the case that I went yesterday,
> I'm not going today.')
> Hu⌐ru⌐i no de, a⌐tarasi⌐i no ḡa ka⌐ita⌐i n̄ desu ḡa— 'Inasmuch as it's
> old I'd like to buy a new one . . . ' (Lit. 'Being the case that it's old,
> I'd like to buy a new one . . . ')
> Byo⌐oki na⌐ no de, kyo⌐o wa ki⌐mase⌐n̄. 'Because he's sick he isn't
> coming today.' (Lit. 'Being a case of being sick, today he won't
> come.')

Thus, the following three sentences all contain causal expressions:

> Ta⌐kakatta kara, ka⌐imase⌐n̄ desita. 'It was expensive so I didn't buy
> it.'
> Ta⌐kakatta no de, ka⌐imase⌐n̄ desita. 'Inasmuch as it was expensive I
> didn't buy it.'
> Ta⌐kakute ka⌐imase⌐n̄ desita. 'It was expensive and [so] I didn't buy it.'

Of the three alternatives, the one with no de is most formal.

An adjectival gerund of cause plus i⌐i 'being ——— , it's nice' or 'it's nice
because it's ——— ' is the closest Japanese equivalent of English 'it's nice and
——— ' (i.e. 'it's ——— in a pleasant way'). Thus, tu⌐meta⌐kute ⌐i⌐i 'it's nice
and cold'; hi⌐rokute ⌐i⌐i 'it's nice and big.'

The gerund of cause may occur in sentence-final position, or pre-final before ne⌐e, in fragments (cf. Lesson 27, Grammatical Note 4). Thus:

> A: I⌐kimase⌐n̄ desita ka— 'Didn't you go?'
> B: E⌐e. A⌐me ḡa ⌐hu⌐tte— 'No. It was raining and [so I didn't].'

2. ——— no ni 'in spite of the fact that ——— '

A verbal, adjectival or copula (non-past or past) + nominal no + particle
ni 'against' or 'in spite of' occurs in expressions of strong contrast: 'in
spite of the fact that ——— .' [3] Thus:

---

[1] Remember that the non-past copula form occurring before no is na.

[2] No may be contracted to n̄.

[3] A non-past verbal + no ni 'in spite of the fact that ——— ' and a non-past
verbal + no ni 'in the process of ——— ' are distinguished by context.

Yóku ha⌐taraita⌐ no ni, ze⌐ñzeñ tukaremaseñ⌐ desita.
  'In spite of the fact that I worked hard, I didn't get at all tired.'
Ta⌐kakatta no ni, su̅gu da⌐me⌐ ni na⌐rima⌐sita.
  'In spite of the fact that it was expensive, it broke right away.'
Byo⌐oki na⌐ no ni, ha⌐taraki ni kima⌐sita.
  'In spite of the fact that he's sick, he came to work.'

Compare the following sentences, representing weak and strong degrees of contrast:

Se⌐tumee-site moraima⌐sita g̅a, ma⌐da wa⌐karimase⌐ñ.
  'I had it explained to me but I still don't understand.'
Se⌐tumee-site moratta⌐ keredo, ma⌐da wa⌐karimase⌐ñ.
  'Although I had it explained to me, I still don't understand.'
Se⌐tumee-site moratta⌐ no ni, ma⌐da wa⌐karimase⌐ñ.
  'In spite of the fact that I had it explained to me, I still don't understand.'

The first two sentences are almost interchangeable, but the third sentence shows much stronger contrast.

Sekkaku frequently occurs within a —— no ni pattern, meaning 'in spite of the fact that I took the trouble to —— .' Thus:

Se⌐kkaku tuku⌐tta no ni, da⌐re mo tabemaseñ⌐ desita.
  'In spite of the fact that I took the trouble to make it, nobody ate it.'

3. Quoted Alternate Questions

Review alternate questions in Lesson 12, Grammatical Note 3.

Alternate questions A ka and B ka occur in the informal style, preceding inflected words like √wa⌐kara⌐nai 'don't understand' or 'isn't clear,' √siranai 'don't know,' √wasureru 'forget,' etc., meaning 'whether A or B'; in such occurrences they are called QUOTED ALTERNATE QUESTIONS. Before ka, the informal non-past da is regularly lost.

Examples:

I⌐ku⌐ ka i⌐kana⌐i ka si⌐rimase⌐ñ.
  'I don't know whether he will go or won't go.'
Kore wa zi⌐buñ de katta⌐ ka, da⌐re ka kara moratta⌐ ka; wa⌐surema⌐sita.
  'I have forgotten whether I bought this myself or got it from someone.' (Lit. 'As for this, did I buy it myself, did I receive it from someone, I have forgotten.')
Sore wa de⌐ki⌐ru ka de⌐ki⌐nai ka, he⌐ñzi⌐ o site kudasai.
  'Please give me an answer [as to] whether it's possible or not.'
A⌐ma⌐i ka su⌐ppa⌐i ka si⌐rimaseñ g̅a, ta⌐bete mimasyoo.
  'I don't know whether it's sweet or sour but let's eat it and see.'
A⌐no⌐ hito no kuruma wa ⌐Ho⌐odo ka Kya⌐dera⌐kku ka, o⌐bo⌐ete i⌐maseñ⌐.
  'I don't remember whether his car is a Ford or a Cadillac.'
A⌐me datta ka, yu⌐ki⌐ datta ka, o⌐bo⌐ete i⌐mase⌐ñ g̅a; sono hi ⌐te⌐ñki g̅a wa⌐rukatta koto wa ⌐yo⌐ku o⌐bo⌐ete imasu.
  'I don't remember whether it was rain or snow, but the fact that the weather was bad that day I remember well.'

When the second of a pair of quoted alternate questions is do⌐o ka (an informal equivalent of do⌐o desu ka) 'how is it?,' the combination is equivalent to 'whether A [or not].' [1] Thus:

> o⌐mosiro⌐i ka tu⌐mara⌐nai ka kĭku 'ask whether it is interesting or dull'

but:

> o⌐mosiro⌐i ka ⌐do⌐o ka kĭku 'ask whether it is interesting [or not]'

Examples:

> Ta⌐naka-sañ wa kima⌐su ḡa, Sa⌐too-sañ wa ⌐ku⌐ru ka ⌐do⌐o ka si⌐rima-se⌐ñ.
> 'Mr. Tanaka is coming but I don't know whether Mr. Sato is coming or not.'
> Sono zassi wa o⌐mosiro⌐i ka ⌐do⌐o ka wa⌐kara⌐nakatta kara, ka⌐imase⌐ñ desita.
> 'I couldn't tell whether that magazine was interesting [or not], so I didn't buy it.'
> O⌐suki ka do⌐o ka ki⌐ite kudasa⌐i.
> 'Ask him whether he likes it [or not].'
> Ho⌐ñtoo ka do⌐o ka si⌐raberare⌐ru desyoo ka.
> 'Could you find out whether it's true [or not]?'

WARNING: Do not confuse quoted alternate questions with gerund + mo + gerund + mo (Lesson 22, Grammatical Note 4); the English equivalents of of both contain 'whether.' Compare:

> Tanaka-san wa i⌐ku⌐ ka i⌐kana⌐i ka si⌐rimase⌐ñ.
> 'I don't know [the answer to the question] whether Mr. Tanaka is going or (is) not (going).' (Lit. 'Is Mr. Tanaka going, is he not going, I don't know.')

and:

> Ta⌐naka-sañ ḡa itte⌐ mo i⌐kana⌐kute mo, wa⌐takusi wa ikimase⌐ñ.
> 'Whether Mr. Tanaka goes or (does) not (go), I'm not going.' (Lit. 'Even if Mr. Tanaka goes, even if he doesn't go, I am not going.')

4. ——to site

To site following a nominal is the Japanese equivalent of 'in the capacity of —— ,' 'as —— ,' 'for —— .' Thus:

> Se⌐ñse⌐e to site i⌐kima⌐sita. 'He went as a teacher.'

A —— to site phrase as an item of comparison is followed by particle wa. Thus:

> Be⌐ñkyoo-suru mono⌐ to si⌐te⌐ wa, o⌐mosiro⌐i desu.
> 'As something to study, it's interesting.'
> A⌐merika⌐ziñ to si⌐te⌐ wa, ni⌐hoñḡo ḡa zyoozu⌐ desu.
> 'His Japanese is good for an American.'

A —— to site phrase may also be followed by particle mo 'even.' Thus:

> A⌐merika no hatake to site⌐ mo o⌐oki⌐i desu.
> 'It's big even for an American farm (lit. field).'

---

[1] Do⌐o ka usually occurs in the Japanese equivalent, whereas 'or not' is optional in English.

5. Enumeration

In enumeration, two or more nominals, with or without preceding modifiers, may follow one another without intervening particles. Each member of the series regularly begins a new accent phrase (i.e. is pronounced as if at the beginning of a sentence).

Examples:

hoˈñ zaˈssi siñbuñ 'books, magazines, newspapers'
Tookyoo Yǒkohama ⌐Kyoˈoto 'Tokyo, Yokohama, Kyoto'
siˈroˈi waˈñpiˈisu, aˈoˈi ˈseˈetaa, koˈñ no kutu 'white dress, blue sweater, navy blue shoes'

DRILLS

A. Substitution Drill

1.	It's never high.	Keˈssite taˈkaku aˈrimaseˈñ.
2.	It's not very high.	Aˈñmari taˈkaku aˈrimaseˈñ.
3.	It's not a bit high.	Tiˈttoˈ mo ˈtaˈkaku aˈrimaseˈñ.
4.	It's not at all high.	Zeˈñzeñ taˈkaku aˈrimaseˈñ.
5.	It's not especially high.	Beˈtu ni taˈkaku aˈrimaseˈñ.
6.	It's really not high.	Hoˈñtoo wa taˈkaku aˈrimaseˈñ.
7.	It's ordinarily not high.	Huˈtuu wa taˈkaku aˈrimaseˈñ.

B. Substitution Drill

1.	It's so cheap that you'll probably be amazed.	Aˈñmari yaˈsukute, biˈkkuˈri-suru desyoo.
2.	It's so simple that you'll probably be amazed.	Añmari kañtañ de, biˈkkuˈri-suru desyoo.
3.	It's so complicated that you'll probably be amazed.	Añmari hukuzatu de, biˈkkuˈri-suru desyoo.
4.	It's so different that you'll probably be amazed.	Añmari tiḡatte (i)te, biˈkkuˈri-suru desyoo.
5.	It's so noisy that you'll probably be amazed.	Aˈñmari yakamaˈsikute, biˈkkuˈri-suru desyoo.
6.	It's so quiet that you'll probably be amazed.	Aˈñmari siˈzuka de, biˈkkuˈri-suru desyoo.
7.	It's so strong that you'll probably be amazed.	Aˈñmari tuˈyokute, biˈkkuˈri-suru desyoo.
8.	It takes so much time that you'll probably be amazed.	Aˈñmari zikañ ḡa kakaˈtte, biˈkkuˈri-suru desyoo.
9.	He's so young that you'll probably be amazed.	Aˈñmari waˈkakute, biˈkkuˈri-suru desyoo.

C. Grammar Drill (based on Grammatical Note 1)

Tutor: A┌tu┐i desu yo⌣ 'It's hot.'
Student: A┐tukute ko┌marima┐su yo⌣ 'I'm bothered by the heat.' (Lit. 'Being hot, I'm bothered.')

1.	Ta┌ka┐i desu yo⌣	Ta┐kakute ko┌marima┐su yo⌣
2.	Hu┐beñ desu yo⌣	Hu┐beñ de ko┌marima┐su yo⌣
3.	Ma┌tiḡaima┐su yo⌣	Ma┌tiḡa┐tte ko┌marima┐su yo⌣
4.	To┌oi┐ desu yo⌣	To┌o┐kute ko┌marima┐su yo⌣
5.	Ta┌rimase┐ñ yo⌣	Ta┌rina┐kute ko┌marima┐su yo⌣
6.	Mu┌siatu┐i desu yo⌣	Mu┌sia┐tukute ko┌marima┐su yo⌣
7.	Hu┌kuzatu de┐su yo⌣	Hukuzatu de ko┌marima┐su yo⌣
8.	Hu┌ru┐i desu yo⌣	Hu┐rukute ko┌marima┐su yo⌣
9.	O┌mo┐i desu yo⌣	O┌mo┐kute ko┌marima┐su yo⌣
10.	Ka┌bi ḡa haema┐su yo⌣	Ka┌bi ḡa ha┐ete ko┌marima┐su yo⌣

D. Grammar Drill (based on Grammatical Note 1)

Tutor: Su┌zusi┐i desu ┌ne┐e. 'Isn't it cool!'
Student: Su┌zu┐sikute ┌i┐i desu ┌ne┐e. 'Isn't it nice and cool!'

1.	Tu┌meta┐i desu ┌ne┐e.	Tu┌meta┐kute ┌i┐i desu ┌ne┐e.
2.	Ha┌rema┐sita ┌ne┐e.	Ha┐rete ┌i┐i desu ┌ne┐e.
3.	Ka┐ñtañ de┐su ┌ne┐e.	Kañtañ de ┌i┐i desu ┌ne┐e.
4.	Ti┌ka┐i desu ┌ne┐e.	Ti┌ka┐kute ┌i┐i desu ┌ne┐e.
5.	Ki┐ree desu ┌ne┐e.	Ki┐ree de ┌i┐i desu ┌ne┐e.
6.	Hi┌ro┐i desu ┌ne┐e.	Hi┐rokute ┌i┐i desu ┌ne┐e.
7.	Be┐ñri desu ┌ne┐e.	Be┐ñri de ┌i┐i desu ┌ne┐e.
8.	Ka┌ru┐i desu ┌ne┐e.	Ka┌ru┐kute ┌i┐i desu ┌ne┐e.
9.	Si┐zuka desu ┌ne┐e.	Si┐zuka de ┌i┐i desu ┌ne┐e.
10.	Yo┐ku ni⊢aima⊣su ┌ne┐e.	Yo┐ku ni⊢a⊣tte ┌i┐i desu ┌ne┐e.

E. Grammar Drill (based on Grammatical Note 1)

Tutor: Mo┐o i┌tta┐ kara, mo┐o i┌kimase┐ñ.
Student: Mo┐o i┌tta┐ no de, mo┐o i┌kimase┐ñ.
'Because I already went, I won't go any more.'

1.	Ha┌zi┐mete so⊢ñna mono⊣ (o) ⊢mi⊣ta kara, bi┌kku┐ri-simasita.	Ha┌zi┐mete so⊢ñna mono⊣ (o) ⊢mi⊣ta no de, bi┌kku┐ri-simasita.
2.	Ki ┌ni irana┐i kara, ya┌meta┐i ñ desu ḡa—	Ki ┌ni irana┐i no de, ya┌meta┐i ñ desu ḡa—
3.	Syo┌oziki┐ da kara, so┌ñna koto┐ wa si┌mase┐ñ.	Syo┌oziki┐ na no de, so┌ñna koto┐ wa si┌mase┐ñ.
4.	Mo┐o se┌tumee-site moratta┐ kara, wa┌ka┐ru hazu desu.	Mo┐o se┌tumee-site moratta┐ no de, wa┌ka┐ru hazu desu.
5.	Ha┌take ḡa sukuna┐i kara, yasai wa ta┌ka┐i ñ desu.	Ha┌take ḡa sukuna┐i no de, yasai wa ta┌ka┐i ñ desu.

6. Be⌐ñkyoo-sina⌐katta kara,
    wa⌐karimaseñ desita.

7. A⌐ñmari hukuzatu da⌐tta
    kara, ze⌐ñbu ka⌐ema⌐sita.

8. Hu⌐ruku ⌐na⌐tta kara,
    a⌐tarasi⌐i no ḡa ka⌐ita⌐i
    ñ desu.

Be⌐ñkyoo-sina⌐katta no de, wa⌐ka-
rimaseñ desita.

A⌐ñmari hukuzatu da⌐tta no de,
ze⌐ñbu ka⌐ema⌐sita.

Hu⌐ruku ⌐na⌐tta no de, a⌐tarasi⌐i
no ḡa ka⌐ita⌐i ñ desu.

F. Grammar Drill (based on Grammatical Note 2)

Tutor: Ha⌐take ḡa sukuna⌐i keredo, yasai wa ya⌐su⌐i ñ desu.
        'Although there aren't many farms (lit. fields), the vegeta-
        bles are cheap.'

Student: Ha⌐take ḡa sukuna⌐i no ni, yasai wa ya⌐su⌐i ñ desu.
          'In spite of the fact that there aren't many farms, the veg-
          etables are cheap.'

1. Tu⌐ka⌐rete (i)⌐ta⌐ keredo,
    tu⌐zukema⌐sita.

2. Ta⌐ ya hãtake ḡa o⌐o⌐i
    keredo, bukka wa ta⌐ka⌐i
    ñ desu.

3. Hu⌐beñ na to⌐koro⌐ da
    keredo, ya⌐tiñ wa ta⌐ka⌐i
    ñ desu.

4. Se⌐tumee-site morawana⌐-
    katta keredo, ze⌐ñbu wa-
    ⌐karima⌐sita.

5. Si⌐tya⌐a i⌐kena⌐i tte ⌐tta⌐
    kedo, sityatta.[1]

6. Mu⌐zukasisuḡi⌐ru keredo,
    ka⌐emase⌐ñ.

7. Mo⌐to wa ka⌐ñtañ da⌐tta
    keredo, i⌐ma wa ⌐zu⌐ibuñ
    hu⌐kuzatu ni na⌐tte (i)ma-
    su.

Tu⌐ka⌐rete (i)⌐ta⌐ no ni, tu⌐zuke-
ma⌐sita.

Ta⌐ ya hãtake ḡa o⌐o⌐i no ni,
bukka wa ta⌐ka⌐i ñ desu.

Hu⌐beñ na to⌐koro⌐ na no ni,
ya⌐tiñ wa ta⌐ka⌐i ñ desu.

Se⌐tumee-site morawana⌐katta
no ni, ze⌐ñbu wa⌐karima⌐sita.

Si⌐tya⌐a i⌐kena⌐i tte ⌐tta⌐ no ni,
sityatta.

Mu⌐zukasisuḡi⌐ru no ni, ka⌐ema-
se⌐ñ.

Mo⌐to wa ka⌐ñtañ da⌐tta no ni,
i⌐ma wa ⌐zu⌐ibuñ hu⌐kuzatu ni
na⌐tte (i)masu.

G. Substitution Drill

1. In spite of the fact that
    I took the trouble to
    come here, there wasn't
    a good house for rent.

2. In spite of the fact that
    I took the trouble to make
    it, nobody ate it.
    /tu⌐ku⌐ru, da⌐re mo ta-
    be⌐nai/

Se⌐kkaku kita⌐ no ni, i⌐i kãsiya
(wa) a⌐rimase⌐ñ desita.

Se⌐kkaku tuku⌐tta no ni, da⌐re
mo tabemase⌐ñ desita.

---

[1] Contracted equivalent of Si⌐te⌐ wa i⌐kena⌐i tte i⌐tta⌐ keredo, site simatta.

3. In spite of the fact that I   Se⌐kkaku okane (o) karita⌐ no ni,
    took the trouble to borrow   i⌐rimase⌐ñ desita.
    money, I didn't need it.
    /okane o kariru, iranai/

4. In spite of the fact that I   Se⌐kkaku katta⌐ no ni, tu⌐kaimase⌐ñ
    took the trouble to buy   desita.
    it, I didn't use it. /kau,
    tukawanai/

5. In spite of the fact that I   Se⌐kkaku motte⌐ kita no ni, da⌐re
    took the trouble to bring   mo mimase⌐ñ desita.
    it, nobody looked at it.
    /mo⌐tte ku⌐ru, da⌐re mo
    mi⌐nai/

6. In spite of the fact that I   Se⌐kkaku ha⌐yaku ⌐o⌐kita no ni,
    took the trouble to get up   da⌐re mo miemase⌐ñ desita.
    early, nobody appeared.
    /ha⌐yaku o⌐ki⌐ru, da⌐re
    mo mie⌐nai/

H. Substitution Drill

1. I can't tell whether he   So⌐no⌐ hito (wa) de⌐ki⌐ru ka ⌐do⌐o
    can do it or not.   ka wa⌐karimase⌐ñ.

2. I don't know whether he   So⌐no⌐ hito (wa) de⌐ki⌐ru ka ⌐do⌐o
    can do it or not.   ka si⌐rimase⌐ñ.

3. I don't remember whether   So⌐no⌐ hito (wa) de⌐ki⌐ru ka ⌐do⌐o
    he can do it or not.   ka o⌐bo⌐ete (i)⌐mase⌐ñ.

4. I've forgotten whether he   So⌐no⌐ hito (wa) de⌐ki⌐ru ka ⌐do⌐o
    can do it or not.   ka wa⌐surema⌐sita.

5. Please tell me whether   So⌐no⌐ hito (wa) de⌐ki⌐ru ka ⌐do⌐o
    he can do it or not.   ka o⌐siete kudasa⌐i.

6. Do you know whether he   So⌐no⌐ hito (wa) de⌐ki⌐ru ka ⌐do⌐o
    can do it or not?   ka go⌐zo⌐ñzi desyoo ka.

I. Grammar Drill (based on Grammatical Note 3)

Tutor: Ta⌐ka⌐i desu ka, ya⌐su⌐i desu ka⌐ 'Is it expensive or is it
         cheap?'
Student: Ta⌐ka⌐i ka ya⌐su⌐i ka si⌐rimase⌐ñ. 'I don't know whether
         it's expensive or cheap.'

1. Hi⌐syo⌐ (o) ya⌐toima⌐sita   Hi⌐syo⌐ (o) ya⌐to⌐tta ka ya⌐towa⌐-
    ka, ya⌐toimase⌐ñ desita   nakatta ka si⌐rimase⌐ñ.
    ka⌐

2. Ka⌐ñtañ de⌐su ka, hu⌐ku-   Kañtañ ka hŭkuzatu ka si⌐rima-
    zatu de⌐su ka⌐   se⌐ñ.

3. Me⌐ğane (o) ⌐ka⌐kete (i)ma-   Me⌐ğane (o) ⌐ka⌐kete (i)ta ka ⌐do⌐o
    sita ka⌐   ka si⌐rimase⌐ñ.

4. A⌐ita uti⌐ (ğa) a⌐rima⌐su   A⌐ita uti⌐ (ğa) ⌐a⌐ru ka ⌐do⌐o ka
    ka⌐   si⌐rimase⌐ñ.

5. Tu⌐yo⌐i desu ka, yo⌐wa⌐i   Tu⌐yo⌐i ka yo⌐wa⌐i ka si⌐rimase⌐ñ.
    desu ka⌐

6. Ta⌐isi⌐kañ desita ka,   Ta⌐isi⌐kañ datta ka ryo⌐ozi⌐kañ
   ryo⌐ozi⌐kañ desita ka⌐   datta ka si⌐rimase⌐ñ.

7. Syo⌐okai-site moraima⌐-   Syo⌐okai-site moratta⌐ ka ⌐do⌐o
   sita ka⌐   ka si⌐rimase⌐ñ.

8. O⌐isi⌐i desu ka⌐   O⌐isi⌐i ka ⌐do⌐o ka si⌐rimase⌐ñ.

9. Gu⌐ñziñ de⌐sita ka⌐   Gu⌐ñziñ da⌐tta ka ⌐do⌐o ka si⌐rima-
                      se⌐ñ.

10. Ka⌐siya de⌐su ka⌐   Ka⌐siya ka do⌐o ka si⌐rimase⌐ñ.

J. Grammar Drill (based on Grammatical Note 3)

> Tutor: A⌐tara⌐sikute mo ⌐hu⌐rukute mo ka⌐maimase⌐ñ. 'It doesn't
> matter whether it's new or old.'
> Student: A⌐tarasi⌐i ka hu⌐ru⌐i ka si⌐rimase⌐ñ. 'I don't know whether
> it's new or old.'

1. Yo⌐yaku-site⌐ mo si⌐na⌐-   Yo⌐yaku-suru⌐ ka si⌐na⌐i ka si⌐ri-
   kute mo ka⌐maimase⌐ñ.   mase⌐ñ.

2. Hi⌐rokute mo ⌐se⌐makute   Hi⌐ro⌐i ka se⌐ma⌐i ka si⌐rimase⌐ñ.
   mo ka⌐maimase⌐ñ.

3. Wa⌐kakute mo to⌐siyori⌐   Wa⌐ka⌐i ka to⌐siyori⌐ ka si⌐rima-
   de mo ka⌐maimase⌐ñ.   se⌐ñ.

4. O⌐nazi de⌐ mo ti⌐gatte   Onazi ka ti⌐gatte (i)ru⌐ ka si⌐ri-
   (i)te⌐ mo ka⌐maimase⌐ñ.   mase⌐ñ.

5. Ka⌐ta⌐kute mo ya⌐wara⌐-   Ka⌐ta⌐i ka ya⌐waraka⌐i ka si⌐rima-
   kakute mo ka⌐maimase⌐ñ. se⌐ñ.

6. Ha⌐taraite⌐ mo a⌐soñde⌐   Ha⌐taraku⌐ ka a⌐sobu⌐ ka si⌐rima-
   mo ka⌐maimase⌐ñ.   se⌐ñ.

7. Be⌐ñri de mo ⌐hu⌐beñ de   Be⌐ñri ka ⌐hu⌐beñ ka si⌐rimase⌐ñ.
   mo ka⌐maimase⌐ñ.

8. Ke⌐ñbutu-site⌐ mo o⌐yo⌐gi Ke⌐ñbutu-suru⌐ ka o⌐yo⌐gi ni i⌐ku⌐
   ni i⌐tte⌐ mo ka⌐maima-   ka si⌐rimase⌐ñ.
   se⌐ñ.

K. Substitution Drill

1. I'm using it as a summer   Sore (o) na⌐tu no uti⌐ to site
   home.   tukatte (i)masu.

2. I'm using it as a cleaning Sore (o) zo⌐okiñ to site tukatte
   rag.   (i)ma⌐su.

3. I'm using it as a baby   Sore (o) ⌐a⌐katyañ no ⌐be⌐tto to
   bed.   site tukatte (i)masu.

4. I'm using it as a furoshiki. Sore (o) hu⌐rosiki to site tukatte
                      (i)ma⌐su.

5. I'm using it as a desk.   Sore (o) tu⌐kue to site tukatte
                      (i)ma⌐su.

6. I'm using it as a mos-   Sore (o) ka⌐ya to site tukatte
   quito net.   (i)ma⌐su.

7. I'm using it as an ashtray. Sore (o) ha⌐iza⌐ra to site tukatte
                      (i)masu.

8. I'm using it as a store.   Sore (o) mi⌐se⌐ to site tukatte
                      (i)masu.

L. Substitution Drill

1. It's nice as a summer home, isn't it.

Na⌐tu no uti¬ to si⌐te¬ wa ⌐i¬i desu ⌐ne¬e.

2. It's big for a farm (lit. field), isn't it.

Ha⌐take to site¬ wa hi⌐ro¬i desu ⌐ne¬e.

3. It's cheap for rent, isn't it.

Ya⌐tiñ to si⌐te¬ wa ya⌐su¬i desu ⌐ne¬e.

4. It's complicated for a plot, isn't it.

Su⌐zi to si⌐te¬ wa hu⌐kuzatu de⌐su ⌐ne¬e.

5. It's long for a winter vacation, isn't it.

Hu⌐yuya⌐sumi to si⌐te¬ wa na⌐ga¬i desu ⌐ne¬e.

6. It's slow for an express, isn't it.

Kyu⌐ukoo to site¬ wa o⌐so¬i desu ⌐ne¬e.

7. He's heavy for a baby, isn't he.

A⌐katyañ to si⌐te¬ wa o⌐mo¬i desu ⌐ne¬e.

8. He's young for a teacher, isn't he.

Se⌐ñse¬e to si⌐te¬ wa wa⌐ka¬i desu ⌐ne¬e.

9. He's nice as a person, isn't he.

Hi⌐to to site¬ wa ⌐i¬i desu ⌐ne¬e.

M. Expansion Drill

1. I couldn't buy any.

Ka⌐emase¬ñ desita.

They were sold out already so I couldn't buy any.

Mo⌐o u⌐rikire da⌐tta kara, ka⌐emase¬ñ desita.

In spite of the fact that I went to buy [them] they were sold out already so I couldn't buy any.

Ka⌐i ni itta¬ no ni; mo⌐o u⌐rikire da⌐tta kara, ka⌐emase¬ñ desita.

In spite of the fact that I went to buy tickets, they were sold out already so I couldn't buy any.

Ki⌐ppu (o) kai ni itta¬ no ni; mo⌐o u⌐rikire da⌐tta kara, ka⌐emase¬ñ desita.

In spite of the fact that I went all the way to the Kabukiza to buy tickets, they were sold out already so I couldn't buy any.

Ka⌐bukiza ma⌐de ki⌐ppu (o) kai ni itta¬ no ni; mo⌐o u⌐rikire da⌐tta kara, ka⌐emase¬ñ desita.

In spite of the fact that I took the trouble to go all the way to the Kabukiza to buy tickets, they were sold out already so I couldn't buy any.

Se⌐kkaku Kabukiza ma⌐de ki⌐ppu (o) kai ni itta¬ no ni; mo⌐o u⌐rikire da⌐tta kara, ka⌐emase¬ñ de-sita.

2. I'd like to go.

I⌐kita¬i ñ desu.

I'd like to go after my summer vacation starts.

Na⌐tuya⌐sumi ni ⌐na⌐tte kara i⌐kita¬i ñ desu.

Because there are lots of houses for rent, I'd like to go there after my summer vacation starts.

Ka⌐siya ḡa oo⌐i no de, na⌐tuya⌐su-mi ni ⌐na⌐tte kara i⌐kita⌐i ñ de-su.

Because the scenery is nice and there are lots of houses for rent, I'd like to go there after my summer vacation starts.

Ke⌐siki mo ⌐i⌐i si, ka⌐siya ḡa oo⌐i no de; na⌐tuya⌐sumi ni ⌐na⌐tte kara i⌐kita⌐i ñ desu.

Because [it] is convenient and the scenery is nice and there are lots of houses for rent, I'd like to go there after my summer vacation starts.

Be⌐ñri da si, ke⌐siki mo ⌐i⌐i si, ka⌐siya ḡa oo⌐i no de; na⌐tuya⌐su-mi ni ⌐na⌐tte kara i⌐kita⌐i ñ desu.

Because that town is convenient and the scenery is nice and there are lots of houses for rent, I'd like to go there after my summer vacation starts.

A⌐no mati⌐ (wa) ⌐be⌐ñri da si, ke⌐-siki mo ⌐i⌐i si, ka⌐siya ḡa oo⌐i no de; na⌐tuya⌐sumi ni ⌐na⌐tte kara i⌐kita⌐i ñ desu.

3. I'll get in touch with you.

Go⌐reñraku-sima⌐su.

Even if I'm not going to rent it I'll get in touch with you.

Ka⌐rina⌐kute mo go⌐reñraku-sima⌐-su.

Whether I rent it or not I'll get in touch with you.

Ka⌐rite⌐ mo ka⌐rina⌐kute mo go⌐reñ-raku-sima⌐su.

I'll think it over a little and whether I rent it or not I'll get in touch with you.

Tyo⌐tto ka⌐ñḡa⌐ete, ka⌐rite⌐ mo ka-⌐rina⌐kute mo go⌐reñraku-sima⌐su.

I can't tell yet, but I'll think it over a little and whether I rent it or not I'll get in touch with you.

Ma⌐da wa⌐karimase⌐ñ ḡa; tyo⌐tto ka⌐ñḡa⌐ete, ka⌐rite⌐ mo ka⌐rina⌐-kute mo go⌐reñraku-sima⌐su.

I can't tell yet whether I'm going to rent it or not, but I'll think it over a little and whether I rent it or not I'll get in touch with you.

Ka⌐riru⌐ ka ⌐do⌐o ka ⌐ma⌐da wa⌐ka-rimase⌐ñ ḡa; tyo⌐tto ka⌐ñḡa⌐ete, ka⌐rite⌐ mo ka⌐rina⌐kute mo go-⌐reñraku-sima⌐su.

4. I think [it] is just fine.

Tyo⌐odo i⌐i to omoimasu.

I think an inn like this is just fine.

Koo iu ryokañ ḡa tyo⌐odo i⌐i to omoimasu.

I've been looking for [one]. I think an inn like this is just fine.

Sa⌐ḡasite (i)ru⌐ ñ desu ḡa, koo iu ryokañ ḡa tyo⌐odo i⌐i to omoimasu.

I've been looking for a
cheaper place. I think
an inn like this is just
fine.

Because it's too expen-
sive I've been looking
for a cheaper place. I
think an inn like this is
just fine.

I wanted to stop [there]
but because it's too ex-
pensive I've been look-
ing for a cheaper place.
I think an inn like this
is just fine.

I wanted to stop at a big
hotel but because they're
too expensive I've been
looking for a cheaper
place. I think an inn
like this is just fine.

Mo⌐tto ya⌐su¬i to⌐koro⌐ (o) sa⌐ḡa-
site (i)ru⌐ ñ desu ḡa, koo iu
ryokañ ḡa tyo⌐odo i⌐i to omoimasu.

A⌐ñmari taka⌐i no de, mo⌐tto ya-
⌐su⌐i to⌐koro⌐ (o) sa⌐ḡasite (i)ru⌐
ñ desu ḡa; koo iu ryokañ ḡa
tyo⌐odo i⌐i to omoimasu.

To⌐marita⌐katta keredo; a⌐ñmari
taka⌐i no de, mo⌐tto ya⌐su⌐i to-
⌐koro⌐ (o) sa⌐ḡasite (i)ru⌐ ñ
desu ḡa; koo iu ryokañ ḡa tyo-
⌐odo i⌐i to omoimasu.

O⌐oki⌐i ⌐ho⌐teru ni to⌐marita⌐ka-
tta keredo; a⌐ñmari taka⌐i no de,
mo⌐tto ya⌐su⌐i to⌐koro⌐ (o) sa⌐ḡa-
site (i)ru⌐ ñ desu ḡa; koo iu ryokañ ḡa tyo⌐odo i⌐i to omoimasu.

QUESTION SUPPLEMENT

(based on the Basic Dialogues)

(a) 1. Su⌐misu-sañ to Ta⌐naka-sañ no hana⌐site iru to⌐koro⌐ wa, do⌐ñna to-
⌐koro⌐ desu ka↲

2. Do⌐o site ⌐Su⌐misu-sañ wa ko⌐no heñ ni ka⌐siya ḡa a⌐ru ka ⌐do⌐o ka
ki⌐kima⌐sita ka↲

3. Ta⌐naka-sañ no heñzi⌐ wa?

4. Su⌐misu-sañ wa ⌐doko e i⌐kita⌐katta ñ desu ka↲ Do⌐o site ya⌐me-
ma⌐sita ka↲ I⌐ma ⌐doñna to⌐koro⌐ o sa⌐ḡasite ima⌐su ka↲

5. Ha⌐zime ni mi⌐ta uti wa ⌐doo site ki ⌐ni irimase⌐ñ desita ka↲

6. So⌐no tuḡi⌐ wa ⌐doñna u⌐ti de⌐sita ka↲ Ka⌐siya de⌐sita ka↲

7. Ke⌐siki wa ⌐doo desu ka↲

8. Tanaka-sañ wa ⌐ya⌐nusi o si⌐tte ima⌐su ka↲

9. Do⌐o site ⌐Su⌐misu-sañ wa syo⌐okai-site moraita⌐i ñ desu ka↲

(b) 10. Su⌐misu-sañ wa ⌐i⌐tu ki⌐ta⌐i ñ desu ka↲

11. Su⌐misu-sañ wa do⌐no-ḡurai natu no uti o karita⌐i ñ desu ka↲

12. Ko⌐no uti no ya⌐tiñ wa ⌐i⌐kura desu ka↲

13. Koko wa To⌐okyoo kara to⌐oi⌐ desu ka, ti⌐ka⌐i desu ka↲

14. To⌐okyoo ma⌐de ka⌐yoema⌐su ka↲

(c) 15. To⌐okyoo no natu⌐ wa ⌐do⌐o desu ka↲

16. Ko⌐ko no natu⌐ wa hu̇tuu ⌐do⌐o desu ka↲ Kyo⌐neñ no na⌐tu⌐ wa ⌐do⌐o
desita ka↲

17. Kono uti kara ⌐e⌐ki made a⌐ru⌐ite do⌐no-ḡurai kakarima⌐su ka↲

18. I⌐tu mo ⌐ba⌐su ḡa a⌐rima⌐su ka↲

19. E⌐ki no ⌐so⌐ba ni ⌐do⌐ñna mi⌐se⌐ ḡa a⌐rima⌐su ka↲

20. Do⌐ñna mi⌐se⌐ ḡa ⌐su⌐ḡu ⌐so⌐ba ni a⌐rima⌐su ka↲

(d) 21. Koko no bukka wa ⌐do̅⌐o desu ka⌐

22. Na⌐ni g̅a to⌐kubetu ni yasu⌐i n̅ desu ka⌐

23. Na⌐tu no bukka wa do̅⌐o desu ka⌐

24. Ko⌐ko no yasai wa yasu⌐i n̅ desu g̅a, sore wa kōno hen̅ wa ha⌐take g̅a oo⌐i kara desu ka⌐

25. Su⌐misu-san̅ wa kōno uti o ka⌐riru ka do̅⌐o ka yānusi ni i⌐ima⌐sita ka⌐

26. Su⌐misu-san̅ wa kōno syuumatu ni ⌐do̅⌐ko e i⌐ku tumori de⌐su ka⌐

27. Su⌐misu-san̅ wa ⌐yānusi ni ⌐do̅n̅na ya⌐kusoku o sima⌐sita ka⌐

(e) 28. Su⌐misu-san̅ wa rāisyuu ⌐do̅⌐o su⌐ru tumori de⌐su ka⌐

EXERCISES

1. You have just met the owner of a house in Karuizawa which you are interested in renting for the summer. Using the Basic Sentences of this lesson as a point of departure, discuss the house, including as many questions and details as possible.

2. Make up six short dialogues each one of which contains one of the following:

a. ta⌐kakatta no ni

b. a⌐me g̅a hu⌐rihazime⌐ta no de

c. hi⌐rune o sita⌐ no ni

d. to⌐siyori⌐ na no de

e. se̩⌐kkaku kita⌐ no ni

f. ka⌐isya g̅a tika⌐i no de

Lesson 30. Renting a House (cont.)

BASIC DIALOGUES: FOR MEMORIZATION

(a)

Tanaka

according to what
Mr. Ueda says

Uᴦeda-sañ no hanasi˥ ni
yoru to

a house for rent that
seems just right for
you

aᴦna˥ta ni tyoᴦodo i˥i yoo
na kāsiya

advertisement

kookoku

an advertisement for
a house for rent

kasiya no kookoku

1. According to (what) Mr. Ueda
(says), in this morning's
paper there was an ad for a
house for rent that seems
just right for you. Did you
see it?

Uᴦeda-sañ no hanasi˥ ni yoru
to, ke˥sa no siñbuñ ni aᴦna˥ta ni
tyoᴦodo i˥i yoo na kaᴦsiya no
kookoku ḡa a˥tta soo desu ḡa;
goᴦrañ ni narima˥sita ka⌐

Smith

2. I just read it.

Yo˥ñda toᴦkoro˥ desu.

(handing over newspaper)

This is it. Here.

Koᴦre de˥su yo. Do˥ozo.

Tanaka (after reading the advertisement)

maybe it's good

i˥i ka mo sirenai

3. Oh, this may be good!

A˥a, i˥i ka mo siremaseñ ᴦne˥e.

agent

buᴦro˥okaa

4. Why don't you ask the agent
and see [about it]?

Buᴦro˥okaa ni kiᴦite mi˥tara ᴦdo˥o
desyoo.

(b)

Smith

facts pertaining to a
house

uᴦti no koto˥

concerning facts per-
taining to a house

uᴦti no koto˥ de

5. I'd like to inquire about a
house . . .

Uᴦti no koto˥ de ᴦtyo˥tto uᴦkaḡai-
ta˥i ñ desu ḡa—

(name of a Japanese
newspaper)

A˥sahi

198

6. I read [about it] in Asahi this morning. What kind of house is that (house)?

    Ke⌐sa ⌐A⌐sahi de yo⌐mima⌐sita ḡa, a⌐no uti⌐ (wa) ⌐do⌐ñna u⌐ti⌐ desu ka⌐

            Agent

    building lot   sikiti
    one tsubo (approximately   hi⌐to⌐-tubo
      6' x 6')
    200 tsubo   ni⌐hyaku⌐-tubo

7. Let's see. The lot is (lit. has) 200 tsubo.

    So⌐o desu ⌐ne⌐e. Sikiti (wa) ni⌐hyaku⌐-tubo a⌐rima⌐su yo⌐

            Smith

8. That's big, isn't it—for in the city . . .

    Hi⌐ro⌐i desu ⌐ne⌐e — ma⌐ti no na⌐ka to si⌐te⌐ wa.

            Agent

    three-mat area <u>or</u> room   sa⌐ñ-zyo⌐o
    four-and-one-half-mat   yo-⌐zyo⌐o-hañ
      area <u>or</u> room
    six-mat area <u>or</u> room   ro⌐ku-zyo⌐o
    eight-mat area <u>or</u> room   ha⌐ti-zyo⌐o
    ten-mat area <u>or</u> room   zyu⌐u-zyo⌐o

9. Yes. The house consists of (lit. is) an eight-mat room, two six-mat rooms, a four-and-one-half-mat room, a three-mat room, and a Western-style room with a ten-mat area . . .

    E⌐e. Uti wa ha⌐ti-zyo⌐o; ro⌐ku-zyo⌐o hu⌐ta⌐-ma; yo-⌐zyo⌐o-hañ; sa⌐ñ-zyo⌐o; sore kara, zyu⌐u-zyo⌐o no yo⌐oma na⌐ ñ desu ḡa⌐

            Smith

10. I see.   A⌐a, so⌐o.

            Agent

    south   minami
    facing south   minamimuki
    exposure to the sun   hiatari
    is sunny   hi⌐atari ḡa i⌐i

11. It's not a very big house, but it faces south so it's sunny, and it has a large beautiful garden.

    A⌐ñmari ooki⌐i u⌐ti⌐ zya ⌐na⌐i ñ desu ḡa; mi⌐namimuki de⌐su kara, hi⌐atari ḡa yo⌐kute; sore kara, hi⌐ro⌐i ⌐ki⌐ree na ni⌐wa ḡa arima⌐su yo⌐

            Smith

    equipment <u>or</u> facilities   se⌐tubi
      <u>or</u> accommodations

12. Oh. How is the equipment?

    So⌐o desu ka. Se⌐tubi (wa) ⌐do⌐o desyoo ka.

Agent

13. It's good—very [good].   I⌐i desu yo⌐ — tottemo⌐

Smith

flushing   suiseñ
14. I suppose the toilet is a   Te⌐a⌐rai (wa) su⌐iseñ desyo⌐o ne?
    flush toilet, isn't it?

Agent

15. Yes, that's right.   E⌐e ⌐so⌐o desu yo⌐

Smith

running water or   suidoo
    water pipes
16. What about gas [and] running   Ga⌐su, suidoo wa?
    water?

Agent

17. Of course it's running water   Mo⌐ti⌐roñ su⌐idoo de⌐su ḡa, ano
    but that area doesn't have gas   heñ (wa) ⌐ma⌐da ⌐ga⌐su wa ⌐na⌐i ñ
    yet.   desu yo.

Smith

18. What about the bath?   O⌐hu⌐ro wa?

Agent

coal   se⌐kita⌐ñ
19. It's [heated with] coal.   Se⌐kita⌐ñ desu.

Smith

heating   dañboo
20. How about the heating?   Dañboo wa?

Agent

Western-style building   yookañ
heating equipment or   da⌐ñboose⌐tubi
    central heating
21. It's not a Western-style   Yo⌐okañ zya na⌐i ñ desu kara,
    building so there's no central   da⌐ñboose⌐tubi (wa) a⌐rimase⌐ñ.
    heating.

    I guess or you might   ma⌐a
    say
    electric heater   de⌐ñkisuto⌐obu
    quilt-covered warming   kotatu
      place
    to the approximate extent   ko⌐tatu-ḡu⌐rai
      of a kotatsu
22. I guess electric heaters, hi-   Ma⌐a; de⌐ñkisuto⌐obu, hi⌐bati,
    bachi, [and] kotatsu are about   ko⌐tatu-ḡu⌐rai de⌐ .
    all [that you could use] . . .

Smith

repairs   syuuzeñ
the tenant (lit. the side   ka⌐riru ho̚o
  that borrows or rents)
do [it] through the tenant   ka⌐riru ho̚o de suru
23. The repairs wouldn't have to   Syuuzeñ (wa) ka⌐riru ho̚o de si-
be made by the tenant, would   ⌐na̍kute mo ⌐i̍i ñ desⓡoo ne?
they?

Agent

24. No (lit. that's right), (because)   E̚e, ya̍nusi ḡa si⌐ma̍su kara__
the landlord makes them.

(c)

Landlord (showing the house)

roof   ya̍ne
fence   ka⌐ki̍ne
wall   hee
become painful <u>or</u>   i⌐ta̍mu /-u/
  damaged <u>or</u> worn out
be painful <u>or</u> damaged   i⌐ta̍ñde (i)ru
  <u>or</u> worn out
25. [Right] now I'm repairing the   I̍ma ⌐ya̍ne (o) na⌐o̍site, ta⌐ta-
roof and (ex)changing the   mi (o) torikaete (i)ma̍su ḡa;
mats. The fence and wall   ka⌐ki̍ne to he̋e mo ⌐tyo̍tto i⌐ta̍-
are also a bit damaged so   ñde (i)masu kara, so⌐re mo na-
I'm thinking of repairing   oso̚o to o⌐mo̍tte (i)ru ñ desu.
them too.

Smith

wall of a room   kabe
26. How about the walls?   Kabe wa?

Landlord

paint   nuru /-u/
repaint   nu⌐rikae̍ru /-ru/
27. The walls are clean so I don't   Ka⌐be wa ki̍ree desu kara, nu-
think they'll have to be re-   ⌐rikae̍nakute mo ⌐i̍i to omoi-
painted (lit. I think it will be   masu.
all right even if I don't re-
paint them).

Smith

screens   a⌐mi̍do
28. Are there screens?   A⌐mi̍do (ḡa) a⌐rima̍su ka__

Landlord

29. There aren't any but I can   Na̍i ñ desu ḡa, su̍ḡu tu⌐kera-
put them on right away.   rema̍su yo.

Smith

trash   go⌐mi¬
30. What about trash?   Go⌐mi¬ wa?

Landlord

trash collector   go⌐mi¬ya
31. The trash collector comes so   Go⌐mi¬ya (ga) ki⌐ma¬su kara, go-
    don't worry about that.   ⌐siṅpai na¬ku.

Smith

day after tomorrow   a⌐sa¬tte
32. Well, I'll bring my wife the   Zya¬a, a⌐sa¬tte ⌐ka¬nai (o) tu⌐rete
    day after tomorrow; (so)   kima¬su kara, mo⌐o iti-do mi¬-
    would you let me see [the   sete i⌐tadakemase¬ṅ ka.
    house] again [then]?

Landlord

maybe [someone] isn't   i⌐na¬i ka mo sirenai
there
33. I may not be in but my wife   Wa⌐takusi wa ina¬i ka mo si-
    will be here so come right   ⌐remase¬ṅ ga; ka⌐nai wa o⌐ri-
    ahead.   ma¬su kara, do⌐ozo.

ADDITIONAL VOCABULARY

1. The chimney is damaged so I   E⌐ṅtotu ga itaṅde (i)masu kara,
    want to have it fixed...   na⌐o¬site mo⌐raita¬i ṅ desu ga—

        floor   yuka
        ceiling   teṅzyoo
        gate   mo¬ṅ

2. I'd like to see the southern   Nihoṅ no mi⌐nami no ho¬o ga
    part of Japan...   mi⌐ta¬i ṅ desu ga—

        north   ki⌐ta¬
        east   hi⌐gasi¬
        west   nisi

NOTES ON THE BASIC DIALOGUES

1. Note again the occurrence of particle ga separating a statement from a
    related question.

6. See preceding note.

9. Ro⌐ku-zyo¬o hu⌐ta¬-ma: note the occurrence of a number directly follow-
    ing a member of an enumerated series.

11. Note also: kitamuki 'facing north,' higasimuki 'facing east,' and nisi-
    muki 'facing west.'

23. Note: <u>syuuzeñ-suru</u> 'repair,' 'fix' is used in reference to houses, ma-
     chines, watches, etc. <u>Na⌐o¬su</u> is a word of more general use.
     For a description of the negative permission pattern, see Lesson 22,
     Grammatical Note 4.

25. <u>Hee</u> is an outdoor wall, for example one surrounding a house; <u>kabe</u> (Basic
     Sentence 26) refers most frequently to the plaster walls in a Japanese
     house.

27. <u>Nu⌐rikae¬ru</u>: compare <u>ki⌐kae¬ru</u> 'change clothes'; <u>no⌐rikae¬ru</u> 'change ve-
     hicles'; <u>torikaeru</u> 'exchange.'
     For a description of the negative permission pattern, see Lesson 22,
     Grammatical Note 4.

GRAMMATICAL NOTES

1. <u>to⌐koro¬</u> [1]

    In many of its occurrences, the nominal <u>to⌐koro¬</u> refers only to spatial lo-
cation and means 'place.' For example:

     Ki¬ree na to⌐koro¬ desu. 'It's a pretty place.'
     Ka̅gu o u⌐tte iru tokoro¬ wa ⌐do¬ko desu ka⌄ 'Where is the place
       where they sell furniture?

    But in other contexts, <u>to⌐koro¬</u> refers to location in time and means 'oc-
casion' or 'moment' or 'point in time.' The words occurring with <u>to⌐ko-
ro¬</u> or the over-all context determines which meaning it has in any given occurrence.

    The following examples illustrate some of the uses of <u>to⌐koro¬</u> as a time
word. Note that in other contexts many of these same combinations would
refer to place.

<u>to⌐koro¬</u> + √da

     Yo¬mu to⌐koro¬ desu. 'I'm just going to read.'
     Yo¬ñde iru to⌐koro¬ desu. 'I'm just reading.'
     Yo¬ñda to⌐koro¬ desu. 'I've just read.'
     Yo¬ñde ita to⌐koro¬ desu. 'I have just been reading.'
     Yo⌐mo¬o to si⌐te iru tokoro¬ desu. 'I'm just on the point of reading.'
       or 'I'm just about to read.'
     Yo¬mu to⌐koro¬ desita. 'I was just going to read.'
     Yo¬ñde iru to⌐koro¬ desita. 'I was just reading.'
     Yo¬ñda to⌐koro¬ desita. 'I had just read.'
     Yo¬ñde ita to⌐koro¬ desita. 'I had just been reading.'
     Yo⌐mo¬o to si⌐te iru tokoro¬ desita. 'I was just about to read.'

<u>to⌐koro¬</u> + o

     Se⌐ñse¬e g̅a ⌐yo¬ñde iru to⌐koro¬ o mi⌐ma¬sita. 'I saw the teacher just
       as he was reading.'
     O⌐isog̅asii tokoro¬ o a⌐ri¬g̅atoo gozaimasita. 'Thank you [for your kind-
       ness] just at a time when you are busy.'

---

[1] The contracted equivalent is <u>toko</u>.

$$\text{to}^{\lceil}\text{koro}^{\rceil} + \left| \frac{\text{e}}{\text{ni}} \right|$$

Se⌐n̄se⌐e ḡa ⌐yon̄de iru to⌐koro⌐ $\left| \begin{array}{c} \text{e} \\ \text{ni} \end{array} \right|$ ki⌐ma⌐sita. 'I came just as the
teacher was reading.'

The gerund of an intransitive verbal of motion + √iru regularly refers to
a state rather than an action:

> ka⌐eru 'return' ~ ka⌐ette iru 'be back'
> ku⌐ru 'come' ~ ki⌐te⌐ iru 'be here' etc.

However, before to⌐koro⌐, such combinations often refer to the actual occurrence of the action: ka⌐ette iru tokoro 'just the time when [someone] is returning,' ki⌐te⌐ iru tokoro 'just the time when [someone] is coming.'

2. ——ka mo sirenai

X + ka mo sirenai (formal, si⌐remase⌐n̄) means 'maybe X,' 'X may be
true.' X consists of, or ends with, a verbal (informal non-past or past), an
adjectival (informal non-past or past, affirmative or negative), a nominal,
da⌐tta, or a particle. In other words, ka mo sirenai is preceded by an informal sentence, non-past or past, but before ka mo sirenai, the informal
non-past copula da is lost.

The accent of inflected words before ka is the same as that before kara,
no, keredo, etc. Following an unaccented word or phrase, the ka of ka mo
sirenai is accented.

Examples:

> Ku⌐ru ka mo siremase n̄. 'Maybe he'll come.'
> Ki⌐ta ka mo siremase n̄. 'Maybe he has come.'
> Mu⌐zukasi⌐i ka mo siremase n̄. 'It may be difficult.'
> Mu⌐zukasi⌐katta ka mo siremase n̄. 'It may have been difficult.'
> I⌐sya ka⌐ mo siremase n̄. 'He may be a doctor.'
>   (Cf. Isya da. 'He is a doctor.')
> Byo⌐oki da⌐tta ka mo siremase n̄. 'Maybe he was sick.'
> Bo⌐ku no ka mo siremase n̄. 'Maybe it's mine.'
>   (Cf. Bo⌐ku no da. 'It is mine.')
> To⌐modati kara ka⌐ mo siremase n̄. 'Maybe it's from a friend.'
>   (Cf. Tomadati kara da. 'It's from a friend.')
> To⌐modati da⌐ kara ka mo siremase n̄. 'Maybe it's because he's a
>   friend.'
>   (Cf. To⌐modati da⌐ kara da. 'It's because he's a friend.')
> Ko⌐nai ka mo siremase n̄. 'Maybe he won't come.'
> Mu⌐zukasiku na⌐i ka mo siremase n̄. 'Maybe it isn't difficult.'
> So⌐o zya ⌐na⌐i ka mo siremase n̄. 'Maybe it isn't so.'

3. ——ni yoru to

A nominal followed by ni yoru to indicates the source of the statement
that follows. The source may be a person (se⌐n̄se⌐e ni yoru to 'according to
the teacher'), but more often it is a thing (ra⌐zio ni yoru to 'according to the
radio'), particularly something said or written (se⌐n̄se⌐e no ha⌐nasi⌐ ni yoru

to 'according to what the teacher says,' a⌐no ho¬n̄ ni yoru to 'according to that book'). —— ni yoru to is a rather formal expression.

Most sentences containing —— ni yoru to also contain so⌐o √da (Lesson 22, Grammatical Note 2) as a further indication that the information is second-hand. Thus:

> Ke⌐sa moratta teḡami ni yoru to, Tookyoo wa ko̅tosi ⌐zu⌐ibun̄ sa⌐mu⌐i soo desu.
> 'According to a letter I received this morning, (the report is that) Tokyo is awfully cold this year.'
> To⌐modati no hanasi¬ ni yoru to, a⌐no buro̅okaa wa syo⌐oziki¬ zya ⌐na⌐i soo desu ḡa; ho⌐n̄too de¬su ka⌐˩
> 'According to what a friend tells me, (the report is that) that agent isn't honest. Is that true?'

4. Counters: -tubo, -zyoo

-Tubo is the most common counter of Japanese area measurement for building lots, gardens, houses, etc. One tsubo equals the area covered by two tatami, i.e. approximately 36 square feet. For combinations with numerals from 1 to 10, see the list below noting the mixture of numerals from both series; from 11 on, -tubo combines with numerals of Series I: zyu⌐ui¬t-tubo '11 tsubo,' zyu⌐uni¬-tubo '12 tsubo,' etc.).

-Zyoo is another Japanese area counter, used in measuring the size of rooms. One jo equals the area covered by one tatami, i.e. approximately 18 square feet or exactly $1/2$-tsubo. -Zyoo combines with numerals of Series I, but only certain combinations occur with any frequency (see the list, following). A numeral compounded with -zyoo, besides indicating an area, may also be used as the name for a room having that area.

Study the following lists:

hi⌐to⌐-tubo	'1 tsubo'	i⌐ti-zyo⌐o	'1-mat area'
hu⌐ta⌐-tubo	'2 tsubo'	ni-⌐zyo⌐o	'2-mat area'
mi¬-tubo	'3 tsubo'	sa⌐n̄-zyo⌐o	'3-mat area' or '3-mat room'
yo¬-tubo	'4 tsubo'	yo-⌐zyo⌐o-han̄	'4 $1/2$-mat area' or '4 $1/2$-mat room'
i⌐tu¬-tubo or			
go¬-tubo	'5 tsubo'		
ro⌐ku¬-tubo	'6 tsubo'	ro⌐ku-zyo⌐o	'6-mat area' or '6-mat room'
na⌐na¬-tubo	'7 tsubo'		
ha⌐t-tubo	'8 tsubo'	ha⌐ti-zyo⌐o	'8-mat area' or '8-mat room'
kyu⌐u-tubo	'9 tsubo'		
to¬-tubo	'10 tsubo'	zyu⌐u-zyo⌐o	'10-mat area' or '10-mat room'
na¬n̄-tubo	'how many tsubo?'	na¬n̄-zyoo	'area of how many mats?'

5. More About -g͟u⌐rai

-G͞u⌐rai 'about' has occurred previously following numbers and indefinite quantity expressions (cf. Lesson 8, Grammatical Note 5). It may also occur following non-quantity expressions indicating approximate extent: 'to the extent of ——,' 'about as much as ——,' ' —— being about all.'

Examples:

> Kyo⌐neñ wa, a⌐no mise no hito⌐ wa, mi⌐ñna eeg͞o g͞a dekima⌐sita g͞a; kotosi wa, Tanaka-sañ, Ya⌐mamoto-sañ-g͞u⌐rai de; ho⌐ka no hito⌐ wa, ze⌐ñzeñ dekimase⌐ñ.
> 'Last year the people in that store could all speak English, but this year Tanaka and Yamamoto are about the only ones and the other people can't speak at all.'
> Hu⌐zisañ-g͞u⌐rai ⌐ki⌐ree na ya⌐ma⌐ wa, do⌐ko ni mo na⌐i to omoimasu.
> 'I don't think there is a mountain as pretty as Fuji (lit. pretty about as much as Fuji) anywhere.'

X-G͞u⌐rai usually occurs with an affirmative inflected expression. Compare:

> Yu⌐ki-g͞u⌐rai si⌐ro⌐i desu. 'It's as white as snow.'

with:

> Yu⌐ki⌐ hodo ⌐si⌐roku a⌐rimase⌐ñ. 'It isn't as white as snow.'

DRILLS

A. Substitution Drill

1. It's big, isn't it—for in the city.
    Hi⌐ro⌐i desu ⌐ne⌐e — ma⌐ti no na⌐ka to si⌐te⌐ wa.

2. It's weak, isn't it—for a wall.
    Yo⌐wa⌐i desu ⌐ne⌐e — he⌐e to site⌐ wa.

3. He's young, isn't he—for a parent.
    Wa⌐ka⌐i desu ⌐ne⌐e — o⌐ya⌐ to si⌐te⌐ wa.

4. It's pretty, isn't it—for an ad.
    Ki⌐ree desu ⌐ne⌐e — ko⌐okoku to site⌐ wa.

5. It's big, isn't it—for a kotatsu.
    O⌐oki⌐i desu ⌐ne⌐e — ko⌐tatu to site⌐ wa.

6. It's out of the ordinary, isn't it—for a Western building.
    To⌐kubetu de⌐su ⌐ne⌐e — yo⌐okañ to site⌐ wa.

7. It's unusual, isn't it—for a gate.
    Me⌐zurasi⌐i desu ⌐ne⌐e — ⌐mo⌐ñ to si⌐te⌐ wa.

8. It's dark, isn't it—for the color of a wall.
    Ko⌐i desu ⌐ne⌐e — ka⌐be no iro⌐ to si⌐te⌐ wa.

9. It's elegant, isn't it—for inn equipment.
    Ri⌐ppa de⌐su ⌐ne⌐e — ryo⌐kañ no se⌐tubi to si⌐te⌐ wa.

B. Substitution Drill

1. I'd like to ask about a house . . .
    U⌐ti no koto⌐ de ⌐tyo⌐tto u⌐kag͞ai-ta⌐i ñ desu g͞a—

2. I'd like to ask about kabuki . . .

Ka⌐buki no koto⌉ de ⌐tyo⌉tto u⌐ka-ḡaita⌉i n̄ desu ḡa_

3. I'd like to ask about kimono . . .

Ki⌐mono no koto⌉ de ⌐tyo⌉tto u⌐ka-ḡaita⌉i n̄ desu ḡa_

4. I'd like to ask about inns . . .

Ryo⌐kan̄ no koto⌉ de ⌐tyo⌉tto u⌐ka-ḡaita⌉i n̄ desu ḡa_

5. I'd like to ask about universities . . .

Da⌐iḡaku no koto⌉ de ⌐tyo⌉tto u⌐ka-ḡaita⌉i n̄ desu ḡa_

6. I'd like to ask about the rainy season . . .

Tu⌐yu no koto⌉ de ⌐tyo⌉tto u⌐kaḡai-ta⌉i n̄ desu ḡa_

C. Substitution Drill

1. The lot is (lit. has) 200 tsubo.

Sikiti (wa) ni⌐hyaku⌉-tubo a⌐rima⌉-su yo_

2. That house has five rooms.

Ano uti (wa) i⌐tu⌉-ma a⌐rima⌉su yo_

3. The parlor is ten mats.

Za⌐siki⌉ (wa) zyu⌐u-zyo⌉o a⌐rima⌉su yo_

4. The garden is 50 tsubo.

Niwa (wa) go⌐zyu⌉t-tubo a⌐rima⌉su yo_

5. That inn has 100 rooms.

Ano ryokan̄ (wa) hya⌐ku⌉-ma a⌐ri-ma⌉su yo_

6. The study is eight mats.

Syosai (wa) ha⌐ti-zyo⌉o a⌐rima⌉su yo_

7. That house for rent is 35 tsubo.

Ano kasiya (wa) ⌐san̄zyuu ⌐go⌉-tubo a⌐rima⌉su yo_

8. The bedroom is six mats.

Sin̄situ (wa) ro⌐ku-zyo⌉o a⌐rima⌉su yo_

D. Substitution Drill (based on Grammatical Note 3)

1. According to what Mr. Ueda says, it's very interesting.

U⌐eda-san̄ no hanasi⌉ ni yoru to, to⌐ttemo omosiro⌉i soo desu.

2. According to a letter from an acquaintance, it's very interesting.

Si⌐riai kara⌉ no teḡami ni yoru to, to⌐ttemo omosiro⌉i soo desu.

3. According to this morning's Asahi, it's very interesting.

Ke⌉sa no ⌐A⌉sahi ni yoru to, to-⌐ttemo omosiro⌉i soo desu.

4. According to the magazine I bought last night, it's very interesting.

Yuube katta zassi ni yoru to, to⌐ttemo omosiro⌉i soo desu.

5. According to what I heard on the radio tonight, it's very interesting.

Kon̄ban̄ kiita ⌐ra⌉zio ni yoru to, to⌐ttemo omosiro⌉i soo desu.

6. According to the book I read yesterday, it's very interesting.

Ki⌐noo yon̄da ⌐ho⌉n̄ ni yoru to, to⌐ttemo omosiro⌉i soo desu.

E. Substitution Drill (based on Grammatical Note 1)

1. I just read the ad.	Ko⌐okoku (o) yo⌐nda to⌐koro⌐ desu.
2. I'm just repainting the walls.	<u>Ka⌐be (o) nurika⌐ete iru to⌐koro⌐</u> desu.
3. I'm just going to take a bath.	<u>O⌐hu⌐ro ni ⌐ha⌐iru</u> to⌐koro⌐ desu.
4. I've just been writing letters.	<u>Te⌐ḡami (o) ka⌐ite (i)ta</u> to⌐koro⌐ desu.
5. I'm just about to go home.	<u>U⌐ti e kaero⌐o to si⌐te (i)ru</u> to-koro⌐ desu.
6. I was just about to go home.	U⌐ti e kaero⌐o to si⌐te (i)ru <u>to-koro⌐</u> desita.
7. I had just had it pressed.	<u>A⌐iroñ (o) ka⌐kete mo⌐ratta</u> toko-ro⌐ desita.
8. I was just looking up the telephone number.	<u>De⌐ñwabaⁿḡoo (o) si⌐ra⌐bete (i)ru</u> to⌐koro⌐ desita.
9. I had just been talking on the telephone.	<u>De⌐ñwa de hana⌐site (i)ta</u> to⌐koro⌐ desita.

F. Grammar Drill (based on Grammatical Note 1)

Tutor: Yo⌐mima⌐sita. 'I read [it].'
Student: Yo⌐nda to⌐koro⌐ desu. 'I just read [it].'

1. Ka⌐be (o) nutte (i)ma⌐su.	Ka⌐be (o) nutte (i)ru tokoro⌐ desu.
2. Ya⌐ne (o) na⌐osima⌐sita.	Ya⌐ne (o) na⌐o⌐sita to⌐koro⌐ desu.
3. Hu⌐toñ (o) siite (i)ma⌐su.	Hu⌐toñ (o) siite (i)ru tokoro⌐ desu.
4. Da⌐iḡaku (o) dema⌐sita.	Da⌐iḡaku (o) de⌐ta to⌐koro⌐ desu.
5. Ku⌐ruma (o) miḡaite (i)ma⌐su.	Ku⌐ruma (o) miḡaite (i)ru tokoro⌐ desu.
6. Ta⌐tami (o) torikaema⌐-sita.	Ta⌐tami (o) torikaeta tokoro⌐ desu.
7. De⌐ñwatyoo (o) saḡasite ima⌐su.	De⌐ñwatyoo (o) saḡasite (i)ru to-koro⌐ desu.
8. Su⌐ñpoo (o) hakarima⌐-sita.	Su⌐ñpoo (o) haka⌐tta to⌐koro⌐ desu.

G. Substitution Drill

1. [He] came just as [I] was reading the ads.	Ko⌐okoku (o) yo⌐nde (i)ru to⌐koro⌐ e ki⌐ma⌐sita.
2. [He] came just when [I] had gone to bed.	<u>Ne⌐ta</u> tokoro⌐ e ki⌐ma⌐sita.
3. [He] came just as [I] was taking a bath.	<u>O⌐hu⌐ro ni ⌐ha⌐itte (i)ru</u> to⌐koro⌐ e ki⌐ma⌐sita.
4. [He] came just as [I] was about to prepare dinner.	<u>Syo⌐kuzi no sitaku (o) siyoo to site (i)ru</u> tokoro⌐ e ki⌐ma⌐sita.
5. [He] came just as [I] was polishing the car.	<u>Ku⌐ruma (o) miḡaite (i)ru</u> tokoro⌐ e ki⌐ma⌐sita.

6. [He] saw me as [I] was polishing the car.

   Ku⌜ruma (o) mi͡gaite (i)ru <u>tokoro⌝ (o) mi⌐ma⌐sita</u>.

7. [He] saw me as [I] was washing the dishes.

   <u>O⌐sara (o) aratte (i)ru</u> tokoro⌝ (o) mi⌐ma⌐sita.

8. [He] saw me as [I] was writing with a brush.

   <u>Hu⌜de de ka⌝ite (i)ru</u> to⌐koro⌐ (o) mi⌐ma⌐sita.

H. Substitution Drill

1. Maybe there's central heating.

   Da⌜ṅboose⌝tubi (g͡a) ⌜a⌝ru ka mo siremaseṅ.

2. There's probably central heating.

   Da⌜ṅboose⌝tubi (g͡a) ⌜a⌝ru desyoo.

3. I think there's central heating.

   Da⌜ṅboose⌝tubi (g͡a) ⌜a⌝ru to omoi-<u>masu</u>.

4. There's supposed to be central heating.

   Da⌜ṅboose⌝tubi (g͡a) ⌜a⌝ru <u>hazu desu</u>.

5. They say there's central heating.

   Da⌜ṅboose⌝tubi (g͡a) ⌜a⌝ru <u>soo desu</u>.

6. There's central heating, isn't there?

   Da⌜ṅboose⌝tubi (g͡a) ⌜a⌝ru desyoo?

I. Grammar Drill (based on Grammatical Note 2)

> Tutor: I⌜kima⌝su. 'He'll go.'
> Student: I⌜ku⌝ ka mo siremaseṅ. 'Maybe he'll go.'

1. To⌜modati (o) turete kima⌝su.

   To⌜modati (o) turete ku⌝ru ka mo siremaseṅ.

2. A⌜no tosiyori⌝ (wa) mi-⌜mi⌝ g͡a to⌜oi⌝ desu.

   A⌜no tosiyori⌝ (wa) mi⌜mi⌝ g͡a to-⌜oi⌝ ka mo siremaseṅ.

3. A⌜no se⌝ki (wa) a⌜ite (i)ma⌝su.

   A⌜no se⌝ki (wa) a⌜ite (i)ru⌝ ka mo siremaseṅ.

4. Si⌜o⌝ (g͡a) ta⌜rimase⌝ṅ.

   Si⌜o⌝ (g͡a) ta⌜rina⌝i ka mo siremaseṅ.

5. Ka⌜rita⌝ no (wa) o⌜to⌝tosi desita.

   Ka⌜rita⌝ no (wa) o⌜to⌝tosi datta ka mo siremaseṅ.

6. De⌜ṅkisuto⌝obu (g͡a) tu⌜ke-raremase⌝ṅ desita.

   De⌜ṅkisuto⌝obu (g͡a) tu⌜kerare⌝na-katta ka mo siremaseṅ.

7. Sore (wa) o⌜oki⌝i moṅdai desu.

   Sore (wa) o⌜oki⌝i mo⌐ṅdai ka⌐ mo siremaseṅ.

8. Sore (wa) ⌜ma⌝da ki⌜me-mase⌝ṅ.

   Sore (wa) ⌜ma⌝da ki⌜mena⌝i ka mo siremaseṅ.

9. A⌜no kami⌝ (wa) u⌜ketori de⌝su.

   A⌜no kami⌝ (wa) u⌜ketori ka⌝ mo siremaseṅ.

10. Ta⌜iya (g͡a) paṅku-sima⌝-sita.

    Ta⌜iya (g͡a) paṅku-sita⌝ ka mo siremaseṅ.

J. Grammar Drill

> Tutor: I⌜ku⌝ ka mo siremaseṅ. 'Maybe he'll go.'
> Student: I⌜kana⌝i ka mo siremaseṅ. 'Maybe he won't go.'

1. Iˤi ka mo siremaseñ.   Yoˤku ˹naˤi ka mo siremaseñ.
2. Aˤru ka mo siremaseñ.   Naˤi ka mo siremaseñ.
3. Deˤkita ka mo siremaseñ.   Deˤkiˤnakatta ka mo siremaseñ.
4. Tuˤmetaˤkatta ka mo si-   Tuˤmetaku naˤkatta ka mo sire-
   remaseñ.   maseñ.
5. Kaˤñtañ daˤtta ka mo si-   Kaˤñtañ zya naˤkatta ka mo sire-
   remaseñ.   maseñ.
6. Beˤñri ka mo siremaseñ.   Beˤñri zya ˹naˤi ka mo sirema-
                                          señ.
7. Niˤhoñɡo (ɡa) kakeˤru ka   Nihoñɡo (ɡa) kaˤkeˤnai ka mo si-
   mo siremaseñ.   remaseñ.
8. Daˤñbooseˤtubi ka mo si-   Daˤñbooseˤtubi zya ˹naˤi ka mo
   remaseñ.   siremaseñ.
9. Syuuzeñ wa suˤruˤ ka mo   Syuuzeñ wa siˤnaˤi ka mo sire-
   siremaseñ.   maseñ.

K. Substitution Drill (based on Grammatical Note 5)

1. There's not a place as   Giˤñza-ɡuˤrai kaˤimono ni iˤi to-
   good as the Ginza for   ko wa ˹naˤi.
   shopping.
2. There's not a place as   Aˤno heñ-ɡuˤrai saˤñpo ni iˤi to-
   good as around there for   ko wa ˹naˤi.
   walking.
3. There's not a place as   Koˤno syosai-ɡuˤrai beˤñkyoo ni
   good as this library for   iˤi toko wa ˹naˤi.
   studying.
4. There's not a place as   Uˤeno-kooeñ-ɡuˤrai haˤnamiˤ ni
   good as Ueno Park for   ˤiˤi toko wa ˹naˤi.
   seeing the cherries.
5. There's not a place as   Iˤnaka-ɡuˤrai yaˤsumiˤ ni ˤiˤi to-
   good as the country for   ko wa ˹naˤi.
   rest.
6. There's not a place as   Aˤno mati-ɡuˤrai keˤñbutu ni iˤi
   good as that town for   toko wa ˹naˤi.
   sightseeing.

L. Expansion Drill

1. He may not be able to   Deˤkiˤnai ka mo siremaseñ.
   do it.
   It's raining (lit. falling)   Huˤtteˤ (i)ru kara, deˤkiˤnai ka
   so he may not be able   mo siremaseñ.
   to do it.
   It's raining so he may not   Aˤme ɡa huˤtteˤ (i)ru kara, de-
   be able to do it.   ˤkiˤnai ka mo siremaseñ.
   [He] said [that] but it's   Iˤtta keredo; aˤme ɡa huˤtteˤ
   raining so he may not   (i)ru kara, deˤkiˤnai ka mo
   be able to do it.   siremaseñ.
   [He] said he'd fix [it]   Naˤoˤsu tte iˤttaˤ keredo; aˤme
   but it's raining so he may   ɡa huˤtteˤ (i)ru kara, deˤkiˤ-
   not be able to do it.   nai ka mo siremaseñ.

[He] said he'd fix [it] today but it's raining so
he may not be able to
do it.

[He] said he'd fix the
damaged places today
but it's raining so he
may not be able to do
it.

[He] said he'd fix the
damaged places in the
roof today but it's
raining so he may not
be able to do it.

The carpenter said he'd
fix the damaged places
in the roof today but
it's raining so he may
not be able to do it.

Kyo'o na⌐o¬su tte i⌐tta¬ keredo;
a¬me ḡa hu⌐tte¬ (i)ru kara, de-
⌐ki¬nai ka mo siremaseñ.

I⌐ta¬ñda to⌐koro¬ (o) ⌐kyo'o na⌐o¬su
tte i⌐tta¬ keredo; a¬me ḡa hu⌐tte¬
(i)ru kara, de⌐ki¬nai ka mo siremaseñ.

Ya¬ne no i⌐ta¬ñda to⌐koro¬ (o)
⌐kyo'o na⌐o¬su tte i⌐tta¬ keredo;
a¬me ḡa hu⌐tte¬ (i)ru kara, de-
⌐ki¬nai ka mo siremaseñ.

Da¬iku-sañ ḡa ⌐ya¬ne no i⌐ta¬ñda
to⌐koro¬ (o) ⌐kyo'o na⌐o¬su tte
i⌐tta¬ keredo; a¬me ḡa hu⌐tte¬
(i)ru kara, de⌐ki¬nai ka mo siremaseñ.

2. Have you seen it?

The report is that they're
doing a play. Have you
seen it?

The report is that they're
doing a very interesting
play. Have you seen it?

The report is that they're
doing a very interesting
play in Nihombashi. [1]
Have you seen it?

According to what the
teacher says, they're
doing a very interest-
ing play in Nihombashi.
Have you seen it?

Go⌐rañ ni narima¬sita ka↲
Si⌐bai (o) site (i)ru so'o desu ḡa,
go⌐rañ ni narima¬sita ka↲

To⌐temo omosiro¬i si⌐bai (o) site
(i)ru so'o desu ḡa, go⌐rañ ni na-
rima¬sita ka↲
Nihoñbasi [1] de to⌐temo omosiro'i
si⌐bai (o) site (i)ru so'o desu
ḡa, go⌐rañ ni narima¬sita ka↲

Se⌐ñse'e no ha⌐nasi¬ ni yoru to,
Nihoñbasi de to⌐temo omosi-
ro¬i si⌐bai (o) site (i)ru so'o
desu ḡa; go⌐rañ ni narima¬sita
ka↲

3. It will probably be all
right, won't it?

I probably don't have to
take it, do I?

I probably don't have to
take an umbrella do I?

The report is that it will
clear so I probably
don't have to take an
umbrella, do I?

I¬i desyoo ne?

Mo⌐tte ikana¬kute mo ⌐i¬i desyoo
ne?
Ka¬sa (o) mo⌐tte ikana¬kute mo
⌐i¬i desyoo ne?
Ha⌐re¬ru soo da kara, ka¬sa (o)
mo⌐tte ikana¬kute mo ⌐i¬i desyoo ne?

---

[1] A section of Tokyo.

The report is that it will
clear tonight so I prob-
ably don't have to take
an umbrella, do I?

According to the news-
paper it's going to clear
tonight so I probably
don't have to take an
umbrella, do I?

Koⁿbañ ha⌐re⌐ru soo da kara, ka˥-
sa (o) mo˥tte ikana˥kute mo ⌐i˥i
desyoo ne?

Siñbuñ ni yoru to, koⁿbañ ha⌐re⌐ru
soo da kara; ka˥sa (o) mo˥tte
ikana˥kute mo ⌐i˥i desyoo ne?

4. I'm looking for [it].

I'm looking for a bigger
one.

It's small so I'm looking
for a bigger one.

Even as a home for the
summer it's small so
I'm looking for a big-
ger one.

The equipment is good
too, but even as a home
for the summer it's
small so I'm looking
for a bigger one.

[It] is sunny and the equipment is good too, but
even as a home for the
summer it's small so
I'm looking for a big-
ger one.

That house for rent is
sunny and the equip-
ment is good too, but
even as a home for the
summer it's small so
I'm looking for a big-
ger one.

Sa⌐ḡasite (i)ru˥ ñ desu.
Mo˥tto o⌐oki˥i no (o) sa⌐ḡasite
(i)ru˥ ñ desu.
Ti⌐isa˥i kara, mo˥tto o⌐oki˥i no (o)
sa⌐ḡasite (i)ru˥ ñ desu.
Na⌐tu no uti˥ to si˥te˥ mo ti⌐isa˥i
kara, mo˥tto o⌐oki˥i no (o) sa-
⌐ḡasite (i)ru˥ ñ desu.

Se⌐tubi mo ⌐i˥i keredo: na⌐tu no
uti˥ to si˥te˥ mo ti⌐isa˥i kara,
mo˥tto o⌐oki˥i no (o) sa⌐ḡasite
(i)ru˥ ñ desu.

Hi⌐atari ḡa i˥i si, se⌐tubi mo ⌐i˥i
keredo; na⌐tu no uti˥ to si˥te˥
mo ti⌐isa˥i kara, mo˥tto o⌐oki˥i
no (o) sa⌐ḡasite (i)ru˥ ñ desu.

Ano kasiya wa hi⌐atari ḡa i˥i si,
se⌐tubi mo ⌐i˥i keredo: na⌐tu no
uti˥ to si˥te˥ mo ti⌐isa˥i kara,
mo˥tto o⌐oki˥i no (o) sa⌐ḡasite
(i)ru˥ ñ desu.

5. You'd better call.

You'd better call a taxi.

If you want to go you'd
better call a taxi.

If you want to go right
away you'd better call
a taxi.

If you want to go right
away you'd better call
a taxi.

It will take all of two or
three hours, so if you

Yo⌐ñda ho˥o ḡa ⌐i˥i desu yo↲
Ta˥kusii (o) yo⌐ñda ho˥o ḡa ⌐i˥i
desu yo↲
I⌐kita˥kattara, ta˥kusii (o) yo⌐ñda
ho˥o ḡa ⌐i˥i desu yo↲
I˥ma ⌐su˥ḡu i⌐kita˥kattara, ta˥kusii
(o) yo⌐ñda ho˥o ḡa ⌐i˥i desu
yo↲
Mo˥si ⌐i˥ma ⌐su˥ḡu i⌐kita˥kattara,
ta˥kusii (o) yo⌐ñda ho˥o ḡa ⌐i˥i
desu yo↲
Ni-⌐sañ-zi˥kañ mo ka⌐ka˥ru kara;
mo˥si ⌐i˥ma ⌐su˥ḡu i⌐kita˥kattara,

<table>
<tr><td>

want to go right away
you'd better call a
taxi.

</td><td>

ta˥kusii (o) yo˥ñda ho˥o ḡa ˥i˥i
desu yo⌐

</td></tr>
<tr><td>

It will take all of two or
three hours more, so
if you want to go right
away you'd better call
a taxi.

</td><td>

Mo˥o ni-sañ-zi˥kañ mo ka˥ka˥ru
kara; mo˥si ˥i˥ma ˥su̅ḡu i˥kita˥-
kattara, ta˥kusii (o) yo˥ñda ho˥o
ḡa ˥i˥i desu yo⌐

</td></tr>
<tr><td>

I'm just fixing [it] but it
will take all of two or
three hours more, so
if you want to go right
away you'd better call
a taxi.

</td><td>

Na˥o˥site (i)ru to˥koro˥ desu ḡa;
mo˥o ni-sañ-zi˥kañ mo ka˥ka˥ru
kara; mo˥si ˥i˥ma ˥su̅ḡu i˥kita˥-
kattara, ta˥kusii (o) yo˥ñda ho˥o
ḡa ˥i˥i desu yo⌐

</td></tr>
<tr><td>

I'm just fixing your car
but it will take all of
two or three hours
more, so if you want
to go right away you'd
better call a taxi.

</td><td>

A˥na˥ta no kuruma (o) na˥o˥site
(i)ru to˥koro˥ desu ḡa; mo˥o
ni-sañ-zi˥kañ mo ka˥ka˥ru kara;
mo˥si ˥i˥ma ˥su̅ḡu i˥kita˥kattara,
ta˥kusii (o) yo˥ñda ho˥o ḡa ˥i˥i
desu yo⌐

</td></tr>
<tr><td>

I'm just fixing your car
now but it will take all
of two or three hours
more, so if you want
to go right away you'd
better call a taxi.

</td><td>

I˥ma a˥na˥ta no kuruma (o) na˥o˥-
site (i)ru to˥koro˥ desu ḡa;
mo˥o ni-sañ-zi˥kañ mo ka˥ka˥ru
kara; mo˥si ˥i˥ma ˥su̅ḡu i˥kita˥-
kattara, ta˥kusii (o) yo˥ñda ho˥o
ḡa ˥i˥i desu yo⌐

</td></tr>
</table>

SUPPLEMENTARY CONVERSATION

(Mr. Smith unexpectedly meets his friend, Mr. Yamada, on the street.)

Smith: Tyo˥tto si˥tu˥ree desu ḡa, Ya˥mada-sañ zya arimase˥ñ ka⌐
Yamada: A˥a, Su˥misu-sañ. Si˥ba˥raku desita ˥ne˥e.
Smith: Si˥ba˥raku desita ˥ne˥e. I˥ma To˥okyoo de otutome de˥su ka⌐
Yamada: E˥e. Ni˥hoñbasi [1] no ḡiñkoo de˥su. Mi˥na˥sañ o˥ge˥ñki? Okosañ ˥zu˥-
          ibuñ ˥o˥okiku ˥na˥tta desyoo ne?
Smith: Okaḡesama de. O˥taku mo mina˥sañ o˥ge˥ñki desyoo?
Yamada: E˥e. A˥ri˥ḡatoo. To˥okyoo e kite˥ kara ni-˥syu˥ukañ ni na˥rima˥su
          ḡa, ma˥da u˥ti ḡa na˥kute ko˥ma˥tte imasu yo.
Smith: I˥ma wa ryo˥kañ de˥su ka⌐
Yamada: Iie. Bo˥ku dake ḡiñkoo no tomodati no uti ni ite, ka˥nai ya ko-
          domo wa ˥ma˥da O˥osaka de ma˥tte iru kara; ha˥yaku u˥ti˥ o ka-
          ˥rita˥i ñ desu ḡa;*kasiya wa a˥rimase˥ñ ˥ne˥e.
Smith: Ho˥ñtoo ni sukuna˥i desu yo — kasiya wa⌐ Ka˥imase˥ñ ka — u˥ti˥ o.
Yamada: Kasiya mo ˥ya˥tiñ ḡa ta˥ka˥i kara, ti˥isa˥i u˥ti˥ o ka˥tte˥ mo ˥i˥i
          keredo; a˥ru desyoo ka.
Smith: Bo˥ku no kaisya no hito˥ ḡa u˥rita˥i ñ desu yo.
Yamada: So˥re wa ke˥kkoo. Do˥ñna u˥ti˥ desyoo.

---

[1] A section of Tokyo.

Smith: Bo⌐ku wa yo⌐ku si⌐rana⌐i kara, so⌐no tomodati to soodañ-sita⌐ra
           ⌐do⌐o desyoo. A⌐to de a⌐ña⌐ta no hoo e o⌐deñwa-simasu kara—
Yamada: Do⌐o mo a⌐ri⌐gatoo. Bo⌐ku no meesi de⌐su. Do⌐ozo. Go⌐-zi made
           gi⌐ñkoo ni orima⌐su kara, o⌐neḡai-sima⌐su.
Smith: Zya⌐a, go⌐-zi made ni o⌐deñwa-simasu kara—
Yamada: O⌐isoḡasi⌐i to⌐koro⌐ o su⌐mimase⌐ñ.
Smith: Iie. Na⌐ñ de mo arimase⌐ñ yo.

   (After Mr. Yamada has received further details on the telephone, he goes
      to see the house that is for sale. He talks to Mr. Goto, the owner.)

Yamada: Go⌐meñ-kudasa⌐i. Su⌐misu-sañ no go⌐⌐syookai de mairima⌐sita. U⌐ti
           no koto⌐ de u⌐kaḡaita⌐i ñ desu ḡa—
Goto: A⌐a, Ya⌐mada-sañ de irassyaima⌐su ne? Yo⌐ku i⌐rassyaima⌐sita.
           Do⌐ozo o⌐hairi-kudasa⌐i. Su⌐ḡu o⌐wakari de⌐sita ka⌐
Yamada: E⌐e. E⌐ki no ⌐ma⌐e no koobañ de yo⌐ku o⌐siete moraima⌐sita ka-
           ra— Kono heñ wa ⌐si⌐zuka de ⌐i⌐i tokoro desu ⌐ne⌐e.
Goto: E⌐ki kara ⌐tyo⌐tto to⌐oi⌐ desu ḡa, u⌐ti ḡa sukuna⌐kute ⌐i⌐i desyoo?
Yamada: Kono otaku wa i⌐tu-ḡoro no⌐ desu ka⌐
Goto: Go-⌐neñ ma⌐e ni tu⌐kurima⌐sita.
Yamada: Oniwa mo na⌐kanaka hiro⌐i desu ⌐ne⌐e.
Goto: E⌐e. Sikiti ḡa ni⌐hyaku⌐-tubo a⌐rima⌐su kara—
Yamada: Uti wa na⌐ñ-tubo-ḡu⌐rai desyoo ka.
Goto: Tyoodo ⌐ni⌐zyuu ⌐ha⌐t-tubo desu.
Yamada: Kono heñ wa ⌐ga⌐su wa ⌐do⌐o desu ka⌐
Goto: Kyo⌐neñ kara ki⌐te⌐ imasu yo⌐ O⌐hu⌐ro mo ⌐ga⌐su desu.
Yamada: Zya⌐a, be⌐ñri de ⌐i⌐i desu ⌐ne⌐e.
Goto: E⌐e. Ga⌐su ḡa ki⌐te⌐ kara zu⌐tto be⌐ñri ni na⌐rima⌐sita yo⌐
Yamada: O⌐heya o mi⌐sete i⌐tadakita⌐i ñ desu ḡa—
Goto: Do⌐ozo ⌐do⌐ozo. . . . Ko⌐tira ḡa zasiki⌐ de, ha⌐ti-zyo⌐o desu. Tona-
           ri ḡa tyanoma de, ro⌐ku-zyo⌐o desu.
Yamada: Kabe mo ta⌐tami mo ⌐ki⌐ree desu ⌐ne⌐e.
Goto: E⌐e. Kyo⌐neñ ka⌐be o nurika⌐ete ta⌐tami mo atara⌐siku si⌐ma⌐sita
           kara— Ko⌐tira ḡa roku-zyo⌐o de, mukoo ni ko̅domo no ti⌐isa⌐i he-
           ⌐ya⌐ ḡa a⌐rima⌐su ḡa; sa⌐ñ-zyoo-ḡu⌐rai desu ḡa, ta⌐tami wa ari-
           mase⌐ñ.
Yamada: Zya⌐a, ta⌐tami no heya⌐ wa ⌐mi⌐-ma desu ne?
Goto: So⌐o desu. Da⌐idokoro to huroba⌐ wa ⌐tyo⌐tto se⌐ma⌐i desu ḡa—
           Do⌐ozo ⌐mi⌐te kudasai.
Yamada: Tyo⌐odo i⌐i desu ⌐ne⌐e. Hi⌐atari mo yo⌐kute, ni⌐wa mo hi⌐rokute—
           Su⌐misu-sañ kara no ha⌐nasi⌐ ni yoru to, o⌐uri ni narita⌐i ñ da
           ⌐so⌐o desu ḡa—
Goto: E⌐e. Mo⌐o su⌐ḡu ⌐Ko⌐obe e i⌐kima⌐su kara, kono uti wa u⌐rita⌐i ñ
           desu yo.
Yamada: I⌐kura-ḡu⌐rai de?
Goto: So⌐o desu ⌐ne⌐e. Su⌐misu-sañ ni mo ⌐tyo⌐tto o⌐hanasi-sima⌐sita
           ḡa; ho⌐ka no kata⌐ ni wa hya⌐ku nizyuu-mañ-ḡu⌐rai [1] de u⌐rita⌐i
           to o⌐mo⌐tte imasita ḡa; Su⌐misu-sañ no o⌐tomodati de⌐su kara,
           mo⌐o suko⌐si ⌐ya⌐suku i⌐tasimasyo⌐o.

_____

[1]   120 ten thousands = 1,200,000. 'Yen' is understood.

Yamada: So⌐re wa do⌐o mo. Zya⌐a, ka⌐nai to dēnwa de ⌐yo⌐ku soodañ-site,
         ka⌐nai to issyo ni mōo iti-do‿
Goto: Do⌐ozo ⌐do⌐ozo. Su⌐mimase⌐ñ ḡa; ho⌐ka no hito⌐ mo mi⌐ema⌐su ka‿
         ra, na⌐rubeku ha⌐yaku o⌐neḡai-sita⌐i ñ desu ḡa‿
Yamada: Mo⌐ti⌐roñ. Ha⌐tu-ka ma⌐de ni go⌐heñzi-sima⌐su kara‿
Goto: O⌐neḡai-itasima⌐su.
Yamada: Do⌐o mo si⌐tu⌐ree-itasimasita. Zya⌐a, ma⌐ta mairima⌐su kara‿
Goto: Do⌐ozo ōtya o. Ka⌐nai ḡa si⌐taku site orima⌐su kara‿
Yamada: O⌐so⌐reirimasu. Do⌐ozo o⌐kamai na⌐ku.

English Equivalents

Smith: Say, excuse me but aren't you Mr. Yamada?
Yamada: Oh, Mr. Smith. I haven't seen you for a long time.
Smith: It <u>has</u> been a long time. Are you working in Tokyo now?
Yamada: Yes. I'm in a bank in Nihombashi. [Is] everyone in your family
         well? Your children must have grown a lot (lit. become very big),
         haven't they?
Smith: [They're fine] thank you. Everyone is well in your family too?
Yamada: Yes, thank you. You know, it's almost (lit. it will become) two
         weeks since I came to Tokyo, but I'm having an awful time because
         I don't have a house yet.
Smith: Are you staying at (lit. is it) an inn now?
Yamada: No. I (only) am staying at the home of a friend from the bank and
         my wife and children are still waiting in Osaka so I'd like to rent a
         house quickly, but there aren't any rentals to be had, are there.
Smith: They're really scarce—houses for rent. Aren't you going to buy (a
         house)?
Yamada: Rented houses are expensive too because of the rent (lit. rented
         houses too, the rent is high) so it would be all right if I bought a
         small house, but I wonder if there are any.
Smith: You know, a man in my company wants to sell [a house].
Yamada: That's wonderful. What kind of house is it?
Smith: I don't know too much about it so why don't you talk it over with
         this (lit. that) friend of mine? I'll put in a call to you later so . . .
Yamada: Thanks very much. Here's my card. Please take it. I'll be at the
         bank until five so would you [call me]?
Smith: Then I'll call you by five (so) . . .
Yamada: I'm sorry [to bother you] when you're so busy.
Smith: Not at all. It's nothing.
. . . .
Yamada: Excuse me. Mr. Smith sent me. (Lit. I've come through the intro-
         duction of Mr. Smith.) I'd like to inquire about the house . . .
Goto: Oh, you're Mr. Yamada, aren't you? I'm so glad you've come.
         Please come in. Did you find [the house] right away?
Yamada: Yes. I got good directions at the police box in front of the station
         so . . . This neighborhood is (a) nice and quiet (place), isn't it.
Goto: It's a bit far from the station, but it's pleasant because there aren't
         many houses, don't you think?

Yamada: About how old is this house? (Lit. This house is of about when?)
Goto: I built it five years ago.
Yamada: The garden is quite big too, isn't it.
Goto: Yes. The lot is (lit. has) 200 tsubo so . . .
Yamada: About how many tsubo is the house?
Goto: It's exactly 28 tsubo.
Yamada: How about gas around here?
Goto: It's been (lit. come) here since last year. The bath is gas too.
Yamada: Then it's nice and convenient, isn't it.
Goto: Yes. Since the gas came it's been (lit. become) much more conven-
          ient.
Yamada: I'd like to have you show me the rooms . . .
Goto: Certainly. This is the parlor and it's eight mats. Next (door) is the
          sitting room and it's six mats.
Yamada: The walls and the tatami are in good shape (lit. clean), aren't they.
Goto: Yes. Last year we repainted the walls and renovated the tatami
          (so) . . . This is a six-mat room and beyond there's a small child's
          room. It's about three mats [in size] but it doesn't have tatami.
Yamada: Then there are three tatami rooms — right?
Goto: That's right. The kitchen and bathroom are a bit small . . . Please
          take a look.
Yamada: It's just right. It's (both) sunny and the garden is big too, and . . .
          According to Mr. Smith, you want to sell . . .
Goto: Yes. We're going to Kobe very soon now so we'd like to sell this
          house.
Yamada: For about how much?
Goto: Hmmm . . . I talked a little [about this] to Mr. Smith too. I was
          thinking that I'd like to sell it for about ¥ 1,200,000 to anyone else
          (lit. other people), but since you're a friend of Mr. Smith's, I'll make
          it a little cheaper.
Yamada: That's very [kind of you]. Well, I'll discuss this with my wife by
          telephone and [then I'd like to come here] once more with her . . .
Goto: By all means. I'm sorry [to mention this] but other people will be
          coming too, so I'd like to ask [that you make it] as soon as possible.
Yamada: Of course. I'll give you an answer by the 20th (so) . . .
Goto: If you would.
Yamada (preparing to leave):   Please excuse my rudeness [in barging in].
          Then I'll come here again (so) . . .
Goto: Please [have] some tea. My wife is getting it ready (so) . . .
Yamada: Thank you. Please don't go to any trouble.

EXERCISES

1. Answer an ad for a summer house, checking on the following points:

        a. Location of the house
        b. Rent for two months
        c. Furniture
        d. Running water, electricity, gas, flush toilet, screens, trash
            disposal
        e. Transportation

2. You are considering a house Mr. Tanaka wants to rent.

      As Mr. Tanaka: Mr. Tanaka replies:

    a. how large the lot is.   150 tsubo.

    b. what kind of house it is.   A new Western-style house
                                            with southern exposure.

    c. how many rooms are   Seven rooms.
        in the house.

    d. if there are any tatami   Yes, two.
        rooms.

    e. about the heating   There is gas in the house
        facilities.   so you use gas heaters.

    f. what kind of bath the   The bath is gas.
        house has.

    g. who takes care of the   The landlord.
        repairs.

    h. when you may see the   How about tomorrow?
        house.

Lesson 31. At a Department Store

BASIC DIALOGUES: FOR MEMORIZATION

(a)

(Mr. Smith and Mr. Brown, accompanied by Mr. Tanaka,
are doing some shopping.)

Smith (at the information desk)

toy	o⌐mo⌐tya
1. Where [is] the place where they sell toys?	O⌐mo⌐tya utte ru toko ⌐do⌐ko?

Clerk

counter <u>or</u> selling place	uriba
toy counter <u>or</u> toy department	o⌐motyau⌐riba
2. The toy department is on the third floor.	O⌐motyau⌐riba (wa) sa⌐ñ-ḡai de gozaima⌐su.

Smith

3. Thanks.	Do⌐o mo.

(to Tanaka)

4. (I think) I'd like to send a Japanese toy to my daughter who's in America . . .	A⌐merika ni iru musume⌐ ni Ni⌐hoñ no omo⌐tya (o) o⌐kutte yaritai to omo⌐tte ⌐ne⌐e.

Tanaka

doll	niñḡyoo
a doll that's wearing kimono	kimono (o) kite (i)ru niñḡyoo
dolls and so forth <u>or</u> a doll for example <u>or</u> something like a doll	ni⌐ñḡyoo na⌐do <u>or</u> ni⌐ñḡyoo na⌐ñka
5. How about something like a doll dressed in kimono?	Ki⌐mono (o) kite (i)ru niñḡyoo na⌐ñka (wa) ⌐do⌐o desyoo.
one time	ik-kai
two or three times	ni-sañ-kai
send, for someone (lit. give sending)	okutte aḡeru
have at some time sent, for someone	o⌐kutte aḡeta koto⌐ ḡa ⌐a⌐ru
become broken	ko⌐ware⌐ru /-ru/
have never been broken	ko⌐wa⌐reta koto wa ⌐na⌐i

218

6. I have sent [them] two or three
times, but there hasn't been a
single case of breakage so I
do think it's safe (but) . . .

Boku (wa) ni-⌐saṅ-kai okutte aḡe-
ta koto⌐ ḡa ⌐a⌐ru ṅ desu ḡa; ko-
⌐wa⌐reta koto (wa) i⌐k-kai mo na⌐i
kara, da⌐izyo⌐obu da to o⌐mo⌐u ṅ
desu ḡa—

Smith

gift
7. It's a girl so a doll would
probably make (lit. become)
a good gift, wouldn't it.

okurimono
O⌐ṅna⌐ no ko da kara, niṅḡyoo
wa ⌐i⌐i o⌐kurimono ni na⌐ru desyoo ⌐ne⌐e.

(b)

(At the doll counter)

Tanaka

second in a series
is second from the left

is cute
8. The big doll that's second
from the left is cute, isn't
it.

ni-⌐baṅ-me⌐
hi⌐dari kara ni-baṅ-me⌐ ni
⌐a⌐ru
ka⌐wai⌐i /-ku/
Hi⌐dari kara ni-baṅ-me⌐ ni ⌐a⌐ru
o⌐oki⌐i niṅḡyoo (wa) ka⌐wai⌐i desu
⌐ne⌐e.

Smith

price
9. Yes. The price is attached,
isn't it?

nedaṅ
E⌐e. Ne⌐daṅ (ḡa) tu⌐ite (i)ru desyoo?

Brown

10. It's ¥ 1500.

Se⌐ṅ go⌐hyaku⌐-eṅ desu.

Smith

comparatively
11. It's comparatively cheap,
isn't it.

wari ni
Wa⌐ri ni yasu⌐i ṅ desu ⌐ne⌐e.

12. I'll take it. (Lit. I guess I'll
make it that one.)

So⌐re ni simasyo⌐o.

Tanaka

wrap
the interval when [some-
one] is having [some-
thing] wrapped
(Japanese game)
(Japanese game)
look in at or peek at
13. While you are having the doll
wrapped, I'll go and take a
look at the go and shogi
counter.

tu⌐tu⌐mu /-u/
tu⌐tu⌐ṅde moratte (i)ru
aida

go⌐
syooḡi
nozoku /-u/
Ni⌐ṅḡyoo (o) tutu⌐ṅde moratte
(i)ru aida ni; tyo⌐tto, go⌐ ya
syooḡi no u⌐riba (o) nozoite
kima⌐su.

Smith

14. Take your time.   Do⌐ozo go⌐yukku⌐ri.

Tanaka

15. I'll be right back.   Su⌐ḡu ki⌐ma⌐su yo⌐

(c)

Tanaka (to Brown)

16. There's something that you   A⌐ha⌐ta mo ⌐na⌐ni ka mi⌐ta⌐i mo-
     want to look at too, isn't   ⌐no⌐ (ḡa) ⌐a⌐ru ñ desyoo?
     there?

Brown

     want   ho⌐si⌐i /-ku/
     I want   bo⌐ku ḡa hosi⌐i
     the thing which I want   bo⌐ku ḡa hosi⌐i no or
                                          bo⌐ku no hosi⌐i no

     is low   hi⌐ku⌐i /-ku/
17. The thing I want is a low   Bo⌐ku no hosi⌐i no (wa) hi⌐ku⌐i
     table.   te⌐eburu na⌐ ñ desu yo.

     the other day or   kono aida or
       recently   konaida
18. I saw [this] recently when   Konaida, to⌐modati no uti e itta
     I went to a friend's house.   to⌐ki /ni/ ⌐mi⌐ta ñ desu ḡa; za-
     He's using a tatami-room   siki no teeburu (o) yo⌐oma de
     table in a Western-style   tukatte (i)ru⌐ ñ desu yo.
     room.

19. You know, I thought it was   Na⌐kanaka i⌐i to o⌐mo⌐tta ñ
     quite nice.   desu yo.

Tanaka

     is round   marui /-ku/
     is square   si⌐kaku⌐i /-ku/
20. Which do you like better,   Ma⌐ru⌐i no to si⌐kaku⌐i no to,
     round ones or square ones?   do⌐tira ḡa o⌐suki de⌐su ka⌐

Brown

     couch or sofa   naḡaisu
     is long and slender or   ho⌐sonaḡa⌐i /-ku/
       is long and narrow
21. I'm going to put it in front   Na⌐ḡaisu no ma⌐e ni o⌐ku⌐ ñ
     of a couch so I'd prefer a   desu kara, ho⌐sonaḡa⌐i hoo ḡa
     long narrow one.   ⌐i⌐i ñ desu yo.

Tanaka

     thing that isn't here or   na⌐i mono
       thing [someone] doesn't
       have
     there isn't a thing they   na⌐i mo⌐no⌐ wa ⌐na⌐i
       don't have

22. It's a big department store so   O⌐oki⌐i de⌐pa⌐ato desu kara, na⌐i
    there probably isn't a thing   mo⌐no⌐ wa ⌐na⌐i desyoo ⌐ne⌐e.
    they don't have.

Brown

    past noon <u>or</u> afternoon   hi⌐ru-suḡi⌐
    time before eating   ta⌐be⌐ru mae
23. It's past noon already, but is   Mo⌐o hi⌐ru-suḡi⌐ desu ḡa, ta⌐be-
    it all right if we go to look   ru mae ni ⌐tyotto ⌐mi⌐ ni i⌐tte⌐
    at [them] for a minute be-   mo ⌐i⌐i desu ka⌐
    fore we eat?

Smith

24. Certainly.   Do⌐ozo ⌐do⌐ozo.

Tanaka

    after having finished   su⌐ma⌐seta ⌐a⌐to de
25. After we've finished our   Ka⌐imono (o) suma⌐seta ⌐a⌐to de,
    shopping, let's take our time   na⌐ni ka u⌐ma⌐i mo⌐no⌐ (o) yu⌐kku⌐-
    and have something good to   ri ta⌐bemasyo⌐o.
    eat.

    vicinity   ti⌐ka⌐ku
    the sushi shop 'Shintomi'   su⌐si⌐ya no Sīntomi
    the tempura shop 'Tenkin'   teñpuraya no Tēñkiñ
    the soba shop 'Yabu'   so⌐ba⌐ya no Yābu
    Yabu and so forth <u>or</u>   Ya⌐bu na⌐do <u>or</u>
      Yabu for example <u>or</u>   Ya⌐bu na⌐ñka
      a place like Yabu
    guide <u>or</u> show the way   a⌐ñna⌐i-suru <u>or</u>
                                           go⌐añna⌐i-suru⌐

26. Near here there are places   Ko⌐no tika⌐ku ni wa, su⌐si⌐ya no
    like the sushi shop 'Shintomi,'   Sīntomi, teñpuraya no Tēñkiñ,
    the tempura shop 'Tenkin,'   so⌐ba⌐ya no Ya⌐bu na⌐ñka (ḡa)
    and the soba shop 'Yabu'; (so)   ⌐a⌐ru kara; o⌐suki na tokoro⌐ e
    I'll take you to a place you'll   go⌐añnai-sima⌐su yo⌐
    like.

(d)

Smith

    writing brush   hude
    ink stick   su⌐mi⌐
    ink stone   su⌐zuri⌐
    ink stone and so forth   su⌐zuri⌐ nado <u>or</u>
      <u>or</u> ink stone for ex-   su⌐zuri⌐ nañka
      ample <u>or</u> a thing like
      an ink stone
27. I just remembered. I'd like   I⌐ma o⌐moida⌐sita ñ desu ḡa; hude,
    to look at things like writing   sumi, su⌐zuri⌐ nañka mo mi⌐ta⌐i
    brushes, ink sticks, and ink   ñ desu ḡa; ka⌐maimase⌐ñ ka⌐
    stones, too. Is that all
    right?

Japanese syllabary	kana
Chinese character	kañzi
practice (noun)	reñsyuu
practice (verb)	reñsyuu o suru **or**
	reñsyuu-suru

28. I want to practice writing
    kana and kanji with a brush.

    Kana ya kañzi (o) hu⌈de de ka⌉ku
    re⌐ñsyuu (g̃a) sita⌐i ñ desu yo.

Tanaka

calligraphy
29. Oh, calligraphy?

    syuuzi
    A⌉a, syu⌈uzi de⌉su ka.

Brown

quote — calligraphy
30. What is 'calligraphy'?

    syuuzi tte
    Syuuzi tte, ⌈na⌉ñ desyoo ka.

Tanaka

way **or** style of
  writing
the meaning 'practice'
31. It means 'practice in writing
    style.'

    ka⌈kika⌉ta

    re⌈ñsyuu tte iu i⌉mi
    Ka⌈kika⌉ta no re⌈ñsyuu tte iu
    i⌉mi desu yo.

(e)

Brown

32. Oh, I'm hungry.

    A⌉a onaka (g̃a) suita.

Smith

33. Me — I'm thirsty.

    Boku wa ⌈no⌉do (g̃a) ka⌈wakima⌉-
    sita yo.

Tanaka

while drinking
34. Well then, let's have some
    beer and eat at the same
    time (lit. while drinking beer
    let's eat).

    no⌈mina⌉g̃ara
    Zya⌉a, bi⌉iru (o) no⌐mina⌉g̃ara
    ta⌈bemasyo⌉o.

ADDITIONAL VOCABULARY

1. Where is the place where they
   sell souvenirs?

   Mi⌈yag̃e (o) utte (i)ru tokoro⌉
   (wa) ⌈do⌉ko desu ka⌐

curios **or** antiques	kottoohiñ
china **or** pottery	setomono
kitchen utensils	da⌈idokorodo⌉og̃u **or**
	ka⌈ttedo⌉og̃u
foodstuffs **or** groceries	syokuryoohiñ
writing materials	bu⌈ñbo⌉og̃u **or** bu⌈ñpo⌉og̃u
yard goods **or** dry goods	gohukumono

2. What I want is a <u>screen</u>.　　Wa⌐takusi no hosi⌐i no (wa) <u>byo-</u>
　　　　　　　　　　　　　　　<u>⌐obu</u> na⌐ ñ desu yo.

       hanging scroll　　　　　　ka⌐ke⌐mono
       fan (folding)　　　　　　　señsu
       fan (non-folding)　　　　　u⌐ti⌐wa
       picture　　　　　　　　　e⌐
       jewel　　　　　　　　　　hooseki
       pearl　　　　　　　　　　siñzyu

3. The average large depart-　　Hutuu no o⌐oki⌐i de⌐pa⌐ato ni
　　ment store has a <u>basement</u>.　　(wa) <u>ti⌐ka⌐situ</u> (ḡa) arimasu.

       roof garden　　　　　　　okuzyoo
       rest room <u>or</u> lounge　　　kyu⌐uke⌐esitu

NOTES ON THE BASIC DIALOGUES

4. 'and—that is why I am going to the toy department.'

6. 'but—I can't be sure.'
   <u>Ko⌐ware⌐ru</u> is the intransitive partner of transitive <u>ko⌐wa⌐su</u> /-<u>u</u>/ 'break
   [something].'

13. Note: <u>X ni tu⌐tu⌐mu</u> 'wrap in X.'
    <u>Go⌐</u> is a complicated game played with markers on a board marked with
    squares. It is extremely popular in Japan. <u>Syooḡi</u> is Japanese chess.
    The verbal √<u>suru</u> occurs with the names of games as the equivalent of
    'play': <u>go⌐ (o) suru</u> 'play go'; <u>syooḡi o suru</u> 'play shogi.'

14. <u>Go⌐yukku⌐ri</u>, the honorific equivalent of <u>yu⌐kku⌐ri</u> 'slowly,' is an invita-
    tion to 'take it easy,' 'don't rush,' 'have a pleasant, unhurried time.'

17. <u>Ho⌐si⌐i</u>: Nominals indicating the person who wants and the thing wanted
    are followed by particle <u>wa</u> or <u>ḡa</u>, depending on emphasis.
    <u>Ho⌐si⌐i</u> is regularly used in expressions of wanting but not in polite re-
    quests. Compare:

    > <u>Ta⌐bako ḡa hosi⌐i kara, ta⌐bakoya e itte kima⌐su.</u>　'I want some
    >   cigarettes so I'm going to the cigar store.'

    with:
    > <u>Ta⌐bako (o) oneḡai-sima⌐su.</u>　'I'd like <u>or</u> May I have some ciga-
    >   rettes.'

    <u>Ta⌐ka⌐i</u> 'is high' is used as the opposite of both <u>ya⌐su⌐i</u> 'is low in price'
    and <u>hi⌐ku⌐i</u> 'is low in height.'

18. <u>Konaida</u> is the contracted, less formal equivalent of <u>kono aida</u>.
    Note the use of <u>ḡa</u> here and in Sentence 27 below, separating an intro-
    ductory statement from a related statement which contains information
    being pointed up or emphasized, or from a related question.

20. Note: <u>maru</u> 'circle' and <u>marui</u> 'is round.'
    　　　<u>si⌐kaku⌐</u> 'square' and <u>si⌐kaku⌐i</u> 'is square.'

21. Ho⌐soˈnaḡaˈi is a compound of the adjectivals ho⌐soˈi 'is thin or small in circumference' and na⌐ḡaˈi 'is long.' The opposite of ho⌐soˈi is hu⌐toˈi /-ku/ 'is thick or big in circumference.'

26. Ti⌐kaˈku 'vicinity' is a nominal derived from an adjectival (ti⌐kaˈi 'is near'). Compare also to⌐okuˈ 'far distance,' 'the far away' (from tooi 'is far'), and o⌐sokuˈ 'late' (from osoi 'is late'), as in o⌐sokuˈ made 'until late.'
The no of su⌐siˈya no Sīntomi, teṅpuraya no Tēñkiñ, and so⌐baˈya no Yābu is the special form of da occurring at the end of a sentence modifier (cf. Lesson 19, Grammatical Note 1).

27. The ink for Japanese brush-writing is made by rubbing an ink stick (su⌐miˈ) against an ink stone (su⌐zuriˈ) containing a small amount of water.

28. Native Japanese writing is usually a combination of kana (symbols representing syllables without reference to meaning) and Chinese characters (symbols representing words or meaningful parts of words). The writing of Japanese with Roman letters — as the Japanese in this text — is called ro⌐omaˈzi 'romanization.'
For particle ḡa, see the end of Note 1 in Lesson 7.

32. Note the informal style. Brown's exclamation is addressed to himself as much as to anyone else.

33. Ka⌐waˈku 'become dry' is the intransitive partner of transitive ka⌐wakaˈsu /-u/ 'dry [something].'

Additional Vocabulary:

Da⌐idokorodoˈoḡu ~ ka⌐ttedoˈoḡu: Katte is an alternate word for 'kitchen.' Do⌐oḡuˈ as an independent word means 'implement,' 'tool,' 'utensil.'

GRAMMATICAL NOTES

1. ―― ko⌐toˈ ḡa ⌐aˈru

The informal past of a verbal + ko⌐toˈ (nominal meaning 'act' or 'fact') + ḡa (or wa) + aˈru means '[someone] has, at some time up to the present, done so-and-so.' In question form, the Japanese sequence is equivalent to 'have [you] ever done so-and-so?' The negative ―― ko⌐toˈ ḡa (or wa) ⌐naˈi means '[someone] has never done so-and-so.' Thus:

(a) Hi⌐koˈoki de i⌐tta kotoˈ ḡa arimasu. 'I have (at some time) gone by plane.'
(b) Hi⌐koˈoki de i⌐tta kotoˈ ḡa a⌐rimaˈsu ka ⌐ 'Have you ever gone by plane?'
(c) Hi⌐koˈoki de i⌐tta kotoˈ wa a⌐rimaseˈñ. 'I have never gone by plane.'

The simple past of a verbal refers to past occurrence and may be equivalent to either 'did do' or 'has done,' depending on context. The -ta ko⌐toˈ ḡa ⌐aˈru sequence means only 'has at some time done.' Thus:

Ka⌐buki o mima⌐sita ka⌐ 'Did you see kabuki?' or 'Have you seen kabuki?'

but:

Ka⌐buki o mi⌐ta koto ḡa a⌐rima⌐su ka⌐ 'Have you ever seen kabuki?'

When a̲ru occurs in one of its past forms in this pattern, the combination means '[someone] had, at some time up to a given point in the past, done so-and-so.' Thus:

Ni⌐ho⌐n e ⌐ku⌐ru made wa, ni⌐hoñḡo o kiita koto⌐ ḡa a⌐rimase⌐n desita. 'Until I came to Japan, I had never heard Japanese.'

A past negative may also precede ko⌐to⌐; the combination means '[some-one] has, at some time, not done so-and-so.' In question form, the Japanese sequence is equivalent to 'have [you] ever not done so-and-so?' If ko⌐to⌐ is preceded AND followed by a negative, the combination means '[someone] has never not done so-and-so,' i.e. 'there has never been a time when [someone] did not do so-and-so' or '[someone] has always done so-and-so.'

(d) Hi⌐ko⌐oki de i⌐kana⌐katta koto ḡa arimasu. 'I have at some time not gone by plane.'

(e) Hi⌐ko⌐oki de i⌐kana⌐katta koto ḡa a⌐rima⌐su ka⌐ 'Have you ever not gone by plane?'

(f) Hi⌐ko⌐oki de i⌐kana⌐katta koto wa a⌐rimase⌐n. 'There has never been a time when I didn't go by plane.'

Corresponding —— ko⌐to⌐ ḡa ⌐a⌐ru patterns preceded by a non-past verbal or negative adjectival also occur, meaning 'there are times (or there is never a time) when [someone] does (or doesn't do) so-and-so.' Thus:

(a) Hi⌐ko⌐oki de i⌐ku koto⌐ ḡa arimasu. 'There are times when I go by plane.'

(b) Hi⌐ko⌐oki de i⌐ku koto⌐ ḡa a⌐rima⌐su ka⌐ 'Do you ever go by plane?'

(c) Hi⌐ko⌐oki de i⌐ku koto⌐ wa a⌐rimase⌐n. 'There is never a time when I go by plane.'

(d) Hi⌐ko⌐oki de i⌐kanai koto⌐ mo[1] arimasu. 'There are times when I don't go by plane.'

(e) Hi⌐ko⌐oki de i⌐kanai koto⌐ mo a⌐rima⌐su ka⌐ 'Do you ever not go by plane?'

(f) Hi⌐ko⌐oki de i⌐kanai koto⌐ wa a⌐rimase⌐n. 'There is never a time when I don't go by plane.'

With the preceding, compare the following, which are similar in meaning:[2]

(a) Tokidoki hi⌐ko⌐oki de ikimasu. 'Sometimes I go by plane.'

> The —— ko⌐to⌐ ḡa ⌐a⌐ru pattern is used whether an action oc-curs frequently or only rarely; tokidoki implies comparative frequency, whether used alone (as in the immediately preceding example) or together with the —— ko⌐to⌐ ḡa ⌐a⌐ru pattern (for

---

[1] Note the use of mo: '[Usually I do go by plane but] there are also times when I don't go by plane.'

[2] Sentence (a) here is to be compared with (a) in the preceding group, (c) with (c), etc.

example: <u>Tokidoki hi⌈ko⌉oki de i⌐ku koto⌉ ḡa arimasu.</u> 'Sometimes (there are times when) I go by plane.')

(c) Kessite hi⌈ko⌉oki de i⌈kimase⌉n̄. 'I never go by plane.'
(d) Taitee hi⌈ko⌉oki de ikimasu. 'Usually I go by plane.'
(f) I⌉tu mo hi⌈ko⌉oki de ikimasu. 'I always go by plane.'

2. 'Before,' 'While,' and 'After'

a. 'Before': <u>ma⌉e</u>

<u>Ma⌉e</u>, a nominal meaning 'time before' or 'place in front,' has pre-
viously occurred in combinations like <u>zi⌉p-puñ ⌐ma⌉e</u> 'ten minutes ago' and
<u>e⌉ki no ⌐ma⌉e</u> 'front of the station.' <u>Ma⌉e</u> may also be preceded by a sentence
modifier, ending with or consisting of an informal, NON-PAST verbal; the
sequence means 'before doing so-and-so' or 'before so-and-so happens <u>or</u>
happened.' The subject of the sentence modifier, if expressed, is followed by
<u>ḡa</u> or <u>no</u>. Thus: <u>ta⌈be⌉ru mae</u> 'before eating'; <u>i⌈ku ma⌉e</u> 'before going'; su-
<u>⌐ru ma⌉e</u> 'before doing'; <u>to⌈modati ḡa</u> (or <u>no</u>) <u>ku⌉ru mae</u> 'before my friend
comes <u>or</u> came.'

What follows <u>ma⌉e</u> depends upon its relation to what follows in the sentence. When the sequence ending in <u>ma⌉e</u> tells WHEN something happened,
it is followed by particle <u>ni</u>; when the <u>ma⌉e</u> sequence modifies a nominal, it
is followed by <u>no</u>; when it is the topic of comparison, it is followed by <u>wa</u>;
etc.

Examples:

De⌈kakeru ma⌉e ni, tyo⌈tto de⌈n̄wa-sita⌉i n̄ desu ḡa—
    'Before I go out, I'd just like to make a phone call . . .'
So⌈no boosi o kau ma⌉e ni, iti-do ka⌈bu⌉tte ⌐mi⌉ta hoo ḡa ⌐i⌉i desyoo?
    'Before you buy that hat, shouldn't you try it on once?' (lit. 'it would
    be better to have tried putting it on once, wouldn't it?')
No⌈bori ḡa (or no) tu⌉ku mae ni, ku⌈dari ḡa tatima⌉sita.
    'Before the up-train arrived, the down-train left.'
Ko⌈no kaisya ni tutome⌉ru ⌐ma⌉e no siḡoto wa, o⌈mosi⌉roku ⌈na⌉katta n̄
    desu.
    'The work [I did] before working for this company wasn't interesting.'
Ni⌈hon̄ e ⌐ku⌉ru mae wa ze⌈n̄zen̄ nihon̄ḡo o kikimase⌉n̄ desita.
    'Before I came to Japan (in comparison with after), I didn't hear Jap-
    anese at all.'
Sore wa ⌐a⌉u ⌐ma⌉e desita.
    'That was before I met [him].'

b. 'While': <u>aida</u> and <u>-naḡara</u>

<u>Aida</u>, a nominal meaning 'interval of time <u>or</u> space,' has previously
occurred in combinations like <u>A to B no aida</u> 'between A and B.' <u>Aida</u> may
also be preceded by a sentence modifier ending with (or consisting of) an informal verbal or negative adjectival, non-past or past; most commonly this
is <u>iru</u>, <u>ita</u>, <u>inai</u>, or <u>i⌈na⌉katta</u> (or a more polite equivalent) preceded by a
verbal gerund. The sequence is equivalent to 'while so-and-so is <u>or</u> was
occurring.' The subject of the sentence modifier, if expressed, is followed

by ḡa or no. Thus: <u>ta⌐bete iru aida</u> 'while [someone] is eating'; <u>no⌐nde ita aida</u> 'while [someone] was drinking'; <u>Tanaka-sañ ḡa</u> (or <u>no</u>) <u>iru aida</u> 'while Mr. Tanaka is here'; <u>tomodati ḡa</u> (or <u>no</u>) <u>inai aida</u> 'while my friend isn't here.'

Such a sequence is regularly used (a) when two actions or conditions having different subjects occur concurrently — 'while A is doing <u>or</u> being one thing, B is doing <u>or</u> being another'; and (b) when one action occurs within the interval during which another action or condition occurs (in which case the subjects may be the same or different) — 'at some point (<u>or</u> on occasions) while A is doing <u>or</u> being one thing, A (<u>or</u> B) does another.'

What follows <u>aida</u> depends upon its relation to what follows in the sentence. When an <u>aida</u> phrase occurs as an extent construction (telling HOW LONG something happens or happened), it occurs without a following particle; an <u>aida</u> phrase followed by particle <u>ni</u> indicates the interval during part of which something else happens.

Examples:

Dekakete iru aida, da⌐re ḡa ru⌐subañ o sima⌐su ka⌐
  'While we're out, who'll watch the house?'
A⌐na⌐ta ḡa beñkyoo-site iru aida ni, watakusi wa ka⌐imono ni itte kima⌐su.
  'While you are studying, I'll go and do some shopping (lit. I'll come having gone for shopping).'
Tanaka-sañ ḡa to⌐modati to hana⌐site ita aida, bo⌐ku wa ku⌐ruma no na⌐ka de ⌐ma⌐tte imasita.
  'While Mr. Tanaka was talking with a friend, I was waiting in the car.'
A⌐na⌐ta ḡa te⌐ḡami o yo⌐nde i⌐rassya⌐ru aida ni, watakusi wa to⌐modati ni deñwa-sima⌐su.
  'While you're reading the letter, I'll telephone a friend.'
Kyo⌐oto ni ita aida, yo⌐ku sa⌐simi⌐ o ta⌐bema⌐sita.
  'While I was in Kyoto, I ate sashimi a good deal.'
Ha⌐ha ḡa i̅nai aida, bo⌐ku ḡa zi̅buñ de syo⌐kuzi no sitaku o sima⌐sita.
  'Throughout the time my mother hasn't been here, I've prepared the meals by myself.'

When two actions are performed concurrently by the same person(s), a compound consisting of a verbal stem + <u>-naḡara</u> 'while doing so-and-so' occurs. If the verbal stem is accented, the derived <u>-naḡara</u> compound is also accented, on syllable <u>na</u>; otherwise, it is regularly unaccented. Thus:

ta⌐be⌐ru (stem: ta⌐be)	'eat'	ta⌐bena⌐ḡara 'while eating'
ha⌐na⌐su (stem: ha⌐na⌐si)	'talk'	ha⌐nasina⌐ḡara 'while talking'
kiku (stem: kiki)	'listen'	kikinaḡara 'while listening'
suru (stem: si)	'do'	sinaḡara 'while doing'

Examples:

Ra⌐zio o kikinaḡara be⌐ñkyoo-sima⌐sita.
  'While listening to the radio, I studied.' or 'I listened to the radio and studied at the same time.'
A⌐rukina⌐ḡara i⌐roiro hanasimasyo⌐o.
  'Let's talk (about various things) as we walk.'

Syu⌐zin wa ⌐ma⌐initi si⌐ñbuñ o yomina⌐gara ⌐go⌐han o tabemasu.
  'Every day my husband eats while reading the paper.'
Ta⌐bena⌐gara ta⌐bako o nomima⌐sita.
  'While I ate I smoked.'

With the last example, compare:

Tomodati ga ⌐ta⌐bete ita aida, watakusi wa ta⌐bako o nomima⌐sita.
  'While my friend was eating, I smoked.'

Remember: when YOU whistle while YOU work, use -nagara; when YOU whistle while SOMEONE ELSE works, use aida.

   c. 'After': a⌐to de

A⌐to de occurred previously meaning 'later on.' A⌐to is a nominal meaning 'later'; de is the gerund of da, meaning 'being.' Preceded by a sentence modifier consisting of or ending with an informal PAST verbal, it means 'after having done so-and-so.' The subject of the sentence modifier, if expressed, is usually followed by particle ga, less commonly by particle no. Thus: tabeta ⌐a⌐to de 'after having eaten'; si⌐ta a⌐to de 'after having done'; to⌐modati ga (or, less commonly, no) itta a⌐to de 'after my friend went.'

   Examples:

Ki⌐ita a⌐to de, o⌐moidasima⌐sita.
  'After I heard it I remembered.'
U⌐tta a⌐to de, ma⌐ta ho⌐siku na⌐rima⌐sita.
  'After I sold it, I began to want it (lit. I became wanting) again.'
Tomodati ga ta⌐isi⌐kañ o ya⌐meta a⌐to de ha⌐irima⌐sita.
  'I joined [the embassy] after my friend quit (the embassy).'

Kara preceded by a verbal gerund, meaning 'after doing so-and-so,' has occurred previously (cf. Lesson 16, Grammatical Note 2). An informal past + a⌐to de and the corresponding gerund + kara are close in meaning; but the pattern with kara usually implies that two actions follow each other directly or immediately, whereas the construction with a⌐to de occurs when one action takes place any time after—that is, not before—another. Thus:

Ga⌐kkoo o de⌐te kara, so⌐no kaisya ni hairima⌐sita.
  'After (i.e. directly after) leaving school, I joined that company.'
but:
Ga⌐kkoo o de⌐ta ⌐a⌐to de, so⌐no kaisya ni hairima⌐sita.
  'I joined that company after (i.e. not before) I left school.' (Something else may or may not have intervened.)

3. na⌐ñka ~ na⌐do

Na⌐ñka, or its more formal equivalent na⌐do, following one or more nominals, indicates that the preceding are mentioned as examples of a longer possible list. It often follows a series of nominals joined by particle ya, which also indicates that the words listed are examples of a longer series.

If the preceding word is accented, na⌐ñka and na⌐do lose their accents.

Examples:

> waˈtakusi naˈn̄ka 'people like me,' 'I, for example'
> kyoˈnen̄ nado 'last year, for example'
> hoˈn̄, zassi, siˈn̄bun̄ naˈdo 'books, magazines, newspapers, etc.'
> peˈn̄ ya eˈn̄pitu naˈn̄ka 'pens and pencils and so on'

A sequence + <u>naˈn̄ka</u> (or <u>naˈdo</u>) occurs in the same kinds of constructions —and followed by the same particles—as the sequence alone.

Examples:

> Toˈkidoki arimaˈsu ḡa, kyoˈnen̄ nado wa zeˈn̄zen̄ arimaseˈn̄ desita.
> 'Sometimes there are some, but last year, for example, there weren't any at all.'
> Koˈko niˈ wa, hoˈn̄, zassi, siˈn̄bun̄ naˈdo o siˈmatte kudasaˈi.
> 'In here, put away the books, magazines, newspapers, and so forth.'
> Peˈn̄ ya eˈn̄pitu naˈn̄ka o kaˈimaˈsita.
> 'I bought pens and pencils and things like that.'

4. Compound Nominals Ending in -kata

A verbal stem (the -maˈsu form minus -maˈsu) + -kata is a nominal meaning 'manner <u>or</u> way <u>or</u> style of doing so-and-so.' If the verbal stem is accented, the derived -kata compound is accented on syllable ka; if the verbal stem is unaccented, the -kata compound is also unaccented. Thus:

kaˈku	(stem: kaˈki)	'write'	kaˈkikaˈta 'way of writing'
yoˈmu	(stem: yoˈmi)	'read'	yoˈmikaˈta 'way of reading'
aˈruˈku	(stem: aˈruˈki)	'walk'	aˈrukikaˈta 'way of walking'
haˈnaˈsu	(stem: haˈnaˈsi)	'talk'	haˈnasikaˈta 'way of talking'
taˈbeˈru	(stem: taˈbe)	'eat'	taˈbekaˈta 'way of eating'
suru	(stem: si)	'do'	sikata 'way of doing'

5. Ordinal Numbers

The addition of the suffix -me to a number changes a cardinal number to its corresponding ordinal (which is accented on its final syllable). Thus:

niˈ-ban̄	'number 2'	and:	ni-ˈban̄-meˈ '2d in a series'
mi-ˈttuˈ	'3 things'	and:	mi-ˈttu-meˈ 'the 3d thing'
yo-nen̄	'4 years'	and:	yo-ˈnen̄-meˈ 'the 4th year'
go-ˈkaḡetu	'5 months'	and:	go-ˈkaḡetu-meˈ 'the 5th month'
roˈku-mai	'6 thin, flat units'	and:	roˈku-mai-meˈ 'the 6th thin, flat unit'

Ordinarily, -me is suffixed to numbers above number 1 in any series. For the first in a series, expressions like <u>hazime (no)</u> are used.

DRILLS

A. Substitution Drill

1. Where is the place where they sell toys?

Oˈmoˈtya (o) uˈtte (i)ru tokoroˈ (wa) ˈdoˈko desu ka⌐

2. Where is the place where they are having the conference?

Ka⌐i¬gi (o) si⌐te (i)ru tokoro⌐ (wa) ⌐do⌐ko desu ka↲

3. Where is the place where the children are playing?

Ko⌐domo ga asoñde (i)ru tokoro⌐ (wa) ⌐do⌐ko desu ka↲

4. Where is the place where your husband is working?

Go⌐syu⌐ziñ ga ha⌐taraite (i)ru tokoro⌐ (wa) ⌐do⌐ko desu ka↲

5. Where is the place where you are buying your groceries?

Syokuryoohiñ[1] (o) ka⌐tte (i)ru tokoro⌐ (wa) ⌐do⌐ko desu ka↲

6. Where is the place where they are making pottery like this?

Ko⌐o iu setomono (o) tuku⌐tte (i)ru to⌐koro⌐ (wa) ⌐do⌐ko desu ka↲

7. Where is the place where you are studying Japanese?

Ni⌐hoñgo (o) beñkyoo-site (i)ru tokoro⌐ (wa) ⌐do⌐ko desu ka↲

8. Where is the place where they are fixing the screen?

Byo⌐obu (o) nao⌐site (i)ru to⌐koro⌐ (wa) ⌐do⌐ko desu ka↲

B. Substitution Drill

1. It's comparatively cheap, isn't it!

Wa⌐ri ni yasu⌐i ñ desu ⌐ne⌐e.

2. It's really cheap, isn't it!

Ho⌐ñtoo ni yasu⌐i ñ desu ⌐ne⌐e.

3. It's really cute, isn't it!

Ho⌐ñtoo ni kawai⌐i ñ desu ⌐ne⌐e.

4. It's quite cute, isn't it!

Na⌐kanaka kawai⌐i ñ desu ⌐ne⌐e.

5. It's quite high, isn't it!

Na⌐kanaka taka⌐i ñ desu ⌐ne⌐e.

6. It's a little high, isn't it!

Tyo⌐tto ta⌐ka⌐i ñ desu ⌐ne⌐e.

7. It's a little low, isn't it!

Tyo⌐tto hi⌐ku⌐i ñ desu ⌐ne⌐e.

8. It's awfully low, isn't it!

Zu⌐ibuñ hi⌐ku⌐i ñ desu ⌐ne⌐e.

9. It's awfully thick (around), isn't it!

Zu⌐ibuñ hu⌐to⌐i ñ desu ⌐ne⌐e.

10. It's very thick (around), isn't it!

To⌐ttemo huto⌐i ñ desu ⌐ne⌐e.

C. Substitution Drill

1. Which do you prefer — a round one or a square one?

Ma⌐ru⌐i no to si⌐kaku⌐i no to, do⌐tira ga o⌐suki de⌐su ka↲

2. Which do you prefer — a thin (around) one or a thick (around) one?

Ho⌐so⌐i no to hu⌐to⌐i no to, do⌐tira ga o⌐suki de⌐su ka↲

3. Which do you prefer — an expensive one or a cheap one?

Ta⌐ka⌐i no to ya⌐su⌐i no to, do⌐tira ga o⌐suki de⌐su ka↲

4. Which do you prefer — a low one or a high one?

Hi⌐ku⌐i no to ta⌐ka⌐i no to, do⌐tira ga o⌐suki de⌐su ka↲

5. Which do you prefer — a simple one or a complicated one?

Ka⌐ñtañ na⌐ no to hu⌐kuzatu na⌐ no to, do⌐tira ga o⌐suki de⌐su ka↲

6. Which do you prefer — a far one or a near one?

To⌐oi⌐ no to ti⌐ka⌐i no to, do⌐tira ga o⌐suki de⌐su ka↲

---

[1] Has accented alternant: syo⌐kuryo⌐ohiñ.

7. Which do you prefer — a bright one or a conservative one?

Ha⌐de¬ na no to zi⌐mi¬ na no to, do¬tira ḡa o⌐suki de⁴su ka⌣

8. Which do you prefer —a dark (in color) one or a light (in color) one?

Ko⌐i¬ no to u⌐su¬i no to, do¬tira ḡa o⌐suki de⁴su ka⌣

9. Which do you prefer —a thin (flat) one or a thick (flat) one?

U⌐su¬i no to a⌐tu¬i no to, do¬tira ḡa o⌐suki de⁴su ka⌣

10. Which do you prefer —a light one or a heavy one?

Ka⌐ru¬i no to o⌐mo¬i no to, do¬tira ḡa o⌐suki de⁴su ka⌣

D. Substitution Drill

1. It's a girl so a doll would probably make a good gift, wouldn't it.

O⌐ñna¬ no ko da kara, niñḡyoo wa ⌐i¬i o⌐kurimono ni na⁴ru desyoo ⌐ne¬e.

2. It's a boy so a knife would probably make a good gift, wouldn't it.

O⌐toko¬ no ko da kara, na⌐ihu wa ⌐i¬i o⌐kurimono ni na⁴ru desyoo ⌐ne¬e.

3. It's a child so a toy would probably make a good gift, wouldn't it.

Ko⌐domo da¬ kara, o⌐mo¬tya wa ⌐i¬i o⌐kurimono ni na⁴ru desyoo ⌐ne¬e.

4. It's a Japanese so something from America would probably make a good gift, wouldn't it.

Ni⌐hoñzi¬ñ da kara, A⌐merika no mono¬ wa ⌐i¬i o⌐kurimono ni na⁴ru desyoo ⌐ne¬e.

5. It's an American so something from Japan would probably make a good gift, wouldn't it.

A⌐merika¬ziñ da kara, Ni⌐hoñ no mono¬ wa ⌐i¬i o⌐kurimono ni na⁴ru desyoo ⌐ne¬e.

6. It's a woman so flowers would probably make a good gift, wouldn't they.

O⌐ñna no hito¬ da kara, ha⌐na¬ wa ⌐i¬i o⌐kurimono ni na⁴ru desyoo ⌐ne¬e.

7. It's a student so a book would probably make a good gift, wouldn't it.

Ga⌐kusee da¬ kara, ho⌐ñ wa ⌐i¬i o⌐kurimono ni na⁴ru desyoo ⌐ne¬e.

E. Substitution Drill [1]

1. I think I'd like to send a toy to my daughter . . .

Mu⌐sume¬ ni o⌐mo¬tya (o) o⌐kutte yaritai to omo⁴tte ⌐ne¬e.

2. I think I'd like to send some candy to my son . . .

Musuko ni o⌐ka¬si (o) o⌐kutte yaritai to omo⁴tte ⌐ne¬e.

3. I think I'd like to send a book to the teacher . . .

Se⌐ñse¬e ni ⌐ho¬ñ (o) o⌐kutte aḡetai to omo⁴tte ⌐ne¬e.

4. I think I'd like to send some pearls to my wife . . .

Ka⌐nai ni si⌐ñzyu (o) okutte yaritai to omo⁴tte ⌐ne⁴e.

---

[1] Be sure to replace <u>yaritai</u> with <u>aḡetai</u> wherever appropriate.

5. I think I'd like to send some Japanese pottery to my (younger) sister in America . . .

A⌐merika no imooto⌐ ni Ni⌐hoñ no setomono (o) okutte yaritai to omo⌐tte ⌐ne⌐e.

6. I think I'd like to send a fan to a foreign friend of mine . . .

Gaiziñ no tomodati ni se⌐ñsu (o) okutte a͟getai to omo⌐tte ⌐ne⌐e.

7. I think I'd like to send some fruit to our maid who is sick . . .

Byooki no zyotyuu ni ku⌐da⌐mono (o) o⌐kutte yaritai to omo⌐tte ⌐ne⌐e.

F. Substitution Drill (based on Grammatical Note 4)

1. What a strange way of writing!

He⌐ñ na ka⌐kika⌐ta desu ⌐ne⌐e.

2. What a strange way of talking! /ha⌐na⌐su/

He⌐ñ na hanasika⌐ta desu ⌐ne⌐e.

3. What a strange way of walking! /a⌐ru⌐ku/

He⌐ñ na a⌐rukika⌐ta desu ⌐ne⌐e.

4. What a strange way of saying [it]! /iu/

He⌐ñ na i⌐ikata de⌐su ⌐ne⌐e.

5. What a strange way of thinking! /ka⌐ñ͟gae⌐ru/

He⌐ñ na ka⌐ñ͟gaeka⌐ta desu ⌐ne⌐e.

6. What a strange way of reading [it]! /yo⌐mu/

He⌐ñ na yo⌐mika⌐ta desu ⌐ne⌐e.

7. What a strange way of calling! /yobu/

He⌐ñ na yo⌐bikata de⌐su ⌐ne⌐e.

- 8. What a strange way of using [it]! /tukau/

He⌐ñ na tu⌐kaikata de⌐su ⌐ne⌐e.

G. Substitution Drill (based on Grammatical Note 5)

1. It's the second from the left.

Hidari kara ni-⌐bañ-me⌐ desu.

2. He's the third person from the right.

Mi͟gi kara sa⌐ñ-niñ-me⌐ desu.

3. It's the fourth thing from the bottom.

Sita kara yo⌐ttu-me⌐ desu.

4. It's the fifth (thin, flat) thing from the top.

Ue kara go-⌐mai-me⌐ desu.

5. It's the sixth (long, cylindrical) thing from the front.

Ma⌐e kara ro⌐p-poñ-me⌐ desu.

6. It's the seventh (vehicle) from the back.

Usiro kara nana-dai-me⌐ desu.

H. Substitution Drill

1. I want to practice writing with a brush.

Hu⌐de de ka⌐ku re⌐ñsyuu (͟ga) sita⌐i ñ desu yo.

2. I want to practice singing this song.

Ko⌐no uta⌐ (o) u⌐tau reñsyuu (͟ga) sita⌐i ñ desu yo.

3. I want to practice talking
   in Japanese.

   Ni⌐hoñḡo de hana⌐su re⌐ñsyuu (ḡa)
   sita⌐i ñ desu yo.

4. I want to practice reading
   French.

   Hu⌐rañsuḡo (o) yo⌐mu re⌐ñsyuu
   (ḡa) sita⌐i ñ desu yo.

5. I want to practice changing
   a tire.

   Ta⌐iya (o) torikaeru reñsyuu (ḡa)
   sita⌐i ñ desu yo.

6. I want to practice tying
   an obi.

   O⌐bi (o) si⌐me⌐ru re⌐ñsyuu (ḡa)
   sita⌐i ñ desu yo.

I. Grammar Drill

Tutor: Ka⌐kika⌐ta (o) re⌐ñsyuu-simasyo⌐o. 'Let's practice writing.'

Student: Ka⌐kika⌐ta no re⌐ñsyuu (o) simasyo⌐o. 'Let's practice
writing.' (Lit. 'Let's do writing practice.')

1. Ni⌐hoñḡo (o) reñsyuu-
   simasyo⌐o.

   Ni⌐hoñḡo no reñsyuu (o) simasyo⌐o.

2. Ka⌐na to kañzi (o) reñ-
   syuu-simasyo⌐o.

   Ka⌐na to kañzi no reñsyuu (o) si-
   masyo⌐o.

3. Syo⌐oḡi (o) reñsyuu-
   simasyo⌐o.

   Syo⌐oḡi no reñsyuu (o) simasyo⌐o.

4. Si⌐bai (o) reñsyuu-
   simasyo⌐o.

   Si⌐bai no reñsyuu (o) simasyo⌐o.

5. Go⌐ (o) re⌐ñsyuu-simasyo⌐o.

   Go⌐ no re⌐ñsyuu (o) simasyo⌐o.

J. Grammar Drill

Tutor: Ma⌐do (o) a⌐kema⌐sita. '[I] opened the window.'
Student: Ma⌐do (ḡa) a⌐kima⌐sita. 'The window opened.'

1. O⌐sara (o) kowasima⌐sita.

   O⌐sara (ḡa) kowarema⌐sita.

2. Se⌐ñtakumono (o) kawa-
   kasima⌐sita.

   Se⌐ñtakumono (ḡa) kawakima⌐sita.

3. A⌐tarasi⌐i siḡoto (o)
   ha⌐zimema⌐sita.

   A⌐tarasi⌐i siḡoto (ḡa) ha⌐zimari-
   ma⌐sita.

4. Hi ⌐(o) kimema⌐sita.

   Hi ⌐(ḡa) kimarima⌐sita.

5. Ko⌐domo (o) okosima⌐sita.

   Ko⌐domo (ḡa) okima⌐sita.

6. De⌐ñki (o) ke⌐sima⌐sita.

   De⌐ñki (ḡa) ki⌐ema⌐sita.

7. Te⌐ḡami (o) todokema⌐-
   sita.

   Te⌐ḡami (ḡa) todokima⌐sita.

8. Ku⌐suri (o) kobosima⌐-
   sita.

   Ku⌐suri (ḡa) koborema⌐sita.

K. Expansion Drill (based on Grammatical Note 3)

Tutor: Ni⌐ñḡyoo (wa) do⌐o desyoo. 'How about a doll?'
Student: Ni⌐ñḡyoo na⌐ñka (wa) ⌐do⌐o desyoo. 'How about something
like a doll?'

1. O⌐mo⌐tya (wa) ⌐do⌐o desyoo.

   O⌐mo⌐tya na⌐ñka (wa) ⌐do⌐o desyoo.

2. Hi⌐bati (wa) ⌐do⌐o desyoo.

   Hi⌐bati na⌐ñka (wa) ⌐do⌐o desyoo.

3. Hu⌐rosiki (wa) do⌐o desyoo.   Hu⌐rosiki na¬ñka (wa) ⌐do⌐o desyoo.
4. O⌐sake (wa) do⌐o desyoo.   O⌐sake na¬ñka (wa) ⌐do⌐o desyoo.
5. O⌐ka⌐si (wa) ⌐do⌐o desyoo.   O⌐ka⌐si nañka (wa) ⌐do⌐o desyoo.

L. Grammar Drill

Tutor: Syu⌐uzi to iu⌐ no (wa) ⌐na¬ñ desyoo. 'What is (the thing
          called) calligraphy?'
Student: Syuuzi tte ⌐na¬ñ desyoo. 'What is "calligraphy"?'

1. Su⌐zuri⌐ to i⌐u⌐ no (wa)   Su⌐zuri⌐ tte ⌐na¬ñ desyoo.
    ⌐na¬ñ desyoo.
2. Ko⌐tatu to iu⌐ no (wa)   Kotatu tte ⌐na¬ñ desyoo.
    ⌐na¬ñ desyoo.
3. Ha⌐nami⌐ to i⌐u⌐ no (wa)   Ha⌐nami⌐ tte ⌐na¬ñ desyoo.
    ⌐na¬ñ desyoo.
4. Syo⌐o⌐gi to iu⌐ no (wa)   Syoo⌐gi tte ⌐na¬ñ desyoo.
    ⌐na¬ñ desyoo.
5. Ka⌐ke⌐mono to i⌐u⌐ no   Ka⌐ke⌐mono tte ⌐na¬ñ desyoo.
    (wa) ⌐na¬ñ desyoo.
6. Tu⌐yu to iu⌐ no (wa) ⌐na¬ñ   Tuyu tte ⌐na¬ñ desyoo.
    desyoo.

M. Grammar Drill

Tutor: Wa⌐takusi no hosi⌐i no (wa) te⌐eburu na⌐ ñ desu. 'What
          I want is a table.'
Student: Te⌐eburu no hosi⌐i no wa wa⌐takusi na⌐ ñ desu. 'I'm
          the one who wants a table.'

1. Mu⌐sume no hosi⌐i no (wa)   Ni⌐ñgyoo no hosi⌐i no (wa) mu-
    ni⌐ñgyoo na⌐ ñ desu.   ⌐sume⌐ na ñ desu.
2. A⌐no⌐ hito no de⌐ki⌐ru no   Ro⌐siago no deki⌐ru no (wa) a⌐no⌐
    (wa) ro⌐siago na⌐ ñ desu.   hito na ñ desu.
3. To⌐modati no zyoozu⌐ na   Syu⌐uzi no zyoozu⌐ na no (wa) to-
    no (wa) o⌐syu⌐uzi[1] na ñ   ⌐modati na⌐ ñ desu.
    desu.
4. Se⌐ñse⌐e no wa⌐ka⌐ru no   Do⌐itugo no waka⌐ru no (wa)
    (wa) do⌐itugo na⌐ ñ desu.   se⌐ñse⌐e na ñ desu.
5. Hi⌐syo no iru⌐ no (wa)   Ka⌐mi no iru⌐ no (wa) hi⌐syo⌐ na
    ka⌐mi⌐ na ñ desu.   ñ desu.
6. Wa⌐tasi no suki⌐ na no   Sa⌐simi no suki⌐ na no (wa) wa-
    (wa) sa⌐simi⌐ na ñ desu.   ⌐tasi na⌐ ñ desu.
7. Ga⌐kusee no sita⌐i no (wa)   E⌐e⌐go no reñsyuu no sita⌐i no
    e⌐e⌐go no reñsyuu na⌐ ñ   (wa) ga⌐kusee na⌐ ñ desu.
    desu.
8. A⌐no gaiziñ no hanase⌐ru   Hu⌐rañsugo no hanase⌐ru no (wa)
    no (wa) hu⌐rañsugo na⌐ ñ   a⌐no gaiziñ na⌐ ñ desu.
    desu.

1
Polite (+) form used more commonly by women.

N. Grammar Drill (based on Grammatical Note 2)

    Tutor: De⌐kakema⌐sita. So⌐no ma⌐e ni, ta⌐bema⌐sita. 'I went out. Before that I ate.'
    Student: De⌐kakeru ma⌐e ni, ta⌐bema⌐sita. 'Before going out, I ate.'

1. Ka⌐erima⌐su.
   So⌐no ma⌐e ni, ka⌐ḡuu⌐riba
   (o) no⌐zoite kima⌐su.

   Ka⌐eru mae ni, ka⌐ḡuu⌐riba (o)
   no⌐zoite kima⌐su.

2. A⌐no isu (o) nurikaema⌐su.
   So⌐no ma⌐e ni, a⌐raima⌐su.

   A⌐no isu (o) nurikae⌐ru mae ni,
   a⌐raima⌐su.

3. Ki⌐mema⌐su.
   So⌐no ma⌐e ni, mo⌐o tyo⌐tto
   so⌐odañ-simasyo⌐o.

   Ki⌐meru ma⌐e ni, mo⌐o tyo⌐tto
   so⌐odañ-simasyo⌐o.

4. To⌐modati ni watasima⌐-
   sita.
   So⌐no ma⌐e ni, hu⌐rosiki
   ni tutumima⌐sita.

   To⌐modati ni watasu ma⌐e ni,
   hu⌐rosiki ni tutumima⌐sita.

5. Sa⌐ñpo ni ikima⌐sita.
   So⌐no ma⌐e ni, o⌐tya (o)
   nomima⌐sita.

   Sa⌐ñpo ni iku ma⌐e ni, o⌐tya (o)
   nomima⌐sita.

6. Ki⌐sya⌐ ni norimasu.
   So⌐no ma⌐e ni, ki⌐ppu (o)
   kaima⌐su.

   Ki⌐sya⌐ ni no⌐ru ma⌐e ni, ki⌐ppu
   (o) kaima⌐su.

O. Grammar Drill (based on Grammatical Note 2)

    Tutor: A⌐na⌐ta wa ni⌐ñḡyoo (o) tutu⌐ñde moraimasu. Watasi wa
    ⌐go⌐ ya syooḡi no u⌐riba o nozoite kima⌐su. 'You will
    have the doll wrapped. I'll go and take a look at the <u>go</u>
    and <u>shogi</u> counter.'
    Student: A⌐na⌐ta ḡa ni⌐ñḡyoo (o) tutu⌐ñde moratte (i)ru aida ni,
    watasi wa ⌐go⌐ ya syooḡi no u⌐riba o nozoite kima⌐su.
    'While you have the doll wrapped, I'll go and take a look
    at the <u>go</u> and <u>shogi</u> counter.'

1. A⌐na⌐ta wa de⌐ñwa (o)
   kakema⌐su.
   Watakusi wa si⌐ñbuñ (o)
   katte kima⌐su.

   A⌐na⌐ta ḡa de⌐ñwa (o) ka⌐kete (i)ru
   aida ni, watakusi wa si⌐ñbuñ
   (o) katte kima⌐su.

2. A⌐na⌐ta wa se⌐ñse⌐e to
   hanasimasu.
   Watakusi wa ta⌐bako (o)
   nomima⌐su.

   A⌐na⌐ta ḡa se⌐ñse⌐e to ha⌐na⌐site
   (i)ru aida ni, watakusi wa ta-
   ⌐bako (o) nomima⌐su.

3. A⌐na⌐ta wa o⌐sara (o)
   araima⌐su.
   Watakusi wa za⌐siki⌐ (o)
   katazukemasu.

   A⌐na⌐ta ḡa o⌐sara (o) aratte (i)ru
   aida ni, watakusi wa za⌐siki⌐
   (o) katazukemasu.

4. A⌐na⌐ta wa ki⌐mono (o)
   kikaema⌐su.
   Watakusi wa te⌐eburu (o)
   yoyaku-site okima⌐su.

   A⌐na⌐ta ḡa ki⌐mono (o) kika⌐ete
   (i)ru aida ni, watakusi wa te⌐e-
   buru (o) yoyaku-site okima⌐su.

5. A⌐na⌐ta wa bu⌐ro⌐okaa to   A⌐na⌐ta ḡa bu⌐ro⌐okaa to soodañ-
    soodañ-simasu.   site (i)ru aida ni, watakusi wa
    Watakusi wa ma⌐ta uti   ma⌐ta uti (o) mi⌐sete morai-
    (o) mi⌐sete moraimasu.   masu.
6. A⌐na⌐ta wa ke⌐ñbutu-   A⌐na⌐ta ḡa keñbutu-site (i)ru aida
    sima⌐su.   ni, watakusi wa hi⌐rune (o)
    Watakusi wa hi⌐rune (o)   sima⌐su.
    sima⌐su.

P. Grammar Drill (based on Grammatical Note 2)

        Tutor: Bi⌐iru (o) nomimasu. Ta⌐bema⌐su. '[We]'ll drink beer.
                 [We]'ll eat.'
        Student: Bi⌐iru (o) no⌐mina⌐ḡara, ta⌐bema⌐su. '[We]'ll eat and
                 drink beer at the same time.'

1. A⌐rukimasyo⌐o. Ha⌐nasi-   A⌐rukina⌐ḡara, ha⌐nasimasyo⌐o.
    masyo⌐o.
2. U⌐ta⌐ (o) u⌐taima⌐sita.   U⌐ta⌐ (o) utaina⌐ḡara, o⌐sake (o)
    O⌐sake (o) nomima⌐sita.   nomima⌐sita.
3. Ta⌐bema⌐sita. To⌐modati   Ta⌐bena⌐ḡara, to⌐modati kara⌐ no
    kara⌐ no te⌐ḡami (o) yo-   te⌐ḡami (o) yomima⌐sita
    mima⌐sita.
4. A⌐sobima⌐sita. Si⌐ḡoto   Asobina⌐ḡara, si⌐ḡoto (o) sima⌐-
    (o) sima⌐sita.   sita.
5. So⌐o iima⌐sita. He⌐ya⌐   Soo iina⌐ḡara, he⌐ya⌐ kara de⌐ma⌐-
    kara de⌐ma⌐sita.   sita.
6. Ra⌐zio (o) ki⌐kimasyo⌐o.   Ra⌐zio (o) kikina⌐ḡara, syo⌐kuzi
    Syo⌐kuzi (o) simasyo⌐o.   (o) simasyo⌐o.

Q. Grammar Drill (based on Grammatical Note 2)

        Tutor: Ka⌐imono (o) suma⌐sete kara, ta⌐bemasyo⌐o. 'After fin-
                 ishing our shopping let's eat.'
        Student: Ka⌐imono (o) suma⌐seta ⌐a⌐to de, ta⌐bemasyo⌐o.' 'Let's
                 eat after (not before) we've finished our shopping.'

1. So⌐odañ-site⌐ kara, ki⌐me-   So⌐odañ-sita a⌐to de, ki⌐mema⌐-
    ma⌐sita.   sita.
2. Ka⌐be (o) nurika⌐ete kara,   Ka⌐be (o) nurika⌐eta ⌐a⌐to de,
    ta⌐tami (o) torikaema⌐sita.   ta⌐tami (o) torikaema⌐sita.
3. Sa⌐kura (o) mi⌐te kara,   Sa⌐kura (o) mi⌐ta ⌐a⌐to de, o⌐beñ-
    o⌐beñtoo (o) tabemasyo⌐o.   too (o) tabemasyo⌐o.
4. Se⌐tumee-site moratte⌐   Se⌐tumee-site moratta a⌐to de,
    kara, yo⌐ñde mimasyoo.   yo⌐ñde mimasyoo.
5. Ni⌐ho⌐ñ e i⌐tte⌐ kara, ni-   Ni⌐ho⌐ñ e i⌐tta a⌐to de, ni⌐ho⌐ñḡo
    ⌐hoñḡo (o) beñkyoo-   (o) beñkyoo-sihazimema⌐sita.
    sihazimema⌐sita.
6. De⌐ñki (o) ke⌐site⌐ kara,   De⌐ñki (o) ke⌐sita a⌐to de, ma⌐do
    ma⌐do (o) a⌐kema⌐sita.   (o) a⌐kema⌐sita.

7. A⌐merika e ka⌐ette kara,
   ta⌐bako (o) yamema⌐sita.

   A⌐merika e ka⌐etta ⌐a⌐to de, ta⌐ba-
   ko (o) yamema⌐sita.

8. Ne⌐dañ (o) kiite⌐ kara,
   ki⌐mema⌐sita.

   Ne⌐dañ (o) kiita a⌐to de, ki⌐mema⌐-
   sita.

R. Grammar Drill (based on Grammatical Note 1)

Tutor: I⌐kima⌐su ka⌐   'Do you (<u>or</u> are you going to) go?'
Student: I⌐tta koto⌐ ḡa a⌐rima⌐su ka⌐   'Have you ever gone?'

1. O⌐sasimi (o) mesiaḡari-
   ma⌐su ka⌐

   O⌐sasimi (o) mesiaḡatta koto⌐ ḡa
   a⌐rima⌐su ka⌐

2. Hi⌐ko⌐oki ni no⌐rima⌐su
   ka⌐

   Hi⌐ko⌐oki ni no⌐tta koto⌐ ḡa a⌐ri-
   ma⌐su ka⌐

3. O⌐kusañ (o) tu⌐rete iki-
   ma⌐su ka⌐

   O⌐kusañ (o) tu⌐rete itta koto⌐ ḡa
   a⌐rima⌐su ka⌐

4. Hu⌐de de kakima⌐su ka⌐

   Hu⌐de de ka⌐ita koto ḡa a⌐rima⌐su
   ka⌐

5. To⌐okyoo ma⌐de ka⌐yoima⌐-
   su ka⌐

   To⌐okyoo ma⌐de ka⌐yotta koto⌐ ḡa
   a⌐rima⌐su ka⌐

6. Yoohukuya ni se⌐biro (o)
   tuku⌐tte mo⌐raima⌐su ka⌐

   Yoohukuya ni se⌐biro (o) tuku⌐-
   tte mo⌐ratta koto⌐ ḡa a⌐rima⌐su
   ka⌐

7. Ko⌐tatu (o) tukaima⌐su ka⌐

   Ko⌐tatu (o) tukatta koto⌐ ḡa a⌐ri-
   ma⌐su ka⌐

8. Hu⌐toñ ni nema⌐su ka⌐

   Hu⌐toñ ni neta koto⌐ ḡa a⌐rima⌐su
   ka⌐

9. A⌐sahi (o) yo⌐mima⌐su ka⌐

   A⌐sahi (o) ⌐yo⌐ñda koto ḡa a⌐ri-
   ma⌐su ka⌐

10. Ka⌐buki (o) mima⌐su ka⌐

    Ka⌐buki (o) mi⌐ta koto ḡa a⌐ri-
    ma⌐su ka⌐

Give the <u>iie</u> answer for each of the questions in the right-hand
column above.

S. Grammar Drill (based on Grammatical Note 1)

(For each sentence on the left, give the approximate meaning equivalent containing <u>tokidoki</u>, <u>i⌐tu mo</u>, <u>taitee</u>, or <u>kessite</u>.)

1. Ni⌐hoñ no siñbuñ (o) yo⌐-
   mu koto wa a⌐rimase⌐ñ.

   Kessite Ni⌐hoñ no siñbuñ (o)
   yomimase⌐ñ.

2. Hu⌐de de ka⌐ku koto ḡa
   arimasu.

   Tokidoki hu⌐de de kakima⌐su.

3. Ku⌐ruma de ikanai koto⌐
   mo arimasu.

   Taitee ku⌐ruma de ikima⌐su.

4. O⌐soku⌐ made ha⌐taraku
   koto⌐ ḡa arimasu.

   Tokidoki o⌐soku⌐ made hatara-
   kimasu.

5. Koko ni da⌐re mo inai
   koto⌐ wa a⌐rimase⌐ñ.

   I⌐tu mo ko̅ko ni ⌐da⌐re ka imasu.

6. O⌐boerare⌐nai koto mo
   arimasu.

   Ta⌐itee oboerarema⌐su.

7. Oˈsake naˈñka (o) ˈnoˈmu   Kessite oˈsake naˈñka (o) noˈmi-
   koto wa aˈrimaseˈñ.   maseˈñ.
8. Gaˈiziñ daˈ keredo, wa-   Gaˈiziñ daˈ keredo, iˈtu mo wa-
   ˈkaraˈnai koto wa aˈri-   karimasu.
   maseˈñ.

QUESTION SUPPLEMENT

(based on the Basic Dialogues)

(a) 1. Deˈpaˈato no oˈmoˈtya o uˈtte iru tokoroˈ wa ˈnaˈñ to iˈimaˈsu ka⌐
     2. Oˈmotyauˈriba wa naˈñ-ḡai deˈsu ka⌐
     3. Suˈmisu-sañ wa ˈnaˈni o ˈdaˈre ni oˈkutte yaritaˈi ñ desu ka⌐
     4. Taˈnaka-sañ no hanasiˈ ni yoru to, naˈni ḡa ˈiˈi oˈkurimono ni
        naˈru desyoo ka.
     5. Tanaka-sañ wa ˈdoˈo site niˈñḡyoo o gaikoku e okutteˈ mo daˈi-
        zyoˈobu da to oˈmoimaˈsu ka⌐
     6. Suˈmisu-sañ wa ˈdoˈo site niñḡyoo wa ˈiˈi oˈkurimono ni naˈru to
        oˈmoimaˈsu ka⌐

(b) 7. Doˈno niñḡyoo ḡa kaˈwaiˈi ñ desu ka⌐
     8. Iˈkura desu ka⌐
     9. Taˈkaˈi ñ desu ka, yaˈsuˈi ñ desu ka⌐
    10. Suˈmisu-sañ wa ˈdoˈñna okurimono ni kiˈmemaˈsita ka⌐
    11. Suˈmisu-sañ ḡa niˈñḡyoo o tutuˈñde moratte iru aïda ni, Tanaka-
        sañ wa ˈnaˈni o siˈmaˈsu ka⌐

(c) 12. Buˈraˈuñ-sañ no miˈtaˈi no wa ˈnaˈñ desu ka⌐
    13. Buˈraˈuñ-sañ no tomodati wa zaˈsiki no teeburu o ˈdoˈko de tuˈka-
        tte imaˈsu ka⌐
    14. Buˈraˈuñ-sañ wa ˈdoˈo oˈmoimaˈsita ka⌐
    15. Buˈraˈuñ-sañ wa ˈdoˈo site hoˈsonaḡaˈi teeburu ḡa kaˈitaˈi ñ desu
        ka⌐
    16. Tanaka-sañ wa kaˈimono o sumaˈsete kara ˈnaˈni o siˈtaˈi ñ desu
        ka⌐
    17. Deˈpaˈato no tiˈkaˈku ni wa ˈdoˈñna taˈbeˈru toˈkoroˈ ḡa aˈrimaˈsu
        ka⌐
    18. Tanaka-sañ wa ˈdoˈko e Buˈraˈuñ-sañ o aˈñnai-simaˈsu ka⌐

(d) 19. Suˈmisu-sañ wa niñḡyoo no hoka ni ˈnaˈni ḡa miˈtaˈi ñ desu ka⌐
    20. Doˈo site soˈñna monoˈ ḡa kaˈitaˈi ñ desu ka⌐
    21. Syuˈuzi to iuˈ no wa ˈnaˈñ to iu ˈiˈmi desu ka⌐

EXERCISES

1. Ask the following questions and make up an appropriate answer for each:

   a. Ask a Japanese friend if he has ever been (lit. gone) to America.
   b. Ask who the third man from the right is.

    c. Ask where the toys you bought yesterday are.

    d. Ask your house guest if he would like to take a bath before having dinner.

    e. Ask a friend if he has ever eaten at the Tenkin Tempura Shop.

    f. Ask the maid who broke the big square plate.

    g. Ask if you should wrap the books and magazines together.

    h. Ask a Japanese friend if he ever writes with a brush.

    i. Ask the meaning of 'na⌈o⌉su.'

    j. Ask Mr. Tanaka if he is going to have dinner AFTER he has telephoned to America.

    k. Ask Mr. Tanaka if you may read his newspaper while he is telephoning.

    l. Ask Mr. Tanaka if he will write his address and telephone number in romanization for you.

   m. A visitor is looking for Mr. Smith's office. Ask if you should show him the way.

    n. A Japanese friend is trying to read an English text. Ask if he understands the meaning.

    o. You have been asked to write your name and address. Ask if romanization will be all right.

    p. Ask a friend if he ever eats while reading the paper.

    q. Ask Mr. Tanaka if he started studying English AFTER he went to America.

    r. Ask a friend if he is hungry.

2. Practice the drills of this lesson, changing to informal style wherever possible.

Lesson 32. Sightseeing

BASIC DIALOGUES: FOR MEMORIZATION

(a)

Smith

all directions <u>or</u>
   everywhere

hoˈoboo

travel

ryokoo-suru

return having traveled

ryoˈkoo-site kaˈeru

1. Since I came all the way to Japan, (I think) I'd like to travel around before I go home (lit. return home having traveled in all directions)...

Sekkaku Niˈhoˈn̄ e kiˈtaˈ n̄ desu kara, hoˈoboo ryoˈkoo-site kaerita'i to oˈmoimaˈsu ḡa—

that being the case <u>or</u>
   accordingly

sore de

troublesome <u>or</u> annoying

meˈewaku /na/ <u>or</u>
   goˈmeˈewaku⁺ /na/

provided it isn't a nuisance for you <u>or</u> unless it's a nuisance for you

goˈmeˈewaku zya haˈkereba

2. That being the case, if it isn't too much trouble, would you tell me what kind of places I should go to?

Sore de; goˈmeˈewaku zya haˈ-kereba, doˈn̄na toˈkoroˈ e iˈttaˈ-ra ˈiˈi ka oˈsiete kudasaimaseˈn̄ ka.

Tanaka

be useful <u>or</u> serve a purpose

yaˈkuˈ ni ˈtaˈtu /-u/ <u>or</u>
oˈyaku ni taˈtu⁺

3. Hmm. Depending on the person, the places one wants to see are different, so I don't know whether I'll be of any use or not...

Saˈa. Hito ni yotte miˈtaˈi toˈkoroˈ ḡa tiˈḡaimaˈsu kara, oˈyaku ni taˈtu ka ˈdoˈo ka waˈkarimaseˈn̄ ḡa—

provided it's a nearby place

tiˈkaˈi toˈkoroˈ nara

famous

yuumee /na/

4. If you mean a nearby place, Nikko is famous.

Tiˈkaˈi toˈkoroˈ nara, Niˈkkoo ḡa yuˈumee deˈsu n̄eˈe.

Smith

5. Oh, that's right.

Aˈa, soˈo desu n̄eˈe.

240

          provided [someone] goes   i⌐ke⌐ba

6. How is it most convenient to go   A⌐soko e iku⌐ no ni wa, na⌐ñ de
    there? (Lit. In going there, it   i⊢ke⊣ba i⊢tibañ be⊣ñri desyoo ka.
    is probably most convenient
    provided you go by what?)

Tanaka

7. I guess the electric train is   Ma⌐a, de⌐ñsya ḡa itibañ i⌐i desɯ
    best—since there's a special   yo⌣ — to⊢kkyuu (ḡa) arima⊣su
    express.   kara.

Smith

          decide to go   i⌐ku koto⌐ ni suru
          provided [someone]   i⌐ku koto⌐ ni su⊢re⊣ba
            decides to go
          unless [someone] buys   ka⌐tte okana⌐kereba
            in advance
          it won't do   na⌐ra⌐nai
          must buy in advance   ka⌐tte okana⌐kereba na⊢ra⊣-
                                nai

8. But if I decide to go by   De⌐ mo; to⌐kkyuu de iku koto⌐ ni
    special express, I suppose   su⊢re⊣ba, to⌐kkyuu⌐ukeñ (o) ka⊢tte
    I'll have to buy a special   okana⊣kereba na⊢ra⊣nai desyoo
    express ticket in advance,   ne?
    won't I.

Tanaka

9. Yes. By the day before   E⌐e. Ma⌐e no hi⌐ made ni.
    [you go].

(b)

Smith

          fishing   turi
          hot spring <u>or</u> hot spring   oñseñ
            resort
          hot spring resort where   tu⌐ri no deki⌐ru oñseñ
            fishing is possible

10. I'd like to try going to a   Tu⌐ri no deki⌐ru ⌐si⌐zuka na
     quiet hot spring resort   oñseñ e i⊢tte mita⊣i ñ desu ḡa⌐
     where I can fish . . .

Tanaka

          provided it's Izu   I⌐zu na⌐ra

11. Oh. If it's Izu, there are   A⌐a ⊢so⊣o. I⌐zu na⌐ra, so⌐ñna
     lots of places like that.   tokoro⌐ (ḡa) ta⌐kusañ arima⌐su
                              yo⌣

Smith (thinking)

          island   si⌐ma⌐

12. Isn't (lit. wasn't) Izu an   Izu (wa), si⌐ma⌐ zya nakatta ñ
    island?   desu ka⌣

Tanaka

fairly or rather   ka⁷nari
peninsula   hañtoo
13. No. It's a fairly large   Iie. Ka⁷nari o⌐oki⌐i ha⌐ñtoo
peninsula.   de⁷su yo.

Smith

14. Oh, was that it.   A⁷a, so⁷o desita ka.

(c)

Smith

Buddhist temple   te⌐ra⁷ or otera⁺
Shinto shrine   zi⁷ñzya
15. I hear that in Kyoto there are   Kyo⁷oto ni wa hu⌐ru⁷i o⌐tera ya
many old temples and shrines.   zi⁷ñzya (ḡa) o⌐o⁷i soo desu ⌐ne⁷e.

Tanaka

16. That's right.   E⁷e.

Smith

Christianity   kirisutokyoo
church   kyookai
17. Aren't there any Christian   Ki⌐risutokyoo no kyookai wa
churches?   arimase⁷ñ ka⌟

Tanaka

do exist or do have   a⁷ru koto wa ⌐a⁷ru
build or erect   ta⌐te⁷ru /-ru/
newly built thing   a⌐tara⁷siku ⌐ta⁷teta mono
18. Well, they do exist but there   Ma⁷a, ⌐a⁷ru koto wa a⌐rima⁷su
are [only a] few and they're   ḡa; su⌐kuna⁷i si, taitee a⌐tara⁷-
usually newly built (things).   siku ⌐ta⁷teta mo⌐no⁷ desu.

Smith

19. Oh? or Really?   Hoo?

Tanaka

Shintoism   si⁷ñtoo
Buddhism   bu⁷kkyoo
flourishing or prosperous   sakañ /na/
or thriving or popular
a place where Buddhism   bu⁷kkyoo to ⌐si⁷ñtoo no
and Shintoism flourish   sakañ na tokoro
20. [That's] because Kyoto is a   Kyo⁷oto wa ⌐bu⁷kkyoo to ⌐si⁷ñ-
place where Buddhism and   too no sa⌐kañ na tokoro⁷ desu
Shintoism flourish.   kara.

Smith

21. I see! or To be sure! or   Naruhodo.
Of course!

(d)

Smith

Honshu	⎫ 4 main	Ho⌐nsyuu
Hokkaido	⎬ islands	Ho⌐kka⌐idoo
Shikoku	⎭ of Japan	Si⌐ko⌐ku
Kyushu		Kyu⌐usyuu

some place to go and see
<u>or</u> some place of
interest

22. Aren't there some places of
interest in Kyushu?

doʼko ka keꜛnbutu-suru
tokoroʼ

Kyuʼusyuu ni wa ⌐doʼko ka keꜛnbutu-suru tokoroʼ (wa) aꜛrima-
seꜜn ka⌐

Tanaka

23. Certainly there are.

Aꜛrimaʼsu to mo.

beginning with Nagasaki
<u>or</u> from Nagasaki on
down <u>or</u> to say nothing
of Nagasaki
(mountain in Kyushu)
(island in Kyushu)
(city in Kyushu)

24. [There are] Aso, Aoshima,
Kagoshima, and so on—to
say nothing of Nagasaki.

Na⌐gaʼsaki o hazime

Aʼso
Aosima
Kagosima

Na⌐gaʼsaki (o) hazime; Aʼso,
Aosima, Ka⌐gosima naʼdo⌐

harbor <u>or</u> port
one of the harbors
a day when the weather
is nice
view
is wonderful

25. Nagasaki is one of the oldest
harbors, and on days when
the weather is nice, the view
of Aso is wonderful.

minato
mi⌐nato no hitoʼ-tu
te⌐nki no ꜛiꜜi hi

na⌐game⌐
su⌐barasiʼi /-ku/

Na⌐gaʼsaki wa iꜛtiban huruʼi mi-
ꜛnato no hitoꜜ-tu da si; te⌐nki no
ꜛiꜜi hi ni wa, Aʼso no naꜛgameꜜ
(wa) su⌐barasiʼi n desu yo⌐

(e)

Smith

26. In Japan, wherever you go,
there are things that are unusual and interesting, aren't
there.

Niꜛhoꜜn ni wa; doʼko e iꜛtteꜜ mo,
me⌐zuraʼsikute oʼmosiroʼi moꜛnoꜜ
ga arimasu ⌐neʼe.

Tanaka

27. There are, aren't there.

Soʼo desu ⌐neʼe.

Smith

souvenir
buy for a souvenir

miyage <u>or</u> omiyage [+]
miyage ni kau

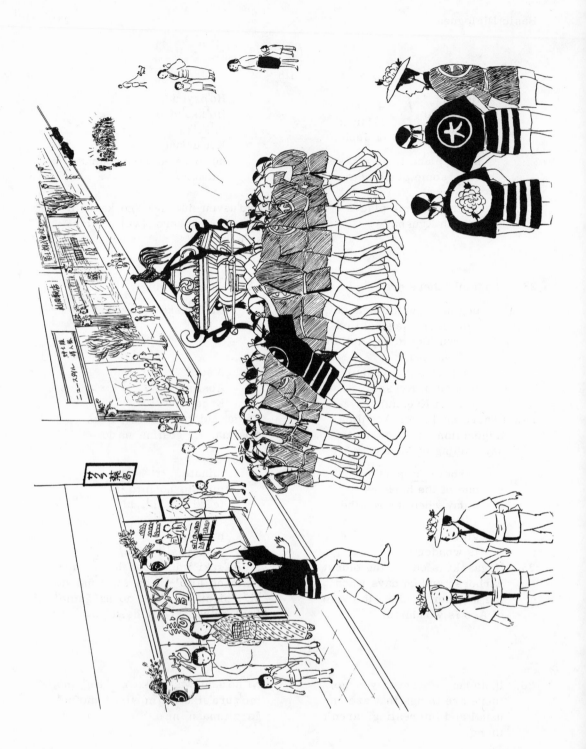

[lit.] become desirous of returning home having bought	ka⌐tte kaerita⌐ku ⌐na⌐ru

28. Whatever I see I want to buy and take home for a souvenir.
Na⌐ni (o) ⌐mi⌐te mo, mi⌐ya͞ge ni katte kaerita⌐ku na⌐rima⌐su yo.

Tanaka

29. I guess so.
So⌐o desyoo ⌐ne⌐e.

a country or one's native land or area	kuni or okuni ↑
of (or from) whatever country things are or	do⌐no kuni no mo⌐no⌐ de mo
things of every country	
respectively or severally	so⌐re⌐zore
flavor or taste	azi
different flavor	ti͞gatta azi

30. [That's] because things of every country have their own different flavor.
Do⌐no kuni no mo⌐no⌐ de mo, so-re⌐zore ti͞gatta azi ͞ga arima⌐su kara_

every time [someone] travels	ryo⌐koo-suru tabi⌐ ni
used to buy	ka⌐tta mono⌐ da or ka⌐tta mo⌐n̄ da

31. You know, I too used to buy souvenirs every time I traveled.
Watasi mo ⌐mo⌐to wa ryo⌐koo-suru tabi⌐ ni o⌐miya͞ge (o) katta mon(o)⌐ [1] desu yo.

(f)

Tanaka

geography	ti⌐ri
history	rekisi
provided [someone] knows	si⌐tte (i)re⌐ba
the more [someone] knows	si⌐tte (i)re⌐ba i͞ru hodo
a trip	ryokoo

32. The more you know Japanese geography and history, the more interesting trips are possible.
Nihon̄ no ⌐ti⌐ri ya rēkisi (o) si⌐tte (i)re⌐ba i͞ru hodo o⌐mosiro⌐i ryo-⌐koo ͞ga deki⌐ru n̄ desu ⌐ne⌐e.

Smith

33. That's true, isn't it.
So⌐re wa so⌐o desu ⌐ne⌐e.

concerning history	re⌐kisi ni tu⌐ite
cause or reason or circumstance	wa⌐ke
isn't the case that [someone] doesn't know	si⌐ranai wa⌐ke zya ⌐na⌐i
in a big hurry	o⌐oi⌐so͞gi de

---

[1] When final o is dropped, mo⌐no⌐ becomes mo⌐n̄.

one time
decide to read

ip-peñ
yo⌐mu koto ni suru

34. It isn't (the case) that I
don't know anything at all
about geography and history,
but I guess I'll (decide to) do
some reading again in a big
hurry before I start out.

Ti⌐ri ya re⌐kisi ni tu⌐ite, ze⌐ñzeñ
siranai wa⌐ke zya ⌐na⌐i ñ desu
ḡa; de⌐kakeru ma⌐e ni o⌐oi⌐soḡi de
mo⌐o ip-peñ yo⌐mu koto ni si⌐ma-
syo⌐o.

Tanaka

35. Oh?

So⌐o desu ka.

provided [someone]
wants to read
guidebook

yo⌐mita⌐kereba or o⌐yomi
ni narita⌐kereba ⌐
a⌐ñnaisyo⌐

36. If you want to read it, I have
a guidebook in English . . .

O⌐yomi ni narita⌐kereba, e⌐eḡo
no añnaisyo⌐ (ḡa) a⌐rima⌐su ḡa—

Smith

borrow

haisyaku-suru ⌐

37. Oh, then I'd like to borrow
it by all means . . .

A. Zya⌐a, ze⌐hi ha⌐isyaku-sita⌐i
ñ desu ḡa—

Tanaka

provided it's all right
or agreeable or con-
venient
hold or take hold of or
have

yo⌐rosi⌐kereba

mo⌐tu /-u/

38. Certainly. Take it now if
you'd like to.

E⌐e, do⌐ozo. Yo⌐rosi⌐kereba, i⌐ma
o⌐moti-kudasa⌐i.

ADDITIONAL VOCABULARY

1. In Japan, wherever you go,
there are lanterns.

Ni⌐ho⌐ñ ni wa ⌐do⌐ko e i⌐tte⌐ mo
to⌐oroo ḡa arima⌐su ⌐ne⌐e.

paper lantern
tower or pagoda
gateway to Shinto shrine
festival
portable shrine carried
about during festivals

tyo⌐oti⌐ñ
to⌐o
torii
maturi or omaturi +
mi⌐kosi or o⌐mi⌐kosi +

2. For sightseers sightseeing
busses are best, aren't
they?

Ka⌐ñko⌐okyaku ni wa ka⌐ñkooba⌐su
ḡa i⌐tibañ i⌐i desyoo?

sightseeing train

ka⌐ñkoore⌐ssya

3. Do you like hiking?

Ha⌐ikiñḡu ḡa o⌐suki de⌐su ka↲

mountain-climbing	ya「mano「bori
swimming	o「yoḡi「
golf	go「ruhu
tennis	te「nisu

4. Isn't (lit. wasn't) that (place) a <u>plain</u>?

Asuko (wa) <u>he「eti</u> zya na「katta ñ desu ka⌣

valley	ta「ni「
beach	ha「ma「
cape <u>or</u> promontory	misaki
bay	wa「ñ

5. For fishing I usually go to a <u>lake</u>.

Tu「ri ni「 wa wǎtasi (wa) tǎitee <u>mi「zuu「mi</u> e ikimasu.

pond	i「ke「
river	ka「wa「
canal	u「ñḡa

6. Does the continent of Asia have many <u>volcanoes</u>?

A「ziya-ta「iriku wa 「ka「zañ ḡa o「o「i ñ desu ka⌣

| forest | hayasi |
| jungle | mituriñ |

7. What (place) is the largest <u>country</u> in the world?

Se「ka「i de i「tibañ hiro「i <u>kuni</u> (wa) 「do「ko desyoo ka.

| desert | sabaku |

8. The more you know <u>politics</u> the more interesting it gets.

<u>Se「ezi</u> (o) sitte (i)re「ba ǐru hodo o「mosi「roku na「rima「su yo⌣

| economics | ke「ezai |
| word <u>or</u> language | ko「toba「 |

NOTES ON THE BASIC DIALOGUES

10. <u>Turi</u> refers to fishing with a line.

12. Note the use of the past. The speaker is trying to recall something from the past: 'Wasn't the information I had the fact that Izu is an island?'

18. From ta「te「ru 'build' is derived ta「te「mono 'building.'

21. <u>Naruhodo</u> means 'of course' following a statement, not in answer to a question.

24. <u>X o hazime</u> singles out X as the most important member of a group, animate or inanimate.

31. <u>Ta「bi「</u> 'time' or 'occurrence' has an alternate form ta「ñbi「.

34. Wa┐ke: Note also Do┐o iu ┝wa┤ke desu ka. 'What is the reason?'

37. Haisyaku-suru is the humble equivalent of kariru. Haisyaku occurs in sentence-final position as an informal polite imperative meaning 'let me borrow.'

38. Mo┐tu: compare motte iku 'take' (lit. 'go holding') and mo┌tte ku┐ru 'bring' (lit. 'come holding'). Note: X o ┌mo┐tte imasu '[I] have X' or '[I] own X' or '[I] am holding X.'

Additional Vocabulary:

3. Note also ya┌ma┐ ni noboru 'climb a mountain.'

6. Note riku 'land'; ta┐iriku 'continent.'

GRAMMATICAL NOTES

1. The Provisional

I┌ke┐ba	is the PROVISIONAL of	iku 'go.'
Su┌re┐ba		suru 'do.'
Yo┌rosi┐kereba		yorosii 'is good.'
Na┐kereba		na┐i 'isn't.'
Na┌rita┐kereba		na┌rita┐i 'want to become.'
Na┐ra		copula da.

Inflected words (verbs, adjectivals, and √da) have PROVISIONAL forms meaning, in the affirmative, 'provided so-and-so happens or is true,' and in the negative, 'provided so-and-so doesn't happen or isn't true' or 'unless so-and-so happens or is true.'

To form the provisional:

Verbals, all groups: Drop the final -u of the informal non-past (the citation form) and add -eba; if the non-past is accented, the provisional is accented on the same syllable, and if the non-past is unaccented, the provisional is accented on the next-to-last syllable.

Examples:

ta┌be┐ru 'eat': ta┌be┐reba 'provided [someone] eats'
kau 'buy': ka┌e┐ba 'provided [someone] buys'
i┌rassya┐ru† 'go,' 'come,' 'be': i┌rassya┐reba 'provided [someone] goes or comes or is'
ku┐ru 'come': ku┐reba 'provided [someone] comes'

Adjectivals: Drop the final -i of the non-past and add -kereba; the adjectival provisional is always accented, on the same syllable as the corresponding adjectival past and conditional.

Examples:

ti┌isa┐i 'is small': ti┐isakereba 'provided [something] is small'
su┌zusi┐i 'is cool': su┌zu┐sikereba 'provided it is cool'
sa┌mu┐i 'is cold': sa┐mukereba 'provided it is cold'
i┐i/yo┐i 'is good': yo┐kereba 'provided [something] is good'

ta⌐be¬nai 'doesn't eat': ta⌐be¬nakereba 'provided [someone] doesn't eat' or 'unless [someone] eats'

ta⌐beta¬i 'want to eat': ta⌐beta¬kereba 'provided [someone] wants to eat'

Copula: The provisional of <u>da</u> is <u>na¬ra</u> or <u>na¬raba</u>; it loses its accent following an accented word or phrase.

A sequence consisting of or ending with a provisional states the provision subject to which something else occurs. The most common English equivalent for both the conditional and the provisional, in the affirmative, is 'if ——,' but there is a slight distinction in meaning between the two. Compare:

Ku⌐ruma o utta¬ra, ryo⌐koo-sima¬su. 'If (<u>or</u> when) I sell the car, I'm going to take a trip.' (This sentence tells what will happen if or when I sell the car.)

and:

Ku⌐ruma o ure¬ba, ryo⌐koo-sima¬su. 'I'm going to take a trip, if (i.e. provided) I sell the car.' (This sentence tells under what circumstances I will take a trip.)

In the negative, the conditional corresponds to English 'if not ——,' whereas the negative provisional is comparable to English 'unless ——.' Compare:

Ta⌐naka-sañ ḡa ko¬nakattara, be⌐ñkyoo-sima¬su. 'If Mr. Tanaka doesn't come, I'll study.' (This sentence tells what will happen if Mr. Tanaka doesn't come.)

and:

Ta⌐naka-sañ ḡa ko¬nakereba, be⌐ñkyoo-sima¬su. 'I'll study unless Mr. Tanaka comes.' (This sentence indicates an intention to study — provided Mr. Tanaka doesn't come.)

While the conditional occurs in sentences referring to past, present, or future time, sentences containing a provisional form usually refer to present or future time only. However, extended predicates (for example, i⌐ku¬ ñ desu 'it is a matter of going') have provisional equivalents consisting of a non-past or past + ñ (or <u>no</u>) <u>nara</u>; and when the combination consists of a past + ñ <u>nara,</u> it refers indirectly to the past (for example, i⌐tta¬ ñ nara 'provided it is a matter of having gone,' 'provided you DID go'). Thus:

A⌐na¬ta ḡa i┗ku┛ ñ nara, wa⌐takusi mo ikimasyo¬o.
   'Provided it involves your going, I'll go too.'
Wa⌐kara¬nakatta ñ nara, do¬o site wa┗kara┛nai tte i┗wana┛katta ñ desu ka⌣
   'If it's a case of not having understood, why is it you didn't say that you didn't understand?' (I.e. 'If you didn't understand, why didn't you say so?')
Ya⌐su¬i ñ nara, ka⌐tte¬ mo ┗i┛i desu.
   'Provided it is cheap, you may buy it.'

A provisional followed by <u>i⌐i desu ḡa</u> [1] —lit. 'provided so-and-so, it is (or will be) fine but' — is a present or future hope or wish, and followed by <u>yo⌐-katta no ni</u>, is a past, contrary-to-fact wish. Thus:

Ha⌐yaku ⌐ku⌐reba ⌐i⌐i desu ḡa ⌐ne⌐e. 'I hope he comes early, don't you.'
I⌐re⌐ba ⌐i⌐i desu ḡa— 'I hope he's in.'
Hu⌐ra⌐nakereba ⌐i⌐i desu ḡa ⌐ne⌐e. 'I hope it doesn't rain, don't you.'
Ki⌐ke⌐ba ⌐yo⌐katta no ni. 'I wish I had asked.' (Lit. 'In spite of the fact that it was good provided I ask [I didn't].')

Additional examples:

A⌐sa ⌐ha⌐yaku i⌐ke⌐ba, a⌐tarasi⌐i sa⌐kana ḡa kaema⌐su.
   'You can buy fresh fish, provided you go early in the morning.'
Te⌐ñki ni ⌐na⌐reba, a⌐ru⌐ite ikimasu.
   'I'll walk there provided it clears (lit. becomes good weather).'
Sa⌐mukereba, su⌐to⌐obu o tu⌐ke⌐te kudasai.
   'Turn on the heater if it's cold.'
Ni⌐hoñḡo ḡa wakara⌐nakereba, e⌐eḡo de itte⌐ mo ka⌐maimase⌐ñ.
   'You may say it in English, unless you understand Japanese.'
Ko⌐ohi⌐i ḡa no⌐mita⌐kereba; a⌐soko de utte iru⌐ kara, do⌐ozo.
   'If you want to drink coffee, they're selling it over there so go right ahead.'
Hu⌐rañsuḡo na⌐ra su⌐ko⌐si yo⌐mema⌐su ḡa, eeḡo wa ze⌐ñzeñ yomema-se⌐ñ.
   'Provided it's French I can read it a little, but English I can't read at all.'
Ba⌐su nara, zyu⌐p-puñ-ḡu⌐rai sika ka⌐karimase⌐ñ.
   'It takes only about ten minutes, if it's the bus.'

2. ' M u s t '

A negative provisional ending in <u>-nakereba</u> followed immediately by the negative √na⌐ra⌐nai is an expression of necessity: 'unless [someone] does so-and-so, it won't do (lit. it doesn't become)': that is '[someone] must do so-and-so.' Thus: <u>ta⌐be⌐nakereba na⌐ra⌐nai</u> '[someone] must eat'; <u>no⌐ma⌐-nakereba na⌐ra⌐nai</u> '[someone] must drink'; <u>si⌐na⌐kereba na⌐ra⌐nai</u> '[some-one] must do.'

The stronger √ikenai 'it won't do' may be used in place of √na⌐ra⌐nai, particularly when it is the person addressed who is required to do some-thing: 'you must —— .'

Alternating with the negative provisional in this pattern is the negative gerund ending in <u>-nakute</u> + particle <u>wa</u>, usually contracted to <u>nakutya[a]</u> (cf. Lesson 25, Grammatical Note 2). Compare:

I⌐ttya⌐a ikenai. 'You mustn't go.' (Lit. 'As for going, it won't do.')

and:

I⌐kana⌐kutyaa ikenai. 'You must go.' (Lit. 'As for not going, it won't do.')

—————————————
[1] Or <u>i⌐i (desu) ke(re)do</u>.

The -nakutyaa alternant is less formal than the -nakereba alternant.

A -nakereba (or -nakutyaa) + naˈraˈnai (or ikenai) sequence often occurs in a strong negative reply to a question which asks, 'Is it all right if [I] don't ────?' (cf. Lesson 22, Grammatical Note 4). Thus:

> Iˈkanaˈkute mo ˈiˈi desu ka⌐ 'Is it all right if I don't go?'
> Iie. Iˈkanaˈkereba (or iˈkanaˈkutyaa) naˈrimaseˈñ (or iˈkemaseˈñ) yo. 'No. You must go.'

Conversely, in the negative reply to a 'must' question, a negative gerund + mo + iˈi 'you don't have to ────' occurs. Thus:

> Iˈkanaˈkereba (or iˈkanaˈkutyaa) naˈrimaseˈñ ka⌐ 'Must I go?'
> Iie. Iˈkanaˈkute mo ˈiˈi desu yo⌐ 'No. You don't have to go.'

Additional examples:

> Koˈñbañ wa oˈsokuˈ made kaˈisya ni inaˈkereba naˈraˈnai ka mo siˈrenaˈi kara, koˈrareˈnai to omoimasu.
> 'Tonight since I may have to be in the office until late I don't think I can come (lit. I think I can't come).'
> Siˈnaˈkereba naˈraˈnai siˈgoto ga aˈru kara, oˈsaki ni situˈree-simasu.
> 'There's work I must do so excuse me for leaving ahead of you.'
> Narubeku niˈhoñgo o tukau yoˈo ni siˈnaˈkereba naˈrimaseˈñ.
> 'One must try to use Japanese as much as possible.'
> Haˈyaku iˈkanaˈkutyaa iˈkemaseˈñ yo. 'You must go early!'
> Kiˈnoˈo wa ˈnoˈdo ga iˈtaˈkute, iti-niti-zyuu neˈte inaˈkereba naˈraˈnakatta ñ desu.
> 'I had to stay in bed all day yesterday with a sore throat.' (Lit. 'Yesterday my throat being sore, I had to be in bed all day long.')
> Aˈsitaˈ mo, kyoˈo no ˈyoˈo ni, ˈhaˈyaku deˈkakenaˈkutyaa naˈraˈnai?
> 'Do you have to go out early tomorrow too, the way [you did] today?'

3. 'The more ────, the more ────'

A sequence containing a provisional + the corresponding citation form + hodo 'extent' occurs in the Japanese equivalent of English sequences having the pattern 'the more X, the more Y' (for example, 'the bigger the better,' 'the higher the fewer,' 'the more I see it the more I want it.'

Examples:

> Aˈtaraˈsikereba aˈtarasiˈi hodo ŏisii. 'The fresher the more delicious.' (Lit. 'Provided it's fresh, to the extent that it's fresh, it's delicious.')
> Oˈokikereba oˈokiˈi hodo ˈiˈi desu. 'The bigger the better.' (Lit. 'Provided it's big, to the extent that it's big, it's good.')
> Kotira no tugoo wa ˈhaˈyakereba haˈyaˈi hodo ˈiˈi ñ desu. 'The earlier the better for me.' (Lit. 'As for the circumstances on this [i.e. my] side, provided it's early, to the extent that it's early, it's good.')
> Kyoˈoto no haˈnasiˈ o kiˈkeˈba kĭku hodo iˈtte miˈtaku narimasu.
> 'The more I hear about Kyoto, the more I want to try and go.' (Lit.

'Provided I hear talk of Kyoto, to the extent that I hear, I become desirous of going and seeing.')

Nihoñgo wa be⌐ñkyoo-sure¬ba sŭru hodo mu⌐zukasiku na¬ru yoo desu. 'The more I study Japanese, the more difficult it seems to become.' (Lit. 'As for Japanese, provided I study, to the extent that I study, it seems to become difficult.')

The corresponding sequence derived from a nominal + √da expression occurs in either of the following forms:

(1) nominal + de ⌐a¬reba ⌐a¬ru hodo ——

(2) nominal + nara + nominal + $\begin{vmatrix} no \\ na \end{vmatrix}$ hodo ——

Thus: be⌐ñri da 'it's convenient':

Be¬ñri de ⌐a⁺reba ⌐a⁺ru hodo ta⌐ka¬i desu.
Be¬ñri nara ⌐be¬ñri na hodo ta⌐ka¬i desu.
'The more convenient it is, the more expensive it is!'

4. —— ko⌐to¬ ni √suru

A nominal X + particle ni of goal + √suru means 'make [it] to be X,' 'decide on X' (cf. Lesson 14, Grammatical Note 6).

When the nominal is ko⌐to¬ 'act' preceded by a verbal in its citation form, the combination is equivalent to 'decide to do so-and-so.' Compare:

Ki⌐ñyo¬obi ni si⁺masyo⁺o. 'Let's decide on Friday'; 'Let's make it Friday.'

and:

I⌐ku koto¬ ni si⁺masyo⁺o. 'Let's decide to go'; 'Let's plan to go.'

When ko⌐to¬ is preceded by a negative, the combination means 'decide not to do so-and-so.' Thus:

I⌐kanai koto¬ ni si⁺masyo⁺o. 'Let's decide not to go'; 'Let's plan on not going.'

The use of ko⌐to¬ ni √suru following a verbal or a negative adjectival implies choosing between two or more alternatives, or deciding on a plan, or changing a plan. Compare:

Ta⌐bemasyo¬o. 'Let's eat.'

and:

Ta⌐be¬ru koto ni si⁺masyo⁺o. '[Of the various possible alternatives] let's decide to eat.'

Examples:

A¬me ḡa hu⁺tta⁺ra, i⌐kanai koto¬ ni si⁺masyo⁺o.
'Let's decide not to go if it rains.'
A⌐soko de tabe¬ru koto ni si⁺ta⁺ra ⁺do⁺o desyoo.
'How would it be if we decided to eat over there?'

Kyo⌐o ⌐ku⌐-zi-hatu Ko⌐obe-iki de ta⌐tu koto ni si⌐ma⌐sita.
'I have decided to leave today on the 9 o'clock train for Kobe.'
Narubeku e⌐eḡo o tukawanai koto⌐ ni si⌐tai to omo⌐tte imasu.
'I've been thinking that I'd like to (decide to) avoid using (lit. not to
use) English as much as possible.'

5. a⌐ru koto wa ⌐a⌐ru

Ko⌐to⌐ wa, preceded by a sentence modifier (consisting of — or ending with
— a non-past or past verbal or adjectival, or a nominal + no or na or datta)
and followed by an independent equivalent of the modifier, is equivalent to 'it
IS so-and-so [but],' 'so-and-so IS true [but],' 'granted so-and-so [but].'
Thus:

ta⌐be⌐ru koto wa ta⌐bema⌐su ḡa_ '[someone] DOES eat but . . .' (for
example, as in: 'he DOES eat but he doesn't eat the right things,'
'he DOES eat but he doesn't eat much,' etc.)
o⌐oki⌐i koto wa o⌐oki⌐i '[it] IS big' (for example, as in: 'it IS big but
it isn't very good')
byo⌐oki no koto⌐ wa byo⌐oki de⌐su '[someone] IS sick' (for example,
as in: 'he IS sick but it isn't serious')
be⌐ñri na ko⌐to⌐ wa ⌐be⌐ñri desu 'it IS convenient' (for example, as
in: 'it IS convenient but it's not a pretty place')

If the inflected word before and after ko⌐to⌐ is a negative, the combination
means 'granted that so-and-so isn't true.' Thus:

A⌐ñmari tabe⌐nai koto wa ta⌐be⌐nai ñ desu ḡa, si⌐ñpai wa arimase⌐ñ.
'Granted he doesn't eat much, but there's nothing to worry about.'

Additional examples:

Bo⌐ku mo i⌐ku koto⌐ wa i⌐kima⌐su ḡa, na⌐ñ-zi ni i⌐ku⌐ ka wa wa⌐kari-
mase⌐ñ.
'I too AM going, but at what time I'm going I can't tell.'
A⌐no e⌐eḡa wa o⌐mosiro⌐i koto wa o⌐mosiro⌐i ñ desu ḡa, na⌐ḡasu⌐ḡite_
'That movie IS interesting, but it's too long . . .'
Ano heñ wa ⌐si⌐zuka na ko⌐to⌐ wa ⌐si⌐zuka desu ḡa, añmari ⌐be⌐ñri
zya a⌐rimase⌐ñ.
'That section IS quiet but it isn't very convenient.'
I⌐ma de mo ⌐ki⌐ree na ko⌐to⌐ wa ⌐ki⌐ree desu ḡa; a⌐ki ni ⌐na⌐ttara,
mo⌐tto ⌐ki⌐ree ni na⌐rima⌐su yo_
'Even now it IS pretty, but when autumn comes, it will be(come)
prettier.'

6. mo⌐no⌐ Referring to Habitual Action

An inflected word in its past-tense form + nominal mo⌐no⌐ (different
from the nominal mo⌐no⌐ 'concrete thing') + √da indicates habitual action:
'used to do or be so-and-so.' The contracted equivalent of mo⌐no⌐ is mo⌐ñ.

Examples:

Ko⌐domo no toki⌐ ni wa, ma⌐ibañ ⌐so⌐hu ni ha⌐nasi⌐ o si⌐te moratta
mono⌐ desu.

'When I was a child, I used to have my grandfather tell me a story every night.'

Mo⌐to wa ⌐zu˩ibuñ sa⌐ke o no⌐nda mo⌐no˩ desu ḡa—

'I used to drink (sake) a great deal (formerly) but [now I don't].'

A⌐kai mono⌐ wa ko⌐domo sika kina⌐katta mo⌐no˩ desu ḡa, i⌐ma wa ke-⌐kkoñ-sita hito⌐ de mo ki⌐te ima⌐su ⌐ne˩e.

'Only children used to wear red (things), but now even married people wear it.'

Deñwa wa mi⌐ñna ku⌐rokatta mo⌐no˩ desu ḡa, kono-ḡoro wa a⌐ka⌐i no ya si⌐ro⌐i no mo a⌐rima⌐su ⌐ne˩e.

'Telephones all used to be black but nowadays there are also red ones and white ones (and others), aren't there.'

7. ―― ni ⌐tu⌐ite

A nominal X + <u>ni ⌐tu⌐ite</u> means 'about X' or 'concerning X.'

A phrase ending with <u>ni ⌐tu⌐ite</u> occurs (1) without following particle, in construction with an inflected word or phrase; (2) followed by particle <u>no</u> in construction with a nominal; (3) followed by particle <u>wa</u> with contrastive meaning; (4) preceded by an interrogative and followed by particle <u>mo</u> + a negative, with an all-exclusive meaning.

Examples:

So⌐re ni tu⌐ite se⌐tumee-site kurema⌐sita. 'He explained to me about that.'

Ko⌐re ni tu⌐ite ⌐do˩o omoimasu ka⌐ 'What do you think about this?'

Na⌐ni ni ⌐tu⌐ite ha⌐nasimasyo⌐o ka. 'What shall we talk about?'

Ni⌐ho˩ñ ni ⌐tu⌐ite desu. 'It's about Japan.'

Ni⌐ho˩ñ ni ⌐tu⌐ite no ⌐ho˩ñ o yo⌐mima⌐sita. 'I read a book about Japan.'

Ka⌐buki ni tu⌐ite wa na⌐ni mo sirimase⌐ñ. 'About kabuki I know nothing.'

Na⌐ni ni ⌐tu⌐ite mo ha⌐nasemase⌐ñ. 'I can't talk about anything.'

8. Particles: Sentence-final <u>to mo</u>

The particle sequence <u>to mo</u> occurs following an inflected word—nonpast or past, informal or formal—at the end of a statement which answers a question. It implies strong emphasis: 'certainly' or 'positively' or 'of course.'

Examples:

A⌐no˩ hito ni⌐hoñḡo ḡa deki⌐ru?. . . De⌐ki⌐ru to mo. To⌐ttemo zyoozu⌐ desu yo⌐

'Can he speak Japanese?. . . Of course he can. He's very good.'

Ano sakana ta⌐berarema⌐su ka⌐. . . Ta⌐berarema⌐su to mo. O⌐isi˩i desu yo⌐

'Can you eat that fish?. . . Of course you can eat it. It's delicious.'

A⌐no ho⌐teru ta⌐ka⌐i?. . . Ta⌐ka⌐i to mo.

'Is that hotel expensive?. . . It certaiⁱ   xpensive.'

Kono teḡami zi⌐buñ de ka⌐ita?. . . So⌐o da to mo.

   'Did you write this letter by yourself?. . . Certainly (that's right).'

Ma⌐da a⌐rima⌐sita ka↵ . . . A⌐rima⌐sita to mo.

   'Was there still some?. . . Of course there was.'

9. Counter -heñ

The counter -heñ combines with the numerals of Series I to count number of times or occurrences. It is similar in meaning to counters -do and -kai.

i⌐p-peñ 'one time'	ro⌐p-peñ 'six times'
ni-⌐he⌐ñ 'two times'	si⌐ti-heñ or na⌐na⌐-heñ 'seven times'
sa⌐ñ-beñ 'three times'	ha⌐p-peñ or ha⌐ti⌐-heñ 'eight times'
yo⌐ñ-heñ 'four times'	kyu⌐u-heñ 'nine times'
go-⌐he⌐ñ 'five times'	zi⌐p-peñ or zyu⌐p-peñ 'ten times'

na⌐ñ-beñ 'how many times?'

DRILLS

A. Substitution Drill

   (Each cue is given in its independent form. In using it as a sentence modifier make any changes necessary.)

1. Isn't there some place of interest?

   Do⌐ko ka ke⌐ñbutu-suru tokoro⌐ (wa) a⌐rimase⌐ñ ka↵

2. Isn't there some famous place? /yuumee da/

   Do⌐ko ka yu⌐umee na tokoro⌐ (wa) a⌐rimase⌐ñ ka↵

3. Isn't there some pretty place? /ki⌐ree da/

   Do⌐ko ka ⌐ki⌐ree na to⌐koro⌐ (wa) a⌐rimase⌐ñ ka↵

4. Isn't there some place with a nice view? /na⌐ḡame⌐ ḡa ⌐i⌐i/

   Do⌐ko ka na⌐ḡame no[1] i⌐i to⌐koro⌐ (wa) a⌐rimase⌐ñ ka↵

5. Isn't there some warm place? /a⌐ttaka⌐i/

   Do⌐ko ka a⌐ttaka⌐i to⌐koro⌐ (wa) a⌐rimase⌐ñ ka↵

6. Isn't there some place [I] can commute to? /kayoeru/

   Do⌐ko ka ka⌐yoeru tokoro⌐ (wa) a⌐rimase⌐ñ ka↵

7. Isn't there some broken place (i.e. part)? /ko⌐wa⌐reta/

   Do⌐ko ka ko⌐wa⌐reta to⌐koro⌐ (wa) a⌐rimase⌐ñ ka↵

8. Isn't there some special place? /tokubetu da/

   Do⌐ko ka to⌐kubetu na tokoro⌐ (wa) a⌐rimase⌐ñ ka↵

9. Isn't there some place that isn't hot? /a⌐tuku ⌐na⌐i/

   Do⌐ko ka ⌐a⌐tuku ⌐na⌐i to⌐koro⌐ (wa) a⌐rimase⌐ñ ka↵

10. Isn't there some place where skiing is popular? /su⌐ki⌐i ḡa sa̅kañ da/

   Do⌐ko ka su⌐ki⌐i no[1] sa⌐kañ na tokoro⌐ (wa) a⌐rimase⌐ñ ka↵

---

[1] Or ḡa.

B. Substitution Drill

1. Since I came all the way
    to Japan, (I think) I'd
    like to travel around be-
    fore I go home.

Sekkaku Ni⌐ho⌐ñ e ki⌐ta⌐ ñ desu
kara, ho⌐oboo ryo⌐koo-site kae-
rita⌐i to omoimasu.

2. Since I came all the way
    to Japan, (I think) I'd
    like to see the sights of
    Kyoto before I go home.

Sekkaku Ni⌐ho⌐ñ e ki⌐ta⌐ ñ desu
kara, <u>Kyo⌐oto (o) ke⌐ñbutu-site</u>
kaerita⌐i to omoimasu.

3. Since I came all the way
    to Japan, (I think) I'd
    like to go to a famous hot
    spring before I go home.

Sekkaku Ni⌐ho⌐ñ e ki⌐ta⌐ ñ desu
kara, <u>yu⌐umee na oñseñ e itte</u>
kaerita⌐i to omoimasu.

4. Since I came all the way
    to Japan, (I think) I'd
    like to see kabuki before
    I go home.

Sekkaku Ni⌐ho⌐ñ e ki⌐ta⌐ ñ desu
kara, <u>ka⌐buki (o) mi⌐te ka⌐eri-</u>
ta⌐i to omoimasu.

5. Since I came all the way
    to Japan, (I think) I'd
    like to climb Mt. Fuji
    before I go home.

Sekkaku Ni⌐ho⌐ñ e ki⌐ta⌐ ñ desu
kara, <u>Hu⌐zisañ ni no⌐botte</u> kae-
rita⌐i to omoimasu.

6. Since I came all the way
    to Japan, (I think) I'd
    like to study Japanese
    before I go home.

Sekkaku Ni⌐ho⌐ñ e ki⌐ta⌐ ñ desu
kara, <u>ni⌐hoñgo (o) beñkyoo-site</u>
kaerita⌐i to omoimasu.

7. Since I came all the way
    to Japan, (I think) I'd
    like to consult with
    Dr. Tanaka before I go
    home.

Sekkaku Ni⌐ho⌐ñ e ki⌐ta⌐ ñ desu
kara, <u>Ta⌐naka-señse⌐e to so⌐o-
dañ-site</u> kaerita⌐i to omoimasu.

8. Since I came all the way
    to Japan, (I think) I'd
    like to buy some sou-
    venirs before I go home.

Sekkaku Ni⌐ho⌐ñ e ki⌐ta⌐ ñ desu
kara, <u>o⌐miyage (o) katte</u> kaeri-
ta⌐i to omoimasu.

C. Substitution Drill

1. The things of every
    country have their own
    flavor, haven't they.

Do⌐no kuni no mo⌐no⌐ de mo,
so⌐re⌐zore ti⌐gatta azi ga ari-
ma⌐su ⌐ne⌐e.

2. The clothing of every
    country has its own flavor,
    hasn't it.

Do⌐no kuni no ki⌐mono de⌐ mo,
so⌐re⌐zore ti⌐gatta azi ga ari-
ma⌐su ⌐ne⌐e.

3. The drinks of every
    country have their own
    flavor, haven't they.

Do⌐no kuni no no⌐mi⌐mono de
mo, so⌐re⌐zore ti⌐gatta azi ga
arima⌐su ⌐ne⌐e.

4. The shops of every
    country have their own
    flavor, haven't they.

Do⌐no kuni no <u>mi⌐se⌐</u> de mo, so-
⌐re⌐zore ti⌐gatta azi ga arima⌐su
⌐ne⌐e.

5. The furniture of every country has its own flavor, hasn't it.

Do⌐no kuni no ⌐ka⌐ḡu de mo, so-⌐re⌐zore ti⌐ḡatta azi ḡa arima⌐su ⌐ne⌐e.

6. The dolls of every country have their own flavor, haven't they.

Do⌐no kuni no ni⌐ñḡyoo de⌐ mo, so⌐re⌐zore ti⌐ḡatta azi ḡa arima⌐su ⌐ne⌐e.

7. The language of every country has its own flavor, hasn't it.

Do⌐no kuni no ko⌐toba⌐ de mo, so⌐re⌐zore ti⌐ḡatta azi ḡa arima⌐su ⌐ne⌐e.

8. The food of every country has its own flavor, hasn't it.

Do⌐no kuni no ta⌐bemo⌐no de mo, so⌐re⌐zore ti⌐ḡatta azi ḡa arima⌐su ⌐ne⌐e.

D. Substitution Drill

1. If it isn't too much trouble, would you tell me what kind of places I should go to?

Go⌐me⌐ewaku zya ⌐ña⌐kereba, do⌐ñ-na to⌐koro⌐ e i⌐tta⌐ra ⌐i⌐i ka o⌐siete kudasaimase⌐ñ ka.

2. If it isn't too much trouble, would you tell me where I should travel? /Do⌐ko e ryo-⌐koo-sita⌐ra ⌐i⌐i desu ka⌐/

Go⌐me⌐ewaku zya ⌐ña⌐kereba, do⌐ko e ryo⌐koo-sita⌐ra ⌐i⌐i ka o⌐siete kudasaimase⌐ñ ka.

3. If it isn't too much trouble, would you tell me how I should wrap it? /Do⌐o iu ⌐hu⌐u ni tu⌐tu⌐ñ-dara ⌐i⌐i desu ka⌐/

Go⌐me⌐ewaku zya ⌐ña⌐kereba, do⌐o iu ⌐hu⌐u ni tu⌐tu⌐ñdara ⌐i⌐i ka o⌐siete kudasaimase⌐ñ ka.

4. If it isn't too much trouble, would you tell me who should explain it to me (lit. by whom I should have it explained)? /Da⌐re ni se⌐tumee-site moratta⌐ra ⌐i⌐i desu ka⌐/

Go⌐me⌐ewaku zya ⌐ña⌐kereba, da⌐re ni se⌐tumee-site moratta⌐ra ⌐i⌐i ka o⌐siete kudasaimase⌐ñ ka.

5. If it isn't too much trouble, would you tell me how it is most convenient to go? /Na⌐ñ de i⌐ke⌐ba i⌐tibañ be⌐ñri desu ka⌐/

Go⌐me⌐ewaku zya ⌐ña⌐kereba, na⌐ñ de i⌐ke⌐ba i⌐tibañ be⌐ñri ka o⌐siete kudasaimase⌐ñ ka.

6. If it isn't too much trouble, would you tell me what (time) train is fastest to ride on? /Na⌐ñ-zi no ki⌐sya⌐ ni no⌐re⌐ba i⌐tibañ haya⌐i desu ka⌐/

Go⌐me⌐ewaku zya ⌐ña⌐kereba, na⌐ñ-zi no ki⌐sya⌐ ni no⌐re⌐ba i⌐tibañ haya⌐i ka o⌐siete kudasaimase⌐ñ ka.

7. If it isn't too much
    trouble, would you tell
    me who those people
    are? /A⌐no hito⌐tati (wa)
    ⌐da⌐re desu ka⌐/

8. If it isn't too much
    trouble, would you tell
    me what kind of things
    Buddhism and Shinto are?
    /Bu⌐kkyoo ya ⌐si⌐ntoo (wa)
    ⌐do⌐nna mo⌐no⌐ desu ka⌐/

Go⌐me⌐ewaku zya ⌐ha⌐kereba, a⌐ho
hito⌐tati (wa) ⌐da⌐re ka o⌐siete
kudasaimase⌐n ka.

Go⌐me⌐ewaku zya ⌐ha⌐kereba, bu⌐-
kkyoo ya ⌐si⌐ntoo (wa) ⌐do⌐nna
mo⌐no⌐ ka o⌐siete kudasaimase⌐n
ka.

E. **Substitution Drill**

1. Every time I travel I buy a
    souvenir.
2. Every time I ride in a
    plane I get sick.
3. Every time I go to Japan,
    I climb Fuji.
4. Every time I rent a house,
    I change the tatami.
5. Every time I go sightsee-
    ing, I get tired.
6. Every time I go out, I
    forget something.
7. Every time I repaint [it],
    I make [it] a different
    color.
8. Every time I smoke, my
    throat hurts.

Ryo⌐koo-suru tabi⌐ ni, o⌐miya⌐ge
(o) kaima⌐su.

Hi⌐ko⌐oki ni no⌐ru tabi⌐ ni, byo-
⌐oki ni narima⌐su.

Ni⌐ho⌐n e i⌐ku tabi⌐ ni, Hu⌐zisan
ni noborimasu.

Kasiya (o) ka⌐riru tabi⌐ ni, ta-
⌐tami (o) torikaema⌐su.

Ke⌐nbutu ni i⌐ku tabi⌐ ni, tu⌐ka⌐-
rete simaimasu.

De⌐kakeru tabi⌐ ni, na⌐ni ka wa-
⌐surete simaima⌐su.

Nu⌐rikae⌐ru ta⌐bi⌐ ni, ti⌐gatta iro⌐
ni simasu.

Tabako (o) ⌐no⌐mu ta⌐bi⌐ ni, no⌐do
⌐ga i⌐ta⌐ku narimasu.

F. **Response Drill** (based on Grammatical Note 6)

Tutor: I⌐tta koto⌐ ⌐ga a⌐rima⌐su ka⌐ 'Have you ever gone [there]?'
Student: E⌐e. Mo⌐to wa ⌐yo⌐ku i⌐tta mono⌐ desu. 'Yes. I used to
         go [there] often.'

1. Ryo⌐koo-sita koto⌐ ⌐ga a⌐ri-
    ma⌐su ka⌐
2. Hu⌐de de ka⌐ita koto ⌐ga
    a⌐rima⌐su ka⌐
3. Ryo⌐kan ni tomatta koto⌐
    ⌐ga a⌐rima⌐su ka⌐
4. Tu⌐ri ni itta koto⌐ ⌐ga
    a⌐rima⌐su ka⌐
5. Go⌐ (o) si⌐ta koto⌐ ⌐ga
    a⌐rima⌐su ka⌐
6. Zi⌐tensya ni notta koto⌐
    ⌐ga a⌐rima⌐su ka⌐

E⌐e. Mo⌐to wa ⌐yo⌐ku ryo⌐koo-
sita mono⌐ desu.

E⌐e. Mo⌐to wa ⌐yo⌐ku /hu⌐de de/
ka⌐ita mo⌐no⌐ desu.

E⌐e. Mo⌐to wa ⌐yo⌐ku /ryo⌐kan ni/
tomatta mono⌐ desu.

E⌐e. Mo⌐to wa ⌐yo⌐ku /tu⌐ri ni/
itta mono⌐ desu.

E⌐e. Mo⌐to wa ⌐yo⌐ku /⌐go⌐ (o)/
si⌐ta mono⌐ desu.

E⌐e. Mo⌐to wa ⌐yo⌐ku /zi⌐tensya
ni/ notta mono⌐ desu.

7. Ka⌐buki (o) mi¬ta koto
    ḡa a⌐rima¬su ka⌟

E¬e. Mo¬to wa ⌐yo¬ku /ka⌐buki (o)/
      mi¬ta mo⌐no¬ desu.

8. Ni⌐hoñ no siñbuñ (o)
    yo¬ñda koto ḡa a⌐rima¬su
    ka⌟

E¬e. Mo¬to wa ⌐yo¬ku /Ni⌐hoñ no
      siñbuñ (o)/ yo¬ñda mo⌐no¬ desu.

G. Substitution Drill (based on Grammatical Note 7)

1. We talked about history.
Re⌐kisi ni tu¬ite ha⌐nasima¬sita.

2. We talked about geography.
Ti¬ri ni tuite ha⌐nasima¬sita.

3. I'd like to read about
    geography . . .
Ti¬ri ni tuite <u>yo⌐mita¬i</u> ñ desu
ḡa⌟

4. I'd like to read about
    Japanese farmers . . .
<u>Ni⌐hoñ no hyakusyo¬o</u> ni tuite
yo⌐mita¬i ñ desu ḡa⌟

5. I'd like to ask about
    Japanese farmers . . .
Ni⌐hoñ no hyakusyo¬o ni tuite <u>ki-
⌐kita¬i</u> ñ desu ḡa⌟

6. I'd like to ask about
    Buddhism . . .
<u>Bu¬kkyoo</u> ni tuite ki⌐kita¬i ñ desu
ḡa⌟

7. Would you give me some
    information about Bud-
    dhism?
Bu¬kkyoo ni tuite o⌐siete kurema-
<u>se¬ñ ka</u>.

8. Would you give me some
    information about politics
    and economics?
<u>Se⌐ezi to ke¬ezai</u> ni tuite o⌐siete
kuremase¬ñ ka.

9. I'm writing a book about
    politics and economics.
Se⌐ezi to ke¬ezai ni tuite ⌐ho¬ñ
(o) ⌐ka¬ite (i)masu.

10. I'm writing a book about
    Christianity.
<u>Ki⌐risutokyoo</u> ni tu¬ite ⌐ho¬ñ (o)
⌐ka¬ite (i)masu.

H. Expansion Drill

Tutor: Tanaka-sañ Ya⌐mamoto-sañ na¬ñka (ḡa) imasu. /Ikeda-
         sañ/ 'Mr. Tanaka, Mr. Yamamoto and others are here.
         /Mr. Ikeda/'
Student: Ikeda-sañ (o) hazime, Tanaka-sañ Ya⌐mamoto-sañ na¬ñ-
         ka (ḡa) imasu. 'Mr. Tanaka, Mr. Yamamoto, and others
         are here, to say nothing of Mr. Ikeda.'

1. Zassi si⌐ñbuñ na¬ñka (o)
    u⌐tte (i)ma¬su. /ho¬ñ/
Ho¬ñ (o) hazime, zassi si⌐ñbuñ
na¬ñka (o) u⌐tte (i)ma¬su.

2. Rekisi ⌐ti¬ri nañka (o)
    be⌐ñkyoo-site (i)ma¬su.
    /ko⌐toba¬/
Ko⌐toba¬ (o) hazime, rekisi ⌐ti¬-
ri nañka (o) be⌐ñkyoo-site
(i)ma¬su.

3. Kotatu de⌐ñkisuto¬obu
    nañka (o) tu⌐katte ima¬su.
    /hi¬bati/
Hi¬bati (o) hazime, kotatu de⌐ñki-
suto¬obu nañka (o) tu⌐katte
(i)ma¬su.

4. O⌐yoḡi¬ ya ⌐te¬nisu mo
    sa⌐kañ ni narima¬sita.
    /go⌐ruhu/
Go⌐ruhu (o) hazime, o⌐yoḡi¬ ya
⌐te¬nisu mo sa⌐kañ ni narima¬-
sita.

5. Hi⌐syo¬ mo zyo⌐tyuu mo
    kima¬sita. /o¬kusañ/
O¬kusañ (o) hazime, hi⌐syo¬ mo
zyo⌐tyuu mo kima¬sita.

6. Ta⌐roo-tyañ mo ⌐Zi⌐roo-
tyañ mo ki┕ma┙sita.
/se⌐ñse⌐e/

Se⌐ñse⌐e (o) hazime, Ta⌐roo-tyañ
mo ⌐Zi⌐roo-tyañ mo ki┕ma┙sita.

I. Response Drill (based on Grammatical Note 4)

Tutor: I⌐kimasyo⌐o ka. 'Shall we go?'
Student: E┐e, i⌐ku koto┐ ni si┕masyo┙o. 'Yes, let's plan to go.'

1. Ya⌐memasyo⌐o ka.
2. Ko⌐domo (o) turete ikima-
syo┐o ka.
3. Mo⌐o suko⌐si so⌐odañ-
simasyo┐o ka.
4. Ki┕mono (o) kimasyo⌐o ka.

5. Teeburu (o) yo⌐yaku-site
okimasyo┐o ka.
6. Yo⌐osyoku (o) tabemasyo⌐o
ka.
7. Hu⌐toñ ni nemasyo⌐o ka.

8. Ka⌐ñkooba⌐su ni no┕rima-
syo┙o ka.

E┐e, ya⌐meru koto┐ ni si┕masyo┙o.
E┐e, ko⌐domo (o) turete iku koto┐
ni si┕masyo┙o.
E┐e, mo⌐o suko⌐si so⌐odañ-suru
koto┐ ni si┕masyo┙o.
E┐e, ki⌐mono (o) kiru koto┐ ni
si┕masyo┙o.
E┐e, teeburu (o) yo⌐yaku-site oku
koto┐ ni si┕masyo┙o.
E┐e, yo⌐osyoku (o) tabe⌐ru koto ni
si┕masyo┙o.
E┐e, hu⌐toñ ni neru koto┐ ni si-
┕masyo┙o.
E┐e, ka⌐ñkooba┐su ni no┕ru koto┐
ni si┕masyo┙o.

J. Response Drill (based on Grammatical Note 5)

Tutor: A⌐rimase┐ñ ka⌐ 'Aren't there any?'
Student: A┕ru koto wa a┕rima┙su ḡa⌐ 'There ARE some but...'

1. Wa┕karimase┐ñ ka⌐

2. Ya⌐ku┐ ni ta⌐timase┐ñ ka⌐

3. Ka⌐wai⌐iku a⌐rimase┐ñ ka⌐

4. Yu⌐umee zya arimase┐ñ
ka⌐
5. Ni⌐hoñzi┐ñ zya a⌐rimase┐ñ
ka⌐
6. Tu⌐yoku a⌐rimase┐ñ ka⌐
7. To⌐kee (o) mo⌐tte (i)⌐ma-
se┐ñ ka⌐
8. Re⌐ñsyuu-site (i)mase┐ñ
ka⌐
9. Yo┐ku a⌐rimase┐ñ ka⌐
10. Syo⌐oziki┐ zya a⌐rimase┐ñ
ka⌐

Wa┕ka⌐ru koto wa wa┕karima┙su
ḡa⌐
Ya⌐ku┐ ni ⌐ta┕tu koto wa ta┕ti-
ma┙su ḡa⌐
Ka┕wai┙i koto wa ka┕wai┙i desu
ḡa⌐
Yu┕umee na koto┐ wa yu┕umee
de┙su ḡa⌐
Ni┕hoñzi┐ñ no koto wa ni┕hoñzi┙ñ
desu ḡa⌐
Tu┕yo┙i koto wa tu┕yo┙i desu ḡa⌐
To┕kee (o) mo⌐tte (i)┕ru koto┐ wa
┕mo⌐tte (i)masu ḡa⌐
Re┕ñsyuu-site (i)ru koto┐ wa si┕te
(i)ma┙su ḡa⌐
I┐i koto wa ┕i┙i desu ḡa⌐
Syo┕oziki┐ na koto wa syo┕oziki┙
desu ḡa⌐

K. Response Drill

Tutor: A⌐rimase┐ñ ka⌐ 'Aren't there any?'
Student: Na┐i ┕wa┙ke zya a⌐rimase┐ñ ḡa⌐ 'It isn't that there aren't
any but [something else is involved].'

1. De⌐ki¬mase⌐n̄ ka↓   De⌐ki¬nai ⌐wa⌐ke zya a⌐rimase⌐n̄
                              ḡa—

2. Hu⌐ben̄ desu ka↓   Hu⌐ben̄ na ⌐wa⌐ke zya a⌐rimase⌐n̄
                              ḡa—

3. A⌐tta⌐kaku a⌐rimase⌐n̄ ka↓ A⌐tta⌐kaku ⌐na⌐i ⌐wa⌐ke zya a⌐ri-
                              mase⌐n̄ ḡa—

4. Ki⌐koemase⌐n̄ ka↓   Ki⌐koenai wa⌐ke zya a⌐rimase⌐n̄
                              ḡa—

5. Ka⌐maimase⌐n̄ ka↓   Ka⌐mawa⌐nai ⌐wa⌐ke zya a⌐rima-
                              se⌐n̄ ḡa—

6. Ki ⌐ni irimase⌐n̄ ka↓   Ki ⌐ni iranai wa⌐ke zya a⌐rima-
                              se⌐n̄ ḡa—

7. Ko⌐marima⌐su ka↓   Ko⌐ma⌐ru ⌐wa⌐ke zya a⌐rimase⌐n̄
                              ḡa—

8. O⌐yoḡemase⌐n̄ ka↓   O⌐yoḡe⌐nai ⌐wa⌐ke zya a⌐rimase⌐n̄
                              ḡa—

9. Hi⌐roku a⌐rimase⌐n̄ ka↓   Hi⌐roku ⌐na⌐i ⌐wa⌐ke zya a⌐rima-
                              se⌐n̄ ḡa—

10. To⌐modati zya arimase⌐n̄   To⌐modati zya na⌐i ⌐wa⌐ke zya
    ka↓   a⌐rimase⌐n̄ ḡa—

11. Ti⌐ḡaima⌐su ka↓   Ti⌐ḡau wa⌐ke zya a⌐rimase⌐n̄ ḡa—

12. He⌐ta⌐ desu ka↓   He⌐ta⌐ na ⌐wa⌐ke zya a⌐rimase⌐n̄
                              ḡa—

L. Substitution Drill (based on Grammatical Note 1)

1. How would it be best to   Na⌐n̄ de i⌐ke⌐ba i⌐tiban̄ i⌐i de-
   go? (Lit. Provided I go   syoo ka.
   how, would it be best?)

2. What would be best to   Na⌐ni (o) ⌐yo⌐meba i⌐tiban̄ i⌐i
   read? /na⌐ni o ⌐yo⌐mu/   desyoo ka.

3. Which would be best to   Do⌐re (o) re⌐n̄syuu-sure⌐ba
   practice? /do⌐re o ren̄-   i⌐tiban̄ i⌐i desyoo ka.
   syuu-suru/

4. What time would it be   Na⌐n̄-zi ni ⌐ku⌐reba i⌐tiban̄ i⌐i
   best to come? /na⌐n̄-zi   desyoo ka.
   ni ⌐ku⌐ru/

5. Who would be best to   Da⌐re ni se⌐tumee-site mora-
   explain it? (Lit. Pro-   e⌐ba i⌐tiban̄ i⌐i desyoo ka.
   vided I have it explained
   by whom, would it be
   best?) /da⌐re ni setumee-
   site morau/

6. When would be best to   I⌐tu to⌐rikaere⌐ba i⌐tiban̄ i⌐i
   exchange [it]? /i⌐tu tori-   desyoo ka.
   kaeru/

7. What day would be best   Na⌐n̄yo⌐obi ni to⌐doke⌐reba i⌐ti-
   to deliver [it]? /na⌐n̄yo-   ban̄ i⌐i desyoo ka.
   obi ni to⌐doke⌐ru/

8. Where would it be best   Do⌐ko ni o⌐ite oke⌐ba i⌐tiban̄
   to put [it] for the time   i⌐i desyoo ka.
   being? /do⌐ko ni oite oku/

9. What month would it be   Naⁿ-ḡatu ni ryoᵏkoo-sureᵈba iᵏti-
    best to travel? /naⁿ-   baⁿ iᵈi desyoo ka.
    ḡatu ni ryokoo-suru/
10. How would it be best to   Doᵓo iᵏeᵈba iᵏtibaⁿ iᵈi desyoo ka.
    say it? /doᵓo iu/

M. Grammar Drill (based on Grammatical Note 1)

    Tutor: Aᵓme ḡa hurimasu. 'It rains.'
    Student: Aᵓme ḡa ˹huˈreba ˈiᵈi desu ḡa ˹neˈe. 'I hope it rains . . .'

1. Oᵓkusaⁿ (o) turete kimasu.   Oᵓkusaⁿ (o) tuᵏrete kuᵏreba ˈiᵈi
                                     desu ḡa ˹neˈe.
2. Yuˈkiᵓ ḡa huˈrimaseⁿ̄.   Yuˈkiᵓ ḡa huˈraˈnakereba ˈiᵈi de-
                                     su ḡa ˹neˈe.
3. Eᵓki de ˹niᵓmotu (o) azu-   Eᵓki de ˹niᵓmotu (o) aᶻukeᵓreba
    kemasu.   ˈiᵈi desu ḡa ˹neˈe.
4. Raˈisyuu maᵓde tuzuki-   Raˈisyuu maᵓde tuᵏzukeᵈba ˈiᵈi
    masu.   desu ḡa ˹neˈe.
5. Niˈhoⁿḡo ḡa dekimaᵓsu.   Niˈhoⁿḡo ḡa dekiᵓreba ˈiᵈi desu
                                     ḡa ˹neˈe.
6. Koᵓⁿbaⁿ ˹yoᵓku beⁿkyoo-   Koᵓⁿbaⁿ ˹yoᵓku beᵏⁿkyoo-sureᵈba
    simasu.   ˈiᵈi desu ḡa ˹neˈe.
7. Kaᵏuᵓ no (o) waˈsuremase-   Kaᵏuᵓ no (o) waˈsurenaᵓkereba ˈiᵈi
    ⁿ̄.   desu ḡa ˹neˈe.
8. Aᵓsa ˹haᵓyaku tukimasu.   Aᵓsa ˹haᵓyaku ᵏtuᵏkeba ˈiᵈi desu
                                     ḡa ˹neˈe.
9. Baⁿ osoku deˈmaseᵓⁿ̄.   Baⁿ osoku ˹deᵓnakereba ˈiᵈi desu
                                     ḡa ˹neˈe.
10. Zyuˈubuᵓⁿ̄ arimasu.   Zyuˈubuᵓⁿ̄ ᵏaᵈreba ˈiᵈi desu ḡa
                                     ˹neˈe.

N. Substitution Drill (based on Grammatical Note 1)

1. If you want to read, I   Yoᵓmitaᵓkereba aˈⁿnaisyoᵓ (ḡa)
    have a guidebook . . .   aᵏrimaᵈsu ḡa_
2. If you want to go, there's   Iᵏkitaᵓkereba, kyoᵓokai (ḡa) ari-
    a church . . . /iku, kyoo-   maᵓsu ḡa_
    kai/
3. If you want to visit [them],   Keˈⁿbutu-sitaᵓkereba, oᵓtera ya
    there are temples and   ziˈⁿzya (ḡa) aᵏrimaᵓsu ḡa_
    shrines . . . /keⁿbutu-
    suru, oᵓtera ya ziᵓⁿzya/
4. If you want to rent [it],   Kaᵓritaᵓkereba, iᵓi kaˈsiya (ḡa)
    there's a nice house for   arimaᵓsu ḡa_
    rent . . . /kariru, iᵓi
    kāsiya/
5. If you want to write [it],   Kaˈkitaᵓkereba, eⁿpitu (ḡa) ari-
    I have a pencil . . .   maᵓsu ḡa_
    /kaᵓku, eⁿpitu/

6. If you want to telephone,
   I have a phone book . . .
   /de⌐ñwa (o) kake⌐ru,
   deñwatyoo/

   De⌐ñwa (o) kaketa⌐kereba, de⌐ñwa-
   tyoo (ḡa) arima⌐su ḡa—

7. If you want to buy [any],
   there are nice souvenirs . . .
   /kau, i⌐i mı̃⌐yaḡe/

   Ka⌐ita⌐kereba, i⌐i mi⌐yaḡe (ḡa)
   arima⌐su ḡa—

8. If you want to stop, there's
   a nice inn . . . /tomaru,
   i⌐i ryŏkañ/

   To⌐marita⌐kereba, i⌐i ryo⌐kañ (ḡa)
   arima⌐su ḡa—

O. Grammar Drill (based on Grammatical Note 3)

> Tutor: Ti⌐ri ya re⌐kisi (o) sitte (i)ma⌐su. '[You] know geography
>   and history.'
>   O⌐mosiro⌐i ryo⌐koo ḡa dekima⌐su. 'Interesting trips are
>   possible.'
> Student: Ti⌐ri ya rēkisi (o) si⌐tte (i)re⌐ba ı̃ru hodo o⌐mosiro⌐i ryo-
>   ⌐koo ḡa dekima⌐su. 'The more [you] know geography and
>   history, the more interesting trips are possible.'

1. Wa⌐ka⌐i desu. Tu⌐yo⌐i desu.

   Wa⌐kakereba wa⌐ka⌐i hodo tu⌐yo⌐i
   desu.

2. O⌐oki⌐i desu. I⌐i desu.

   O⌐okikereba o⌐oki⌐i hodo ⌐i⌐i desu.

3. Añna tokee wa ti⌐isa⌐i
   desu. Ta⌐ka⌐i desu.

   Añna tokee wa ⌐ti⌐isakereba ti-
   ⌐isa⌐i hodo ta⌐ka⌐i desu.

4. Sikiti wa ma⌐ti⌐ kara
   to⌐oi⌐ desu. Ya⌐su⌐i desu.

   Sikiti wa ma⌐ti⌐ kara to⌐o⌐kereba
   to⌐oi⌐ hodo ya⌐su⌐i desu.

5. Re⌐ñsyuu-sima⌐su. Zyo-
   ⌐ozu⌐ ni na⌐rima⌐su yo—

   Re⌐ñsyuu-sure⌐ba su̇ru hodo zyo-
   ⌐ozu⌐ ni na⌐rima⌐su yo—

6. Hu⌐kuzatu de⌐su. Mu-
   ⌐zukasi⌐i desu.

   Hu⌐kuzatu de a⌐reba ⌐a⌐ru hodo
   mu⌐zukasi⌐i desu. [1]

7. Ryo⌐koo-sima⌐su. Ku⌐ni
   e kaerita⌐ku narimasu.

   Ryo⌐koo-sure⌐ba su̇ru hodo ku⌐ni
   e kaerita⌐ku narimasu.

8. O⌐kane wa arima⌐su.
   Ho⌐siku ⌐na⌐ru mo⌐no⌐
   desu. [2]

   Okane wa ⌐a⌐reba ⌐a⌐ru hodo
   ⌐ho⌐siku ⌐na⌐ru mo⌐no⌐ desu. [2]

P. Response Drill (based on Grammatical Note 2)

> Tutor: Si⌐na⌐kute mo ⌐i⌐i desu ka— 'Is it all right if [I] don't do
>   it?'
> Student: Iie, si⌐na⌐kereba na⌐rimase⌐ñ yo. 'No, [you] must do it.'

1. Tu⌐tuma⌐nakute mo ⌐i⌐i
   desu ka—

   Iie, tu⌐tuma⌐nakereba na⌐rimase⌐ñ
   yo.

2. Mi⌐nato ni haira⌐nakute mo
   ⌐i⌐i desu ka—

   Iie, /mi⌐nato ni/ haira⌐nakereba
   na⌐rimase⌐ñ yo.

---

[1] Another alternant: Hu⌐kuzatu na⌐ra hu̇kuzatu na hodo mu⌐zukasi⌐i desu.

[2] Mo⌐no⌐ de su in this context means 'it's natural,' 'it's to be expected,' 'it's usual.'

3. Ma⌐initi ka⌐yowana⌐kute   Iie, /ma⌐initi/ ka⌐yowana⌐kereba
    mo ⌐i⌐i desu ka⌐   na⌐rimase⌐ñ yo.
4. A⌐sa⌐tte zya ⌐na⌐kute mo   Iie, a⌐sa⌐tte zya ⌐na⌐kereba na-
    ⌐i⌐i desu ka⌐   ⌐rimase⌐ñ yo.
5. Tu⌐metaku na⌐kute mo ⌐i⌐i   Iie, tu⌐metaku na⌐kereba na⌐ri-
    desu ka⌐   mase⌐ñ yo.
6. Mo⌐o ip-peñ iwana⌐kute mo   Iie, /mo⌐o ip-peñ/ iwana⌐kereba
    ⌐i⌐i desu ka⌐   na⌐rimase⌐ñ yo.
7. Te⌐eburu (o) yoyaku-sina⌐-   Iie, /te⌐eburu (o)/ yoyaku-sina⌐-
    kute mo ⌐i⌐i desu ka⌐   kereba na⌐rimase⌐ñ yo.
8. E⌐eḡo zya na⌐kute mo ⌐i⌐i   Iie, e⌐eḡo zya na⌐kereba na⌐ri-
    desu ka⌐   mase⌐ñ yo.
9. Ma⌐ruku na⌐kute mo ⌐i⌐i   Iie, ma⌐ruku na⌐kereba na⌐rima-
    desu ka⌐   se⌐ñ yo.
10. Ka⌐be (o) nurikae⌐nakute   Iie, /ka⌐be o/ nurikae⌐nakereba
    mo ⌐i⌐i desu ka⌐   na⌐rimase⌐ñ yo.

Repeat the drill above, asking the questions in informal style (i. e.
ending in i⌐i?) and answering informally, using the -nakutyaa na-
⌐ra⌐nai pattern.

Q. Response Drill

    (Give the iie answer for each of the following questions, using a
    'may,' 'must,' 'must not,' or 'don't have to' pattern.)

1. Bu⌐kkyoo to ⌐si⌐ñtoo no   Iie. /Bu⌐kkyoo to ⌐si⌐ñtoo no
    ko⌐to⌐ (o) be⌐ñkyoo-sina⌐-   ko⌐to⌐ wa/ be⌐ñkyoo-sina⌐kute
    kereba na⌐rimase⌐ñ ka⌐   mo ⌐i⌐i desu yo⌐
2. Tu⌐ri ni itte⌐ mo ⌐i⌐i   Iie. /Tu⌐ri ni/ ittya⌐a i⌐kema-
    desu ka⌐   se⌐ñ yo.
3. A⌐ñna⌐i-sinakute mo ⌐i⌐i   Iie. A⌐ñna⌐i-sinakereba na⌐ri-
    desu ka⌐   mase⌐ñ yo.
4. No⌐zoitya⌐a i⌐kemase⌐ñ   Iie. No⌐zoite⌐ mo ⌐i⌐i desu yo⌐
    ka⌐
5. Hu⌐de de ka⌐ite mo ⌐i⌐i   Iie. /Hu⌐de de/ ka⌐ityaa i⌐ke-
    desu ka⌐   mase⌐ñ yo.
6. Ha⌐rawa⌐nakute mo ⌐i⌐i   Iie. Ha⌐rawa⌐nakereba na⌐rima-
    desu ka⌐   se⌐ñ yo.
7. O⌐ñseñ zya na⌐kereba na⌐-   Iie. O⌐ñseñ zya na⌐kute mo ⌐i⌐l
    ⌐rimase⌐ñ ka⌐   desu yo⌐
8. Go⌐mi⌐ (o) i⌐retya⌐a i⌐ke-   Iie. Go⌐mi⌐ (o) i⌐rete⌐ mo ⌐i⌐i
    mase⌐ñ ka⌐   desu yo⌐

SUPPLEMENTARY DIALOGUES

1. Tanaka: I⌐i ⌐te⌐ñki da kara, tu⌐ri ni ikimase⌐ñ ka⌐
    Smith: Se⌐kkaku⌐ da keredo; kyo⌐o wa ba⌐ñ ma⌐de ni si⌐te simawana⌐-
             kereba na⌐ra⌐nai ⌐yo⌐o ga ⌐a⌐tte, i⌐karena⌐i ñ desu yo.
    Tanaka: Zya⌐a, hi⌐to⌐ri de i⌐ku koto⌐ ni si⌐ma⌐su yo.
    Smith: Su⌐mimase⌐ñ.

2. Tanaka: Ho⸢oryuuzi[1] tte iu otera go⸢zo⸣ñzi desu ka⌐

    Smith: Iti-do ni⸢hoñzi⸣ñ no tomodati ni tu⸣rete itte moratta koto⸣ ḡa
             ⸢a⸣ru ñ desu ḡa, zu⸣ibuñ ri⸢ppa na mono⸣ da to o⸣mo⸣tta ñ de-
             su.

    Tanaka: Watasi wa ⸢mo⸣o go-⸢roku-do itta⸣ ñ desu ḡa; mi⸣reba ⸢mi⸣ru
             hodo su⸢barasi⸣i to o⸣mo⸣tte, mata ⸢su⸣ḡu i⸣tte mi⸣taku ⸢na⸣ru
             ñ desu yo⌐

    Smith: Watasi wa a⸢ñmari yo⸣ku ⸢mi⸣nakatta kara, ze⸣hi ma⸣ta ikita⸣i
             ñ desu. I⸢tu ka i⸣ssyo ni tu⸣rete itte kudasaimase⸣ñ ka⌐

    Tanaka: A⸣a, i⸣i desu to mo. I⸢ssyo ni ikimasyo⸣o.

3. Tanaka: Kono heñ ni ka⸢siya ḡa na⸣i desyoo ka ⸢ne⸣e.

    Agent: A⸢rima⸣su ḡa; kono heñ wa ⸢beñri na to⸢koro⸣ na no de, ya⸣tiñ
             ḡa ⸢ka⸣nari ta⸢ka⸣i ñ desu yo⌐

    Tanaka: So⸣o desyoo ⸢ne⸣e. Ya⸣tiñ ḡa a⸢ñmari ta⸣kaku ⸢na⸣kute, beñri na
             to⸢koro⸣ ḡa ⸢a⸣reba ⸣i⸣i ñ desu ḡa⌐

    Agent: Mu⸢zukasi⸣i desu ⸢ne⸣e. Ya⸣tiñ wa ⸢e⸣ki kara to⸢oku na⸣reba ⸢na⸣-
             ru hodo ⸢ya⸣suku ⸢na⸣tte imasu ḡa, hu⸣beñ ni mo na⸢rima⸣su
             kara ⸢ne⸣e.

4. Tanaka   (filling out a form): Su⸢mimase⸣ñ. Tyo⸣tto u⸢kaḡaita⸣i ñ desu
             ḡa⌐

    Clerk: Na⸣ñ desyoo ka⌐

    Tanaka: Ko⸢no kami⸣ ni ⸢pe⸣ñ de ka⸢ka⸣nakereba na⸢ra⸣nai ka e⸢ñpitu de
             ka⸣ite mo ⸣i⸣i ka u⸢kaḡaita⸣i ñ desu ḡa⌐

    Clerk: Na⸣ñ de ⸢ka⸣ite mo ka⸢maimase⸣ñ ḡa, ha⸢kki⸣ri ⸢ka⸣ite kudasai⌐

5. Tanaka: Ki⸢noo no ka⸣iḡi ni i⸢rassyaima⸣sita ka⌐

    Smith: E⸣e. I⸢tta koto⸣ wa i⸢tta⸣ ñ desu ḡa; yo⸣o ḡa ⸢a⸣tte, ha⸣yaku
             ⸢ka⸣ette si⸢matta⸣ kara, kyo⸣o ⸢da⸣re ka ni ⸢do⸣ñna ko⸢to⸣ o ki⸣-
             ⸣meta⸣ ka ki⸢kana⸣kereba na⸢ra⸣nai to o⸣mo⸣tte iru ñ desu yo⌐
             A⸢na⸣ta wa?

    Tanaka: Watasi wa ⸢ka⸣iḡi no owaru su⸢ko⸣si ⸣ma⸣e ni ka⸢isya e ka⸣ette
             ki⸣ta⸣ no de, ka⸣iḡi no ko⸢to⸣ wa na⸢ni mo kikana⸣katta ñ desu
             yo⌐

6. Smith: Se⸢tona⸣ikai[2] wa to⸣temo ⸢ke⸣siki ḡa ⸢i⸣i soo desu ḡa, si⸢ma⸣ ḡa
             ta⸢kusañ a⸣ru ñ desyoo?

    Tanaka: E⸣e. A⸣wazi[3] o hazime, Syo⸢odo⸣sima[3] nado⌐ Sa⸢ñ-zeñ-ḡu⸣rai
             ⸣a⸣ru soo desu.

    Smith: Sa⸢ñ-byaku zya ⸣na⸣i ñ desu ka⌐

    Tanaka: Sa⸢ñ-zeñ desu yo⌐ Miñna ti⸢isa⸣i si⸣ma⸣ desu ḡa⌐

    Smith: I⸢tta koto⸣ ḡa ⸢a⸣ru ñ desyoo?

    Tanaka: E⸣e. Mo⸣to wa, ya⸢sumi no toki⸣ ni wa, yo⸣ku i⸣tta mono⸣ de-
             su.

7. Smith: I⸣ma ka⸢erima⸣su ka⌐

    Tanaka: E⸣e, ka⸢ero⸣o to o⸣mo⸣tte imasu ḡa⌐

---

[1] Name of a famous Buddhist temple.

[2] 'Inland Sea.'

[3] Name of island.

Smith: Su⌐gu ⌐ka⌐eru ñ nara, e⌐ki made no⌐tte ikimase⌐ñ ka↵
Tanaka: A⌐ri⌐gatoo. Zya⌐a, e⌐ñryo na⌐ku o⌐negai-sima⌐su.

8. Smith: Ke⌐ñbutu-suru ma⌐e ni ka⌐buki ni tu⌐ite yo⌐mita⌐i ñ desu ga, i⌐i
             ⌐ho⌐ñ ga ⌐a⌐ru desyoo ka.
    Tanaka: E⌐e⌐go no⌐ desu ne?
    Smith: Mo⌐ti⌐roñ ⌐so⌐o desu yo.
    Tanaka: I⌐roiro arima⌐su ga; do⌐no ⌐ho⌐ñ mo so⌐re⌐zore ⌐i⌐i to⌐koro⌐ mo
             wa⌐ru⌐i to⌐koro⌐ mo ⌐a⌐tte, ko⌐re ga itibañ i⌐i to i⌐eru mono⌐
             wa ⌐na⌐i ñ desu yo↵
    Smith: Watasi wa si⌐bai ya e⌐ega no be⌐ñkyoo o sita koto⌐ wa ⌐na⌐i
             si; ma⌐a, kañtañ ni ka⌐buki to iu mono⌐ wa ⌐do⌐ñna mo⌐no⌐ ka
             ⌐yo⌐ñde mi⌐ta⌐i ñ desu ga↵
    Tanaka: Zya⌐a, wa⌐tasi ga mo⌐tte ru a⌐ñnaisyo⌐ ga tyo⌐odo i⌐i ka mo
             si⌐remase⌐ñ yo↵ E⌐ mo ⌐ha⌐itte ru si; u⌐sui hoñ da kara,
             su⌐gu yo⌐me⌐ru si↵
    Smith: Na⌐ñ te iu ⌐ho⌐ñ desyoo. Hu⌐tuu no ho⌐ñya de ka⌐eru⌐ desyoo
             ne?
    Tanaka: E⌐e, ka⌐eru to omoima⌐su ga; wa⌐tasi no⌐ o ⌐yo⌐ñdara ⌐do⌐o
             desu ka↵ I⌐ma da⌐re mo yo⌐ñde i⌐mase⌐ñ kara↵
    Smith: Ha⌐isyaku-dekima⌐su ka↵
    Tanaka: Mo⌐ti⌐roñ desu to mo. Tyo⌐tto o⌐mati ni nare⌐reba; o⌐oi⌐sogi
             de ⌐uti e itte, su⌐gu to⌐tte kima⌐su yo↵
    Smith: Do⌐o mo ⌐i⌐tu mo go⌐me⌐ewaku na o⌐negai o site, su⌐mimase⌐ñ.

English Equivalents

1. Tanaka: Since it's [such] nice weather, won't you go fishing?
    Smith: It's kind of you to ask me but I can't go today because I have
             some business I must finish up (lit. do completely) by evening.
    Tanaka: Then I'll plan to go alone.
    Smith: I'm sorry.

2. Tanaka: Do you know the Horyuji Temple?
    Smith: I have had a Japanese friend take me once. I thought it was an
             awfully impressive thing.
    Tanaka: I've gone there five or six times already, but the more I see it
             the more I think that it's wonderful and I (get to) want to try and
             go again soon.
    Smith: Since I didn't see it too well, I want to go again by all means.
             Won't you take me along some time?
    Tanaka: Oh, certainly! Let's go together.

3. Tanaka: I wonder if there aren't any houses for rent around here.
    Agent: There are, but since this section is a convenient location the
             rents are rather high.
    Tanaka: I guess that's right. I hope there's a place where the rents
             aren't too high that's convenient. (Lit. It will be fine if there's
             a place [described by saying] the rents aren't too high and it's
             convenient.)
    Agent: That's difficult. The farther you get from the station the cheaper
             the rent gets, but it gets inconvenient too so—you know . . .

4. Tanaka: Excuse me. I'd like to ask you something . . .
   Clerk: What is it?
   Tanaka: I'd like to inquire whether I must write with a pen on this paper,
           or whether I may write with a pencil . . .
   Clerk: It doesn't matter what you write with but please write clearly.

5. Tanaka: Did you go to yesterday's conference?
   Smith: Yes, I did go, but I had some business to attend to and I went
           home early so I've been thinking that I must ask someone today
           what kind of things [they] decided. How about you?
   Tanaka: Since I came back to the office [just] a little before the confer-
           ence ended, I didn't hear anything about the conference.

6. Smith: I hear that the Inland Sea has very beautiful scenery. (Lit. As
           for the Inland Sea, I hear that the scenery is very good.) There
           are lots of islands, aren't there?
   Tanaka: Yes. [There's] Shodoshima, for example, to say nothing of
           Awaji. They say there are about three thousand.
   Smith: Don't you mean three hundred?
   Tanaka: It's three thousand. They're all small islands but [it is three
           thousand].
   Smith: You've gone there, haven't you?
   Tanaka: Yes. I used to go often at vacation time.

7. Smith: Are you going home now?
   Tanaka: Yes, I've been thinking I would . . .
   Smith: If you're going home right away, wouldn't you [like to] ride as
           far as the station?
   Tanaka: Thanks. I'll take you up on that. (Lit. Well, I'll ask you without
           holding back.)

8. Smith: I'd like to read about kabuki before I see it. Is there a good
           book?
   Tanaka: You mean an English one, don't you?
   Smith: Of course (that's right).
   Tanaka: There are all different kinds, but every book has its own good
           points (lit. places) and bad points, and there is no book (lit. thing)
           about which you can say, 'This one is best.'
   Smith: I've never made a study of plays and movies, and I just want to try
           reading briefly what kind of thing (the thing called) 'kabuki' is . . .
   Tanaka: In that case, the guidebook I have may be just right. There are
           pictures in it and it's a thin book so you can read it in no time
           and . . .
   Smith: What's the name of the book? (Lit. It's a book called what?) You
           can probably buy it at a regular bookstore, can't you?
   Tanaka: Yes, I think you can buy it but how about reading mine? No one
           is reading it now so . . .
   Smith: Can I borrow it?
   Tanaka: Of course! If you can wait a minute, I'll rush home (lit. go
           home in a big hurry) and get it (lit. come having picked it up).
   Smith: I hate to bother you all the time. (Lit. I'm very sorry to make
           troublesome requests all the time.)

BASIC DIALOGUES: RESTATEMENT

(as contained in a letter from Tanaka to Smith)

Sekkaku Ni⌐ho⌐n e o⌐ide ni na⌐tta no de, ho⌐oboo ryo⌐koo-nasa⌐tte o⌐kaeri ni narita⌐i kara, do⌐nna to⌐koro⌐ e i⌐tta⌐ra ⌐i⌐i ka o⌐siete moraita⌐i to iu o⌐hanasi de⌐su ga; hito ni yotte mi⌐ta⌐i to⌐koro⌐ ga ti⌐gau⌐ no de, o⌐yaku ni ta⌐tu ka ⌐do⌐o ka wa⌐karimase⌐n ga; mo⌐osiagete¹ mimasyo⌐o.

Ti⌐ka⌐i to⌐koro⌐ nara, Ni⌐kkoo ga yu⌐umee de⌐su. Ni⌐kkoo e i⌐ku⌐ no ni wa, to⌐kkyuu ga arima⌐su kara, de⌐nsya de i⌐ku⌐ no ga i⌐tiban be⌐nri desu. Ke⌐redomo, to⌐kkyuu de iku koto⌐ ni su⌐re⌐ba, ma⌐e no hi⌐ made ni to⌐kkyu-uke⌐n o ka⌐tte okana⌐kereba na⌐rimase⌐n.

Tu⌐ri no deki⌐ru ⌐si⌐zuka na o⌐nse⌐n ni itte mita⌐i to o⌐ssyaima⌐su ga, I⌐zu na⌐ra so⌐nna tokoro⌐ ga ta⌐kusan arima⌐su. Izu wa ⌐ka⌐nari o⌐oki⌐i ha-⌐ntoo de⌐su.

A⌐na⌐ta ga o⌐kiki ni na⌐tta yoo ni, Kyo⌐oto wa hu⌐ru⌐i o⌐tera ya zi⌐nzya ga ta⌐kusan arima⌐su. Kyo⌐oto wa ⌐bu⌐kkyoo to ⌐si⌐ntoo no sa⌐kan na tokoro⌐ desu kara, kirisutokyoo no kyookai mo ⌐a⌐ru ko⌐to⌐ wa a⌐rima⌐su ga; su⌐ku-na⌐i si, taitee a⌐tara⌐siku ⌐ta⌐teta mo⌐no⌐ desu.

Kyu⌐usyuu ni wa, do⌐ko ka ke⌐nbutu-suru tokoro⌐ ga ⌐a⌐ru ka to iu go⌐si-tumo⌐n² de⌐su ga; mo⌐ti⌐ron arimasu. Na⌐ga⌐saki o hazime; A⌐so, Aosima, Ka⌐gosima na⌐do desu ga; Na⌐ga⌐saki wa i⌐tiban huru⌐i mi⌐nato no hito⌐tu da si, te⌐nki no ⌐i⌐i hi ni wa, A⌐so no na⌐game⌐ wa su⌐barasi⌐i mo⌐no⌐ desu.

O⌐hanasi no yo⌐o ni, Ni⌐ho⌐n ni wa ⌐do⌐ko e i⌐tte⌐ mo me⌐zura⌐sikute o⌐mosiro⌐i mo⌐no⌐ ga arimasu. Na⌐ni o ⌐mi⌐te mo mi⌐yage ni katte kaeri-ta⌐ku ⌐na⌐ru to o⌐ssya⌐ru keredo; do⌐no kuni no mo⌐no⌐ de mo so⌐re⌐zore ti⌐gatta azi ga arima⌐su kara, a⌐na⌐ta ga so⌐o oomoi ni na⌐ru no wa a⌐tari-mae³ da to omoima⌐su. Wa⌐takusi mo mo⌐to wa ryo⌐koo-suru tabi⌐ ni mi-⌐yage o katta mono⌐ desu.

Ni⌐ho⌐n no ti⌐ri ya re⌐kisi ni tu⌐ite, mo⌐o go⌐zo⌐nzi ka mo si⌐remase⌐n ga; ti⌐ri ya re⌐kisi wa si⌐tte ire⌐ba i⌐ru hodo o⌐mosiro⌐i ryo⌐koo ga deki⌐ru kara, o⌐dekake ni na⌐ru ⌐ma⌐e ni, so⌐re ni tu⌐ite ⌐na⌐ni ka i⌐ti-do o⌐yomi ni na⌐ttara i⌐ka⌐ga desyoo ka. Yo⌐rosi⌐kattara; wa⌐takusi no tokoro⌐ ni ⌐eego no a⌐nnaisyo⌐ ga a⌐rima⌐su kara, i⌐tu de⌐ mo o⌐moti-kudasa⌐i.

EXERCISES

1. Plan a trip to Kyoto with a friend. Have your conversation cover the fol-
    lowing points:

---

¹ Moosiaḡeṛu ⁺ /-ru/ 'say (to you).'

² Situmoñ (gositumoñ ⁺) 'question.'

³ Atarimae 'natural,' 'proper,' 'reasonable.'

    a. when you will leave
    b. how long you will stay
    c. how you will go
    d. where you will stay (tomaru)
    e. what you want to see
    f. what souvenirs you want to buy

2. Make up 15 short conversations, each one of which contains one of the
following:

    a. ya⌐ku˥ ni ┌ta┤tu
    b. o⌐oi˥soḡi de
    c. ta⌐be˥ru koto wa ta┌bema┤su
    d. yo⌐rosi˥kereba
    e. se⌐ñse˥e o hazime
    f. go⌐me˥ewaku zya ┌na┤kereba
    g. sekkaku ni⌐hoñ˥go o beñkyoo-site iru˥ ñ desu kara
    h. o˥okikereba o⌐oki˥i hodo
    i. sore de
    j. si⌐na˥kereba na┌ra┤nai
    k. ryo⌐koo-suru koto˥ ni si┌ma┤sita
    l. i⌐tta mono˥ desu
    m. Ni⌐ho˥ñ ni tuite
    n. de⌐ki˥nai ┌wa┤ke zya ┌na┤i
    o. ku˥ru ta┌bi┤ ni

Lesson 33. House Repairs

BASIC DIALOGUES: FOR MEMORIZATION

(a)

Mr. Smith

specialty

señmoñ

specialist <u>or</u> expert

se⌐ñmoñ no hito⌐

isn't so much that
[someone] hires (lit.
isn't the extent of
hiring)

ta⌐no⌐mu hodo zya ˥na˦i

1. It's not worth hiring an expert, but I do have all kinds of work that I can't do by myself.

Se⌐ñmoñ no hito⌐ (o) ta⌐no⌐mu hodo zya ˥na˦i keredo, zi⌐buñ zya deki⌐nai sigoto (g̃a) i⌐roiro a⌐ru ñ desu.

for example

ta⌐to⌐eba

shelf

tana

suspend <u>or</u> hang by a
string

turu /-u/

move [something]

u⌐g̃oka⌐su /-u /

a grass <u>or</u> weed

ku⌐sa⌐

weed a garden (lit. remove garden weeds)

ni⌐wa no kusa⌐ o ⌐to⌐ru

do such things as suspending, moving,
weeding

tu⌐tta⌐ri u⌐g̃oka⌐sitari
⌐to⌐ttari suru

2. For example, they're (lit. being) things like putting up shelves, moving heavy furniture, weeding the garden . . .

Ta⌐to⌐eba; ta⌐na (o) tutta⌐ri, o⌐moi ka⌐g̃u (o) u⌐g̃oka⌐sitari, ni⌐wa no kusa⌐ (o) ⌐to⌐ttari su⌐ru yo˦o na ko⌐to˦ de—

Tanaka

handyman

beñriya

3. Then you should call in a handyman.

Zya⌐a, be⌐ñriya (o) yoñda⌐ra ˥i˦i desyoo.

Mr. Smith

what?

e?

business <u>or</u> occupation

syo⌐obai

4. What? Handyman? Is there such a business?

E? Beñriya? So⌐ñna syo⌐obai (g̃a) ⌐a⌐ru ñ desu ka˩

270

Tanaka

so-and-so	na⌐ninani
service	sa⌐abisu
so-and-so service	na⌐ninani-sa⌐abisu
with the name "So-and-so Service"	na⌐ninani-sa⌐abisu tte iu namae de
do	yaru /-u/
[someone] does for you [1]	yatte kureru

5. Yes. Nowadays there are places of business with the name "So-and-so Service" that do everything for you.

E⌐e. Kono-ḡoro, na⌐ninani-sa⌐a-bisu tte iu namae de, na⌐n̄ de⌐ mo ya⌐tte kureru mise⌐ ḡa ⌐a⌐ru n̄ desu yo⌋

Mr. Smith

6. Really? or You don't say! or No kidding!

Hee?

Tanaka

things that are impossible except for (lit. unless it is) an expert	se⌐n̄mon̄ no hito⌐ zya ⌐na⌐kereba de⌐ki⌐nai koto
suitable or appropriate	tekitoo /na/
[someone] makes con-tact for you [1]	ren̄raku-site kureru
way or manner	to⌐ori
like its name or in accordance with its name	na⌐mae no to⌐ori

7. Of course, [for] things that can't be done except by an expert, they put you in touch with a suitable place in each case, so like their name, they are handy.

Mo⌐ti⌐ron̄, se⌐n̄mon̄ no hito⌐ zya ⌐na⌐kereba de⌐ki⌐nai koto wa, so⌐re⌐zore te⌐kitoo na tokoro⌐ e re⌐n̄raku-site kureru⌐ kara; na⌐mae no to⌐ori ⌐be⌐n̄ri desu yo⌋

(b)

(A man from Chiyoda Service comes to see Mr. and Mrs. Smith)

Man

Chiyoda Service	Ti⌐yoda-sa⌐abisu
person	mo⌐no⌐ ↓

8. I'm (a person) from Chiyoda Service. I've come to in-quire about what you want done.

Ti⌐yoda-sa⌐abisu no mo⌐no⌐ de gozaimasu ḡa, go⌐yo⌐o (o) u⌐ka-ḡai ni mairima⌐sita.

Mr. Smith

a good deal or a good many	daibu

---

[1] 'You' here may refer literally to the person addressed, or it may mean 'you' in the indefinite sense of 'one' or 'anyone.'

	one thing at a time	hi⌐to-tu-zu⌝tu
9.	Oh, there are a good many things that I want to have done so I'll explain them one at a time.	A⌝a, ya⌐tte moraitai koto⌝ (ḡa) da⌐ibu a⌝ru kara, hi⌐to-tu-zu⌝tu se⌐tumee-simasyo⌝o.

Man

10.	Certainly.	Ha⌝a ⌐ha⌝a.

Mr. Smith (pointing to fusuma)

	tear [something]	ya⌐bu⌝ku /-u/
	hole	a⌐na⌝
11.	We've torn the fusuma so I'd like to have the holes re-paired.	Hu⌐suma (o) yabu⌝ite si⌐matta⌐ kara, tyo⌝tto a⌐na⌝ (o) na⌐o⌐site mo⌐raita⌐i ñ desu.

Man

	cause to repair	na⌐osase⌝ru /-ru/
	make someone repair	da⌝re ka ni na⌐osase⌝ru
12.	Certainly. This I'll have someone repair right away.	Ha⌝a ⌐ha⌝a. Kore wa ⌐sūḡu ⌐da⌝re ka ni na⌐osasema⌝su.

Mr. Smith (pointing to a chair)

	screw	ne⌝zi
	come off <u>or</u> come out <u>or</u> be taken	to⌐re⌝ru /-ru/
13.	Next—the screws of this chair have come out too so . . .	Sore kara ne? Ko⌐no isu no ne⌝zi mo ⌐to⌐rete si⌐matta⌐ kara—

Man

14.	Oh, this is simple.	A⌝a, ko⌐re wa kañtañ de gozai-ma⌝su.

15.	I'll bring some new screws.	A⌐tarasi⌐i ⌐ne⌝zi (o) mo⌐tte mairima⌐su.

Mr. Smith

	chimney	eñtotu
	become blocked <u>or</u> clogged	tu⌐ma⌝ru /-u/
	before it gets clogged (lit. in the non-clogged interval)	tu⌐mara⌝nai uti ni
	cause to clean	soozi-saseru /-ru/
16.	And the chimney—before it gets clogged would you have [someone] clean it (for me)?	Eñtotu mo, tu⌐mara⌝nai uti ni so⌐ozi-sasete kuremase⌝ñ ka⌟
	when it is after clogging	tu⌐ma⌝tte kara da to
17.	Because it's awful, (when it is) after it's clogged . . .	Tu⌐ma⌝tte kara da to, ta⌐iheñ de⌝su kara⌟

Man

18. Yes. Certainly.   Ha⌐a ⌐ha⌐a. Ka⌐sikomarima⌐sita.

Mr. Smith

      care or repair (noun)   te⌐ire⌐
      care for or repair (verb)   te⌐ire⌐ o suru
19. I guess I'll have the garden   Ni⌐wa no teire⌐ mo si⌐te morai-
    taken care of, too.   masyo⌐o.

      lawn   siba
      circumference   mawari
      around the fence   ka⌐ki⌐ne no mawari ni
      plant (verb)   ueru /-ru/
      [do things like] clipping   ka⌐tta⌐ri u⌐eta⌐ri
        and planting
20. Cutting the lawn, planting   Si⌐ba (o) katta⌐ri, ka⌐ki⌐ne no
    some trees around the fence . . .   mawari ni ⌐ki⌐ (o) u⌐eta⌐ri—

Man

21. Yes, certainly.   Ha⌐a, syo⌐oti-itasima⌐sita.

      gardener   uekiya
      within the morning   asa no uti /ni/
      cause to visit   ukaḡawaseru /-ru/
22. There's a good gardener [I   I⌐i u⌐ekiya (ḡa) orima⌐su kara,
    know] so I'll have him come   asita a⌐sa no uti /ni/ ukaḡawa-
    and see you tomorrow, during   semasyo⌐o.
    the morning.

(c)

Mrs. Smith

    curtain   ka⌐ateñ
23. Say! I'd like to have this   Ano ne! Ko⌐no ki⌐zi (o) so⌐ko
    material made into curtains   no ka⌐ateñ ni si⌐te moraita⌐i
    for [over] there. Do you   ñ desu kedo, ta⌐riru⌐ desyoo ka.
    think it's enough?

Man

    isn't any insufficiency   ta⌐rinai koto⌐ wa ⌐na⌐i
    back or lining or   u⌐ra⌐
      wrong side
    when [someone] doesn't   tu⌐ke⌐nai to
      attach
24. Yes, it's enough all right,   Ha⌐a. Ta⌐rinai koto⌐ wa go⌐zai-
    but I don't think it looks right   mase⌐ñ ḡa; u⌐ra⌐ (o) tu⌐ke⌐nai
    without a lining (lit. I think   to, gu⌐ai ḡa waru⌐i to omoimasu.
    the condition is bad when you
    don't attach a lining.)

Mrs. Smith

oh!   a⌐ra ¹

25. Oh, really? Well then, make   A⌐ra, soᐟo? Zyaᐟa, u⌐raᐟ (o) tu-
    (lit. attach) a lining, would   ⌐keᐧte ne?
    you?

        whenever it falls   huᐟru to
        leak (verb)   moᐟru /-u/
        maid's room   zyotyuubeya

26. Also, I hear that the rain   Sore kara; hiᐟdoku ⌐huᐧru to,
    leaks in whenever it rains   aᐟme ḡa ⌐moᐟru soo desu kara;
    hard, so please look at the   zyo⌐tyuubeya no yaᐟne mo ⌐miᐧte
    roof of the maid's room too,   kudasai ne?
    would you?

Mr. Smith (to Mrs. Smith)

27. Oh, there's still [more to be   A. Maᐟda ⌐aᐧru ne?
    done], isn't there?

        smell or odor   ni⌐oᐟi
        have an odor   ni⌐oᐟi ḡa suru
        box for refuse   gomibako
        lid or cover   huta

28. Let's have the lid of the rub-   Heᐟñ na ni⌐oᐟi ḡa su⌐ruᐧ kara,
    bish box (ex)changed because   go⌐mibako no huta (o) torikaete
    it has a strange smell.   moraoᐟo.

Mrs. Smith

29. That's right. We must have   Soᐟo desu ⌐neᐧe. Na⌐rubeku haᐟ-
    that done as quickly as pos-   yaku si⌐te morawanaᐧkereba_
    sible.

Mr. Smith (to man from Chiyoda Service)

        for the most part or by   daitai
          and large or generally
        estimate   mitumori
        rough estimate   daitai no mitumori
        cause to know or let   siraseru /-ru/
          [someone] know

30. Please let me know your rough   A⌐sita no bañ maᐟde ni da⌐ritai
    estimate by tomorrow night.   no mitumori (o) sirasete kudasaᐟi.

        on the basis of that   so⌐no ueᐟ de

31. Let's talk things over again on   So⌐no ueᐟ de maᐟta soodañ-sima-
    the basis of that.   syoᐧo.

Man

32. Certainly.   Haᐟa, syo⌐oti-itasimaᐟsita.

_____

¹ Woman's exclamation of surprise.

Mrs. Smith

feed <u>or</u> cause to eat
ta⌐besase⌐ru /-ru/

33. At noon I'll feed the gardener
so... (Lit. As for the gardener's noontime, I on my
part will feed him so...)
U⌐ekiya no ohi⌐ru wa ko⌐tira de
tabesasema⌐su kara—

Man

cause to have
mo⌐tase⌐ru /-ru/

send here <u>or</u> hand over
to speaker
yo⌐ko⌐su /-u/

send here with a lunch
be⌐ñto⌐o o mo⌐ta⌐sete yo-
⌐ko⌐su

cause to drink <u>or</u> let
[someone] drink
no⌐mase⌐ru /-ru/

would you make <u>or</u> let
[someone] drink?
(lit. can't I receive
your causing [someone]
to drink?)
no⌐ma⌐sete i⌐tadakemase⌐ñ
ka

34. No, no! I'll send him here
with his lunch so would you
give him (lit. let him drink)
just tea?
Iie iie. Be⌐ñto⌐o (o) mo⌐ta⌐sete
yo⌐kosima⌐su kara, o⌐tya dake
noma⌐sete i⌐tadakemase⌐ñ ka—

ADDITIONAL VOCABULARY

1. In repairing that you need a
<u>stick</u>.
A⌐re o nao⌐su no ni wa, <u>bo⌐o</u>
ḡa irima⌐su yo—

board	i⌐ta
ladder	hasiḡo
rope	na⌐wa⌐
hammer	ka⌐nazu⌐ti
hatchet <u>or</u> ax	o⌐no
pliers	pe⌐ñti <u>or</u> yattoko
saw	no⌐koḡiri⌐
screwdriver	ne⌐zima⌐wasi
nail	kuḡi
tool	do⌐oḡu⌐

2. This kind of thing is made of
<u>wood</u>.
Ko⌐o iu mono⌐ wa ⌐ki⌐ de tuku-
rimasu.

brick	re⌐ñḡa
tile	ta⌐iru
sand	suna
dirt	tu⌐ti⌐
gravel	zyari

3. Please put this in the <u>closet</u>.   Kore (o) o⌐siire ni irete kudasa⌐i.

       storeroom   mo⌐nooki¬
       storehouse <u>or</u> godown   ku⌐ra¬

4. When [you] <u>pull</u> [it] there's   Hi⌐ku to koma⌐ru kara, ki⌐otuke⌐te.
    trouble so be careful.

[you] push [it]	osu /-u/	T [1]
[you] raise [it]	aḡeru /-ru/	T
[you] lower [it]	sa⌐ḡe⌐ru /-ru/	T
[you] bend [it]	maḡeru /-ru/	T
[you] turn [it] <u>or</u> send [it] around	mawasu /-u/	T
[it] goes around	mawaru /-u/	I [1]
[you] drop [it]	o⌐to⌐su /-u/	T
[it] falls <u>or</u> drops	o⌐ti⌐ru /-ru/	I
[you] throw [it] down <u>or</u> knock [it] down	ta⌐o⌐su /-u/	T
[it] falls over <u>or</u> collapses	ta⌐ore⌐ru /-ru/	I
[you] pick [it] <u>up</u>	hirou /-u/	T
[you] lift [it]	mo⌐tiaḡe⌐ru /-ru/	T
[you] grasp [it]	niḡiru /-u/	T
[you] hit <u>or</u> strike [it]	u⌐tu /-u/	T
[you] mix [it]	ma⌐ze⌐ru /-ru/	T
[it] mixes <u>or</u> mingles	ma⌐zi⌐ru /-u/	I
[you] tie <u>or</u> bind [it]	si⌐ba⌐ru /-u/	T
[you] let [it] go <u>or</u> set [it] free	ha⌐na⌐su /-u/	T
[it] separates <u>or</u> parts (from) <u>or</u> falls apart	ha⌐nare⌐ru /-ru/	I

NOTES ON THE BASIC DIALOGUES

1. <u>Zya</u> is the contracted equivalent of <u>de wa</u>: zi⌐buñ zya deki⌐nai siḡoto
'work which by myself I can't do.'

2. Ta⌐to⌐eba is the provisional of a verbal ta⌐toe⌐ru /-<u>ru</u>/ 'give an example'
or 'illustrate.'
U⌐ḡoka⌐su is the transitive partner of intransitive u⌐ḡo⌐ku /-<u>u</u>/ '[some-
thing] moves.'

5. Na⌐ninani: note also da⌐redare 'so-and-so (a person)' and do⌐kodoko
'such-and-such a place.'
<u>Kureru</u> 'give' occurs with these three meanings: (a) 'someone gives
to me'; (b) 'someone else gives to you'; and (c) 'someone gives to
someone undefined'—cf. Lesson 17, Grammatical Note 1.
<u>Yaru</u> 'do' is a less formal word than <u>suru</u>. The two verbals are often
interchangeable, but <u>yaru</u> does not occur in compounds like beñkyoo-
<u>suru</u>, <u>kekkoñ-suru</u>, etc.

---

[1] T = transitive; I = intransitive.

7. Yo⌐o means 'way' or 'manner' with emphasis on resemblance, but to⌐-ori means 'way' or 'manner' in the sense of accordance or agreement.

>   Compare: Ya⌐kusoku no yo⌐o desu. 'It's like (i. e. resembles) a promise.' and: Ya⌐kusoku no to⌐ori desu. 'It's as [someone] promised,' 'It's in accordance with a promise.' To⌐ori usually occurs without a following particle when it modifies an inflected word or phrase.

8. Note the polite style of speech used by a beñriya in addressing his prospective employer.

11. Ya⌐bu⌐ku: another transitive verbal meaning 'tear [something]' is ya⌐bu⌐ru /-u/. The intransitive partner is ya⌐bure⌐ru /-ru/ '[something] tears.'
    Note the combinations a⌐na⌐ o akeru 'make a hole' and a⌐na⌐ ḡa aku 'get a hole [in something].'

12. Kore wa 'this — in comparison with other jobs.'

13. To⌐re⌐ru is the intransitive partner of transitive to⌐ru 'take' or 'take away.'

16. The transitive partner of intransitive tu⌐ma⌐ru is tu⌐me⌐ru /-ru/ 'cram' or 'stuff' or 'stop up.'

24. The opposite of u⌐ra⌐ is o⌐mote⌐ 'front surface' or 'outside' or 'right side.'

26. Note: ya⌐ne ḡa ⌐mo⌐ru 'the roof leaks'; ḡa⌐su ḡa ⌐mo⌐ru 'gas escapes'; ya⌐ne kara ⌐a⌐me ḡa ⌐mo⌐ru 'the roof leaks rain.'

28. With ni⌐o⌐i ḡa suru, compare azi ḡa suru 'have a flavor.' Note the combinations huta o suru 'put a lid on' and X no huta o suru 'put a lid on X.'

29. Lit. 'Unless we have that done as quickly as possible, [it won't do].'

34. Yo⌐ko⌐su refers to the sending of people or things to the place where the speaker now is.

Additional Vocabulary, 4. The intransitive partner of transitive aḡeru is aḡaru /-u/ 'go up' (Lesson 18); of transitive sa⌐ḡe⌐ru, sa⌐ḡa⌐ru /-u/ 'go down'; and of transitive maḡeru, maḡaru /-u/ 'make a turn' (Lesson 7).

GRAMMATICAL NOTES

1. The Causative

Ta⌐besase⌐ru		ta⌐be⌐ru 'eat.'
Na⌐osase⌐ru		na⌐o⌐su 'repair.'
Ukaḡawaseru		ukaḡau 'visit.'
Siraseru	is the CAUSATIVE of	siru 'come to know.'
Mo⌐tase⌐ru		mo⌐tu 'have.'
No⌐mase⌐ru		no⌐mu 'drink.'
Soozi-saseru		soozi-suru 'clean.'

Most verbals have corresponding CAUSATIVE verbals meaning 'cause [someone] to do so-and-so' or 'make [someone] do so-and-so' or, in some circumstances, 'let [someone] do so-and-so.'

An informal non-past causative is accented if the verbal from which it is derived is accented, and the accent occurs on the next-to-last syllable. To form the causative:

<table>
<tr><td>-ru verbals:</td><td>substitute -sase-ru for the final -ru of the informal non-past (the citation form)</td></tr>
<tr><td></td><td>Example: akeru 'open': akesaseru 'make [someone] open'</td></tr>
<tr><td>-u verbals:</td><td>substitute -ase-ru for the final -u of the informal non-past; when the informal non-past ends in two vowels, substitute -wase-ru for the final -u</td></tr>
<tr><td></td><td>Examples: ka'ku 'write': ka⌐kase⌐ru 'make [someone] write'
tukau 'use': tukawaseru 'make [someone] use'</td></tr>
<tr><td>-aru verbals:</td><td>causative does not occur</td></tr>
<tr><td>Irregular verbals:</td><td>ku'ru 'come': ko⌐sase'ru 'make [someone] come'
suru 'do': saseru 'make [someone] do'</td></tr>
</table>

All causatives are themselves verbals of the -ru group. Thus, the causative of akeru has such forms as:

Informal non-past:	akesaseru
Stem:	akesase
Informal past:	akesaseta
Gerund:	akesasete
Conditional:	a⌐kesaseta'ra
Provisional:	a⌐kesasere'ba

The person acted upon (i.e. made to do something) is usually followed by particle ni:

U⌐nte'nsyu ni ku⌐ruma o miḡakasema'sita. 'I made the driver polish the car.'

However, with some causatives based on intransitive verbals—namely, those that never occur with direct object particle o—the person made to do something is followed by particle ni or o:

Ta'roo ni i⌐kasema'sita.
    or   'I made Taro go.'
Ta'roo (o) i⌐kasema'sita.

But with a few causatives, the person made to do something is followed by o but not ni:

U⌐ti no zyotyuu (o) yamesasema'sita. 'I fired our maid.' (Lit. 'I caused our maid to quit.')

The causative is sometimes equivalent to 'let [someone] do so-and-so,' particularly when a causative gerund is followed by a verbal of giving or receiving. Thus:

Yo⌐ma¬sete kudasai. 'Please let me read [it].'

Tu⌐kawasete kurema¬sita. '[He] let me use [it].' (Lit. '[He] gave me letting [me] use.')

Ha⌐ikeñ-sasete itadakima¬su. '(Lit.) I accept your letting me look.' (Said by a person about to look at something he has been given permission to see.)

Ka⌐era¬sete i⌐tadakemase¬ñ ka⌐ 'May I go home?' or 'Would you let me go home?' (Lit. 'Can't I receive your letting me go home?')

The latter sentence is an extremely polite way of asking permission.

However, depending on context, a causative in combination with a word of giving or receiving may still mean 'make [someone] do so-and-so.' For example, the first sentence of the preceding group may also mean 'Please make [someone] read [it].'

In some contexts, a causative which is not followed by a word of giving or receiving is equivalent to 'let [someone] do so-and-so.' For example:

Kodomo o ni⌐wa de asobasema¬sita. 'He let the children play in the garden.'

Tu⌐kawasete¬ wa i⌐kemase¬ñ. 'You mustn't let [them] use [it].'

Be sure to distinguish among the following three kinds of examples:

(a) I⌐kasema¬sita. 'I had [him] go.'
(b) I⌐tte moraima¬sita. 'I had [him] go.'
(c) I⌐kasete moraima¬sita. '[He] let me go.' or 'I had [him] have [someone] go.'

Sentence (a) implies that he went because I told him to. Other English equivalents would be 'I made him go' and 'I let him go.' Sentence (b) states that 'I received his going'—that is, 'he went for me.' There is no indication in the Japanese whether or not he was told to go; the sentence tells only what was done for me. Sentence (c) also tells what I received: depending on context, either permission to go, or the causing of someone else to go.

The causative and representative may occur together in either one of two ways:

(a) causative representative verbal(s) + √<u>suru</u>
   or
(b) non-causative representative verbal(s) + √<u>saseru</u>

Example:

ma⌐do o a⌐kesaseta¬ri si⌐mesa¬setari suru 'make [someone]
   or   keep opening and
ma⌐do o a⌐keta¬ri ⌐si¬metari saseru   shutting the window'

Additional examples:

Zyotyuu ni syo⌐kuzi no sitaku o sasema¬sita.
   'I had the maid get dinner ready.'

Kodomo ni ⌐gohañ o ta⌐besase¬nakereba na⌐ra¬nai kara, si⌐tu¬ree-simasu.
   'I must feed the children so please excuse me.'

Naǹ-do mo ka⌐ka¬seta ñ desu ḡa, ma¬da ⌐yo¬ku o⌐boe¬nai yoo desu.
  'I made him write it any number of times, but he doesn't seem to
  have learned it yet.'
Sono a⌐tarasi¬i zyotyuu wa ze⌐ñzeñ deki¬nakatta kara, mo⌐o ya⌐mesa-
  sema¬sita.
  'That new maid couldn't do anything so I've fired her (lit. made her
  quit) already.'
U⌐ñte⌐ñsyu o ⌐ma¬initi kosasemasu.
  'I have the driver come every day.'
A⌐buna¬i kara, ti⌐isa¬i ko ni ⌐ma¬tti o mo⌐ta¬sete wa i⌐kemase¬ñ yo.
  'You mustn't let small children have matches, because it's danger-
  ous.'
I⌐itai koto¬ ḡa ⌐a¬ru kara, wa⌐takusi ni¬ mo i⌐wasete moraita¬i ñ de-
  su.
  'There are things I'd like to say so I want you to let me speak, too.'
Wa⌐takusi ni¬ mo ko⌐no deñwa o tukawasete kuremase¬ñ ka↲
  'Would you let me use this phone, too?'
O⌐kusama, tyo¬tto gu⌐ai ḡa wa⌐ruku na⌐rima¬sita kara, ka⌐era¬sete i⌐ta-
  dakemase⌐ñ ka↲
  'Madam, I don't feel well, so may I go home?'
A⌐buna¬i kara, i⌐so¬ide na⌐osa¬sete kudasai.
  'It's dangerous so please have [someone] fix it in a hurry.'

2. Particle _to_ 'with' Following Inflected Words

Particle _to_ 'with' has previously occurred following nominals: for example, to⌐modati to hana¬sita 'I talked with a friend.'

Particle _to_ may also follow a NON-PAST inflected form—formal or, more
commonly, informal—when one action or state accompanies (or accompanied)
another: X to Y 'with the occurrence of X, Y' or 'when _or_ if X, Y' or
'whenever _or_ if ever X, Y.' Y may be non-past, past, imperative, etc.; it
has no restrictions as to form. Thus:

  Wa⌐ka¬ru to, o⌐mosiro¬i. 'Whenever I understand (lit. with being clear),
    it's interesting.'
  Go¬-zi ni ⌐na¬ru to, de⌐ma¬sita. 'When it got to be 5 o'clock (lit. with
    becoming 5 o'clock), I left.'
  Sa⌐mu¬i to, u⌐ti o demase¬ñ. 'Whenever it's cold (lit. with being cold),
    I don't leave the house.'
  Ki⌐otuke¬nai to, ko⌐warema¬su yo↲ 'If you're not careful (lit. with not
    being careful), it will break!'
  Hima da to, ho¬ñ o yomimasu. 'When I'm free (lit. with being free), I
    read (a book).'

A non-past inflected form + _to_ + _su¬ḡu_ means 'as soon as so-and-so happens _or_ happened' (lit. 'immediately with the occurrence of so-and-so'):

  De¬ñki o kesu to ⌐su¬ḡu ne⌐te simaima¬su. 'As soon as I turn off the
    lights (lit. immediately with turning off the lights), I fall asleep.'
  Byo⌐oki ni na¬ru to ⌐su¬ḡu o⌐isyasañ o yobima¬sita. 'As soon as I got
    sick, I called the doctor.'

Compare and study the following groups of examples:

Past:

    (a) Ma˦do o a˥keta˦ra, sa˦muku na˥rima˦sita. 'When I opened the window, it got cold.'

    (b) Ma˦do o a˥keta toki˦ ni, ko˥tori ḡa ha˦itte ki˥ma˦sita. 'When I opened the window, a bird flew in.'

    (c) Ma˦do o akeru to, ku˥sya˦mi¹ o si˥hazimema˦sita. 'When I opened (lit. with the opening of) the window, I started sneezing.'

Habitual:

    (a) Ma˦do o a˥keru toki˦ ni wa, ki˥otuke˦te kudasai. '(At times) when you open the windows, be careful.'

    (b) Ma˦do o akeru to, so˦to de asonde iru ko˥domo no ko˦e ḡa ⌐yo˥ku kikoemasu. 'When I open (lit. with the opening of) the windows, I can hear the voices of the children playing outside, very clearly.'

Future:

    (a) Ma˦do o a˥kere˦ba, sa˦muku narimasu. 'It will get cold if (i.e. provided) you open the window.'

    (b) Ma˦do o a˥keta˦ra, sa˦muku narimasu. 'If you [should] open the window, it will get cold.'

    (c) Ma˦do o akeru to, sa˦muku na˥rima˦su yo⌐ 'If you open (lit. with the opening of) the window, it will get cold!'

To is also used in expressions indicating 'hope':

    Iru to ⌐i˦i desu ḡa ⌐ne˦e.
      'I hope he's in, don't you.'
    Wa˥ka˦ru to ⌐i˦i desu ḡa ⌐ne˦e.
      'I hope he understands, don't you.'

Additional examples:

    Go-˥zi-suḡi˦ ni ˥na˦ru to, kono miti wa zi˥do˦osya de i˥ppai ni narima˦su.
      'When it gets to be after five, this street becomes filled with cars.'
    O˥mosiro˦i to, yo˦ru o˥soku na˦ru made ⌐ho˦ñ ya za˥ssi o yo˦ñde imasu.
      'When they're interesting, I read (lit. am reading) books and magazines in the evening until it gets late.'
    Wa˥kara˦nai to, wa˥ka˦ru made ˥na˦ñ-do mo se˥ñse˦e ni ki˥kima˦su.
      'Whenever I don't understand, I ask the teacher over and over again, until I do (understand).'
    Ha˦yaku dekakenai to, o˥soku narima˦su yo⌐
      'If you don't start out in a hurry, you'll be late!'
    A˥mai mono˦ da to, i˥kura de˦ mo tabemasu.
      'When it's something sweet, I eat any (large) amount.'
    Te˦ñki no ˥i˦i hi da to, ko˥ko kara de˦ mo ˥Hu˦zisañ ḡa ˥yo˦ku miemasu.
      'When it's a nice day, you can see Fuji very well, even (being) from here.'
    Syokuzi ḡa owaru to ⌐su˦ḡu zi˥mu˦syo e ka˥erima˦sita.
      'As soon as dinner was over, I returned to the office.'

---

¹ Ku˥sya˦mi 'a sneeze'; ku˥sya˦mi o suru 'sneeze (verb).'

3. -zu⌐tu

-Zu⌐tu occurs immediately following numbers and indefinite quantity expressions, meaning 'each' or 'of each' or 'for each' or 'at a time.' Thus,
hi⌐to-tu-zu⌐tu ya⌐rima⌐sita means 'I gave one of each' or 'I gave one for
each [of them]' or 'I gave one at a time.'

Before -zu⌐tu, a word which is normally accented loses its accent.

Examples:

Na⌐ihu to ⌐ho⌐oku to su⌐pu⌐uñ o, i⌐p-poñ-zu⌐tu o⌐tori-kudasa⌐i.
    'Take one each of the knives, forks, and spoons.'
Ma⌐initi nĩhoñḡo to ẽeḡo o ni-⌐zikañ-zu⌐tu beñkyoo-simasu.
    'Every day I study Japanese and English two hours each.'
Wa⌐surenai yo⌐o ni ⌐ma⌐iasa kŭsuri o hi⌐to-tu-zu⌐tu no⌐ma⌐sete kudasai.
    'Don't forget to have him take one of each of the medicines every
        morning.'
Mi⌐na⌐sañ so⌐no kami⌐ o sa⌐ñ-mai-zu⌐tu ⌐to⌐tte kudasai.
    'Everybody, please take three sheets each of that paper.'
Su⌐kosi-zu⌐tu i⌐rete kudasa⌐i.
    'Put in a little at a time.'

4. uti Preceded by Negative

Uti occurs as a time word meaning 'interval' in combinations like wa⌐ka⌐i
uti ni 'in the interval when [someone] is young,' asa no uti ni 'within the
morning,' etc.

Uti is also frequently preceded by a sentence modifier consisting of, or
ending with, a non-past negative. The combination means literally 'the interval during which so-and-so has not happened'—i.e. 'before so-and-so
happens.'

Examples:

Byo⌐oki na⌐ra; hi⌐doku na⌐ra⌐nai uti ni, i⌐sya ni mi⌐te mo⌐rawana⌐ke-
    reba na⌐rimase⌐ñ.
    'If you're sick, you must have the doctor see you before it gets se-
        rious (lit. during the interval when it hasn't become serious).'
O⌐kyakusañ ḡa ko⌐nai uti ni, kodomo ni ⌐go⌐hañ o ta⌐besa⌐sete si⌐ma-
    imasyo⌐o.
    'I guess I'll finish feeding the children before the guests come (lit.
        during the interval when the guests haven't come).'
Deñsya ḡa tomarañai uti ni, o⌐rite wa i⌐kemase⌐ñ.
    'You mustn't get off before the train stops (lit. during the interval
        when the train hasn't stopped).'

5. ——ko⌐to⌐ wa ⌐na⌐i

Ko⌐to⌐ wa √⌐na⌐i preceded by a sentence modifier means 'there isn't any
matter of ——,' 'it isn't that ——.' The sequence is frequently followed by
ḡa or keredo meaning 'but.'

Examples:

I⌐kanai koto⌐ wa a⌐rimase⌐ñ ḡa, i⌐ku⌐ no wa o⌐soku na⌐ru to omoimasu.

      'It isn't that I'm not going, but I think I'll go late (lit. the going will
        be late).'
I⌐kitai koto⌐ wa ⌐na⌐i keredo, i⌐kana⌐kereba na⌐rimase⌐ñ.
      'It isn't that I want to go but I must go.'
O⌐naka ḡa ita⌐i koto wa ⌐na⌐i ñ desu ḡa, tyo⌐tto ⌐he⌐ñ na ñ desu.
      'It isn't that my stomach hurts, but it feels (lit. is) a little strange.'
De⌐ki⌐nai koto wa ⌐na⌐i to omoimasu.
      'I don't think it's impossible.' (Lit. 'I think that there isn't im-
        possibility.')

    In this pattern, the negative following ko⌐to⌐ wa ordinarily has medium-
high [⌐] pitch. Compare:

    i⌐kanai koto⌐ wa ⌐na⌐i 'it isn't that I'm not going'

and:

    i⌐kanai koto⌐ wa ⌐na⌐i 'there's never a time when I don't go'

    The first sequence—ending with ⌐na⌐i—is an example of the pattern de-
scribed in this note, but the second sequence—ending with ⌐na⌐i—is an example of a pattern described in Lesson 31, Grammatical Note 1. The contrast in accents is usual but not invariable.

DRILLS

A. Substitution Drill

      1. I'm (a person) from Chi-   Ti⌐yoda-sa⌐abisu no mo⌐no⌐ de
          yoda Service . . .   gozaimasu ḡa—
      2. I'm (a person) from the   A⌐merika-taisi⌐kañ no mo⌐no⌐ de
          American Embassy . . .   gozaimasu ḡa—
      3. I'm (a person) from the   Ko⌐otuuko⌐osya no mo⌐no⌐ de go-
          JTB . . .   zaimasu ḡa—
      4. I'm (a person) from the   Ho⌐keñḡa⌐isya no mo⌐no⌐ de go-
          insurance company . . .   zaimasu ḡa—
      5. I'm (a person) from the   Mo⌐ñbu⌐syoo no mo⌐no⌐ de gozai-
          Ministry of Education . . .   masu ḡa—
      6. I'm (a person) from the   Ni⌐hoñ-gi⌐ñkoo no mo⌐no⌐ de go-
          Bank of Japan . . .   zaimasu ḡa—
      7. I'm (a person) from the   A⌐sahi-si⌐ñbuñ no mo⌐no⌐ de go-
          Asahi Shimbun . . .   zaimasu ḡa—
      8. I'm (a person) from the   De⌐ñkiḡa⌐isya no mo⌐no⌐ de goza-
          electric company . . .   imasu ḡa—

B. Substitution Drill

      1. I'll send [him] here with   O⌐beñtoo (o) mota⌐sete yokosi-
          his lunch.   masu.
      2. I'll send [him] here with   Mi⌐tumori (o) mota⌐sete yokosi-
          the estimate.   masu.
      3. I'll send [him] here with   A⌐ñnaisyo⌐ (o) mo⌐ta⌐sete yoko-
          a guide book.   simasu.
      4. I'll send [him] here with   Ki⌐ppu (o) mota⌐sete yokosimasu.
          the tickets.

5. I'll send [him] here with the receipt.

U⌐ketori (o) mota⌐sete yokosima-su.

6. I'll send [him] here with a letter.

Te⌐g̃ami (o) mota⌐sete yokosima-su.

7. I'll send [him] here with the money.

O⌐kane (o) mota⌐sete yokosimasu.

8. I'll send [him] here with the key.

Ka⌐g̃i⌐ (o) mo⌐ta⌐sete yokosima-su.

C. Substitution Drill

1. Please pull that rope.

A⌐no nawa⌐ (o) hi⌐ite kudasa⌐i.

2. Please let go that rope. /ha⌐na⌐su/

A⌐no nawa⌐ (o) ha⌐na⌐site kudasai.

3. Please grab that rope. /nig̃iru/

A⌐no nawa⌐ (o) ni⌐g̃itte kudasa⌐i.

4. Please pick up that rope. /hirou/

A⌐no nawa⌐ (o) hi⌐rotte kudasa⌐i.

5. Please lower that rope. /sa⌐g̃e⌐ru/

A⌐no nawa⌐ (o) ⌐sa⌐g̃ete kudasai.

6. Please tie that rope. /si⌐ba⌐ru/

A⌐no nawa⌐ (o) si⌐ba⌐tte kudasai.

7. Please take away that rope. /to⌐ru/

A⌐no nawa⌐ (o) ⌐totte kudasai.

8. Please hold that rope. /mo⌐tu/

A⌐no nawa⌐ (o) ⌐motte kudasai.

9. Please raise that rope. /ag̃eru/

A⌐no nawa⌐ (o) a⌐g̃ete kudasa⌐i.

10. Please drop that rope. /o⌐to⌐su/

A⌐no nawa⌐ (o) o⌐to⌐site kudasai.

11. Please hand over that rope. /watasu/

A⌐no nawa⌐ (o) wa⌐tasite kudasa⌐i.

12. Please lend me that rope. /kasu/

A⌐no nawa⌐ (o) ka⌐site kudasa⌐i.

D. Substitution Drill

1. The <u>carpenter</u> collapsed.

Da⌐iku-sañ g̃a ta⌐orema⌐sita.

2. The <u>carpenter</u> knocked [it] over.

Da⌐iku-sañ g̃a ta⌐osima⌐sita.

3. [He] knocked over the ladder.

Ha⌐sig̃o o taosima⌐sita.

4. [He] stood the ladder up.

Ha⌐sig̃o o tatema⌐sita.

5. <u>I</u> stood [it] up <u>or</u> built [it].

Wa⌐takusi g̃a tatema⌐sita.

6. <u>I</u> stood up.

Wa⌐takusi g̃a tatima⌐sita.

7. I bent [it].

Wa⌐takusi g̃a mag̃ema⌐sita.

8. [I] bent a nail.

Ku⌐g̃i o mag̃ema⌐sita.

9. [I] dropped a nail.

Ku⌐g̃i o otosima⌐sita.

10. The <u>gardener</u> dropped [it].

U⌐ekiya g̃a otosima⌐sita.

E. Substitution Drill

1. I'd like to make this material into curtains . . .

Ko⌐no ki⌐zi (o) ⌐ka⌐ateñ ni si⌐ta⌐i ñ desu g̃a—

2. I'd like to make this room into a study . . .

Ko⌐no <u>heya⌐</u> (o) <u>syo⌐sai</u> ni sita⌐i ñ desu g̃a—

3. I'd like to make this board into a shelf . . .

Ko⌐no <u>i⌐ta</u> (o) <u>ta⌐na</u> ni sita⌐i ñ desu g̃a—

4. I'd like to make this Japanese room into a Western-style room . . .

Ko⌐no <u>zasiki⌐</u> (o) <u>yo⌐oma</u> ni sita⌐i ñ desu g̃a—

5. I'd like to make this house into a school . . .

Kono <u>uti</u> (o) <u>ga⌐kkoo</u> ni sita⌐i ñ desu g̃a—

6. I'd like to make this meat into sukiyaki . . .

Ko⌐no <u>niku⌐</u> (o) <u>su⌐kiyaki</u> ni sita⌐i ñ desu g̃a—

7. I'd like to make this kimono into a dress . . .

Kono <u>kimono</u> (o) <u>wa⌐ñpi⌐isu</u> ni si⌐ta⌐i ñ desu g̃a—

8. I'd like to make this fish into sashimi . . .

Kono <u>sakana</u> (o) <u>o⌐sasimi</u> ni si- ta⌐i ñ desu g̃a—

F. Substitution Drill

1. It doesn't warrant hiring an expert but . . .

Se⌐ñmoñ no hito⌐ (o) ta⌐no⌐mu hodo zya ⌐na⌐i keredo—

2. It doesn't warrant building a new house but . . .

A⌐tarasi⌐i uti (o) ta⌐te⌐ru hodo zya ⌐na⌐i keredo—

3. It doesn't warrant repainting the whole wall but . . .

<u>Kabe (o) ⌐ze⌐ñbu nu⌐rikae⌐ru</u> hodo zya ⌐na⌐i keredo—

4. It doesn't warrant calling a doctor but . . .

<u>O⌐isyasañ (o) yobu</u> hodo zya na⌐i keredo—

5. It doesn't warrant quitting that company but . . .

<u>Ano kaisya (o) ya⌐meru</u> hodo zya na⌐i keredo—

6. It doesn't warrant firing him but . . .

<u>A⌐no⌐ hito (o) ya⌐mesaseru</u> hodo zya na⌐i keredo—

7. It doesn't warrant going all the way back there but . . .

<u>A⌐suko ma⌐de mo⌐do⌐tte iku</u> hodo zya ⌐na⌐i keredo—

8. It doesn't warrant being in bed from morning till night but . . .

<u>A⌐sa kara ba⌐ñ ma⌐de ne⌐te (i)ru</u> hodo zya na⌐i keredo—

G. Substitution Drill

1. They're things like putting up shelves and moving heavy furniture.

Ta⌐na (o) tutta⌐ri, o⌐moi ka⌐g̃u (o) u⌐g̃oka⌐sitari su⌐ru yo⌐o na ko- ⌐to⌐ desu.

2. They're things like planting trees and weeding.
/ki⌐ (o) ueru, ku⌐sa⌐ (o) ⌐to⌐ru/

Ki⌐ (o) u⌐eta⌐ri, ku⌐sa⌐ (o) ⌐to- ttari su⌐ru yo⌐o na ko⌐to⌐ desu.

3. They're things like re-
    pairing old houses and
    putting up new houses.
    /hu⌐ru˺i uti (o) na⌐o˺su,
    a⌐tarasi˺i uti (o) ta⌐te˺-
    ru/

    Hu⌐ru˺i uti (o) na⌐o˺sitari, a⌐tara-
    si˺i uti (o) ⌐ta˺tetari su⌐ru yo˺o
    na ko⌐to˺ desu.

4. They're things like tak-
    ing care of the garden
    and cleaning the house.
    /ni⌐wa no teire˺ (o)
    suru, uti no soozi (o)
    suru/

    Ni⌐wa no teire˺ (o) si⌐ta˺ri, u⌐ti
    no soozi (o) sita⌐ri su⌐ru yo˺o
    na ko⌐to˺ desu.

5. They're things like see-
    ing the sights and buy-
    ing souvenirs. /keñbutu-
    suru, omiyaḡe (o) kau/

    Ke⌐ñbutu-sita˺ri, o⌐miyaḡe (o) ka-
    tta˺ri su⌐ru yo˺o na ko⌐to˺ desu.

6. They're things like tak-
    ing walks and going fish-
    ing. /sañpo-suru, turi
    ni iku/

    Sa⌐ñpo-sita˺ri, tu⌐ri ni itta˺ri su⌐ru
    yo˺o na ko⌐to˺ desu.

7. They're things like
    studying the language
    and reading history and
    geography books. /ko-
    ⌐toba˺ (o) beñkyoo-suru,
    re⌐kisi ya ti˺ri no ⌐ho˺ñ
    (o) ⌐yo˺mu/

    Ko⌐toba˺ (o) be⌐ñkyoo-sita˺ri, re-
    ⌐kisi ya ti˺ri no ⌐ho˺ñ (o) ⌐yo˺ñ-
    dari su⌐ru yo˺o na ko⌐to˺ desu.

8. They're things like read-
    ing advertisements and
    telephoning agents.
    /ko⌐okɔku (o) yo˺mu, bu-
    ⌐ro˺okaa ni deñwa-suru/

    Ko⌐okoku (o) yo⌐ñdari, bu⌐ro˺okaa
    ni de⌐ñwa-sita˺ri su⌐ru yo˺o na
    ko⌐to˺ desu.

H. Substitution Drill

    (Add <u>no</u> following the substitution item, as required.)

1. It's like its name.   Na⌐mae no to˺ori desu.
2. It's as I said.   I⌐tta to˺ori desu.
3. It's as you said.   O⌐ssya˺tta ⌐to˺ori desu.
4. It's as I explained.   Se⌐tumee-sita to˺ori desu.
5. It's as you know.   Go⌐zo˺ñzi no ⌐to˺ori desu.
6. It's as I promised.   Ya⌐kusoku no to˺ori desu.
7. It's as you ordered.   Go⌐tyuumoñ no to˺ori desu.
8. It's as I thought.   O⌐mo˺tta ⌐to˺ori desu.
9. It's like always.   I⌐tu mo no ⌐to˺ori desu.

I. Response Drill (based on Grammatical Note 5)

        Tutor: Si⌐mase˺ñ ka↲ /mo⌐ñdai ḡa a˺ru/ 'Aren't you going to
                do it? /there are problems/'

Student: Si⌐nai koto⌐ wa ⌐na⌐i ñ desu ḡa, mo⌐ñdai ḡa a⌐ru ñ desu.
'It isn't that I'm not going to do it, but there are problems.'

1. Ta⌐rimase⌐ñ ka⌐ /gu⌐ai   Ta⌐rinai koto⌐ wa ⌐na⌐i ñ desu
   ḡa waru⌐i/   ḡa, gu⌐ai ḡa waru⌐i ñ desu.

2. Wa⌐karimase⌐ñ ka⌐   Wa⌐kara⌐nai koto wa ⌐na⌐i ñ desu
   /o⌐mosi⌐roku ⌐na⌐i/   ḡa, o⌐mosi⌐roku ⌐na⌐i ñ desu.

3. Ki⌐koemase⌐ñ ka⌐ /wa-   Ki⌐koenai koto⌐ wa ⌐na⌐i ñ desu
   ⌐kara⌐nai/   ḡa, wa⌐kara⌐nai ñ desu.

4. Mi⌐emase⌐ñ ka⌐ /yo⌐me-   Mi⌐e⌐nai koto wa ⌐na⌐i ñ desu
   nai/   ḡa, yo⌐me⌐nai ñ desu.

5. I⌐karemase⌐ñ ka⌐ /i⌐ki-   I⌐karenai koto⌐ wa ⌐na⌐i ñ desu
   taku na⌐i/   ḡa, i⌐kitaku na⌐i ñ desu.

6. Si⌐rimase⌐ñ ka⌐ /su⌐ki⌐   Si⌐ranai koto⌐ wa ⌐na⌐i ñ desu ḡa,
   zya ⌐na⌐i/   su⌐ki⌐ zya ⌐na⌐i ñ desu.

7. De⌐kimase⌐ñ ka⌐ /si⌐ta-   De⌐ki⌐nai koto wa ⌐na⌐i ñ desu
   ku na⌐i/   ḡa, si⌐taku na⌐i ñ desu.

J. Substitution Drill (based on Grammatical Note 4)

1. Before the chimney gets   E⌐ñtotu ḡa tumara⌐nai uti ni, na-
   clogged (lit. in the non-   ⌐osimasyo⌐o.
   clogged interval), let's
   fix it.

2. Before the nails come   Ku⌐ḡi ḡa tore⌐nai uti ni, na⌐osi-
   out, let's fix it.   masyo⌐o.

3. Before the handyman   Be⌐ñriya ḡa ko⌐nai uti ni, na⌐osi-
   comes, let's fix it.   masyo⌐o.

4. Before it goes bad, let's   Da⌐me⌐ ni na⌐ra⌐nai uti ni, na⌐osi-
   fix it.   masyo⌐o.

5. Before it breaks, let's   Ko⌐ware⌐nai uti ni, na⌐osimasyo⌐o.
   fix it.

6. Before the children wake   Ko⌐domo ḡa oki⌐nai uti ni, na⌐osi-
   up, let's fix it.   masyo⌐o.

7. Before it collapses, let's   Ta⌐ore⌐nai uti ni, na⌐osimasyo⌐o.
   fix it.

8. Before it falls, let's fix   O⌐ti⌐nai uti ni, na⌐osimasyo⌐o.
   it.

9. Before it falls apart,   Ha⌐nare⌐nai uti ni, na⌐osimasyo⌐o.
   let's fix it.

10. Before the secretary   Hi⌐syo⌐ ḡa ka⌐era⌐nai uti ni, na-
    goes home, let's fix it.   ⌐osimasyo⌐o.

K. Substitution Drill (based on Grammatical Note 2)

1. When it rains hard, it   Hi⌐doku ⌐hu⌐ru to, a⌐me ḡa ⌐mo⌐ru
   leaks.   ñ desu.

2. When I move heavy fur-   O⌐moi ka⌐ḡu (o) u⌐ḡoka⌐su to, se-
   niture, my back hurts.   ⌐naka ḡa i⌐taku ⌐na⌐ru ñ desu.
   /o⌐moi ka⌐ḡu (o) u⌐ḡo-
   ka⌐su, se⌐naka ḡa i⌐taku
   ⌐na⌐ru/

3. When I break something,   Na⌐ni ka ko⌐wa⌐su to, na⌐o⌐site
   I have it fixed. /na⌐ni   mo⌐rau⌐ n̄ desu.
   ka ko⌐wa⌐su, na⌐o⌐site
   morau/

4. When I have time, I   Hima da to, hi⌐rune (o) suru⌐ n̄
   take a nap. /hima da,   desu.
   hirune (o) suru/

5. When I don't understand,   Wa⌐kara⌐nai to, se⌐n̄se⌐e ni ki-
   I ask the teacher. /wa-   ⌐ku⌐ n̄ desu.
   ⌐kara⌐nai, se⌐n̄se⌐e ni
   kiku/

6. When it's cold, I don't   Sa⌐mu⌐i to, de⌐kakena⌐i n̄ desu.
   go out. /sa⌐mu⌐i, de-
   kakenai/

7. When I drink, I don't   O⌐sake (o) no⌐mu to, gu⌐ai ḡa
   feel well. /o⌐sake (o)   wa⌐ruku ⌐na⌐ru n̄ desu.
   no⌐mu, gu⌐ai ḡa wa⌐ruku
   ⌐na⌐ru/

L. Grammar Drill (based on Grammatical Note 1)

        Tutor: Si⌐ma⌐sita. /da⌐re ka/ 'I did it. /someone/'
        Student: Da⌐re ka ni sa⌐sema⌐sita. 'I had someone do it.'

1. Ta⌐na (o) turima⌐sita.   Da⌐iku ni ta⌐na (o) turasema⌐-
   /da⌐iku/   sita.

2. Ki⌐ (o) u⌐ema⌐sita.   Uekiya ni ⌐ki⌐ (o) u⌐esasema⌐-
   /uekiya/   sita.

3. Na⌐ḡaku ma⌐tima⌐sita.   Ya⌐nusi ni ⌐na⌐ḡaku ma⌐tasema⌐-
   /ya⌐nusi/   sita.

4. Hu⌐de de kakima⌐sita.   Se⌐eto ni hu⌐de de kakasema⌐-
   /se⌐eto/   sita.

5. Ku⌐ruma (o) miḡakima⌐-   U⌐n̄te⌐n̄syu ni ku⌐ruma (o) miḡa-
   sita. /u⌐n̄te⌐n̄syu/   kasema⌐sita.

6. Syo⌐kuzi no sitaku (o)   Zyotyuu ni syo⌐kuzi no sitaku
   sima⌐sita. /zyotyuu/   (o) sasema⌐sita.

7. Mo⌐nooki⌐ no ka⌐ḡi⌐ (o)   Ka⌐nai ni mo⌐nooki⌐ no ka⌐ḡi⌐
   ka⌐kema⌐sita. /ka⌐nai/   (o) ka⌐kesasema⌐sita.

8. Ni⌐hon̄ḡo de hanasima⌐-   A⌐no⌐ hito ni ni⌐hon̄ḡo de hana-
   sita. /a⌐no⌐ hito/   sasema⌐sita.

9. A⌐sa ⌐ha⌐yaku ki⌐ma⌐sita.   Hi⌐syo⌐ ni ⌐a⌐sa ⌐ha⌐yaku ko⌐sa-
   /hi⌐syo⌐/   sema⌐sita.

10. Ki⌐mono (o) kima⌐sita.   Kodomo ni ki⌐mono o kisasema⌐-
    /kodomo/   sita.

11. U⌐suku kirima⌐sita.   Ni⌐ku⌐ya ni u⌐suku kirasema⌐-
    /ni⌐ku⌐ya/   sita.

12. Ze⌐n̄bu ki⌐kima⌐sita.   Tomodati ni ⌐ze⌐n̄bu ki⌐kasema⌐-
    /tomodati/   sita.

    a. For each of the causative sentences in the above exercise, give
        the corresponding sentence using a gerund + morau.

Example:

Tutor: A⌐no¬ hito ni sa⌐sema¬sita   'I had him do it.'
Student: A⌐no¬ hito ni si⌐te moraima¬sita. 'I had it done by him.' or 'He did it for me.'

M. Completion Drill (based on Grammatical Note 1)

Tutor: Si⌐ta¬katta n̄ desu ḡa, 'I wanted to do it but —'
Student: a⌐no¬ hito wa sa⌐sete kuremase¬n̄ desita. 'he didn't let me (do).'

1. Ka¬ḡu (o) u⌐ḡokasita¬katta n̄ desu ḡa,
   a⌐no¬ hito wa u⌐ḡokasa¬sete ku⌐mase⌐n̄ desita.

2. Ryo⌐koo-sita¬katta n̄ desu ḡa,
   a⌐no¬ hito wa ryo⌐koo-sasete ku-remase¬n̄ desita.

3. Siḡoto (o) tu⌐zuketa¬katta n̄ desu ḡa,
   a⌐no¬ hito wa tu⌐zukesasete kure-mase¬n̄ desita.

4. Eeḡo de i⌐ita¬katta n̄ desu ḡa,
   a⌐no¬ hito wa i⌐wasete kuremase¬n̄ desita.

5. A⌐no dooḡu¬ (o) tu⌐kaita¬-katta n̄ desu ḡa,
   a⌐no¬ hito wa tu⌐kawasete kurema-se¬n̄ desita.

6. Yoohuku (o) ki⌐ta¬katta n̄ desu ḡa,
   a⌐no¬ hito wa ki⌐sasete kurema-se¬n̄ desita.

7. Geta (o) ha⌐kita¬katta n̄ desu ḡa,
   a⌐no¬ hito wa ha⌐kasete kurema-se¬n̄ desita.

8. Osasimi (o) ta⌐beta¬katta n̄ desu ḡa,
   a⌐no¬ hito wa ta⌐besa¬sete ku⌐re-mase⌐n̄ desita.

9. Sono teḡami (o) yo⌐mita¬-katta n̄ desu ḡa,
   a⌐no¬ hito wa yo⌐ma¬sete ku⌐rema-se⌐n̄ desita.

10. Ra¬zio (o) ki⌐kita¬katta n̄ desu ḡa,
    a⌐no¬ hito wa ki⌐kasete kuremase¬n̄ desita.

11. Se⌐n̄se¬e ni a⌐ita¬katta n̄ desu ḡa,
    a⌐no¬ hito wa a⌐wa¬sete ku⌐rema-se⌐n̄ desita.

N. Grammar Drill (based on Grammatical Note 1)

Tutor: Si⌐te¬ mo ⌐i¬i desu ka◡ 'May I do it?'
Student: Sa⌐sete itadakemase¬n̄ ka◡ 'Would you let me do it?'

1. Ko⌐ko de ma¬tte mo ⌐i¬i desu ka◡
   Ko⌐ko de mata¬sete i⌐tadakema-se¬n̄ ka◡

2. Ha¬yaku ⌐ka⌐ette mo ⌐i¬i desu ka◡
   Ha¬yaku ka⌐era¬sete i⌐tadakema-se¬n̄ ka◡

3. E⌐n̄pitu de ka¬ite mo ⌐i¬i desu ka◡
   E⌐n̄pitu de kaka¬sete i⌐tadake-mase¬n̄ ka◡

4. Ni⌐ho¬n̄ ni tuite ki⌐ite¬ mo ⌐i¬i desu ka◡
   Ni⌐ho¬n̄ ni tuite ki⌐kasete itada-kemase¬n̄ ka◡

5. De⌐n̄wa (o) ka¬kete mo ⌐i¬i desu ka◡
   De⌐n̄wa (o) kakesa¬sete i⌐tadake-mase¬n̄ ka◡

6. A⌐na¬ta no ⌐se⌐etaa (o) ki⌐te¬ mo ⌐i¬i desu ka◡
   A⌐na¬ta no ⌐se⌐etaa (o) ki⌐sasete itadakemase¬n̄ ka◡

7. Asita ya⌐su¬nde mo ⌐i¬i
   desu ka⌟
8. Hi⌐rune (o) site¬ mo ⌐i¬i
   desu ka⌟
9. A⌐na¬ta no zi⌐biki¬ (o)
   tu⌐katte¬ mo ⌐i¬i desu
   ka⌟
10. Raisyuu kara ⌐tyo¬tto
    ya⌐sumi¬ (o) ⌐to¬tte mo
    ⌐i¬i desu ka⌟

Asita ya⌐suma¬sete i⌐tadakemase¬ñ
ka⌟
Hi⌐rune (o) sasete itadakemase¬ñ
ka⌟
A⌐na¬ta no zi⌐biki¬ (o) tu⌐kawasete
itadakemase¬ñ ka⌟

Raisyuu kara ⌐tyo¬tto ya⌐sumi¬ (o)
to⌐ra¬sete i⌐tadakemase¬ñ ka⌟

O. Expansion Drill

1. [He] had [him] do [it].
   [He] had [him] do work.
   [He] had [him] do work
   in the kitchen.
   [He] had the carpenter
   do work in the kitchen.
   The handyman had the
   carpenter do work in
   the kitchen.

Sa⌐sema¬sita.
Si⌐ḡoto (o) sasema¬sita.
Daidokoro de si⌐ḡoto (o) sase-
ma¬sita.
Da¬iku ni da̅idokoro de si⌐ḡoto
(o) sasema¬sita.
Beñriya wa ⌐da¬iku ni da̅idokoro
de si⌐ḡoto (o) sasema¬sita.

2. I made [them] drink [it].
   I made [them] drink
   medicine.
   I made [them] drink the
   medicine a little at a
   time.
   I made [them] drink the
   medicine I had re-
   ceived, a little at a
   time.
   I made [them] drink the
   medicine I had re-
   ceived from the doctor,
   a little at a time.
   I made the children drink
   the medicine I had re-
   ceived from the doctor,
   a little at a time.

No⌐masema¬sita.
Ku⌐suri (o) nomasema¬sita.

Kusuri (o) su⌐kosi-zu¬tu no⌐ma-
sema¬sita.

Moratta kusuri (o) su⌐kosi-zu¬tu
no⌐masema¬sita.

Oisyasañ ni moratta kusuri (o)
su⌐kosi-zu¬tu no⌐masema¬sita.

Kodomo ni o̅isyasañ ni moratta
kusuri (o) su⌐kosi-zu¬tu no⌐ma-
sema¬sita.

3. I had [him] plant [them].
   I had [him] plant trees.
   I had [him] plant tall
   trees.
   I had [him] plant trees
   taller than the fence.
   I had [him] plant trees
   taller than the fence,
   [all] around.

U⌐esasema¬sita.
Ki¬ (o) u⌐esasema¬sita.
Ta⌐ka¬i ⌐ki¬ (o) u⌐esasema¬sita.

Ka⌐ki¬ne yori ta⌐ka¬i ⌐ki¬ (o)
u⌐esasema¬sita.
Mawari ni, ka⌐ki¬ne yori ta⌐ka¬i
⌐ki¬ (o) u⌐esasema¬sita.

I had [him] plant trees taller than the fence, [all] around the fence.	Ka⌐ki⌉ne no mawari ni, ka⌐ki⌉ne yori ta⌐ka⌉i ˻ki˥ (o) u˻esasema˥sita.
I had the gardener plant trees taller than the fence, [all] around the fence.	Uekiya ni, ka⌐ki⌉ne no mawari ni, ka⌐ki⌉ne yori ta⌐ka⌉i ˻ki˥ (o) u˻esasema˥sita.

4.

I had [her] exchange [it].	To⌐rikaesasema⌉sita.
I had [her] exchange a necktie.	Ne˻kutai (o) to⌐rikaesasema˥sita.
I had [her] exchange a loud necktie.	Ha⌐de⌉ na ˻ne˥kutai (o) to⌐rikaesasema˥sita.
I had [her] exchange a loud necktie I had received from a friend.	Tomodati ni moratta ha⌐de⌉ na ˻ne˥kutai (o) to⌐rikaesasema˥sita.
I had [her] exchange a loud necktie I had received from a friend, for a more conservative one.	Tomodati ni moratta ha⌐de⌉ na ˻ne˥kutai (o) ⌐mo⌉tto zi⌐mi⌉ na no to to⌐rikaesasema⌉sita.
I had my wife exchange a loud necktie I had received from a friend, for a more conservative one.	Ka⌉nai ni tŏmodati ni moratta ha⌐de⌉ na ˻ne˥kutai (o) ⌐mo⌉tto zi⌐mi⌉ na no to to⌐rikaesasema⌉sita.

SUPPLEMENTARY DIALOGUES

1. Smith: De⌉kitara, i⌉ma ⌐tyo⌉tto te⌐gami o ka⌉ite mo⌐raita˥i ñ desu ḡa↲
   Secretary: Ha⌉a, ka⌐sikomarima⌉sita.
   Smith: Hazime ni wa⌐tasi no iu to⌉ori ˻ka⌉ite ˻mi˥te kudasai↲ So⌐no ue⌉ de na˻osima˥su kara‿ I⌉i desu ka↲
   Secretary: Ha⌐i. Do⌉ozo o⌐ssya⌉tte kudasai.

2. Mrs. Smith: O⌐isii oka⌉si desu ⌐ne⌉e. Do⌐ko de o˻kai ni narima˥sita ka↲
   Mrs. Yamamoto: Ta⌐naka-sañ no o⌐kusañ ḡa go⌐zibuñ de otukuri ni na⌉tte, zyo⌐tyuusañ ni mota⌉sete yo˻ko⌉site ku˻dasa˥tta ñ desu yo↲
   Mrs. Smith: *Zu⌐ibuñ o⌐zyoozu de⌉su ⌐ne⌉e.

3. Tanaka: Haisyaku-sita zassi ya⌐bu⌉ite si˻maima˥sita. Do⌉o mo su⌐mi⌉mase⌉ñ desita.
   Smith: Ka⌐maimase⌉ñ. Sore wa ⌐mo⌉o ⌐yo⌉ñde si˻matta˥ ñ desu kara‿
   Tanaka: Na⌐ḡa⌉i aida o⌐kari-sita⌉ri ya⌐bu⌉itari, hoñtoo ni gŏmeñ-nasai↲[1]
   Smith: Ho⌐ñtoo ni kamawa⌉nai ñ desu yo. Tu⌐ḡi⌉ no ḡa ki˻te˥ masu kara, yo⌐mimase⌉ñ ka↲
   Tanaka: Kore kara ki⌐otukema⌉su kara, ha⌐isyaku-sasete kudasa⌉i.

4. Smith: Ni⌐hoñ no rekisi o beñkyoo-sita⌉i ñ desu ḡa, da⌉re ka te⌐kitoo na señse⌉e o syo⌐okai-site kudasaimase⌉ñ ka↲

---

[1] Go⌐meñ-nasa⌉i. 'Excuse me.'

Tanaka: Zya⸍a, Ya⌐mada-sañ to iu hito⸍ o si˥tte ima⸍su ḡa⎽ A⌐no⸍ hito
wa bĕtu ni re⌐kisi ḡa señmoñ to iu hodo zya na⸍i ñ desu ḡa; na-
⌐kanaka yo⌐ku si˥tte iru⸍ si, sono ue, e⸍ḡo mo daibu hanase⌐ru
hi˥to⸍ desu kara⎽
Smith: Ze⌐hi so⌐no kata⸍ o syo⌐okai-site kudasaimase⸍ñ ka⎦
Tanaka: E⸍e, i⸍i desu to mo. Su⌐ḡu re˥ñraku-simasyo⸍o.

5. Tanaka: Ma⸍initi do⌐no-ḡurai-zu⸍tu be˥ñkyoo-site ru⸍ ñ desu ka⎦
Smith: Ga⌐kkoo de⸍ wa go-⌐zikañ-zu⸍tu desu.
Tanaka: Kañzi wa?
Smith: Kañzi wa ⌐ma⸍initi i⌐ti-zikañ-zu⸍tu de, taitee to⌐o-ḡurai-zu⸍tu
naraimasu.

6. Tanaka: Kono siḡoto kyo⌐o-zyuu ni site simaita⸍i ñ desu ḡa, zi⌐kañ
ḡa tarina⸍i ka mo sirenai to o˥mo⸍tte, si⌐ñpai-site iru⸍ ñ desu.
Smith: So⌐ñna ni isoḡa⸍nakute mo ⌐i⸍i ñ desu yo⎦ Ko⌐ñsyuu no uti ni
sure⸍ba ˥i⸍i ñ desu kara⎽
Tanaka: A⌐sita-zyuu ni sumase⸍nai to, do⌐yoo ma⸍de ni si⌐ha⸍kereba na-
˥rana⸍i hŏka no siḡoto ḡa o⌐soku narima⸍su kara⎽
Smith: Ma⸍a, de⌐ki⸍nai mono de⌐ki⸍nai ñ desu kara. A⌐ñmari hata-
rakisuḡi⸍ru to, byo⌐oki ni narima⸍su kara ⌐ne⸍e.

7. Smith: Ko⌐no ki⸍zi wa ⌐do⸍tira ḡa o˥mote⸍ de, do⌐tira ḡa u⌐ra⸍ ka wa-
⌐karimase⸍ñ ⌐ne⸍e.
Tanaka: A⌐kai ho⌐o ḡa o⌐mote⸍ zya ˥na⸍i desyoo ka.
Smith: Sa⸍a. Wa⌐takusi ni⸍ wa wa⌐karimase⸍ñ ḡa⎽

8. Smith: Hutuu no ni⌐hoñḡo no ho⌐ñ no o⌐mote⸍ ni ˥na⸍ru no wa, e⸍ḡo
no hoñ no u⌐ra⸍ ni ˥na⸍ru ñ desu ḡa, ro⌐omazi de ka⌐ita ˥ho⌐ñ wa
˥do⸍o desyoo.
Tanaka: Ro⌐omazi no ho⸍ñ wa su⌐kuna⸍i ñ desu ḡa, daitai e⸍ḡo no ho⸍ñ
to o⌐nazi⸍ da to omoima⸍su ḡa⎽

9. Mrs. Tanaka: Tyo⸍tto ko⌐no osakana ta⸍bete ˥mi⸍te ne? He⸍ñ na a⸍zi ḡa
suru⸍ desyoo?
Maid: Ko⌐marima⸍sita ⌐ne⸍e. Mo⸍o ⌐Ta⌐roo-tyañ ni ta⌐besa⸍sete si˥matta⸍
ñ desu keredo⎽ Ho⌐ñtoo ni tyo⸍tto ˥he⸍ñ desu ⌐ne⸍e. Byo⌐oki ni na-
ra⸍nakereba ⌐i⸍i desu ḡa⎽
Mrs. Tanaka: Ki⌐otuke⸍te ite; gu⸍ai ḡa waru⸍i yoo dattara, su⸍ḡu o˥isya-
sañ ni turete ikimasyo⸍o.

10. Smith: O⌐isyasañ de⸍ mo ⌐da⸍redare sa⌐ñ te iu⸍ ñ desu ka⎦
Tanaka: Da⌐redare-señse⸍e tte i⸍u⸍ ñ desu yo⎦

11. Employee: Tyo⸍tto gu⸍ai ḡa waru⸍i ñ desu ḡa, ha⸍yaku ka⌐era⸍sete i˥ta-
dakemase⸍ñ ka⎦
Employer: Gu⸍ai ḡa waru⸍i? Zya⸍a, hi⸍doku na˥ra⸍nai uti ni ˥ka⸍etta
hoo ḡa ˥i⸍i yo⎦
Employee: Sore kara; a⸍sita⸍ mo, su⌐mimase⸍ñ ḡa, ya⌐suma⸍sete ku⌐da-
saimase⸍ñ ka⎦ O⌐isyasañ ni mi⸍te mo⌐raita⸍i ñ desu ḡa⎽
Employer: A⌐sita⸍ wa be⌐tu ni isoḡa⸍siku ˥na⸍i kara, ka⌐mawa⸍nai yo⎦
Employee: Zya⸍a; su⌐mimase⸍ñ ḡa, ka⌐era⸍sete itadakimasu. Si⌐tu⸍ree-
simasu.
Employer: Odaizi ni.

12. Tanaka: Eego wa wa⌐ka¬ru to o⌐mosiro¬i ñ desu ḡa, wa⌐kara¬nai to i⌐ya¬
     ni ⌐na¬tte simatte_
     Smith: Na⌐ñ de mo ⌐so¬o desyoo? Ma¬a ⌐to¬nikaku, ma¬initi su⌐kosi-zu¬tu
     be⌐ñkyoo-sita¬ra, su⌐ḡu zyo⌐ozu¬ ni na⌐rima¬su yo↲

13. Smith: I⌐ñki¬[1] no bi⌐ñ no hu⌐ta o site okana¬i to, ko⌐bosima¬su yo↲
     Tanaka: Sono huta wa ⌐ko¬ruku[2] ḡa ⌐to¬rete si⌐matta¬ kara, da⌐me¬ na
     ñ desu.
     Smith: Zya¬a, ho⌐ka no bi⌐ñ no hu⌐ta o tukatta¬ra ⌐do¬o desu ka↲
     Tanaka: A¬ru ka ⌐do¬o ka sa⌐ḡasite mimasyo¬o.

14. Mrs. Smith: Ta⌐iheñ ke¬kkoo na o⌐ka¬si de gozaimasu ⌐ne¬e. Do¬tira no
     de gozaimasu ka↲
     Mrs. Tanaka: Do¬kodoko no ⌐na¬ninani to i⌐u yo¬o na yu⌐umee na mono¬
     de wa go⌐zaimase¬ñ. U⌐ti no so⌐ba no o⌐ka¬siya no mo⌐no¬ de go-
     zaimasu ḡa, na⌐kanaka i¬i azi de gozaimasyoo?

English Equivalents

1. Smith: If you can, I'd like to have you write a letter now . . .
   Secretary: Yes, certainly.
   Smith: First, please try writing it as I say it. On the basis of that, I'll
     correct it (so . . .) All right?
   Secretary: Yes. Please go ahead (lit. say [it]).

2. Mrs. Smith: What delicious cake! Where did you buy it?
   Mrs. Yamamoto: Mrs. Tanaka made it herself and was kind enough to
     send the maid here with it.
   Mrs. Smith: She's very good [at baking], isn't she.

3. Tanaka: I've torn the magazine I borrowed from you. I'm very sorry.
   Smith: It doesn't matter. I've already finished reading that one (so . . .)
   Tanaka: What with borrowing it for a long time and tearing it, [I] really
     [must ask you to] excuse me.
   Smith: It really doesn't matter. The next [issue] has come. Wouldn't
     you [like to] read it?
   Tanaka: From now on I'll be careful so do let me borrow it.

4. Smith: I'd like to study Japanese history. Would you be kind enough to
     introduce [me to] some suitable teacher?
   Tanaka: Well, I know a man named Mr. Yamada . . . He isn't a real
     specialist in history (lit. he isn't especially so much that you say
     history [is] a specialty) but he knows it quite well and, what is more,
     he is a person who can speak a considerable amount of English too,
     so . . .
   Smith: By all means would you introduce [me to] him?
   Tanaka: Yes, of course, that will be fine. I'll get in touch with him
     right away.

---

[1] 'Ink.'

[2] 'Cork.'

5. Tanaka: About how long (each [day]) are you studying every day?
    Smith: At school, it's five hours (each [day]).
    Tanaka: What about kanji?
    Smith: Kanji is one hour (each time) every day, and we usually learn
       about ten each time.

6. Tanaka: I'd like to finish doing this work (within) today, but I've been
       worrying, thinking that there may not be enough time.
    Smith: You don't have to hurry so much. (Because) it will be all right
       provided you do it sometime this week.
    Tanaka: If I don't finish it (within) tomorrow, other work that I must do
       by Saturday will be late (so. . .)
    Smith: Well, things that are impossible are impossible (so. . .) When
       you overwork (too much), you get sick so—you know.

7. Smith: You can't tell which is the right side and which is the wrong side
       of this material, can you.
    Tanaka: Wouldn't the redder side be the right side?
    Smith: Hmm . . . It isn't clear to me but [maybe you can tell].

8. Smith: What is (lit. becomes) the front of the normal Japanese book is
       (lit. becomes) the back of an English book, but what about books
       written in romaji?
    Tanaka: There aren't many romaji books but I think that for the most
       part they are the same as English books . . .

9. Mrs. Tanaka: Say, taste (lit. try eating) this fish, would you? Doesn't
       it have a funny taste?
    Maid: Oh dear. I've already fed it to Taro . . . It really is a little
       strange, isn't it. I hope he doesn't get sick . . .
    Mrs. Tanaka: Let's be careful, and if he seems to have something the
       matter with him, let's take him to the doctor right away.

10. Smith: Even in the case of a doctor do you say 'So-and-so-san'?
    Tanaka: You say 'So-and-so-sensei.'

11. Employee: I don't feel well. May I go home early?
    Employer: You don't feel well? Then you'd better go home before you
       feel worse (lit. in the interval when it hasn't become bad).
    Employee: And I'm sorry but would you let me take tomorrow off too?
       I'd like to have the doctor look me over . . .
    Employer: Tomorrow we're not especially busy so it will be all right.
    Employee: Well then, I'm sorry but I'll leave now (lit. I'll accept your
       letting me go home). Goodbye.
    Employer: Take care of yourself.

12. Tanaka: English is fun when I understand it, but when I don't under-
       stand, I end up hating it . . .
    Smith: Isn't everything like that? In any case, if you study every day
       a little at a time, you'll get to be good at it very soon.

13. Smith: If you don't put the top on the ink bottle (now, for future refer-
       ence), you'll spill it.
    Tanaka: That top is no good because the cork has come out of it.
    Smith: Then why don't you use the top of another bottle?
    Tanaka: I'll look and see if there is [one] or not.

14. Mrs. Smith: This is very fine cake. Where is it from?
     Mrs. Tanaka: This isn't anything famous that you can describe as "so-
         and-so from such-and-such a place." (Lit. This isn't a famous thing
         of the kind "so-and-so from such-and-such a place.") It's something
         from a pastry shop near the house, but it has (lit. is) quite a nice
         flavor, hasn't it?

EXERCISES

1. You have just bought a house and are discussing repairs and changes to
    be made, with a handyman. Cover the following work which you want
    him to have done for you:

    a. putting up shelves in the kitchen
    b. replacing (i.e. exchanging) the mats in the zashiki and the fusuma
        that are torn
    c. cleaning the chimney
    d. repairing the wall in front of the house and the fence around the
        garden
    e. planting some big trees toward the back of the garden
    f. repairing the places in the roof that leak

    Ask the handyman to give you a rough estimate by Saturday, and tell him
    you will talk to him again next week, on the basis of that.

2. Tell Haruko:

    a. that your overcoat button (botañ) has come off.
    b. that your overcoat has a hole.
    c. that your overcoat is torn.
    d. that the screws in the door have come out.
    e. that this fish has a funny taste.
    f. that this milk has a funny smell.
    g. to put the lid on this box.
    h. to lock this box.
    i. to stuff some paper in this box.
    j. to put up the mosquito nets.

3. Make up ten short conversations, each one of which contains one of the
    following phrases:

    a. so⌐no ue⌐ de
    b. ka⌐era⌐nai uti ni
    c. su⌐kosi-zu⌐tu
    d. ya⌐kusoku no to⌐ori
    e. ya⌐meru hodo zya na⌐i
    f. mo⌐ta⌐sete yokosimasu
    g. uti no mawari ni
    h. i⌐kasete itadakemaseñ ka
    i. a⌐me ḡa ⌐hu⌐ru to
    j. ta⌐to⌐eba

Lesson 34. Personal History

BASIC DIALOGUES: FOR MEMORIZATION

(a)

(An applicant for a position has come for an interview)

Applicant

a personal history record	ri⌐reki⌐syo

1. I've brought my personal history record.

Ri⌐reki⌐syo (o) mo⌐tte mairi-ma⌐sita.

Employer

2. I'll take a look at it.

Tyo⌐tto haikeñ-simasu.

birth or place of birth (name of city and pre-fecture near Tokyo)	umare or oumare ⌐ Ti⌐ba

3. Oh, you were born in Chiba (lit. your place of birth is Chiba)—right?

A⌐a, oumare (wa) ⌐Ti⌐ba desu ne?

Applicant

be born	umareru /-ru/
grow up	so⌐da⌐tu /-u/

4. Yes. Chiba is the place (lit. one) where I was born, but the place where I grew up is not Chiba.

Ha⌐a. U⌐mareta⌐ no wa ⌐Ti⌐ba desu ḡa, so⌐da⌐tta no wa ⌐Ti⌐ba zya a⌐rimase⌐ñ.

Employer

5. What do you mean by that?

To iu to?

Applicant

in reality or the fact is	zi⌐tu⌐ wa
both parents	ryo⌐osiñ or go⌐ryo⌐osiñ ⌐
substitute	kawari
instead of parents	ryo⌐osiñ no kawari ni
grandfather	so⌐hu or o⌐zi⌐isañ ⌐
grandmother	so⌐bo or o⌐ba⌐asañ ⌐
bring up or raise	so⌐date⌐ru /-ru/
be brought up	so⌐daterare⌐ru /-ru/
be brought up by one's grandmother	so⌐bo ni so⌐daterare⌐ru

6. The fact is that until I entered school, I was brought up by my grandmother instead of my parents.

Zi⌐tu⌐ wa, ga⌐kkoo e ha⌐iru made wa, ryo⌐osiñ no kawari ni ⌐so⌐bo ni so⌐daterarema⌐sita.

place of one's permanent
  residence
         ho⌐n̄seki⌐ti

live <u>or</u> reside   su⌐mu /-u/

be living in the country   i⌐naka ni su⌐n̄de (i)ru

7. Therefore I lived in the   De⌐su kara, ho⌐n̄seki⌐ti no i⌐naka
   country, where our permanent ni su⌐n̄de (i)masita.
   residence place is.

Employer

8. Oh, of course.   A⌐a, naruhodo.

one's permanent residence   hon̄seki
Saitama Prefecture   Sa⌐itama⌐-ken̄
Konosu City   Ko⌐onosu⌐-si
Ningyo Cho   Ni⌐n̄gyo⌐o-tyoo
Lot No. 8   ha⌐ti-ba⌐n̄ti

9. Your permanent residence   Hon̄seki (wa) Sa⌐itama⌐-ken̄, Ko-
   is (Lot) No. 1638, Ningyo   onosu⌐-si, Ni⌐n̄gyo⌐o-tyoo, sen̄
   Cho, Konosu City, Saitama   roppyaku ⌐san̄-zyuu ha⌐ti-ba⌐n̄ti
   Prefecture—right?   desu ne?

Applicant

10. Yes, that's right.   Ha⌐i, so⌐o desu.

Employer

oh! <u>or</u> my word! <u>or</u>   oya?
  hold on!
elementary school   syo⌐oga⌐kkoo
middle school   tyu⌐ugaku
Kansai (the Kyoto-Osaka   Ka⌐n̄sai
  area, western Honshu)
Kanto (the Kanto plain,   Ka⌐n̄too
  central Honshu)

11. Oh! But [you went to] ele-   Oya? Si⌐ka⌐si; syo⌐oga⌐kkoo wa
   mentary school [in] Kansai, ⌐Ka⌐n̄sai, tyu⌐ugaku wa Si⌐ko⌐ku,
   middle school [in] Shikoku, daigaku wa To⌐okyoo na⌐ n̄ desu
   and university [in] Tokyo— ne?
   right?

Applicant

Japan Broadcasting   Ni⌐hon̄hoosookyo⌐okai
  Company (NHK)
often   tabitabi
change one's post   ten̄kin̄-suru
be made to change one's   ten̄kin̄-saserareru /-ru/
  post <u>or</u> be transferred

12. Yes. That's because my   Ha⌐i. Ti⌐ti⌐ ga Ni⌐hon̄hoosoo-
   father worked for NHK and kyo⌐okai ni tu⌐tto⌐mete (i)te, ta-
   was transferred often.   ⌐bitabi ten̄kin̄-saserareta⌐ kara
                          desu.

Employer

13.   I see.   Naruhodo.

(b)

Smith

(Smith is asking Tanaka about his military experiences.)

let me see or well now   eeto
armed forces   gu⌐ntai
join the armed forces   gu⌐ntai ni ʳhaˈiru

14.   Well now . . . Did you join the   Eeto⌐ Daʳiḡaku (o) deʳru to ʳsuˈ-
      armed forces immediately   ḡu, gu⌐ntai ni ʳhaˈitta ñ desu
      upon leaving the university?   ka⌐

Tanaka

army   riʳku⌐ḡuñ
be taken   toʳrareˈru /-ru/

15.   Yes. I was taken into the   Eˈe. Suˈḡu riʳku⌐ḡuñ ni toʳrare-
      army right away.   maˈsita.

Smith

during the war   señzityuu

16.   During the war what kind of   Señzityuu wa ʳdo⌐ñna siḡoto (o)
      work were you doing?   siʳte (i)maˈsita ka⌐

Tanaka

soon after or in no time   maʳmo⌐naku
war   señsoo
summon or draft   syoosyuu-suru
be drafted   syoosyuu-sareru /-ru/

17.   I came back from military   Gu⌐ntai kara ʳkaˈette maʳmo⌐-
      [service] and in no time the   naku seʳñsoo ḡa hazimattaˈ no
      war began, so I was drafted   de, suˈḡu maʳta syoosyuu-sare-
      again right away.   maˈsita.

be defeated or be beaten   makeru /-ru/
the end of war   syuuseñ
the war ends (lit. become   syuʳuseñ ni naˈru
   the end of war)
be made to work   hatarakaserareru /-ru/

18.   I was made to work in the   Niʳho⌐ñ ḡa mǎkete, syuʳuseñ ni
      armed forces without inter-   naˈru made; zuʳtto gu⌐ntai de
      ruption until Japan was de-   haʳtarakaseraremaˈsita.
      feated and the war ended.

Smith

19.   Oh.   Aˈa, soˈo.

Tanaka

unfortunate or   ainiku
   unfortunately

Manchuria	Maꜛñsyuu
Siberia	Siberiya
be taken (of living beings)	turete ikareru /-ru/
give back <u>or</u> send back <u>or</u> return [something]	kaꜛesu /-u/
be returned	ka⌐esareꜛru /-ru/

20. Unfortunately I was in Man-
churia so I was taken to
Siberia, and I was finally
returned [to Japan] in Showa
28 [1953].

Ainiku ⌐Maꜛñsyuu ni iᵇtaꜙ no de,
Siberiya e turete ikarete; syoowa
ꜛniꜛzyuu haᶜtiꜛ-neñ ni yaᶜtto kaesa-
remaꜛsita.

Smith

hardship <u>or</u> troubles <u>or</u> an ordeal	kuꜛroo <u>or</u> go⌐kuꜛroo ꜛ
restricted <u>or</u> uncom-fortable <u>or</u> incon-venient	huꜛziyuu /na/

21. What an ordeal! It must have
been awfully uncomfortable,
wasn't it?

So⌐re wa gokuꜛroo desita ᵇneᶜe.
Zuꜛibuñ ⌐huꜛziyuu datta desyoo?

Tanaka

indeed <u>or</u> really <u>or</u> honestly	mattaku
too awful to talk about (lit. is severe to the extent that it doesn't become talk)	ha⌐nasiꜛ ni na⌐raꜛnai hodo hiᵇdoᶜi
life <u>or</u> existence	seekatu
family	kaꜛzoku <u>or</u> go⌐kaꜛzoku ꜛ
one's family at home	ku⌐ni no kaꜛzoku
be patient <u>or</u> put up with	gaꜛmañ-suru

22. Yes. Honestly, it was too
awful a life to talk about,
but I thought about my family
at home, and managed to put
up with it.

Eꜛe. Mattaku, ohanasi ni na-
⌐raꜛnai hodo hiᵇdoᶜi seᵇekatu deᶜ-
sita ḡa; ku⌐ni no kaꜛzoku no koᵇtoᶜ
(o) kaᵇñḡaᶜete, yaᶜtto gaꜛmañ-site
(i)masita.

Smith

23. Really! How terrible that was!
How about after you came back?

Sore wa sore wa. Ta⌐iheñ deꜛ-
sita ᵇneᶜe. Kaꜛette kara wa?

Tanaka

uh—	anoo
is ashamed <u>or</u> is shy	ha⌐zukasiꜛi /-ku/ or o⌐hazukasiꜛi ꜛ /-ku/
burn [something]	yaku /-u/
be unfavorably affected by burning	yakareru /-ru/

have one's home burn	uti o yakareru
have a shop	mi⌐se⌐ o yaru
live <u>or</u> make a living	seekatu-suru

24. Uh—the fact is that I'm ashamed [to say it], but because our home was wiped out by fire and there was no suitable work, I lived by having my wife run a small shop.

Anoo— Zi⌐tu⌐ wa, o⌐hazukasi⌐i ñ desu ḡa; u⌐ti (o) yakarete si-matta⌐ si, te⌐kitoo na siḡoto mo na⌐katta no de; ka⌐nai ni ti⌐isa⌐i mi⌐se⌐ (o) yarasete se⌐ekatu-sima⌐sita.

Smith

25. I see.

Naruhodo.

(c)

(Jones is interviewing Ikeda for a position as translator and has just finished discussing his experience and qualifications.)

Jones

by the way <u>or</u> well now	to⌐koro⌐ de
translation	hoñyaku

26. Well now, we want a person here now who will do translating for us (lit. a person from whom we'll receive the doing of translation).

To⌐koro⌐ de ⌐i⌐ma ko⌐tira de⌐ wa, ho⌐ñyaku (o) site morau[1] hito⌐ ḡa ho⌐si⌐i ñ desu.

Ikeda

27. I see.

Ha⌐a.

Jones

circumstances <u>or</u> case	baai
in hurrying circumstances <u>or</u> in cases where [someone] is in a hurry	i⌐so⌐ḡu baai ni
middle of the night	yo⌐naka⌐

28. In cases where we're in a hurry, there may be times when we have [people] work until the middle of the night. Even so, would it be all right?

I⌐so⌐ḡu baai ni wa, yo⌐naka⌐ made ha⌐taraite morau koto⌐ ḡa ⌐a⌐ru ka mo si⌐remase⌐ñ ḡa; so⌐re de⌐ mo ka⌐maimase⌐ñ ka⌐

Ikeda

be made to do	saserareru /-ru/
complaint	huhee
complain	huhee o iu

29. Certainly. No matter what kind of work I'm made to do [and when [I'm made to do it], I'll never complain.

Ha⌐a. Do⌐ñna siḡoto (o) ⌐i⌐tu sa⌐serarete⌐ mo, ke⌐ssite huhee wa moosimase⌐ñ.

---

[1] Some native speakers prefer <u>kureru</u> here.

a hundred times as many (or much) or hundred-fold	hyaku-bai
a thousand times as many (or much) or thousandfold	señ-bai
is hard to bear	turai /-ku/
even a hundred times even a thousand times as hard	hyaku-bai mo señ-bai mo ˈturai

30. [That's] because I used to do work a hundred times and a thousand times as hard.

Hyaku-bai mo seˈñ-baiˈ mo turai siḡoto (o) sita monoˈ desu kara＿

Jones

compare   kuraberu /-ru/

31. If you compare it to that [I guess it's not so bad], is it.

Soˈre ni kurabereˈba ˈneˈe.

within one hour   iˈti-zikañ-iˈnai ni
translate   hoñyaku-suru
translate into Japanese   nihoñgo ni hoñyaku-suru

32. Well then, please try translating this into Japanese within one hour.

Zyaˈa, kore (o) iˈti-zikañ-iˈnai ni niˈhoñgo ni hoñyaku-site miˈte kudasai.

question   situmoñ

33. If you have any questions, please ask me.

Naˈni ka siˈtumoñ (ḡa) aˈttara kiˈite kudasaˈi.

Ikeda

34. All right. I don't have anything to inquire about especially.

Haˈi. Betu ni uˈkaḡau kotoˈ (wa) aˈrimaseˈñ.

Jones

35. Well then, please begin right away.

Zyaˈa, suḡu haˈzimete kudasaˈi.

ADDITIONAL VOCABULARY

Supplementary Questions:

live or exist   iˈkiˈru /-ru/

1. Are your parents living?

Goˈryoˈosiñ (ḡa) ˈiˈkite (i)masu ka⌟

die   sinu /-u/
die or pass on   nakunaru[1] /-u/

---

[1] Less abrupt word than sinu.

2. When did your father die?   Oˈtoˈosañ (wa) ˈiˈtu naˈkunarimaˈ-
                                                sita ka↵

        education or schooling   kyooiku
        undergo   uˈkeˈru /-ru/
3. What kind of schooling have   Doˈñna kyoˈoiku (o) ukemaˈsita
    you had?   ka↵

        graduate (verb)   sotuḡyoo-suru
4. When did you graduate from   Iˈtu daˈiḡaku (o) sotuḡyoo-simaˈ-
    college?   sita ka↵

        experience   keekeñ or gokeekeñˈ
5. Do you have experience?   Goˈkeekeñ (ḡa) arimaˈsu ka↵

        interpreting   tuˈuyaku
6. Is(n't) there someone here   Tuˈuyaku no deˈkiˈru hito (wa)
    who can interpret?   iˈmaseˈñ ka↵

7. Did you join the navy?   Kaˈiḡuñ ni haˈirimaˈsita ka↵

        air force   kuuḡuñ
        marines   rikuseñtai
        Self-Defense Forces   zieetai

8. Were you a soldier?   Heˈetai deˈsita ka↵

        navy sailor   suˈihee
        military officer   syoˈokoo

Definitions:

1. Schooling which you are re-   Uˈkeˈnakereba naˈraˈnai kyooiku
    quired to have is called   wa giˈmukyoˈoiku to iu.
    "compulsory education."

2. (The act of) boys (or men)   Oˈtokoˈ mo oˈñnaˈ mo iˈssyo ni
    and girls (or women) getting   kyooiku o ukeˈru koto wa daˈñ-
    their education together is   zyokyoˈoḡaku to iu.
    called "coeducation."

3. The dress (i.e. clothing)   Guˈñziñ no kiru hukuˈ wa ḡǔñ-
    that military personnel wear   puku to iu.
    is called a "(military) uni-
    form."

NOTES ON THE BASIC DIALOGUES

1. One's riˈrekiˈsyo is regularly presented in Japan when applying for a
    job. It is written according to a standard form, and includes one's
    name, present address and permanent address, and a record of educa-
    tion, professional experience, awards, and punishments.

4. So⌐da⌐tu is the intransitive partner of transitive so⌐date⌐ru (Sentence 6).

5. **To iu to:** The first **to** is the quotative and the second **to** is the particle of accompaniment. The phrase means literally 'with saying quote'—that is, 'when one says what has just been said, what does one mean?' The quotative applies to what immediately precedes—in this case, Basic Sentence 4: 'When you say "Chiba is the place . . . is not Chiba," what do you mean?'

6. Remember that o⌐zi⌐isañ and o⌐ba⌐asañ are also used as polite words for 'old man' and 'old woman' respectively.

7. The verbal ⌐su⌐mu occurs most commonly in its gerund form suñde + √iru.

9. **Hoñseki** denotes the permanent address of a Japanese—often the residence of his or her parents and/or grandparents or her husband's family. It designates the place where a Japanese is formally registered. Addresses in Japanese, like dates, begin with the largest division that is mentioned and end with the smallest; the parts follow each other directly without intervening particles (but note the contrast between Mi⌐nato⌐-ku, Si⌐ba 'Shiba, Minato Ward' and Mi⌐nato⌐-ku no ⌐Si⌐ba 'Shiba in Minato Ward'). Cities are si⌐, but Tokyo is a special kind of city called to⌐ (hence To⌐okyo⌐o-to but Yo⌐kohama⌐-si). Some other divisions which occur frequently in addresses are gu⌐ñ 'county,' mu⌐ra⌐ 'village,' ku⌐ 'ward,' ma⌐ti⌐ 'town' or 'machi' (part of a city, same as 'cho'), and, of course, tyoome 'chome.' Most—but not necessarily all— parts of an address consist of compounds made up of a proper name plus the type of division. Thus: X-guñ 'X County,' X-mura 'X Village,' etc. Note, however, the following typical Tokyo address, which includes a proper name without a division suffix: To⌐okyo⌐o-to Mi⌐nato⌐-ku Ázabu Tǎkeya-tyoo na⌐na-ba⌐ñti 'No. 7, Takeya-cho, Azabu, Minato Ward, (City of) Tokyo.'

11. The Japanese pre-war and post-war education systems differ considerably. Roughly speaking, they compare as follows:

	Pre-war	Post-war
Syo⌐oǧa⌐kkoo	6 years	6 years
Tyu⌐uǧaku	5 years	3 years
Kookoo	3 years	3 years
Daiǧaku	3 years	4 years

There were six years of compulsory education before the war, nine years after.
Kookoo is an abbreviated form of ko⌐otooǧa⌐kkoo.

12. 'Change one's post' as applied to military personnel is teñniñ-suru.

16. With señzityuu, compare señzeñ 'before the war' and señgo 'after the war.'

17. A verbal gerund + ma⌐mo⌐naku means 'soon after doing so-and-so,' 'after doing so-and-so, in no time —— .'

18. Note: X ni makeru 'be defeated in X.' The past maketa (lit. 'I have been beaten') often occurs as the equivalent of 'I give up!' or 'You win!'

The transitive partner of intransitive <u>makeru</u> is <u>makasu</u> /-u/ 'beat [someone]' (<u>X de makasu</u> 'beat [someone] at X'). The opposite of <u>makeru</u> is <u>ka⌐tu</u> /-u/ 'win' (<u>X ni ⌐ka⌐tu</u> 'win in X' or 'win over X').

20. <u>Ka⌐esu</u> is the transitive partner of intransitive <u>ka⌐eru</u> /-u/ 'go back.'

21. <u>Hu⌐ziyuu</u> is the opposite of <u>zi⌐yu⌐u</u> /na/ 'free' or 'unrestricted.'

24. <u>Yaku</u> is also the equivalent of 'bake,' 'roast,' 'toast.' <u>Yaku</u> is the transitive partner of intransitive <u>yakeru</u> /-ru/ 'be burned,' 'be baked,' 'be roasted,' 'be toasted.'

26. <u>To⌐koro⌐ de</u> usually introduces a shift in subject.

31. Note also: <u>X to kuraberu</u> 'compare with X.'

33. Note also: <u>situmoñ-suru</u> 'question' (verb) or 'ask questions.'

GRAMMATICAL NOTES

1. The Passive

So⌐daterare⌐ru		so⌐date⌐ru 'bring up.'
Ka⌐esare⌐ru		ka⌐esu 'give back.'
Yakareru	is the PASSIVE of	yaku 'burn.'
Umareru		umu 'give birth to.'
To⌐rare⌐ru		to⌐ru 'take.'
Sareru		suru 'do.'

Most verbals have corresponding PASSIVE verbals meaning basically 'be affected by such-and-such an action or state.'

An informal non-past passive is accented if the verbal from which it is derived is accented; the accent of the citation form occurs on the next-to-last syllable.

To form the passive:

-ru Verbals: Substitute <u>-rare-ru</u> for the final <u>-ru</u> of the informal non-past.

                    Example: <u>mi⌐ru</u> 'see': <u>mi⌐rare⌐ru</u> 'be affected by [someone's] seeing'

-u Verbals: Substitute <u>-are-ru</u> for the final <u>-u</u> of the informal non-past. When the informal non-past ends in two vowels, substitute <u>-ware-ru</u> for the final <u>-u</u>.

                    Examples: <u>to⌐ru</u> 'take': <u>to⌐rare⌐ru</u> 'be affected by [someone's] taking'
                    <u>iu</u> 'say': <u>iwareru</u> 'be affected by [someone's] saying'

-aru Verbals: Passive does not ordinarily occur.

Irregular Verbals: <u>ku⌐ru</u> 'come': <u>ko⌐rare⌐ru</u> 'be affected by [someone's] coming'
                    <u>suru</u> 'do': <u>sareru</u> 'be affected by [someone's] doing'

The passives of verbals belonging to the -ru group and of iku and ku⌐ru
are identical in form with the commonly occurring alternants of the corresponding potentials.

All passives are themselves verbals belonging to the -ru group. Thus,
the passive of to⌐ru has such forms as:

Informal non-past: to⌐rare⌐ru
Stem: to⌐ra⌐re
Informal past: to⌐ra⌐reta
Gerund: to⌐ra⌐rete
Conditional: to⌐rare⌐tara
Provisional: to⌐rare⌐reba

What we call a passive in English is not the same as a Japanese passive.
The basic meaning of a Japanese passive is 'someone is directly or indirectly, often unfavorably, affected by the action of someone else.' In conversational Japanese, the subject of a passive—i.e. the one who is affected—is
almost invariably a person;[1] if expressed, it is followed by particle wa or
ḡa. The agent by whom the action is performed, if expressed, is followed
by particle ni. The direct object of a non-passive verbal occurs as the direct object (followed by particle o) of the corresponding passive. Study the
following pairs:

1. (a) O⌐kosima⌐sita. 'I woke [someone] up.'
    (b) O⌐kosarema⌐sita. 'I was awakened.' (Lit. 'I was [directly] af-
        fected—perhaps unfavorably—by [someone's] waking [me] up.')

2. (a) Ko⌐domo o okosima⌐sita. 'I woke the children up.'
    (b) Ko⌐domo o okosarema⌐sita. 'The children were awakened and I
        was annoyed.' (Lit. 'I was unfavorably affected by the waking of
        the children [by someone].')

3. (a) Zyo⌐tyuu ḡa kodomo o okosima⌐sita. 'The maid woke the chil-
        dren up.'
    (b) Zyotyuu ni ko⌐domo o okosarema⌐sita. 'The children were awak-
        ened by the maid and I was annoyed.' (Lit. 'I was unfavorably af-
        fected by the waking of the children by the maid.')

4. (a) Zyo⌐tyuu ḡa yamema⌐sita. 'The maid quit.'
    (b) Zyo⌐tyuu ni yamerarema⌐sita. 'The maid quit and I was annoyed.'
        (Lit. 'I was unfavorably affected by quitting by the maid.')

The subject of every passive form in the preceding examples is the speaker
('I'), and if it were expressed, it would be followed by wa or ḡa, depending
on emphasis.

It is important to note the following contrast between English and Japanese
passives: if an English passive is transformed to the corresponding active,
the subject of the passive becomes the object of the active:

'I (subject) was awakened by my mother' = 'My mother woke me (object).'
'My son (subject) was awakened by the maid' = 'The maid woke my
    son (object).'

---

[1] A few passives occur with inanimate subjects in conversation. Thus: Kore
wa na⌐ni ni tu⌐kawarete ima⌐su ka◡ 'What is this being used for?'

In Japanese this is usually not true: see examples under 2, 3, and 4 above.

Even intransitive verbals have passive equivalents. Compare:

U⌐ñte⌐ñsyu wa o⌐soku kima⌐sita. 'The driver came late.'
and:
U⌐ñte⌐ñsyu ni o⌐soku korarema⌐sita. 'The driver came late and I was
    annoyed.' (Lit. 'I was unfavorably affected by coming late on the
    part of the driver.')

Passives based on intransitive verbals, and on transitive verbals denoting
an action which is never done to people, regularly have the unfavorable shade
of meaning. Thus:

ka⌐erare⌐ru 'be unfavorably affected by someone's returning'
ikareru 'be unfavorably affected by someone's going'
ta⌐berare⌐ru 'be unfavorably affected by someone's eating'
no⌐mare⌐ru 'be unfavorably affected by someone's drinking'

However, a passive based on a verbal which denotes an action which can be
directed toward a person, may or may not have the unfavorable shade of
meaning, depending on the individual verbal and/or on context. Thus:

sirareru 'come to be known' or 'be unfavorably affected by someone's
    finding out'
yobareru 'be called' or 'be unfavorably affected by someone's calling'
kikareru 'be asked' or 'be unfavorably affected by someone's asking'
o⌐kosare⌐ru 'be awakened' or 'be unfavorably affected by the waking of
    someone'

In English, an unfavorable shade of meaning is sometimes denoted by the
use of the pattern 'have so-and-so done.' Compare the following three examples:

Tanaka-sañ ni de⌐ñwa o ka⌐kete mo⌐raima⌐sita.
    'I had Mr. Tanaka telephone.' (he did it for me)
Tanaka-sañ ni de⌐ñwa o kakesasema⌐sita.
    'I had Mr. Tanaka telephone.' (I caused him to do it)
Tanaka-sañ ni de⌐ñwa o kakerarema⌐sita.
    'I had Mr. Tanaka telephone.' (I didn't want him to call)

In the few cases where the doer of the action of a Japanese passive is inanimate, it is regularly followed by particle de. Thus:

de⌐ñwa de okosare⌐ru 'be awakened by the telephone'

A commonly occurring exception is:

a⌐me ni hu⌐rare⌐ru 'be rained on'

Remember that in the Japanese equivalent of a sentence like 'My watch
was taken by a child,' the subject is the person affected, the direct object is
the thing taken, and the agent is the person who did the taking. Thus:

(Watakusi wa) kŏdomo ni to⌐kee o torarema⌐sita.

In the Japanese equivalent of a sentence like 'The windows were opened by
the maid,' no passive occurs unless an unfavorable reaction is implied.
Thus:

Zyotyuu ḡa ⌜ma⌝do o a⊢kema⊣sita. 'The maid opened the windows.' or 'The windows were opened by the maid.'

but:

Zyotyuu ni ⌜ma⌝do o a⊢kerarema⊣sita. 'The maid opened the windows and I was annoyed' or 'The windows were opened by the maid—but I didn't want them opened.'

In the Japanese equivalent of sentences like 'The windows are opened,' which contain an English passive that describes a state of being resulting from an action, rather than the action itself, a transitive gerund + a⌝ru occurs (cf. Lesson 16, Grammatical Note 1). Thus:

Ma⌝do ḡa a⊢kete arima⊣su. 'The windows are opened.' or 'The windows have been opened.'

Additional examples:

Ta⌜noma⌝reta ⊢yo⊣o ḡa ⊢a⊣ru kara, Ta⌜naka-sañ no uti ni yorana⌝kereba na⊢rimase⊣ñ.
'There's a matter I've been asked to attend to so I must stop in at Mr. Tanaka's house.'

Gaiziñ ni mi⌜ti o kikarema⌝sita ḡa, e⌜eḡo de setumee-dekimase⌝ñ desita.
'I was asked the way by an American (i.e. Westerner) but I couldn't explain in English.'

A⌝sa ⌜ha⌝yaku de⌜ñwa de okosa⌝reta kara, ne⌜mu⌝i ñ desu.
'I'm tired because I was awakened early in the morning by the telephone.'

Watakusi wa na⌜ni mo iwana⌝katta no ni, he⌝ñ na ko⊢to⊣ o i⌜tta yo⌝o ni o⊢mowa⊣rete; ko⌜marima⌝sita.
'I'm upset because [people] think I said something strange when I didn't say anything at all.' (Lit. 'I have become upset, being affected by [someone's] thinking as if I said a strange thing in spite of the fact that I said nothing.')

Kyo⌝neñ u⌜ti o yakarete⌝ kara, a⌜pa⌝ato ni imasu.
'I've been in an apartment from the time my house burned last year (lit. after being unfavorably affected by the burning of my house last year).'

Se⌜kkaku ka⌝ita teḡami o ko⌜domo ni yabukarema⌝sita.
'The children tore up the letters I took such trouble to write.' (Lit. 'I was unfavorably affected by the tearing of the specially written letters, by the children.')

Sa⌝too-sañ wa ⌜da⌝re ka ni ku⌜ruma o tora⌝reta soo desu.
'I hear that Mr. Sato had his car taken by someone.'

Ha⌜nami⌝ ni i⌜ku tumori da⌝tta no ni, a⌝me ni hu⊢ra⊣rete i⌜karemase⌝ñ desita.
'Although I planned to go to see the cherry blossoms, I couldn't go because it rained (lit. I was unfavorably affected by the falling of rain).'

2. The Passive Causative

Hatarakaserareru } is the PASSIVE CAUSATIVE of { hataraku 'work.'
Saserareru   }   { suru 'do.'

Most verbals have a causative equivalent (cf. Lesson 33, Grammatical
Note 1) and most causatives, in turn, have a passive equivalent, made (as
are all passives derived from verbals of the -ru group) by replacing the final -ru of the informal non-past with -rare-ru. The resulting verbal,
which ends in -(s)ase-rare-ru, is called the PASSIVE CAUSATIVE and
means 'be affected by someone's making [me] do so-and-so,' 'be made to
do so-and-so.' A passive causative based on an accented causative is also
accented; the accent of the citation form is on the next-to-last syllable.
Thus:

	Causative	Passive Causative
ta⌐be¬ru 'eat'	ta⌐besase¬ru 'cause to eat'	ta⌐besaserare¬ru 'be made to eat'
no¬mu 'drink'	no⌐mase¬ru 'cause to drink'	no⌐maserare¬ru 'be made to drink'
iu 'say'	iwaseru 'cause to say'	iwaserareru 'be made to say'
iku 'go'	ikaseru 'cause to go'	ikaserareru 'be made to go'
ku⌐ru 'come'	ko⌐sase¬ru 'cause to come'	ko⌐saserare¬ru 'be made to come'
suru 'do'	saseru 'cause to do'	saserareru 'be made to do'

Some speakers of Japanese also use a slightly abbreviated form of the
passive causative in which the -(s)aserareru ending is replaced by -(s)asa-
reru. Thus: ta⌐besasare¬ru 'be made to eat,' no⌐masare¬ru 'be made to
drink,' etc.

When expressed, the subject of a passive causative — that is, the nominal
denoting the person who is made to do something — is followed by particle wa
or ḡa, and the agent — the person who causes the action — is followed by particle ni. Thus:

(Watakusi wa) se⌐ñse¬e ni i⌐waserema¬sita.
'I was made to say [it] by the teacher.'

The meaning of a passive causative resembles, but is not identical with,
that of a -nakereba na⌐ra¬nai pattern. Compare:

(a) Ka⌐imono ni ikana⌐kereba na⌐rimase¬ñ desita. 'I had to go shop-
        ping.'

and:

(b) Ka⌐imono ni ikaserema¬sita. 'I was made to go shopping.'

Sentence (a) states simply that it was necessary for me to go shopping; anything from a shortage of supplies to a direct order may have been the cause
of my going. Sentence (b), however, implies that some person(s) made me
go, even though they are not necessarily identified in the sentence.

Some situations may be described in terms of either a causative or a passive causative, with the personal nominals occurring as subject and before particle <u>ni</u> reversed. Thus:

Ta⌐roo wa ⌐Zi⌐roo ni saʰsema⁴sita. 'Taro made Jiro do it.'

Zi⌐roo wa ⌐Ta⌐roo ni saʰserarema⁴sita. 'Jiro was made to do it by Taro.'

However, when the person made to do something is the speaker, the passive causative is regularly used:

Ta⌐roo ni saʰserarema⁴sita. 'I was made to do it by Taro' or 'Taro made me do it.'

Additional examples:

Ya⌐kusoku no zikañ ni itta⌐ no ni, i⌐ti-zi⌐kañ mo ma⌐tasera⌐rete si-ʰmaima⁴sita.

'In spite of the fact that I went at the appointed time, I ended up being made to wait all of an hour.'

I⌐soḡasera⌐reta no de, ho⌐ñ o moʰtte ku⁴ru no o wa⌐surema⌐sita.

'Because I was made to hurry, I forgot to bring my book.'

Tanaka-sañ wa ka⌐isya o yamesasera⌐reta soo desu.

'I hear that Mr. Tanaka was fired (lit. was made to quit the company).'

Nihoñḡo de ha⌐nasi⌐ o saʰserarema⁴sita.

'I was made to give a talk in Japanese.'

Yuube tōmodati ni ⌐bi⌐iru o ta⌐kusañ nomasera⌐reta no de, ma⌐da o⌐naka no guai ḡa he⌐ñ desu.

'I was made to drink lots of beer by a friend last night so my stomach still feels strange.'

3. -i⌐nai ～ -i⌐ḡai

-I⌐nai 'within' or 'up to' or 'not more than' occurs directly following a number — most commonly one denoting a period of time or an amount of money.

The opposite of -i⌐nai is -i⌐ḡai 'outside of,' 'except for.' It occurs following nominals in general.

Before -i⌐nai and -i⌐ḡai, a word which is normally accented loses its accent.

Examples:

I⌐s-syuukañ-i⌐nai ni Ni⌐ho⌐ñ e ʰta⁴tu tumori desu.

'I expect to leave for Japan within a week.'

Se⌐ñ-eñ-i⌐nai dattara, ka⌐tte⌐ mo ʰi⁴i desu.

'If it should be not more than ¥1000, you may buy it.'

Zyu⌐u-niñ-i⌐nai no ʰka⁴iḡi ni wa, ko⌐no heya⌐ o tukaimasu.

'For conferences of up to ten people, we use this room.'

Mo⌐kuyoobi-i⌐ḡai nara, i⌐tu de⌐ mo uʰti ni ima⁴su.

'I'll be at home anytime, if it's not Thursday (lit. provided it's outside of Thursday).'

To⌐okyoo-i⌐ḡai ni wa i⌐kitaku arimase⌐ñ.

'I don't want to go outside of Tokyo.'

Ni⌐hoñgo-i¬ḡai wa wa⌐karimase¬ñ.
'I don't understand [any language] except Japanese.'

4. C o u n t e r s :   -bai and -bañti

-Bai is the counter for multiples, meaning 'so-and-so many times (as much or as many).' It combines with numerals of Series I, from 'two' on:

ni-bai	'2 times (as much or as many)'
sañ-bai	'3 times (as much or as many)'
yoñ-bai	'4 times (as much or as many)'
go-bai	'5 times (as much or as many)'
roku-bai	'6 times (as much or as many)'
nana-bai or siti-bai	'7 times (as much or as many)'
hati-bai	'8 times (as much or as many)'
kyuu-bai	'9 times (as much or as many)'
zyuu-bai	'10 times (as much or as many)'
na¬ñ-bai	'how many times (as much or as many)?'

A nominal X + particle no + a number ending in -bai means 'so-and-so many times as much or as many as X.' Thus:

Zyu¬u wa ⌐ni¬ no go-⌐bai de¬su. '10 is 5 times 2.'
A⌐tarasi¬i zi⌐biki⌐ wa i⌐ma ma¬de tu⌐katta zibiki⌐ no sa⌐ñ-bai a¬ru
    soo desu. 'I hear that the new dictionary has 3 times [as much as]
    the dictionary I've used until now.'

Bai occurs as an independent word meaning 'double,' in combinations like
ba⌐i ni na¬ru 'become double,' '[something] doubles' and ba⌐i ni su¬ru 'double [something].'

-Bañti combines with numerals of Series I to name lot numbers. The numbers from one to ten are:

i⌐ti-ba¬ñti	'lot number one'
ni-⌐ba¬ñti	'lot number two'
sa⌐ñ-ba¬ñti	'lot number three'
yo⌐ñ-ba¬ñti	'lot number four'
go-⌐ba¬ñti	'lot number five'
ro⌐ku-ba¬ñti	'lot number six'
na⌐na-ba¬ñti	'lot number seven'
ha⌐ti-ba¬ñti	'lot number eight'
kyu⌐u-ba¬ñti	'lot number nine'
zyu⌐u-ba¬ñti	'lot number ten'
na⌐ñ-ba¬ñti	'lot number what?'

DRILLS

A. Substitution Drill

1. [We] beat Tokyo University.   To⌐odai o makasima¬sita.
2. [We] beat [them] at tennis.   Te¬nisu de ma⌐kasima⌐sita.

3. Tokyo University beat [us].   To⌐odai ḡa makasima⌐sita.
4. Tokyo University won.   To⌐odai ḡa katima⌐sita.
5. Tokyo University lost.   To⌐odai ḡa makema⌐sita.
6. [We] lost in war.   Se⌐ñsoo ni makema⌐sita.
7. [We] won in war.   Se⌐ñsoo ni katima⌐sita.
8. [We] won over Tokyo   To⌐odai ni katima⌐sita.
    University.

B. Substitution Drill

1. We want someone (lit. a   Ho⌐ñyaku (o) site morau hito⌐
    person) who will do trans-   ḡa ho⌐si⌐i ñ desu.
    lating for us (lit. [from
    whom] we will receive
    translating).
2. We want someone who   Ya⌐ne (o) na⌐o⌐site mo⌐rau hito⌐
    will repair the roof for   ḡa ho⌐si⌐i ñ desu.
    us.
3. We want someone who will   Ka⌐be (o) nurika⌐ete mo⌐rau hito⌐
    repaint the walls for us.   ḡa ho⌐si⌐i ñ desu.
4. We want someone who will   Ko⌐re (o) setumee-site morau
    explain this for us.   hito⌐ ḡa ho⌐si⌐i ñ desu.
5. We want someone who will   Pi⌐ano (o) uḡoka⌐site mo⌐rau hi-
    move the piano for us.   to⌐ ḡa ho⌐si⌐i ñ desu.
6. We want someone who will   E⌐ñtotu (o) soozi-site morau hi-
    clean the chimney for us.   to⌐ ḡa ho⌐si⌐i ñ desu.
7. We want someone who will   Ni⌐wa no kusa⌐ (o) ⌐to⌐tte mo⌐rau
    weed the garden for us.   hito⌐ ḡa ho⌐si⌐i ñ desu.
8. We want someone who will   Ta⌐na (o) tutte morau hito⌐ ḡa
    put up some shelves for   ho⌐si⌐i ñ desu.
    us.
9. We want someone who will   Tu⌐uyaku (o) si⌐te morau[1] hito⌐
    do interpreting for us.   ḡa ho⌐si⌐i ñ desu.

C. Substitution Drill

1. Instead of fish I used   Sakana no kawari ni ni⌐ku⌐ (o)
    meat.   tu⌐kaima⌐sita.
2. Instead of screws I used   Ne⌐zi no kawari ni ku⌐ḡi (o)
    nails.   tukaima⌐sita.
3. Instead of milk I used   Mi⌐ruku no kawari ni mi⌐zu (o)
    water.   tukaima⌐sita.
4. Instead of kanji I used   Kañzi no kawari ni ka⌐na (o)
    kana.   tukaima⌐sita.
5. Instead of gas I used   Ga⌐su no kawari ni ⌐deñki (o)
    electricity.   tu⌐kaima⌐sita.
6. Instead of a heater I   Su⌐to⌐obu no kawari ni ⌐hi⌐bati
    used a hibachi.   (o) tu⌐kaima⌐sita.
7. Instead of gasoline I   Gasoriñ no kawari ni ⌐o⌐iru (o)
    used oil.   tu⌐kaima⌐sita.

---

[1] Some native speakers prefer _kureru_ here.

8. Instead of a (dusting) cloth I used a cleaning rag.

Hu⌐ki⌐n̄ no kawari ni zo⌐okin̄ (o) tukaima⌐sita.

9. Instead of hot water I used cold water.

Oyu no kawari ni mi⌐zu (o) tukaima⌐sita.

10. Instead of chopsticks I used a fork.

O⌐ha⌐si no kawari ni ⌐ho⌐oku (o) tu⌐kaima⌐sita.

D. Substitution Drill

1. It was too awful a life to talk about.

Ha⌐nasi⌐ ni na⌐ra⌐nai hodo hi⌐do⌐i se⌐ekatu de⌐sita.

2. It was too tough a life to talk about.

Ha⌐nasi⌐ ni na⌐ra⌐nai hodo tu⌐rai seekatu de⌐sita.

3. It was too upsetting a life to talk about.

Ha⌐nasi⌐ ni na⌐ra⌐nai hodo ko⌐ma⌐-tta se⌐ekatu de⌐sita.

4. It was too restricted a life to talk about.

Ha⌐nasi⌐ ni na⌐ra⌐nai hodo ⌐hu⌐zi-yuu na se⌐ekatu de⌐sita.

5. It was too dangerous a life to talk about.

Ha⌐nasi⌐ ni na⌐ra⌐nai hodo a⌐bunai seekatu de⌐sita.

6. It was too boring a life to talk about.

Ha⌐nasi⌐ ni na⌐ra⌐nai hodo tu⌐mara⌐-nai se⌐ekatu de⌐sita.

7. It was too troublesome a life to talk about.

Ha⌐nasi⌐ ni na⌐ra⌐nai hodo ⌐ku⌐roo no o⌐o⌐i se⌐ekatu de⌐sita.

E. Substitution Drill

1. The place where I was born is Chiba but the place where I grew up is not (Chiba).

U⌐mareta⌐ no wa ⌐Ti⌐ba desu ḡa, so⌐da⌐tta no wa ⌐Ti⌐ba zya a⌐ri-mase⌐n̄.

2. The place where I worked is the country but the place where I lived is not (country).

Ha⌐taraita⌐ no wa i⌐naka de⌐su ḡa, su⌐n̄da no wa i⌐naka zya arima-se⌐n̄.

3. The one I read is English but the one I wrote is not (English).

Yo⌐n̄da no wa e⌐eḡo de⌐su ḡa, ka⌐-ita no wa e⌐eḡo zya arimase⌐n̄.

4. The one I checked is mine but the one I took is not (mine).

A⌐zu⌐keta no wa wa⌐takusi no⌐ de-su ḡa, mo⌐tte i⌐tta no wa wa⌐ta-kusi no⌐ zya a⌐rimase⌐n̄.

5. The one who asked the question is a student but the one who answered is not (a student).

Si⌐tumon̄-sita⌐ no wa ga⌐kusee de⌐-su ḡa, he⌐n̄zi⌐-sita no wa ga⌐ku-see zya arimase⌐n̄.

6. The one who broke it is a child but the one who fixed it is not (a child).

Ko⌐wa⌐sita no wa ko⌐domo de⌐su ḡa, na⌐o⌐sita no wa ko⌐domo zya arimase⌐n̄.

7. The place where they made it is a factory but the place where they sold it is not (a factory).

Tu⌐ku⌐tta no wa ko⌐oba⌐ desu ḡa, u⌐tta⌐ no wa ko⌐oba⌐ zya a⌐rima-se⌐n̄.

F. Substitution Drill

1. This one is simple if
    you compare it to that
    one . . .

    Kore wa a⌐re ni kurabere¬ba ka-
    ⌐ntañ na¬ ñ desu ḡa—

2. Kana is easy if you com-
    pare it to kanji . . .

    Kana wa ka⌐ñzi ni kurabere¬ba
    ya⌐sasi¬i ñ desu ḡa—

3. The post-war [period] is
    free if you compare it to
    pre-war . . .

    Señgo wa se⌐ñzeñ ni kurabere¬ba
    zi⌐yu¬u na ñ desu ḡa—

4. This kind of cloth wears
    well if you compare it
    to that kind of cloth . . .

    Ko⌐ñna ki¬zi wa a⌐ñna ki¬zi ni
    ku⌐rabere¬ba zyo⌐obu na¬ ñ desu
    ḡa—

5. Life in the country is
    hard if you compare it
    to life in the city . . .

    Inaka no seekatu wa ma⌐ti no se-
    ekatu ni kurabere¬ba tu⌐ra¬i ñ
    desu ḡa—

6. This house is big if you
    compare it to that house . . .

    Kono uti wa a⌐no uti ni kurabere¬-
    ba hi⌐ro¬i ñ desu ḡa—

7. The Japanese are small
    if you compare them to
    the Americans . . .

    Ni⌐hoñzi¬ñ wa A⌐merika¬ziñ ni ku-
    ⌐rabere¬ba ti⌐isa¬i ñ desu ḡa—

8. This book is easy to
    read if you compare it
    to the newspapers . . .

    Ko⌐no ho¬ñ wa si⌐ñbuñ ni kurabe-
    re¬ba yo⌐miyasu¬i ñ desu ḡa—

G. Substitution Drill

1. In case you're in a hurry,
    what do you do?

    I⌐so¬ḡu ba⌐tai ni¬ wa ⌐do¬o simasu
    ⌐ka⌡

2. In case you want to ask a
    question, what do you
    do?

    Si⌐tumoñ-sitai baai ni¬ wa ⌐do¬o
    simasu ka⌡

3. In case you've been beaten,
    what do you do?

    Ma⌐keta baai ni¬ wa ⌐do¬o sima-
    su ka⌡

4. In case you haven't under-
    stood, what do you do?

    Wa⌐kara¬nakatta ba⌐ai ni¬ wa ⌐do¬o
    simasu ka⌡

5. In case you can't translate,
    what do you do?

    Ho⌐ñyaku-deki¬nai ba⌐ai ni¬ wa
    ⌐do¬o simasu ka⌡

6. In case of typhoon, what
    do you do?

    Ta⌐ihu¬u no ba⌐ai ni¬ wa ⌐do¬o
    simasu ka⌡

7. In case you want to go
    home early, what do you
    do?

    Ha¬yaku ka⌐erita¬i ba⌐ai ni¬ wa
    ⌐do¬o simasu ka⌡

8. In case you can't hear,
    what do you do?

    Ki⌐koenai baai ni¬ wa ⌐do¬o si-
    masu ka⌡

9. In that case, what do you
    do?

    So⌐no baai ni¬ wa ⌐do¬o simasu
    ka⌡

10. In case of rain, what do
    you do?

    A¬me no ba⌐ai ni¬ wa ⌐do¬o sima-
    su ka⌡

H. Substitution Drill (based on Grammatical Note 4)

        (Insert the appropriate numeral with counter -bai.)

1. Four is twice two.   Si⌐ wa ⌐ni⌐ no ni-⌐bai de⌐su.
2. Three is three times one.   Sañ wa i⌐ti⌐ no sa⌐ñ-bai de⌐su.
3. Twelve is six times two.   Zyu⌐uni⌐ wa ⌐ni⌐ no ro⌐kù-bai de⌐-
                                        su.
4. Twenty is four times five.   Ni⌐zyuu wa ⌐go⌐ no yo⌐ñ-bai de⌐su.
5. Sixteen is eight times two.   Zyu⌐uroku⌐ wa ⌐ni⌐ no ha⌐ti-bai
                                        de⌐su.
6. Fifty is five times ten.   Go⌐zyu⌐u wa ⌐zyu⌐u no go-⌐bai de⌐-
                                        su.
7. Thirty-five is seven times   Sa⌐ñzyuu ⌐go⌐ wa ⌐go⌐ no na⌐ha-bai
    five.   de⌐su.
8. One hundred is ten times   Hya⌐ku⌐ wa ⌐zyu⌐u no zyu⌐u-bai de⌐-
    ten.   su.

I. Substitution Drill

1. I plan to leave for Kyoto   I⌐s-syuukañ-i⌐nai ni ⌐Kyo⌐oto e
    within a week.   ⌐ta⌐tu tumori desu.
2. I plan to leave for Kyoto   Raisyuu ⌐Kyo⌐oto e ⌐ta⌐tu tumori
    next week.   desu.
3. I plan to leave for Kyoto   Mo⌐kuyo⌐o made ni ⌐Kyo⌐oto e
    by Thursday.   ⌐ta⌐tu tumori desu.
4. I plan to leave for Kyoto   Do⌐yoobi-ḡo⌐ro ⌐Kyo⌐oto e ⌐ta⌐tu
    about Saturday.   tumori desu.
5. I plan to leave for Kyoto   Tooka ni ⌐Kyo⌐oto e ⌐ta⌐tu tumo-
    on the tenth.   ri desu.
6. I plan to leave for Kyoto   Koñgetu-zyuu ni ⌐Kyo⌐oto e ⌐ta⌐tu
    before this month is over.   tumori desu.
7. I plan to leave for Kyoto   Asa no uti ni ⌐Kyo⌐oto e ⌐ta⌐tu
    during the morning.   tumori desu.
8. I plan to leave for Kyoto   Yo⌐-zi ⌐tyo⌐tto ⌐ma⌐e ni ⌐Kyo⌐oto
    a little before four.   e ⌐ta⌐tu tumori desu.
9. I plan to leave for Kyoto   Si⌐ti-zi-ha⌐ñ ni ⌐Kyo⌐oto e ⌐ta⌐tu
    at 7:30.   tumori desu.
10. I plan to leave for Kyoto   Tyo⌐odo ku⌐-zi ni ⌐Kyo⌐oto e ⌐ta⌐tu
    at nine sharp.   tumori desu.

J. Level Drill [1]

1. Ri⌐reki⌐syo (o) mo⌐tte   Ri⌐reki⌐syo (o) mo⌐tte kima⌐sita.
    mairima⌐sita.
2. Ke⌐site huhee wa moosi-   Ke⌐site huhee wa iimase⌐ñ.
    mase⌐ñ.

---

[1] In each case, the sentence on the right is a plain formal equivalent of the
polite formal sentence on the left.

3. Ha⌐isyaku-site¬ mo yo⌐ro-
   si¬i desu ka⌐   Ka⌐rite¬ mo ⌐i¬i desu ka⌐

4. Ya⌐suma¬sete i⌐tadakema-
   se⌐ñ ka⌐   Ya⌐suma¬sete mo⌐raemase⌐ñ ka⌐

5. To o⌐ssya¬ru to?   To iu to?

6. Do¬tira de o⌐sodati ni
   narima¬sita ka⌐   Do⌐ko de so⌐datima¬sita ka⌐

7. Ni⌐hoñḡo ni hoñyaku-
   nasaima¬sita ka⌐   Ni⌐hoñḡo ni hoñyaku-sima¬sita
                                     ka⌐

K. Expansion Drill

1. [She] was born.   U⌐marema¬sita.
   [She] was born in Tokyo.   To⌐okyoo de umarema¬sita.
   [She] was born in Tokyo   Syoowa ⌐zyu¬ugo-neñ ni To⌐okyoo
   in Showa 15.   de umarema¬sita.
   Mrs. Tanaka was born   Ta⌐naka-sañ no o⌐kusañ wa syo̊-
   in Tokyo in Showa 15.   owa ⌐zyu¬ugo-neñ ni To⌐okyoo
                                        de umarema¬sita.

2. Would you translate [it]   Ho⌐ñyaku-site kudasaimase⌐ñ ka⌐
   for me?
   Would you translate [it]   E⌐ḡo ni hoñyaku-site kudasai-
   into English for me?   mase¬ñ ka⌐
   Would you translate this   Kono kookoku (o) e⌐ḡo ni hoñ-
   advertisement into   yaku-site kudasaimase¬ñ ka⌐
   English for me?
   Would you translate this   Kono ni̊hoñḡo no kookoku (o)
   Japanese advertisement   e⌐ḡo ni hoñyaku-site kudasai-
   into English for me?   mase¬ñ ka⌐

3. [It] was defeated.   Ma⌐kema¬sita.
   [It] was defeated in war.   Se⌐ñsoo ni makema¬sita.
   [It] was defeated in war   Syoowa ni⌐zyu¬u-neñ ni se⌐ñsoo
   in Showa 20.   ni makema¬sita.
   Germany was defeated   Do̊itu (wa) syo̊owa ni⌐zyu¬u-neñ
   in war in Showa 20.   ni se⌐ñsoo ni makema¬sita.

4. Somebody broke some-   Ko⌐wasarema¬sita.
   thing and I was annoyed.
   I had three plates broken.   Sara (o) ⌐sa¬ñ-mai ko⌐wasarema¬-
                                        sita.
   I had three plates broken   A⌐tarasi¬i zyotyuu ni såra (o)
   by the new maid.   ⌐sa¬ñ-mai ko⌐wasarema¬sita.
   I had three plates broken   I⌐ti-zikañ-i¬nai ni a⌐tarasi¬i zyo-
   by the new maid within   tyuu ni såra (o) ⌐sa¬ñ-mai ko-
   an hour.   ⌐wasarema¬sita.

5. I used to be made to work.   Ha⌐tarakaserareta mon(o)¬ desu.
   I used to be made to work   Hatake de ha⌐tarakaserareta
   in the fields.   mon(o)¬ desu.

I used to be made to work in the fields from morning till night.	A⌐sa kara ba⌐ñ ma⌐de hǎtake de ha⌐tarakaserareta mon(o)⌐ desu.
My father used to make me work in the fields from morning till night.	Ti⌐ti⌐ ni ⌐a⌐sa kara ba⌐ñ ma⌐de hǎtake de ha⌐tarakaserareta mon(o)⌐ desu.

L. Grammar Drill (based on Grammatical Note 1)

    Tutor: Da⌐re ka si⌐ma⌐sita. 'Somebody did it.'
    Student: Da⌐re ka ni sa⌐rema⌐sita. 'I was [unfavorably] affected
               by someone's doing it.' or 'I had someone do it.'

1. Tomodati ḡa o⌐soku kima⌐sita.
    Tomodati ni o⌐soku korarema⌐sita.
2. Hi⌐syo⌐ ḡa ya⌐mema⌐sita.
    Hi⌐syo⌐ ni ya⌐merarema⌐sita.
3. Kodomo ḡa to⌐kee (o) torima⌐sita.
    Kodomo ni to⌐kee (o) torarema⌐sita.
4. Zyotyuu ḡa o⌐ka⌐si (o) ta⌐bema⌐sita.
    Zyotyuu ni o⌐ka⌐si (o) ta⌐berarema⌐sita.
5. Da⌐re ka ma⌐do (o) a⌐kema⌐sita.
    Da⌐re ka ni ma⌐do (o) a⌐kerarema⌐sita.
6. Ta⌐roo-tyañ ḡa to ⌐(o) simema⌐sita.
    Ta⌐roo-tyañ ni to ⌐(o) simerarema⌐sita.
7. Ga⌐kusee ḡa kikima⌐sita.
    Ga⌐kusee ni kikarema⌐sita.
8. O⌐ba ḡa sodatema⌐sita.
    O⌐ba ni sodaterarema⌐sita.
9. A⌐katyañ ḡa o⌐kosima⌐sita.
    A⌐katyañ ni o⌐kosarema⌐sita.
10. Se⌐ñse⌐e ḡa ko⌐re (o) yomima⌐sita.
    Se⌐ñse⌐e ni ko⌐re (o) yomarema⌐sita.

M. Grammar Drill (based on Grammatical Note 2)

    Tutor: Si⌐ma⌐sita. /da⌐re ka/ 'I did it. /someone/'
    Student: Da⌐re ka ni | sa⌐serareta / sa⌐sareta | mon(o)⌐ desu. [1] 'Someone used
        to make me do it.'

1. Ya⌐sai (o) tabema⌐sita. /ha⌐ha/
    Ha⌐ha ni ya⌐sai (o) | tabesasera⌐reta / tabesasa⌐reta | mo⌐n(o)⌐ desu.

2. Hu⌐de de kakima⌐sita. /se⌐ñse⌐e/
    Se⌐ñse⌐e ni hu⌐de de | kakasera⌐reta / kakasa⌐reta | mo⌐n(o)⌐ desu.

3. Pa⌐ñku-sita taiya (o) torikaema⌐sita. /ti⌐ti⌐/
    Ti⌐ti⌐ ni pa⌐ñku-sita taiya (o) | torikaesaserareta / torikaesasareta | mon(o)⌐ desu.

4. E⌐ḡo de hanasima⌐sita. /oba/
    Oba ni e⌐ḡo de | hanasasera⌐reta / hanasasa⌐reta | mo⌐n(o)⌐ desu.

---
[1] Give the long and short forms for each.

5. Mi⌐ruku (o) no┌mima⌐sita.
   /ryo⌐osiñ/

   Ryo⌐osiñ ni ⌐mi⌐ruku (o)
   | no┌masera⌐reta
   | no┌masa⌐reta | mo┌n(o)⌐ desu.

6. Pi┌ano no reñsyuu (o)
   sima⌐sita. /ha⌐ha/

   Ha⌐ha ni pi┌ano no reñsyuu (o)
   | saserareta
   | sasareta | mon(o)⌐ desu.

7. Yo⌐ku ha┌tarakima⌐sita.
   /so⌐hu/

   So⌐hu ni ⌐yo⌐ku | ha┌tarakaserareta
                   | ha┌tarakasareta |
   mon(o)⌐ desu.

8. Ga┌kkoo ni aru┌ite i┌ki-
   ma⌐sita. /ti┌ti⌐/

   Ti┌ti⌐ ni ga┌kkoo ni aru┌ite
   | i┌kaserareta
   | i┌kasareta | mon(o)⌐ desu.

9. Ma⌐initi ko┌ko e kima⌐-
   sita. /se┌ñse⌐e/

   Se┌ñse⌐e ni ⌐ma⌐initi ko┌ko e
   | kosasera⌐reta
   | kosasa⌐reta | mo┌n(o)⌐ desu.

10. Ma⌐iasa ma┌tima⌐sita.
    /tomodati/

    Tomodati ni ⌐ma⌐iasa
    | ma┌tasera⌐reta
    | ma┌tasa⌐reta | mo┌n(o)⌐ desu.

For each sentence of the above exercise, give the corresponding sentence meaning 'I had to —— ' with no reference to any person as the cause.

Example:
   Tutor: Ha⌐ha ni ya┌sai (o) tabesasera⌐reta mo┌no(o)⌐ desu.
   Student: Ya┌sai (o) tabe⌐nakereba na┌rimase┌ñ desita.

N. Substitution Drill (based on Grammatical Note 2)

1. No matter what kind of work I'm made to do, I'll never complain.

   Do⌐ñna sigoto (o) sa┌serarete⌐ mo, ke┌site huhee wa iimase⌐ñ.

2. No matter when I'm made to work, I'll never complain.

   I⌐tu ha┌tarakaserarete⌐ mo, ke┌site huhee wa iimase⌐ñ.

3. No matter where I'm made to go, I'll never complain.

   Do⌐ko e i┌kaserarete⌐ mo, ke┌site huhee wa iimase⌐ñ.

4. No matter what time I'm made to come, I'll never complain.

   Na⌐ñ-zi ni ko┌sasera⌐rete mo, ke┌site huhee wa iimase⌐ñ.

5. No matter what town I'm transferred to, I'll never complain.

   Do⌐no ma┌ti⌐ ni te┌ñkiñ-saserarete⌐ mo, ke┌site huhee wa iimase⌐ñ.

6. No matter what kind of tough life I'm made to live, I'll never complain.

   Do⌐ñna tu┌rai seekatu (o) saserarete⌐ mo, ke┌site huhee wa iimase⌐ñ.

7. No matter what I'm made to eat, I'll never complain.

Na⌐ni (o) ta⌐besasera⌐rete mo, ke⌐site huhee wa iimase⌐ñ.

8. No matter what kind of medicine I'm made to take, I'll never complain.

Do⌐ñna kusuri (o) no⌐masera⌐rete mo, ke⌐site huhee wa iimase⌐ñ.

Do the above drill, with the tutor reading each of the sentences on the right and the student repeating, substituting the short form of the passive causative.

Example:

Tutor: Do⌐ñna siḡoto (o) sa⌐serarete⌐ mo, ke⌐site huhee wa iimase⌐ñ.

Student: Do⌐ñna siḡoto (o) sa⌐sarete⌐ mo, ke⌐site huhee wa iimase⌐ñ.

O. Substitution Drill

1. I came back and in no time war began.

Ka⌐ette ma⌐mo⌐naku se⌐ñsoo ḡa hazimarima⌐sita.

2. I came back and in no time I began this.

Ka⌐ette ma⌐mo⌐naku ko⌐re (o) hazimema⌐sita.

3. I came back and in no time I joined the army.

Ka⌐ette ma⌐mo⌐naku ḡu⌐ñtai ni ha⌐irima⌐sita.

4. I came back and in no time I was taken into the army.

Ka⌐ette ma⌐mo⌐naku ri⌐ku⌐ḡuñ ni to⌐rarema⌐sita.

5. I came back and in no time I was drafted.

Ka⌐ette ma⌐mo⌐naku syo⌐osyuu-sarema⌐sita.

6. I came back and in no time I quit.

Ka⌐ette ma⌐mo⌐naku ya⌐mema⌐-sita.

7. I came back and in no time he quit on me.

Ka⌐ette ma⌐mo⌐naku a⌐no⌐ hito ni ya⌐merarema⌐sita.

8. I came back and in no time I fired him.

Ka⌐ette ma⌐mo⌐naku a⌐no⌐ hito (o) ya⌐mesasema⌐sita.

9. I came back and in no time I was fired by him.

Ka⌐ette ma⌐mo⌐naku a⌐no⌐ hito ni ya⌐mesaserarema⌐sita.

10. I came back and in no time I was transferred.

Ka⌐ette ma⌐mo⌐naku te⌐ñkiñ-saserarema⌐sita.

SUPPLEMENTARY DIALOGUES

1. Tanaka: Ta⌐bako ika⌐ḡa desu ka⌐

   Yamamoto: Se⌐kkaku⌐ desu ḡa, sake to tabako o to⌐merarete iru⌐ ñ de-su yo⌐

   Tanaka: Gobyooki de?

   Yamamoto: E⌐e. I⌐k-kaḡetu-ḡu⌐rai ⌐ma⌐e made ti⌐ti⌐ no mu⌐ra⌐ de ya-⌐su⌐ñde i⌐ta⌐ ñ desu yo⌐

   Tanaka: So⌐o desu ka. I⌐kemase⌐ñ desita ⌐ne⌐e. Si⌐rimase⌐ñ desita ka-ra, si⌐tu⌐ree-simasita.

Yamamoto: Iie, do᷈o itasimasite. Kono-ḡoro wa zēñzeñ gu᷉ai no wa-
ru᷉i to᷅koro᷄ wa ⌐na᷉i ñ desu ḡa, ma᷉da su᷅ki᷄ na sake to tabako wa no⌐ma᷉sete mo᷅raena᷄i ñ de ⌐ne᷉e.

Tanaka: Sore wa sore wa. Ma᷉a, byo᷉oki ni᷄ wa ka⌐temase᷄ñ kara,
mo᷉o suko᷉si ᷅ga᷄mañ-suru ñ desu ⌐ne᷉e.

2. Tanaka: Do᷈o desu ka⌐ —a᷅na᷄ta no beñkyoo wa.
   Smith: Mo᷈o i᷅ya᷄ ni ᷅na᷄tte si᷅maima᷄sita yo.
   Tanaka: Do᷈o site desu ka.
   Smith: Ma᷉initi ⌐ma᷉initi ᷅a᷄sa kara ba᷅ñ ma᷄de ni⌐hoñḡo o kakasera᷄re-
   tari, ha⌐nasasera᷄retari, ki⌐kasera᷄retari su⌐ru᷄ ñ desu kara⌐
   Tanaka: De᷈ mo, so᷉o sure᷉ba ⌐ha᷉yaku o᷅boerare᷄ru desyoo?
   Smith: So⌐re wa so᷉o desu ḡa⌐

3. Tanaka: Ho᷈ñyaku-sina᷅kere᷄ba na⌐ra᷄nai teḡami ḡa ⌐a᷄ru ñ desu ḡa,
   o᷅siete kudasaimase᷄ñ ka⌐
   Smith: E⌐eḡo ni hoñyaku-suru᷄ ñ nara, o᷅te᷄tudai-sima᷄su yo⌐
   Tanaka: Hi⌐to᷄ri de si⌐ta᷄ra; go-bai mo zyu᷉u-bai mo zikañ ḡa kaka᷄-
   tte, yo⌐naka᷄ ni ⌐na᷄tte mo de⌐ki᷄nai ka mo si⌐remase᷄ñ kara⌐
   Smith: Zya, su᷉ḡu ha⌐zimemasyo᷄o.
   Tanaka: Zya᷉a, su᷅mimase᷄ñ ḡa, o᷅neḡai-sima᷄su.

4. Yamamoto: Tanaka-sañ. O⌐kosañ ḡa oumare ni na᷄tta soo de, o᷅mede-
   too gozaima᷄su.
   Tanaka: A᷅ri᷄ḡatoo gozaimasu.
   Yamamoto: Do᷄tira de irassyaimasu ka⌐
   Tanaka: Mu⌐suko de gozaima᷄su.
   Yamamoto: So⌐re wa i᷅i desu ⌐ne᷉e.

5. Mr. Smith: O⌐tokoro o itte kudasa᷄i. Bo᷄ku ḡa ka⌐kima᷄su kara. A.
   Ainiku ka⌐mi᷄ ḡa i⌐ti-mai mo na᷄kute⌐
   Mr. Tanaka: Bo⌐ku arima᷄su. Do᷄ozo. To⌐okyo᷄o-to, Mi⌐nato᷄-ku, Azabu,
   Ho⌐ñmura᷄-tyoo, sa⌐ñ-ba᷄ñti desu yo⌐
   Mr. Smith: Mo᷉o suko᷉si yu⌐kku᷄ri i⌐tte kudasaimase᷄ñ ka. Ka⌐kika᷄ta
   o᷅so᷄i kara⌐

6. Smith: Tanaka-sañ wa ⌐ma᷉da go⌐byooki de᷄su ka⌐
   Yamamoto: E᷉e. Mo᷉o ro⌐k-kaḡetu ne⌐tte ima᷄su yo⌐ Uti de ⌐na᷄ni ka
   ho᷉ñyaku no siḡoto o site, so᷉re de seekatu-site iru so᷄o desu
   ḡa⌐
   Smith: Go⌐ka᷄zoku wa?
   Yamamoto: Ohanasi ni na⌐ra᷄nai hodo tu⌐rai so᷄o desu yo. Okane wa
   ta⌐rina᷄i si, byo᷅oki no koto᷄ o si⌐ñpai-site iru᷄ si⌐

7. Smith: I᷉ma ⌐su᷉ñde iru tokoro ho⌐ñseki᷄ti desu ka⌐
   Mr. Tanaka: Iie .iie. Ho⌐ñseki wa inaka no ho᷄o de, su᷉ñda koto wa
   a⌐rimase᷄ñ.
   Smith: To iu to?
   Mr. Tanaka: Bo᷉ku ḡa u⌐mareru ma᷄e ni ti⌐ti᷄ ḡa To᷄okyoo e teñkiñ-
   saserarete, bo᷉ku ·wa zu⌐tto Tookyoo de sodatima᷄sita. So᷉hu
   ya ⌐so᷄bo wa ⌐ma᷉da ᷅inaka ni ite, so᷅tira ḡa ma᷉da ho⌐ñseki
   na᷄ ñ desu.
   Smith: Naruhodo.

8. Conductor (announcing): Ma⌐mo⌐naku Yo⌐kohama de gozaima⌐su. O⌐ori
     ni na⌐ru ka⌐ta⌐ wa o⌐sitaku neḡaima⌐su.
    Male Passenger: Ni⌐motu ḡa o⌐o⌐i ñ da ḡa, a⌐kaboo wa iru daro⌐o ne?
    Conductor: Ha⌐a. Ho⌐omu³ ni o⌐rima⌐su kara, go⌐siñpai na⌐ku.

9. Smith: A⌐na⌐ta wa ḡo⌐zibuñ no o⌐ka⌐asañ ni tuite ha⌐na⌐su toki, na⌐ñ te
          yo⌐bu⌐ ñ desu ka⌐
    Mr. Tanaka: Ba⌐ai ni yotte tiḡau⌐ ñ desu ḡa; tyu⌐uḡaku no tomodati to
          ha⌐na⌐su ba⌐ai ni⌐ wa o⌐hukuro⌐¹ tte itte, ka⌐zoku to ha⌐na⌐su
          ba⌐ai ni⌐ wa o⌐ka⌐asañ te itte, se⌐ñse⌐e nado ni ⌐te⌐enee² ni ha-
          ⌐nasa⌐nakereba na⌐ra⌐nai ba⌐ai ni⌐ wa ⌐ha⌐ha tte i⌐u⌐ ñ desu.
    Smith: Naruhodo. O⌐ka⌐asañ ni wa a⌐na⌐ta tte i⌐u⌐ ñ desu ka⌐
    Mr. Tanaka: Iie. Ti⌐ti⌐ ya ⌐ha⌐ha o a⌐na⌐ta tte yo⌐bu koto⌐ wa a⌐rima-
          se⌐ñ. Taitee o⌐to⌐osañ o⌐ka⌐asañ te yo⌐bu⌐ ñ desu.

10. Smith: Se⌐ñse⌐e ni ri⌐reki⌐syo o mo⌐tte ku⌐ru yoo ni i⌐wareta⌐ ñ desu
          ḡa, ri⌐reki⌐syo tte i⌐u⌐ no wa ⌐do⌐ñna mo⌐no⌐ desu ka⌐
    Mr. Tanaka: Sore wa ⌐ne⌐e. So⌐no⌐ hito no u⌐mareta tokoro⌐ ya u⌐mareta
          hi, sore kara ⌐de⌐ta gakkoo ya ⌐do⌐ñna siḡoto o si⌐ta⌐ ka to i⌐u
          yo⌐o na koto o ⌐ka⌐ita mo⌐no⌐ na ñ desu.
    Smith: Zya⌐a, i⌐ma ma⌐de no ke⌐ekeñ o ka⌐keba ⌐i⌐i ñ desu ne?
    Mr. Tanaka: Ma⌐a ⌐so⌐o desu ḡa; da⌐itai no kakika⌐ta ḡa wa⌐kara⌐nai to
          o⌐komari desyo⌐o kara, bo⌐ku no o o⌐mise-simasyo⌐o ka.
    Smith: Yo⌐rosi⌐kereba, ha⌐ikeñ-sasete kudasa⌐i.

                        English Equivalents
1. Tanaka: How about a cigarette?
    Yamamoto: It's kind of you to ask but I'm not allowed to drink or smoke
              (lit. I am affected by the stopping of sake and cigarettes).
    Tanaka: Because you're ill?
    Yamamoto: Yes. Until about a month ago I was away from work (lit.
              resting), in my father's village.
    Tanaka: Really. That was too bad. I didn't know so excuse my rude-
            ness.
    Yamamoto: That's all right. There's nothing wrong with me (lit. there
              are no places at all where the condition is bad) these days but
              they won't let me drink or smoke yet—things I love to do (lit. I
              cannot yet receive their letting me take in sake and cigarettes
              which I love). . .
    Tanaka: Oh dear. I guess you should be patient a little longer since
            you can't have the upper hand when it comes to sickness (lit.
            over sickness you can't win). . .

2. Tanaka: How goes it—your studying?
    Smith: I'm fed up with it already.
    Tanaka: Why?

---

¹ Familiar way of referring to one's mother, comparable to English 'the old
lady.' Used by young men.

² Te⌐enee /na/ 'polite.'

³ Ho⌐omu 'platform.'

Smith: Because day after day, day after day, from morning until night, I'm made to write Japanese and speak it and listen to it.

Tanaka: But if you do that, you'll be able to learn it quickly, won't you?

Smith: That's true but . . .

3. Tanaka: I have a letter that I must translate. Would you show me how?

Smith: If it's a matter of translating into English, I'll help you.

Tanaka: If I do it alone, it will take me five and ten times as much time, and even if I keep on until the middle of the night (lit. even if it becomes the middle of the night), I may not be able to finish it (so . . .)

Smith: Well, let's begin right away.

Tanaka: (Well) I'm sorry [to bother you] but would you [help me]?

4. Yamamoto: Mr[s]. Tanaka! I hear that your baby has been born. Congratulations.

Tanaka: Thank you.

Yamamoto: Is it a boy or a girl? (Lit. Which is it?)

Tanaka: It's a boy.

Yamamoto: Isn't that nice!

5. Mr. Smith: Please tell me your address. (Because) I'll write it down. Oh. Unfortunately I don't have a single sheet of paper . . .

Mr. Tanaka: I have. Here you are. It's No. 3, Hommura Cho, Azabu, Minato Ward, Tokyo (City).

Mr. Smith: Would you say it a little more slowly? (Because) I write slowly (lit. my way of writing is slow).

6. Smith: Is Mr. Tanaka still sick?

Yamamoto: Yes. He's been in bed six months now. He is doing some translation work at home and is making his living with that, they say, but . . .

Smith: What about his family?

Yamamoto: I hear that they are having too difficult a time to talk about. They don't have enough money and they are worrying about his illness and . . .

7. Smith: Is the place where you are living now your permanent residence (place)?

Mr. Tanaka: No no. My permanent residence is in the country and I've never lived there.

Smith: What do you mean by that?

Mr. Tanaka: My father was transferred to Tokyo before I was born and I grew up (all the time) in Tokyo. My grandfather and grandmother are still in the country and that is still our permanent residence.

Smith: I see.

8. Conductor: Next stop Yokohama. (Lit. In no time it will be Yokohama.) All passengers getting off, please get ready. (Lit. I request preparation [from] persons who will get off.)

Male Passenger: I have a lot of luggage. I suppose there will be porters, won't there?

Conductor: Yes. They'll be on the platform so don't worry.

9. Smith: When you speak about your own mother, what is it you call her?
    Tanaka: It's different depending on circumstances. In cases where I'm
            speaking with friends from middle school, I say "ofukuro," and
            in cases where I'm speaking with the family, I say "okāsan,"
            and in cases where I must speak politely, to people like teach-
            ers, I say "haha."
    Smith: I see. [When speaking] to your mother do you say "anata"?
    Tanaka: No. There's never a time when I address my mother and fa-
            ther as "anata." I usually address them as "otōsan," "okāsan."

10. Smith: I was told by the teacher to bring my personal history; (but) what
            sort of thing is a personal history?
     Mr. Tanaka: Oh, that. It's a thing [that has] written [on it] things like
            the place where the person was born and the day when he was
            born, and then the schools he graduated (lit. went out) from and
            what kind of work he's done.
     Smith: Then as long as I write my experience up to now it will be all
            right, won't it?
     Mr. Tanaka: That's about it, but you'll probably have difficulty if you
            don't understand the general way of writing it, so shall I show
            you mine?
     Smith: If it's all right, please let me see it.

EXERCISES

1. Interview an applicant for a job. Check on his name, present address,
    permanent residence, educational background, military service, and
    experience. Tell him you will get in touch with him by next Monday.

2. Make up twelve short conversations, each one of which contains one of
    the following phrases:

        a. huhee o iu
        b. i⌐s-syuukañ-i⌐nai ni
        c. wa⌐kara⌐nai ba⌐ai ni⌐ wa
        d. o⌐hazukasi⌐i ñ desu ḡa
        e. to⌐koro⌐ de
        f. ma⌐mo⌐naku
        g. ha⌐nasi⌐ ni na⌐ra⌐nai hodo turai
        h. ——— no kawari ni
        i. ainiku
        j. uti o yakareru
        k. To⌐okyoo-i⌐ḡai
        l. saserareru

Lesson 35. Among Friends

BASIC DIALOGUES: FOR MEMORIZATION

(a)

(Matsumoto and Tanaka are young men who are close friends.)

Tanaka

game <u>or</u> match   siai
do you go? <u>or</u> are you   iku kai⌟
   gonna go?
1. Matsumoto. Are you gonna   Matumoto-kuñ. Asita no siai
go and see the game tomor-   ⌜mi⌝ ni iku kai⌟
row?

Matsumoto

2. Did you say (it's) a game?   Siai da tte?

   baseball   yakyuu
3. You mean baseball, don't   Yakyuu daro?
you?

Tanaka

4. Yeah.   N̄.

Matsumoto

   it's tiresome, don't you   tu⌜ma⌝ññai zya nai ka
    agree?
5. Aren't you bored stiff by   Ya⌜kyuu na⌝ñka tu⌜ma⌝ññai zya
 things like baseball?   nai ka.

   generally speaking, on the   oyoso
    whole, as a rule
   interest   kyo⌜omi⌝ [1]
   have an interest   kyo⌜omi⌝ ḡa ⌐a⌝ru
6. As a rule, they don't appeal   Oyoso | kyo⌜omi na⌝i ⌐ne⌝e.
to me!

Tanaka

   oh, dear! <u>or</u> good   ma⌝a
    heavens!
   don't say (imperative)   i⌜u⌝ na
7. Oh, don't say that!   Ma⌝a, so⌜o iu⌝ na yo.

   seems to be good <u>or</u>   i⌜i rasi⌝i /-ku/
    is likely to be good
8. The one [i.e. game] tomor-   A⌜sita no⌝ (wa) i⌜i rasi⌝i yo⌟
row is likely to be good.

---

[1] Alternate accent: <u>kyo⌝omi</u>.

    once in a while <u>or</u>   tama ni
    now and then
    associate with   tu⌐kia⌐u /-u/
    associate with (imperative)   tu⌐kia⌐e

9. Keep me company once in a   Ta⌐ma ni⌐ wa tu⌐kia⌐e yo.
     while.

Matsumoto

10. What time does it begin?   Naⁿ-zi kara dai.
     (Lit. From what time is it?)

Tanaka

11. Wasn't it (from) about one?   I⌐ti-zi-ḡo⌐ro kara zya ⌐na⌐katta
                              ka na?

Matsumoto

12. I'm already booked up for   A⌐sita⌐ wa ⌐mo⌐o ya⌐kusoku-sitya-
     tomorrow—to go swimming.   tta⌐ ⁿ da yo—o⌐yo⌐ḡi ni iku tte.

    swim (imperative)   o⌐yo⌐ḡe

13. You come (lit. go) along and Kimi mo issyo ni itte, o⌐yo⌐ḡe
     swim!   yo.

    sports   su⌐po⌐otu
    as for not being a sport   su⌐po⌐otu de ⌐na⌐kutyaa
    it's no fun, don't you   o⌐mosi⌐roku ⌐na⌐i zya nai ka
      agree?

14. When it's not a sport you take Zi⌐buⁿ de yaru supo⌐otu de ⌐na⌐-
     part in (lit. do) yourself,   kutyaa, o⌐mosi⌐roku ⌐na⌐i zya nai
     don't you agree it's no fun?   ka.

Tanaka

15. I wonder what I should do!   Do⌐o siyoo ka ⌐na⌐a＿

    after all   ya⌐ha⌐ri <u>or</u> ya⌐ppa⌐ri

16. I'm going to make it baseball   Boku (wa) ya⌐ppa⌐ri ya⌐kyuu no
     (lit. the baseball alternative) ho⌐o ni su⌐ru⌐ yo.
     after all.

(b)

Wife

    stoppage of electricity   teedeⁿ

17. Oh! The electricity is off!   A⌐ra, teedeⁿ yo‿

Husband

18. Again?   Ma⌐ta⌐ kai‿

Wife

    always <u>or</u> at all hours   syo⌐ttyuu
     <u>or</u> constant(ly)
    because it is constant   syo⌐ttyuu desu mono

19. I hate it because it keeps   Syo⌐ttyuu desu mono, i⌐ya¬a ⌐ne¬e.
    happening.

Husband

    almost   ho⌐to¬ndo
    it's every night, don't   ma⌐iban zya¬ nai ka
      you agree?
20. It's almost every night —   Ho⌐to¬ndo ma⌐iban zya¬ nai ka.
    isn't it.

Wife

    I wonder if it will   tu⌐ku¬ ka sira
      become attached
21. I wonder if it will go on soon.   Su¬gu tu⌐ku¬ ka sira.

Husband

    don't understand <u>or</u>   wa⌐ka¬rya sinai
      can't tell
22. I can't tell.   Wa⌐ka¬rya si¬na¬i sa.

    is dark   kurai /-ku/
    candle   ro⌐osoku¬
23. In any case, it's dark so let's   To¬nikaku ku⌐ra¬i kara, ro⌐osoku¬
    light a candle.   tu⌐keyo¬o.

Wife

    household altar (Shinto)   kamidana
    household altar (Buddhist)   butudan
    kamidana or butsudan   kamidana ka butudan
24. I think there's a big (lit. thick)   Kamidana ka butudan ni hu⌐to¬i
    candle (placed) in the kamidana   roosoku o⌐ite a¬ru to o⌐mo¬u no
    or the butsudan.   yo⌐

Husband

    is it left?   no⌐ko¬tte ru kai⌐
25. Is that still left?   Are ⌐ma¬da no⌐ko¬tte ru kai⌐

Wife

    probably   ta¬bun
    one-third   sa⌐n-bun no iti¬
    about as much as one-third   sa⌐n-bun no iti¬ hodo
26. Yes. Probably there should   E¬e. Ta¬bun sa⌐n-bun no iti¬
    be about a third [of it] left.   hodo no⌐ko¬tte ru hazu yo⌐

Husband

    go <u>or</u> come <u>or</u> be   oide
      (imperative)
    go and get (lit. come   tott(e) oide
      having taken) (impera-
      tive)
27. (Then) would you go and get   Zya¬a, tott(e) oide⌐
    it?

Wife (bringing candle)

accept <u>or</u> receive	tyoodai-suru ↓
let me have (imperative)	tyoˋodaˉi
attach for me (imperative)	tuˋkeˉte tyoodai

28. Light it, would you?   Tuˋkeˉte tyoodai ne?

(c)

(Mrs. Yamamoto has just run into her good friend, Mrs. Ikeda.)

Mrs. Yamamoto

neglect to write or visit	gobusata-suru ↓
excuse me	goˋmeñ-nasaˉi

29. Forgive me for not getting in   Gobusata-sityatte goˋmeñ-nasaˉi
touch with you.   ne?

Mrs. Ikeda

nothing but neglect	goˋbusata baˉkari
to write or visit	

30. <u>I'm</u> the one who keeps neglect-   Koˋtira koˉso goˊbusata baˊkari
ing to get in touch with <u>you</u>.   site—

Mrs. Yamamoto

while thinking <u>or</u>	oˋmoinaˉḡara
although thinking	
unintentionally <u>or</u>	tuˉi
carelessly	

31. While I kept thinking of tele-   Oˋdeñwa siˋyoˉo siˋyoˉo to oˊmoinaˊ-
phoning (lit. while thinking,   ḡara ˊtuˊi—
'I'll make a call, I'll make
[it]'), I unintentionally [let
it slip my mind].

make a business trip	syuttyoo-suru
exam <u>or</u> test	siˋkeˉñ
entrance exam	nyuˋḡakusikeˉñ

32. My husband was away on   Syuˉziñ ḡa syuˊttyoo-sitaˊri, ko-
business, and there were   ˋdomo no nyuuḡakusikeˉñ ḡa ˊaˊtta-
my child's entrance exams,   ri site ˉneˉe.
and so on—you know . . .

Mrs. Ikeda

33. How did your son do?   Boˉttyañ ˋdoˉo nasutte?

Mrs. Yamamoto

thanks to you <u>or</u>	okaḡe de
thanks for asking	
parent	oˋyaˉ
grow thin	yaseru /-ru/

34. He was finally able to get   Okaḡe de, yaˋtto hairemaˉsita
into [school], thank you, but   kedo; siñpai-site, oˋyaˉ mo ko
parents and child wasted away   mo yaˋsetyaimaˉsita wa—
worrying!

Mrs. Ikeda

35. Wasn't it nice that he was   O⌐hairi┐ ni na⌐rete, yo⌐katta wa
      able to get in!   ⌐ne┐e.

      have a good head <u>or</u>   a⌐tama┐ ḡa ⌐i┐i
         be smart <u>or</u> be <u>bright</u>
36. [It's] because your son is   Bo⌐ttyañ (wa) a⌐tama┐ ḡa ⌐i┐i kara_
      bright.

Mrs. Yamamoto

37. Oh, heavens no!   Ma┐a, to⌐ñde mo na┐i.

Mrs. Ikeda

      a relief   hi⌐toa┐ñsiñ [1]
38. You must be relieved [that the   Ko⌐re de hitoa┐ñsiñ ⌐ne┐e.
      got in]. (Lit. With this, a
      relief, isn't it.)

      high school   kookoo
      with each passing year   i⌐ti-neñ-ḡo┐to ni
        <u>or</u> each year
      competition <u>or</u> contest   kyoosoo
39. Isn't it awful how the competi-   Kookoo mo da⌐iḡaku mo i⌐ti-neñ-
      tion for both high school and   ḡo┐to ni kyo⌐osoo ḡa hi⌐doku
      university gets [more] severe   ⌐na⌐tte, ko⌐ma┐ru wa ⌐ne┐e.
      each year.

Mrs. Yamamoto

      unless [someone] leaves   de┐nakeryaa
        <u>or</u> graduates
      find employment <u>or</u> get   syuusyoku-suru
        a job
      because it's a matter of   syu⌐usyoku-deki┐nai ñ
        not being able to find   desu mono
        a job
40. [It's] because you can't get a   I┐i gakkoo (o) ⌐de┐nakeryaa, i┐i
      job in a good place unless you   toko e syu⌐usyoku-deki┐nai ñ
      graduate from a good school,   desu mono ⌐ne┐e.
      isn't it . . .

Mrs. Ikeda

      with this being the trend   ko⌐ñna hu┐u de wa <u>or</u>
        (lit. as for being this   ko⌐ñna hu┐u zya
        kind of manner)
      pathetic <u>or</u> pitiful   ka⌐waiso┐o /na/
41. But with this being the trend,   De┐ mo; ko⌐ñna hu┐u zya, kodo-
      it's hard on the children·(lit.   mo ḡa ka⌐waiso┐o da wa ⌐ne┐e.
      the children are pitiful),
      isn't it.

---

[1] Alternate accent: hi⌐to┐añsiñ.

Mrs. Yamamoto

be that as it may <u>or</u>
to change the subject

so⌐re wa so⌐o to

42. To change the subject, your
baby must be (lit. have become) big by now, isn't he?

So⌐re wa so⌐o to, o⌐taku no a⌐ka-
tyañ ⌐mo⌐o ⌐zu⌐ibuñ ⌐o⌐okiku onari
desyoo?

Mrs. Ikeda

something <u>or</u> anything
act as if wanting to say

na⌐ñ ka
i⌐itaso⌐o ni suru

43. Yes. He has begun to eat
(food) already, and he often
acts as if he wants to say
something.

E⌐e. Mo⌐o ⌐go⌐hañ (o) ta⌐behazi-
meta⌐ si, yo⌐ku ⌐na⌐ñ ka i⌐itaso⌐o
ni su⌐ru⌐ no yo⌐

a word

hitokoto

44. But as far as language goes,
he doesn't say a single word
yet . . .

De⌐ mo, ko⌐toba⌐ wa ⌐ma⌐da hi-
⌐tokoto mo hanasa⌐nai kedo⌐

Mrs. Yamamoto

birthday

ta⌐ñzyo⌐obi <u>or</u> o⌐tañzyo⌐-
obi †

45. Is his birthday soon now?

O⌐tañzyo⌐obi mo⌐o su⌐gu na no?

Mrs. Ikeda

46. No, not yet (not yet).

Iie, ma⌐da ⌐ma⌐da.

because he's nine months

ku-⌐ka⌐ḡetu desu mono

47. (Because) he's nine months
old now.

I⌐ma ku-⌐ka⌐ḡetu desu mono.

Mrs. Yamamoto

in that case

so⌐re de⌐ wa <u>or</u> so⌐re
zya⌐a

unreasonable <u>or</u> beyond
one's power

mu⌐ri /na/

48. In that case, you can't expect
him to talk yet (lit. talk is
still unreasonable), can
you . . .

So⌐re zya⌐a, ohanasi wa ⌐ma⌐da
⌐mu⌐ri ⌐ne⌐e.

rapidly
pleasure <u>or</u> enjoyment

do⌐ñdoñ
ta⌐nosi⌐mi [1] or otanosimi †

49. Babies grow up rapidly so
they're fun [to watch], aren't
they.

A⌐katyañ wa ⌐do⌐ñdoñ ⌐o⌐okiku
o⌐nari da⌐ kara, otanosimi ⌐ne⌐e.

go to someone else's home
go to see

aḡaru /-u/ †
haikeñ ni aḡaru †

---

[1] Or <u>ta⌐nosimi⌐</u>.

50. I'll come (lit. go) to see him   Iti-do ha⌐ikeñ ni aḡaru⌐ wa ne?
    some (lit. one) time—all
    right?

Mrs. Ikeda

51. Yes. Come, by all means.   E⌐e. Ze⌐hi i⌐ra⌐site.

ADDITIONAL VOCABULARY

1. There was an <u>earthquake</u> this   Ke⌐sa <u>zi⌐siñ</u> ḡa arima⌐sita yo⌣
   morning.

        fire   ka⌐zi
        accident   zi⌐ko

2. Help!   Ta⌐suke⌐te.

3. It's set at about <u>5 per cent.</u>   Go⌐-bu hodo ni ⌐na⌐tte (i)masu.

        10 per cent   i⌐ti⌐-wari
        15 per cent   i⌐ti-wari go⌐-bu

4. That baby <u>cries</u> a lot, doesn't   A⌐no a⌐katyañ (wa) ⌐yo⌐ku <u>nᾱku</u>
   he?   desyoo?

        laugh   warau /-u/

5. What a <u>frightening</u> expression!   Ko⌐wa⌐i ka⌐o de⌐su ⌐ne⌐e.
   <u>or</u> What an angry look!

        is dreadful <u>or</u> terrible   su⌐ḡo⌐i /-ku/
          <u>or</u> terrific <u>or</u> extra-
          ordinary
        is lonesome <u>or</u> cheer-   sa⌐bisi⌐i /-ku/
          less
        is happy   u⌐resi⌐i /-ku/

NOTES ON THE BASIC DIALOGUES

3. The loan-word be⌐esubo⌐oru is another word for 'baseball.'

9. Note: <u>hi⌐to to tukia⌐u</u> 'associate with a person.' The derivative nominal
   <u>tukiai</u> means 'association' or 'acquaintance.'

11. Note the use of the past. Compare English: 'Didn't I hear that it started
    at one?'

12. <u>Sityatta</u> is the contracted equivalent of <u>site simatta</u>. <u>Tte</u> is the quota-
    tive: lit. 'I've already made a promise for tomorrow—quote to go swim-
    ming.'

13. <u>Kimi</u> is an informal man's word used in reference to one's equals or in-
    feriors. It is also used as an informal term of address.

Note all the following less formal equivalents of <u>watakusi</u> and <u>aˉnaˉta</u>:

'I':   <u>watasi</u> (men and women)
       <u>boˉku</u> (men only)
       <u>atasi</u> (women only)
       <u>wasi</u> (older men only)
       <u>ore</u> (rough word; men only)

'you': <u>aˉnta</u> (men and women)
       <u>omae</u> (used more commonly by men, in addressing inferiors, particularly children)

14. <u>Naˉkutya/a/</u> is the contracted equivalent of <u>naˉkute wa</u>. The combination <u>e</u> + consonant + <u>a</u> (in the same word or consecutive words) is regularly contracted to <u>ya/a/</u> in contracted speech. When such a contraction yields the combination <u>d</u> + <u>ya</u>, it is regularly spelled <u>zya</u> in this text. Thus:

      sore wa   >   sorya/a/
      —eba [1]   > ⌐—ya/a/
      —kereba [1] > ⌐—kerya/a/ (cf. Sentence 40, below)
      deˉ wa   >   zyaˉ/a/

The <u>zya</u> which occurs in the negative equivalent of a nominal + <u>da</u> combination (for example, <u>hoˉ n zya ˉnaˉi</u> 'it isn't a book') is also a contraction of <u>de</u> + <u>wa</u>. The <u>wa</u> is sometimes omitted, leaving <u>de</u> alone: <u>soˉo de ˉnaˉkereba</u> 'unless it's so'; <u>suˉpoˉotu de ˉnaˉkute wa</u> 'as for not being a sport.'

15. In men's speech, <u>naˉa</u> occurs as an alternant of <u>neˉe</u>, and <u>na</u> as an alternant of <u>ne</u>, particularly in deliberative questions addressed to oneself.

16. <u>Yaˉppaˉri</u> is an informal, more emphatic alternant of <u>yaˉhaˉri</u>.

19. <u>Iˉyaˉa</u> is an alternant of <u>iˉyaˉ</u>.

23. The opposite of <u>kurai</u> is <u>akarui</u> /-<u>ku</u>/ 'is light.'

26. Following a number, <u>hodo</u> regularly means 'about (as much as).'

29. <u>Gobusata-sityau</u> is the contracted equivalent of <u>gobusata-site simau</u>.

32. Note: <u>siˉkeˉn-suru</u> 'test' 'put [something] to a test' and <u>siˉkeˉn o uˉkeˉru</u> /-<u>ru</u>/ 'undergo a test,' 'take a test.'

33. The use of a sentence-final gerund with question intonation as a substitute for a past-tense form is typical of women's informal speech. <u>Naˉsuˉtte</u> is an alternant of <u>naˉsaˉtte</u>, gerund of <u>naˉsaˉru</u> †.

34. <u>Okaˉge de</u> is a less polite equivalent of <u>okaˉgesama de</u>.
The opposite of <u>yaseru</u> is <u>huˉtoˉru</u> /-<u>u</u>/ 'grow fat.' Note: <u>yaˉseta hitoˉ</u> 'thin person'; <u>huˉtoˉtta hito</u> 'fat person.'
<u>Yaˉsetyaimaˉsita</u> is the contracted equivalent of <u>yaˉsete simaimaˉsita</u>.

37. As an expression of pleasure, <u>maˉa</u> is typical of women's speech. In its various other uses (for example, Sentence 7 above), it occurs in the speech of both men and women.

---

[1] Ending of the provisional.

39. Note: kyoosoo-suru 'compete.'

40. See note on Sentence 14 above. The -kerya⌐a⌐ ending may be further contracted to -kya⌐a⌐. Thus, na⌐kereba has as its contracted equivalents na⌐kerya⌐a⌐ and na⌐kya⌐a⌐.

43. Na⌐ñ ka is a contraction of na⌐ni ka and is used by men and women. I⌐itaso⌐o is made up of the stem of iitai 'want to speak,' and -soo 'looking as if ——— .'

48. Note: mu⌐ri ni saseru 'force [someone] to do.'

49. Note also the verbal ta⌐nosi⌐mu /-u/ 'take pleasure in,' 'enjoy' and the adjectival ta⌐nosi⌐i 'is merry or pleasant or enjoyable.'

50. Do not confuse plain ag̃aru 'go up' with humble polite ag̃aru↓ 'go to someone else's home.'

Additional Vocabulary

2. Ta⌐suke⌐ru /-ru/ is a transitive verbal meaning 'save' or 'rescue' or 'help.' Its intransitive partner is ta⌐suka⌐ru /-u/ 'be saved' or 'be helped' or 'survive.'

3. The counter for units of per cent is -bu and for tens of per cent is -wari. Both counters take numerals of Series I. Examples:

i⌐ti⌐-bu	'1%'	i⌐ti⌐-wari	'10%'
ni⌐-bu	'2%'	ni⌐-wari	'20%'
sa⌐ñ-bu	'3%'	sa⌐ñ-wari	'30%'
yo⌐ñ-bu	'4%'	yo⌐ñ-wari	'40%'
go⌐-bu	'5%'	go⌐-wari	'50%'
ro⌐ku⌐-bu	'6%'	ro⌐ku⌐-wari	'60%'
na⌐na⌐-bu or		na⌐na⌐-wari or	
si⌐ti⌐-bu	'7%'	si⌐ti⌐-wari	'70%'
ha⌐ti⌐-bu	'8%'	ha⌐ti⌐-wari	'80%'
ku⌐-bu	'9%'	ku⌐-wari	'90%'
		zyu⌐u-wari [1]	'100%'

na⌐ñ-bu 'how many per cent?'   na⌐ñ-wari 'how many tens of per cent?'

Percentages equaling ten or more, which are not multiples of ten, are regularly expressed in terms of -wari and -bu. Thus, '38 per cent' is sa⌐ñ-wari hati⌐-bu.

4. Naku is a verbal of the -u group.

5. Ko⌐wa⌐i is an adjectival.

GRAMMATICAL NOTES

1. ra⌐si⌐i

X ra⌐si⌐i means 'is apparently or evidently X,' 'is typical of X.' X may be:

---

[1] Rare.

(1) a sentence consisting of (or ending with) a non-past or past infor-
    mal verbal or adjectival
(2) a sentence ending with da⌐tta
(3) a nominal, with or without preceding modifiers
(4) a sequence ending with a particle

Ra⌐si¬i is itself an adjectival, but unlike other adjectivals, it never occurs
at the beginning of a phrase. The word or phrase that immediately precedes
ra⌐si¬i regularly loses its accent.

Ra⌐si¬i resembles -soo and yo⌐o, but there are specific differences:

(1) Grammar

    (a) -Soo is a suffix which enters into compounds with verbal and ad-
        jectival stems and a few nominals. -Soo compounds are them-
        selves na nominals.
    (b) Ra⌐si¬i is an adjectival (ra⌐siku, ra⌐sikute, ra⌐sikatta, etc.). For
        what precedes it, see above.
    (c) Yo⌐o is a na nominal. It is preceded by a demonstrative (kono,
        sono, etc.), a phrase ending in particle no, or a sentence mod-
        ifier (cf. Lesson 24, Grammatical Note 1).

(2) Meaning

    (a) -Soo words usually refer to physical appearance, whereas ra⌐si¬i
        and yo⌐o patterns rely on any kind of evidence.
    (b) For a comparison of -soo and yo⌐o, see Lesson 26, Grammatical
        Note 5.
        Yo⌐o refers to similarity or likeness, whereas ra⌐si¬i indicates
        apparent equivalence. Ko⌐domo no yo⌐o, for example, can refer
        only to someone who is childlike BUT NOT A CHILD, whereas
        ko⌐domo rasi¬i refers ONLY TO A CHILD who is 'just like a
        child.' Similarly, a male can be o⌐nna no yo⌐o 'like a woman,'
        but only a female can be o⌐nna rasi¬i 'ladylike'; summer, fall,
        and winter can be ha⌐ru no ⌐yo⌐o, but only spring can be ha⌐ru
        rasi¬i.

Examples:

    De⌐pa⌐ato ni wa, na⌐n de mo aru rasi¬i desu ⌐ne¬e.
        'Apparently there is everything in department stores, isn't there.'
    Kinoo no siai wa ma⌐ketyatta rasi¬i ⌐ne⌐e.
        'Apparently they lost yesterday's game, didn't they.'
    A⌐no zibiki¬ wa na̅kanaka i⌐i rasi¬i.
        'That dictionary is apparently quite good.'
    Ta⌐kakatta rasi¬i kedo, ka⌐tta so⌐o desu ⌐ne¬e.
        'They say he bought it, although apparently it was expensive.'
    Amerika no he⌐etai rasi¬i hi⌐to⌐ g̅a ki⌐ma⌐sita yo⌐
        'Someone who is evidently an American soldier is here (lit. has
        come).'
    A⌐merika⌐zin̅ desu g̅a, A⌐merikazin̅ ra⌐siku a⌐rimase⌐n̅ ⌐ne¬e.
        'He's an American but he doesn't seem like one (lit. like an Amer-
        ican).'
    Kono teg̅ami wa A⌐merika kara rasi¬i desu ⌐ne¬e.
        'This letter is apparently from America.'

2. ――zya nai ka

X + zya nai[1] ka means 'X is true, isn't it'; 'surely you agree that X is true, don't you'; 'you see, don't you, that X is true!'; 'I knew that X was true!' X, in this construction, is usually a non-past or past verbal or adjectival, the past copula da˺tta, a nominal, or a sequence ending with a particle.

Be sure to distinguish among the following kinds of sentences:

(a) O˹mosi˺roku ˹na˺i? 'Isn't it interesting?' or 'It's not interesting?'
(b) O˹mosiro˺i zya nai ka. 'It is interesting, isn't it.' or 'Surely you agree it's interesting, don't you.'
(c) O˹mosi˺roku ˹na˺i zya nai ka. 'It isn't interesting, is it.' or 'Surely you agree it isn't interesting, don't you.'

In general, ―― zya nai ka in sentence-final position occurs in men's speech. Women use ―― zya nai no as an equivalent. Both men and women also use more polite and more formal equivalents (―― zya arimaseñ ka and ―― de˹ wa gozaimaseñ ka).

Examples:

Gu˹ai ḡa waru˺i soo da ḡa, yo˹ku ta˹berare˺ru zya nai ka.
   'I hear you don't feel well, but you can eat well, can't you!'
Bo˹ku ḡa itta to˺ori, Kyo˹ziñ[2] ḡa katta zya˺ nai ka.
   'Just as I told you, the Giants did win, didn't they.'
So˹ñna ni isoḡa˺nakute mo ˹i˺i zya nai ka.
   'Surely you don't have to hurry so much, do you.'
Ha˹ya˺i ⌐ne˹e. Sa˹ñzyu˺p-puñ sika ka˹kara˺nai zya nai ka.
   'It's early, isn't it. It does take only 30 minutes, doesn't it.'
Tanaka-sañ wa tu˹mara˺nai tte i⌐tta˺ keredo, na˹kanaka omosiro˺i ⌐ho˹ñ zya nai ka.
   'Mr. Tanaka said it was dull, but surely you agree that it is an interesting book, don't you.'
Sa˺ñ-zi kara da tte i⌐tta˺ keredo, ni˺-zi kara zya nai ka.
   'He said it started at (lit. was from) three but it does start at two, doesn't it.'

3. Honorific and Humble Nominals

A nominal consisting of polite prefix o- + a verbal stem is an HONORIFIC NOMINAL. (Examples: omati from ma˺tu 'wait,' oake from akeru 'open,' etc.) An honorific nominal is unaccented.

Honorific nominals occur:

(1) + ni √˹na˺ru (Lesson 9, Grammatical Note 2)
(2) + √da (Lesson 23, Grammatical Note 2)
(3) + √-suru (Lesson 13, Grammatical Note 4)
(4) + -kudasa˺i(ma˺se) (Lesson 18, Grammatical Note 3)
(5) In sentence-final position as a request (Lesson 18, Grammatical Note 3).

---

[1] Regularly unaccented in this construction. The accent pattern of X + zya nai ka is parallel to that of X + ka mo sirenai.

[2] Kyoziñ 'giant.'

Some honorific nominals are irregular. For example, goran̄ (occurring in patterns 1, 4, 5 above) is the honorific nominal for the verbal mi⌐ru, and oide (occurring in patterns 1, 2, 4, and 5) is the honorific nominal for verbals ku⌐ru 'come,' iku 'go,' and iru 'be.'

Note also the nominal gomen̄ 'your pardon,' which occurs in patterns 2, 4, and 5, although it is not directly linked with any particular verbal.

Contrasting with the above honorific nominals is a small group of HUMBLE NOMINALS which occur in patterns 3 and 5 above, and refer politely (i. e. humbly) to the actions of the speaker:

tyo⌐oda⌐i: tyoodai-suru (humble equivalent of morau 'receive,' 'accept,' 'eat,' 'drink'; usage resembles that of itadaku)
              Tyo⌐oda⌐i. 'Let me have [it].'
haiken̄:   haiken̄-suru (humble equivalent of mi⌐ru 'see')
              Haiken̄. 'Let me see [it].'
haisyaku: haisyaku-suru (humble equivalent of kariru 'borrow'; usage resembles that of okari-suru)
              Haisyaku. 'Let me borrow [it].'

4. Informal Imperatives

  A. Affirmative

    The affirmative informal imperative of a verbal consists of:

      (1) -ru Group: the citation form with final -u changed to -o[2]
                            (but note ku⌐re⌐ 'give me!' from kureru).

                            Example: ta⌐be⌐ru 'eat': ta⌐be⌐ro 'eat!'

      (2) -u Group: the citation form with final -u changed to -e[2]

                            Example: ma⌐tu 'wait': ma⌐te 'wait!'

      (3) -aru Group: the stem alone

                            Example: na⌐sa⌐ru 'do': na⌐sa⌐i 'do!'

      (4) Irregular Group: suru 'do': si⌐ro⌐ 'do!'
                             ku⌐ru 'come': ko⌐i 'come!'

All may be followed by particle yo.

Except for those of Group (3), all the imperatives listed above are used only by men, in abrupt speech, when they are addressing close friends, intimates, and inferiors. As a slightly less abrupt imperative, men use a verbal gerund + ku⌐re⌐ (the informal imperative of kureru 'give me'):[3]

    Ta⌐bete kure. 'Eat (for me).' (Lit. 'Give me eating.')
    No⌐n̄de kure. 'Drink (for me).'
    Itte kure. 'Go (for me).'

_____

[1] For further comments on tyo⌐oda⌐i see Grammatical Note 4, following.

[2] An imperative of an unaccented verbal is accented on the final syllable.

[3] This is less polite than gerund + honorific nominal okure.

These differ from gerund + ku⌐dasa⌐i only in that ku⌐re⌐ 'give me' is plain informal, whereas ku⌐dasa⌐i 'give me' is polite informal.

Informal imperatives based on honorific verbals of Group (3) above (i⌐ra-
ssya⌐i, na⌐sa⌐i, o⌐ssya⌐i, and ku⌐dasa⌐i) are used by men and women. They
are informal but polite.

Another informal affirmative imperative pattern, used by women and,
less commonly, men, consists of a verbal stem or an honorific nominal
(Note 3 above) + -nasa⌐i. Examples:

    Ta⌐benasa⌐i. or O⌐tabe-nasa⌐i. 'Eat!'
    No⌐minasa⌐i. or O⌐nomi-nasa⌐i. 'Drink!'
    I⌐kinasa⌐i.   or O⌐ide-nasa⌐i.[1] 'Go!'

Such imperatives occur most commonly in addressing children, close rela-
tives, maids, etc. They are never used in addressing a superior. Other examples of the pattern, which—as polite clichés—can be used in addressing
anyone, are:

    O⌐yasumi-nasa⌐i. 'Goodnight.' (Lit. 'Rest!')
and
    O⌐kaeri-nasa⌐i. 'Welcome home.' (Lit. 'Return!')

Remember that verbal gerunds and honorific and humble nominals in sentence-final position[2] also occur as informal affirmative requests (cf. Lesson 18, Grammatical Note 3, and Note 3 above). Tyo⌐oda⌐i, like ku⌐dasa⌐i,
may be preceded by a nominal object or a verbal gerund:

    O⌐ka⌐si (o) tyoodai. 'Give me (lit. let me have) some candy.'
    Ma⌐tte tyoodai. 'Wait (for me).' (Lit. 'Let me have waiting.')

Tyo⌐oda⌐i requests are informal and familiar. They are frequently used by
men and women in addressing children, but in general occur much more
commonly in the speech of women.

B. Negative

A verbal in its citation form (the informal non-past) + particle na is an
abrupt, informal negative imperative used by men in addressing close friends,
intimates, and inferiors. An accented verbal retains its original accent before na, but a normally unaccented verbal acquires an accent on its final syllable. Na may be followed by yo.

Examples:

    Ta⌐be⌐ru na. 'Don't eat!'
    No⌐mu na.   'Don't drink!'
    Su⌐ru⌐ na.   'Don't do [it]!'

Corresponding negative imperatives of honorific verbals are rare.

The following kinds of negative requests, consisting of—or including—a
-nai negative + de, are less abrupt but still informal:

---

[1] Also means 'Come!' or 'Stay!'

[2] Or pre-final before yo and ne.

——nai de.   (Men and women)
——nai de kure.   (Men only)
——nai de okure.   (Men and older women)
——nai de kudasai.   (Men and women)
——nai de tyoodai.   (See tyoˋodaˊi under affirmative above)

5. -naga̅ra 'although'

Reread Lesson 31, Grammatical Note 2.

-Naga̅ra, like English 'while,' has two different meanings: (1) 'while' = 'during' and (2) 'while' = 'although.' It is introduced with the first meaning in Lesson 31, and with the second meaning in this lesson.

-Naga̅ra meaning 'although' is compounded not only with verbal stems but also with some nominals (particularly na words). It is sometimes followed by particle mo 'even.'

The accent of -naga̅ra words is the same, regardless of which meaning -naga̅ra has.

Examples:

Oˋtaku no maˊe o ˋmaˊiniti toˋorinaˊga̅ra, hiˋma g̅a naˋkute oˋyori-dekiˊ-
    nai ñ desu.
    'While I pass (the front of) your house every day, I can't stop in be-
        cause I have no (free) time.'
Oˋisiku naˊi to iinaga̅ra, miˋñna taˋbete siˋmaimaˊsita.
    'While he said it wasn't good, he ended up eating everything.'
Uˋti no maˊe made ikinaga̅ra, haˋirimaseˊñ desita.
    'While he walked all the way to (the front of) the house, he didn't
        come in.'
Siˋtureenaˊg̅ara, oˋtosi o ukag̅aimasyoˋo.
    'While it's rude, let's ask his age.'

6. Fractions

The Japanese equivalent of an English fraction X/Y is Y-buñ no X: lit. 'X-many of Y-many parts,' in which X and Y are numerals of Series I, and -buñ is the counter for 'parts.'

A numeral + counter -buñ is unaccented.

    1/3   saˋñ-buñ no itiˊ
    1/4   yoˋñ-buñ no itiˊ or si-ˋbuñ no itiˊ
    2/5   go-ˋbuñ no niˊ
    5/6   roˋku-buñ no goˊ
    3/7   siti-buñ no sañ or nana-buñ no sañ
    5/8   haˋti-buñ no goˊ
    2/9   kyuˋu-buñ no niˊ
    9/10 zyuˋu-buñ no kyuˊu

Ni-ˋbuñ no itiˊ is the equivalent of mathematical '1/2'; for conversational 'half,' there is the special word haˋñbuˊñ.

A nominal + particle <u>no</u> + a fraction means 'a fraction of so-and-so.' Thus: <u>roosoku no sa⌐n̄-buñ no iti⌐</u> 'one-third of the candle(s).'

<u>Kono</u> + a fraction means 'a fraction of this' and <u>sono</u> + a fraction means 'a fraction of that': for example, <u>kono sa⌐n̄-buñ no ni⌐</u> 'two-thirds of this.'

Additional examples:

Ni⌐ wa ro⌐ku⌐ no sa⌐n̄-buñ no iti⌐ desu.
    'Two is one-third of 6.'
Ro⌐ku⌐ no sa⌐n̄-buñ no ni⌐ wa ⌐si⌐ desu.
    'Two-thirds of 6 is 4.'
So⌐no ho⌐n̄ no yo⌐n̄-buñ no sañ hodo yomima⌐sita.
    'I read about three-quarters of that book.'
Ko⌐no hañbu⌐n̄ wa so⌐no sa⌐n̄-buñ no iti⌐ yori su⌐kuna⌐i desu.
    'Half of this is less than one-third of that.'

7. Particles: <u>ka</u> 'or,' <u>ba⌐kari</u> 'only,' <u>mono</u> 'because'

a. <u>ka</u> 'or'

<u>Ka</u> connects nominals and means 'or':

    kore ka so⌐re 'this or that'
    nihoñḡo ka ⌐eeḡo 'Japanese or English'
    pe⌐ñ ka ⌐eñpitu 'a pen or pencil'

Be sure to distinguish between the following two kinds of sentences:

Pe⌐ñ ka e⌐ñpitu o tukaima⌐sita ka⌐ 'Did you use (either) a pen or a pencil?' (anticipating answer 'yes' or 'no')
Pe⌐ñ o tu⌐kaima⌐sita ka, e⌐ñpitu o tukaima⌐sita ka⌐ 'Did you use a pen—or (did you use) a pencil?' (i.e. which one did you use?)

Examples:

Ho⌐ñ ka za⌐ssi o kasite kudasa⌐i.
    'Please let me borrow a book or a magazine.'
Kyo⌐o wa Ta⌐naka-sañ ka Ya⌐mamoto-sañ ḡa ku⌐ru hazu desu.
    'Today Mr. Tanaka or Mr. Yamamoto is supposed to come.'
A⌐sita⌐ ka a⌐sa⌐tte i⌐kimasyo⌐o.
    'Let's go tomorrow or the next day.'
Raisyuu ⌐Ni⌐kkoo ka ⌐Kyo⌐oto e i⌐ku tumori de⌐su.
    'I plan to go to Nikko or Kyoto next week.'

b. <u>Ba⌐kari</u> 'only'

<u>Ba⌐kari</u> (or, more emphatic, <u>ba⌐kkari</u>) means 'little else but,' 'just.' Some of its more common occurrences are:

   1.   Preceded by a non-past or past verbal and followed by √<u>da</u>.

        Examples: Be⌐ñkyoo-suru ba⌐kari desu. 'He just studies.' or 'All he does is study.' or 'He does little else but study.'
                  Tu⌐ita ⌐ba⌐kari desu. 'He (only) just arrived.'

2. Preceded by a verbal gerund and followed by √iru.

Examples: A⌐sa kara ba⌐ñ ma⌐de ha⌐taraite ba⌐kari imasu. 'All
I'm doing is working, from morning till night.'
Te⌐rebi o ⌐mi⌐te ⌐ba⌐kari i⌐ma⌐sita. 'All he was do-
ing was watching television.'

3. Preceded by a nominal.

A verbal compound consisting of a nominal + <u>suru</u>—for example,
<u>beñkyoo-suru</u> 'study'—occurs as two independent words with <u>ba⌐ka-
ri</u> between them: for example, <u>be⌐ñkyoo ba⌐kari suru</u> 'do nothing
but study.'

Examples:

Ku⌐-zi kara be⌐ñkyoo-suru⌐ no wa, Ta⌐naka-sañ ba⌐kari desu.
'Mr. Tanaka is about the only one who studies at (lit. from)
nine o'clock.'
Kodomo wa o⌐ka⌐si ⌐ba⌐kari ta⌐bema⌐sita. 'The children ate
little else but sweets.'
Ueda-sañ wa ryo⌐koo ba⌐kari simasu. 'Mr. Ueda does little
else but travel.'

Following a nominal, the meaning of <u>ba⌐kari</u> resembles that of <u>dake</u>
and <u>sika</u>. Compare the following examples:

Ta⌐naka-sañ dake tabema⌐sita. 'Just Mr. Tanaka (no one
else) ate.'
O⌐ka⌐si ⌐ba⌐kari ta⌐bema⌐sita. 'I ate little else but candy.'
(i.e. lots of candy, a little of other things)
O⌐ka⌐si sika ta⌐bemase⌐ñ desita. 'I didn't eat anything except
candy.' (a negative approach, emphasizing that nothing else
was eaten)

Following a nominal which is a number or indefinite quantity word, [1]
<u>ba⌐kari</u> means 'about,' 'only about': <u>mi-⌐ttu ba⌐kari</u> 'about 3 (units),'
<u>ni-⌐neñ ba⌐kari</u> 'about 2 years.' Compare:

Zyu⌐u-niñ ba⌐kari ki⌐ma⌐sita. '(Only) about ten people came.'
Zyu⌐u-niñ-ḡu⌐rai ki⌐ma⌐sita. 'About ten people came.'
Zyu⌐u-niñ hodo ki⌐ma⌐sita. 'About (as many as) ten people
came.'

c. <u>mono</u> 'because'

The particle <u>mono</u> occurs as a more familiar, informal equivalent of
<u>kara</u> 'because,' in sentences where the emphasis is on the reason or justifi-
cation for an action which is contrary to expectation. It occurs more commonly, though not exclusively, in the speech of women.

Examples:
Are ka⌐ita⌐katta kedo, ya⌐meta⌐ no yo⌐—ta⌐ka⌐i ñ desu mono— (W)
'I wanted to buy it but I gave up the idea—because it's expensive.'

---

[1] An accented number or quantity expression loses its accent before <u>ba⌐kari</u>.

Ko⌐ńna e⌐e̅ga tu⌐ma⌐ńnai mono, mo⌐o de⌐yo⌐o yo. (M)
  'This kind of movie is boring so let's leave now.'
I⌐ti-zi⌐kań mo a⌐ru⌐ku ń nara, i⌐kana⌐i wa⌣—tu⌐kare⌐ru mono⌣ (W)
  'If it's a matter of walking for all of an hour I'm not going—because
  I'll get tired.'

8. Sentence Particles: <u>kai</u>, <u>sa</u>

 a. <u>kai</u>

<u>Kai</u> is an interrogative sentence particle used by men in informal
speech, as a more conversational, less abrupt equivalent of <u>ka</u>. It follows
non-past, past, and tentative informal inflected words (but <u>da</u> is lost before
<u>kai</u> just as it is lost before <u>ka</u>).

Examples:

Formal (MW)	Informal (M; abrupt)	Informal (M)	Informal (Predominantly W)	Informal (MW)
Wa⌐ka⌐rima⌐su ka⌣	Wa⌐ka⌐ru ka.	Wa⌐ka⌐ru kai⌣	Wa⌐ka⌐ru no?	Wa⌐ka⌐ru?
Sa⌐mu⌐i desu ka⌣	Sa⌐mu⌐i ka.	Sa⌐mu⌐i kai⌣	Sa⌐mu⌐i no?	Sa⌐mu⌐i?
So⌐o desu ka⌣	So⌐o ka.	So⌐o kai⌣	So⌐o na no?	So⌐o?
So⌐o desita ka⌣	So⌐o datta ka.	So⌐o datta kai⌣	So⌐o datta no?	So⌐o datta?

In informal questions containing a question word (<u>na</u>ni, <u>da</u>re, i<u>tu</u>, etc.),
<u>dai</u> occurs in men's speech in sentence-final position as a more conversa-
tional, less abrupt equivalent of sentence-final <u>da</u>.

Examples:

Formal (MW)	Informal (M; abrupt)	Informal (M)	Informal (Predominantly W)	Informal (MW)
Do⌐o desu ka⌣	Do⌐o da.	Do⌐o dai⌣	Do⌐o na no?	Do⌐o?
Do⌐ko desu ka⌣	Do⌐ko da.	Do⌐ko dai⌣	Do⌐ko na no?	Do⌐ko?
Da⌐re no desu ka⌣	Da⌐re no da.	Da⌐re no dai⌣	Da⌐re no na no?	Da⌐re no?
Na⌐ń-zi kara desu ka⌣	Na⌐ń-zi kara da.	Na⌐ń-zi kara dai⌣	Na⌐ń-zi kara na no?	Na⌐ń-zi kara?

 b. <u>sa</u>

<u>Sa</u> is a sentence particle of emphasis which occurs, in the standard
language, in men's informal speech. Its meaning is similar to that of <u>yo</u> but
it is softer and less assertive. It does not follow imperative form.

Before <u>sa</u>, <u>da</u> is lost:

 So⌐o da yo.
 So⌐o da ne?

   but:

 So⌐o sa.

9. -ḡo⌐to ni

-Ḡo⌐to ni, directly following a nominal—particularly a number denoting a period of time—means 'each so-and-so,' 'each and every so-and-so,' 'with the occurrence of each so-and-so.' Before -ḡoto ni, a word which is regularly accented loses its accent. Thus:

> hu⌐tu-ka-ḡo⌐to ni 'every two days'
> sa⌐ñ-syuukañ-ḡo⌐to ni 'every three weeks'
> hi-⌐ḡo⌐to ni 'with each passing day'

Examples:

> Sa⌐ñ-neñ-ḡo⌐to ni ku⌐ni e kaerima⌐su.
>   'Every three years, I return to my country.'
> Yo-⌐zikañ-ḡo⌐to ni ko⌐no kusuri o no⌐ñde kudasai.
>   'Please take this medicine every four hours.'
> Ba⌐su wa sa⌐ñzyup-puñ-ḡo⌐to ni ⌐de⌐ru soo desu.
>   'They say the bus leaves every 30 minutes.'
> Tanaka-sañ no eēgo wa hi-⌐ḡo⌐to ni zyo⌐ozu⌐ ni na⌐rima⌐su yo⌐
>   'Mr. Tanaka's English improves with each passing day.'
> Tu⌐kia⌐u hi⌐to-ḡo⌐to ni so⌐o iima⌐su yo⌐
>   'He says that to every person he associates with.'

10. —— ka sira

Ka sira occurs at the end of sentences following inflected words—nonpast, past, and tentative—and means 'I wonder if —— .' It occurs more commonly, but not exclusively, in the speech of women. The more common men's equivalent is ka na (cf. Sentence 11 of the Basic Dialogues).

For accentuation, see ka mo siremaseñ (Lesson 30, Grammatical Note 2).

Remember that before ka, da is lost.

Examples: [1]

> Wa⌐ka⌐ru ka sira. 'I wonder if he understands.'
> Wa⌐ka⌐tta ka sira. 'I wonder if he understood.'
> I⌐ko⌐o ka sira. 'I wonder if I should go.'
> Sa⌐mu⌐i ka sira. 'I wonder if it's cold.'
> Sa⌐mukatta ka sira. 'I wonder if it was cold.'
> So⌐o ka sira.[2] 'I wonder if that's so.'
> So⌐o datta ka sira. 'I wonder if it was like that.'

11. wa⌐ka⌐rya sinai

A verbal stem + wa + √sinai occurs as a more emphatic equivalent of the corresponding negative of the verbal. The stem of an unaccented verbal acquires an accent on its final syllable.

---

[1] The examples are all in the informal style. Formal inflected forms also occur before ka sira.

[2] So⌐o da + ka sira = So⌐o ka sira.

Examples:

    ta⌐be¬nai: ta⌐be¬ wa sinai 'doesn't eat'
    no⌐ma¬nakatta: no⌐mi wa si┐na┘katta 'didn't drink'
    ko⌐nai: ki¬ wa sinai 'doesn't come'
    si⌐mase¬n̄:   si¬ wa si┌mase┘n̄ 'doesn't do'

In more familiar speech, <u>wa</u> becomes <u>ya</u>, resulting in combinations like:

    ta⌐be¬ ya sinai
    no¬mi ya si┐na┘katta
    ki¬ ya sinai

In contracted speech, a verbal stem of two or more syllables ending in <u>i</u> loses its final -<u>i</u>; the -<u>a</u> of particle <u>ya</u> is often lengthened.

Examples:

    no¬mya[a] sinai 'doesn't drink'
    ha┌na┘sy[a] sinai 'doesn't talk'

DRILLS

A. Substitution Drill

    1. I'm so glad (lit. wasn't it nice) that you were able to get into that school!

        A⌐no gakkoo ni ha┐irete ⌐yo┐katta desu ┌ne┘e.

    2. I'm so glad that you were able to buy tickets for tomorrow's game!

        <u>Asita no siai no kippu ḡa kaete ⌐yo┐katta desu ┌ne┘e.</u>

    3. I'm so glad that you passed the entrance examination!

        <u>Nyu⌐uḡakusike┐n̄ ni ┌pa┐su-site</u> [1] ⌐yo┐katta desu ┌ne┘e.

    4. I'm so glad that you got a job at a good place!

        <u>I┐i to┌koro┘ e syu̅usyoku-site</u> ⌐yo┐katta desu ┌ne┘e.

    5. I'm so glad that there wasn't a fire!

        <u>Ka┐zi ḡa ⌐na┐kute</u> ⌐yo┐katta desu ┌ne┘e.

    6. I'm so glad that you didn't get sick!

        <u>Byo⌐oki ni nara┐nakute</u> ⌐yo┐katta desu ┌ne┘e.

    7. I'm so glad that Tokyo University won!

        <u>To⌐odai ḡa ka┐tte</u> ⌐yo┐katta desu ┌ne┘e.

    8. I'm so glad that you transferred to a place where it's pleasant to live!

        <u>Su⌐mii┐i to┌koro┘ e te̅nkin̄-site</u> ⌐yo┐katta desu ┌ne┘e.

B. Substitution Drill

    1. Once in a while we go together.

        Ta⌐ma ni¬ wa i┌ssyo ni ikima┘su.

---

[1] <u>Pasu-suru</u> 'pass (an examination).'

2. We sometimes go to-   To⌐kidoki¬ issyo ni ikima⌐su.
    gether.

3. We go together almost   Ho⌐toñdo¬ ┌ma┤initi i┌ssyo ni iki-
    every day.   ma┤su.

4. We often go together.   Ta⌐bitabi issyo ni ikima⌐su.

5. We always go together.   I¬tu mo i┌ssyo ni ikima┤su.

6. We usually go together.   Ta⌐itee issyo ni ikima⌐su.

7. We ordinarily go together. Hu⌐tuu issyo ni ikima⌐su.

8. We go together a good   Yo¬ku i┌ssyo ni ikima┤su.
    deal.

C. Substitution Drill

1. I'm already booked up   A⌐sita¬ wa ⌐mo¬o ya⌐kusoku-sityai-
    for tomorrow — to go   ma¬sita yo—o┌yo┤ḡi ni i┌ku┤ tte.
    swimming.

2. I'm already booked up   A⌐sita¬ wa ⌐mo¬o ya⌐kusoku-sityai-
    for tomorrow — to come   ma¬sita yo—<u>ma┌ta koko e ku┤ru</u>
    here again.   tte.

3. I'm already booked up   A⌐sita¬ wa ⌐mo¬o ya⌐kusoku-sityai-
    for tomorrow — to go to   ma¬sita yo—<u>se┌ñse┤e no otaku ni</u>
    the teacher's house.   <u>a┌ḡaru┤</u> tte.

4. I'm already booked up   A⌐sita¬wa ⌐mo¬o ya⌐kusoku-sityai-
    for tomorrow — to go   ma¬sita yo—<u>ha┌nami┤ ni i┌ku┤</u>
    to see the cherry blos-   tte.
    soms.

5. I'm already booked up   A⌐sita¬ wa ⌐mo¬o ya⌐kusoku-sityai-
    for tomorrow — to work   ma¬sita yo—<u>i┌tiniti-zyuu hataraku┤</u>
    all day.   tte.

6. I'm already booked up   A⌐sita¬ wa ⌐mo¬o ya⌐kusoku-sityai-
    for tomorrow — to play   ma¬sita yo—<u>te┤nisu (o) su┌ru┤</u>
    tennis.   tte.

7. I'm already booked up   A⌐sita¬ wa ⌐mo¬o ya⌐kusoku-sityai-
    for tomorrow — to take   ma¬sita yo—<u>ko┌domo (o) oisyasañ</u>
    the children to the   <u>no toko┤ e tu┌rete iku┤</u> tte.
    doctor's (place).

8. I'm already booked up   A⌐sita¬ wa ⌐mo¬o ya⌐kusoku-sityai-
    for tomorrow — to go   ma¬sita yo—<u>Gi┌ñza e kaimono ni</u>
    to the Ginza to shop.   <u>iku┤</u> tte.

D. Level Drill [1]

1. So⌐o sitya¬a i⌐kemase¬ñ   So⌐o site¬ wa i⌐kemase¬ñ yo⌴
    yo⌴

2. A¬me ḡa hu⌐ra¬nakeryaa   A¬me ḡa hu⌐ra¬nakereba ┌i┤i desu
    ┌i┤i desu ḡa ⌐ne¬e.   ḡa ⌐ne¬e.

---

[1] Each sentence on the right is the uncontracted equivalent of the sentence on
the left.

3. Kodomo (wa) ⌐mo⌐o ne-   Kodomo (wa) ⌐mo⌐o ne⌐te simai-
   ⌐tyaima⌐sita yo⌐   ma⌐sita yo⌐
4. A⌐ñna hiko⌐oki nya no⌐rya⌐a   A⌐ñna hiko⌐oki ni wa no⌐ri⌐ wa
   si⌐na⌐i yo.   si⌐na⌐i yo.
5. Ze⌐ñzeñ waka⌐ñnai.   Ze⌐ñzeñ wakara⌐nai.
6. Ko⌐ñna hu⌐u zya tu⌐ma⌐-   Ko⌐ñna hu⌐u de wa tu⌐mara⌐nai
   ñnai zya nai ka.   zya[1] nai ka.
7. Si⌐ti⌐-zi made ni ⌐ko⌐-   Si⌐ti⌐-zi made ni ⌐ko⌐nakereba
   nakyaa a⌐wa⌐nai.   a⌐wa⌐nai.
8. Sa⌐ke (o) no⌐ñzyatta.   Sa⌐ke (o) no⌐ñde simatta.

E. Grammar Drill (based on Grammatical Note 1)

   Tutor: Wa⌐karima⌐su ⌐ne⌐e. 'He understands, doesn't he.'
   Student: Wa⌐karu rasi⌐i desu ⌐ne⌐e. 'He apparently understands,
            doesn't he.'

1. Kinoo no siai (wa) ⌐yo⌐-   Kinoo no siai (wa) yo⌐katta rasi⌐i
   katta desu ⌐ne⌐e.   desu ⌐ne⌐e.
2. Kyo⌐o (wa) si⌐keñ de-   Kyo⌐o (wa) si⌐keñ datta rasi⌐i desita ⌐ne⌐e.   su ⌐ne⌐e.
3. A⌐no⌐ ko (wa) ⌐i⌐tu mo   A⌐no⌐ ko (wa) ⌐i⌐tu mo wa⌐ratte
   wa⌐ratte (i)ma⌐su ⌐ne⌐e.   (i)ru rasi⌐i desu ⌐ne⌐e.
4. Ko⌐no zibiki⌐ (wa) ho⌐ñ-   Ko⌐no zibiki⌐ (wa) ho⌐ñyaku-sita
   yaku-sita hito⌐ no desu   hito no rasi⌐i desu ⌐ne⌐e.
   ⌐ne⌐e.
5. Zi⌐ko (ḡa) a⌐rima⌐sita   Zi⌐ko (ḡa) a⌐tta rasi⌐i desu
   ⌐ne⌐e.   ⌐ne⌐e.
6. Ze⌐ñzeñ ga⌐mañ de⌐ki-   Ze⌐ñzeñ ga⌐mañ de⌐kinai rasi⌐i
   mase⌐ñ ⌐ne⌐e.   desu ⌐ne⌐e.
7. Añna seekatu (wa) sa-   Añna seekatu (wa) sa⌐bisii rasi⌐i
   ⌐bisi⌐i desu ⌐ne⌐e.   desu ⌐ne⌐e.
8. O⌐to⌐osañ no si⌐riai de⌐su   O⌐to⌐osañ no si⌐riai rasi⌐i desu
   ⌐ne⌐e.   ⌐ne⌐e.
9. Kono mati no otera (wa)   Kono mati no otera (wa) yu⌐u-
   yu⌐umee de⌐su ⌐ne⌐e.   mee rasi⌐i desu ⌐ne⌐e.
10. A⌐suko no oso⌐ba (wa)   A⌐suko no oso⌐ba (wa) o⌐isii ra-
    o⌐isi⌐i desu ⌐ne⌐e.   si⌐i desu ⌐ne⌐e.
11. Su⌐po⌐otu ni wa kyo⌐omi⌐   Su⌐po⌐otu ni wa kyo⌐omi⌐ ḡa na⌐i
    ḡa a⌐rimase⌐ñ ⌐ne⌐e.   rasi⌐i desu ⌐ne⌐e.

F. Substitution Drill

1. Apparently golf has be-   Ni⌐ho⌐ñ de wa ⌐go⌐ruhu ḡa sa⌐kañ
   come popular in Japan.   ni natta rasi⌐i desu.
2. They say that golf has   Ni⌐ho⌐ñ de wa ⌐go⌐ruhu ḡa sa⌐kañ
   become popular in Japan.   ni <u>na⌐tta soo desu.</u>

---

[1] This <u>zya</u> rarely occurs in its uncontracted equivalent in informal conversation.

3. Golf is supposed to have become popular in Japan.

Ni⌐ho˥n̄ de wa ⌐go˥ruhu ḡa sa⌐kañ ni na˥tta hazu desu.

4. I think that golf has become popular in Japan.

Ni⌐ho˥n̄ de wa ⌐go˥ruhu ḡa sa⌐kañ ni na˥tta to omoimasu.

5. Don't you agree that golf has become popular in Japan?

Ni⌐ho˥n̄ de wa ⌐go˥ruhu ḡa sa⌐kañ ni na˥tta n̄ zya arimaseñ ka.

6. Golf seems to have become popular in Japan.

Ni⌐ho˥n̄ de wa ⌐go˥ruhu ḡa sa⌐kañ ni na˥tta yoo desu.

G. Substitution Drill

1. I'm to go on a business trip every month from now on.

Kore kara ma⌐ituki syuttyoo-suru˥ n̄ desu.

2. I plan to go on a business trip every month from now on.

Kore kara ma⌐ituki syuttyoo-suru tumori de˥su.

3. I've decided to go on a business trip every month from now on.

Kore kara ma⌐ituki syuttyoo-suru koto˥ ni si┗ma┛sita.

4. I think he'll go on a business trip every month from now on.

Kore kara ma⌐ituki syuttyoo-suru˥ to omoimasu.

5. They say he's going to go on a business trip every month from now on.

Kore kara ma⌐ituki syuttyoo-suru so˥o desu.

6. He's supposed to go on a business trip every month from now on.

Kore kara ma⌐ituki syuttyoo-suru hazu de˥su.

7. Apparently he's going to go on a business trip every month from now on.

Kore kara ma⌐ituki syuttyoo-sùru rasi˥i desu.

H. Grammar Drill (based on Grammatical Note 2)

Tutor: I˥i desu ⌐ne˥e. 'Isn't it nice!'
Student: I˥i zya arimaseñ ka. 'Don't you agree that it's nice?' or 'Isn't it true that it's nice?'

1. Añna ⌐ma˥do no su┗kuna┛i uti (wa) ku⌐ra˥i desu ┗ne┛e.

Añna ⌐ma˥do no su┗kuna┛i uti (wa) ku⌐ra˥i zya arimaseñ ka.

2. Tu⌐rai seekatu de˥su ⌐ne˥e.

Tu⌐rai seekatu zya˥ arimaseñ ka.

3. Ma˥e yori zu⌐tto yase-ma˥sita ┗ne┛e.

Ma˥e yori zu⌐tto yaseta˥ zya ari-maseñ ka.

4. Añna hi⌐do˥i zisiñ (wa) ko⌐wa˥i desu ┗ne┛e.

Añna hi⌐do˥i zisiñ (wa) ko⌐wa˥i zya arimaseñ ka.

5. A⌐na⌉ta no tokee (wa)   A⌐na⌉ta no tokee (wa) ⌐da⌉re ka
   ⌐da⌉re ka ni to⌐rarema⌉-   ni to⌐ra⌉reta zya arimaseñ ka.
   sita ˥ne˥e.

6. A⌐merika⌉ziñ to ze⌐ñzeñ   A⌐merika⌉ziñ to ze⌐ñzeñ tukiawa⌉-
   tukiaimase˥ñ ˥ne˥e.   nai zya arimaseñ ka.

7. A⌐no⌉ hito (wa) ⌐yo⌉ku   A⌐no⌉ hito (wa) ⌐yo⌉ku te⌐ñkiñ-
   te⌐ñkiñ-saserarema⌉su   saserareru⌉ zya arimaseñ ka.
   ⌐ ⌉ne⌉e.

8. Soñna siḡoto (wa) to⌐si⌉-   Soñna siḡoto (wa) to⌐siyori⌉ ni wa
   yori⌉ ni wa ⌐mu⌉ri desu   ⌐mu⌉ri zya arimaseñ ka.
   ⌐ne⌉e.

I. Substitution Drill (based on Grammatical Note 5)

1. While he said he under-   Wa⌐ka⌉ru tte iinaḡara, hoñtoo wa
   stood, he really didn't   wa⌐kara⌉nakatta ñ desu.
   (understand).

2. While he said he'd do it,   Su⌐ru⌉ tte iinaḡara, hoñtoo wa
   he really didn't (do).   si⌐na⌉katta ñ desu.

3. While he said he didn't   Si⌐rana⌉i tte iinaḡara, hoñtoo wa
   know, he really did   si⌐tte (i)ta⌉ ñ desu.
   (know).

4. While he said he'd give   Ku⌐reru⌉ tte iinaḡara, hoñtoo wa
   it to me, he really didn't   ku⌐rena⌉katta ñ desu.
   (give).

5. While he said he could   Ga⌉mañ de⌐ki⌉ru tte iinaḡara, hoñ-
   stand it, he really   too wa ⌐ga⌉mañ de⌐ki⌉nakatta ñ
   couldn't (stand it).   desu.

6. While he said he could   U⌐ḡokase⌉ru tte iinaḡara, hoñtoo
   move it, he really   wa u⌐ḡokase⌉nakatta ñ desu.
   couldn't (move it).

7. While he said he hadn't   Wa⌐surena⌉katta tte iinaḡara, hoñ-
   forgotten, he really had   too wa wa⌐sureta⌉ ñ desu.
   (forgotten).

8. While he said it would   Ya⌐ku⌉ ni ⌐ta⌉tu tte iinaḡara, hoñ-
   be useful, it really   too wa ya⌐ku⌉ ni ta⌐ta⌉nakatta ñ
   wasn't (of use).   desu.

J. Level Drill (based on Grammatical Note 4)

   Tutor: No⌉ñde kudasai. 'Please drink.'

   Male Student: No⌉me yo. 'Drink!'
   Female Student: No⌐minasa⌉i yo. 'Drink!'

1. Ta⌐ma ni⌉ wa tu⌐kia⌉tte   Ta⌐ma ni⌉ wa tu⌐kia⌉e yo.
   kudasai.   Ta⌐ma ni⌉ wa tu⌐kiainasa⌉i yo.

2. Tyo⌉tto ⌐ma⌉tte kudasai.   Tyo⌉tto ⌐ma⌉te yo.
                                  Tyo⌉tto ma⌐tinasa⌉i yo.

3. Ko⌐no sakana (o) yaite   Ko⌐no sakana (o) yake⌉ yo.
   kudasa⌉i.   Ko⌐no osakana (o) yakinasa⌉i yo.

4. Ta⌐bako (o) katte⌐ kite   Ta⌐bako (o) katte ko⌐i yo.
    kudasai.   Ta⌐bako (o) katte kinasa⌐i yo.
5. A⌐sita ha⌐yaku yo⌐ko⌐site   A⌐sita ha⌐yaku yo⌐ko⌐se yo.
    kudasai.   A⌐sita ha⌐yaku yo⌐kosinasa⌐i yo.
6. Ro⌐osoku⌐ (o) tu⌐ke⌐te   Ro⌐osoku⌐ (o) tu⌐ke⌐ro yo.
    kudasai.   Ro⌐osoku⌐ (o) tu⌐kenasa⌐i yo.
7. U⌐ta⌐ (o) u⌐tatte kudasa⌐i.   U⌐ta⌐ (o) u⌐tae⌐ yo.
                                     U⌐ta⌐ (o) u⌐tainasa⌐i yo.
8. Ko⌐re kara sitaku (o)   Ko⌐re kara sitaku (o) siro⌐ yo.
    site kudasa⌐i.   Ko⌐re kara sitaku (o) sinasa⌐i yo.
9. A⌐ma⌐do (o) a⌐kete ku-   A⌐ma⌐do (o) a⌐kero⌐ yo.
    dasa⌐i.   A⌐ma⌐do (o) a⌐kenasa⌐i yo.
10. Kore (o) ka⌐midana ni   Kore (o) ka⌐midana ni oke⌐ yo.
    oite kudasa⌐i.   Kore (o) ka⌐midana ni okinasa⌐i
                                     yo.

K. Level Drill (based on Grammatical Note 4)

         Tutor: So⌐o iwana⌐i de kudasai. 'Please don't say that.'

         Male Student: So⌐o iu⌐ na yo. 'Don't say that!'
         Female Student: So⌐o iwana⌐i de yo. 'Don't say that!'

1. Wa⌐surena⌐i de kudasai.   Wa⌐sureru⌐ na yo.
                                     Wa⌐surena⌐i de yo.
2. Sore wa ⌐mi⌐nai de ku-   Sore wa ⌐mi⌐ru na yo.
    dasai.   Sore wa ⌐mi⌐nai de yo.
3. Dare ni mo mi⌐se⌐nai   Dare ni mo mi⌐se⌐ru na yo.
    de kudasai.   Dare ni mo mi⌐se⌐nai de yo.
4. Sa⌐waḡa⌐nai de kudasai.   Sa⌐waḡu⌐ na yo.
                                     Sa⌐waḡa⌐nai de yo.
5. Si⌐ṅpai-sina⌐i de kudasai.   Si⌐ṅpai-suru⌐ na yo.
                                     Si⌐ṅpai-sina⌐i de yo.
6. Ma⌐kena⌐i de kudasai.   Ma⌐keru⌐ na yo.
                                     Ma⌐kena⌐i de yo.
7. Kore wa tu⌐kawana⌐i de   Kore wa tu⌐kau⌐ na yo.
    kudasai.   Kore wa tu⌐kawana⌐i de yo.
8. A⌐no sakana (o) tabe⌐nai   A⌐no sakana (o) tabe⌐ru na yo.
    de kudasai.   A⌐no osakana (o) tabe⌐nai de yo.
9. O⌐kane (o) karina⌐i de   O⌐kane (o) kariru⌐ na yo.
    kudasai.   O⌐kane (o) karina⌐i de yo.
10. O⌐kane (o) kasana⌐i de   O⌐kane (o) kasu⌐ na yo.
    kudasai.   O⌐kane (o) kasana⌐i de yo.

L. Response Drill (based on Grammatical Note 4)

         Tutor: So⌐re (o) site aḡemasyo⌐o ka. 'Shall I do that one
                           for you?'

         Male Student: Ṅ, si⌐te kure⌐ yo. 'Yes, please do.'
         Female Student: E⌐e, si⌐te tyooda⌐i.[1] 'Yes, please do.'

---

[1] Remember that <u>tyoodai</u> imperatives are familiar and informal.

1. De⌐ṅwaba⌐ṅḡoo (o) ki⌐ite
   aḡemasyo⌐o ka.

   N̄, ki⌐ite kure⌐ yo.
   E⌐e, ki⌐ite tyooda⌐i.

2. Na⌐mae (o) ka⌐ite a⌐ḡe-
   masyo⌐o ka.

   N̄, ka⌐ite ku⌐re⌐ yo.
   E⌐e, ka⌐ite tyoodai.

3. Syo⌐ozi (o) si⌐mete a⌐ḡe-
   masyo⌐o ka.

   N̄, si⌐mete ku⌐re⌐ yo.
   E⌐e, si⌐mete tyoodai.

4. A⌐ṅna⌐i-site a⌐ḡemasyo⌐o
   ka.

   N̄, a⌐ṅna⌐i-site ku⌐re⌐ yo.
   E⌐e, a⌐ṅna⌐i-site tyoodai.

5. Ku⌐suri (o) aḡemasyo⌐o
   ka.

   N̄, ku⌐re⌐ yo.
   E⌐e, tyo⌐oda⌐i.

6. Hu⌐rosiki ni tutu⌐ṅde
   a⌐ḡemasyo⌐o ka.

   N̄, tu⌐tu⌐ṅde ku⌐re⌐ yo.
   E⌐e, tu⌐tu⌐ṅde tyoodai.

7. So⌐no ni⌐motu (o) ⌐mo⌐tte
   a⌐ḡemasyo⌐o ka.

   N̄, mo⌐tte ku⌐re⌐ yo.
   E⌐e, mo⌐tte tyoodai.

8. Ka⌐ya (o) tutte aḡema-
   syo⌐o ka.

   N̄, tu⌐tte kure⌐ yo.
   E⌐e, tu⌐tte tyooda⌐i.

M. Level Drill [1]

> Tutor: Ka⌐erima⌐sita ka⌐ 'Has he gone home?'
> Student: O⌐kaeri ni narima⌐sita ka⌐ 'Has he gone home?'

1. Mo⌐o mi⌐ma⌐sita ka⌐

   Mo⌐o go⌐raṅ ni narima⌐sita ka⌐

2. Do⌐ko e i⌐kima⌐sita ka⌐

   Do⌐tira e o⌐ide ni narima⌐sita
   ka⌐

3. Ho⌐ṅ (o) ka⌐esima⌐sita
   ka⌐

   Ho⌐ṅ (o) o⌐kaesi ni narima⌐sita
   ka⌐

4. Ta⌐naka-saṅ ima⌐su ka⌐

   Ta⌐naka-saṅ oide ni narima⌐su
   ka⌐

5. Na⌐ṅ-zi-ḡo⌐ro de⌐ma⌐su
   ka⌐

   Na⌐ṅ-zi-ḡo⌐ro o⌐de ni narima⌐su
   ka⌐

6. A⌐sita mata kima⌐su ka⌐

   A⌐sita mata oide ni narima⌐su
   ka⌐

7. Na⌐ṅ-zi ni o⌐kima⌐su
   ka⌐

   Na⌐ṅ-zi ni o⌐oki ni narima⌐su
   ka⌐

8. Do⌐ko de so⌐datima⌐sita
   ka⌐

   Do⌐tira de o⌐sodati ni narima⌐-
   sita ka⌐

N. Substitution Drill (based on Grammatical Note 6)

1. One-third of three is one.

   Saṅ no sa⌐ṅ-buṅ no iti⌐ wa i⌐ti⌐
   desu.

2. Two-fifths of five is two.

   Go⌐ no go-⌐buṅ no ni⌐ wa ⌐ni⌐
   desu.

3. One-fifth of ten is two.

   Zyu⌐u no go-⌐buṅ no iti⌐ wa ⌐ni⌐
   desu.

4. One-fourth of eight is two.

   Ha⌐ti⌐ no yo⌐ṅ-buṅ no iti⌐ wa ⌐ni⌐
   desu.

---

[1] In each case, the sentence on the right contains √na⌐ru and is the polite
equivalent of the sentence on the left.

5. Two-thirds of six is   Ro⌐ku⌐ no sa⌐n̄-buñ no ni⌐ wa ⌐si⌐
   four.   desu.
6. Three-fourths of four   Si⌐ no yŏn̄-buñ no san̄ wa sa⌐n̄
   is three.   de⌐su.
7. One-third of twelve is   Zyu⌐uni⌐ no sa⌐n̄-buñ no iti⌐ wa
   four.   ⌐si⌐ desu.
8. One-tenth of twenty is   Ni⌐zyuu no zyu⌐u-buñ no iti⌐ wa
   two.   ⌐ni⌐ desu.

O. Expansion Drill (based on Grammatical Note 7)

        Tutor: So⌐re (o) kudasa⌐i. /are/ 'Give me that. /that one over
                 there/'
        Student: So⌐re ka are (o) kudasa⌐i. 'Give me that one or that one
                 over there.'

1. Ka⌐midana ni oite ari-   Ka⌐midana ka butudañ ni oite
   ma⌐su. /butudañ/   arima⌐su.
2. Ko⌐ohi⌐i (o) tyo⌐oda⌐i.   Ko⌐ohi⌐i ka o⌐tya (o) tyooda⌐i.
   /otya/
3. E⌐ñpitu de ka⌐ite kuda-   E⌐ñpitu ka pe⌐ñ de ⌐ka⌐ite kudasai. /pe⌐ñ/   sai.
4. Re⌐kisi (ḡa) beñkyoo-   Re⌐kisi ka ti⌐ri (ḡa) be⌐ñkyoo-
   sita⌐i ñ desu. /ti⌐ri/   sita⌐i ñ desu.
5. Ne⌐zi (ḡa) irimasu.   Ne⌐zi ka ku⌐ḡi (ḡa) irima⌐su.
   /kuḡi/
6. Maineñ ya⌐ma⌐ e ikima-   Maineñ ya⌐ma⌐ ka ⌐u⌐mi e iki-
   su. /u⌐mi/   masu.
7. Ge⌐tuyo⌐o ni i⌐ku tumori   Ge⌐tuyo⌐o ka ka⌐yo⌐o ni i⌐ku tu-
   de⌐su. /ka⌐yo⌐o/   mori de⌐su.
8. Ka⌐iḡuñ ni ha⌐irita⌐i ñ   Ka⌐iḡuñ ka ku⌐uḡuñ ni . hairita⌐i
   desu. /kuuḡuñ/   ñ desu.

P. Level Drill (based on Grammatical Note 8)

        Tutor: I⌐kima⌐su ka⌐ 'Are you going?'

        Male Student: I⌐ku⌐ kai⌐ 'Are you going?'
        Female Student: I⌐ku⌐ no?[1] 'Are you going?'

1. Wa⌐karima⌐sita ka⌐   Wa⌐ka⌐tta kai⌐
                                Wa⌐ka⌐tta no?
2. Ta⌐sukarima⌐sita ka⌐   Ta⌐suka⌐tta kai⌐
                                Ta⌐suka⌐tta no?
3. I⌐tu desu ka⌐   I⌐tu dai⌐
                                I⌐tu na no?
4. Ko⌐wa⌐i desu ka⌐   Ko⌐wa⌐i kai⌐
                                Ko⌐wa⌐i no?

---
[1] Remember that this pattern is used more frequently, but not exclusively
by women.

5. Syo⌐ttyuu desu ka⌐   Syo⌐ttyuu kai⌐
                                    Syo⌐ttyuu na no?

6. Tu⌐ra⌐katta desu ka⌐   Tu⌐ra⌐katta kai⌐
                                    Tu⌐ra⌐katta no?

7. Ma⌐kema⌐sita ka⌐   Ma⌐keta⌐ kai⌐
                                    Ma⌐keta⌐ no?

8. Mu⌐ri desita ka⌐   Mu⌐ri datta kai⌐
                                    Mu⌐ri datta no?

Q. Grammar Drill (based on Grammatical Note 7)

    Tutor: Ha⌐irima⌐sita. 'He came in.'
    Student: Ha⌐itta ⌐ba⌐kari desu. 'He (only) just came in.'

1. Ku⌐suri (o) nomima⌐sita.   Ku⌐suri (o) no⌐ñda ⌐ba⌐kari desu.
2. Da⌐iḡaku (o) dema⌐sita.   Da⌐iḡaku (o) de⌐ta ⌐ba⌐kari desu.
3. Nyu⌐uḡakusike⌐ñ (o) u⌐ke-   Nyu⌐uḡakusike⌐ñ (o) ⌐u⌐keta ⌐ba⌐-
   ma⌐sita.   kari desu.
4. I⌐i to⌐koro⌐ ni syu⌐usyoku-   I⌐i to⌐koro⌐ ni syu⌐usyoku-sita
   sima⌐sita.   ba⌐kari desu.
5. Ri⌐ku⌐ḡuñ ni syo⌐osyuu-   Ri⌐ku⌐ḡuñ ni syo⌐osyuu-sareta
   sarema⌐sita.   ba⌐kari desu.
6. Ku⌐ni ni kaerima⌐sita.   Ku⌐ni ni ka⌐etta ⌐ba⌐kari desu.
7. So⌐no kookoku (o) mima⌐-   So⌐no kookoku (o) mi⌐ta ⌐ba⌐kari
   sita.   desu.
8. Ni⌐ho⌐ñ ni tu⌐kima⌐sita.   Ni⌐ho⌐ñ ni ⌐tu⌐ita ⌐ba⌐kari desu.

R. Grammar Drill (based on Grammatical Note 7)

    Tutor: Mi-⌐ttu hodo kaima⌐sita. 'I bought about (as many as)
             three.'
    Student: Mi-⌐ttu ba⌐kari ka⌐ima⌐sita. 'I bought (only) about
             three.'

1. Zyu⌐u-niñ hodo mi⌐ema⌐-   Zyu⌐u-niñ ba⌐kari mi⌐ema⌐sita.
   sita.
2. Ro⌐osoku⌐ (ḡa) ⌐sa⌐ñ-boñ   Ro⌐osoku⌐ (ḡa) sa⌐ñ-boñ ba⌐kari
   hodo no⌐ko⌐tte (i)masu.   no⌐ko⌐tte (i)masu.
3. Sore wa sa⌐ñzeñ-eñ hodo   Sore wa sa⌐ñzeñ-eñ ba⌐kari ka-
   kaka⌐ru to omoimasu.   ⌐ka⌐ru to omoimasu.
4. Kippu (o) ha⌐ti⌐-mai hodo   Kippu (o) ha⌐ti-mai ba⌐kari ka-
   ka⌐ima⌐sita.   ⌐ima⌐sita.
5. Ta⌐kusii ḡa go-⌐dai hodo   Ta⌐kusii ḡa go-⌐dai ba⌐kari na-
   narañde (i)ma⌐su.   ⌐rañde (i)ma⌐su.
6. Ki⌐ (ḡa) go-⌐hoñ hodo   Ki⌐ (ḡa) go-⌐hoñ ba⌐kari u⌐ete
   uete arima⌐su.   arima⌐su.

S. Substitution Drill (based on Grammatical Note 9)

1. Each year the competi-   I⌐ti-neñ-ḡo⌐to ni kyo⌐osoo ḡa hi⌐-
   tion gets more severe.   doku narimasu.

2. Each month the competition gets more severe.

Iᶠk-kaḡetu-ḡoᵗto ni kyoᶠosoo ḡa hiᵗ-doku narimasu.

3. Each month the teacher
changes.

Iᶠk-kaḡetu-ḡoᵗto ni se͞nseᶦe ḡa ka-warimasu.

4. Every two hours the
teacher changes.

Ni-ᶜzikañ-ḡoᵗto ni se͞nseᶦe ḡa ka-warimasu.

5. Every two hours I take
medicine.

Ni-ᶜzikañ-ḡoᵗto ni kuᶠsuri (o) nomi-maᵗsu.

6. Every thirty minutes I
take medicine.

·Saᶠñzip-puñ-ḡoᵗto ni kuᶠsuri (o) no-mimaᵗsu.

7. They say there's an accident every thirty min-
utes.

Saᶠñzip-puñ-ḡoᵗto ni ziᶦko ḡa ᵗaᵗru soo desu.

T. Grammar Drill

Tutor: Waᶠkarimaseᵗn̄. 'I don't understand.'
Student: Waᶠkaᵗrya sinai.¹ 'I don't understand.'

1. Iᶠkimaseᵗn̄.
2. Kiᶠmaseᵗn̄.
3. Siᶠmaseᵗn̄.
4. Taᶠbemaseᵗn̄.
5. Noᶠmimaseᵗn̄.
6. Siᶠrimaseᵗn̄.
7. Miᶠmaseᵗn̄.
8. Yoᶠmimaseᵗn̄.
9. Kaᶠkimaseᵗn̄.
10. Haᶠnasimaseᵗn̄.

Iᶠkyaᵗa sinai.
Kiᵗ ya sinai.
Siᵗ ya sinai.
Taᶠbeᵗ ya sinai.
Noᵗmya sinai.
Siᶠryaᵗa sinai.
Miᵗ ya sinai.
Yoᵗmya sinai.
Kaᵗkya sinai.
Haᶠnaᵗsya sinai.

U. Variation Drill² (based on Grammatical Note 10)

Left Column: Iᵗi ka sira. 'I wonder if it's all right.'
Right Column: Iᵗi ka na? 'I wonder if it's all right.'

1. Daᶠizyoᵗobu ka sira.
2. Iᶠkoᵗo ka sira.
3. Saᶠbisiᵗi ka sira.
4. Doᵗko ni ᵗsuᵗñde (i)ru
ka sira.
5. Muᵗri datta ka sira.
6. Yaᶠmesaseraretaᵗ ka sira.

Daᶠizyoᵗobu ka na?
Iᶠkoᵗo ka na?
Saᶠbisiᵗi ka na?
Doᵗko ni ᵗsuᵗñde (i)ru ka na?
Muᵗri datta ka na?
Yaᶠmesaseraretaᵗ ka na?

---

¹ Emphatic, informal, contracted form. Based on Grammatical Note 11.

² The sentences on the left occur more commonly (though not exclusively) in
women's speech, and the sentences on the right are typical of men's speech.
For men students, the tutor reads the sentences on the left and the student
gives the sentences on the right. For women students, the reverse procedure is used.

7. De⌐ki¬ru ka sira.   De⌐ki¬ru ka na?
8. Te⌐edeñ ka¬ sira.   Teedeñ ka na?

SUPPLEMENTARY DIALOGUES

1. Mr. Tanaka (meeting Mr. Yamada late at night): Yamada-kuñ, i¬ma oka-
        eri kai⌐

   Mr. Yamada: Ma¬iban, ka⌐isya no okyaku no tukia¬i de, o⌐soku na¬ru ñ
        da yo.

   Mr. Tanaka: Ya⌐ppa¬ri ki¬mi mo so¬o kai. Bo¬ku mo ⌐syo⌐ttyuu na ñ de,
        i⌐ya¬ ni ⌐na⌐ttyau yo. Ka⌐isya no okyaku to tukia¬u yori, uti
        de ⌐ka¬nai ya ko̅do̅mo to yu⌐kku¬ri ta⌐beta⌐i yo.

   Mr. Yamada: So¬o da yo. Hito o ryoo̅ori¬ya e a⌐ñna⌐i-saseraretari,
        syu⌐ttyoo-saserareta¬ri, i⌐ya¬ da ⌐ne¬e—kaisyaiñ wa.

   Mr. Tanaka: De¬ mo; ho⌐ka no toko¬ e syu⌐usyoku-site¬ mo, onazi sa⌐

2. Mr. Tanaka: Do¬ñdoñ mo⌐no⌐ no nedañ g̅a ag̅aru ⌐ne¬e.

   Mr. Yamamoto: Sa⌐to¬o nañka i⌐s-syuukañ-g̅o¬to ni ⌐go¬-eñ mo ag̅atte
        iru yo⌐

   Mr. Tanaka: Na⌐ñ de¬ mo so⌐o ta⌐kaku ⌐na⌐ttyaa ko⌐ma¬ru ⌐ne¬e.

   Mr. Yamamoto: Gekkyuu wa o⌐nazi na¬ ñ da kedo—

3. Mr. Tanaka: Bu⌐ra¬uñ-sañ [1] a⌐merika¬ziñ na no ni hi⌐tokoto mo eeg̅o
        tukawana¬katta yo⌐

   Mr. Yamamoto: Ze¬ñbu ni⌐hoñg̅o de hana⌐sita no kai⌐

   Mr. Tanaka: So¬o da yo. Sono ue, na⌐kanaka uma¬i kotoba tu⌐kau⌐
        ñ da yo. Bi⌐kku¬ri-sityatta.

   Mr. Yamamoto: Taitee g̅a¬iziñ no hanasi ⌐he¬ñ na mo⌐no⌐ da g̅a ⌐ne¬e.

4. Mrs. Tanaka: Tyo¬tto zi⌐biki tyooda¬i.
   Maid: Ko⌐re de gozaima¬su ka⌐
   Mrs. Tanaka: A¬a, so⌐re zya na¬i no yo. Mo¬tto a̅tui ku⌐ro¬i no da ke-
        do, so⌐ko ni na¬i?
   Maid: Ku⌐ro¬i no wa ko⌐re sika gozaimase¬ñ g̅a, ko⌐re de go-
        zaima¬su ka⌐
   Mrs. Tanaka: So¬o ⌐so⌐o, sore. Do¬o mo.

5. Father: O⌐mosiroso¬o na ⌐e⌐eg̅a g̅a ⌐a⌐ru yo⌐ O¬mae mo itte mi¬nai
        kai⌐
   Son: Do¬ñna ⌐e⌐eg̅a? O⌐to¬osañ tu⌐rete¬ tte ku⌐reru⌐ no?
   Father: A¬a. Kyo¬o wa hi¬ma da¬ kara ne?
   Son: I¬i ⌐na¬a. O⌐to¬osañ g̅a ⌐i¬i to o⌐mo⌐u mo⌐no⌐ nara, na⌐ñ de mo
        i¬i yo⌐ Bo¬ku ⌐su̅g̅u ki⌐kae¬ru kara, ma¬tte te ne?
   Father: I¬i to mo. Yu⌐kku¬ri ki⌐ka⌐ete oide⌐

6. Mrs. Tanaka: Bo¬ttyañ o⌐ge¬ñki?
   Mrs. Yamamoto: Okag̅esama de. De¬ mo, ze⌐ñzeñ beñkyoo-sina¬i ñ de,
        ko⌐ma¬ttyau·no yo⌐
   Mrs. Tanaka: Ma¬da ti⌐isa¬i kara desyoo?

---

[1] 'Brown.'

Mrs. Yamamoto: Mo┐o zyu┌uni┐ na ñ desu mono, su┌ko┌si wa be┌ñkyoo-
　　　　　　　sasena┌kutyaa—

Mrs. Tanaka:　　Si┌taku na┐i no ni ┌mu┐ri ni sa┌sete┐ mo, da┌me┐ zya
　　　　　　　nai ka sira.

Mrs. Yamamoto: So┐o ┌ne┐e. Syu┐ziñ mo, beñkyoo si┌ro┐ si┌ro┐ tte ┌mu┐ri
　　　　　　　ni sa┌sete┐ mo o┌boe┐nai kara, na┌ni mo iwanai ho┐o ga ┌i┐i
　　　　　　　tte i┌u┐ ñ da kedo; mo┐o su┌ḡu ┌tyu┌uḡaku desyoo? Si┌ñpai
　　　　　　　na┐ no yo.

Mrs. Tanaka:　　Soñna ni si┌ñpai-sina┌kute mo da┌izyo┐obu yo⌐

7. Mr. Tanaka:　　Mu┐ri ka mo si┌rena┐i kedo, a┌sita ma┐de ni ko┐no te-
　　　　　　　ḡami ho┌ñyaku-site kurena┐i kai.

Mr. Yamamoto: Do┌ñna ñ dai. Ya┌sasi┐i ñ nara de┌ki┐ru yo⌐

Mr. Tanaka:　　Ki┌mi ni┐ nara mu┐zukasiku na┐i sa. Bo┌ku ni wa ze┌ñ-
　　　　　　　zeñ waka┌ñnai kedo sa⌐

Mr. Yamamoto: Ma┐a, si┌te mi┌ru yo.

Mr. Tanaka:　　I┐tu mo ki┐mi ni yarasetyatte, su┌ma┐nai[1] kedo; ta┌no┐-
　　　　　　　mu yo.

Mr. Yamamoto: Ya┌raserareru┐ no wa ┌i┐i beñkyoo sa. De┐ mo; si┌te
　　　　　　　mi┐nakutya, de┌ki┐ru ka ┌do┐o ka wa┌kara┐nai yo⌐—hoñtoo
　　　　　　　ni. De┌kitara a┌sita no a┐sa mo┌tte ku┐ru yo.

Mr. Tanaka:　　Su┌ma┐nai[1] kedo, ze┌hi ta┌no┐mu yo.

8. Taro: Ano hu┌to┐tta hito ┌da┐re ka na?
　Jiro: Si┌rana┐i kai⌐ Masao-kuñ da yo⌐
　Taro: Masao-kuñ? Hu┌to┐ttyatta ┌na┐a.
　Jiro: Kinoo ga┌kkoo de a┐tta ñ da kedo, boku mo bi┌kku┐ri-sityatta yo.
　　　　I┐k-ka┐ḡetu hodo ┌Ni┐kkoo de ya┌su┐ñde, ta┌be┐ru no ḡa i┌ti-
　　　　bañ tanosimi┐ datta tte.
　Taro: Ha┐yaku ya┌seta ho┐o ḡa ┌i┐i ┌na┐a.

9. Mr. Smith:　　Kono-ḡoro i┌s-syuukañ-ḡo┐to ni ka┌ñzi go-┌zyuu hodo oboe-
　　　　　　　saserare┐ru ñ da ḡa, mu┐ri da to o┌mo┐u yo.
　Mr. Tanaka: So┐o daroo ┌ne┐e.
　Mr. Smith:　　Be┌ñkyoo ba┌kari site, tyo┐tto a┌tama┐ ḡa ┌he┐ñ ni ┌na┐tta
　　　　　　　yo.

10. Man:　　Ueda-kuñ o┌mosiro┐i hito da ┌na┐a.
　Woman: E┐e. Tu┌kia┌eba tu┌kia┌u hodo ┌i┐i hito da wa⌐
　Man:　　A┌no┐ hito to ha┌na┌su no ḡa tanosimi┐ da ┌ne┐e. O┌mosiro┐i
　　　　　ko┌to ba┌kari itte—

11. Tanaka: O┐zyo┐osañ o┌ge┐ñki?
　Smith:　Okaḡesama de. Ma┌initi ┌so┐to de ya┌kyuu ba┌kari site—
　Tanaka: Yakyuu o?
　Smith:　E┐e. A┌no┐ ko wa o┌ñna rasi┐i koto wa ze┌ñzeñ sina┐i de, i┐tu
　　　　　mo o┌toko┐ no ko to a┌sobu┐ ñ desu yo⌐

12. Tanaka: *I┐i o┌te┐ñki desu ┌ne┐e.
　Smith:　Hoñtoo ni ha┌ru ra┌siku na┌rima┌sita ┌ne┐e.
　Tanaka: Mo┐o sa┌kura ḡa sakihazime┐ta soo desu yo⌐
　Smith:　So┐o desu ka. Kotosi wa ┌tyo┐tto ha┌ya┐i yoo zya arimaseñ ka⌐

---

[1] Informal equivalent of su┌mimase┌ñ.

13. American Student (male): Mo˺o ni˹hoñgo na˺ñka be˹ñkyoo-sitaku na˺i yo.
    Japanese Friend (male):   Na˺ze dai.
    American: Su˹re˺ba su˹ru hodo muzukasiku na˺tte, i˹ya˺ ni ˹na˺ttyatta ñ
       ˹da˺ yo.
    Japanese: Ma˺a, so˹o iu˺ na yo. Kimi wa i˹tibañ ñma˺i ñ zya nai ka.
       Ki˹mi ḡa yametyatta˺ra, mi˹ñna yametyau˺ zya nai ka.
    American: Do˹o site ko˹ñna meñdookusa˹i ka˹ñzi na˹ñka tu˹kau˹ ñ da-
       roo ˹na˺a.
    Japanese: Boku mo ˹do˺o site ka si˹rya˺a si˹na˺i kedo_

14. (Mr. Tanaka and his wife have dropped in to see Mr. and Mrs. Yamamo-
    to. Mr. Yamamoto is Mr. Tanaka's former boss. [1])

    Mrs. Yamamoto: A˺ra i˹rassya˹i. A˹ha˺ta,[2] me˹zurasi˹i kata o˹mie ni
       na˹tta wa_
    Mr. Yamamoto: A˺a, Ta˹naka-ku˹ñ ka. O˺kusañ mo ḡo˺issyo? Yo˺ku
       ˹ki˹ta ˹ne˺e. E˹ñryo na˹ku a˹ḡatte kure˹ yo.
    Mr. Tanaka: Do˺o mo go˹busata-itasima˺sita. Mi˹na˺sama o˹ge˺ñki
       de irassyaimasu ka_
    Mr. Yamamoto: A˺a, okaḡe de. Ki˹mi ñ[3] toko˺ mo mi˹ñna ge˺ñki kai_
    Mr. Tanaka: Ha˺a, okaḡesama de.
    Mrs. Tanaka: O˹bo˺ttyama mo o˹ge˺ñki de irassyaimasyoo?
    Mrs. Yamamoto: E˺e. Ma˹sao mo ge˺ñki yo_ De˺ mo ˹ne˺e. Mo˺o su˹ḡu
       ko˹okoo no nyuuḡakusike˹ñ desyoo? Ma˺ibañ yo˹naka ma˺de
       be˹ñkyoo-sina˺kereba na˹ra˺nai no de, ka˹waiso˺o na no yo.
    Mrs. Tanaka: Gakkoo wa ˹i˺i to˹koro˺ ni ˹na˺reba ˹na˺ru hodo kyo-
       osoo ḡa ˹hi˺doo gozaimasu kara ˹ne˺e.
    Mr. Yamamoto: Mu˺ri ni ˹i˺i gakkoo e i˹rete˺ mo, a˺to de ko˹ma˺ru ñ
       da kara; mu˹ri na beñkyoo wa su˹ru˺ na tte i˹u˺ ñ da ḡa_
    Mrs. Yamamoto: Kono-ḡoro ˹syo˺ttyuu teedeñ-suru desyoo? Se˹kkaku
       beñkyoo-site ru˺ no ni, ko˹ma˺ttyau no yo_
    Mr. Yamamoto: Ro˹osoku zya be˹ñkyoo-deki˺nai kara ˹na˺a.
    Mrs. Tanaka: O˹bo˺ttyama wa ˹yo˺ku o˹deki ni na˹ru kara, go˹siñ-
       pai-nasara˺nakute mo_
    Mrs. Yamamoto: To˹ñde mo na˺i wa_ Si˹ke˺ñ ḡa ˹su˺meba hi˹toa˺ñsiñ
       de˹ki˺ru kedo; so˹re ma˺de wa, o˹ya no ho˺o mo ˹i˺tu mo
       si˹ke˺ñ no ko˹to ba˹kari ka˹ñḡa˺ete i˹na˺kerya na˹ra˺nai ñ
       de, ra˹ku˺ zya ˹na˺i no yo_
    Mr. Yamamoto: So˺re wa so˹o to, ki˹mi no oto˺osañ kono-ḡoro ˹do˺o?
    Mr. Tanaka: Okaḡesama de, da˹ibu yo˺ku na˹rima˺sita. I˺ma wa
       I˹zu no oñseñ de yasu˹ñde orimasu.
    Mr. Yamamoto: So˹re wa yo˺katta ˹ne˺e.
    Mr. Tanaka: Su˹ko˺si ya˹seta yo˺o desu ḡa; isya wa ˹mo˺o si˹ñpai
       na˺i to i˹tte orima˺su no de, hi˹toa˺ñsiñ-itasimasita.
    Mrs. Yamamoto: A˺katyañ wa? Tu˹rete ku˺reba ˹yo˺katta no ni_
    Mrs. Tanaka: No˹rimono ḡa komima˺su no de, kyo˺o wa tu˹rete mai-
       rimase˹ñ desita. Ma˹ta aḡarasete itadakima˺su kara_

---

1 Note the differences of politeness and formality level in the Japanese text,
reflecting the difference of position.

2 A wife regularly addresses her husband as a˹na˺ta.

3 Contraction of no.

Mrs. Yamamoto: Ze⌐hi tu⌐rete⌐ kite tyoodai⌐ Mo⌐o o⌐tañzyo⌐obi wa
                ⌐su⌐ñda no ne?
Mrs. Tanaka: Ha⌐a, se⌐ñgetu de gozaimasita.
Mrs. Yamamoto: A⌐katyañ wa ta⌐hosi⌐mi ⌐ne⌐e. . . . I⌐ma ⌐go⌐hañ tu⌐ku-
                ra⌐sete ru kara, ta⌐bete itte tyoodai ne?
Mr. Tanaka: A⌐ri⌐gatoo gozaimasu ga, ko⌐domo ga ma⌐tte orimasu
                kara⌐
Mr. Yamamoto: Ma⌐a, soñna koto iwazu ni, ta⌐bete itte ku⌐re⌐ yo.
                Su⌐gu daroo?
Mrs. Yamamoto: E⌐e, su⌐gu yo⌐ Da⌐ kara, ta⌐bete ra⌐ssya⌐i yo.
Mr. Tanaka: O⌐so⌐reirimasu. Se⌐kkaku⌐ de gozaimasu kara, tyo-
                ⌐odai-site mairima⌐su.
Mrs. Yamamoto: So⌐o site⌐ ne? Na⌐rubeku iso⌐ide sa⌐seru⌐ kara⌐

English Equivalents

1. Mr. Tanaka: Yamada, are you going home now?
    Mr. Yamada: I'm (lit. I get) late every night entertaining (lit. because
                of association of) company clients.
    Mr. Tanaka: Then it's the same with you? I get sick of it too because
                it's happening all the time. Instead of mixing with company
                clients, I'd prefer to eat leisurely at home, with my wife
                and children.
    Mr. Yamada: That's right. Having to take (lit. lead) people to restau-
                rants and go away on business trips is awful, isn't it—for
                company employees.
    Mr. Tanaka: But even if you take a job in another place it will be just
                the same.

2. Mr. Tanaka: Prices (of things) go up fast, don't they.
    Mr. Yamamoto: Sugar, for example, is going up as much as ¥ 5 every
                week.
    Mr. Tanaka: With everything getting expensive like that, it's awful,
                isn't it.
    Mr. Yamamoto: Salaries are the same but [nothing else is].

3. Mr. Tanaka: Even though Mr. Brown is an American, he didn't use
                a single word of English.
    Mr. Yamamoto: Did he say everything in Japanese?
    Mr. Tanaka: That's right. What's more, he uses quite good (lit.
                skillful) language. I was amazed.
    Mr. Yamamoto: Usually Westerners' speech is (something) strange
                (but)—you know.

4. Mrs. Tanaka: Say, let me have the dictionary.
    Maid: Do you mean this one?
    Mrs. Tanaka: Oh, not that. It's a thicker, black one. Isn't it right
                over there?
    Maid: If it's (lit. as for) a black one, there's only this one. Is
                this the one?
    Mrs. Tanaka: That's right, that's right, that one. Thanks.

5. Father: There's an interesting(-looking) movie. Wouldn't you like to go
             and see it (too)?
    Son: What kind of movie? Will you (lit. father) take me?
    Father: Yes, I'm free today so . . .
    Son: That's wonderful. Everything is good that you think is good
             (lit. provided it's a thing that father thinks is good). I'll
             change clothes right away so wait (lit. be waiting) for me,
             will you?
    Father: Sure. Take your time changing. (Lit. Come having changed
             slowly.)

6. Mrs. Tanaka: Is your son well?
    Mrs. Yamamoto: Yes, thank you. But I get upset because he doesn't
                    study at all.
    Mrs. Tanaka: Isn't that because he's still young (lit. small)?
    Mrs. Yamamoto: He's twelve already, so unless I make him study a
                    little [there will be trouble — i.e. I must make him study a
                    little].
    Mrs. Tanaka: I wonder if it isn't bad, forcing him to do it (lit. even
                    forcibly making him do it) when (lit. in spite of the fact that)
                    he doesn't want to (do).
    Mrs. Yamamoto: Hmmm. My husband too says that even if you force
                    him to do it by saying 'Study! Study!' he won't learn, so
                    it's better not to say anything, but soon now it will be [time
                    for] middle school — right? It's a worry.
    Mrs. Tanaka: You don't have to worry like that.

7. Mr. Tanaka: This may be unreasonable but would you translate this
                   letter for me by tomorrow?
    Mr. Yamamoto: What kind (of one) is it? If it's an easy one I can do it.
    Mr. Tanaka: For you it won't be hard. It's completely beyond me . . .
                   (Lit. For me, it's completely incomprehensible but . . .)
    Mr. Yamamoto: Well, I'll try and do it.
    Mr. Tanaka: I'm sorry, always ending up having you do it, but would
                   you?
    Mr. Yamamoto: Having to do it is good practice (lit. study). But unless
                   I try doing it, I can't tell whether I can or not — really. If I
                   can, I'll bring it tomorrow morning.
    Mr. Tanaka: I'm sorry to bother you, but I really need it (lit. I re-
                   quest it by all means).

8. Taro: I wonder who that fat fellow is.
    Jiro: Don't you know? It's Masao.
    Taro: Masao? Hasn't he put on weight!
    Jiro: I saw him at school yesterday. I was surprised too. He took a
           vacation at Nikko for about (as much as) a month and eating
           was his greatest pleasure, he says.
    Taro: He'd better get thin in a hurry!

9. Mr. Smith: We have to learn about (as many as) fifty kanji each week
                 nowadays. I think it's unreasonable.
    Mr. Tanaka: It probably is.
    Mr. Smith: My head is reeling (lit. has become strange) because all I
                 do is study.

10. Man: Isn't Ueda an interesting man!
     Woman: Yes. The more you see of him the nicer (person) he is.
     Man: Talking with him is a pleasure, isn't it! (Because) everything
                 he says is interesting. (Lit. Saying nothing but interesting
                 things.)

11. Tanaka: How is your daughter?
     Smith: Fine, thank you. She does nothing every day but [play] base-
                 ball outside . . .
     Tanaka: Baseball?
     Smith: Yes. Instead of doing anything at all that's ladylike, she al-
                 ways plays with the boys.

12. Tanaka: Isn't it nice weather!
     Smith: It's really (become) like spring, isn't it.
     Tanaka: I hear that the cherry trees have begun to bloom already.
     Smith: Really? Don't they seem a little early this year?

13. American Student (male): I don't want to study anything like Japanese
                 any more.
     Japanese Friend (male):   Why?
     American: The more I do it the harder it gets, and I'm good and sick of
                 it.
     Japanese: Come now, don't say that! Aren't you the best[in the group]?
                 If you quit, you know that everybody will quit.
     American: I wonder why you use things like these kanji that are such a
                 nuisance.
     Japanese: I don't know why either . . .

14. Mrs. Yamamoto: Oh, come in! /To Mr. Yamamoto/ (You,) someone
                 unexpected has come.
     Mr. Yamamoto: Oh, Tanaka? Is your wife with you? I'm glad you
                 came. Come right in (lit. up).
     Mr. Tanaka: Excuse us for not having been in touch with you. Are
                 you all well?
     Mr. Yamamoto: Yes, thanks. Is everyone well at your place, too?
     Mr. Tanaka: Yes, thank you.
     Mrs. Tanaka: Your son is well too, isn't he?
     Mrs. Yamamoto: Yes, Masao is fine, too. But you know—[he'll be tak-
                 ing] entrance exams for high school soon now. He has to
                 study every night until the middle of the night; (so) I feel
                 sorry for him.
     Mrs. Tanaka: [That's] because the better the school is, the keener
                 the competition.
     Mr. Yamamoto: (Even) if you do get him into a good school with a
                 struggle, you have trouble later on, so I say 'Don't do
                 studying that's too much for you,' but [it does no good].
     Mrs. Yamamoto: The electricity goes off constantly these days, doesn't
                 it? It gets to be annoying just when he is taking the trouble
                 to study.
     Mr. Yamamoto: (Because) you can't study with candles!
     Mrs. Tanaka: Your son does very well so you don't have to worry.
     Mrs. Yamamoto: Heavens no! We'll be able to relax once the test is
                 over, but until then, even (the side of) the parents must al-
                 ways be thinking of nothing but the exams so it's not easy.

Mr. Yamamoto: To change the subject, how is your father these days?

Mr. Tanaka: He's much better, thank you. Right now, he's taking it easy at an Izu hot spring.

Mr. Yamamoto: Wasn't it fine [that it turned out that way].

Mr. Tanaka: He seems a little thin but the doctor keeps saying there's nothing more to worry about so we are relieved.

Mrs. Yamamoto: How is the baby? I wish you had brought him.

Mrs. Tanaka: The trains (and busses, etc.) are crowded so we didn't bring him today . We'll (accept your letting us) come again so [we'll bring him then].

Mrs. Yamamoto: Please do bring him.   His birthday has passed (lit. finished) already, hasn't it?

Mrs. Tanaka: Yes, it was last month.

Mrs. Yamamoto: What a joy babies are! . . . I'm having dinner made now so do eat before you go (lit. go having eaten), won't you?

Mr. Tanaka: Thank you but the children are waiting, so . . .

Mr. Yamamoto: Oh, don't say that. Do eat before you go. (Lit. Without saying that kind of thing, go having eaten.) (To Mrs. Yamamoto) It will be [ready] soon, won't it?

Mrs. Yamamoto: Yes, right away. That's why [you should] eat before you go.

Mr. Tanaka: Thank you very much. Since you've been so kind as to ask us, we will (eat and then go).

Mrs. Yamamoto: Fine. (Lit. Do that, will you?) I'll have it made as quickly as possible (so . . .)

EXERCISES

1. Read the following in Japanese:

a.	2/3	k.	10%
b.	3/4	l.	3%
c.	1/2	m.	14%
d.	9/10	n.	68%
e.	3/5	o.	50%
f.	4/7	p.	72%
g.	3/10	q.	99%
h.	1/9	r.	85%
i.	5/6	s.	90%
j.	3/8	t.	11%

2. Go through the Supplementary Dialogues of this lesson, changing all the typically feminine utterances to corresponding men s utterances if you are a man, and vice versa if you are a woman.

3. Make up twelve short conversations, each of which contains one of the following:

a. ta⌐ma ni⌐ wa   g. to⌐ñde mo na⌐i
b. ya⌐ppa⌐ri   h. i⌐k-kaḡetu-ḡo⌐to ni
c. ho⌐to⌐ñdo   i. so⌐re wa so⌐o to
d. otya ka ko⌐ohi⌐i   j. mu⌐ri ni saseru
e. tu⌐i   k. do⌐ñdoñ
f. be⌐ñkyoo ba⌐kari   l. wa⌐ka⌐ru to iinaḡara

4. Make up informal conversations according to the following outlines:

   a. You have just met a close friend whom you haven't seen for a long
       time. Discuss what you've been doing, why you haven't been in
       touch, how the family is, when you can get together again, etc.
       Use your imagination and keep the conversation lively!

   b. You are planning a weekend trip with a close friend. He wants to
       go to Kyoto, stay at a Western-style hotel, visit temples and
       shrines, and shop for souvenirs. You want to go to Izu, stay at a
       Japanese inn, and swim and fish and rest. Have a friendly discus-
       sion and reach some final agreement.

   c. There is to be a baseball game next Saturday. You want a close
       friend of yours to go to the game with you, but he wants to watch
       it on television. Argue about the matter until one of you gives in.

Appendix I

A. Summary of Verbals

Every Japanese verbal is assigned to one of four sub-classes: -ru, -u, -aru, or irregular. Most verbals belong to one of the first two classes, since there are only five -aru verbals (go⌐za⌐ru⁺, i⌐rassya⌐ru⁺, ku⌐dasa⌐ru⁺, na⌐sa⌐ru⁺, and o⌐ssya⌐ru⁺) and two irregular verbals (ku⌐ru and suru). Verbals belonging to the -u class are further divided according to the sound that precedes final -u: k, ḡ, b, m, n, s, r, t, or a vowel.

The following is a summary of informal forms introduced in this text, with samples of each subclass. Where possible, an accented and unaccented sample are given for each. In every row across, Forms 2–9 are derived forms of the verbal whose citation form (the informal non-past) is Form 1; Form 10 is a verbal derivative but is itself an adjectival whose inflection is summarized in Appendix I B below; Forms 11–14 are verbal derivatives and are themselves the citation forms of verbals belonging to the -ru group, having their own inflected forms 2–9. When a particular form of a sample verbal occurs only rarely (or never)—for example, yo⌐roko⌐bu 'take pleasure in' does not ordinarily occur in the imperative—the rare (or hypothetical) form is enclosed in parentheses in the chart on pages 360–61.

SAMPL

	1.	2.	3.	4.	5.	6.	7.
Subclass	Non-past	Stem	Gerund	Past	Conditional	Representative	Provision

-ru

(accented)	ta'be'ru 'eat'	ta'be	ta'bete	ta'beta	ta'betara	ta'betari	ta'be'reba
(unaccented)	ireru 'insert'	ire	irete	ireta	i'reta'ra	i'reta'ri	i'rere'ba

-u

-ku

(accented)	a'ru'ku 'walk'	a'ru'ki	a'ru'ite	a'ru'ita	a'ru'itara	a'ru'itari	a'ru'keba
(unaccented)	kiku 'ask	kiki	kiite	kiita	ki'ita'ra	ki'ita'ri	ki'ke'ba

-gu

(accented)	o'yo'gu 'swim'	o'yo'gi	o'yo'ide	o'yo'ida	o'yo'idara	o'yo'idari	o'yo'geba

-bu

(accented)	yo'roko'bu 'take pleasure in'	yo'roko'bi	yo'roko'nde	yo'roko'nda	yo'roko'ndara	yo'roko'ndari	yo'roko'be
(unaccented)	yobu 'call'	yobi	yonde	yonda	yo'nda'ra	yo'nda'ri	yo'be'ba

-mu

(accented)	no'mu 'drink'	no'mi	no'nde	no'nda	no'ndara	no'ndari	no'meba
(unaccented)	yamu 'cease'	yami	yande	yanda	ya'nda'ra	ya'nda'ri	ya'me'ba

-nu

(unaccented)	sinu 'die'	sini	sinde	sinda	si'nda'ra	si'nda'ri	si'ne'ba

-su

(accented)	ha'na'su 'talk'	ha'na'si	ha'na'site	ha'na'sita	ha'na'sitara	ha'na'sitari	ha'na'seba
(unaccented)	kasu 'lend'	kasi	kasite	kasita	ka'sita'ra	ka'sita'ri	ka'se'ba

-ru

(accented)	tu'ku'ru 'make'	tu'ku'ri	tu'ku'tte	tu'ku'tta	tu'ku'ttara	tu'ku'ttari	tu'ku'reba
(unaccented)	noru 'ride'	nori	notte	notta	no'tta'ra	no'tta'ri	no're'ba

-tu

(accented)	ma'tu 'wait'	ma'ti	ma'tte	ma'tta	ma'ttara	ma'ttari	ma'teba

Vowel + -u

(accented)	ha'ra'u 'pay'	ha'ra'i	ha'ra'tte	ha'ra'tta	ha'ra'ttara	ha'ra'ttari	ha'ra'eba
(unaccented)	arau 'wash'	arai	aratte	aratta	a'ratta'ra	a'ratta'ri	a'rae'ba

-aru [1]

(accented)	o'ssya'ru⌐ 'say'	o'ssya'i	o'ssya'tte	o'ssya'tta	o'ssya'ttara	o'ssya'ttari	o'ssya'reb

Irregular

(accented)	ku'ru 'come'	ki'	ki'te'	ki'ta'	ki'ta'ra	ki'ta'ri	ku'reba
(unaccented)	suru 'do'	si	site	sita	si'ta'ra	si'ta'ri	su're'ba

---

[1] Go'za'ru belongs to this subclass but occurs only in the formal style — i.e. the stem go'zai compounds with √-ma'su. I'rassya'ru has alternate gerunds i'rassya'tte ~ i'ra'site, na'sa'ru has alternate gerunds na'sa'tte ~ na'su'tte, and ku'dasa'ru has alternate gerunds ku'dasa'tte ~ ku'dasu'tte. Parallel alternation occurs in Form 4–6 of these three verbals.

ERBALS

8. Tentative	9. Imperative	10. Negative Non-past	11. Potential Non-past	12. Causative Non-past	13. Passive Non-past	14. Passive Causative Non-past
a⌐beyo¬o	ta⌐be¬ro	ta⌐be¬nai	ta⌐berare¬ru	ta⌐besase¬ru	ta⌐berare¬ru	ta⌐besaserare¬ru
reyoo	i⌐rero¬	irenai	irerareru	iresaseru	irerareru	iresaserareru
a⌐ruko¬o	a⌐ruke	a⌐ruka¬nai	a⌐ruke¬ru	a⌐rukase¬ru	a⌐rukare¬ru	a⌐rukaserare¬ru
ikoo	ki⌐ke¬	kikanai	kikeru	kikaseru	kikareru	kikaserareru
o⌐yogo¬o	o⌐yoḡe	o⌐yoḡa¬nai	o⌐yoḡe¬ru	o⌐yoḡase¬ru	o⌐yoḡare¬ru	o⌐yoḡaserare¬ru
yo⌐rokobo¬o)	(yo⌐roko¬be)	yo⌐rokoba¬nai	(yo⌐rokobe¬ru)	(yo⌐rokobase¬ru)	(yo⌐rokobare¬ru)	(yo⌐rokobaserare¬ru)
oboo	yo⌐be¬	yobanai	yoberu	yobaseru	yobareru	yobaserareru
o⌐mo¬o	no⌐me	no⌐ma¬nai	no⌐me¬ru	no⌐mase¬ru	no⌐mare¬ru	no⌐maserare¬ru
(yamoo)	(ya⌐me¬)	yamanai	(yameru)	(yamaseru)	yamareru	(yamaserareru)
sinoo)	(si⌐ne¬)	sinanai	(sineru)	(sinaseru)	sinareru	(sinaserareru)
a⌐naso¬o	ha⌐na¬se	ha⌐nasa¬nai	ha⌐nase¬ru	ha⌐nasase¬ru	ha⌐nasare¬ru	ha⌐nasaserare¬ru
kasoo	ka⌐se¬	kasanai	kaseru	kasaseru	kasareru	kasaserareru
u⌐kuro¬o	tu⌐ku¬re	tu⌐kura¬nai	tu⌐kure¬ru	tu⌐kurase¬ru	tu⌐kurare¬ru	tu⌐kuraserare¬ru
oroo	no⌐re¬	noranai	noreru	noraseru	norareru	noraserareru
ma⌐to¬o	ma⌐te	ma⌐ta¬nai	ma⌐te¬ru	ma⌐tase¬ru	ma⌐tare¬ru	ma⌐taserare¬ru
a⌐rao¬o	ha⌐ra¬e	ha⌐rawa¬nai	ha⌐rae¬ru	ha⌐rawase¬ru	ha⌐raware¬ru	ha⌐rawaserare¬ru
raoo	a⌐rae¬	arawanai	araeru	arawaseru	arawareru	arawaserareru
o⌐ssyaro¬o	o⌐ssya¬i	o⌐ssyara¬nai	o⌐ssyare¬ru	(o⌐ssyarase¬ru)	(o⌐ssyarare¬ru)	(o⌐ssyaraserare¬ru)
ko⌐yo¬o	ko¬i	ko¬nai	ko⌐rare¬ru	ko⌐sase¬ru	ko⌐rare¬ru	ko⌐saserare¬ru
iyoo	si⌐ro¬	sinai	de⌐ki¬ru	saseru	sareru	saserareru

Remarks on accent:

FORM 1 (Non-past): Before particles ḡa, ka, kara, keredo, si, and yori, [1]
sentence particles ka, kai, sa, and wa, nominal no, and various forms
of the copula, [2] an unaccented non-past acquires a final-syllable accent.
Examples: noꜝruꜝ kara, aꜛrauꜝ keredo, kiꜝkuꜝ kai, suꜝruꜝ no, etc.

FORM 3 (Gerund): Before particles mo and wa, and sentence particle yo,
an unaccented gerund acquires a final-syllable accent. Examples: noꜛtteꜝ
mo, aꜛratteꜝ wa, kiꜛiteꜝ yo, etc.

FORM 4 (Past): See remarks under Form 1 above. Examples: noꜛttaꜝ kara,
aꜛrattaꜝ keredo, kiꜛitaꜝ kai, siꜛtaꜝ no, etc.

FORM 8 (Tentative): The informal tentative of an unaccented verbal has an
accented alternant. Thus: noꜛroꜝo, aꜛraoꜝo, etc.

GENERAL: When, according to the regular pattern, an accent would occur on
the voiceless syllable of a verbal, it may shift to a neighboring voiced
syllable.

Examples:

kuꜝru 'come':	gerund	kiꜛteꜝ
huꜝru 'fall, rain':	gerund	huꜛtteꜝ (or huꜝtte)
kiꜝru 'cut':	gerund	kiꜛtteꜝ (or kiꜛtte)

Formal verbals are made by combining the stem (Form 2 above) with
√-maꜝsu. The inflection of √-maꜝsu is as follows:

1	2	3	4	5	6	7
-maꜝsu	——	-maꜝsite	-maꜝsita	-maꜝsitara	-maꜝsitari	(⁓masuꜝreba)

8	9	10
-masyoꜝo	-maꜝse	-maseꜝn̄

---

[1] Alternate accent: unaccented verbal + accented yoꜝri.

[2] Alternate accent: unaccented verbal and accented √da. Example: iꜛkuꜝ desyoo or iꜛku desyoꜝo.

B. Summary of Adjectivals

An adjectival is an inflected word which ends in -<u>ai</u>, -<u>ii</u>, -<u>ui</u>, or -<u>oi</u> in its citation form (informal non-past) and has a derivative form (the adverbial) ending in -<u>ku</u>.

Negative adjectivals end in -<u>nai</u> and are derived from verbals; they have, in addition to a -<u>ku</u> adverbial, an alternate adverbial ending in -<u>zu</u>, but they have no polite adverbial form.

-<u>Tai</u> 'want to' adjectivals are also derived from verbals; except for accent differences, they are identical with -<u>ai</u> adjectivals in general.

The following is a summary of adjectival forms introduced in this text, with samples of each type. Note that Form 11, the negative form of non-negative adjectivals, is the adverbial + <u>na͘i</u>; <u>na͘i</u> is itself inflected like any negative adjectival except that it has no -<u>zu</u> adverbial.

SAMPLE

	1.	2.	3.	4.	5.
	Non-past	Adverbial	Alternate Negative Adverbial	Polite Adverbial	Gerund

-ai

(accented)	ta˹ka˺i 'is high'	ta˹kaku	——	ta˹koǫ	ta˹kakute
(unaccented)	tumetai 'is cold'	tumetaku	——	tumetoo	tu˹meta˺kute

-ii

(accented)	su˹zusi˺i 'is cool'	su˹zu˺siku	——	suzusyuu	su˹zu˺sikute
(unaccented)	oisii 'is delicious'	oisiku	——	oisyuu	o˹isi˺kute

-ui

(accented)	a˹tu˺i 'is hot'	a˹tuku	——	a˹tuu	a˹tukute
(unaccented)	atui 'is thick'	atuku	——	atuu	a˹tu˺kute

-oi

(accented)	hi˹ro˺i 'is wide'	hi˹roku	——	hi˹roo	hi˹rokute
(unaccented)	tooi 'is far'	tooku	——	tooo	to˹o˺kute

-tai

(accented)	ta˹beta˺i 'want to eat'	ta˹beta˺ku	——	ta˹beto˺o	ta˹beta˺kute
(unaccented)	ikitai 'want to go'	ikitaku	——	ikitoo	i˹kita˺kute

-nai

(accented)	ta˹be˺nai 'doesn't eat'	ta˹be˺naku	ta˹be˺zu	——	ta˹be˺nakute
(unaccented)	ikanai 'doesn't go'	ikanaku	ikazu	——	i˹kana˺kute

ADJECTIVALS

6.	7.	8.	9.	10.	11.
Past	Conditional	Represen-tative	Provisional	Tentative [1]	Negative
ta⌐kakatta	ta⌐kakattara	ta⌐kakattari	ta⌐kakereba	ta⌐kakaro⌐o	ta⌐kaku ⌐na⌐i
tu⌐meta⌐katta	tu⌐meta⌐kattara	tu⌐meta⌐kattari	tu⌐meta⌐kereba	tu⌐metakaro⌐o	tu⌐metaku na⌐i
su⌐zu⌐sikatta	su⌐zu⌐sikattara	su⌐zu⌐sikattari	su⌐zu⌐sikereba	su⌐zusikaro⌐o	su⌐zu⌐siku ⌐na⌐i
o⌐isi⌐katta	o⌐isi⌐kattara	o⌐isi⌐kattari	o⌐isi⌐kereba	o⌐isikaro⌐o	o⌐isiku na⌐i
a⌐tukatta	a⌐tukattara	a⌐tukattari	a⌐tukereba	a⌐tukaro⌐o	a⌐tuku ⌐na⌐i
a⌐tu⌐katta	a⌐tu⌐kattara	a⌐tu⌐kattari	a⌐tu⌐kereba	a⌐tukaro⌐o	a⌐tuku na⌐i
hi⌐rokatta	hi⌐rokattara	hi⌐rokattari	hi⌐rokereba	hi⌐rokaro⌐o	hi⌐roku ⌐na⌐i
to⌐o⌐katta	to⌐o⌐kattara	to⌐o⌐kattari	to⌐o⌐kereba	to⌐okaro⌐o	to⌐oku na⌐i
ta⌐beta⌐katta	ta⌐beta⌐kattara	ta⌐beta⌐kattari	ta⌐beta⌐kereba	ta⌐betakaro⌐o	ta⌐beta⌐ku ⌐na⌐i
i⌐kita⌐katta	i⌐kita⌐kattara	i⌐kita⌐kattari	i⌐kita⌐kereba	i⌐kitakaro⌐o	i⌐kitaku na⌐i
ta⌐be⌐nakatta	ta⌐be⌐nakattara	ta⌐be⌐nakattari	ta⌐be⌐nakereba	ta⌐benakaro⌐o	——
i⌐kana⌐katta	i⌐kana⌐kattara	i⌐kana⌐kattari	i⌐kana⌐kereba -	i⌐kanakaro⌐o	——

---

[1] The alternate informal tentative adjectival pattern — consisting of a non-past adjectival + daroo — is the pattern regularly drilled in the text.

Remarks on accent:

FORM 1 (Non-past): Before particles g̲a̲, k̲a̲, k̲a̲r̲a̲, k̲e̲r̲e̲d̲o̲, s̲i̲, and y̲o̲r̲i̲, [1]
sentences particles k̲a̲, k̲a̲i̲, s̲a̲, and w̲a̲, nominal n̲o̲, and forms of the
copula, an unaccented non-past acquires an accent on its next-to-last syl-
lable. [2] Examples: t̲u̲⌐m̲e̲t̲a̲⌐i̲ k̲a̲r̲a̲, i̲⌐k̲i̲t̲a̲⌐i̲ k̲e̲r̲e̲d̲o̲, i̲⌐k̲a̲n̲a̲⌐i̲ n̲o̲, etc.

In sentence-final position, a normally unaccented non-past adjectival occurs with both accented and unaccented alternants. Example: A̲b̲u̲n̲a̲i̲. or
A̲⌐b̲u̲n̲a̲⌐i̲.

GENERAL: Many of the accented adjectival forms in the chart above have
alternate accents in current use in the Tokyo area. Some of these have
occurred in the text.

Examples:

t̲a̲⌐k̲a̲k̲u̲t̲e̲	or	t̲a̲⌐k̲a̲⌐k̲u̲t̲e̲
h̲i̲⌐r̲o̲k̲u̲t̲e̲	or	h̲i̲⌐r̲o̲⌐k̲u̲t̲e̲
m̲i̲⌐z̲i̲⌐k̲a̲k̲u̲	or	m̲i̲⌐z̲i̲k̲a̲⌐k̲u̲
u̲⌐r̲e̲⌐s̲y̲u̲u̲	or	u̲⌐r̲e̲s̲y̲u̲⌐u̲

In each case, the second form is a newer form.

---

[1] Alternate accent: unaccented adjectival + accented y̲o̲⌐r̲i̲.

[2] But t̲o̲o̲i̲ acquires an accent on its final syllable.

C. Summary of the Copula da

The following forms of √da have been introduced:

	1. Non-past	2. Pre-nominal	3. Gerund	4. Past	5. Condi-tional	6. Repre-sentative	7. Provi-sional	8. Ten-tative
Inform-al	da	na~no	de	da˺tta	da˺ttara	da˺ttari	nara⌊ba⌋	da⌈ro˺o
Form-al	de˺su	——	de˺site	de˺sita	de˺si-tara	de˺si-tari	de˺sita-raba	de⌈syo˺o

Remarks on accent:

accented form of √da regularly loses its accent following an accented word or phrase.

FORM 2 (Pre-nominal) is regularly unaccented except that na following an unaccented word or phrase and preceding nominal no acquires an accent. Example: byo⌈oki na˺ no.

FORM 3 (Gerund) following an unaccented nominal (or nominal + particle) acquire an accent before particles mo and wa. Examples: so⌈re de˺ mo, so⌈re de˺ wa, ko⌈ko kara de˺ mo, etc.

FORM 8 (Tentative) following an unaccented verbal has alternate accents: either the verbal remains unaccented (with da⌈ro˺o/de⌈syo˺o accented) or the verbal acquires a final-syllable accent (with daroo/desyoo unaccented).

Examples:

i⌈ku daro˺o	or	i⌈ku˺ daroo
i⌈ku desyo˺o	or	i⌈ku˺ desyoo
i⌈tta daro˺o	or	i⌈tta˺ daroo
i⌈tta desyo˺o	or	i⌈tta˺ desyoo

Appendix II

A. na Nominals [1]

beꜛnri	'convenient'	meꜛewaku	'troublesome'
betu [2]	'separate'	muꜛri	'unreasonable'
daꜛisuki	'very pleasing'	oꜛoki [3]	'big'
daˈiziˈ	'valuable,' 'important'	rippa	'splendid'
daˈizyoˈobu	'safe'	sakañ	'flourishing'
daˈmeˈ	'no good'	siˈtuˈree	'rude'
geꜛñki	'good health,' 'high spirits'	siꜛzuka	'quiet'
		-soo [4]	'looking as if'
haˈdeˈ	'bright,' 'loud,' 'flashy'	suˈkiˈ	'pleasing'
heeki	'unconcerned'	syoꜛoziki	'honest'
heꜛñ	'strange'	taiheñ	'dreadful,' 'awful'
hima	'free time'	taisetu	'important'
huꜛbeñ	'inconvenient'	teꜛenee	'polite'
hukuzatu	'complicated'	tekitoo	'suitable'
huꜛu	'manner'	tiꜛisa [3]	'small'
huꜛziyuu	'inconvenient,' 'restricted'	yoꜛo	'manner'
		yuumee	'famous'
iroiro [2]	'various'	ziˈmiˈ	'subdued,' 'conservative'
iˈyaˈ	'unpleasant'		
kañtañ	'simple'	ziˈyuˈu	'free'
kaˈwaisoˈo	'pitiful'	zyoobu	'sturdy'
keꜛkkoo	'fine'	zyoˈozuˈ	'proficient'
kiɾai	'dislike'	zyuˈubuˈñ	'enough'
kiꜛree	'pretty,' 'clean'		

Examples of usage:

Kiꜛree desu. '[It]'s pretty.'

Kiꜛree zya aˈrimaseˈñ. '[It] isn't pretty.'

Kiꜛree na oˈzyoˈosañ desu. '[She]'s a pretty girl.'

Kiꜛree ni naˈrimaˈsita. '[She]'s grown to be pretty.'

Kiꜛree ni kaˈkimaˈsita. '[He] wrote beautifully.'

---

[1] The list below includes all na nominals introduced in this text.

[2] Occurs with na or no as the modifier of a following nominal.

[3] With following na, alternates with -i form of related adjectival as modifier of a following nominal. Thus: $\left|\frac{\text{tiꜛisa na}}{\text{tiˈisaˈi}}\right|$ ˈkoˈe 'low voice'; $\left|\frac{\text{oꜛoki na}}{\text{oˈoki ˈi}}\right|$ ˈkoˈe 'loud voice.'

[4] For example, deˈkisoˈo 'looking as if it would be possible,' aˈtusoˈo 'looking as if it would be hot,' zyoˈobusoˈo 'sturdy-looking,' etc.

B. Counters [1]

Counter for:	Numerals of Series I[2]	Numerals of Series II[3]	Irregular	Counts	Names	Counts and Names
		Occurs with:			Usage: [4]	
-bai (34)	multiples	X			X		
-bañ (12)	serial numbers	X				X	
-bañ (21)	nights		X		X		
-bañ-señ (19)	track numbers	X				X	
-baˈñti (34)	lot numbers	X				X	
-bu (35)	units of per cent	X			X		
-buñ (35)	fraction denominators	X				X	
-dai (20)	vehicles	X			X		
-do (1)	number of times	X			X		
-eñ (3)	yen	X			X		
-ḡatu (8)	months of the year	X				X	
-ḡoˈo-sya (19)	train car numbers	X				X	
-guˈramu (22)	grams	X			X		
-hai (14)	glassfuls	X			X		
-heñ (32)	number of times	X			X		
-hoñ (5)	long, cylindrical objects	X			X		
-huñ (8)	minutes	X					X
-ka/-niti (8)	days			X			X
-kaˈḡetu (8)	months	X			X		
-kai (16)	floors	X					X
-kai (32)	number of times	X			X		
-ma (21)	rooms		X		X		
-mai (5)	thin, flat objects	X			X		
-neñ (8)	years	X					X
-niñ-mae (15)	portions	X			X		
-ri/-niñ (10)	people			X	X		
-riˈttoru (20)	liters	X			X		
-satu (5)	volumes	X			X		
-syuˈukañ (8)	weeks	X			X		
-too (19)	classes	X				X	
-tu (5, 10)	units of inanimate objects; years of age (people)		X		X		

---

[1] The list below includes all the counters introduced in this text. The parenthesized numbers tell in what lesson each appeared first. An accent mark indicates a consistently accented counter.

[2] Iˈti⌐, ni⌐, sañ, etc.

[3] Hiˈto⌐, huta, mi⌐, etc.

[4] A number which counts tells how many; a number which names tells which one. Thus: ni-ˈkaˈḡetu '2 months' counts, ni⌐-ḡatu 'February' names, and ni⌐-neñ '2 years' or 'the year 2' counts and names.

Counters (cont.)

	Counter for:	Occurs with:			Usage:		
		Numerals of Series I	Numerals of Series II	Irreg- ular	Counts	Names	Counts and Names
-tubo (30)	tsubo (app. 6' x 6')		X[1]		X		
-tyoome⌐ (7)	chome	X				X	
-wari (35)	tens of per cent	X			X		
-zi (8)	hours of the day	X				X	
-zi⌐kañ (8)	hours	X			X		
-zyo⌐o (30)	jo (app. 3' x 6')	X			X[2]		

---

[1] Also occurs with some numerals of Series I.

[2] Also occurs as a name for a room having the given number of mats.

C. Table of Time Expressions [1]

		Present	Next	Next-after-next	Last	Last-before-last	Every
'day'	hi	kyo̅o 'today'	a⌐sita⌐ 'tomorrow'	a⌐sa⌐tte 'day after tomorrow'	ki⌐no̅o 'yesterday'	o⌐toto̅i 'day before yesterday'	ma⌐initi 'every day'
'morning'	⌐asa	ke⌐sa 'this morning'	a⌐sita no a̅sa 'tomorrow morning'	a⌐sa⌐tte no ⌐a⌐sa 'morning after next'	ki⌐noo no a̅sa 'yesterday morning'	o⌐totoi no a̅sa 'morning before last'	ma⌐iasa 'every morning'
'night'	bañ	ko⌐ñbañ 'tonight'	asita no bañ 'tomorrow night'	a⌐sa⌐tte no bañ 'night after next'	kinno no bañ or yuube 'last night'	ototoi no bañ 'night before last'	ma⌐ibañ [2] 'every night'
'week'	syu⌐u	koñsyuu 'this week'	raisyuu 'next week'	saraisyuu 'week after next'	señsyuu 'last week'	se⌐ñse⌐ñsyuu 'week before last'	maisyuu 'every week'
'month'	tu⌐ki⌐	koñḡetu 'this month'	raiḡetu 'next month'	saraiḡetu 'month after next'	señḡetu 'last month'	se⌐ñse⌐ñḡetu 'month before last'	maituki or maiḡetu 'every month'
'year'	to⌐si⌐	kotosi 'this year'	raineñ 'next year'	saraineñ 'year after next'	kyo⌐neñ 'last year'	o⌐to̅tosi 'year before last'	maitosi or maineñ 'every year'

[1] There are many formal alternants which are not listed here; only the more common conversational expressions are included.

[2] Has unaccented alternant.

Japanese-English Glossary

Except for proper names, the following list contains all the vocabulary introduced in this text, Parts I and II—words occurring in the Notes and as additional vocabulary as well as those occurring in the Basic Dialogues. Numbers following the entries refer to lessons: a number alone means that the entry first occurs in the Basic Dialogues of that lesson; a number followed by '-A' refers to the Additional Vocabulary of that lesson; a number followed by '-N' indicates that the item first occurs in the Notes or any later section of that lesson. CI, Int, and App. refer to Classroom Instructions, [1] Introductory Lesson, and Appendix respectively. An asterisk means that the item is included in the Index to the Grammatical Notes, with a reference to the location of the appropriate note(s).

Except in special cases, verbals and adjectivals are listed in their citation form only. Every verbal—except a compound ending in -suru—is identified as transitive /tr/ or intransitive /intr/ [2] and is assigned to the appropriate subclass; [3] its gerund is also given. For example, akeru /tr:-ru: akete/ identifies akeru as a transitive verbal belonging to the -ru subclass (i.e. the subclass to which ta⌐be⌐ru 'eat' and mi⌐ru 'see' belong), with gerund akete. All compound verbals ending in -suru have the same inflection as that of suru alone; accordingly, they are identified only as /tr/ or /intr/.

Every adjectival is identified by '/-ku/' [4] after the citation form. Thus, the adjectival meaning 'is big' appears as o⌐oki⌐i /-ku/.

All forms of the copula which occur in the text are listed and identified.

Nominals occur with no special designation, except that the members of the subclass of na-nominals [5] are identified by a following '/na/.'

Particles and quotatives are so identified. All are marked with asterisks, since all are included in the index.

Pre-nominals are identified by the designation '/+ nom/.'

Counters are so identified and are listed with a preceding hyphen.

---

[1] Words designated as CI are those which occur only in the Classroom Instructions.

[2] For a description of transitive and intransitive verbals, see Part I, Lesson 16, Grammatical Note 1.

[3] For a description of verbal subclasses, see Part I, Lesson 11, Grammatical Note 1.

[4] See Part I, Lesson 2, Grammatical Note 1.

[5] See Part I, Lesson 12, Grammatical Note 4.

373

'/M/' and '/W/' follow entries typical of men's or women's speech respectively.

Except in a few special cases, words having a polite alternant that differs from the plain alternant only in the addition of the polite prefix o- or go- are listed only in the plain alternant.

For purposes of alphabetizing, hyphens and the macron of $\bar{g}$ are ignored. Syllabic $\bar{n}$ is assigned to the position immediately following nonsyllabic n.

In most cases, combinations occurring as indented sublistings match the first occurrence in the lessons; but a simpler, more generally occurring example of the pattern is cited in cases where the combination which occurs first in the lessons seems less desirable as the model for a pattern of wide general use.

A

a   oh!   4
aˀa   oh!   Int.
aˀa   that way   29-N
aˀa   yes   16
abunai   /-ku/   is dangerous   7
aḡaru   /intr:-u:aḡatte/   go up, come
    up, enter   18
aḡaruꜜ   /intr:-u:aḡatte/   go to some-
    one else's home   35
aḡeru*   /tr:-ru:aḡete/   give (to some-
    one other than the speaker)   17;
    raise   29-N
  site aḡeru   do for someone   17
aida*   space between   7; interval of
    time, while   31
  kono aida   the other day, recently
    31
  Tookyoo to Yokohama no aida
    between Tokyo and Yokohama   7
  tu˹tuꜜnde moratte (i)ru aida   while
    [someone] is having [something]
    wrapped   31
ainiku   unfortunate(ly)   34
airoñ   pressing iron, pressing   21
  a˹iroñ o kakeꜜru   iron, press   21
akaboo   porter, redcap   20
akai   /-ku/   is red   4
akañboo   baby   26-N
akarui   /-ku/   is light (i. e. not dark)
    35-N ·
aˀkatyañ   baby   26
akeru   /tr:-ru:akete/   open [some-
    thing]   16
aˀki   autumn, fall   18
a˹kiyaꜜsumi   autumn vacation   25-N
aku   /intr:-u:aite/   [something] opens
    16; become vacant   29
  aite (i)ru   be open   16; be free for
    use or unoccupied   21
a˹maꜜdo   sliding storm-door   18
a˹maḡaꜜsa   rain umbrella   29-N
amai   /-ku/   is sweet or sugary or
    insufficiently salted   14-A
aˀme   rain   18
  aˀme ga ˻huꜜru   it rains   18
a˹merikaꜜziñ   an American   10
a˹miꜜdo   screens   30
aˀnaꜜ   hole   33
  aˀnaꜜ o akeru   make a hole   33-N
  aˀnaꜜ ḡa aku   get a hole in some-
    thing   33-N
aˀnaꜜta   you   Int

ane   older sister   11-A
aˀni   older brother   11-A
ano*   /+ nom/   that — over there   3
Ano ne!   Say! Hey there!   13
anoo   uh . . .   34
añmari   /+ negative/   not very much,
    not so much, not too much   3;
    /+ affirmative/   so much, too
    much   14
añna*   that kind, that kind of   5
  añna ni   to that extent   28-N
a˹ññaꜜi-suru   /tr/   guide, show the way
    31
a˹ññaisyoꜜ   guidebook   32
aññaizyo, a˹ññaizyoꜜ   information booth
    19
aˀñta   you   35-N
aˀo   blue, green   16
a˹oꜜi   /-ku/   is blue or green   4; is
    pale   14
a˹paꜜato   apartment house   16
aˀra   /W/   oh! you don't say! not
    really!   33
arare   hail   26-A
aˀrasi   storm   26-A
arau   /tr:-u:aratte/   wash   17
are*   that thing over there   2
A˹riꜜḡatoo (gozaimasita).ꜜ   Thank you
    (for what you did).   Int.
A˹riꜜḡatoo (gozaimasu).ꜜ   Thank you.
    Int.
aˀru*   /intr:-u:aꜜtte;neg-naꜜi/   be lo-
    cated (of inanimate objects), have
    2
  siꜜmete ˻aꜜru   have been closed
    16
a˹ruꜜku   /intr:-u:a˹ruꜜite/   walk   20
aˀsa   morning   9
a˹saꜜ   flax, linen   23-A
a˹sagoꜜhañ   breakfast   15-N
asamesi   /M/   breakfast   24-N
a˹saꜜtte   day after tomorrow   30
a˹siꜜ   leg, foot   17-A
a˹sitaꜜ, asita   tomorrow   1
asobu   /intr:-u:asoñde/   play, amuse
    oneself, be at leisure, have a
    good time; visit (for pleasure);
    loaf, be unemployed   27
asoko   that place over there, over
    there   6
asuko   /see asoko/   6
a˹tamaꜜ   head   17

aᴦtamaᴀ (cont.)
    aᴦtamaᴀ g̃a ᴴiᴀi have a good head,
        be smart or bright 35
    aᴦtamaᴀ g̃a iᴦtaᴀi have a headache 17
aᴦtarasiᴀi /-ku/ is new or fresh 2
atarimae natural, proper, reasonable
        32-N
atasi /W/ I, me 35-N
aᴦt(a)takaᴀi /-ku/ is warm 16
atira that one (of two); that way,
        thereabouts, over there 6
aᴀto* later, afterward 4
    aᴀto de later, at a later time 4
    suᴦmaᴀseta ato de after having
        finished 31
    aᴀto no iᴴk-kaᴀg̃etu the remaining
        month 29
    Aᴀto ᴴnaᴀni o simasyoo ka. What

aᴀto* (cont.)
        shall I do next? 17
aᴦttiᴀ /see atira/ 6
atui /-ku/ is thick (of flat objects) 22-N
aᴦtuᴀi /-ku/ is hot 14
aᴦtusug̃iᴀru /intr:-ru:aᴦtusuᴀg̃ite/ be
        too hot 21
aᴀu /intr:-u:aᴀtte/ meet, see (and talk
        to) a person 11
    Yaᴦmada-sañ ni aᴀu meet or see
        Mr. Yamada 11
azi flavor, taste 32
    azi g̃a suru have a flavor 33-N
aᴢukaᴀru /tr:-u:aᴢukaᴀtte/ receive in
        custody, take charge of, keep 20-N
aᴢukeᴀru /tr:-ru:aᴢukete/ put into some-
        one else's keeping temporarily,
        check, deposit 20

B

baai circumstances, case 34
    iᴦsoᴀg̃u baai ni in case [someone]
        is in a hurry 34
bai double 34-N
    baᴦi ni naᴀru [something] doubles
        34-N
    bai ni suru double [something] 34-N
-bai /counter for multiples/ 34
baᴀkari* /particle/ nothing but,
        little else but, only, just 35
    goᴦbusata baᴀkari nothing but
        neglect to write or visit 35
baᴀkkari /see baᴀkari/ 35-N
bañ night 19
-bañ /counter for nights/ 21
-bañ /counter for naming numbers
        in a series/ 12
bañdo (man's) belt 23-A
    bañdo o suru wear a belt 23-A
baᴦñg̃oᴀhañ evening meal, dinner 15-N
baᴦñg̃oᴀo number 12
bañmesi /M/ dinner 24-N
-bañ-señ /counter for naming track
        numbers/ 19
-bañti /counter for naming lot
        numbers/ 34
baᴀree ballet 28-A
baᴀsu bus 8
baᴀta butter 14-A
baᴀtterii battery 20-N
beᴦekokuᴀziñ an American 10-A
beᴦesuboᴀoru baseball 35-N
beᴦñg̃oᴀsi lawyer 24-A

beñkyoo-suru /tr/ study 11
beᴀñri /na/ convenient 29-N
beñriya handyman 33
beᴦñtoᴀo box lunch 27
beᴦñzyoᴀ /M/ toilet 6-A
beruto (woman's) belt 23-A
    beruto o suru wear a belt 23-A
beᴀtto bed 17-A
betu /na ~ no/ separate 21
betu ni /+ negative/ not especially 13
biᴀiru beer 14
biᴦkkuᴀri-suru /intr/ be surprised, be
        amazed, be startled 29
biᴀru building (Western style) 6
boᴀku, boku /M/ I, me 5
boᴀkutati /M/ we, us 27
boo stick 33-A
boᴦoekiᴀsyoo foreign trader 24-A
boᴦohuᴀu gale 26-A
booi waiter, steward, barboy, office
        boy 24-A
boosi hat 23
botañ button 33-N
boᴀttyañ† son 11-A
bu part 28
    hiru no bu daytime performance
        28-N
    yoᴀru no bu evening performance 28
-bu /counter for units of per cent/ 35
bukka commodity prices 29
buᴀkkyoo Buddhism 32
-buñ /counter for fraction denominator/
        35

-buñ (cont.)

    sa⌐n-buñ no iti⌐   one third   35

bu⌐nbo⌐ogu   writing materials   31-A

bu⌐npo⌐ogu   writing materials   31-A

bu⌐nraku   (traditional Japanese puppet
    theater)   28-A

bu⌐ra⌐usu   blouse   23-A

bu⌐re⌐eki   brakes   20

da*   /copula: informal non-past/

    da⌐ kara   therefore, so, for that
    reason, that is why   27

dai   charge, cost   22

dai*   /M/   /interrogative alternant of
    <u>da</u>/   35

-dai   /counter for vehicles/   20

daibu   a good deal, a good many   33

daidokoro   kitchen   17

da⌐idokorodo⌐ogu   kitchen utensils
    31-A

daigaku   university   13

da⌐iku   carpenter   24-A

da⌐isuki   /na/   very pleasing   15

daitai   for the most part, by and large,
    generally   33

da⌐izi⌐   /na/   important, valuable
    11-N

    Odaizi ni.⌐   Take care /of your-
    self/!   11

da⌐izyo⌐obu   /na/   safe, all right   7

da⌐ke*   just, only   4

    so⌐re dake⌐   just that, that's all   4

    mi-⌐ttu⌐ dake   just three (units)   5

da⌐kuroñ   dacron   23

da⌐me⌐   /na/   no good, bad, broken   2

dañboo   heating   30

da⌐nboose⌐tubi   heating equipment,
    central heating   30

dañdañ   gradually   27

da⌐nnasa⌐ma⌐   master   12

da⌐nsu   dance, dancing (Western style)
    28-A

da⌐nzyokyo⌐ogaku   coeducation   34-A

da⌐re   who?   10

    da⌐re ka   someone, somebody   25

    dare mo   /+ negative/   nobody   13

da⌐redare   so-and-so (a person)   33-N

da⌐ro⌐o*   /copula: informal tentative/   24

da⌐su   /tr:-u:da⌐site/   put out, send out,
    take out   17

    te⌐gami o da⌐su   mail a letter   25-N

da⌐tta*   /copula: informal past/

bu⌐ro⌐okaa   agent   30

buta   pig   17-A

butaniku   pork   22-N

butudañ   household altar (Buddhist)
    35

byoobu   screen   31-A

byooiñ   hospital   7

byooki   sickness, sick   11

D

de*   /copula: gerund/

    de⌐ mo   however, but, even so   29

    zyo⌐tyuu no hanasi⌐ de wa   accord-
    ing to what the maid says   22

    si⌐na⌐i de   without doing, instead of
    doing   24

    wa⌐surena⌐i de /kudasai/   don't for-
    get   22

de*   /particle/   by means of   7; at, in
    7

de⌐guti   exit   20

dekakeru /intr:-ru:dekakete/   set out,
    go out   13

de⌐ki⌐ru /intr:-ru:de⌐kite/   be possible,
    can do   9; come into being,
    be(come) completed   15

    ko⌐maka⌐ku de⌐ki⌐ru   can change
    [money]; can make into small
    units   22

    ni⌐hongo ga deki⌐ru   can [speak]
    Japanese   9

de⌐nki   electricity, electric light   16

de⌐nkiga⌐isya   electric company   24

de⌐nkisuto⌐obu   electric heater   30

de⌐nsya, deñsya   electric train, street
    car   8

deñwa   telephone   6

    de⌐nwa o kake⌐ru   telephone (verb)
    12

de⌐nwaba⌐ngoo   telephone number   12

deñwa-suru /intr/   make a telephone
    call   12

deñwatyoo   telephone book   12

de⌐pa⌐ato   department store   6

de⌐ru /intr:-ru:de⌐te/   go out, leave   9;
    go out (for a special occasion)   27

    de⌐te kuru   emerge   26

de⌐sita*   /copula: formal past/

de⌐su*   /copula: formal non-past/

    de⌐su kara   /formal equivalent of
    da⌐ kara/   27

de⌐syo⌐o*   /copula: formal tentative/

de⌐te kuru   emerge   26

-do /counter for number of times/ 1
do˹a door (Western-style) 16
doituḡo German language 11-A
do˹itu˺ziñ a German 10-A
do˹ko what place? where? 6
   do˹ko ka somewhere, some place 25
   do˹ko e mo ikanai not go anywhere 27
do˹kodoko such-and-such a place 33-N
do˹nata↑ who? 10
do˹no* /+ nom/ which —— ? 3
dono-ḡurai about how long? about how much? 8
do˹ñdoñ rapidly 35
do˹nna* what kind? what kind of? 5
   do˹ñna ni to what extent? 28-N
do˹o how? what way? 2
   Do˹o itasimasite.↑ Don't mention it. You're welcome. Int.
   do˹o mo in every way Int.
   Do˹o mo. [Thanks] very much. Int.
   do˹o sita what happened? 14
   do˹o site why? how? 11
   do˹o site˺ mo whatever happens, by all means 26
   do˹o suru do what? act how? 13
   a˹ru ka ˻do˹o ka wa˹kara˺nai isn't

do˹o (cont.)
   clear whether there are or not 29
doobutu animal 17-A
do˹oḡu˺ implement, tool, utensil 31-N
-doori /see to˹ori˺/ avenue, street 7-N
-doori in accordance with 19·
   zi˹kañ-do˺ori on time 19
do˹ozo please Int.
dorai dry cleaning 23-N
do˹raikuri˺iniñḡu dry cleaning 23
do˹re* which thing (of three or more)? 2
   do˹re de˺ mo whichever (of three or more) it is, any one at all 15
   do˹re ka any one (of three or more) 25-N
do˹tira which one (of two)?; which way? whereabouts? where? 6
   do˹tira de˺ mo whichever one (of two) it is, either one 15
   do˹tira ka either one 25-N
   do˹tira mo both 10
   do˹tira no ˻ho˹o which alternative? 15
do˹tirasama↑ who? 12
do˹tti /see do˹tira/ 6
do˹yo˺o(bi), doyoo Saturday 8

E

e˺ picture 31-A
e* /particle/ to, into, onto 7
e? what? 33
ebi shrimp, prawn 14
e˺e yes; that's right Int.
e˺eḡa movie 25
e˹eḡa˺kañ movie theater 7
eeḡo English language 11-A
e˹ekoku˺ziñ Englishman 10-A

eeto let me see, well now 34
e˺ki station 6
-eñ /counter for yen/ 3
eñpitu pencil 2
eñryo reserve, restraint 18
   Go˹eñryo na˺ku.↑ Don't hold back. Don't stand on ceremony. 18
eñtotu chimney 30-A
e˹ñziñ engine 20-N

G

ḡa* /particle/
   Ha˹iza˺ra ḡa arimasu. There's an ashtray. 4
   Ki˹ree desu ḡa— It's pretty but . . .' 4
gaikoku foreign country 11-N
gaikokuḡo foreign language 11
ga˹ikoku˺ziñ foreigner 11-N
ga˹iko˺okañ diplomat 24-A
ga˹imu˺syoo Foreign Office 11
-ḡaisya /see kaisya/ company 12-N

gaiziñ foreigner, Westerner, American 11-N
gakkoo school 6-A
gakusee student 24-A
ga˹mañ-suru /intr/ be patient, put up with 34
ga˹ñneñ the year 1, first year of an emperor's reign 8-N
gara pattern 23
ga˹re˺ezi garage (commercial) 20
gasoriñ gasoline 20

ga⌐soriñsuta⌐ndo   gas station   20
ga⌐suḡa⌐isya   gas company   12-N
-ḡata ⌐   /pluralizing suffix/   27-N
   a⌐nataḡa⌐ta   you (plural)   27-N
-ḡatu   /counter for naming the months
   of the year/   8
geesya   geisha   28-N
gekizyoo   theater   6-A
ge⌐ñkañ   entry hall   16
ge⌐ñki /na/   health, pep, good spirits
   Int.
      (O)⌐ge⌐ñki desu ka⌐   Are you well?
      How are you?   Int
geta   wooden clogs   23-A
ge⌐tuyo⌐o(bi), getuyoo   Monday   8
gi⌐mukyo⌐oiku   compulsory education   34-A
giñkoo   bank   6
gi⌐ñko⌐oiñ   bank employee   24-A
go⌐   five   3
go⌐   (Japanese game)   31
gobusata-suru ⌐   /intr/   neglect to
   write or visit   35
Go⌐eñryo na⌐ku. ⌐   Don't hold back.
   Don't stand on ceremony.   18
go⌐ḡo   afternoon, p.m.   9
go⌐hañ   cooked rice; food   14-A; meal
   15
gohukumono   yard goods, dry goods
   31-A
Go⌐ku⌐roosama (desita). ⌐   Thanks for
   your trouble.   1
Go⌐meñ-kudasa⌐i(ma⌐se).   Excuse me
   (for breaking away or interrupting).
   12; Is anybody here?   22
Go⌐meñ-nasa⌐i.   Excuse me.   33-N
go⌐mi⌐   trash   30
gomibako   box for trash   33
go⌐mi⌐ya   trash collector   30
-ḡoo-sya   /counter for naming train
   car numbers/   19

go⌐rañ ni na⌐ru ⌐   see (a thing); look at
   28
-go⌐ro*   approximate point of time,
   about   8
   ha⌐ti-ḡatu-go⌐ro   about August   8
go⌐ruhu   golf   32-A
Go⌐siñpai na⌐ku. ⌐   Don't worry.   30
gotisoo   a feast, delicious food and/or
   drink   14-N
   Go⌐tisoosama (de⌐sita). ⌐   It was a
   feast. Thank you for the delicious
   refreshments.   14
-ḡo⌐to ni*   every ——   35
   i⌐ti-neñ-ḡo⌐to ni   with every passing
   year   35
Go⌐yukku⌐ri. ⌐   Take it easy. Don't rush.
   Have a pleasant, unhurried time.
   31
go⌐za⌐ru+ *   /intr:-aru/   be located (of
   inanimate objects); have   Int.
go⌐zeñ   a.m.   9-N
go⌐zo⌐ñzi da ⌐   know   13
guai   condition   20
   gu⌐ai ḡa i⌐i   be in good condition, be
      fine, be in good health   20-N
   gu⌐ai ḡa waru⌐i   be in bad condition, be
      out of order, feel unwell, feel sick
      20
guñ   county   34-N
guñpuku   military uniform   34-A
gu⌐ñtai   armed forces   34
guñziñ   serviceman (i.e. man in the
   armed forces)   24-A
-ḡu⌐rai*   approximate extent, about   8
   dono-ḡurai   about how much?   8
   ni-⌐syuukañ-ḡu⌐rai   about two weeks   8
   ko⌐tatu-ḡu⌐rai   about as much as a ko-
      tatsu   30
-guramu   /counter for grams/   22
gyuuniku   beef   22
gyuunyuu   cow's milk   14-A

H

ha⌐   tooth   17-A
ha⌐a+   yes; that's right   4
ha⌐de /na/   gaudy, bright, loud   23
ha⌐e⌐ru /intr:-ru:ha⌐ete/   come out,
   spring up, grow   26
ha⌐ha   mother   11-A
ha⌐i   yes; that's right   Int; here you
   are   3
-hai   /counter for glassfuls and cup-
   fuls/   14

haiiro   gray   16
haikeñ-suru ⌐   /tr/   see (a thing); look at
   28
ha⌐ikiñḡu   hiking   32-A
ha⌐iru /intr:-u:ha⌐itte/   enter, go in
   17
   ha⌐itte (i)ru   be inside   17; be in-
      cluded   21
ha⌐isya   dentist   24-A
haisyaku-suru ⌐   /tr/   borrow   32

haiyuu   actor, actress   28-A

ha⌐iza⌐ra   ashtray   3

ha⌐ka⌐ru /tr:-u:ha⌐ka⌐tte/   measure   23
   su⌐ṅpoo o haka⌐ru   take measure-
      ments   23

ha⌐kki⌐ri   clearly, distinctly, precisely
   18

hako   box   17

haku /tr:-u:haite/   put on, wear (on
   feet or legs)   23

ha⌐ma⌐   beach   32-A

hameru /tr:-ru:hamete/   put on, wear
   (on hands)   23-A

hana   nose   17-A

ha⌐ha⌐   flower   6-A; flower arrange-
   ment   18

ha⌐hami⌐   cherry-blossom viewing   27

ha⌐hare⌐ru /intr:-ru:ha⌐ha⌐rete/   become separated, part from, fall
   apart   33-A

ha⌐hasi⌐   talking, a talk, a story   13
   a⌐ho⌐ hito no ha⌐hasi⌐ de wa   ac-
      cording to what he says   22

hanasi-tyuu   in the middle of talking;
   the line is busy   13

ha⌐ha⌐su /tr:-u:ha⌐ha⌐site/   speak, talk
   13

ha⌐ha⌐su /tr:-u:ha⌐ha⌐site/   let go, set
   free   33-A

ha⌐ha⌐ya   flower shop, florist   6-A

hanazi   nosebleed   24-N

-haṅ   half   8
   sa⌐ṅ-zikaṅ-ha⌐ṅ   three hours and a
      half   8
   go-⌐zi-ha⌐ṅ   5:30   9

ha⌐ṅbu⌐ṅ   half, half part   14

ha⌐ṅdoba⌐kku   handbag   23-A

haṅkati   handkerchief   23-A

ha⌐ṅniti⌐   half-day   25

haṅtai   opposite   19

haṅtai-suru /intr/   oppose   19-N

haṅtoo   peninsula   32

haori   coat (Japanese style)   23-A

ha⌐ra⌐u /tr:-u:ha⌐ra⌐tte/   pay   22

ha⌐re⌐ru /intr:-ru:ha⌐re⌐te/   clear up   26

ha⌐reso⌐o /na/   looking as if it would
      clear up   26

ha⌐ru   spring (season)   18-N

ha⌐ruya⌐sumi   spring vacation   25-N

ha⌐si   chopsticks   14-A

ha⌐si⌐   bridge   20

hasiḡo   ladder   33-A

hatake   non-rice field, dry field   29

ha⌐tarakisuḡi⌐ru /intr:-ru:ha⌐tarakisu⌐-
      ḡite/   overwork   25

hataraku /intr:-u:hataraite/   work   24

ha⌐tati   twenty years of age   10-N

ha⌐ti⌐   eight   3

ha⌐ti-zyo⌐o   eight-mat area or room   30

hatu   leaving   19
   zyu⌐uiti⌐-zi hatu   leaving at eleven
      o'clock   19
   Ko⌐obe hatu   leaving Kobe, coming
      from Kobe   19

hatu-ka   twenty days; twentieth day of
   the month   8

ha⌐ya⌐i /-ku/   is fast or early   9

ha⌐ya⌐ru /intr:-u:ha⌐ya⌐tte/   become
      prevalent   26

hayasi   forest   32-A

hazimaru /intr:-u:hazimatte/   [some-
      thing] begins   26-N

hazime   beginning   24

Ha⌐zimema⌐site. How do you do?   11

hazimeru* /tr:-ru:hazimete/   begin
      [something]   26
   hu⌐rihazime⌐ru   begin raining or
      snowing   26
   Naḡasaki o hazime   beginning with
      Nagasaki, from Nagasaki on down,
      to say nothing of Nagasaki   32

ha⌐zi⌐mete   the first time   11
   Ha⌐zi⌐mete ome ni kakarimasu. ↓
      How do you do?   11

hazu*   expectation   22
   kasu hazu da   is supposed to rent,
      is expected to rent   22
   na⌐i hazu wa ⌐ha⌐i   there's no reason
      to suppose that there isn't any,
      there should be some   22-N

ha⌐zukasi⌐i /-ku/   is shamed, is shy
      34

he⌐bi   snake   17-A

hee   wall   30

hee?   really? you don't say! no kid-
      ding!   33

heeki /na/   unconcerned, indifferent,
      unmoved   27
   heeki de suru   do with unconcern,
      make nothing of [it]   27-N
   heeki na kao o suru   look uncon-
      cerned   27-N

heetai   soldier   34-A

heeti   a plain   32-A

heṅ   area, section, part   6
   kono heṅ   this area, around here   6

heñ (cont.)
    do⌐no heñ   what part? what section?
       19
he⌐ñ /na/   strange   13
-heñ   /counter for number of times/
       32
he⌐ñzi⌐   a reply, an answer   24
    he⌐ñzi⌐ o suru   answer, reply (verb)
       24
he⌐ta /na/   unskilled, poor at   18
he⌐ya   room   13
hi, hi⌐   day   15; sun   26
hiatari   exposure to the sun   30
    hi⌐atari ga i⌐i   is sunny   30
hi⌐bati   brazier   21
hidari   left   6
    hi⌐dari no ho⌐o   left side; toward the
       left   6
hi⌐do⌐i /-ku/   is severe   21
hi⌐gasi⌐   east   30-A
higasimuki   facing east   30-N
hige   beard, hair on the face   22
hikidasi   drawer   17
hi⌐ko⌐oki   airplane   8
hikoozyoo   airport   20
hiku /tr:-u:hiite/   pull   33-A
    kaze o hiku   catch a cold   26-N
hi⌐ku⌐i /-ku/   is low   31
hima /na/   free time, leisure   12
    hi⌐ma na toki⌐   time when [someone]
       is free   12
hi⌐ro⌐i /-ku/   is broad or wide or
       spacious or big in area   21
hi⌐rosa   area; width   23-N
hirou /tr:-u:hirotte/   pick up   33-A
hi⌐ru⌐   noon, daytime   15-N
    hiru no bu   daytime performance
       28-N
hi⌐rugo⌐han   noon meal, lunch   15
hirumesi /M/   lunch   24
hirune   nap   27
    hirune o suru   take a nap   27
hi⌐ru-sugi⌐   past noon, afternoon   31
hi⌐syo⌐   secretary   24
hito, hi⌐to⌐   person   10
    o⌐ñna⌐ no hito   woman   10
    o⌐toko⌐ no hito   man   10
hi⌐to⌐añsiñ, hi⌐toa⌐ñsiñ   a relief   35
hi⌐to⌐koto   a word   35
hi⌐to⌐-ri   one person, single (person)
       10
    hi⌐to⌐-ri de   alone, by oneself   17
hi⌐to⌐-tu   one unit   5

hodo*   approximate extent   15
    sa⌐ñ-buñ no iti⌐ hodo   about as much
       as one-third   35
    teñpura hodo su⌐ki⌐ zya ⌐na⌐i   [I] don't
       like [it] as much as tempura   15
    ta⌐no⌐mu hodo zya ⌐na⌐i   isn't worth
       hiring, doesn't warrant hiring   33
    ha⌐nasi⌐ ni na⌐ra⌐nai hodo hi⌐do⌐i   is
       too awful to talk about   34
    si⌐tte (i)re⌐ba i⌐ru hodo   the more
       someone knows   32
hoka   other, another, other than   4
    hoka ni   in addition   4
    Tanaka-sañ no hoka ni   in addition
       to Mr. Tanaka, other than Mr. Ta-
       naka   15-N
    hoka no hi   another day   15
ho⌐keñga⌐isya   insurance company   24
ho⌐ñ   book   2
-hoñ   /counter for long, cylindrical
       units/   5
ho⌐ñbako   bookcase   24-N
ho⌐ñdana   bookshelf   17
hoñseki   one's permanent residence   34
ho⌐ñseki⌐ti   place of one's permanent
       residence   34
hoñtoo   truth, true   3
ho⌐ñya   book store, book dealer   6-A
hoñyaku   translation   34
hoñyaku-suru /tr/   translate   34
ho⌐o*   side; direction; alternative   6
    hi⌐dari no ho⌐o   left side, toward
       the left   6
    ko⌐tira no ho⌐o   this side, this di-
       rection   6
    mi⌐gi no ho⌐o   right side, toward
       the right   6
    i⌐i hoo no ryokañ   rather good inn,
       inn on the good side   21
    si⌐ta ho⌐o ga ⌐i⌐i   it will be better to
       have done [it], [you]'d better do [it]
       20
hoo?   oh? really?   32
ho⌐oboo   all directions, everywhere   32
ho⌐oku   fork   14-A
ho⌐omu   platform   34-N
ho⌐oñ   horn   20-N
hooseki   jewel   31-A
hosi   star   26-A
ho⌐si⌐i /-ku/   want   31
    bo⌐ku ga hosi⌐i   I want [it]   31
    te⌐eburu ga hosi⌐i   [I] want a table   31
ho⌐so⌐i /-ku/   is thin or small in circum-
       ference   31-N

ho˹sonaḡa˺i /-ku/   is long and slender
     or long and narrow   31
ho˺su /tr:-u:ho˺site/   dry [something]
     out, air [something]   23
ho˹teru   hotel   6
ho˹to˺ndo   almost   35
hu˹beñ /na/   inconvenient   29
hu˹buki   snow storm   26-A
hude   writing brush   31
huhee   complaint   34
     huhee o iu   complain   34
hu˹ki˺ñ   dishrag, dish cloth, cloth   17
huku /tr:-u:huite/   wipe   17
hu˹ku /intr:-u:hu˺ite/   blow   26
hu˹ku˺   clothing   34-A
hukuzatu /na/   complicated   28
hu˹ne   ship, boat   8
-huñ   /counter for naming and counting
     minutes/   8
hurañsuḡo   French language   11-A
hu˹rañsu˺ziñ   Frenchman   10-A
hu˹rihazime˺ru /intr:-ru:hu˹rihazi˺mete/
     begin falling (of rain or snow)   26
hu˹ro˺   bath   21-N
hu˹roba˺   bathroom (not toilet)   17-A
huroba-tuki   with bath   21
hurosiki   furoshiki (cloth square for
     wrapping)   4

-i˹ḡai*   outside of, except for   34-N
   mo˹kuyoobi-i˺ḡai   except for Thurs-
     day   34-N
i˹ḡirisu˺ziñ   Englishman   10-A
-i˹ḡo   later than, after   28
   so˹re-i˺ḡo   after that, later than
     that   28
i˹i /yo˺ku/   is good or fine or all
     right; never mind   2
   i˹tte˺ mo ˹i˺i   is all right to go,
     [someone] may go   22
   i˹kana˺kute mo ˹i˺i   is all right not
     to go, [someone] doesn't have to
     go   22-N
   su˹zu˺sikute ˹i˺i   is nice and cool   29
   ku˹reba ˹i˺i desu ḡa ˹ne˺e   [I] hope
     [someone] comes   32-N
-i˹i* /-yo˺ku/   is easy to ——   28-N
   tu˹kaii˺i   is easy to use   28-N
iie   no; that's not right   Int.
i˹ka˹ḡa+   how?   4
   I˹ka˹ḡa desu ka˩   How are you? How
     are things? How about it (offering
     something)?   4

hu˹ru /intr:-u:hu˺tte, hu˺tte˺/   fall (of
     rain or snow)   18
   a˺me ḡa ˹hu˺ru   it rains   18
hu˹ru˺i /-ku/   is old (i.e. not new) or
     stale   2-A
hu˹suma˺, husuma   sliding door (opaque)
     18
huta   lid, cover   33
   huta o suru   put a lid on   33
hu˹ta-tu˺   two units   5
hu˹to˺i /-ku/   is thick or big in circum-
     ference   31-N
hutoñ   Japanese quilt   21
   hutoñ o siku   spread the quilts (for
     sleeping)   21
hu˹to˺ru /intr:-u:hu˹to˺tte/   grow fat   35-N
   hu˹to˺tta hito   fat person   35-N
hutuu   usual, regular, ordinary   21
hu˹u /na/   manner, style   22
   do˺ñna huu   what (kind of) style?   22
hu˹yu˺   winter   18-N
hu˹yuya˺sumi   winter vacation   25-N
hu˹ziyuu /na/   restricted, uncomfortable,
     inconvenient   34
hya˹ku˺   one hundred   3
-hyaku   /counter for hundreds/   3
hya˹kusyo˺o   farmer   24-A
hyo˺o   hail   26-A

I

i˹ke˺   pond   32-A
I˹kemase˺ñ ˹ne˺e.   That's too bad.   11
ikenai   it won't do, that's too bad
     11
   si˹te˺ wa i˹kenai   must not do   25
   si˹na˺kereba i˹kenai   must do   32-N
   si˹na˺kute wa (or si˹na˺kutya/a/)
     i˺kenai   must do   32-N
-iki   -bound   19
   Kyooto-iki   bound for Kyoto   19
i˹ki˺ru /intr:-ru:i˹kite/   live, exist,
     be alive   34-A
iku* /intr:-u:itte/   go   1
i˺kura   how much?   3
i˺kutu   how many units?   5; how old
     (of people)?   10
i˺ma   now   7
i˹ma˺   living room   17-A
i˺mi   meaning   21
   do˺o iu ˹i˺mi   what meaning?   21
i˹mo˺oto   younger sister   11-A
i˹nabi˺kari   lightning   26-A
   i˹nabi˺kari ḡa suru   there is light-
     ning   26-A

-iꜛnai* within 34
  iꜛti-zikañ-iꜛnai within one hour 34
inaka the country 27
iꜛnuꜜ dog 17
iꜛñdoꜜziñ an Indian (from India) 10-A
iꜛñki ink 33-N
ippai full 20
  iꜛppai ni naꜜru become full 20-N
  ippai ni suru fill [something] 20
  hiꜛtoꜜ de ippai filled with people 27
iꜛrassyaꜜru ꜝ* /intr:-aru:iꜛrassyaꜜtte ~
  iꜛraꜜsite/ be 6; go 7; come 8
  Iꜛrassyaꜜi(maꜜse). Welcome! 4
  Doꜜnata de (i)rassyaimasu kaↃ ꜝ
  Who is it? Who are you? 10
ireru /tr:-ru:irete/ put in, insert 17
iriḡuti entrance 20-N
iꜛroꜜ color 5
  doꜜñna iro what (kind of) color? 5
iroiro /na~no/ various[ly] 25
iroñ na various 28
iru* /intr:-ru:ite/ be located (of
  animate beings) 6
  beñkyoo-site (i)ru be studying 11
  huꜜtte (i)ru be raining 18
  kekkoñ-site (i)ru be married 10
iru /intr:-u:itte/ be necessary, need,
  want 4
iru /intr:-u:itte/ enter 29
  ki ni iru be pleasing, appeal 29
iꜛsoḡasiꜜi /-ku/ is busy 13
iꜛsoꜜḡu /intr:-u:iꜛsoꜜide/ be in a hurry 7
issyo together 15
  Saꜜitoo-sañ to issyo together with
  Mr. Saito 15
isu chair 17-A
isya doctor (medical) 24-A
iꜛta board 33-A
itadaku ꜝ* /tr:-u:itadaite/ eat, drink
  14; receive, accept 17

itadaku ꜝ* (cont.)
  siꜛte itadakemaseꜜñ ka ꜝ would you be
  kind enough to do [it]? 25
  saꜛsete itadakemaseꜜñ ka ꜝ would you
  be kind enough to let me do [it]
  33
iꜛtaꜜi /-ku/ is painful 17
iꜛtaꜜmu /intr:-u:iꜛtaꜜñde/ be(come) hurt
  or spoiled or damaged or worn
  out or painful 14
  iꜛtaꜜñda ebi spoiled shrimp 14
itasu ꜝ /tr:-u:itasite/ make, do 13
  Doꜜo itasimasite. Don't mention it.
  You're welcome. Int.
iꜛtiꜜ one (numeral) 3
itibañ, iꜛtiꜜbañ* to the highest degree 15
  iꜛtibañ takaꜜi is most expensive 15
iti-niti-zyuu all day long 25
iꜛtoꜜko cousin 11-A
Iꜛtte irassyaꜜi. Goodbye. (Lit. Go and
  come.) 20
Iꜛtte kimaꜜsu. Goodbye. (Lit. I'll go
  and come.) 20-N
Iꜛtte mairimaꜜsu. ꜝ Goodbye. (Lit. I'll
  go and come.) 20
iꜛttoꜜosya first-class car 19-A
iꜛtu when? 8
  iꜛtu ka some time 25-N
  iꜛtu mo always 9
iꜛtuꜜ-tu five units 5
iu /tr:-u:itte/ say, be named, be
  called 1
  To iu to? What do you mean by that?
  34
  suꜛru yoꜜo ni iu tell [someone] to do
  24
iꜛya /M/ no; that's not right 16
iꜛyaꜜ /na/ unpleasant 26
-iꜛzeñ before 28-N
  soꜛre-iꜜzeñ before that 28-N

K

ka* /particle/ (question) Int.
  Oꜛgeꜜñki desu kaↃ ꜝ Are you well?
  Int.
  doꜜo iu ka siꜛranai not know how one
  says it 18
  aꜜru ka ꜝdoꜜo ka waꜛkaraꜜnai isn't
  clear whether there are or not 29
ka* /particle/ or 35
  peꜜñ ka eꜜñpitu pen or pencil 35
ka mo sirenai* maybe — 30
  iꜜi ka mo sirenai maybe it's good,
  it may be good 30

ka sira* I wonder — 35
  suꜛruꜜ ka sira I wonder if [someone]
  will do [it] 35
-ka ~ -niti /counter for naming and
  counting days/ 8
kaꜜateñ curtain 33
kabe wall of a room 30
kabi mildew 26
kabuki (form of traditional Japanese
  theater) 28
kaꜛbuꜜru /tr:-u:kaꜛbuꜜtte/ put on or
  wear (on head) 23

kaˈdo   street corner   7
kaˈeriˈ   return (noun)   27
kaˈeru /intr:-u:kaˈette/   return (home)
    9
kaeru /tr:-ru:kaete/   change [something]   21-N
kaˈesu /tr:-u:kaˈesite/   give back, send
    back, return [something]   34
kaˈette kuru   come back   22
kaˈg̃eki   opera   28-A
-kag̃etu /counter for number of months/
    8
ka⌐g̃i˥   key   16
    ka⌐g̃i˥ g̃a ka˥kaˈru   [something]
        locks   16
    ka⌐g̃i˥ o ka˥keˈru   lock [something]
        16
kaˈg̃u   furniture   17-A
kai* /M/ /sentence particle/   (question)   35
    I⌐ku˥ kai⌐   Are you gonna go?   35
-kai /counter for naming and counting
    floors/   16
-kai /counter for number of times/   31
kaidañ   stairway   17-A
kaˈig̃i, kaˈig̃iˈ   conference   25
    kaig̃i-tyuu   in the middle of a conference, in conference   25
kaˈig̃uñ   navy   34-A
kaikee   bill, accounting, check   15
kaimono   shopping   26
ka⌐inikuˈi /-ku/   is difficult to buy   28
kaisya   business company, company
    office   12
ka⌐isyaˈiñ   company employee   24
ka⌐kaˈru /intr:-u:kaˈkaˈtte/   be required, take   8; be suspended   11
    ka⌐g̃i˥ g̃a ka˥kaˈru   [something]
        locks   16
    oˈme ni kakaˈru⌐   see (a person),
        meet   11
    Haⁱziˈmete ome ni kakarimasu.⌐
        How do you do.   11
    zi⌐kañ g̃a kakaˈru   take time   8
ka⌐keˈmono   hanging scroll   31-A
ka⌐keˈru /tr:-ru:kaˈkete/   hang, suspend, apply [something]   12; sit
    down   25
    aˈiroñ o kakeˈru   press with an iron
        21
    deˈñwa o kakeˈru   telephone (verb)
        12
    ka⌐g̃i˥ o ka˥keˈru   lock [something]
        16

ka⌐keˈru (cont.)
    meˈg̃ane o ka˥keˈru   wear eyeglasses
        23-A
ka⌐kikaˈta   way or style of writing   31
ka⌐kiˈne   fence   30
kaˈku /tr:-u:kaˈite/   write, draw   7
kaˈmaˈu /intr:-u:kaˈmaˈtte/   mind, care
    about   18-N
    kaˈmawaˈnai   doesn't matter, makes
        no difference, is all right   9
ka⌐miˈ   paper   5
ka⌐miˈ   hair (on head)   22
kamidana   household altar (Shinto)   35
ka⌐minariˈ   thunder   26-A
    ka⌐minariˈ g̃a naru   it thunders   26-A
kana   Japanese written syllabary   31
kaˈnai   (one's own) wife   11
kaˈnari   fairly, rather   32
kaˈnazuˈti   hammer   33-A
kane   money   22
ka⌐ñg̃aeˈru /tr:-ru:kaⁿg̃aˈete/   consider,
    think over   29
ka⌐ñg̃oˈhu   nurse   24-A
ka⌐ñkokuˈziñ   a South Korean   10-A
kañkoo   sightseeing   32-N
    kañkoo ni iku   go sightseeing   32-N
ka⌐ñkoobaˈsu   sightseeing bus   32-A
ka⌐ñkoˈokyaku   sightseer   32-A
ka⌐ñkooreˈssya   sightseeing train   32-A
kañtañ /na/   simple   28
kañzi   Chinese written character   31
kao   face; expression   14
    aˈoˈi kao o suru   be pale   14
kara* /particle/   from   8; because   11;
    after   16
    sore kara   from that point, after that,
        and then, and   4
ka⌐raˈ   empty   20-N
karada   body   17-A
ka⌐raˈi /-ku/   is spicy or salty   14
kariru /tr:-ru:karite/   borrow, rent
    [from someone]   13
karu /tr:-u:katte/   clip, mow   22
karui /-ku/   is light (i.e. not heavy)   20-N
kaˈsa   umbrella   23
kaseñ   synthetic fibers   23
Ka⌐sikomarimaˈsita.   Certainly.   I'll do
    as you have asked.   4
kasiya   house for rent   29
kasu /tr:-u:kasite/   lend, rent [to someone]   22
ka⌐taˈ⌐   person   10
    o⌐ñna no kataˈ⌐   woman   10
    o⌐toko no kataˈ⌐   man   10
ka⌐taˈ   shape, style   23

katai /-ku/ is hard or tough or stiff
   or firm 22-N
katamiti one-way 19
katati shape, style 23
ka⌐tazuke⌐ru /tr:-ru:ka⌐tazu⌐kete/
   straighten up, put in order 16
katte kitchen 31-N
ka⌐ttedo⌐oḡu kitchen utensils 31-A
ka⌐tu /intr:-u:ka⌐tte/ win 34-N
kau /tr:-u:katte/ buy 4
ka⌐wa⌐ river 32-A
ka⌐wai⌐i /-ku/ is cute 31
ka⌐waiso⌐o /na/ pathetic, pitiful 35
ka⌐waka⌐su /tr:-u:ka⌐waka⌐site/ dry
   [something] 31-N
ka⌐wa⌐ku /intr:-u:ka⌐wa⌐ite/ become
   dry 15
   no⌐do ḡa ka⌐wa⌐ita I'm thirsty 15
kawari a change; a substitute 34; a
   second helping 18
   ryo⌐osiñ no kawari ni instead of
   parents 34
kawaru /intr:-u:kawatte/ undergo
   change 24
kaya mosquito net 21
ka⌐yo⌐o(bi), kayoo Tuesday 8
kayou /intr:-u:kayotte/ commute 29
ka⌐zañ volcano 32-A
kaze wind 21
   ka⌐ze ḡa hu⌐ku the wind blows 26
kaze a cold 26
   kaze o hiku catch a cold 26
ka⌐zi a fire 35-A
ka⌐zoku family 11-A
ke wool 23-A
kedo /see keredo/ 20
ke⌐do /see ke⌐redo/ 22
keekeñ experience 34-A
ke⌐ezai economics 32-A
kekkoñ-suru /intr/ marry 10
   kekkoñ-site (i)ru be married 10
ke⌐kkoo /na/ fine, all right 9
   Mo⌐o ⌐ke⌐kkoo desu. I'm fine as I am.
   I've had enough already. 14
-keñ prefecture 34
   Sa⌐itama⌐-keñ Saitama Prefecture 34
keñbutu-suru /tr/ see the sights, go
   sightseeing 27
ke(re)do* /particle/ although 20
ke⌐(re)do however 22
ke⌐sa this morning 9
ke⌐siki scenery 29
kessite never 29

kesu /tr:-u:kesite/ turn off, extinguish,
   erase 16
ki⌐ tree 27; wood 33-A
ki spirit, mind, attention 25
   ki ⌐ḡa tu⌐ku notice 25
   ki ni iru be pleasing, appeal 29
kieru /intr:-ru:kiete/ become extin-
   guished, go out 16-N
kiiroi /-ku/ is yellow 4
ki⌐kae⌐ru, ki⌐ka⌐eru /tr:-ru:ki⌐ka⌐ete/
   change clothes 23
kikoeru /intr:-ru:kikoete/ be audible,
   can hear 13
kikoo climate 26
kiku /tr:-u:kiite/ ask a question, listen,
   hear 12
kimaru /intr:-u:kimatte/ be(come) decided 23-N
kimeru /tr:-ru:kimete/ decide [some-
   thing] 23
kimi you 27
kimono kimono, Japanese clothing 23-A
kimoti feeling, mood 18
   ki⌐moti ḡa i⌐i is pleasant or agreeable 18
ki⌐ho⌐o, kinoo yesterday 1
ki⌐nu silk 23-A
ki⌐ñyo⌐o(bi), kiñyoo Friday 8
ki⌐otuke⌐ru /intr:-ru:ki⌐otuke⌐te/ be
   careful 17
kippu ticket 19
kirai /na/ displeasing 15
ki⌐ree /na/ pretty, clean 3
kirisutokyoo Christianity 32
kiru /tr:-ru:kite/ put on, wear (on
   body) 23
ki⌐ru /tr:-u:ki⌐tte, ki⌐tte/ cut, cut off,
   hang up (the telephone) 13
ki⌐ssa⌐teñ, kissateñ tearoom 14-A
ki⌐sya⌐ (steam) train 8
ki⌐sya⌐ newspaperman 24-A
ki⌐ta⌐ north 30-A
kitamuki facing north 30-N
ki⌐tana⌐i /-ku/ is dirty 16
kitto surely, positively, certainly 24
kitui /-ku/ is tight 23
ki⌐zi material, cloth 23
ko child 10
   o⌐ñna⌐ no ko little girl 10
   o⌐toko⌐ no ko little boy 10
ko⌐bore⌐ru /intr:-ru:ko⌐bo⌐rete/ [some-
   thing] spills 17
   ko⌐bo⌐rete (i)ru be spilled 17

ko⌐bo⌐su /tr:-u:ko⌐bo⌐site/   spill [some-
    thing]   17-N
kodomo   child   10
ko⌐e   voice   13
    o⌐oki⌐i ⌐ko⌐e de or o⌐oki na ⌐ko⌐e
    de   with a loud voice   13
ko⌐i /-ku/   is strong or thick (of liq-
    uids); is dark (of colors)   14-A
koko   this place, here   6
ko⌐ko⌐no-tu   nine units   5
ko⌐maka⌐i /-ku/   is small or fine or
    detailed   17
ko⌐ma⌐ru /intr:-u:ko⌐ma⌐tte/   be(come)
    distressing or troublesome or
    annoying or inconvenient or
    perplexing   9
    a⌐tukute ko⌐ma⌐ru   be annoying be-
    cause it's hot   29
ko⌐me⌐   uncooked rice   14-A
ko⌐mu /intr:-u:ko⌐nde/   be(come)
    crowded   20
    ko⌐nde (i)ru   be crowded   20
konaida   the other day, recently   31
kono* /+ nom/   this ―   3
kono aida   the other day, recently   31
kono-goro   these days, nowadays   18
ko⌐n   navy blue   23
ko⌐nbañ   this evening, tonight   13
    Koñbañ wa.   Good evening.   Int.
koñdo   this time (i.e. this next time or
    this last time)   28
koñgetu   this month   10
koñna*   this kind, this kind of   5
    koñna ni   to this extent   28-N
Koñniti wa.   Good afternoon.   Int.
koñsyuu   this week   App.
ko⌐o   thus, this way   29
    ko⌐o iu tokoro⌐   place like this   29
ko⌐oba⌐   factory   24
koobañ   police box   7
kooeñ   park   6-A
kooiñ   factory worker   24-A
ko⌐ohi⌐i   coffee   14
ko⌐ohiizya⌐wañ   cup (with handles)   14-A
kookoku   advertisement   30
ko⌐oka⌐ñsyu   telephone operator   12
kookoo   high school   34-N
ko⌐omu⌐iñ   government employee   24
koori   ice   14-A
kooru   freeze   26
    kootte (i)ru   be frozen   26
ko⌐otooga⌐kkoo   high school   34-N
ko⌐otuuko⌐osya   Japan Travel Bureau   12

kootya   black tea   14-A
koozyoo, ko⌐ozyo⌐o   factory   24
koppu   glass for drinking   14-A
kore*   this thing   2
ko⌐ruku   cork   33-N
ko⌐sa   strength or thickness (liquids);
    darkness (colors)   23-N
ko⌐si⌐   lower part of the back   17-A
ko⌐syo⌐o   pepper   14-A
kosyoo   out of order   13
kosyoo-suru /intr/   break down   13-N
ko⌐tae⌐ru, ko⌐ta⌐eru /intr:-ru:ko⌐ta⌐ete/
    answer   CI
kotatu   quilt-covered warming place   30
kotira   this one (of two); this way, here-
    abouts, here   6; this person   11;
    the person speaking   12
    ko⌐tira no ho⌐o   this side, this di-
    rection   6
ko⌐to⌐*   thing (intangible), act, fact   24
    a⌐ru⌐ku koto ga de⌐ki⌐ru   can walk   25-N
    sa⌐ñpo-suru koto ga su⌐ki⌐ da   like to
    take walks   24-N
    i⌐ku koto ga ⌐a⌐ru   do sometimes go
    31-N
    i⌐tta koto ga ⌐a⌐ru   have at some
    time gone   31
    i⌐ku koto ni suru   decide to go   32
    a⌐ru koto wa ⌐a⌐ru   do exist, do have   32
    ta⌐rinai koto⌐ wa ⌐na⌐i   isn't that it's
    not enough   33
ko⌐toba⌐   word, language   32-A
kotori   bird   17-A
kotosi   this year   8
kotozuke   message; the giving of a mes-
    sage   13
ko⌐tti⌐ /see kotira/   6
kottoohiñ   curios, antiques   31-A
ko⌐wa⌐i /-ku/   is frightening   35-A
ko⌐wareru /intr:-ru:ko⌐wa⌐rete/   be-
    come broken   31
    ko⌐wa⌐rete (i)ru   be broken   31
ko⌐wa⌐su /tr:-u:ko⌐wa⌐site/   break [some-
    thing]   31-N
ku⌐   nine   3
ku⌐   ward   34-N
    Mi⌐nato⌐-ku   Minato Ward   34-N
kubi   neck   17-A
ku⌐da⌐mono   fruit   14-A
kudari   down-train (i.e. going away from
    Tokyo)   19
ku⌐dasa⌐i* /imperative of ku⌐dasa⌐ru/
    give me   1

kuˈdasaˈi* (cont.)

   Koˈre o kudasaˈi. Please give me
    this one. 4

   Maˈtte kudasai. Please wait. 1

   Iˈsoḡaˈnai de kudasai. Please don't
    hurry. 7

kuˈdasaˈru ꜔* /tr:-aru:kuˈdasaˈtte ~ ku-
   dasuˈtte/ give me 4

   kaˈite kuˈdasaimaseˈn̄ ka ꜔ would
    (lit. won't) you be kind enough to
    write (or draw) for me? 7

kuḡi nail 33

kuˈmo cloud 26-A

kuˈmoˈru /intr:-u:kuˈmoˈtte/ cloud up
   26

kuni a country; one's native land <u>or</u>
   area 32

-kun̄ /M/ /suffix attached to men's
   and boys' names; familiar/ 13

kuˈraˈ storehouse, godown 33-A

kuraberu /tr:-ru:kurabete/ compare
   34

kurai /-ku/ is dark 35

kureru* /tr:-ru:kurete/ give me 17

   taˈnoˈnde kureru request (<u>or</u> order)
    for me 17, ~ for you 33

   oˈkoˈsite kurenai ka would(n't) you
    wake me? 21

kuˈroˈi /-ku/ is black 4

kuˈroo hardship, troubles, ordeal 34

   Goˈkuˈroosama (desita). Thanks for
    your trouble. 1

kuˈru* /intr:irreg:kiˈteˈ/ come 8

   huˈtte kuru begin to fall 26

   taˈnoˈnde kuru come having en-
    gaged, go and engage 20

kuruma car, cart 7

kuˈsaˈ a grass, weed 33

   niˈwa no kusaˈ o ꜔toˈru weed the
    garden 33

kuˈsiˈ a comb 23-A

kusuri medicine 6-N

kusuriya drugstore, druggist 6-A

kuˈsyaˈmi a sneeze 33-N

   kuˈsyaˈmi o suru sneeze (verb)
    33-N

kuti mouth 17-A

kuˈtuˈ shoes 21

kuˈtuˈsita socks, stockings 23

kuuḡun̄ air force 34-A

kuˈuki air 20

kyaˈburettaa carburetor 20-N

kyaku guest, customer 18

kyoˈo today 1

kyoˈodai brothers and/or sisters 11-A

kyooiku education, schooling 34

kyookai church 32

kyoˈomiˈ, kyoˈomi an interest 35

   kyoˈomiˈ ḡa ꜔aˈru have an interest
    35

kyoosoo competition, contest 35

kyoosoo-suru /intr/ compete 35-N

kyoozyu professor 24-A

kyozin̄ giant 35-N

kyuˈu nine 3

kyuuˈukeˈesitu rest room, lounge 31-A

kyuukoo express 19

kyuuˈkoˈoken̄ express ticket 19-A

kyuˈuryoo salary 24

kyuˈuzi waiter/waitress, steward[ess],
   barboy, office boy 24-A

M

-ma /counter for number of rooms/
   21

maˈa oh well, I guess, you might say
   4; oh dear, good heavens 35

maˈda* /+ affirmative/ still, yet 18;
   /+ negative/ not yet 14

   maˈda da it is yet to happen; not
    yet 14

made* /particle/ as far as 7;
   until 9

   Toˈokyoˈo-eki made as far as Tokyo
    Station 7

   naˈn̄-zi made until what time? 9

   zyuˈu-ḡatuˈ made ni by October 9

   tuˈku made until arriving 27

maˈdo window 16

maˈdoˈḡuti ticket window 19

maˈe* front 6; before 8

   eˈki no ꜔maˈe front of the station 6

   maˈe no kaisya previous company
    24

   ziˈp-puˈn̄ mae ten minutes before
    the hour 8

   ziˈp-pun̄ maˈe, ziˈp-pun̄ ꜔maˈe ten
    minutes ago 8

   taˈbeˈru ꜔maˈe (time) before eating
    31

maeuri advance sale 28

maḡaru /intr:-u:maḡatte/ make a turn
   7

maꞌgaru (cont.)
    kaꞌdo o magaru   turn at the corner,
      turn the corner 7
mageru /tr:-ru:magete/ bend [some-
    thing] 33-A
maꞈgoꞋ grandchild 11-A
-mai /counter for thin, flat units/ 5
maꞋiasa every morning 9-N
maꞋiban every night 19-N
maido every time 4
    Maꞈido ariꞈgatoo gozaimasu. Thank
      you again and again. 4
maigetu every month 9-N
mainen every year 9-N
maꞋiniti every day 9
    maꞋiniti no ꞈyoꞋo ni almost every
      day 24
maꞋiru ꞈ* /intr:-u:maꞋitte/ go 7;
    come 8
maisyuu every week 9-N
maitosi every year 9-N
maituki every month 9-N
makasu /tr:-u:makasite/ beat [some-
    one in something] 34-N
makeru /intr:-ru:makete/ be defeated,
    be beaten 34
    maketa I give up! you win! 34-N
maꞈkitaꞋbako cigarette 3-N
maꞈkuꞋ curtain, act 28
    maku no aida between acts 28
makuai between acts 28
maꞈmaꞋ condition 16
    soꞈno mamaꞋ de being that condition
      as it is 16
maꞈmoꞋnaku soon after, in no time 34
-man /counter for ten thousands/ 3
mannaka middle 23
maru circle 31-N
marui /-ku/ is round 31
maꞈssuꞈgu straight 7
mata again 4
    Maꞈta doꞋozo. Please [come] again.
      4
maꞈtiꞋ town 29; machi (part of a city)
    34-N
maꞈtiaꞋisitu waiting room 20
maꞈtigaeꞋru /tr:-ru:maꞈtigaꞋete/ make
    a mistake 24
maꞈtigaꞋu /intr:-u:maꞈtigaꞋtte/ be
    wrong 24-N
maꞋtinee daytime performance 28-N
mattaku indeed, really, honestly 34
maꞋtti match 3

maꞋtu /tr:-u:maꞋtte/ wait, await, wait
    for 1
maturi festival 32
mawari circumference 33
    kaꞈkiꞋne no mawari ni around the
      fence 33
mawaru /intr:-u:mawatte/ go around
    20
mawasu /tr:-u:mawasite/ send around,
    turn [something] around 20
maꞈzeꞋru /tr:-ru:maꞋzete/ mix [some-
    thing] 33-A
maꞈziꞋru /intr:-u:maꞈziꞋtte/ [some-
    thing] mixes 33-A
maꞈzuꞋi /-ku/ is bad-tasting 14
meꞋ eye 17-A
-me* /ordinal number suffix/ 31
meꞋe niece 11-A
meꞋegosan ꞈ niece 11-A
meesi name card, calling card 13
meꞋewaku /na/ troublesome, annoy-
    ing 32
    goꞈmeꞋewaku zya ꞈnaꞋkereba ꞈ if it
      isn't [too much] trouble for you
      32
meꞋezi Meiji Era (1868–1912) 8
meꞈgane eyeglasses 23-A
    meꞈgane o kaꞈkeꞋru wear eye-
      glasses 23-A
meꞋisya eye doctor, oculist 24-A
meꞈndookusaꞋi /-ku/ is troublesome,
    tiresome 27
meꞋsi cooked rice, meal 24-N
mesiagaru ꞈ /tr:-u:mesiagatte/ eat;
    drink; smoke 14
meꞈzurasiꞋi /-ku/ is amazing, unusual,
    unexpected 27
    meꞈzuraꞋsiku ꞈiꞋi is unusually good
      27
miꞋdori green 16-N
miꞈeꞋru* /intr:-ru:miꞋete/ be visible,
    can see; put in an appearance,
    show up, come 18; appear, seem,
    look 26
migaku /tr:-u:migaite/ shine <u>or</u>
    polish [something] 21
migi right (i.e. not left) 6
    miꞈgi no hoꞋo right side, toward
      the right 6
miꞋkosi portable shrine carried about
    during festivals 32
miꞈmiꞋ ear 17-A
    miꞈmiꞋ ga toꞋoi is hard of hearing 27

minami   south   30

minamimuki   facing south   30

miꞈnaꞈsañ┤   everyone   11

minato   harbor, port   32

miꞈñnaꞈ   everyone; everything   11

miꞈruꞈ*   /tr:-ru:miꞈteꞈ/   look at, see   12

  siꞈte miꞈru   try doing, do and see
    19

miꞈruku   milk   14

misaki   cape, promontory   32-A

miꞈseꞈ   store, shop   6-A

  miꞈse no hitoꞈ   shop employee   24-A

  miꞈseꞈ o yaru   have a shop   34

miꞈseꞈru   /tr:-ru:miꞈsete/   show, let
    [someone] see   4

miti   street, road, way   7

mi-ꞈttuꞈ   three units   5

mitukaru   /intr:-u:mitukatte/   be(come)
    found   24

mitukeru   /tr:-ru:mitukete/   find [some-
    thing]   24-N

mitumori   estimate   33

  daitai no mitumori   rough estimate
    33

mituriñ   jungle   32-A

miyaꞇge   souvenir   31-A

miꞈzikaꞈi   /-ku/   is short   22

mizu   cold water   14

miꞈzuuꞈmi   lake   32-A

mo*   /particle/   also, too   4; even
    22

  aꞈoꞈi no mo   blue one(s) too   4

  deꞈpaꞈato ni mo   in the department
    store too   6

  oꞈokiꞈi no mo tiꞈisaꞈi no mo   both
    big ones and small ones   5

  iti-neñ mo   /+ affirmative/   all of
    a year, a whole year   24;
    /+ negative/   not even a year   24

  iꞈtteꞈ mo   even if [someone] goes
    22

  iꞈtteꞈ mo ꞈiꞈi   is all right to go,
    [someone] may go   22

  iꞈtteꞈ mo iꞈkanaꞈkute mo   whether
    [someone] goes or not   22

  doꞈko e iꞈtteꞈ mo   wherever [some-
    one] goes   27

  doꞈo mo   in every way   Int.

  iꞈtu mo   always   9

  dotira mo   both   10

  dare mo   /+ negative/   nobody   13

moꞈdoꞈru   /intr:-u:moꞈdoꞈtte/   go back,
    back up   7

moꞈkuyoꞈo(bi), mokuyoo   Thursday   8

momeñ   cotton   23

momoiro   pink   16-N

moꞈnoꞈ*   thing (tangible)   14; used to
    32

  kaꞈtta monoꞈ da   used to buy   32

moꞈnoꞈ┤   person   33

mono*   /particle/   because   35

  syoꞈttyuu desu mono   because it's
    all the time   35

moꞈnooki ꞈ   storeroom   33-A

moꞈñ   gate   30-A

moꞈñ   /see moꞈnoꞈ/   32

moꞈñbuꞈsyoo   Ministry of Education   25

moñdai   problem   28

moo*   /+ quantity expression/   more,
    additional   1

  moo iti-do   one time more   1

  moꞈo sukoꞈsi   a little more, a few
    more   4

moꞈo*   /+ affirmative/   already, yet,
    now already, soon now   14;
    /+ negative/   no more   18

  moꞈo suꞇgu   soon now, any minute
    now   15

moosiaꞇgeru┤   /tr:-ru:moosiaꞇgete/   say
    (to you)   32-N

moꞈosu┤   /tr:-u:moꞈosite/   say, be
    named, be called   18

morau*   /tr:-u:moratte/   receive, get
    17

  site morau   have [someone] do [it],
    have [something] done   17

  kiꞈteꞈ moraenai?   can('t) I have you
    come? would you come?   25

moꞈru   /intr:-u:moꞈtte/   leak   33

moꞈsi   supposing   28

moꞈsimosi   hello (on the telephone); say
    there!   12

moꞈtaseꞈru   /tr:-ru:moꞈtaꞈsete/   cause
    [someone] to have   33

  beꞈñtoꞈo o moꞈtaꞈsete yoꞈkoꞈsu
    send [someone] here with a lunch
    33

moꞈtiaꞇgeꞈru   /tr:-ru:moꞈtiaꞇgete/   lift
    33-A

moꞈtiꞈroñ   of course   15

moꞈto   former time   24

motte iku   take [something somewhere]
    14-N

moꞈtte kuꞈru   bring [something]
    14

moꞈtto*   more   5

mo˺tu /tr:-u:mo˺tte/ hold, take hold
   of, have 32
mukoo beyond, over there; the far
   side 6
   bi˺ru no mukoo beyond the build-
      ing 6
   mu˹koo no bi˺ru the building over
      there 6
mu˹ne˺ chest (part of the body) 17-A
mu˹ra˺ village 34-N
mu˹ra˺saki purple 16-N

N

na* /pre-nominal alternant of da/ 12
   hi˹ma na toki˺ time when [someone]
      is free 12
na* /negative imperative particle/ 35
   i˹u˺ na don't say 35
na? /sentence particle/ /M/ isn't
   it true? do you agree? 35
na˺a /sentence particle/ /M/ isn't
   it true! don't you agree! 35
na˺do* and so forth, etc. 31
   ni˹ŋgyoo na˺do dolls and so forth,
      a doll for example, something
      like a doll 31
naḡaḡutu boots 24-N
na˹ḡa˺i /-ku/ is long 22
naḡaisu couch, sofa 17-A
na˹ḡame˺ view 32
-naḡara* while, during 31; while,
      although 35
   no˹mina˺ḡara while drinking 31
   o˹moina˺ḡara while or although
      thinking 35
na˺ḡasa length 23
na˹ḡasi˺ a sink 17-A
na˺i /-ku/ there isn't 15
na˺ihu knife 14-A
naiseñ telephone extension 12
na˺ka inside 17
   hi˹kidasi no na˺ka inside the
      drawer 17
na˹kaba˺ middle 26
nakanaka /+ affirmative/ consider-
      ably, more than expected 11;
      /+ negative/ not easily, not
      readily 28
naku /intr:-u:naite/ cry 35-A
nakunaru /intr:-u:nakunatte/ die,
      pass away 34-A
namae name 10
na˺na seven 3

mu˺ri /na/ unreasonable, beyond one's
      power 35
   mu˺ri ni saseru force [someone] to
      do 35
musi bug, insect 21
mu˹siatu˺i /-ku/ is muggy, sultry 26
musuko son 11-A
mu˹sume˺ daughter 11-A
mu-˹ttu˺ six units 5
mu˺zi solid color 23
muzukasii /-ku/ is difficult 11

na˹na˺-tu seven units 5
na˺ni what? 2
   na˺ni ka something, anything 4
   na˺ni ka ɏo˺o some business, some
      matter to be attended to 25
   nani mo /+ negative/ nothing 18
naniiro what color? 5-N
na˺ninani so-and-so 33
naniziñ what nationality? 10-A
na˺ñ /alternant of na˺ni/ what? 2
   na˹ñ de˺ mo no matter what it is,
      anything at all 15
   na˹ñ de mo a˺ru there's every-
      thing 29
   na˹ñ de mo na˺i it's nothing 29
   na˺ñ ka something, anything 35
   na˺ñ te i˥tte˺ mo whatever [some-
      one] says 27
na˺ñ-do mo any number of times 27
na˺ñka* /alternant of na˺do/ 31
nañni mo /see nani mo/ 18
na˹o˺ru /intr:-u:na˹o˺tte/ get well, re-
      cover 14
na˹o˺su /tr:-u:na˹o˺site/ fix, repair 13
na˺pukiñ napkin 14-A
nara(ba) /provisional of da/ 32
naraberu /tr:-ru:narabete/ line [some-
      thing or someone] up 20-N
narabu /intr:-u:narañde/ [something
      or someone] lines up 20
na˹ra˺nai* it won't do 32
   si˹na˺kereba na˺ra˥nai must do 32
na˹ra˺u /tr:-u:na˹ra˺tte/ learn, take
      lessons 18
na˺ru* /intr:-u:na˺tte/ become, get
      to be 10
   na˺tte (i)ru it has become or been
      set at or been made into 29
   o˺okiku na˹ru˥ get big 10
   ya-˹ttu˺ ni ˹na˥ru get to be eight

na⌐ru* (cont.)

years old10

o⌐kaeri ni na⌐ru ⁺ /honorific equivalent of ka⌐eru/9

naru /intr:-u:natte/sound, ring, roar,
rumble26-A

ka⌐minari¬ ḡa naruit thunders
26-A

narubekuas much as possible22

na⌐rubeku usuku ki⌐rucut as thin
as possible22

naruhodoI see, to be sure, of course
32

na⌐sa⌐ru ⁺ /tr:-aru:na⌐sa⌐tte ~ na⌐su⌐tte/
do, make13

na⌐tu¬summer18-N

na⌐tuya⌐sumisummer vacation25

na⌐wa¬rope33-A

ne?* /sentence particle/isn't it
true? do you agree?13

nedañprice31

ne⌐e* /sentence particle/isn't it
true! don't you agree!1

Do⌐ko desyoo ka ⌐ne⌐e.Where would
it be! I wonder where it is!11

ne⌐esañ ⁺older sister11-A

ne⌐ḡa⌐u ⁺ /tr:-u:ne⌐ḡa⌐tte/request Int.

O⌐negai-sima⌐su. ⁺I'd like it. Please
let me have it. Please do so. I have
a request to make of you. Int.

ne⌐kocat - 17-A

ne⌐kutainecktie23-A

ne⌐kutai o suruwear a necktie
23-A

nemui /-ku/is sleepy21

-neñ /counter for naming and counting
years/8

neru /intr:-ru:nete/go to bed, go to
sleep21

nete (i)rube in bed, be asleep21

ne⌐ziscrew33

ne⌐zima⌐wasiscrewdriver33-A

ni¬two3

ni* /particle/in, on, at6; into,
onto, to7; by17

hoka niin addition4

sezu niwithout doing, instead of
doing24

To⌐okyoo ni a⌐rube in Tokyo6

sa⌐n-zi ni ikugo at three o'clock8

ya-⌐ttu¬ ni ⌐na⌐rubecome eight
years old10

ni* (cont.)

teñpura ni surumake it tempura,
decide on tempura14

koko ni okuput here17

tomodati ni iusay to a friend18

a⌐i ni ⌐ku⌐rucome to see25

da⌐re ka ni na⌐osase⌐rumake someone fix33

to⌐modati ni tuku⌐tte morauhave a
friend make [it]17

so⌐bo ni so⌐daterare⌐rube brought
up by one's grandmother34

da⌐re ka ni saserarerube made to
do [something] by someone34-N

ni⌐a⌐u /intr:-u:ni⌐a⌐tte/suit, be be-
coming23

ni⌐ḡa⌐i /-ku/is bitter14-A

niḡiru /tr:-u:niḡitte/grasp33-A

nihoñḡoJapanese language11

Ni⌐hoñ-hoosookyo⌐okaiJapan Broadcasting Company34

nihoñmaJapanese-style room21

ni⌐hoñzi⌐ña Japanese10

ni⌐isañ ⁺older brother11-A

ni⌐ku¬meat6-N

-niku⌐i* /-ku/cause difficulty in do-
ing28

ka⌐iniku⌐iis difficult to buy28

ni⌐ku¬yameat market, butcher6-A

ni¬motubaggage, things to carry20

-niñ /counter for people/10

niñḡyoodoll31

-niñmae /counter for portions/15

ni⌐o¬ismell, odor33

ni⌐o¬i ḡa suruhave an odor33

nippoñḡoJapanese language11

ni⌐ppoñzi⌐ña Japanese10-A

nisiwest30-A

nisimukifacing west30-N

nisyoku-tukiwith two meals, including
two meals21

-niti /counter for naming and counting
days/10

ni⌐tiyo⌐o(bi), nitiyooSunday8

ni⌐to⌐osyasecond-class car19

niwagarden17-A

ni⌐wakaa⌐mesudden shower26-A

ni⌐zi¬, nizirainbow26-A

no*one, ones4; act, fact28; matter, case7-N

a⌐ka⌐i nored one(s)4

kyo⌐o no waas for today's (one)5

no* (cont.)

    ka⌐u¬ no   the act of buying, the buy-
ing, buying 28

    ka⌐u¬ no ni   in the process of buy-
ing, for buying 28; in spite of
the fact that [someone] buys 29

    i⌐kita¬i no desu   it is a case of want-
ing to go, I want to go 7-N

    ka⌐rita¬i no de   being a case of want-
ing to rent, because [someone]
wants to rent 29

no* /particle/

    To⌐okyoo no ti¬zu   map of Tokyo 5

    kyo⌐o no siñbuñ   today's newspaper
5

    watakusi no siñbuñ   my newspaper
5

    ni⌐to¬osya no tomaru tokoro   the
place where the second-class cars
stop 19

no* /pre-nominal alternant of da/
19-N

    byooki no kodomo   sick child 19-N

nobori   up-train (i. e. going toward
Tokyo) 19

noboru /intr:-u:nobotte/   climb 32-N

    ya⌐ma¬ ni noboru   climb a mountain
32-N

no⌐do   throat 15

    no⌐do ḡa ka⌐wa¬ku   become thirsty
15

no⌐koḡiri¬   saw (tool) 33-A

no⌐ko¬ru /intr:-u:no⌐ko¬tte/   be(come)
left over or left behind 20

no⌐ko¬su /tr:-u:no⌐ko¬site/   leave behind,
leave over (for another time) 20-N

no⌐mi¬mizu   drinking water 21

no⌐mi¬mono   a drink, beverage 15

no⌐mu /tr:-u:noñde/   drink; smoke; take
(medicine) 14

no⌐o   (form of classical Japanese drama)
28-A

noriba   place for boarding vehicles 20

norikae   a transfer (from one vehicle
to another) 19

no⌐rikae¬ru, no⌐rika¬eru /intr:-ru:no⌐ri-
ka¬ete/   change vehicles, transfer
19-N

norimono   vehicle 29

noru /intr:-u:notte/   get on (a vehicle),
take (a vehicle), ride 19

noseru /tr:-ru:nosete/   give [someone]
a ride, carry, take on board
19-N

notihodo   later 12

nozoku /tr:-u:nozoite/   look in at, peek
at 31

nu⌐rikae¬ru, nu⌐rika¬eru /tr:-ru:nu⌐rika¬-
ete/   repaint 30

nuru /tr:-u:nutte/   paint 30

nu⌐ru¬i /-ku/   is lukewarm 21

nya/a/ /contraction of ni wa/ 27

nyu⌐uḡakusike¬ñ   entrance exam 35

ñ /M/   yeah 14

ñ* /contraction of no/ 7

    i⌐kita¬i ñ desu   it is a matter of want-
ing to go, I want to go 7

    de⌐kakeru¬ ñ da   it is a matter of go-
ing out, [someone] goes out 23

ñ⌐ma¬ /see u⌐ma¬/ 17-A

ñ⌐ma¬i /see u⌐ma¬i/ 22

O

o* /particle/

    Hu⌐rosiki o mi¬sete kudasai. Please
show me a furoshiki. 4

    Kono miti o ma⌐ssu¬ḡu i⌐tte kudasa⌐i.
Please go straight along this
street. 7

oba   aunt 11-A

o⌐ba¬asañ⁺   grandmother; old lady 11-A

obasañ⁺   aunt; woman 11-A

o⌐bi   Japanese sash 23-A

    o⌐bi o si⌐me⌐ru   tie an obi 23-A

o⌐boe¬ru /tr:-ru:o⌐bo¬ete/   commit to
memory 24

    o⌐bo¬ete (i)ru   remember 24

oboñ⁺   tray 14-A

Odaizi ni.⁺   Take care [of yourself]!
11

odori   dance, dancing (Japanese style)
28-A

O⌐hayoo (gozaima¬su).⁺   Good morning.
Int.

ohukuro /M—familiar/   my mother,
the old lady 34-N

o⌐hu¬ro⁺   bath 21

    o⌐hu¬ro ni ⌐ha⌐iru   go into the bath,
take a bath 21

oi   nephew 11-A

oide⁺ /honorific nominal/ 9-N

    Oide. Come! Go! Stay! 35

    o⌐ide ni na⌐ru⁺   be, come, go 9-N

oiꟷgosañ ᵗ nephew   11-A
oimotosañ ᵗ younger sister   11-A
oꟷiru   oil (for automobiles)   20
oisii /-ku/ is delicious   14
oisyasañ ᵗ doctor (medical)   24-A
oite iku   leave behind   26-N
oˤkaꟷasañ ᵗ mother   11-A
Oˤkaeri-nasaꟷi. Welcome home. Hello.
    20
okaꟷge de ᵗ /informal equivalent of
    okaꟷgesama de/   35
okaꟷgesama de ᵗ thanks to you; thanks
    for asking   Int.
Oˤkamai naˤku. ᵗ Don't bother. Don't
    go to any trouble.   18
okane ⁺ money   22
oˤkaꟷsi ⁺ cake, sweets   14-A
oˤkasiꟷi /-ku/ is funny (either strange
    or amusing)   20
oˤkiꟷru /intr:-ru:oꟷkite/ get up, wake
    up   21
    oꟷkite (i)ru be up, be awake   21
okosañ ᵗ child   10
oˤkoꟷsu /tr:-u:oˤkoꟷsite/ wake [some-
    one] up   21
oku* /tr:-u:oite/ put, place   17
    site oku do in advance, do now for
    later reference   17
okureru /intr:-ru:okurete/ fall behind,
    become late   19
    okurete (i)ru be late   19
okurimono   gift   31
okuru /tr:-u:okutte/ send   23
oꟷkusañ ᵗ wife; madam; mistress   11
okuzyoo   roof garden   31-A
omae /M/ you   35-N
Oˤmatase-(ita)simaꟷsita. ᵗ I'm sorry to
    have kept you waiting.   4
Oˤmatidoosama deꟷsita. ᵗ I'm sorry you
    were kept waiting.   20
oˤme ni kakaꟷru ᵗ see (a person), meet
    11
    Haˤziꟷmete ome ni kakarimasu. ᵗ
    How do you do?   11
omoi /-ku/ is heavy   20
oˤmoidaꟷsu /tr:-u:oˤmoidaꟷsite/ call to
    mind, recall   24
oˤmosiroꟷi /-ku/ is interesting, is un-
    usual, is fun   2
oˤmoteꟷ front surface, outside, right
    side   33-N
oˤmoꟷtya   toy   31
oˤmotyauꟷriba   toy counter, toy depart-
    ment   31

oˤmoꟷu* /tr:-u:oˤmoꟷtte/ think   26
    iꟷi to oˤmoꟷu think it's good   26
    iˤkoo to omoꟷu think I'll go   26
    iˤkoꟷo ka to oˤmoꟷu wonder if I
    should go   26-N
    Doꟷo omoimasu ka⌐ What do you
    think?   26
onaka   stomach   15
    onaka ꟷga suku become hungry   15
onazi   same   2
    onazi kusuri   same medicine   17
    kore to onazi   same as this   17
Oˤneꟷgai-simaꟷsu. ᵗ Please (speaker re-
    questing something; lit. I make a
    request).   Int.
oꟷno   hatchet, ax   33-A
oꟷñgaku   music   28-A
oꟷñgakuka   musician   28-A
oˤñgakuꟷkai   concert   28-A
oˤñnaꟷ female   10
    oˤñnaꟷ no hito woman   10
    oˤñna no kataꟷ ᵗ woman   10
    oˤñnaꟷ no ko little girl   10
oñseñ   hot spring, hot-spring resort
    32
oˤoaꟷme   heavy rain   26-A
oˤobaa   (full-length) coat   23
oohuku   round trip   19
oˤoꟷi /-ku/ is frequent, is much, are
    many   21
oˤoiꟷsoꟷgi de in a big hurry   32
oˤokaꟷze   strong wind   26-A
oˤokeꟷsutora   orchestra   28-A
oꟷoki* /na/ big   13
    oꟷoki na ˤkoꟷe loud voice   13
oˤokiꟷi /-ku/ is big   2
ookisa   size   23-N
ooyuki   heavy snow   26-A
oꟷpera   opera   28-A
ore /M/ I, me   35-N
oˤriꟷru /intr:-ru:oꟷrite/ go down, de-
    scend, get off (a vehicle)   20
oˤroꟷsu /tr:-u:oˤroꟷsite/ lower, let
    down, discharge (from a vehicle)
    20-N
oꟷru ᵗ* /intr:-u:oꟷtte/ be located (of
    animate beings)   6
    keˤkkoñ-site oꟷru ᵗ be married   10
    beˤñkyoo-site oꟷru ᵗ be studying   11
    huˤtte ˤoꟷru ⁺ be raining   18
Osaki ni. ⁺ [Excuse me for going] ahead.
    18
    Doꟷozo, osaki ni. ⁺ Please [go] ahead.
    18-N

osieru /tr:-ru:osiete/   teach, inform
     7
osiire   closet (for clothing, quilts, etc.)
     17-A
osoi /-ku/   is late or slow   11
osoku   late   31-N
Osoreirimasu.   Thank you.   I'm sorry.
     18
ossyaru † /tr:-aru:ossyatte/   say, be
     named, be called   13
osu /tr:-u:osite/   push   33-A
otaku †   home, household   9
     otaku no †   pertaining or belonging
        to your household   10
otiru /intr:-ru:otite/   fall, drop
     33-A
otoko   male   10
     otoko no hito   man   10
     otoko no kata † †   man   10
     otoko no ko   little boy   10
otoosañ †   father   11
otooto   younger brother   11-A
otosu /tr:-u:otosite/   drop [some-
     thing]   33-A

pañ   bread   14-A
pañku-suru /intr/   become punctured
     20
     taiya ga pañku-suru   have a flat
        tire   20

raigetu   next month   16-N
raineñ   next year   16-N
raisyuu   next week   16
raitaa   lighter   4
rasii * /-ku/   seems to be   35
     ii rasii   seems to be good   35
razio   radio   16
ree   zero   12
reezooko   refrigerator   17-A
rekisi   history   32
reñga   brick   33-A
reñraku-suru /tr/   get in touch, con-
     tact, communicate   24
reñsyuu   practice   31
reñsyuu-suru /tr/   practice (verb)   31
reñzi   stove (for cooking)   17-A
reñzu   lens   24
resutorañ   restaurant   14-A
-ri ~ niñ   /counter for people/   10
riku   land   32-N

ototoi, ototoi   day before yesterday
     8
ototosi   year before last   24
otya +   tea   14
owari   the end   28
owaru /intr:-u:owatte/   come to an
     end   28
oya   parent   11-A
oya?   oh! my word! hold on!   34
oyagosañ †   parent   11-A
Oyasumi-nasai.   Good night.   Int.
oyogi   swimming   32-A
oyogu /intr:-u:oyoide/   swim   27
oyoso   generally speaking, on the
     whole, as a rule   35
oyu +   hot water   14-A
ozeñ +   eating tray   21
     ozeñ o dasu   bring out the trays,
        serve dinner   21
ozi   uncle   11-A
oziisañ †   grandfather; old man   11-A
ozisañ †   uncle; man   11-A
ozyoosañ †   daughter; young girl; little
     girl   11-A

P

pasu-suru /intr/   pass (an exam)
     35-N
peñ   pen   2
peñti   pliers   33-A
puroguramu   program   28-N

R

rikuguñ   army   34
rikuseñtai   marines   34-A
rippa /na/   fine, handsome, magnificent,
     imposing   18
rirekisyo   personal history record   34
-rittoru   /counter for liters/   20
roku   six   3
roku-zyoo   six-mat area or room   30
roodoosya   laborer   24-A
rooka   hall, corridor   17-A
roomazi   romanization   31-N
roosoku   candle   35
rosiago   Russian language   11-A
rosiaziñ   a Russian   10-A
rusu   away from home   12
     rusu-tyuu ni   during [someone's] ab-
        sence from home   18
rusubañ   care-taking   27
     rusubañ o suru   take care of house
        during absence of others   27

ryokañ   inn (Japanese style)   6-A
ryokoo   a trip   32
ryokoo-suru /intr/   take a trip, travel
     32

S

sa* /sentence particle/   /M/   35
sa⌐a   hmm . . .   6
sa⌐abisu   service   33
sabaku   desert   32-A
sa⌐bisi⌐i /-ku/   is lonesome or cheer-
     less   35-A
sa⌐ḡa⌐ru /intr:-u:saⁿḡa⌐tte/   go down
     29-N
saḡasu /tr:-u:saḡasite/   look for   22
sa⌐ḡe⌐ru /tr:-ru:saⁿḡete/   lower [some-
     thing]   29-N
sakaba   saké bar   29-N
sakana   fish   6-N
sakanaya   fish market, fish man   6-A
sakañ /na/   flourishing, prosperous,
     thriving, popular   32
sakaya   saké shop   29
sake   rice wine   14
sakezuki   saké lover, drinker   24-N
saki   ahead   6
     kono saki   up ahead from here   7
saku /intr:-u:saite/   bloom   27
     saite (i)ru   be in bloom   27
sakura   cherry tree, cherry blossom
     27
-sama ⁺   (more polite alternant of -sañ)
     12
sa⌐mu⌐i /-ku/   is cold (of weather or
     atmosphere)   14
sañ   three   3
-sañ ⁺   Mr., Mrs., Miss   Int.
sa⌐ñdoi⌐tti   sandwich   28-N
sañpo   a walk   18
sañpo-suru /intr/   take a walk   18-N
sa⌐ñto⌐osya   third-class car   19-A
sa⌐ñ-zyo⌐o   three-mat area or room
     30
sara   plate, dish   14-A
saraiḡetu   month after next   App.
saraineñ   year after next   App.
saraisyuu   week after next   App.
sa⌐rari⌐imañ   salaried man, white-
     collar worker   24-A
sa⌐simi⌐   sashimi (raw fish)   14-A
sa⌐to⌐o   sugar   14-A
-satu /counter for books, magazines,
     etc./   5

ryo⌐ori⌐ya   restaurant (Japanese style) 14-A
ryo⌐osi   fisherman   24-A
ryo⌐osiñ   both parents   11-A
ryo⌐ozi⌐kañ   consulate   6

sa⌐wa⌐ḡu /intr:-u:sa⌐wa⌐ide/   make noise,
     be boisterous   27
Sayonara.   Goodbye.   Int.
sayoo   that way, thus, so   12
Sayoonara.   Goodbye.   Int.
sebiro   man's suit   21
-see   -made   23
     Amerika-see   American-made   23
seekatu   life, existence   34
seekatu-suru /intr/   live, make a living
     34
seereki   Western calendar, Christian
     Era   8-N
se⌐etaa   sweater   23
se⌐eto   pupil   24-A
seezi   politics   32-A
se⌐ka⌐i   world   32-A
se⌐ki, seki   seat, assigned place   12
se⌐kita⌐ñ   coal   30
se⌐kkaku⌐   with much trouble, on pur-
     pose; with special kindness   26
     se⌐kkaku⌐ desu ḡa   it's kind of you
     to ask [me] but   26
     se⌐kkaku ku⌐ru   come on purpose,
     take the trouble to come, come
     specially   26
sekkeñ   soap   17
se⌐ma⌐i /-ku/   is narrow or cramped
     or small in area   21-N
senaka   back (part of the body)   17-A
se⌐ñ   thousand   3
-señ /counter for thousands/   3
se⌐ñḡetu   last month   14
señḡo   post-war   34-N
se⌐ñkyo⌐osi   missionary   24-A
se⌐ñme⌐ñki   wash basin   17-A
señmeñzyo   washroom, lavatory   17-A
señmoñ   specialty   33
     señmoñ no hito   specialist, expert
     33
se⌐ñse⌐e   teacher, doctor   16
se⌐ñse⌐ñḡetu   month before last   App.
se⌐ñse⌐ñsyuu   week before last   App.
señsoo   war   34
señsu   (folding) fan   31-A
señsyuu   last week   26
señtaku   laundering   23-N

señtakumono laundry (i. e. things to be
    laundered) 23-N
señtaku-suru /tr/ launder 23
señtakuya laundry (store), laundryman
    23-N
señzeñ pre-war 34-N
señzitu the other day 18
señzi-tyuu during war 34
setomono china, pottery 31-A
se'tubi equipment, facilities, accom-
    modations 30
setumee explanation 28-N
setumee-suru /tr/ explain 28
se'wa' helpful service 25
    Iroiro o'se'wa ni na'rima'sita. ꜛ
    I'm much obliged to you. 25
si' four 3
si' city 34
    Ko'onosu'-si Konosu City 34
si* /particle/ and 23
    zyo'obu da' si it is strong and what
    is more 23
siai game, match 35
siba lawn 33
sibai a play, show 28
si'ba'raku a while (short or long) 11
    Si'ba'raku desita. It's been a long
    time [since I last saw you]. 11
si'ba'ru /tr:-u:si'ba'tte/ tie, bind
    33-A
sigoto work 10
    sigoto-tyuu in the middle of work
    12
si'ha'iniñ manager 24-A
sika* /particle/ /+ negative/ nothing
    but, only 21
    ko're sika na'i there's nothing but
    this, there's only this 21
si'kaku' square 31-N
si'kaku'i /-ku/ is square 31
si'ka'si however, but 15
sikata method, way of doing 23
    si'kata ga na'i it can't be helped,
    nothing can be done 23
si'ke'ñ exam, test 35
    si'ke'ñ o u'ke'ru take an exam 35
sikeñ-suru /tr/ put to a test, examine
    35-N
sikiti building lot 30
siku /tr:-u:siite/ spread out (on floor,
    ground, etc.) 21
    hutoñ o siku spread out the futon
    (for sleeping) 21

si'ma' island 32
si'ma'ru /intr:-u:si'ma'tte/ [something]
    closes or shuts 16
simau* /tr:-u:simatte/ put away, store
    17
    irete simau finish putting in, put in
    for good, end up by putting in 17
si'me'ru /tr:-ru:si'mete/ close or shut
    [something] 16
    o'bi o si'me'ru wear an obi 23
sinu /intr:-u:siñde/ die 34-A
siñbuñ newspaper 2
si'ñbuñki'sya newspaperman 24-A
siñdai bed 17-A
si'ñda'ikeñ berth ticket 19-A
si'ñda'isya sleeping car 19-A
siñgeki modern drama 28-A
siñpai worry 23
    Go'siñpai na'ku. ꜛ Don't worry. 23
siñpai-suru /tr/ worry 23-N
siñsitu bedroom 17-A
si'ñtoo Shintoism 32
siñzyu pearl 31-A
si'o' salt 14-A
si'rabe'ru /tr:-ru:si'ra'bete/ look into,
    check, investigate 20
siraseru /tr:-ru:sirasete/ cause to
    know, let [someone] know 33
sirenai* it can't be known 30
    i'i ka mo sirenai maybe it's good,
    it may be good 30
siriai acquaintance 29
si'ro'i /-ku/ is white 4
siru /tr:-u:sitte/ come to know 10
    sitte (i)ru know 10
sita under, below, bottom, youngest
    10
    si'ta no ho'ñ bottom book 10-N
    ho'ñ no sita under the book 10-N
sitagi underwear 23-A
sitaku preparation 16
    sitaku o suru prepare 16
si'ti' seven 3
situmoñ question 32-N
situmoñ-suru /intr/ question, ask
    questions 34-N
si'tu'ree /na/ rudeness, rude 10
    Si'tu'ree desu ga— Excuse me
    but . . . 10
    Si'tu'ree(-simasu). Excuse me (on
    leaving). Int.
    Si'tu'ree(-simasita). Excuse me
    (for what I did). Int.

siyoo /see syoo/ 23-N
si'zuka /na/ quiet 21
so'ba vicinity 6
    e'ki no 'so'ba near the station 6
    so'ba no 'e'ki a nearby station 6
    su'gu 'so'ba immediate vicinity 6
so'ba noodles 14-A
so'ba'ya noodle shop 14-A
so'bo grandmother 11-A
so'date'ru /tr:-ru:so'da'tete/ bring up,
    raise 34
so'da'tu /intr:-u:so'da'tte/ grow up 34
so'hu grandfather 11-A
soko that place, there 6
sono* /+ nom/ that— 3
    sono ue on top of that, what is
      more 23
    so'no ue' de on the basis of that 33
sonna* that kind, that kind of 5
    sonna ni to that extent 28
so'o that way, thus, so 2
    So'o desu. That's right. 2
    So'o desu ka. Is that right? Oh? 2
    So'o desu 'ne'e. That's right, isn't it.
      2; Let me see . . . Hmmm . . . 4
so'o da* it is said 22
    i'ku so'o da it is said that [he] is
      going to go; they say that [he] is
      going to go; I hear that [he] is go-
      ing to go 22
-soo* /na/ looking as if 26
    ha'reso'o /na/ looking as if it would
      clear up 26
soodan discussion 28-N
soodan-suru /tr/ discuss, talk over
    28
soozi-suru /tr/ clean (verb) 16
so'ra sky 26-A
sore* that thing 2
    sore de that being the case, accord-
      ingly 32
    so're de' wa in that case 35
    sore kara after that, and then,
      and 4
    so're wa so'o to be that as it may,
      to change the subject 35
Sore wa sore wa. Oh, my goodness!
    You don't say! Really! 27
sorezore respectively, severally 32
so'ru /tr:-u:so'tte/ shave 22
sosite and, then, and then 27
sotira that one (of two); that way,
    thereabouts, there 6; that per-
    son 11; the person addressed 12

so'to outside 17
so'tti' /see sotira/ 6
sotugyoo-suru /tr/ graduate 34-A
su'barasi'i /-ku/ is wonderful 32
su'gi' past, after 8
    ni-'hu'n sugi two minutes after the
      hour 8
su'gi'ru* /intr:-ru:su'gite/ exceed
    21-N
    a'tusugi'ru be too hot 21
su'go'i /-ku/ is dreadful, terrible,
    terrific, extraordinary 35-A
su'gu soon, any minute, right away 5;
    readily, easily 28
    su'gu 'so'ba immediate vicinity 6
suidoo running water, water pipes 30
su'ihee navy sailor 34-A
suisen flushing 30
su'iyo'o(bi), suiyoo Wednesday 8
su'ka'ato skirt 23-A
su'ki' /na/ pleasing; like [something] 15
sukiyaki sukiyaki (stew of vegetables
    with meat or chicken or fish) 14-A
su'kka'ri completely 27
su'ko'si a little, a few 4
    mo'o suko'si a little more, a few
      more 4
suku /intr:-u:suite/ become empty 15
    onaka ga suku become hungry 15
su'kuna'i /-ku/ is rare, scarce; are
    few 21-N
su'mai residence 16
su'mase'ru /tr:-ru:su'ma'sete/ finish
    [something] 26
su'mi corner (of a room) 17
su'mi' ink stick 31
Su'(m)imase'n. I'm sorry. Thank you
    for your trouble. Int.
Su'(m)imase'n desita. I'm sorry (for
    what I did). Thank you (for the
    trouble you took). Int.
su'mu /intr:-u:su'nde/ come to an end
    26-N
su'mu /intr:-u:su'nde/ live, reside 34
suna sand 33-A
sunpoo measurements 23
supeingo Spanish language 11-A
su'po'otu sports 35
su'ppa'i /-ku/ is acid or sour 14-A
su'pu'un spoon 14-A
suru* /tr:irreg:site/ do, perform,
    make 1; make into, decide on 14;
    practice a profession 24; play (a
    game or instrument) 31-N

suru* (cont.)

   ikoo to suru   be about to go; try to
     go 26

   iˈitasoˈo ni suru   act as if wanting to
     say 35

   teñpura ni suru   make it tempura,
     decide on tempura 14

   iˈku kotoˈ ni suru   decide to go 32

   uti to site   as a house 29

   uˈti to siteˈ mo   even as a house 29

suˈsiˈ   sushi (rice with fish, seaweed,
     egg, etc.) 14-A

suˈsiˈya   sushi shop 14-A

suˈtaˈa   star (i.e. leading player) 28-A

sutañdo   lamp 17-A

suteru /tr:-ru:sutete/   throw away 17

suˈtoˈobu   heater 16

suu /tr:-u:sutte/   smoke (cigarettes,
     cigars, etc.) 14

suˈutu   woman's suit 23-A

suwaru /intr:-u:suwatte/   sit (Japanese
     style, on floor or ground) 25-N

suˈzi   plot 28

suˈzuriˈ   ink stone 31

suˈzusiˈi /-ku/   is cool 18

syasyoo   train conductor 19

syatyoo   company president 24-A

syokudoo   dining room 14-A

syoˈkudoˈosya   dining car 19-A

syokuryoohiñ, syoˈkuryoˈohiñ   food-
     stuffs, groceries 31-A

syoku-tuki   with meals 21

syokuzi   dining, a meal 15

   syokuzi o suru   dine, eat a meal 15

syoo   method, way of doing 23

   syoˈo ḡa naˈi   it can't be helped,

syoo (cont.)

   nothing can be done 23

syoobai   business, occupation 33

syoˈoḡaˈkkoo   elementary school 34

syooḡi   shogi (Japanese chess) 31

syookai   introduction 25

syookai-suru /tr/   introduce 25-N

syookoo   military officer 34-A

syoˈoniñ   merchant, shopkeeper 29

syoˈosyoo   a little 4

syoosyuu-suru /tr/   summon; draft 34

syooti-suru /tr/   consent to, agree to
     21

   Syoˈoti-(ita)simaˈsita. Certainly. I
     agree to your request. 21

syoowa   Showa Era (1926-) 8

syooyu   soy sauce 14-A

syoozi   sliding door (translucent) 18

syoˈoziziˈ /na/   honest 29

syosai   study (i.e. a room) 17

syoˈttyuu   always, at all hours, con-
     stantly 35

syuttyoo-suru /intr/   make a business
     trip 35

syuu   week App.

-syuukañ   /counter for number of weeks/
     8

syuumatu   weekend 29

syuuseñ   end of war 34

   syuˈuseñ ni naˈru   war ends 34

syuusyoku-suru /intr/   find employment,
     get a job 35

syuuzeñ   repairs 30

syuuzeñ-suru /tr/   repair, fix 30-N

syuuzi   calligraphy 31

syuˈziñ   husband 11-A

T

taˈ   rice field 29-N

tabako   cigarette, tobacco 3

tabakoya   cigar store 6-A

taˈbemoˈno, taˈbemonoˈ   food, edibles
     15-N

taˈbeˈru /tr:-ru:taˈbete/   eat 14

taˈbesaseˈru /tr:-ru:taˈbesaˈsete/   feed 33

taˈbi   socks (Japanese style) 23-A

taˈbiˈ   time, occasion 32

   ryoˈkoo-suru tabiˈ ni   everytime
     [someone] travels 32

tabitabi   often 34

taˈbuñ   probably 35

Tadaima. Hello, I'm back. 20

taiheñ /na/   awful, dreadful, terrible,
     a nuisance; very 20

taˈihuˈu   typhoon 26-A

taˈiriku   continent 32-A

taˈiru   tile 33-A

taisetu /na/   important 20

taˈisiˈkañ   embassy 6

taisyoo   Taisho Era (1912-1926) 8

taitee   usual, usually 9

   taˈitee no amerikaˈziñ   most Ameri-
     cans 15

taiya, taˈiya   a tire 20

taˈkaˈi /-ku/   is expensive 3; is high
     31-N

taˈkusaˈñ, takusañ   much, many 5

taˈkusii   taxi 7

tama ni   once in a while, now and then
     35

ta⌐ma⌐go egg 14-A

tana shelf 17-A

ta⌐hi⌐ valley 32-A

ta⌐ho⌐mu /tr:-u:ta⌐ho⌐nde/ make a request, place an order 14; engage, hire 20

ta⌐hosi⌐i /-ku/ is merry <u>or</u> pleasant or enjoyable 35-N

ta⌐hosi⌐mi, ta⌐hosimi⌐ pleasure, enjoyment 35

ta⌐hosi⌐mu /tr:-u:ta⌐hosi⌐nde/ take pleasure in, enjoy 35-N

ta⌐nbi⌐ /<u>see</u> ta⌐bi⌐/ 32-N

tansu chest of drawers 17-A

ta⌐nze⌐n quilted kimono 23-A

ta⌐nzyo⌐obi birthday 35

ta⌐ore⌐ru /intr:-ru:ta⌐o⌐rete/ fall over, collapse 33-A

ta⌐o⌐su /tr:-u:ta⌐o⌐site/ throw over, knock down 33-A

tariru /intr:-ru:tarite/ be sufficient 20

ta⌐suka⌐ru /intr:-u:ta⌐suka⌐tte/ be saved, be helped, survive 35-N

ta⌐suke⌐ru /tr:-ru:ta⌐suke⌐te/ rescue, save 35-N

    Tasukete⌐ Help! 35-A

tatami rice-straw floor mat 18

    ta⌐tami no heya⌐ room with tatami 18

ta⌐temo⌐no; ta⌐te⌐mono building 6

ta⌐te⌐ru /tr:-ru:ta⌐tete/ build, erect 32

-tati /pluralizing suffix/ 27

    bo⌐kutati we, us 27

ta⌐to⌐eba for example 33

ta⌐toe⌐ru /tr:-ru:ta⌐to⌐ete/ give an example 33-N

ta⌐tu /intr:-u:ta⌐tte/ depart, leave for a trip 19

ta⌐tu /intr:-u:ta⌐tte/ stand up 27

    ta⌐tte (i)ru be standing 27

    ya⌐ku⌐ ni ⌐ta⌐tu be useful, serve a purpose 32

te⌐ hand 17-A

te⌐a⌐rai toilet 6-A

te⌐bu⌐kuro gloves 23

    te⌐bu⌐kuro o hameru put on <u>or</u> wear gloves 23-A

teeburu table 17

teeden stoppage of electricity 35

te⌐enee /na/ polite 34-N

tegami letter 25

    te⌐gami o da⌐su mail a letter 25-N

te⌐ire⌐ care, repair 33

    te⌐ire⌐ o suru care for, repair 33

tekitoo /na/ suitable, appropriate 33

temae this side 6

    byooin no temae this side of the hospital 6

te⌐nisu tennis 32-A

tenin shop employee 24-A

te⌐nki weather; good weather 18

tenkin-suru /intr/ change one's post 34

tennin-suru /intr/ change one's post (military) 34-N

tenpura tempura (batter-fried fish or vegetables) 14

tenpuraya tempura shop 14-A

tenzyoo ceiling 30-A

te⌐ra⌐ Buddhist temple 32

te⌐rebi television 16

te⌐tuda⌐u /tr:-u:te⌐tuda⌐tte/ help, lend a hand 17

ti blood 24-N

tigau /intr:-u:tigatte/ be wrong; be different 2

    tigatta azi different taste 32

    sore to tigau be different from that 17

    Ti⌐gaima⌐su. Wrong number (on the telephone). 13

ti⌐isa /na/ small 13-N

    ti⌐isa na ⌐ko⌐e a low voice 13-N

ti⌐isa⌐i /-ku/ is small 2

ti⌐ka⌐i /-ku/ is near 20

ti⌐ka⌐ku vicinity 31

ti⌐ka⌐situ basement 31-A

tikatetu subway 20

ti⌐ri geography 32

ti⌐ti⌐ father 11

ti⌐tto⌐ **mo** /+ negative/ not a bit 24

ti⌐zu map 5

to* /particle/ and 4; with 15; as 29

    ho⌐n to zassi book and magazine 4

    Sa⌐itoo-san to issyo together with Mr. Saito 15

    sa⌐muku ⌐na⌐ru to when it gets cold (lit. with getting cold) 33

    uti to site as a house 29

    u⌐ti to site⌐ mo even as a house 29

to* /quotative/ 18

    na⌐n to iu say what? be named <u>or</u> called what? 18

to door 16

to⌐ city, metropolis (Tokyo only) 34-N
   To⌐okyo⌐o-to the city of Tokyo 34-N
to mo* /particle sequence/ certainly,
   positively, of course 32
   A⌐rima⌐su to mo. Certainly there
   are. 32
todana cupboard (with shelves) 17
to⌐doke⌐ru /tr:-ru:to⌐do⌐kete/ deliver
   22
to⌐do⌐ku /intr:-u:to⌐do⌐ite/ reach, be
   delivered 22-N
to⌐ire(tto) toilet 6-A
tokee clock, watch 8
to⌐ki⌐* time, occasion 12
   no⌐ru toki⌐ /ni/ when [someone]
   rides 19
to⌐kidoki⌐ sometimes 9
tokkyuu special express 19
to⌐kkyu⌐uken special-express ticket
   19-A
tokonoma Japanese-style alcove 18
to⌐ko(ro)⌐* place 18; place where one
   lives 22; time, occasion 25
   yo⌐nda to⌐koro⌐ da just read 30
   to⌐koro⌐ de by the way, well now 34
   O⌐isoḡasii tokoro⌐ (o) ⌐do⌐o mo a⌐ri⌐-
   ḡatoo gozaimasu. Thank you for
   your time when you are [so] busy.
   25
tokoya barber, barbershop 22
to⌐ku ni in particular 29
tokubetu special 19-N
to⌐kubetukyu⌐ukoo special express 19
to⌐kubetuni⌐too special second class
   19-N
tokuni special second class 19-N
tomaru /intr:-u:tomatte/ come to a
   halt; stop at, lodge 19
tomeru /tr:-ru:tomete/ bring to a
   halt 7
tomodati friend 10
tonari next door, adjoining 6
   e⌐ki no tonari next door to the
   station 6
to⌐nikaku anyway, at any rate 28
To⌐nde mo na⌐i. Heavens no! 8
to⌐o ten units 5
to⌐o tower, pagoda 32
-too /counter for naming classes/ 19
Toodai Tokyo University 13
tooi /-ku/ is far 13
   denwa ḡa tooi have trouble hearing
   (on the telephone) 13

tooi (cont.)
   mi⌐mi⌐ ḡa tooi is hard of hearing
   27
to⌐oku⌐ far distance, the far away 31-N
to⌐ori⌐ avenue, wide street 7
to⌐ori way, manner 33
   na⌐mae no to⌐ori like its name, in
   accordance with its name 33
tooroo lantern 32-A
to⌐oru /intr:-u:to⌐otte/ pass through, go
   through, pass in front of 19
to⌐osuto toast 14-A
to⌐otoo finally, in the end 24
to⌐re⌐ru /intr:-ru:to⌐rete/ come off,
   come out, be taken 33
tori bird 17-A; chicken, fowl 14-A
torii gateway to Shinto shrine 32-A
torikaeru /tr:-ru:torikaete/ exchange
   20
to⌐ru /tr:-u:to⌐tte/ take up, take away,
   remove, take off, pass [to some-
   one] 17
   na⌐tuya⌐sumi o ⌐to⌐ru take a summer vacation 25
to⌐si⌐ year 26
to⌐siyori⌐, to⌐siyo⌐ri old person 27
totemo exceedingly, very 8
to⌐tte oku put aside for future use 28
tottemo exceedingly, very 8
to⌐zi⌐ru /tr:-ru:to⌐zite/ close [some-
   thing] CI
/t/te* /quotative/ 18
   na⌐n te iu say what? be named <u>or</u>
   called what? 18
-/t/tu /counter for number of units/ ·5;
   /counter for years of people's
   age/ 10
-tubo /counter for tsubo [approximately
   6' x 6']/ 30
tu⌐ḡi⌐ next 7
   tu⌐ḡi⌐ no ⌐ka⌐do next corner 7
tuḡoo circumstances, conditions 25
   tu⌐ḡoo ḡa i⌐i is convenient [for
   someone] 25-N
   tu⌐ḡoo ḡa waru⌐i is inconvenient [for
   someone] 25-N
tu⌐i unintentionally, carelessly 35
tu⌐itati⌐ first day of the month 8
tu⌐ite* concerning 32
   re⌐kisi ni tu⌐ite concerning history
   32
tu⌐kare⌐ru /intr:-ru:tu⌐ka⌐rete/ become
   tired 17

tukau /tr:-u:tukatte/   use 22
 sukiyaki ni takau   use for sukiyaki
  22
tu⌐ke⌐ru /tr:-ru:tu⌐ke⌐te/   attach, turn
  [something] on 16
tu⌐ki⌐   moon; month 26-A
tukiai   association, acquaintance 35-N
tukiatari   end of a street or corridor
  7
tu⌐kia⌐u /intr:-u:tu⌐kia⌐tte/   associate
  with 35
tu⌐ku /intr:-u:tu⌐ite/   arrive 9; [some-
  thing] becomes attached or turned
  on 16
 ki ⌐ga tu⌐ku   notice 25
tukue   desk 17
tu⌐ku⌐ru /tr:-u:tu⌐ku⌐tte/   make 23
tu⌐ma⌐nnai /see tu⌐mara⌐nai/ 24
tu⌐mara⌐nai /-ku/   is dull or boring; is
  trifling 2
tu⌐ma⌐ru /intr:-u:tu⌐ma⌐tte/   become
  blocked or clogged 33
tu⌐me⌐ru /tr:-ru:tu⌐mete/   cram, stuff,
  stop up 33-N
tumetai /-ku/   is cold 14
tumori*   intention, plan 20
 iku tumori da   [I] intend to go, [I]
  plan to go 20
turai /-ku/   is hard to bear 34
tureru /tr:-ru:turete/   lead 28
 turete (i)ku   take (people or animals) 28
turi   fishing 32
turu /tr:-u:tutte/   suspend, hang by a
  string 33
 tana o turu   hang a shelf 33
tutaeru /tr:-ru:tutaete/   report, com-
  municate, convey a message 13
tu⌐ti⌐   dirt 33-A
tu⌐tome⌐ru /intr:-ru:tu⌐to⌐mete/   become employed 10
 tu⌐to⌐mete (i)ru   be employed 10
tu⌐tu⌐mu /tr:-u:tu⌐tu⌐nde/   wrap 31

tu⌐uyaku   interpreting 34-A
tu⌐yo⌐i /-ku/   is strong 17
tuyu   rainy season 26
tuzukeru /tr:-ru:tuzukete/   continue
  [something] 24
tuzuku /intr:-u:tuzuite/   [something]
  continues 24-N; adjoin 28
 tu⌐zuita se⌐ki   adjoining seats 28
tyairo   brown 16
tyaku   arriving 19
 i⌐ti⌐-zi tyaku   arriving at one o'clock
  19
tyanoma   family room (Japanese style)
  17-A
-tyañ↑   /suffix added to children's given
  names/ 10
tyawañ   cup or small bowl (Japanese
  style) 14-A
-tyoo   cho (section of a city) 34
 Ni⌐ñgyo⌐o-tyoo   Ningyo Cho 34
tyoodai-suru↓*   accept, receive 35
 Tyo⌐oda⌐i.   Let me have [it]. 35
 Tu⌐ke⌐te tyoodai.   Attach for me.
  35
tyoodo   exactly 8
-tyoome   /counter for naming chomes/
  7
tyoosengo   Korean language 11-A
tyo⌐osenzi⌐ñ   a Korean 10-A
tyo⌐oti⌐ñ   paper lantern 32-A
tyo⌐tto   a bit, a little 1; just 5
 Tyo⌐tto.   Say there! 4
 tyo⌐tto_   I'm afraid it won't do . . .
  4
-tyuu   in the middle of ——, now busy
  with —— 12
 si⌐goto-tyuu   in the middle of work
  12
tyu⌐ugaku   middle school 34
tyuugokugo   Chinese language 11-A
tyu⌐ugoku⌐ziñ   a Chinese 10-A
tyuumoñ-suru /tr/   place an order
  14

U

u⌐de⌐   arm 17-A
u⌐e⌐, ue   over, above, top, topmost,
  oldest 10
 u⌐e no ho⌐ñ   top book 10-N
 ho⌐ñ no ue   top of the book 10-N
 sono ue   on top of that, what is
  more 23
 so⌐no ue⌐ de   on the basis of that 33

uekiya   gardener 24-A
ueru /tr:-ru:uete/   plant 33
u⌐goka⌐su /tr:-u:u⌐goka⌐site/   move
  [something] 33
u⌐go⌐ku /intr:-u:u⌐go⌐ite/   [someone
  or something] moves 33-N
ukagau↓ /tr:-u:ukagatte/   inquire
  6

ukağau ↓ (cont.)
tyo⌉tto u⌈kağaima⌉su ğa excuse me but; I'm just going to ask [you something] but 6
ukağau ↓ /intr:-u:ukağatte/ visit 16
u⌈ke⌉ru /tr:-ru:u⌉kete/ undergo 34-A
uketori receipt 22
uketuke reception desk 25
u⌈ma⌉ horse 17-A
u⌈ma⌉i /-ku/ is delicious; is skilled 22
umare birth, place of birth 34
umareru /intr:-ru:umarete/ be born 34
u⌉mi sea, ocean 18
u⌉ñğa canal 32-A
u⌈ñte⌉ñsyu driver, chauffeur 24-A
u⌈ra⌉ back, lining, wrong side 33
u⌈resi⌉i /-ku/ is happy 35-A
uriba counter, selling place 31
urikire sellout 28
uriko salesgirl 24-A
uru /tr:-u:utte/ sell 22
usaği rabbit 17-A
usi bull, cow 17-A
usiro back, rear 7
ta⌈isi⌉kañ no usiro back of the embassy 7
usui /-ku/ is weak or thin (of liquids); is light (of colors) 14; is thin (of flat objects) 22
u⌈ta⌉ song 27
utau /tr:-u:utatte/ sing 27
u⌈ti⌉, uti home, house, household 9
uti no our household's, our 10
uti* among 15; interval, within, during 27; /preceded by negative/ before 33
A to B to C no uti [de] [being] among A and B and C 15
asa no uti [ni] within the morning, during the morning 33
tu⌈mara⌉nai uti ni before it gets clogged 33
wa⌈ka⌉i uti while [someone] is young 27
u⌈ti⌉wa (non-folding) fan 31-A
u⌉tu /tr:-u:u⌉tte/ hit, strike 33-A
u⌉uru wool 23-A
uwağı jacket 23

W

wa* /sentence particle/ /W/ 16
wa* /particle/ as for, comparatively speaking Int.
A⌈na⌉ta wa? How about you? Int.
Sore wa ⌈na⌉ñ desu ka⌣ What is that? (Lit. As for that, what is it?) 2
Si⌈ñbuñ wa kaimase⌉ñ desita. A newspaper I didn't buy. 4
Ko⌈ko ni⌉ wa a⌈rimase⌉ñ. Here there isn't one. 6
si⌈te⌉ wa ikenai must not do 25
si⌈na⌉kute wa ikenai must do 32-N
wahuku Japanese-style clothing 23-A
waisyatu shirt 23
wa⌈ka⌉i /-ku/ is young 27
wa⌈ka⌉ru /intr:-u:wa⌈ka⌉tte/ be comprehensible, understand, can tell 1
wa⌉ke cause, reason, circumstance 32
si⌈ranai wa⌉ke zya ⌈na⌉i isn't the case that I don't know 32
Do⌉o iu ⌈wa⌉ke desu ka⌣ What is the reason? 32-N
wañ bowl 14-A
wa⌉ñ bay 32-A
wa⌈ñpi⌉isu (one-piece) dress 23-A
warau /tr:-u:waratte/ laugh 35-A
-wari /counter for units of ten per cent/ 35-A
i⌈ti-wari go⌉-bu 15 per cent 35-A
wari ni comparatively 31
wa⌈ru⌉i /-ku/ is bad 2-A
wasi /M/ I, me 35-N
wasureru /tr:-ru:wasurete/ forget 4
wasyoku Japanese-style food 21
wata(ku)si I, me 5
wata(ku)si no my, mine 5
wataru /intr:-u:watatte/ go over, go across 20
watasu /tr:-u:watasite/ hand over 20-N

Y

ya* /particle/ and 17
  hoꟾn ya zassi books and magazines
    and the like 17
yaꟾbuꟾku /tr:-u:yaꟾbuꟾite/ tear [some-
    thing] 33
yaꟾbureꟾru /intr:-ru:yaꟾbuꟾrete/ [some-
    thing] tears 33-N
yaꟾbuꟾru /tr:-u:yaꟾbuꟾtte/ tear [some-
    thing] 33-N
yaꟾgi goat 17-A
yaꟾhaꟾri after all 35
yaꟾkamasiꟾi /-ku/ is noisy 21
yakeru /intr:-ru:yakete/ be burned
    or baked or roasted or toasted
    34-N
yaku /tr:-u:yaite/ burn, bake, roast,
    toast [something] 34
yaꟾkuꟾ ni ꟾtaꟾtu be useful, serve a
    purpose 32
yakusoku promise, appointment, en-
    gagement, reservation 21
yakusoku-suru /tr/ promise 21-N
yakusya actor, actress 28-A
yakyuu baseball 35
yaꟾmaꟾ mountain 18
yaꟾmanoꟾbori mountain-climbing 32-A
yameru /tr:-ru:yamete/ quit, give up
    14
yamu /intr:-u:yaꟾnde/ cease 26
yaꟾne roof 30
yaꟾnusi, yanusi home owner, landlord 29
yaoya vegetable store 6-A
yaꟾppaꟾri after all 35
yaru* /tr:-u:yatte/ give (to someone
    other than the speaker) 17
  site yaru do for someone 17-N
yaru /tr:-u:yatte/ do 33
  miꟾseꟾ o yaru have a shop 34
yasai vegetable 14-A
yasasii /-ku/ is easy 11
yaseru /intr:-ru:yasete/ grow thin
    35
  yaꟾseta hitoꟾ thin person 35-N
yaꟾsuꟾi /-ku/ is cheap 3
-yasuꟾi* /-ku/ is easy to do 28-N
  kaꟾiyasuꟾi is easy to buy 28-N
yaꟾsumiꟾ vacation, holiday, time off
    8
  yaꟾsumi no hiꟾ day off 27
yaꟾsuꟾmu /tr:-u:yaꟾsuꟾnde/ rest, re-
    lax, take time off 17

yaꟾtiꟾn the rent 29
yaꟾtoꟾu /tr:-u:yaꟾtoꟾtte/ employ 24
yatto finally, barely, with difficulty
    24
yattoko pliers 33-A
ya-ꟾttuꟾ eight units 5
yaꟾwarakaꟾi /-ku/ is soft or tender or
    pliable 22
yo* /sentence particle/ 2
  Peꟾn desu yo. It's a pen (I tell you).
    2
yobu /tr:-u:yonde/ call, summon 13
yoꟾi /-ku/ is good 2-N
yoko side 6
  deꟾpaꟾato no yoko the side of the de-
    partment store 6
yokosu /tr:-u:yokosite/ send here,
    hand over to speaker 33
yoꟾku /adverbial of iꟾi ～ yoꟾi/ well, a
    good deal, often 1
yoꟾmu /tr:-u:yoꟾnde/ read 13
yoꟾnakaꟾ middle of the night 34
yoꟾn four 3
yoꟾo business affairs, matter to attend
    to 22
yoꟾo* /na/ manner, way; seem, look
    24
  aꟾnaꟾta no ꟾyoꟾo na hito a person
    like you 24
  muꟾzukasii yoꟾo da seem to be dif-
    ficult 24
  deꟾkiꟾru yoo ni ꟾnaꟾru reach the
    point where it is possible 24
  kiꟾite miꟾru yoo ni iu tell [some-
    one] to try asking 24
  maꟾiniti no yoꟾo ni almost every
    day 24
yoohuku Western-style clothing 23
yookaꟾn Western-style building 30
yooma Western-style room 21
yoosyoku Western-style food 21-N
yoozi business affairs, matter to
    attend to 22
yori* /particle/ more than 15
  koꟾre yoꟾri ꟾiꟾi is better than
    this 15
yoꟾrokoꟾbu /intr:-u:yoꟾrokoꟾnde/ take
    pleasure in 16
yoꟾrokoꟾnde /gerund of yoꟾrokoꟾbu/
    gladly, with pleasure
    16

yorosii /-ku/ is good or fine or all
    right; never mind 5
  Doozo yorosiku. (Lit.) Please
    (treat me) favorably. 11
  Miña saň ni yorosiku. Give my
    regards to everyone. 11
  yorosi kereba provided it's all
    right or agreeable or convenient
    32
yoru night, night-time 16
  yoru no bu evening performance
    28
yoru /intr:-u:yotte/ stop in 22
yoru* /intr:-u:yotte/ depend, rely 26
  to si ni yotte depending on the
    year, according to the year 26
  zyo tyuu no hanasi ni yoru to
    according to what the maid says
    30
yo-ttu four units 5
yotukado intersection 20
yowa i /-ku/ is weak or frail or
    delicate or in poor health 26

za siki Japanese-style room or
    parlor 21
zassi magazine 2
ze hi by all means 28
zeñ Japanese eating tray 21-N
ze ñbu all, the whole thing 1
zeñzeñ /+ negative/ not at all 22
ze ro zero 12
-zi /counter for naming o'clocks/ 8
zi biki dictionary 2
zibuñ oneself 20
  zibuñ de by oneself 20
  zibuñ no one's own 20
zi do osya, zidoosya automobile 7
zieetai Self-Defense Forces 34-A
zikañ time 18
  zi kañ ga a ru have time 18
  zi kañ-do ori on time 19
-zikañ /counter for number of hours/
    8
zi ko an accident 35-A
zi mi /na/ plain, subdued, quiet 23
zi mu iñ office worker 24-A
zi mu syo office 9
zi ñzya Shinto shrine 32
zisiñ earthquake 35-A
zi syo dictionary 2
zi te ñsya, ziteñsya bicycle 22

yoyaku-suru /tr/ reserve 28
yo zyo o-hañ four-and-a-half-mat
    area or room 30
yu bi finger 17-A
yuka floor 30-A
yukata summer kimono 23-A
yu ki snow 23
-yuki -bound 19
  Yokosuka-yuki Yokosuka-bound
    19
yu kku ri slowly 13
yuku /alternant of iku/ 19-N
yu ube last night 11
yuubiñ mail 24
yu ubi ñkyoku post office 6
yuudati sudden (evening) shower
    26-A
yuu gata early evening 23
yuumee /na/ famous 32
yu za masi water which has been
    boiled 21-N

Z

ziteñsyaya bicycle shop, bicycle
    dealer 22
zi tu wa in reality, the fact is 34
zi yu u /na/ free, unrestricted 34-N
zo ñzi nai /-ku/ don't know 13
zo ñzite o ru know 13
zookiñ cleaning rag 17
zoori sandals 23-A
zu bo ñ trousers 23
zu ibuñ extremely, to a considerable
    degree 3
zutto by far 15; without interruption
    24
  zu tto ma e kara since a long time
    ago 15
-zu tu* each, of each, for each, at a
    time 33
  hi to-tu-zu tu one of each, one for
    each, one at a time 33
zya /contraction of de wa/ 2
  e ñpitu zya na i it isn't a pencil 2
  tu ma ñnai zya nai ka it's tire-
    some—don't you agree? surely
    you agree that it's tiresome 35
zya [a] then, well then, in that case 2
zyama /na/ hindrance, bother 17
  zya ma ni na ru become a bother,
    get in the way 17

zyari   gravel   33-A

-zyoo   /counter for number of units of
    one-tatami area [= 1/2 tsubo or
    app. 18 sq. ft.] and for naming
    rooms/   30

zyoobu /na/   strong, firm, durable,
    healthy   23

zyoꜜobusoꜜo /na/   sturdy-looking,
    healthy-looking   26

zyoꜜosyaꜜkeñ   passenger ticket   19-A

zyoꜜozuꜜ /na/   skilled, skillful   18

zyotyuu   maid   22

zyotyuubeya   maid's room   33

zyoyuu   actress   28-A

zyuꜜñsa, zyuñsa   policeman   7

zyuꜜu   ten   3

-zyuu*   throughout   25
    iti-niti-zyuu   all day long   25
    kyoo-zyuu ni   within today, before
        today is over   25

zyuꜜubuꜜñ /na/   enough   20

zyuꜜu-zyoꜜo   ten-mat area or room
    30

Index to the Grammatical Notes

References are to Lesson and Grammatical Note; for example, 26.4 refers to Lesson 26, Grammatical Note 4. Lessons from 1 through 20 are to be found in Beginning Japanese, Part I.